RESEARCH HANDBOOK ON THE INTERNATIONAL PENAL SYSTEM

RESEARCH HANDBOOKS IN INTERNATIONAL LAW

This highly original series offers a unique appraisal of the state-of-the-art of research and thinking in international law. Taking a thematic approach, each volume, edited by a prominent expert, covers a specific aspect of international law or examines the international legal dimension of a particular strand of the law. A wide range of sub-disciplines in the spheres of both public and private law are considered; from international environmental law to international criminal law, from international economic law to the law of international organisations, and from international commercial law to international human rights law. The *Research Handbooks* comprise carefully commissioned chapters from leading academics as well as those with an emerging reputation. Taking a genuinely international approach to the law, and addressing current and sometimes controversial legal issues, as well as affording a clear substantive analysis of the law, these *Handbooks* are designed to inform as well as to contribute to current debates.

Equally useful as reference tools or introductions to specific topics, issues and debates, the *Handbooks* will be used by academic researchers, post-graduate students, practicing lawyers and lawyers in policy circles.

Titles in this series include:

Research Handbook on International Law and Terrorism
Edited by Ben Saul

Research Handbook on the Law Treaties
Edited by Christian J. Tams, Antonios Tzanakopoulos and Andreas Zimmermann

Handbook of Space Law
Edited by Frans von der Dunk

Research Handbook on International Law and Cyberspace
Edited by Nicholas Tsagourias and Russell Buchan

Research Handbook on Transnational Labour Law
Edited by Adelle Blackett and Anne Trebilcock

Research Handbook on Jurisdiction and Immunities in International Law
Edited by Alexander Orakhelashvili

Research Handbook on the Theory and Practice of International Lawmaking
Edited by Catherine Brölmann and Yannick Radi

Research Handbook on the International Penal System
Edited by Róisín Mulgrew and Denis Abels

Research Handbook on the International Penal System

Edited by

Róisín Mulgrew
University of Nottingham, UK

Denis Abels
University of Amsterdam, the Netherlands

RESEARCH HANDBOOKS IN INTERNATIONAL LAW

Edward Elgar
PUBLISHING

Cheltenham, UK • Northampton, MA, USA

Published by
Edward Elgar Publishing Limited
The Lypiatts
15 Lansdown Road
Cheltenham
Glos GL50 2JA
UK

Edward Elgar Publishing, Inc.
William Pratt House
9 Dewey Court
Northampton
Massachusetts 01060
USA

A catalogue record for this book
is available from the British Library

Library of Congress Control Number: 2015959654

This book is available electronically in the **Elgar**online
Law subject collection
DOI 10.4337/9781783472161

MIX
Paper from
responsible sources
FSC® C013056

ISBN 978 1 78347 215 4 (cased)
ISBN 978 1 78347 216 1 (eBook)

Typeset by Columns Design XML Ltd, Reading
Printed and bound in Great Britain by TJ International Ltd, Padstow

Contents

Contributors

Denis Abels is an Associate Professor of Criminal Law at the University of Amsterdam and an Honorary Judge at the Noord-Holland District Court. He holds a PhD in law (2012, *cum laude*) from the University of Amsterdam. He specializes in (international) sanctioning law. He has published extensively on international sentencing (see various contributions to the Series of *Annotated Leading Cases of International Criminal Tribunals*), international detention law (see, in particular, *Prisoners of the International Community*, 2012) and is a member of the editorial team of the Dutch legal journal 'Sancties'. He is responsible for and teaches various courses on Dutch criminal law and prison law in Bachelor and Master's Programmes of the University of Amsterdam.

Kai Ambos is Chair of Criminal Law, Criminal Procedure, Comparative Law and International Criminal Law at the Georg-August-Universität Göttingen, Germany (since May 2003). Head of the Department of 'Foreign and International Criminal Law', Institute of Criminal Law and Justice at the University of Göttingen. Director of the Centro de Estudios de Derecho Penal y Procesal Penal Latinoamericano (CEDPAL) of Georg-August-Universität Göttingen. Judge at the Provincial Court (*Landgericht*) of Lower Saxony in Göttingen (since 24 March 2006); delegated to the Higher Regional Court (*Oberlandesgericht*) Braunschweig (since 1 January 2015). Dean of Students of the Faculty of Law at the University of Göttingen between April 2008 and 2010; responsible for the Master Programs 'MLE' and 'LLM' from April 2006 to June 2014.

Olympia Bekou is Professor of Public International Law and Head of the International Criminal Justice Unit at the University of Nottingham's Human Rights Law Centre. A qualified lawyer, she specializes in international criminal law. Olympia has undertaken numerous capacity-building missions, including in post-conflict situations (such as Uganda, the DRC and Sierra Leone), has provided legislation drafting assistance to Samoa (with legislation enacted in November 2007) and Jamaica, and has been involved in training the Thai judiciary. She is responsible for the National Implementing Legislation Database (NILD) of the ICC Legal Tools Project and has taught extensively worldwide. In 2014, she was awarded the University of Nottingham Knowledge Exchange and Innovation Award for Societal Impact in Social Sciences for her work 'Fighting Impunity through Technology: Strengthening the Capacity of National and International Criminal Justice Institutions to Investigate and Prosecute the Most Serious International Crimes'.

Silvia D'Ascoli is an Italian lawyer and international criminal attorney with expertise in the fields of International Criminal Law and Human Rights. Since 2007, Silvia has served as Legal Officer for the Office of the Prosecutor (OTP) of the ICTY. In this capacity, she has worked for both the Trial and the Appeals Section of the OTP, focusing on war crime cases concerning Kosovo and Bosnia. She is currently working on the *Mladić* case. She is currently working as an Assistant Appeals Counsel in the UN Mechanism for International Criminal Tribunals (MICT). Silvia received her Ph.D in Law from the European University Institute (Florence, Italy) in 2008. She regularly publishes in international legal journals and is the author of a monograph on *Sentencing in International Criminal Law* (2011). Since 2011, she has been a visiting lecturer in human rights and international tribunals at the Université Catholique de Lille and Paris (Faculté Libre de Droit de Lille, France). Silvia is also a member of the Justice Rapid Response's Roster of Experts for human rights investigations in conflict zones.

Teresa Anne Doherty CBE is from Northern Ireland and worked as a civil servant and volunteer in Zambia before studying law. With other students she worked in legal aid clinics during the 'troubles' in Northern Ireland. She was admitted to the Bars of Northern Ireland, New South Wales and Papua New Guinea. From 1976–87, she practiced law in Northern Ireland and Papua New Guinea and was noted for her work for women's rights and for prisoners. She made a weekly broadcast on legal issues in Tok Pidgin. In 1987, she was appointed Principal Magistrate in Papua New Guinea and, from 1988–97, she served as a Judge of the Supreme and National Courts. She was the first woman Judge in the South Pacific Islands region. In 1998, she returned to private law practice in Northern Ireland, where she worked until 2003. Most recently, from 2003–04, Judge Doherty has served as a Judge of the High Court and the Court of Appeals of Sierra Leone, at the request of the Commonwealth following the civil war. In 2005, she was appointed by the UN to the SCSL. Her dissenting opinion declaring forced marriage as a crime against humanity was upheld on appeal and is the first declaration in international law on this crime. Since 2002, she has served as Parole Commissioner for Northern Ireland.

Mark A. Drumbl is the Class of 1975 Alumni Professor at Washington & Lee University School of Law, where he also serves as Director of the Transnational Law Institute. He has held visiting appointments on several law faculties, including Oxford University, Université de Paris II (Panthéon-Assas), University of Melbourne, University of Sydney, University of Ottawa, Monash University, and Trinity College-Dublin. Professor Drumbl's research and teaching interests include public international law, international criminal law, global environmental governance, and transitional justice. His book, *Atrocity, Punishment, and International Law* (2007) has received critical acclaim and has won commendations from the International Association of Criminal Law (US national section) and the American Society of International Law. In 2012, he published *Reimagining Child Soldiers in International Law and Policy*, which has also been extensively and enthusiastically reviewed. Professor Drumbl has worked in criminal defence in Rwanda, lectures widely, and serves as an expert in US courts. His research has been cited by courts in Canada, the US and the UK. He has degrees in law and political science from McGill, Toronto and Columbia universities.

Shireen Avis Fisher (BA, JD, LLM, PhD) is a Judge of the RSCSL to which she was appointed by Secretary-General Ban Ki-moon in October 2013. Justice Fisher previously served as an Appeals Judge at the SCSL from 2009 through 2013, and as its President in 2012 and 2013. Prior to her appointment to the Special Court, she served as an International Judge of the War Crimes Chamber of the Court of Bosnia and Herzegovina (2005–08). She was called to the Bar in 1976 and appointed as a Judge of the US State of Vermont in 1986. She is the recipient of the *2014 Global Jurist of the Year Award*, presented annually by the Center for International Human Rights of Northwestern University School of Law 'for lifelong dedication to human rights and the rule of law'.

Barbora Holá works as Assistant Professor at the Department of Criminal Law and Criminology, VU University Amsterdam. She is a fellow at the Center for International Criminal Justice and a member of the steering committee of the Africa-Low Countries Network. In 2006 Barbora received her Law degree (summa cum laude) at the Faculty of Law, Charles University in Prague. In 2007 she received LLM in International and European Law at the University of Amsterdam. In 2012 Barbora obtained her PhD in supranational criminology at the VU University Amsterdam. In the past, Barbora worked as a legal counsel at the Public International Law and Policy Group and as part of defence at the ICTY. In her research Barbora focuses on issues of transitional justice, in particular (international) criminal trials, sentencing of international crimes and enforcement of international sentences. In 2013, the Netherlands Organization for Scientific Research awarded Barbora the prestigious VENI grant for a project on vertical (in)consistency of international sentencing.

Annika Jones is a Lecturer in International Law at the University of Durham. Her research is situated within the field of international criminal law and focuses, in particular, on the role of judges and courts in the development of international law. Annika holds a first class degree in Law (LLB) and an LLM in International Criminal Justice and Armed Conflict with distinction. Both were obtained from the University of Nottingham. Her doctoral thesis, which examines the use of external case law at the ICC, was completed at the same institution. In 2012, Annika was awarded the University of Nottingham Endowed Postgraduate Award for her doctoral research. Prior to her appointment at the University of Durham, Annika held posts at the University of Exeter and the University of Nottingham. In 2009, she also spent a period of time at the ICC, working in both the Appeals and Trial Divisions.

Nik Kiefer is a researcher at the Centre for International Law, Free University of Brussels. Previously, he worked for the Council of the European Union, the ICTY as well as for the Council of Europe, where he was a human rights consultant.

Conor McCarthy is a barrister practicing at the Bar of England and Wales and a Member of Monckton Chambers. He was formerly a visiting fellow at the British Institute of International and Comparative Law and has published widely on questions of international law, in particular on questions of remedies under international law. His book *Reparations and Victim Support under the Rome Statute of the International Criminal Court*, was published in 2012.

Lorna McGregor is a Professor in Essex Law School and Director of the Human Rights Centre at the University of Essex. She researches and teaches in the areas of public international law, particularly international human rights law, international criminal law and transitional justice. Her work has appeared in journals such as the *American Journal of International Law*, the *European Journal of International Law*, the *International and Comparative Law Quarterly*, the *Journal of International Criminal Justice* and the *International Journal of Transitional Justice* and has been cited by the UK House of Lords and International Court of Justice. She is a co-chair of the European Society of International Law's Interest Group on International Human Rights Law, a co-chair of the International Law Association's Study Group on Individual Responsibility under International Law, a Commissioner of the UK Equality and Human Rights Commission and a member of REDRESS Legal Advisory Council. From 2012–14, she was a co-chair of an expert group of academics and human rights practitioners on the review of the UNSMR. Prior to becoming an academic, Lorna was the International Legal Adviser at REDRESS where she litigated cases on torture and detention before the ACmHPR, the ECtHR, the I-ACtHR and the HRC and the ICC Programme Lawyer at the International Bar Association focusing on complementarity.

Róisín Mulgrew (BCorp Law and LLB (Galway), LLM in International Criminal Justice and Armed Conflict, MA in Socio-Legal and Criminological Research and PhD (Nottingham)), has been an Assistant Professor in Law at the University of Nottingham since 2010. Her research focuses on international penal law, policy and practice. Her doctoral research exploring issues related to the enforcement of international punishment was published in 2013 (*Towards the Development of the International Penal System*). She has served as a scientific expert for the Council of Europe's Council for Penological Cooperation (helping to draft the 2012 Recommendation concerning foreign prisoners) and a consultant for the UN Office of Drugs and Crime (helping to produce the *Handbook on the International Transfer of Sentenced Persons*). She is currently a member of an Expert Steering Group on Foreign Nationals in Prison established by the European Organisation of Prison and Correctional Services (EuroPris) and the European Society for Probation (CEP).

Jan Christoph Nemitz (Dr. iur. (Freiburg i.Br., 2002), Ass. iur. (Konstanz, 1999), JM (Stockholm, 1996)), works for the German Federal Foreign Office in Berlin. Prior to this, he worked as (Associate) Legal Officer in the Appeals Chamber of the ICTY in The Hague (2002–2015). Previously, he was a research assistant at the Max Planck Institute for Foreign and International Criminal Law in Freiburg im Breisgau (1999–2002). He has taught classes on international criminal procedure at the Universities of Bonn, Münster, and Lund. He has given over 40 presentations on topics of international criminal law at international seminars and conferences, and he has published more than 30 publications in academic books and journals on various legal issues, including international criminal law and public international law.

Margaret M. Penrose received her Juris Doctorate from Pepperdine School of Law in 1993. Following law school, she served as a Senior Law Clerk to the Honourable Jerry Buchmeyer, United States District Judge and as Staff Attorney to the Honourable Jane J. Boyle, United States District Judge. In 1999, she received her LLM from Notre Dame Law School at the Centre for Civil and Human Rights. Since then she has held academic positions at the University of Oklahoma and Texas A&M University School of Law, teaching Constitutional Law and Criminal Procedure. She continues to practice as a civil rights attorney and is currently court appointed counsel at the federal level in several Texas Death Penalty cases.

Göran Sluiter is Professor of International Criminal Law, in particular the Law of International Criminal Procedure at the University of Amsterdam, Amsterdam, the Netherlands and a partner at Prakken d'Oliveira Human Rights Lawyers (Amsterdam). Previously, he has worked nine years as an *ad litem* Judge in the Netherlands, including the adjudication of international crimes in the specialized Chamber of the Hague District Court, and he has worked as a Senior Lecturer in Criminal Law at the University of Amsterdam and Lecturer in International Law at Utrecht University. His research focuses on procedure and practice of international criminal tribunals. He has published extensively in this field.

Sonja Snacken is Professor of Criminology, Penology and Sociology of Law at the Vrije Universiteit Brussel (Belgium), where she holds a 'Research Fellowship' (2006–16). She has master degrees in law and criminology and a PhD in criminology. Her research focuses on penality in Belgium and Europe and on forms of (extreme) institutional dependency, and integrates empirical methods with human rights concerns. She has acted since 1994 as an expert to the European Committee for the Prevention of Torture (CPT) and was a member (2001–12) and President (2006–12) of the Council for Penological Cooperation of the Council of Europe, drafting Recommendations such as the European Prison Rules (2006). She was awarded the Belgian Francqui Chair (2008–09), the Ernest-John Solvay Prize for Scientific Excellence in the Human and Social Sciences by the National Science Foundation (FWO, 2010) and the European Criminology Award 2015 (European Society of Criminology).

Andrew Trotter (BA, LLB QUT; BCL Oxon) is an Associate in Litigation and International Arbitration at White & Case LLP in London. Previously, he practised as a criminal defence lawyer in Australia after internships at the ICTY and ECCC, and an associateship with the Chief Justice of Australia.

Harmen van der Wilt is Professor of International Criminal Law at the Amsterdam School of Law, University of Amsterdam. His research interests include concepts of criminal responsibility in International Criminal Law; domestic prosecutions of international crimes, legal reaction to terrorism, International Criminal Law and legal philosophy, history in the courtroom, European Arrest warrant and transnational crimes. Van der Wilt is a member of the editorial board of the Journal of International Criminal Justice and the Netherlands Yearbook of International Law. He has been a member of the Research council of the EU(F7)-project on the European Arrest Warrant and was a member of the Steering Committee of F7 project DOMAC (Impact of International Courts on Domestic Procedures in Mass Atrocity cases). Van der Wilt has been an *ad litem* Judge in the Criminal Court of Roermond and is currently an *ad litem* Judge in the Extradition Chamber of the District Court in Amsterdam. He is acting president of the Nino Cassese Foundation.

Joris van Wijk is Associate Professor of Criminology at the Department of Criminal Law and Criminology at VU University Amsterdam. He directs the Master's programme International Crimes and Criminology and co-directs the Center for International Criminal Justice (CICJ). His research focuses on international criminal justice and migration related issues.

Dirk van Zyl Smit holds BA and LLB degrees from the University of Stellenbosch, a PhD from the University of Edinburgh and an honorary doctorate in law from the University of Greifswald. He is currently Professor of Comparative and International Penal Law at the University of Nottingham and is Emeritus Professor of Criminology of the University of Cape Town. In 2012 he was Global Visiting Professor of Law at New York University. His publications include *Principles of European Prison Law and Policy: Penology and Human Rights* (with Sonja Snacken) (2009) and *Taking Life Imprisonment Seriously in National and International Law* (2002). Professor van Zyl Smit is currently project leader of a study of life imprisonment worldwide.

Rebecca Young is a Legal Officer in the Legal and Enforcement Unit in the immediate office of the President at the ICC. She has previously been an Associate Legal Officer within the same unit and at the International Court of Justice. She holds an LLM with Distinction from the University of Edinburgh and an LLB with Honours and BA from the University of Adelaide.

Preface

Since the establishment of the ICTY, ICTR and ICC legal scholars have increasingly shown an interest in the field of international criminal justice. Much research has been done on both substantive international criminal law and the law of international criminal procedure. These two components of international criminal law have gradually developed into separate bodies of law. In the domestic context, however, criminal law is usually recognized as having not just a dual, but a tripartite structure, consisting of substantive law, procedural law and sanctioning law. Sanctioning law consists of such aspects as theories and objectives of punishment, penalties, sentencing, enforcement and release. This book analyses these issues from an international criminal justice perspective. It sets out the sanctioning law of the international criminal tribunals and courts, examines its boundaries and explores its core themes.

This Handbook recognizes the social reality that international criminal courts must deal with detainees and prisoners without the developed legal framework, specialist expertise or infrastructure present in domestic penal systems. Accordingly, the international criminal justice context poses unique challenges for international criminal courts. They must deal with a high-profile population of detained persons in a system entirely dependent on the voluntary cooperation of host States, enforcing States and international organizations. Given the proliferation of international courts and the increasing number of cases before them, international penal law, policy and practice are rapidly expanding. The difficulties involved in implementing this law often pose practical and political dilemmas for international criminal courts. Its implementation also has very real and often long-term consequences for international detainees, international prisoners and their families. Indeed, how international prisoners are treated can have an impact on transition in post-conflict States. Accordingly, this book critically analyses the penal methods used by the international penal system to respond to international crime. Looking beyond the rhetoric to the reality of international detention, punishment and imprisonment, the book highlights a range of contemporary challenges and areas where there is a clear need for improvement and makes recommendations for the development of the current system. The book also identifies areas of international penal law and practice that call for a sui generis approach.

Accordingly, this book adopts a broader approach than examining international sanctioning law; it examines the operation of the international penal system. For the purposes of this book, the term 'international penal system' is not a term of art with a specific sociological definition. Nor is it restricted to particular international criminal courts. Rather it is a term that incorporates all issues related to detention and imprisonment by international criminal courts. For example, it includes such issues as non-custodial sanctions, monitoring of conditions of detention, the protection of prisoners under international law and the transfer of prisoners. The different aspects of, and pertinent themes related to, the international penal system will be discussed in chronological order, linking up with the sequence of the international criminal justice process. The book then proceeds to address more normative questions relating to standards, before exploring contemporary and alternative mechanisms for punishing and overseeing punishment, and possible avenues for development. Each Part will begin with a brief introduction to the theme under discussion and the chapters contained therein.

The first theme that will be discussed is remand detention, with a focus on the internal legal position of persons detained at international courts and their provisional release (Part I). Next, we will consider the range of penalties that can be imposed on individuals by international criminal courts and their normative basis (Part II). This is followed by an outline of the sentencing law and practice of the international courts and an exploration of the judicial practice of cross-referencing in the various courts' sentencing jurisprudence (Part III). Since international courts do not have their own prisons, they are dependent on States for the enforcement of their sentences. Part IV evaluates the international system for transferring prisoners to cooperating States in light of inter-State practice and the Rule 11*bis* system. International custodial sanctions are enforced in domestic prisons. The applicable legal regimes are governed primarily by the domestic law of the State of enforcement, but are also subject to supervision by the international courts. Part V explores the legal regimes and principles that govern the enforcement of international sentences of imprisonment with a focus on the penal objective of rehabilitation. The deprivation of liberty by international criminal courts must be governed by international human rights and penal standards. Part VI asks whether, and to what extent, international penal law aligns with contemporary human rights law, and examines the role and methods used by an international body that oversees the implementation of international sentences (CPT). This section also analyses a new system for the conditional release and monitoring of prisoners introduced by the Residual Special Court for Sierra Leone. It is not necessarily the case, however, that international punishment should be restricted to the deprivation of liberty. Part VII asks whether a more prominent role should be accorded to transitional and restorative justice perspectives and explores the role of victim redress in international criminal justice. The final substantive section looks to the future. Part VIII examines arguments for and against creating an international prison and explores issues related to the Rome Statute's scheme for compensating acquitted persons.

The editors would like to thank Edward Elgar Publishing for making this work possible. We would especially like to thank Ben Booth and Laura Mann for their enthusiasm and patience.

This Handbook would, of course, not have been possible without the individual contributors, who have dedicated much time and effort to writing the various chapters. Throughout the process, the editors have been impressed by, and grateful for, the contributors' readiness to enter into a dialogue on many aspects related to this new field of law. Their openness, dedication and the high quality of their contributions have ensured that this work truly deserves to be called a *research* handbook.

Finally, the editors wish to thank Aimel Yousfi-Roquencourt and especially Mike Jonk, for their outstanding work in assisting with the editing of this book.

Róisín Mulgrew and Denis Abels

Abbreviations

ACHPR	African Charter on Human and Peoples' Rights
ACHR	American Convention on Human Rights
ACmHPR	African Commission on Human and Peoples' Rights
ASO	Agreement on Security and Order
BEA	Bilateral Enforcement Agreement
CPT	European Committee for the Prevention of Torture
CRC	Convention on the Rights of the Child
ECCC	Extraordinary Chambers in the Courts of Cambodia
ECHR	European Convention on Human Rights
ECtHR	European Court of Human Rights
EPR	European Prison Rules 2006
GARes	General Assembly Resolution
HQA	Headquarters Agreement
HRC	Human Rights Committee
I-ACmHR	Inter-American Commission on Human Rights
I-ACtHR	Inter-American Court of Human Rights
ICC	International Criminal Court
ICCDC	ICC Detention Centre
ICCPR	International Covenant on Civil and Political Rights
ICCSt	ICC Statute ('Rome Statute')
ICESR	International Covenant on Economic and Social Rights
ICRC	International Committee of the Red Cross
ICTR	International Criminal Tribunal for Rwanda
ICTRSt	ICTR Statute
ICTY	International Criminal Tribunal for the former Yugoslavia
ICTYSt	ICTY Statute
IMTFE	International Military Tribunal, Far East
IMTN	International Military Tribunal, Nuremberg
MICT	Mechanism for International Criminal Tribunals
MICTSt	MICT Statute
OSCE	Organisation for Security and Co-operation in Europe
PDD	Practice Direction on Designation
ROC	Regulations of the Court
ROD	Rules of Detention

ROR	Regulations of the Registry
RPE	Rules of Procedure and Evidence
RSCSL	Residual Special Court for Sierra Leone
RSCSLSt	RSCSL Statute
SCA	Agreement Between the UN and the Government of Sierra Leone on the Establishment of a Special Court for Sierra Leone
SCRes	Security Council Resolution
SCSL	Special Court for Sierra Leone
SCSLDF	SCSL Detention Facility
SCSLSt	SCSL Statute
SPT	Subcommittee for the Prevention of Torture
STL	Special Tribunal for Lebanon
TFV	Trust Fund for Victims
UDHR	Universal Declaration on Human Rights
UN	United Nations
UNBOP	UN Body of Principles on the Protection of all Persons under Any Form of Detention or Imprisonment
UNBP	UN Basic Principles for the Treatment of Prisoners
UNDF	UN Detention Facility (ICTR)
UNDU	UN Detention Unit (ICTY)
UNMIK	UN Interim Administration Mission in Kosovo
UNSC	UN Security Council
UNSMR	UN Standard Minimum Rules on the Treatment of Prisoners

PART I

INTERNATIONAL REMAND DETENTION

This first section of the Research Handbook on the International Penal System focuses on the legal position of persons detained on remand at international criminal courts and tribunals. Little is known about the law governing detention at the Nuremberg remand centre, which housed the Nazi leaders during their trials and before the execution of their sentences.[1] Important developments in the field of human rights law after World War II meant that the drafters of the detention rules of the international criminal tribunals and courts that were established from the 1990s onwards could not draw lessons from the way the Nuremberg detainees had been treated back in the 1940s. A new law of international remand detention had to be created, laying down the rights and obligations of detainees at the UNDU in Scheveningen, the Netherlands, and at the UNDF in Arusha, Tanzania.

Creating an international detention regime was by no means an easy task, although inspiration was sought in soft-law penal standards that had been developed in the context of the UN and the Council of Europe.

The contemporary international remand institutions may consist of separate wings in domestic prisons that are being rented by the tribunal or court concerned (ICTY, ICC), stand-alone detention facilities that are located within a domestic prison (ICTR) or facilities located within the court's compound (SCSL).[2] The daily management is entrusted to a Commanding or Chief Custody Officer, who answers to the Registrar of the international tribunal or court concerned. All of the remand institutions' detention regulations provide for internal complaint mechanisms. Most of these place the ultimate decision-making power for such complaints in the hands of the President/Presidency of the tribunal/court concerned (the notable exception is the SCSL where the (Acting) Registrar was the ultimate arbiter on most detention complaints. Only

---

1 See, in some detail, N.J.W. Goda, *Tales from Spandau. Nazi Criminals and the Cold War* (Cambridge University Press 2007).

2 The ICTY UNDU consists of different floors within the host prison and has held more than 180 detainees to date. The ICTR UNDF contains 56 cells and has held more than 80 persons to date. The SCSLDF, which was located within the Court's compound in Freetown, has in total detained approximately 20 persons.

some narrowly described detention issues could be brought before the President.[3] At all of the mentioned tribunals' and courts' detention facilities, treatment of detained persons is supervised by the ICRC by way of conducting periodic visits. The international remand institutions have held persons accused and convicted of committing international crimes, but also detained witnesses and persons accused and convicted of contempt of court. The ground for an individual detainee's incarceration has, in principle, no bearing upon the detention regime; all persons detained at the institution are subject to the same detention regulations.

The term international remand detention refers to detention at international criminal courts and tribunals before sentencing. International detention law governs the legal position of international remand detainees. Their legal position consists, just like that of international prisoners, of both an internal and an external component. The internal component, or the detainees' internal legal position, refers to the modalities of detention, i.e., the facilities provided to international detainees, the principles guiding their treatment and their rights and duties inside the remand institution. Their internal legal position consists of both substantive rights and procedural rights.

The external legal position of international detainees concerns their rights in procedures relating to their actual deprivation of liberty, i.e., procedures leading to decisions on the basis of which they are sent to and released from the remand institution.

In the first section of this Handbook, both the international remand detainees' internal legal position and an important aspect of their external legal position are discussed in detail.

An overview of the former is presented by Jan Christoph Nemitz in Chapter 1. After discussing the applicable detention law and standards, Nemitz zooms in on such substantive and procedural rights of detainees as the right to contact with the outside world, the right to medical care and the right to complain about the modalities of detention. Nemitz further discusses such safety and security issues as discipline, the use of solitary confinement and suspension of the rules of detention.

In Chapter 2, Andrew Trotter discusses provisional release from international remand detention as an example of the external legal position of international detainees. Trotter describes how, when the *ad hoc* Tribunals were first established, provisional release was seen as an exception to the rule, and explains how this viewpoint changed in later years when more consideration was given to the possibility of release. Trotter examines difficulties related to provisional release that result from characteristics of the context in which international criminal courts and tribunals must operate. He further sets out the differences between the various international courts' and tribunals' release criteria and studies the main provisional release criteria in more depth. He concludes by comparing the role of provisional release in international criminal justice to its role in domestic jurisdictions.

---

[3] See, in more detail, D. Abels, *Prisoners of the International Community. The Legal Position of Persons Detained at International Criminal Tribunals* (TMC Asser Press 2012) Chapter 5.

1. The legal position of international detainees: applicable law and standards

Jan Christoph Nemitz

1. INTRODUCTION

This chapter will present a comprehensive overview of the law governing the detention of individuals who are accused by the ICC, the ICTR and the ICTY and who are detained in the respective detention facilities of these institutions. The reasons for choosing these three international judicial bodies is that over the past years they have gained extensive experience in relation to the legal and practical aspects of detaining persons who are awaiting trial or appeal proceedings or are otherwise detained on the authority of an international tribunal or court.[1]

The chapter will analyse the respective Statutes, RPE, Rules of Detention (ROD), Practice Directions, international instruments and the relevant jurisprudence of these judicial bodies. When analysing this body of law, the chapter will pay due attention to the inherent tension in the relationship between the need to govern, on the one hand, the administration of a detention unit for accused persons who are detained during their proceedings and, on the other hand, the need to ensure the continued application and protection of their individual rights during their time in detention.

The chapter will first define the term 'International Detainee' as being distinct from, for instance, a convicted person or a person on provisional release. It will then set out the various legal sources that form the applicable law of the respective courts and tribunals (Section 2). Thereafter it will address the legal standards that provide the framework in which International Detainees spend their days in the respective detention units. This will include, inter alia, communications and visits, accommodation, personal hygiene, clothing, food, access to medical services, spiritual welfare, recreational activities, and personal possessions of detainees (Section 3). The subsequent part of the chapter will deal with the law governing the maintenance of security in the detention units. In this context the chapter will analyse the respective rules on discipline, segregation and isolation, disturbances and the use of instruments of restraint (Section 4). Further, the applicable procedure to file complaints will be considered, including complaints to the Registry and to the Chambers (Section 5). In addition, the chapter

[1] Due to the necessary limitations in the scope of this chapter, the laws on detention of the ECCC and of the STL will not be analysed. Furthermore, the laws on detention of these two institutions can be substantially distinguished from the detention laws of the three judicial organisations that will be analysed. As to the ECCC, their detainees are held in accordance with national Cambodian law. With respect to the STL, this Tribunal has currently (last update: 17 November 2014) no detainees which means that any analysis of its detention law appears to be a rather theoretical exercise.

will discuss to what extent other specific rights of the detainees of international courts and tribunals are protected, such as the right to receive (or extend) a passport and the right to vote (Section 6). Finally, the chapter will address the possibilities for international detainees to cooperate with their counsel and legal assistants as well as the situation of a self-represented accused who is working on his defence from within the detention unit (Section 7).

Where appropriate the chapter will consider relevant jurisprudence of the various international institutions, including decisions, orders and reports. Reference will also be made to applicable legal standards with respect to detainees.

2. INTERNATIONAL DETAINEES AND THE APPLICABLE SOURCES OF LAW GOVERNING THEIR DETENTION

For the purposes of this chapter an International Detainee is a person detained awaiting trial or appeal proceedings, or held pending transfer to another institution, or any other person detained on the authority of the ICC, ICTR or ICTY. This definition of an International Detainee therefore includes persons who have been finally convicted by an international tribunal but who are still held in the respective detention unit pending the determination of a State in which the sentence can be enforced. While these judicial bodies aim to transfer convicted persons as soon as possible to enforcement States, practice has shown that many months (even years) can pass until such transfers can be achieved.[2] During that time the detention regime remains applicable to them.[3]

---

[2] At the ICC, the sentenced person shall be delivered to the State of enforcement as soon as possible after the designated State of enforcement accepts (Rule 206 ICC RPE). See also D. Abels, *Prisoners of the International Community* (TMC Asser Press 2012) 461. At the ICTY Johan Tarčulovski, a national of the Former Yugoslav Republic of Macedonia, had his conviction for violations of international criminal law affirmed by the Appeals Chamber of the ICTY on 19 May 2010. It took, however, until 7 July 2011 until he could be transferred to Germany to have his 12-year sentence enforced. The ICTY President had designated Germany on 23 August 2010 as the enforcement State, but it took more than ten months to finally send him to Germany. Until 2006 convicted detainees were not even separated from non-convicted detainees. After the suicide of Milan Babić, a convicted person who had returned to the ICTY as a witness in the proceedings against Milan Martić, Swedish independent investigators recommended a separation of convicted and non-convicted individuals in the detention unit (Independent Audit of the UNDU, 4 May 2006). In response the then President of the ICTY stated such practice 'is consistent with principles of human rights' ('Order to the Registrar to Separate Convicted and Non-Convicted Detainees held in the Detention Unit', IT-06-89-Misc. 1 (President) 2).

[3] On the other hand, this definition of an International Detainee means that suspects or accused persons who have not yet been transferred to any of the international courts and tribunals fall outside the scope of this chapter. Similarly, it will not address the legal position of persons who have been (finally) convicted by these courts and tribunals and subsequently transferred to the national authorities of the enforcement State. In both situations, the governing law is not that of the international courts but national law. Neither will this chapter address in any detail the legal position of individuals who have been finally acquitted by the ICTR but who are staying in so-called safe houses as they do not wish to return to Rwanda and no other country is willing to accept them. At the time of writing (24 April 2014), there were still seven

In this context it is important to note that the applicable law governing the detention of International Detainees in the so-called UNDU and ICCDC in The Hague (ICTY and ICC, respectively) and in Arusha (ICTR) is truly international in character, being devised in accordance with the applicable international legal standards. The detention regime for International Detainees inside the detention units is thus, in general, not influenced by national detention laws.[4] Instead the ICTY and the ICTR have adopted detention laws that are in line with UN standards, even where such standards cannot necessarily be seen as customary international law and might be considered as non-binding on States.[5] Those standards are included in the UNSMR,[6] the UNBOP[7] and the UNBP.[8] Similarly, these standards are in line with international legal instruments on detention on the regional level.[9]

The standards set out in these international instruments have been incorporated in the respective detention laws of the ICC, ICTR and ICTY. From a purely legal standpoint it is difficult to see how it could be any other way, given that these tribunals are bound by international legal standards,[10] and that their acceptance by the global public depends, in part, on the perception that their respective detention regimes are operated in a lawful and fair manner. It is in line with a modern understanding of human rights law to accept that minimum detention standards apply to every detainee at an international tribunal, irrespective of the fact that he (or she) is charged with the most serious violations of international humanitarian law. This applies even in cases in which the detention conditions of a high-ranking alleged war criminal surpass those of an alleged criminal of a minor rank who has been detained by national authorities and under national detention laws. Similarly, the fact that many victims of wartime atrocities may receive less medical care than alleged war criminals cannot alter an international court's obligation to provide its International Detainees with appropriate food and with medical services to the extent practically possible,[11] including consultation with a doctor or dentist of their choice[12] and specialist or in-patient treatment in the respective host country.[13] While this may contribute to an unwanted perception of the international tribunals' detention facilities being the 'Scheveningen Hilton' and the

acquitted persons and three ex-convicts who are de facto homeless as they have nowhere to go. Previously, there were 14 individuals in safe houses in Arusha, but the ICTR managed in bilateral negotiations to find countries willing to receive some of them.

4 However, when drafting the ICTY ROD the ICTY Judges ensured that the detention regime was consistent with the Dutch prison system. See Abels (n 2) 178.

5 See Abels (n 2) 148.

6 Approved by ECOSOC Resolutions 663 (XXIV) of 31 July 1957 and 2067 (LXII) of 13 May 1977.

7 GARes 43/173, adopted by the General Assembly on 9 December 1988.

8 GARes 45/111, adopted by the General Assembly on 14 December 1990.

9 See Council of Europe Recommendation no R (87) 3 of 12 February 1987, referred to in *Plavšić* IT-00-39 and 40/1 (Order of the President on the Defence Request to Modify the Conditions of Detention of the Accused, 18 January 2001).

10 For a detailed analysis of the applicability of human rights law in the legal detention regimes of the ICC, the ICTR and the ICTY see Abels (n 2) 134 *et seq*.

11 Rule 27 ICTR ROD, See also Rule 30 ICTY ROD and Reg 103 ICC ROC.

12 Rule 28 ICTR ROD; Rule 31 ICTY ROD; Reg 103(3), (5) ICC ROC.

13 Rule 29 ICTR ROD; Rule 32 ICTY ROD; Reg 103(5) ICC ROC.

'Arusha Hilton', respectively,[14] this is the price to be paid lest the international community falls behind its own widely accepted international standards.[15]

The above-mentioned international detention standards were translated into the respective detention regulations of the ICC, ICTR and ICTY. These are not so much to be found in the respective Statutes or RPE, but rather in their own ROD in which the ICTR, ICTY and ICC have provided detailed provisions on all aspects of the legal duties and rights of International Detainees. As stated above, these provisions reflect legal standards that are truly international in character, which means that an International Detainee in a detention unit of an international court or tribunal has the rights and duties under those international rules, and not under the respective national regulations.[16] These ROD are complemented by Practice Directions, issued by the respective President of the court, which provide further detailed provisions with respect to the position of the International Detainee in a detention unit as well as on the determination of the enforcement State.[17] Finally, the jurisprudence of the international tribunals and courts is an important source for the regulation of the detention of an International Detainee. On the pre-trial, trial and appeal level, many Chambers have already had the opportunity to rule on detention-related issues. Apart from the motions for provisional release that have been filed by detainees on a regular basis, Chambers have had to deal with subject-matters as diverse as requests for interviews,[18] motions to grant political engagement in the country of origin,[19] and a request to be placed under house arrest.[20] Of particular importance is the report that was written by Judge Kevin Parker after the death of Milan Babić who, after having returned to the ICTY as a witness, committed suicide in the UNDU in 2006.[21] In this report Judge Parker made a large number of recommendations in relation to the factual and legal regime of

---

[14] Abels (n 2) 2.

[15] Considerable criticism was also raised by the detention conditions for Biljana Plavšić who had her sentence enforced in a women's prison in Örebro, Sweden. This prison has a sauna, a massage room, sporting facilities and a horse-riding paddock, 'facilities that would be the envy of any holiday camp'. 'Luxury Prison for Bosnia's Iron Lady' (*The Telegraph*, 7 June 2003) <http://www.telegraphindia.com/1030607/asp/foreign/story_2044806.asp> accessed 24 April 2014.

[16] However, during the transfer of an International Detainee from the UNDU to the respective court and tribunal or to any other location outside the detention facilities, the law of the Host State applies.

[17] For instance the UNDU House Rules for Detainees (IT/99) and the UNDU Regulations to Govern the Supervision of Visits to and Communications With Detainees (IT/98/Rev.4). For further legal texts see website of the ICTY at <www.icty.org>. For the ICC see the ICC ROR (ICC-BD/03-03-13), which further regulate, inter alia, the management of the Detention Centre and the Complaints Procedure.

[18] See Part 3.

[19] See *Haradinaj et al* IT-04-84-T (Judgment, 3 April 2008); *Vojislav Šešelj* IT-03-67-PT (Decision on Defence Motion for Provisional Release, 23 July 2004).

[20] In 2005 the then President of the ICTY denied a request for house arrest instead of detention as 'the presence on Dutch territory is likely to pose a danger to public order and peace, if only because of the presence in the Netherlands of thousands of refugees from the former Yugoslavia', *Halilović* IT-01-48-PT (Order of the President on the Renewed Defence Motion Concerning Conditions of Detention During Trial, 24 January 2005) para 21.

[21] Judge K. Parker, *Report to the President – Death of Milan Babić* (ICTY, 8 June 2006).

International Detainees which were aimed at preventing a similar situation in the future.[22] Fortunately, no International Detainee has died in the UNDU since then.

3. LEGAL STANDARDS GOVERNING THE MANAGEMENT OF INTERNATIONAL DETENTION UNITS

The following section will deal with legal provisions governing the day-to-day routine in the detention units, including, inter alia, communications of the International Detainees with their family and friends, the legal regime applicable to visits and the available medical services.

3.1 Communications With the Outside World

An important feature of the life of an International Detainee concerns his or her communications with the outside world. In general detainees are entitled to communicate with their families and other persons with whom it is in their legitimate interest to correspond by letter and by telephone.[23] For security reasons, however, the staff of the detention unit will generally inspect all correspondence and mail for explosives or other restricted materials.[24] Further restrictions have been established, for instance, in the 'Regulations to Govern the Supervision of Visits to and Communications with Detainees' of the ICTY.[25] But communications with their fellow detainees is also of major importance to International Detainees. In this context it is important to bear in mind that the special circumstances of international courts and tribunals often lead to the situation that several detainees are accused of crimes that have been committed at the same crime sites, but by members of the different parties to the armed conflict. In so-called 'flip-side' cases accused from those warring parties may find themselves as being part of the same, or substantially related, proceedings before the court or tribunal. Unless this situation causes potential conflict in the detention unit, those detainees can spend their leisure time with each other in the detention unit. This also means that they can, if they so wish, discuss their case with each other.

---

22 While Judge Parker's report concluded that Milan Babić hung himself with his own belt, he stated that there had not been any threat that had required the belt to be removed and he recommended that '[t]he events of this case are isolated and provide no justification for a change to the policy in this respect of the present Rules of Detention' (Parker (n 21) para 60(m)). Further Judge Parker recommended 'that a record be maintained in the medical records of a detainee at [the UNDU] of any assessment, whether formal or informal, or treatment of a detainee by the [UNDU] psychiatrist', which was not the practice at the time (Ibid., para 60(o)).

23 Rule 58 ICTR ROD; Rule 58(A) ICTY ROD. This right can be restricted by the Registrar or, in cases of emergency, the Commanding Officer, if the Prosecutor has reasonable grounds for believing that such contact is for the purposes of attempting to arrange the escape of the International Detainee, or if such contact could prejudice the outcome of proceedings (Rule 64 ICTR ROD). See also in general Rules 58–64*bis* ICTY ROD; Reg 99(1)(h)–(i) ICC ROC.

24 Rule 59 ICTR ROD; Rule 59(A) ICTY ROD.

25 UNDU, Regulations to Govern the Supervision of Visits to and Communications with Detainees (IT/98/Rev. 4).

In particular, International Detainees enjoy the right to communicate with, and receive visits from, the consular or diplomatic representative of the State to which they belong.[26] Apart from those communications some International Detainees have requested more specific benefits from the international tribunals and courts. It is important to point out that in line with the specific nature of the statutory crimes of which they are accused, which usually require an element of implication of State organs, many International Detainees before the ICC, ICTR and ICTY have exercised important political functions before they came to The Hague or Arusha, respectively. In some instances they had requested to pursue, at least to some extent, their political work from inside the detention unit.

Perhaps the most well-known case before the ICTY in which the political activities of an accused were discussed was the *Haradinaj* case. At the time when he was indicted by the ICTY, Haradinaj was the Prime Minister of Kosovo within the provisional democratic self-governing institutions under SCRes 1244 (1990). From this post he stepped down and surrendered to the ICTY.[27] Like other accused persons, Haradinaj was not allowed to engage in political activities while he was an International Detainee at the UNDU. Then, on 6 June 2005, he was allowed provisional release, but under the condition that he was not permitted 'to make any political appearances or in any way get involved in any public political activity' during the first 90 days of his provisional release.[28] However, he was allowed to 'take up administrative or organizational activities in his capacity of the President of the Alliance for the Future of Kosovo', provided that such activities would not violate the conditions of provisional release.[29] These conditions were changed about five months later when Trial Chamber II allowed Haradinaj to appear in public and engage in political activities, provided that UNMIK found them important for 'a positive development of the political and security situation in Kosovo'.[30] On 1 February 2007, due to the upcoming trial the Trial Chamber recalled Haradinaj from provisional release.[31] During the trial, when he was again an International Detainee, he was not allowed to participate in political activities.[32]

---

[26] Rule 63 ICTR ROD; Rule 63 ICTY ROD; Reg 98 ICC ROC.

[27] *Haradinaj et al* IT-04-84-T (Judgment, 3 April 2008) Appendix A para 3.

[28] Ibid., para 10.

[29] Ibid., para 10, referring to *Haradinaj et al* IT-04-84-PT (Decision on Ramush Haradinaj's Motion for Provisional Release, 6 June 2005) para 53(5).

[30] See *Haradinaj et al* IT-04-84-T (Judgment, 3 April 2008) Appendix A para 11.

[31] Ibid.

[32] Another important case in this respect is the case against Uhuru Muigai Kenyatta, the President of Kenya, who is facing proceedings before the ICC. On 18 October 2013, Trial Chamber V(b) of the ICC granted Kenyatta conditionally to be excused from continuous presence at his trial, with the exception of the opening and closing statements, hearing when victims present their views and concerns in person, the delivery of the Judgment, and any other attendance ordered by the Chamber. This was motivated by the wish of the Chamber to accommodate the functions of his office as President of Kenya. See *Kenyatta*, ICC-01/09-02/11 (Decision on Defence Request for Conditional Excusal from Continuous Presence at Trial, 18 October 2003). See also *Ruto and Sang* ICC-01/09-01/11 (Reasons for the Decision on Excusal from Presence at Trial under Rule 134*quater*, 18 February 2014).

An important case in this context is the *Šešelj* case. In 2004 the Deputy Registrar of the ICTY decided on the communication privileges of Šešelj at the UNDU and:

> [p]rohibit[ed], unless otherwise authorised by the Commanding Officer of the Detention Unit, all communication between the Accused with person(s) except for his legal counsel (if applicable) and diplomatic and consular representatives and his immediate family, provided that his contact with his family shall be subject to live monitoring under conditions prescribed by the Commanding Officer of the Detention Unit.[33]

However, the accused showed a 'defiant disposition' with respect to this decision when he sent a letter to the Deputy President of his political party, which was published in the press on 21 April 2004, and in which he alleged serious misconduct by officials of the ICTY, including Judges, Prosecutors and staff members.[34] The Deputy Registrar found these allegations to be unfounded and of such a grave nature that they amounted to a serious abuse of his communication privileges, in particular as Šešelj had encouraged that the letter be distributed to the media and to supporters of his political party prior to the Serbian presidential elections campaign that was ongoing at the time.[35] As a result, the Deputy Registrar struck a reasonable balance between Šešelj's rights to communicate or receive visits with that of the ICTY to effectively perform its mandate and functions, and he found that the circumstances of the case continued to require the imposition of measures aimed at avoiding 'potentially deleterious media coverage resulting from unrestricted communication entitlements and visits'.[36]

International Detainees have at times requested permission to be interviewed by media outlets that had contacted them with such requests. The ICTY has established a 'Procedure for Contacts with the Media' pursuant to Rule 64*bis*(A) ICTY ROD which is distributed to International Detainees. Any contact between an International Detainee and a media outlet needs to be requested by the detainee and approved by the Registrar.[37] However, face-to-face contacts are not allowed and other forms of contacts with the media can be prevented if the Registrar has reason to believe that the particular

---

33 *Šešelj* IT-03-67-PT (Restrictions on Vojislav Šešelj's Communication Privileges Extended from 10 May to 13 June 2004, 7 May 2004).

34 Ibid.

35 Ibid.

36 Ibid. In June 2004, the Deputy Registrar rendered a subsequent decision in which he considered 'that there is a strong likelihood that the political party and the supporters of the Accused will seek his further involvement in political activities associated with the forthcoming Serbian presidential elections until the anticipated second round of elections, for example, by issuing a letter of support to his political party and its supporters'. *Šešelj* IT-03-67-PT (Restrictions on Vojislav Šešelj's Communication Privileges Extended from 13 June to 1 July 2004, 9 June 2004). Consequently the above-mentioned restrictions were extended. On 7 November 2014 Trial Chamber III ordered *proprio motu* the provisional release of Šešelj on the basis of compelling humanitarian reasons, *Šešelj* IT-03-67-T (Order on the Provisional Release of the Accused *Proprio Motu*, 7 November 2014).

37 *Karadžić* IT-95-05/18-T (President, Deputy Registrar's Submission Regarding the Accused's Request for Reversal of Limitations of Contact with Journalist: Süddeutsche Zeitung Magazin, 21 August 2013).

contact could disturb the good order of the detention unit or could interfere with the administration of justice.[38]

For instance, in 2013, the German *Süddeutsche Zeitung Magazin* requested a face-to-face interview with Radovan Karadžić. The application of the latter to be granted the right to participate in the interview was rejected by the ICTY Tribunal, and the President, to whom Karadžić had appealed, approved the Decision of the Registrar. The reason given was, inter alia, that 'the risk of potential disclosure of confidential information to a journalist in a direct conversation between a detainee and a journalist – even if inadvertent – is inacceptable'.[39] The President upheld the decision of the Registrar, finding that it was reasonable and in compliance with the relevant legal requirements.[40] In light of the risk at stake for the disclosure of confidential information this decision did not disproportionally curtail any right of the accused as an International Detainee.

3.2 Visits

The right to receive visits from family and friends at regular intervals is an important right of an International Detainee, as it is vital to his well being in the detention unit. This is all the more so as International Detainees are usually detained in a country which is neither their country of origin nor the country in which their family and friends are living. In order to allow the International Detainee to keep in contact with his family the ICCDC and the UNDU and UNDF even allow for conjugal visits in a room specifically designed for this purpose. During visits in this room no supervision will be conducted.[41] In general, other visits by family members and friends are conducted within the sight of the security officers at the Detention Units.[42] However, all visitors must comply with the requirements of the visiting regime of the Host State, as they will have to pass through the national prison in order to reach the detention unit. Such procedure may include personal searches of clothing and X-ray examination prior to entering the detention unit.[43]

3.3 Accommodation, Personal Hygiene, Clothing and Food

Unlike many national detention facilities, the international detention units, in general, do not foresee more than one International Detainee in one cell. It is only in exceptional circumstances or in cases where the Commanding Officer, with the

---

[38] Ibid.

[39] *Karadžić* IT-95-05/18-T (Decision on Request for Reversal of Limitations of Contact with Journalist: Süddeutsche Zeitung Magazin, 7 October 2013) para 10.

[40] Ibid., para 17.

[41] Abels (n 2) 573. Abels quotes from an interview with the Commanding Officer of the UNDU who states that '[o]ne of the issues for having people a long way from their home is maintaining family and relationships which makes somebody psychologically stronger'.

[42] Ibid. See also Reg 100 ICC ROC.

[43] Rule 61(1) ICTR ROD; Rule 61(C) ICTY ROD. See also Reg 100(3) ICC ROC. On the issue of financial assistance to family members of the International Detainee, see Abels (n 2) 577–8 (for ICTY), 590–93 (for ICTR), 632–51 (for ICC).

approval of the Registrar, considers that there are advantages to the sharing of accommodation that such a measure can be applied.[44] Further, the detention unit must meet, at all times, all requirements of health and hygiene with regard to climatic conditions, lighting, heating and ventilation.[45] This is closely related to the issue of personal hygiene of the International Detainees. While it is the primary responsibility of the staff of the respective detention unit to ensure that all requirements of health and hygiene are fulfilled, it is for the detainee himself to ensure that his cell is kept clean and tidy at all times.[46] In addition, each International Detainee must keep himself clean and will be provided with the necessary toilet articles.[47] In contrast to many national prisons, International Detainees may wear their own civilian clothing.[48]

A very important aspect of the daily life of the International Detainees is their food. Taking into account their religious beliefs, their age and their health status, the respective ROD provide that their food shall satisfy the standards of dietetics and modern hygiene, and they shall take into consideration the above-mentioned issues as well as any cultural requirements.[49] In addition, International Detainees can use the kitchen facilities in the respective detention units, which also serve as an important place to meet with the other detainees, regardless of their nationality and ethnicity. Furthermore, they can enjoy card games together in the meeting room.

3.4 Medical Services

The provision of health care to International Detainees is of utmost importance both to the detainee and to the conduct of his criminal proceedings. Many decisions and orders have been rendered with respect to the fitness of the detainee to stand trial, his inability to attend proceedings for medical reasons, and surgery and dental treatment. In general International Detainees have the right to consult with a doctor or dentist of their own choice and at their own expense.[50] If a Detainee requires specialist or in-patient treatment, he will be treated within the host prison or transferred to a civil hospital of the Host State.[51] Of particular importance were cases in which the International Detainee requested to be provisionally released to another country in order to receive medical treatment. Such requests have at times been granted. For instance, Pavle Strugar requested provisional release in order to undergo surgery for a total hip prosthesis implantation in the Republic of Montenegro.[52] At first the Appeals Chamber denied this request and found that Strugar had not shown that the medical aid he

44 Rule 14 ICTR ROD; Rule 17 ICTY ROD; Reg 105(3) ICC ROC.

45 Rule 16 ICTR ROD; Rule 19 ICTY ROD. See also Reg 103(1) ICC ROC.

46 Rule 18 ICTR ROD; Rule 21 ICTY ROD.

47 Rule 20 ICTR ROD; Rule 22 ICTY ROD; Reg 197 ICC ROR.

48 Rule 21 ICTR ROD; Rule 24 ICTY ROD; Reg 198 ICC ROR.

49 Rule 23 ICTR ROD; Rule 26 ICTY ROD; Reg 199 ICC ROR.

50 Rule 27 ICTR ROD; Rule 30 ICTY ROD; Reg 157 ICC ROR.

51 Rule 29 ICTR ROD; Rule 32 ICTY ROD; Reg 154(2) ICC ROR.

52 *Strugar* IT-01-42-A (Request for Providing Medical Aid in the Republic of Montenegro in Detention Conditions, 14 November 2005).

needed could not be adequately provided in health institutions in the Netherlands.[53] Shortly thereafter, however, Strugar filed another request for provisional release based on medical reasons, and this time it was granted, as he no longer asked that the time spent on provisional release be credited as time spent in custody.[54] The most well-known example in which such a request had been rejected by a Chamber of the ICTY was in the *Milošević* case in which the accused had sought to be transferred to Russia for proper medical treatment.[55] Here the request was rejected by the competent Trial Chamber for essentially two reasons. First, the Chamber held that Milošević's assigned counsel had not made a real attempt to demonstrate that his medical needs could not be met in the Netherlands, stating that a request for provisional release could not be granted unless such a showing was made.[56] The Trial Chamber further held that in case the accused wanted to be treated by non-Dutch specialists, they could come to the Netherlands to treat him.[57] Second, the Trial Chamber found that Milošević, at the time of the decision, was facing the possibility of life imprisonment if he was convicted. In light of this consideration, it held that notwithstanding the guarantees of the Russian Federation to send him back to The Hague after the medical treatment, it was not satisfied that, if provisionally released, he would indeed return for the continuation of his trial.[58] Only a few weeks later, on 11 March 2006, Milošević was found dead in his cell in the UNDU.

3.5 Spiritual Welfare

As part of the psychological well being of an International Detainee, a qualified representative of each religion or system of beliefs held by any detainee is to be appointed (at the ICTR and ICTY: subject to approval by the Bureau).[59] Access to such an approved representative cannot be refused to any International Detainee.[60] Similarly, detainees are allowed, so far as is practicable, to satisfy the needs of their spiritual and

---

[53] *Strugar* IT-01-42-A (Decision on 'Defence Motion: Request for Providing Medical Aid in the Republic of Montenegro in Detention Conditions', 8 December 2005).

[54] *Strugar* IT-01-42-A (Decision on 'Defence Motion: Defence Request for Provisional Release for Providing Medical Aid in the Republic of Montenegro', 16 December 2005). On 12 January 2006, the Appeals Chamber filed the Corrigendum to 'Decision on "Defence Motion: Defence Request for Provisional Release for Providing Medical Aid in the Republic of Montenegro"'.

[55] *Milošević* IT-02-54-T (Decision on Assigned Counsel Request for Provisional Release, 23 February 2006).

[56] Ibid., para 17.

[57] Ibid.

[58] Ibid., para 18.

[59] Rule 67 ICTR ROD. The Bureau is a body that comprises the President, Vice-President and the Presiding Judges of the Trial Chambers established pursuant to Rule 23 ICTR RPE. At the ICTY, any minister or spiritual adviser has to be accredited by the Registrar, Rule 66(A) ICTY ROD. See also Reg 102 ICC ROC.

[60] Rule 68 ICTR ROD. This right is subject only to any restrictions or supervision as the Commanding Officer, in consultation with the Registrar, may deem necessary. Those restrictions may include personal searches of clothing and X-ray examination of possessions on entry to the detention facility. Rule 61 ICTR ROD. See also Rule 67 ICTY ROD and Reg 100(3) ICC ROC.

moral life by attending services or meetings held in the detention unit and by possessing the necessary books or literature.[61]

3.6 Recreational Activities

In general, each International Detainee is allowed to procure at his own expense books, newspapers and other means of occupation as long as they are compatible with the good order of the respective detention unit.[62] In addition, International Detainees are entitled to follow the news by radio and television broadcasts.[63] This right, however, is not unrestricted. If the Prosecutor believes that the interests of justice would not be served if a particular International Detainee had unrestricted access to the news, or that such unrestricted access could prejudice the outcome of proceedings, he can request that the Registrar, or in cases of urgency, the Commanding Officer, to restrict such access.[64] International Detainees are also entitled to physical exercise and sports activities, including remedial or therapeutic treatment.[65]

3.7 Personal Possessions of Detainees

Unless the clothing or any other personal item in the International Detainee's possession constitutes a threat to the security or the good order of the detention unit or the host prison, or to the health or safety of any person therein, it can remain in the possession of the detainee for his own use.[66] Any item that is taken away from the International Detainee is to be put in an inventory which is to be signed by the detainee.[67] If an item comes from the outside, for instance because it was introduced by a visitor, separate security controls can be implemented by the respective detention unit. Upon release of the International Detainee from the detention unit, after having been acquitted or finally convicted, all articles and money which belong to him shall be returned.[68]

4. MAINTENANCE OF SECURITY IN THE DETENTION UNITS

One of the most important sections of the respective provisions regulating the management of the detention units deals with the maintenance of the security. The status of the International Detainees, the character of the serious violations of international humanitarian law with which they are charged as well as the severe sentences that can be meted out by the international judges may contribute to a possible situation in which the security of the detention unit is endangered. It is therefore of

---

61 Rule 69 ICTR ROD; Rule 68(B) ICTY ROD; Reg 102 ICC ROC and Reg 153 ICC ROR.
62 Rule 72 ICTR ROD; Rule 71 ICTY ROD; Reg 99(1)(c) ICC ROC.
63 Rule 73 ICTR ROD; Rule 72(A) ICTY ROD; Reg 99(1)(d) ICC ROC.
64 Rule 74 ICTR ROD. See also Rule 73 ICTY ROD; Reg 99(1)(d) ICC ROC.
65 Rule 24 ICTR ROD; Rules 27–29 ICTY ROD; Reg 99(1)(f)–(g) ICC ROC.
66 Rule 76 ICTR ROD; Rule 74(A) ICTY ROD; Reg 99(1)(b) ICC ROC.
67 Rules 11–12, 76 ICTR ROD; Rules 13–14, 74(B) ICTY ROD.
68 Rule 81 ICTR ROD; Rule 79 ICTY ROD.

utmost importance to give the respective Registrars and Commanding Officers the legal tools to reinstate law and order once these have been breached.

4.1 Discipline: Segregation, Isolation and Other Means to Maintain Security

Of particular importance for the legal position of International Detainees are the applicable rules on discipline. These provisions are characterised by their balancing between the rights of International Detainees and their duties vis-à-vis the detention unit and the Tribunal. For instance, the detainee has the right to be heard on the subject of any (disciplinary) offence which he is alleged to have committed.[69] On the other hand an International Detainee has the duty to comply with the applicable ROD, and any violation of these rules can be punished.[70] An important non-punitive measure to ensure discipline is the right of the Registrar, either upon request by the Prosecutor or on his own initiative, to order that an International Detainee be segregated from all or some of the other detainees.[71] Such measures, however, can only be imposed in order to avoid any potential conflict in the detention unit or danger to the detainee in question.[72] For example, in the *Čelebići* case, segregation had been imposed on two co-accused in the UNDU. This was not done in order to prevent them from generally communicating with each other in relation to their case. However, the staff of the Detention Unit had become aware that they had exchanged notes and that they hid them in an area in order to circumvent any monitoring by the staff of the UNDU.[73] Similarly, in the *Katanga and Chui* case before the ICC, the Prosecution requested the segregation of both accused;

> because it had reasonable grounds to believe that such contact could prejudice or otherwise affect the outcome of the proceedings against each of the Detainees, adversely impact ongoing or further investigations, harm victims or witnesses or any other person, or be used by the Detainees to breach an order for non-disclosure made by a Judge.[74]

The Single Judge who had to decide on the Prosecution's request considered that this would amount to a de facto segregation of Mathieu Ngudjolo Chui from all other detainees, and that the accused had the right pursuant to Article 67(1) ICCSt to discuss

---

[69] Rule 37 ICTR ROD; Rule 41(iv) ICTY ROD; Reg 95(2) ICC ROC.

[70] Rule 36 ICTR ROD. Such punishment should, in general, be limited to disciplinary measures or, in more severe cases, fines. It is hardly conceivable that violations of the Detention Rules can lead to a sentence of imprisonment. See also Rule 41 ICTY ROD. See also Regulations for the Establishment of a Disciplinary Procedure for Detainees, (IT/97), April 1995. For the ICC see Regs 207–208 ICC ROR.

[71] Rule 38 ICTR ROD. This can only be done after having sought medical advice. See also Rule 42(A) ICTY ROD; Reg 209 ICC ROR.

[72] Rule 38 ICTR ROD; Rule 42(B) ICTY ROD; Reg 201 ICC ROR. For temporary segregation see Reg 209 ICC ROR.

[73] *Delalić et al* IT-96-21-T (Decision of the President on the Prosecutor's Motion for the Production of Notes Exchanged Between Zejnil Delalić and Zdravko Mucić, 11 November 1996) para 25.

[74] *Katanga et al* ICC-01/04-01/07 (Decision revoking the prohibition of contact and communication between Germain Katanga and Mathieu Ngudjolo Chui, 13 March 2008) 7.

the evidence on which the Prosecution intended to rely in order to properly prepare his defence.[75] As the Judge found the allegations of the Prosecution merely speculative, she did not see a need to address the proportionality requirement which would have been necessary for a restriction of the rights of the International Detainees under the detention regime.[76]

It is important to stress that in cases where an International Detainee has requested to be segregated from all or some of the other detainees,[77] the Commanding Officer has to consult with the medical officer to determine whether such segregation would be injurious to the mental or physical health of the detainee, in which case it shall not be ordered.[78] Once segregation has been ordered, the Commanding Officer has to review it at least once a week and report to the Registrar thereon.[79]

A specific situation arose when Jelena Rasić, a former case manager in the *Lukić and Lukić* case, was detained in the UNDU after having pleaded guilty to several charges of contempt.[80] As she was the only female International Detainee at the time in the UNDU, she felt that she had insufficient interactions with the other inmates, and she complained about what she considered to be de facto solitary confinement.[81] As a consequence, she requested provisional release, arguing that her limited communications with some of the male International Detainees for two hours or less per day were insufficient for her well being.[82] The Trial Chamber granted her request to be provisionally released, and her detention situation was later taken into consideration when meting out her sentence.[83]

Another non-punitive measure in particularly severe cases, such as in order to prevent an International Detainee from inflicting injury on any other detainee, is the Commanding Officer's order that a detainee be confined to the isolation unit.[84] It must be noted that, due to the severity of the measure, no International Detainee shall be kept in the isolation unit for more than seven consecutive days. In practice, however, detention in the isolation unit can be significantly longer than seven days. If the

---

75 Ibid., 10.

76 Ibid., 9, 13.

77 While an International Detainee can request to be segregated from other detainees (see, for instance, Rule 40 ICTR ROD), there is no right of an International Detainee to request the segregation of other detainees. *Šešelj* IT-03-67-PT (Decision on Šešelj's Request that the ICTY President Order that Honourable Serbs in Detention and those who have Arranged a Plea Bargain with the Prosecution and Agreed to Give False Testimony be Segregated in the Detention Unit and Prevented from Being Able to Contact Each Other, 15 June 2006). Also, in general, International Detainees who are accused of the same or similar crimes are not per se segregated from each other.

78 Rule 40 ICTR ROD; see also Rule 43(A) ICTY ROD; Reg 201(1) ICC ROR.

79 Rule 41 ICTR ROD. See also Rule 43(D) ICTY ROD; Regulation 201(4) ICC ROR.

80 *Rasić* IT-98-32/1-R77.2 (Written Reasons for Oral Sentencing Judgment, delivered orally 7 February 2012, filed 6 March 2012).

81 *Rasić* IT-98-32/1-R77.2-A (Judgment, 16 November 2012) para 39.

82 Ibid.

83 Ibid., paras 30, 39.

84 Rule 43(b) ICTR ROD. Such a measure can also be imposed by order of the Registrar, acting in consultation with the President, and as a punishment pursuant to Rule 36 ICTR ROD. See also Rule 45(A)(ii) ICTY ROD; Reg 212 ICC ROR.

Commanding Officer decides that further isolation is necessary, the isolation can be ordered to continue for a further period not to exceed seven days, provided that the medical officer has confirmed the physical and mental fitness of the detainee.[85] The relevant rule does not provide for any limit of isolation. To the contrary, it states that '[e]ach and every extension of use of the isolation unit shall be subject to the same procedure'.[86] In light of the serious character of an order to go to the isolation unit it is necessary that any such assignment must be subject to the general principles limiting any administrative decision of the Registrar and the Commanding Officer.[87] In particular it is important to note that no isolation should be ordered if the relevant situation could be solved by a less severe measure or punishment. Further, it must be stressed that the International Detainee's right to make a complaint at any time to the Commanding Officer and, if necessary, ultimately to the President applies of course as well to complaints against being placed in isolation.[88]

4.2 Disturbances and Suspension of the Rules of Detention

While the outer security of the detention units is guaranteed by the law enforcement authorities of the respective Host State, the proper functioning of the good order within the detention units of the ICTR and the ICTY is the duty of the Commanding Officer, the Registrar and the relevant staff members working in the units. If the Commanding Officer opines that a situation carries a risk that would threaten the security and good order of the detention unit, he can contact the head of the host prison and request the immediate assistance of the authorities of the Host State in order to maintain control within the detention unit.[89] While the authorities of the Host State, in general, should not interfere within the detention unit, this provision takes due account of the fact that any disturbance within a detention unit may get out of hand and thus threaten the security and good order of the Host State. If there is such danger of disturbances occurring within a detention unit, the Commanding Officer or the head of the host prison, as appropriate, can suspend the ROD for a maximum of two days.[90] Again, in accordance with the general principle that the discretion to order administrative measures is not unfettered, such suspension of the Rules can only be imposed if no

---

[85] Rule 47 ICTR ROD; Rule 49 ICTY ROD; Reg 212(5) ICC ROR.

[86] Rule 47 ICTR ROD; Rule 49 ICTY ROD; Reg 212(6) ICC ROR.

[87] Pursuant to ICTY jurisprudence, a decision of the Registrar can be quashed if he has: (1) failed to comply with the relevant legal requirements; (2) failed to observe basic rules of natural justice or to act with procedural fairness toward the accused; (3) taken into account irrelevant material or failed to take into account relevant material; or (4) has reached a conclusion that no reasonable person could have reached on the material before him (*Šešelj* IT-03-67-PT (Decision on Vojislav Šešelj's Request for Review of Registrar's Decision of 10 September 2009, 21 October 2009) para 19. As to the relevant procedure before the ICC see Abels (n 2) 322.

[88] See Rules 82–83 ICTR ROD; Rules 80–81 ICTY ROD; Reg 216*bis*–222 ICC ROR.

[89] Rule 54 ICTR ROD; Rule 56 ICTY ROD; Reg 96 ICC ROC.

[90] Rule 55 ICTR ROD. Such suspension has to be reported immediately to the Registrar. Subsequently the President, acting in consultation with the Bureau, must consult with the relevant authorities of the Host State and take such action 'as may be seen fit at the time'. See also Rule 57 ICTY ROD and Reg 96(2) ICC ROC.

other, less severe measures would be effective. Furthermore, during the period in which the ROD are suspended the International Detainees are not without rights, and every discretionary decision has to fulfil the applicable standard of proportionality. Thus, even if the ROD are not directly applicable during that time, any measure imposed on International Detainees must be compatible with applicable human rights law. If necessary, International Detainees must also be able to retroactively file a complaint on the basis of measures taken against them during this time once the suspension of the ROD is terminated. In addition, the severity of the suspension of the ROD requires that as soon as the underlying reason for its imposition has fallen away, the suspension shall be terminated and the ROD shall be applicable as previously.

Similarly, before the ICC, the Chief Custody Officer may take such actions in order to ensure the safety of the detainees and staff, and the security of the detention facility.[91]

4.3 Instruments of Restraint and the Use of Force; Transport of Detainee

As a general rule, International Detainees should not be handcuffed, either in the respective detention unit or in the tribunals and courts. Therefore, handcuffs or other instruments of restraint can only be used in specific, exceptional circumstances such as a precautionary measure against escape during transfer from the detention unit to any other place; on medical grounds by direction and under the supervision of the medical officer and to prevent an International Detainee from self-injury, injury to others or to prevent serious damage to property.[92] If used, such instruments of restraint must be removed as soon as possible.[93] While these provisions on the use of instruments of restraint regulate the use of passive force vis-à-vis an International Detainee, the applicable law of detention also grants the staff of a detention unit the right to use active force. This, however, is only possible in very specific circumstances, namely in self-defence against an International Detainee or in cases of an attempted escape or active or passive resistance to an order.[94] Also, staff must not use more force than is strictly necessary to achieve the desired result, and the incident must be immediately reported to the Commanding Officer who shall provide a report to the Registrar.[95] While the use of force appears to be easily understandable when it comes to the prevention of escape, it is less obvious as a measure against 'active or passive resistance of an order'.[96] In such situations, it is important that force shall only be used if it is not disproportionate to both the order and the nature of the resistance to it. As against any other administrative decision which impacts on the rights of an International Detainee, the latter has the right to file a complaint against the use of force by a staff member of the detention unit. In addition, each International Detainee shall have

---

91 Reg 96(1) ICC ROC.

92 Rule 48 ICTR ROD. The restrained detainee shall be kept under constant and adequate supervision (Rule 50 ICTR ROD). See also Rule 50 ICTY ROD; Reg 203(2) ICC ROR.

93 Rule 49 ICTR ROD; Rule 51 ICTY ROD; Reg 203 ICC ROR.

94 Rule 51 ICTR ROD; Rule 53 ICTY ROD; Reg 204 ICC ROR.

95 Rule 51 ICTR ROD; Rule 53 ICTY ROD; Reg 204(1) ICC ROR.

96 Rule 51 ICTR ROD; Rule 53(A)(ii)(b) ICTY ROD; Reg 204(2)(b)(ii) ICC ROR.

the right to be examined by the medical officer, in the absence of any non-medical staff.[97] The result of this examination as well as any relevant statement of the International Detainee shall be made available to the detainee, the Commanding Officer, the Registrar, the Prosecutor and the President.[98]

5. COMPLAINTS

One of the most important rights of International Detainees of the ICC, ICTR and ICTY is their right to make, at any time, a complaint to the Commanding Officer or his representative.[99] The respective ROD do not explicitly provide for any time period within which the Commanding Officer has to respond to the complaint. However, they do provide for a deadline within which every complaint to the Registrar shall be dealt with, namely 'promptly and (…) within a reasonable period of time'.[100] The same principle should apply with respect to the response by the Commanding Officer. In particular, the more the decision against which the complaint is made affects the rights of the International Detainee, the sooner, it is suggested, the Commanding Officer should respond to it. For instance, if an International Detainee has been confined to the Isolation Unit and has filed a complaint against this assignment, the Commanding Officer or his representative should deal with it without undue delay, bearing in mind the seriousness of the decision. If the detainee is not satisfied with the response of the Commanding Officer, he has the right to file a written complaint to the Registrar, who shall forward it to the President.[101] This ensures that the right to complain against

---

[97] Rule 52 ICTR ROD; Rule 54(A) ICTY ROD; Reg 204(4) ICC ROR.

[98] Rule 52 ICTR ROD; Rule 54(B) ICTY ROD; Reg 204(5) ICC ROR.

[99] Rule 82 ICTR ROD; Rule 80 ICTY ROD. This provision further states that each International Detainee on admission should be provided in a language which he understands the Regulations for the Establishment of a Complaints Procedure for Detainees. See also Reg 106 ICC ROC.

[100] Rule 86 ICTR ROD; Rule 84 ICTY ROD: 'without undue delay'. Reg 219(1) ICC ROR: 'where possible (…) within seven calendar days (…) and in any event, no more than 14 calendar days of the date of receipt'. See also Abels (n 2) 290–92.

[101] Rule 83 ICTR ROD. The complaint to the Registrar, and ultimately to the President, shall be without any censorship (ibid); Rule 81 ICTY ROD. This procedure is further developed in the Regulations for the Establishment of a Complaints Procedure for Detainees (IT/96) (ICTY) which sets out, for instance, the division of responsibilities between the Registrar and the President. An International Detainee may make a formal complaint concerning the conditions of his detention to the Registrar at any time, whether or not such complaint has already been raised with the Commanding Officer, provided that not more than two weeks have elapsed since the incident. The Registrar shall examine the substance of the complaint and determine whether it should be dealt with by the Registrar, being a complaint about an administrative matter or a matter of general concern, or whether it relates to an alleged breach of the rights of the individual detainee, in which case it shall be referred to the President for consideration. In any event the Registrar shall forward a copy of each and every complaint to the President. The Registrar or the President shall investigate the complaint promptly and efficiently and shall seek the views of all relevant persons or bodies, including the Commanding Officer. The detainee shall be permitted to communicate freely and without censorship on the matter with the

matters of detention are not limited to a non-judicative, exclusively administrative procedure. In light of the seriousness of the consequences that decisions against detainees may have, it is imperative that, if necessary, a judicial organ of the international court or tribunal takes the final decision on the issue. This is all the more so as administrative decisions against International Detainees may have a direct impact on the ability of the detainee to conduct his own defence or to assist his counsel and follow the proceedings. Whenever the fair trial rights of the International Detainee are influenced and possibly thwarted, it is of crucial importance that, if necessary, Judges decide on the issue in question.[102] This follows, for instance, from Article 20 ICTYSt which provides that a Trial Chamber 'shall ensure that a trial is fair and expeditious and that proceedings are conducted in accordance with the rules of procedure and evidence, with full respect for the rights of the accused'. Pursuant to the jurisprudence of the ICTY, a Trial Chamber cannot appropriate the power to review a decision of the Registrar if this is specifically conferred on the President of the ICTY. However, in light of a Trial Chamber's statutory obligation to ensure that the trial of the accused is fair, it is the Trial Chamber that has the authority to review a Registrar's decision. In this respect, the President of the ICTY has held that 'review of a decision by the Registrar on allocation of funds in terms of its impact upon the right of an accused to "equality of arms" with the Prosecution lies with the relevant Chamber'.[103] While this decision did not explicitly deal with a detention-related issue, the same principle applies in such a scenario in case the principle of 'equality of arms' is on the line. However, the International Detainee has first to exhaust all available remedies.[104]

Registrar during this period and the Registrar shall, where appropriate, pass all such communications to the President without delay. If the complaint is justified, action to rectify it shall be taken within that two-week period if possible and the detainee advised accordingly.

If the Registrar or the President finds the complaint to be unfounded, the Registrar shall notify the detainee in writing, giving reasons for rejection of the complaint. Rejection of a complaint by the Registrar or the President does not bar the detainee from raising such complaint again. In such cases, the Registrar, in consultation with the President, may reject the complaint without further enquiry if it reveals no additional matters not already considered. These Regulations only apply to the ICTY.

[102] See, for instance, *Šešelj* IT-03-67-PT (Decision on Vojislav Šešelj's Request for Review of Registrar's Decision of 10 September 2009, 21 October 2009) para 19.

[103] *Stanišić and Simatović* IT-03-69-T (Decision on Stanišić Defence Motion for Equality of Arms and Immediate Suspension of the Trial and on Association of Defence Counsel (ADC-ICTY) Motion for Leave to Appear as *Amicus Curiae*, 10 March 2011) para 14.

[104] Ibid., para 14. Pursuant to Reg 106 ICC ROC, '[a] detained person shall have the right to file a complaint against any administrative decision or order or with regard to any other matter concerning his or her detention'. More specifically, a detained person can make an oral or written complaint on any matter concerning his or her detention to the Chief Custody Officer at any time and he or she may be represented by their counsel. Reg 217(1)&(6) ICC ROR. During the investigation of a complaint, the International Detainee has the right to freely communicate with the Chief Custody Officer (Reg 218(2) ICC ROR). Where possible, the complaint shall be dealt with within seven calendar days of its receipt and, in any event, no more than 14 calendar days of the date of receipt (Reg 219(1) ICC ROR). Similarly, if a complaint is deemed to be justified, action to rectify the matter shall be taken, if possible, within 14 days (Reg 219(3) ICC ROR). If the complaint is found to be unjustified, the International Detainee and counsel shall be notified in writing, with reasons for the decision (Reg 219(5) ICC ROR). The International

In this context, it is important to note that each International Detainee has the right to freely communicate with the competent inspecting authority.[105] The ICRC has the right to inspect the respective Detention Units.[106] During such inspections an International Detainee shall have the right to talk to the inspector.[107]

6. PROTECTION OF OTHER SPECIFIC RIGHTS OF INTERNATIONAL DETAINEES

Over the past years, the jurisprudence of the international tribunals has had the opportunity to adjudicate on further rights of International Detainees which are not explicitly mentioned in the respective ROD. For instance, an International Detainee before the ICTY had requested the Appeals Chamber to allow him to extend his identity card. In order to pursue this request he had to ask the Appeals Chamber to grant him leave to physically go to the embassy of his home country in The Hague and to apply for it there.[108] However, the Netherlands, who, like Serbia, had been invited to make submissions on this request, stated that granting such a custodial visit to the embassy would present 'very serious challenges to public order and national security', not the least because the Host State feared an 'unwanted precedent' in relation to other detainees of other international courts and tribunals in The Hague.[109] The Appeals

---

Detainee has the possibility to address the Registrar with respect to a decision of the Chief Custody Officer, and the Presidency in relation to a decision of the Registrar (Regs 220–221 ICC ROR).

[105] Rule 84 ICTR ROD; Rule 82 ICTY ROD. At the ICC, the Presidency can at any time appoint a Judge to inspect the detention centre and to report on its conditions. Further, there shall be regular and unannounced visits by an independent inspecting authority (Reg 94(1), (2) ICC ROC).

[106] Since 1995, the ICRC has been doing annual inspections of the UNDU. During these inspections it holds, inter alia, individual meetings with ICTY International Detainees. See ICTY, 'ICRC completes annual inspection of Detention Unit' (*ICTY*, 17 December 2012) <www.icty.org/sid/11177> accessed 7 May 2014.

[107] Rule 84 ICTR ROD. See also Rule 82 ICTY ROD. Such meetings between International Detainees and the inspector shall be out of the sight and hearing of the staff of the respective detention unit (ibid). None of its content should be disclosed to the Commanding Officer or any other representative of the international court or tribunal, unless this is the wish of the International Detainee. Also, an International Detainee may at any time during an inspection of the detention unit by inspectors appointed by the Tribunal raise a complaint concerning the conditions of his detention, see Regulations for the Establishment of a Complaints Procedure for Detainees (IT/96) (ICTY). With respect to inspections by the ICRC, however, it shall be noted that ICRC staff members enjoy the right not to testify: 'the right to non-disclosure of information relating to the ICRC's activities in the possession of its employees in judicial proceedings is necessary for the effective discharge by the ICRC of its mandate'. *Simić et al* IT-95-9 (Decision on the Prosecution Motion Under Rule 73 for a Ruling Concerning the Testimony of a Witness, 27 July 1999) para 73. See also Reg 94 ICC ROC.

[108] *Popović et al* IT-05-88-A (Public Redacted Version of 22 July 2011 Decision on Vinko Pandurević's Motion for Temporary Alteration of the Conditions of his Detention, 10 November 2011).

[109] Ibid., 2.

Chamber dismissed the request and recalled that matters relating to the rights of International Detainees and conditions of their detention are regulated by the ROD and fall primarily under the authority of the ICTY Registrar and the ICTY President.[110]

Another important right that an International Detainee shall be generally allowed to exercise is the right to vote, that is to participate as a voter in elections in his home country. An International Detainee who has not been finally convicted will in general retain his right to vote in his national elections, in accordance with the respective national election provisions. Thus, as long as the exercise of this right does not conflict with the interests of the administration of justice and the security and good order of the respective detention unit, the international courts and tribunals should enable the detainee to exercise his right to vote.[111] The fact that many International Detainees have been charged with offences which are related to their political position within the State system does not change this. An International Detainee who has not been finally convicted must be presumed to be innocent. And an innocent person must be guaranteed the right to vote.

A more complex issue is the question whether an International Detainee should be allowed to actively take part in political activities in his home country. This issue was given particular attention in the case against Ramush Haradinaj, who, at the time of his arrest, was Prime Minister in Kosovo.[112]

7. COOPERATION OF INTERNATIONAL DETAINEES WITH THEIR COUNSEL

Part of an International Detainee's right to have the opportunity to entertain contacts with the outside world is his or her entitlement to communicate freely with his legal representative.[113] At the ICTY, as a concession to the detention regime, however, visits of the legal representative must be pre-arranged with the Commanding Officer.[114] Furthermore, in general, the International Detainee at the ICTY can address his or her correspondence to counsel without interference. However, where the Commanding Officer or the Registrar has reasonable grounds for believing that this privilege is being used in order to, inter alia, arrange escape or obstruct justice, they can interfere in the correspondence and, for instance, give it to the Registrar who can request counsel to open the correspondence in his presence.[115] Similarly, the lawyer-client privilege is not guaranteed without exceptions when it comes to telephone contacts between an International Detainee and his counsel. Pursuant to Rule 65 ICTY ROD, they can be recorded and monitored. Again, such monitoring can only be ordered if the Registrar

---

[110] Ibid., 4.

[111] For jurisprudence of the European Court on Human Rights on the right to vote of detainees see, for instance *Soyler v Turkey* App no 29411/07 (ECtHR, 17 September 2013).

[112] *Haradinaj et al* IT-04-84-T (Judgment, 4 April 2008).

[113] See Rule 65(A) ICTY ROD; Article 67(1)(b) ICCSt; Rule 73(1) ICC RPE; Reg 151 ICC ROR and Reg 97(1) ICC ROC.

[114] Rules 61, 65(D) ICTY ROD.

[115] See Abels (n 2) 678. For the situation at the ICTR see ibid., 691–706.

has reasonable grounds to believe that the privilege is being abused in an attempt to, for instance, interfere with or intimidate witnesses or interfere with the administration of justice.[116] Pursuant to the same Rule, the International Detainee can request the President to reverse any such decision by the Registrar. While such a requirement is not included in the ROD, it is important to note that any such request should be dealt with expeditiously so that the negative effect on the preparation of the International Detainee's defence is reduced to a minimum. Furthermore, the security requirements regarding the entry to the Detention Unit apply to legal counsel, too.[117]

The legal regime applicable to the cooperation between International Detainees and their counsel before the ICC is of an essentially similar nature.[118]

8. CONCLUSION

In light of the foregoing, it can be summarised that the current detention regimes in these three international courts and tribunals largely protect the legal position of International Detainees and respect and guarantee their rights while being detained during their legal proceedings. The fact that all three detention units are far away from the country of origin of the International Detainees constitutes a systemic hardship for them. However, as the above-mentioned analysis has shown, the applicable rules and regulations, in general, manage to alleviate this hardship to the extent possible. In fact, the proper treatment of the International Detainees in the Detention Rules may cause perceptions of preferential treatment and double standards as detainees of the ICTR, the ICTY and the ICC are detained in accordance with legal standards which may be higher than those standards governing national detention regimes in which lower-ranking accused are detained. However, this almost inevitable mismatch can never be a reason for curtailing the rights of an International Detainee to be detained in accordance with the applicable international standards.

116 Rule 65(B) ICTY ROD.

117 Rule 61 ICTY ROD. For instance, when suspicions arose that some of Slobodan Milošević's legal associates were misusing the lawyer-client privilege by smuggling material in and out of the UNDU, additional security measures included the searching of these legal associates. See Abels (n 2) 683–4.

118 See Abels (n 2) 713–15.

2. Provisional release from international remand detention

Andrew Trotter

1. INTRODUCTION

Provisional release is the mechanism by which a defendant in detention for the purposes of international criminal proceedings may be released for a particular period and sometimes for a particular purpose. It loosely corresponds with bail in Anglo-Saxon criminal systems, but fulfils a slightly different role in internationalized jurisdictions, where release is less common. At the IMTN the option of release was not available.[1] International trials have come a long way since then, as exhibited by the advent of the right against self-incrimination and the abolition of the death penalty, among other developments in procedural fairness.[2]

On the establishment of the ICTR and ICTY provision was made for provisional release in exceptional circumstances only. In the early days of the tribunal it was openly regarded as an exception to the 'preventative detention' of accused prior to their sentence.[3] It was generally utilized to allow the temporary release of defendants when their severe illness or other compassionate circumstances required. The requirement for exceptional circumstances was later removed, and as other UN-assisted tribunals and the ICC have been established the role of provisional release has taken on a form more similar to bail in domestic jurisdictions. There have, however, been some important limitations on that proposition. Many of those limitations are dictated by the exceptional circumstances under which international tribunals operate. Others cannot so easily mobilize that defence and have been the subject of ongoing criticism and reform.

Some tribunals, despite having produced considerable jurisprudence on the matter, are yet to grant provisional release to a defendant. The ICTY has granted provisional release on several occasions. However, no defendant against whom proceedings are active has yet been released at the ICTR, SCSL, ECCC (where Ieng Thirith was granted release only once declared unfit to stand trial), STL (where trials are proceeding in absentia) or ICC (where the release of Bemba Gombo was reversed because no suitable Host State had been found). Naturally, therefore, the most developed jurisprudence on the matter emanates from the ICTY. Most recently the ICC

[1] M. Fairlie, 'The Precedent of Pretrial Release at the ICTY: A Road Better Left Less Travelled' (2010) 33 *Fordham International Law Journal* 1101, 1117.

[2] S. Zappalà, *Human Rights in International Criminal Proceedings* (Oxford University Press 2003) 21.

[3] *Blaskić* IT-95-14-T (Rejection Provisional Release, 25 April 1996) 4.

has signed an agreement with Belgium to facilitate the provisional release of ICC accused persons.[4] What practical effect this will have is yet to be seen.

This chapter commences by examining the key contextual considerations against which pre-conviction detention in international trials must be considered: the characteristic delay and the tension between the presumption of innocence and the need to secure convictions. Section 3 then details the notable differences in the legal criteria, practice and procedure at the various internationalized jurisdictions. Section 4 explores the two common legal criteria – risk of flight and dangers associated with release – in more detail, and then in Section 4.3 examines other notable requirements or criteria that have found their way into the formulation from time to time. Finally, Section 5 conducts a comparison with the position in domestic jurisdictions.

2. CONTEXTUAL CONSIDERATIONS

The detention of accused persons before international tribunals before their conviction may conflict with a number of internationally recognized human rights. Most obviously, the legitimate application of criminal justice requires that the accused be presumed innocent until proven guilty.[5] Additionally, while presumed innocent defendants have a prima facie right to liberty. It is only as an exception to that right that a person may be detained.[6] Detention has therefore been considered a last resort by the ECtHR and is justified only for as long as it remains appropriate for the administration of criminal justice.[7] The provisions of the ICCPR and ECHR entitling the detainee to a prompt trial[8] operate 'essentially to require his provisional release once his continuing detention ceases to be reasonable'.[9] The jurisprudence of the ECtHR suggests that that is a measure that is inextricably tied up with the presumption of innocence: the question being whether it has 'imposed a greater sacrifice than could, in the circumstances of the case, reasonably be expected of a person presumed to be innocent'.[10]

---

4 ICC, 'Press Release, Belgium and ICC sign agreement on interim release of detainees' (10 April 2014).

5 Art. 14(2) ICCPR; Art. 6(2) ECHR; Art. 8(2) AmCHR; Art. 7(2) ACHPR.

6 Art. 5(1)(c) ECHR.

7 Eg *Jablonski v Poland* App no 33492/96 (ECtHR, 20 December 2000) para 84; *Wemhoff v Germany* App no 2122/64 (ECtHR, 27 June 1968) para 15; *Matznetter v Austria* App no 2178/64 (ECtHR, 10 November 1969) para 11.

8 Art. 9(3) ICCPR; Art. 5(3) ECHR.

9 *Neumeister v Austria* App no 1936/63 (ECtHR, 12 July 1968) para 4; see also *Wemhoff v Germany* App no 2122/64 (ECtHR, 27 June 1968) para 5; *Ciulla v Italy* App no 11152/84 (ECtHR, 22 February 1989) para 38; *Rosenbaum v Federal Republic of Germany* App no 3376/67 (ECtHR, 4 February 1969) YB12 250, 274.

10 *Wemhoff v Germany* App no 2122/64 (ECtHR, 27 June 1968) para 5; *Clooth v Belgium* 12718/87 (ECtHR, 12 December 1991) para 36; *Kemmache v France (no 1 and no 2)* App no 12325/86&14992/89 (ECtHR, 27 November 1991) para 52.

Ensuring that justice is done 'also means respect for the alleged perpetrators' fundamental rights'.[11]

On the other hand, there is no generally guaranteed right to bail: detention is justifiable when it is necessary to ensure the administration of justice, where the defendant's flight or interference with evidence or witnesses might otherwise preclude it. It may also be necessary to stem the commission of offences, so the objective of the trial is not frustrated.[12]

Detention has several consequences for an accused person,[13] including the loss of income and economic hardship, stress on family and marital relationships, and associated mental health problems. Aside from the interests of the accused, the interests of justice are also compromised if detention obstructs his ability to properly prepare a defence and confer with counsel,[14] or results in pressure to plead guilty, impacting on the right to a fair trial.[15] This is arguably even more relevant in the context of international criminal trials, where the defendants are typically older, in poorer health, detained for longer periods of time, further from home, under 'long-term stress, which is well-known to induce or exacerbate health conditions'.[16]

It is essential to a proper understanding of the importance of provisional release in international criminal trials to recognize that extensive delays are routinely experienced.[17] Pre-conviction detention is not a substitute for the proper administration of justice.[18] One theme of the *ad hoc* Tribunals' jurisprudence is the effort to appear to be attempting to avoid pre-conviction detention that might 'be perceived as an anticipatory sentence'.[19]

On average, trials from arrest to completion have taken three and a half years at the ICTY and four and a half at the ICTR.[20] Of this, the combined average time in

---

[11] *Limaj* IT-03-66 (Decision on Limaj's Request for Provisional Release, 31 October 2003) para 11. See Art. 21(3) ICCSt; *Lubanga* ICC-01/04-01/06-1487 (Judgment, 21 October 2008) 37.

[12] See Art. 60(2)&58(1)(b)(iii) ICCSt.

[13] See further J. Schnittker and A. John, 'Enduring Stigma: The Long-Term Effects of Incarceration on Health' (2007) 48 *Journal of Health and Social Behaviour* 115.

[14] See for example submissions of the Defence in *Perišić* IT-04-81-T (Decision on Mr. Perišić Motion for Provisional Release during the Court's Winter Recess, 17 December 2008) para 15; cf. *Stanišić and Župljanin* IT-08-91-T (Decision Granting Mićo Stanišić's Request for Provisional Release, 6 June 2012) para 22.

[15] C. Davidson, 'No Shortcuts on Human Rights: Bail and the International Criminal Trial' (2010) 60 *American University Law Review* 1, 6.

[16] Report of Registrar of the ICTY, delivered at ICTY Diplomatic Seminar of 10 June 2008 3, 7.

[17] See eg War Crimes Research Office (ICC Legal Analysis and Education Project), *Expediting Proceedings at the ICC* (June 2011) 11; see generally J. Galbraith, 'The Pace of International Criminal Justice' (2009) 31 *Michigan Journal of International Law* 79, 82.

[18] *Letellier v France* App no 12369/86 (ECtHR, 26 June 1991) paras 38–39.

[19] *Prlić* IT-04-74-T (Decision on Jadranko Prlić's Motion for Provisional Release, 21 April 2011) para 38.

[20] L. Barria and S. Roper, 'How Effective are International Criminal Tribunals?' (2005) 9 *International Journal of Human Rights* 349, 362.

detention from arrest to conviction is roughly 1,000 days.[21] Sometimes the period of pre-trial detention has been so lengthy that there is little or no sentence to be served once a conviction has become final.[22] In one case at the ICTR, pre-trial detention extended over more than six years.[23] Two other defendants were held in custody for ten years before being acquitted.[24]

Although international courts and tribunals have sporadically[25] considered the length of an accused's detention in determining an application for provisional release, its significance has invariably been confined to a discretionary factor,[26] and it has never of itself constituted a ground for release,[27] although it has from time to time been used to support the conclusion that release is appropriate.[28] The ICTR has found no 'unjustified prejudice' in the lack of release over extensive periods of pre-trial detention.[29] One defendant's detention was maintained pending his retrial after he was acquitted on four of five counts, even though he had been in detention for eight years, and there was considered to be 'no risk that he will flee'.[30]

---

21 W. Schomburg, 'The Role of International Criminal Tribunals in Promoting Respect for Fair Trial Rights' (2009) 8 *North-Western University Journal of International Human Rights* 1, 14.

22 The detention of some defendants has been so long that they were either released on the same day that their convictions became final (eg Tihomir Blaškić, Enver Hadžihasanović) or within a few months of being sentenced to several years (eg Miroslav Kvočka, Zdravko Mucić, Dragoljub Prcać, Simo Zarić, Dražden Erdemović). At the ICTR, consider Decision on the Defence Motion for Release, *Bagosora* (ICTR-98-41-T), Trial Chamber I, 12 July 2002, para. 3 (held in custody for six and a half years before proper commencement of trial); and the trial of Ferdinand Nahimana, in custody for four and a half years before commencement of trial.

23 *Bagosora* ICTR-98-41-T (Decision on the Defence Motion for Release, 12 July 2002) paras 4, 28.

24 *Bizimungu et al* ICTR-99-50-T (Judgment, 30 September 2011) paras 4–17.

25 Some decisions, which appear not to have been followed, have rejected the proposition that the length of detention is relevant: *Rukundo* ICTR-2001-70-I (Appeal Regarding Temporal Jurisdiction, 12 July 2004) para 16. Others have considered, conversely, that lengthy detention might heighten the risk of absconding and weigh against release: *Muvunyi* ICTR-00-55-AR65 (Decision on Defence Motion for Reconsideration of Decision Denying Provisional Release, 3 April 2009) para 15. In particular, the length of detention alone does not constitute a 'compelling humanitarian reason' for release: *Prlić* IT-04-74-T (Decision on Jadranko Prlić's Motion for Provisional Release, 21 April 2011) para 38; *Prlić* IT-04-74-AR65.24 (Decision on Jadranko Prlić's Appeal against the Trial Chamber Decision on his Motion for Provisional Release, 8 June 2011) para 10.

26 *Haradinaj* IT-04-84-AR65.2 (Decision on Lahi Brahimaj's Interlocutory Appeal against the Trial Chamber's Decision Denying his Provisional Release, 9 March 2006) para 23.

27 Cf. *Delalić et al* IT-96-21-T (Decision on Motions for Separate Trial, 25 September 1996) para 30; *Delić* IT-96-21-T (Decision on Motion for Provisional Release, 24 October 1996) para 24.

28 See *Delalić* (Decision on Motions for Separate Trial), ibid., para 21.

29 See for example *Nsengimana* ICTR-01-69-T (Judgment, 17 November 2009) paras 45, 53.

30 *Muvunyi* ICTR-00-55-AR65 (Decision on Defence Motion for Provisional Release, 29 January 2009) para 5.

At the ICTY, it has not been considered unreasonable to detain various accused persons for periods ranging from 19 months up to five years before trial commences.[31] Ivan Čermak, for example, was detained for a further seven and a half months from the close of argument while a judgment was finalized which acquitted him on all charges.[32] Generally speaking there is no remedy for an accused in this position. Article 85(3) ICCSt provides for compensation in 'exceptional circumstances' where there is a 'grave and manifest miscarriage of justice'. However, unlike some domestic jurisdictions, no compensation is available for accused who are acquitted following lengthy detention.[33] There have been requests made by the Presidents of the ICTR and the ICTY for amendments to the respective statutes to allow for such compensation,[34] but in the absence of an amendment to their constituting document, there is no authority to grant redress.[35]

The first defendant tried by the hybrid Cambodian Court was also detained for eight years before being formally charged, and a further 18 months before his trial.[36] When raised on appeal, the Supreme Court Chamber held that there could be no remedy for violations of such human rights abuses as they were perpetrated by its predecessor Military Court and therefore not attributable to the ECCC.[37]

Although the period of detention tends to be longer in the international system, both bail in domestic systems and provisional release in the international context are designed to balance the need to detain and human rights standards. To resolve this tension it might be argued that pre-conviction detention is justifiable only by procedural necessity, not as pre-emptive punishment, or based on the seriousness of the charges alone. In broad terms that is a suitable starting point for the analysis of pre-conviction detention in international criminal law. As will be observed in this chapter, however, there are a number of practical constraints and differences in the nature of international criminal trials that have led the tribunals to be somewhat more stringent in the application of those principles.

---

31 *Zarić* IT-95-9-PT (Decision on Zarić's Application for Provisional Release, 4 April 2000) para 3.

32 See eg *Čermak* IT-06-90-T (Decision on Motion for Provisional Release, 27 February 2009); cf. *Halilović* IT-01-48-T (Decision on Motion for Provisional Release, 1 September 2005).

33 On arguments for the introduction of such a compensatory scheme, see J. Michels, 'Compensating Acquitted Defendants for Detention before International Criminal Courts' (2010) 8 *Journal of International Criminal Justice* 407; cf. Art. 85(3) ICCSt.

34 Letter dated 28 September 2000 from the Secretary General annexing letter from President Pillay of the ICTR to the President of the UNSC, 28 September 2000 UN Doc S/2000/925; Letter dated 26 September 2000 from the Secretary General annexing letter from President Jorda of the ICTY to the President of the UNSC, UN Doc S/2000/904 (26 September 2000).

35 *Rwamakuba* ICTR-98-44C-AC (Decision on Appeal against Decision on Appropriate Remedy, 13 September 2007) para 15.

36 *Duch* 001/18-07-2007/ECCC (15 June 2009) paras 2–4.

37 *Duch* 001/18-07-2007/ECCC (3 February 2012) paras 46–48.

3. THE LAW OF PROVISIONAL RELEASE AT THE INTERNATIONAL TRIBUNALS

3.1 ICTY and ICTR

The *ad hoc* Tribunals have produced by some margin the greatest amount of jurisprudence on provisional release. For the most part, the position at the ICTR has mirrored that at the ICTY, although amendments to the applicable rules have from time to time created some divergence.

3.1.1 Procedure

A warrant for arrest may be issued and an accused person brought into custody if a prima facie case is established.[38] In urgent cases the Prosecutor may direct a country to provisionally detain a person before a warrant is issued,[39] and a judge may order their transfer and provisional detention if 'there is a reliable and consistent body of material which tends to show that the suspect may have committed a crime' and it is necessary to avoid a risk of flight or the endangerment of witnesses or victims.[40] That provisional detention can continue for 60 days, or 90 days in exceptional circumstances.[41]

Unlike at the ICC there is no provision for provisional release prior to transfer,[42] probably because there is an independent duty on the custodial State to make that transfer without delay.[43] In cases where such a delay does eventuate without release, the accused may be able to apply for release through domestic courts,[44] but there is no redress for the accused at the Tribunal.[45]

The rules at each of the Tribunals mandate the detention of the accused upon their transfer to the seat of the Tribunal.[46] It is then for the accused to apply for provisional release. There is no mechanism for mandatory review of detention.[47] Unlike common practice in Anglo-Saxon jurisdictions, the question of release is 'rarely, if at all, raised (…) at the initial appearance'.[48] This can have the consequence that the process can be

---

38 Art. 19 ICTYSt; Art. 20 ICTRSt.

39 Rule 40 ICTY RPE; Rule 40 ICTR RPE.

40 Rule 40bis (A) ICTY RPE; Rule 40bis (A) ICTR RPE.

41 Rule 40bis (D) ICTY RPE; Rule 40bis (D) ICTR RPE.

42 Rule 57 ICTY RPE; Rule 57 ICTR RPE.

43 Art. 29 ICTYSt; Art. 28 ICTRSt.

44 See for example in France: *Wenceslas Munyeshyaka* Paris Court of Appeal No 2007/05357 (Decision on Request for Release, 19 September 2007); and the United States: *Surrender of Elizaphan Ntakirutimana* [1997] 988 F Supp 1038; cf *Ntakirutimana v Reno* [1999] 988 5th Cir.

45 *Barayagwiza* ICTR-97-19AC (Decision, 3 November 1999) para 42.

46 Rule 64 ICTY RPE; Rule 64 ICTR RPE.

47 Rule 65(B) ICTY RPE; Rule 65(B) ICTR RPE. Provisional release can also be sought by a suspect transferred and provisionally detained by the Tribunal under Rule 40: see Rule 40bis (H) ICTY RPE; Rule 40bis(H) ICTR RPE.

48 *Ademi* IT-01-46-PT (Order on Motion for Provisional Release, 20 February 2002) para 17.

delayed for some months while written submissions are exchanged.[49] The defendant can also apply to the President for changes in their conditions of detention.[50]

It is well established that the onus in provisional release applications at the ICTY and ICTR falls on the defendant;[51] even decisions that have considered that position to be dubious appear to have accepted it as good law.[52] However, there is a pattern of granting release due to a lack of concrete evidence of risk, which suggests at least some degree of evidentiary burden on the prosecution.[53]

The standard of proof is generally thought to be on the balance of probabilities,[54] although there has been conjecture about whether the task of the detainee should be made even more onerous by raising it to a 'substantial burden' – an intermediate standard between balance of probabilities and beyond reasonable doubt.[55] This position is at odds with the jurisprudence of the ECtHR, which has consistently held that it is for the State to show that the public interest in detaining the defendant is sufficient – in light of these risks – to reverse the general assumption that he should be granted provisional release.[56]

---

49 Consider, for example, the case of Prlić and Čorić: Davidson (n 15) 6.

50 Rule 64 ICTY RPE; Rule 64 ICTR RPE.

51 *Haradinaj et al* IT-04-84-T (Decision on Motion for Provisional Release, 20 July 2007) para 8; see also *Perišić* IT-04-81-T (Decision on Motion for Provisional Release, 31 March 2010) para 12; cf. the minority view in *Krajišnik* IT-00-39 and 40-PT (Decision on Appeal against Refusal to Grant Provisional Release, 8 October 2001) per Robinson J para 16.

52 *Pavković* IT-05-87-PT (Second Decision on Provisional Release, 18 November 2005) para 12; *Krajišnik* IT-00-39 and 40-PT (Decision on Appeal against Refusal to Grant Provisional Release, 8 October 2001) per Robinson J.

53 Eg *Simatović* IT-03-69-PT (Decision on Provisional Release, 28 July 2004) para 32; *Ljubičić* IT-00-41-PT (Decision on Second Application for Provisional Release, 26 July 2005) para 29. Note however that where Trial Chambers have gone so far as to transfer the onus to the prosecution their decisions have been overturned on appeal on that basis: *Pavković* IT-05-87-AR65.1 (Prosecution Appeal on Decision on Provisional Release, 1 November 2005) para 11; *Prlić* IT-04-74-AR65.1-3 (Decision on Provisional Release, 15 December 2012) para 27.

54 *Galić* IT-98-29-T (Decision on Second Defence Request for Provisional Release, 31 October 2005) para 12.

55 *Brđanin* IT-99-36-PT (Decision on Motion for Provisional Rclcasc, 25 July 2000) para 18, interpreted to indicate a higher standard by Shahabuddeen J in his separate opinion in *Šainović* IT-05-87-T (Decision on Provisional Release, 30 October 2002) para 40; see also to the same effect, *Tolimir* IT-04-80-PT (Decision on Defence Motion for Provisional Release, 19 July 2005) para 8. However, Hunt J clarified that by 'substantial burden', he simply meant that in practical terms, meeting the burden of proof on the balance of probabilities is a substantial task for the accused: *Šainović* IT-05-87-T (Decision on Provisional Release, 30 October 2002) per Hunt J (dissenting) para 30.

56 See for example *Neumeister v Austria* App no 1936/63 (ECtHR, 12 July 1968) para 4; *Letellier v France* App no 12369/86 (ECtHR, 26 June 1991) para 35; *W v Switzerland* App no 14379/88 (ECtHR, 26 January 1993) para 30; *Smirnova v Russia* App no 46133/99&48183/99 (ECtHR, 24 July 2003) paras 61–62; *Wemhoff v Germany* App no 2122/64 (ECtHR, 27 June 1968) para 5.

3.1.2 Criteria for release

A Chamber can grant provisional release to an accused 'if it is satisfied that the accused will appear for trial and, if released, will not pose a danger to any victim, witness or other person'.[57] This ICTY Rule has undergone several permutations, and at present also requires that procedural fairness be afforded to the host and receiving States, and permits Chambers to consider humanitarian reasons for release.[58] Whether these factors weigh in favour of release or detention is a question of fact to be resolved in each particular case. The ICTY has confirmed that 'motions for provisional release are fact intensive and cases are considered on an individual basis in light of the particular circumstances of the individual accused'.[59]

A defendant seeking to overturn a denial of a provisional release application was, from July 1997, required to show 'serious cause'.[60] That standard was reduced to 'good cause' in November of the same year.[61] Since July 2005 an appeal against the interlocutory decision of a Trial Chamber on provisional release will succeed if it can be shown that there was an error of law occasioning a miscarriage of justice, according to ordinary appellate principles, without the need to demonstrate any such additional requirement.[62]

The common wording of the Rules governing provisional release at the *ad hoc* Tribunals also retains a residual discretion – that is, to deny release when the legal requirements are otherwise satisfied, rather than to grant release in appropriate cases where they are not.[63] That discretion has been criticized as tending to produce arbitrary results.[64] Factors affecting the exercise of that discretion have included whether detention is in the public interest,[65] and the length of time the accused has been in

---

[57] Rule 65(B) ICTY RPE.

[58] Ibid.

[59] *Ademi* IT-01-46-PT (Order on Motion for Provisional Release, 20 February 2002) para 18.

[60] Rule 65(D) ICTY RPE (Rev. 11, 25 July 1997); interpreted as requiring a 'grave error in the decision': *Delić* IT-96-21 (Motion for Provisional Release, 24 October 1996) para 12(3).

[61] Rule 65(D) ICTY RPE (Rev. 12, 12 November 1997).

[62] Rule 65(D) ICTY RPE (Rev. 36, 8 August 2005).

[63] *Delalić* IT-96-21-T (Decision on Motion for Provisional Release, 25 September 1996) para 18; *Čermak* IT-06-90-T (Decision on Motion for Provisional Release, 24 March 2010) para 5; *Haradinaj et al* IT-04-84-T (Decision on Motion for Provisional Release, 20 July 2007) para 8; *Ademi* IT-01-46-PT (Order on Motion for Provisional Release, 20 February 2002) para 21.

[64] *Krajišnik* IT-00-39 and 40-T (Decision on Motion for Provisional Release, 8 October 2001) per Robinson J (dissenting) para 27.

[65] *Ademi* IT-01-46-PT (Order on Motion for Provisional Release, 20 February 2002) para 22. Other considerations include the potential for conspiracy with accused at large and the proximity of a prospective trial or Judgment date (ibid) and the length of detention (*Brđanin* IT-99-36-PT (Decision on Motion for Provisional Release, 25 July 2000)) para 24.

detention.[66] That discretion has survived recent amendments to the provision at the ICTY.[67]

Once convicted, provisional release will only be granted pending appeal in exceptional circumstances.[68]

3.1.3 Practice – ICTY

At the ICTY there has developed a pattern of granting provisional release during court recess periods, where the presence of the accused is not required. That trend has withstood the observations of some judges that it 'would in practical terms convey the impression (…) that accused (…) are let out on holidays'.[69] No accused has been allowed to remain on bail during the conduct of proceedings,[70] although the Appeals Chamber recently ordered the provisional release of Stanišić and Simatović to Serbia, after ordering a retrial following a prosecution appeal against their acquittal.[71]

Naturally, this situation, as with that of the ICTR, is attributable largely to practical difficulties. Tribunals that are set up on the territory of a third State require the detainees' presence in the country to attend their trials, but are also unlikely to be able to secure, or inclined to negotiate, long-term residential visas for alleged war criminals, many of whom may yet to be captured or even identified at the establishment of the tribunal. In the case of the ICTY the Host State Agreement provides for such contingencies as capture and rearrest in the case of escape, but does not contemplate the possibility of detainees being released into the Host State.[72]

3.1.4 Practice – ICTR

Although the ICTR has produced much jurisprudence on the matter, no application for provisional release before that Tribunal has succeeded. This includes in contempt cases, where the provisional release of defendants on those comparatively minor charges has been refused.[73] The Appeals Chamber has noted the significance of medical grounds,[74] but even grounds that amounted to 'exceptional circumstances', such as serious illness of a family member, have not warranted release at the ICTR.

---

66 *Brahimaj* IT-04-84-AR65.2 (Decision on Motion for Provisional Release, 9 March 2006) para 23; *Petković* IT-04-74-T (Decision on Motion for Provisional Release, 31 March 2008) 7; *Milutinović* IT-99-37-PT (Decision on Motion for Provisional Release, 14 April 2005) para 32; *Bagosora* ICTR-98-41-T (Defence Motion for Release, 12 July 2002) para 22; *Muhimana* ICTR-95-1-B-1 (Provisional Release, 1 October 2002) para 7.

67 *Simatović* IT-03-69-T (Decision on Request for Provisional Release, 13 December 2011) para 7.

68 Rule 65(I) ICTY RPE (Rev. 46, 20 October 2011).

69 *Pusić* IT-04-74-AR65.6 (Decision on Motion for Provisional Release, 23 April 2008) per Schomburg J (dissenting) para 17.

70 See eg *Kordić* IT-95-14/2 (Decision on Motion for Provisional Release, 17 December 1999) 4.

71 *Stanišić and Simatović* IT-03-69 (Decision on Stanišić's Urgent Motion for Provisional Release, 22 December 2015).

72 Art. 17 ASO, signed by ICTY and Kingdom of the Netherlands 14 July 1994.

73 See for example *Nshogoza* ICTR-07-91-PT (Decision on Defence Motion for Provisional Measures, 17 November 2008).

74 *Ngirumpatse* ICTR-99-44-AR65 (Decision on Provisional Release, 7 April 2009) para 14.

This is largely attributable to the circumstances surrounding the latter tribunal. Several decisions have highlighted the function of pre-conviction detention to ensure the accused's presence at trial, given the lack of provision for trials in absentia, and the fact that there is generally no other practically available accommodation in the Host State.[75] Further, the political climate in Rwanda prevents the release of defendants back to their home State, as is common practice at the ICTY.[76] This practical issue has proved prohibitive even in clear cases. Even when the ICTR unanimously acquitted Ignace Baglishema of all charges, it took four months to find a country in which he could resettle.[77] Five other men acquitted by the ICTR spent some years in a safe house in Arusha, awaiting transfer to countries that will accept them, some for as long as ten years.[78]

The ICTR has not been prepared to make any order to a State to accept an accused who is entitled to but cannot practicably attain release, although it has been sought on occasion.[79]

3.2 ICC

3.2.1 Procedure

The first stage of arrest proceedings at the ICC is the State Party executing the arrest warrant. There is a right to apply to the State Party for interim release pending surrender,[80] although only in 'urgent and exceptional circumstances' and only if 'necessary safeguards exist to ensure' that the person can be surrendered.[81] The Pre-Trial Chamber has jurisdiction to make recommendations on such applications[82] and to receive periodic reports on the status of the release.[83]

Once the accused has been transferred to the Court, the Rules governing provisional release are somewhat more generous to the accused than those of the *ad hoc* Tribunals. They require that provisional release be considered at the initial proceedings and reviewed every 120 days thereafter.[84] In practical terms the period of detention may be slightly longer than this, because the period for review commences at the refusal of a specific request for interim release filed by the defendant, not from the issuance of an

---

75 *Nahimana* ICTR-99-52-T (Decision on Provisional Release, 5 September 2002) para 14; *Ndayambaje* ICTR-96-8-A (Motion for Appeal against Provisional Release, 10 January 2003) 5.

76 See *Nshogoza* ICTR-07-91-PT (Decision on Defence Motion for Provisional Release, 17 December 2008) paras 15–16; the same applies to some defendants at the ICC: see for example *Bemba Gombo* ICC-01/05-01/08 OA 2 (Interim Release of Jean-Pierre Bemba Gombo, 2 December 2009) para 10.

77 *Baglishema* ICTR-95-1A-T (Judgment, 7 June 2001); ICTR Press Release, 'Baglishema Leaves for France' (ICTR/INFO-9-2-288.EN, 9 October 2001).

78 Z. Ubwani, 'Rwanda ex-convicts, freed suspects stuck in Arusha' (*The Citizen*, 15 April 2014) <http://www.thecitizen.co.tz/News/Rwanda-ex-convicts–freed-suspects-stuck-in-Arusha-/-/1840392/2280008/-/2tj6mk/-/index.html> accessed 6 June 2015.

79 See for example *Nahimana* ICTR-96-11-I (6 September 2002) para 154.

80 Art. 59(3) ICCSt.

81 Art. 59(4) ICCSt.

82 Art. 59(5) ICCSt.

83 Art. 59(6) ICCSt.

84 Arts. 60(2), 58(1)(b) ICCSt.; Rule 118(2) ICC RPE.

arrest warrant or denial of other motions that might have the effect of remanding the defendant in custody.[85]

Although it is considered an application by the accused, the burden is phrased the opposite way: the person is to be detained only '[i]f the Pre-Trial Chamber is satisfied that the conditions [necessary for detention] are met'.[86] The ICC has declined to interpret this in line with the approach of the *ad hoc* Tribunals, noting that the reversal of the onus in those jurisdictions arises more out of the specific legal framework adopted at the ICTY than from anything inherent in provisional release.[87] Instead, it has confirmed that 'unlike the situation at the *ad hoc* Tribunals, pre-trial detention is not the general rule, but it is the exception', and can only be ordered for enumerated reasons, not discretionary ones.[88] However, the Appeals Chamber has recognized that the assessment 'necessarily involves an element of prediction', granting the Trial Chambers some degree of autonomy in its judgment of the evidence.[89]

Once detention has been ordered, it may be varied only 'if it is satisfied that changed circumstances so require'.[90] This varies the onus, such that the prosecution is not charged with establishing the same criteria on each review or application, but simply establishing that there has been no change in circumstances of the nature raised by the defendant.[91]

3.2.2 Criteria and practice

The substantive requirements of Article 58(1)(b) are similar to those of Rule 65(B): where necessary 'to ensure the person's appearance at trial, to ensure that the person does not obstruct or endanger the investigation or the court proceedings, or where applicable, to prevent the person from continuing with the commission of that crime or a related crime which is within the jurisdiction of the Court and which arises out of the same circumstances'. The decision to release an accused to a certain State affects the interests of that State, and so provision is made for that State to be heard on the conditions that should be imposed in such an order.[92] Unlike at the *ad hoc* Tribunals, where there is a residual discretion to deny release, if these criteria have been satisfied at the ICC, release is mandatory.[93]

Voluntary surrender has been more common at the ICC than the other tribunals, and several accused have been permitted to remain at liberty during the pre-trial stage of

---

85 *Lubanga* 01/04-01/06 (OA 7) (Judgment, 13 February 2007) paras 78–102.

86 Art. 60(2) ICCSt. The ICC has confirmed that the onus is on the Prosecutor: *Katanga* ICC-01/04-01/07-330 (Decision on the powers of the Pre-Trial Chamber to Review *Proprio Motu* the Pre-Trial Detention, 18 March 2008) 6–7. The detention of the accused is also to be reviewed every 120 days: Rule 118(2) ICC RPE.

87 *Katanga*, ibid.

88 *Lubanga* 01/04-01/06 (OA 7) (Judgment, 13 February 2007) para 134.

89 Ibid., para 136.

90 *Bemba Gombo* ICC-01/05-01/08 (OA 2) (Judgment, 2 December 2009) para 60.

91 *Bemba Gombo* ICC-01/05-01/08-1088 (Defence Urgent Motion for Provisional Release, 17 December 2010) para 51.

92 Rule 119(3) ICC RPE; *Bemba Gombo* ICC-01/05-01/08-1626 (Decision on Application for Provisional Release, 19 August 2011) para 55.

93 *Lubanga* 01/04-01/06 (OA 7) (Judgment, 13 February 2007) para 134.

their case. However, orders for the release of certain accused once detained have been attended with some practical difficulty. For example, in *Bemba Gombo* a decision to order provisional release was overturned, largely due to the absence of a willing receiving State. The Pre-Trial Chamber granted provisional release to Bemba Gombo[94] after six countries were proposed.[95] However, the Appeals Chamber reversed this decision on the merits of the request, and because no 'State willing to accept Mr. Bemba and enforce the conditions of release had been identified by the decision'.[96] There is a general obligation on States Parties to cooperate in the 'investigation and prosecution of crimes'.[97] The wording of the *Gombo* decision suggests that this obligation may not extend to accommodating accused on release. In April 2014 the ICC signed an agreement with Belgium to facilitate the provisional release of ICC accused persons,[98] which may assist to overcome this practical obstacle.

3.3 Other Internationalized Jurisdictions

The other tribunals established with the assistance of the UN have produced less jurisprudence on the matter, but warrant a brief mention.

3.3.1 Extraordinary Chambers in the Courts of Cambodia

The ECCC's Co-Investigating Judges may order provisional detention based on broadly the same considerations as the *ad hoc* Tribunals.[99] In addition, detention may be ordered to 'protect the security of the Charged Person'[100] or to 'preserve public order'.[101] These latter grounds are more far-reaching and include the risk of mob attack or public demonstrations.[102] Detention must be reviewed annually and is for a maximum of three years.[103] The defendant can apply at any time for release,[104] provided three months have passed since any previous application.[105] There is provision for the posting of bail, which has been borrowed from the SCSL, but like that tribunal, never used.[106] Once the trial has commenced, the defendant cannot file a further

---

94 *Bemba Gombo* ICC-01/05-01/08-475 (Decision on Interim Release, 14 August 2009).

95 Ibid., para 35.

96 *Bemba Gombo* ICC-01/05-01/08 (OA 2) (Judgment, 2 December 2009) para 105.

97 Art. 86 ICCSt.

98 ICC, 'Press Release, Belgium and ICC sign agreement on interim release of detainees' (10 April 2014).

99 Rule 63(3) ECCC IR.

100 Rule 63(3)(iv) ECCC IR; cf. *IA v France* App no 28213/95 (ECtHR, 23 September 1998) para 108.

101 Rule 63(3)(v) ECCC IR.

102 See *Khieu Samphan* 002/19-09-2007-ECCC/OCIJ (Decision on Motion for Release and Provisional Detention Order, 3 July 2009) paras 50–63.

103 Rule 63(6)(a) ECCC IR (for cases involving charges of genocide, war crimes and crimes against humanity, which in practice encompasses all cases at the ECCC).

104 Rule 64(2) ECCC IR.

105 Rule 64(3) ECCC IR.

106 Rule 65 ECCC IR.

application unless there has been a change of circumstances,[107] and, if in detention at the initial appearance is to remain so until judgment is handed down.[108]

The ECCC employs a presumption in favour of liberty.[109] However, the practical experience has differed. Its first defendant, Kaing Guek Eav (Duch), was detained by the Cambodian Military Court for 11 years before the ECCC was established, and remained in custody until ultimately convicted and sentenced.[110] His sentence was initially discounted for this illegal detention,[111] but on appeal this was reversed on the basis that those violations were not attributable to the ECCC.[112]

The provisional detention of all four defendants in Case 2 was ordered in 2007.[113] Ieng Thirith was released after being found unfit to stand trial in September 2012.[114] Ieng Sary died in March 2013, leaving only Nuon Chea and Khieu Samphan on trial. They both remain in custody.

3.3.2 Special Tribunal for Lebanon

At the STL, unlike the *ad hoc* Tribunals, there is provision for a summons to appear to issue[115] unless the interests of justice require a warrant for arrest.[116] The former mechanism is not available at the ICTY. Provisional detention may be ordered on the same grounds as at the *ad hoc* Tribunals.[117] That detention must be reviewed at least every six months.[118] To successfully appeal such a decision, there is a requirement that defendants show 'good cause',[119] the same requirement that has been removed at the ICTY and the ICTR.

---

107 Rule 82(4) ECCC IR.

108 Rule 82(1) ECCC IR.

109 Rule 82(1) ECCC IR; see also Rule 72(4)(d).

110 *Duch* 001/18-07-2007/ECCC (Judgment, 26 July 2010) 198.

111 Ibid., 215.

112 *Duch* 001/18-07-2007/ECCC (Summary of Appeal Judgment, 3 February 2012). Cf. dissenting opinions of the two international judges, Agnieszka-Klonowiecka-Milart and Chandra Nihal Jayasinghe at 324–7.

113 *Chea* 002/19-09-2007/ECCC (Decision on Appeal against Provisional Detention Order, 20 March 2008); *Ieng Thirith* 002/19-09-2007/ECCC (Decision on Appeal against Provisional Detention Order, 9 July 2008); *Ieng Sary* 002/19-09-2007/ECCC (Decision on Appeal against Provisional Detention Order, 17 October 2008); *Khieu Samphan* 002/19-09-2007/ECCC (Decision on Appeal against Provisional Detention Order, 15 October 2008).

114 *Ieng Thirith* 002/19-09-2007/ECCC (Decision on Prosecutor's Request for Stay of Release Order, 13 September 2012).

115 Rule 78 STL RPE.

116 Rule 79 STL RPE.

117 Rule 63(B)(iii) STL RPE.

118 Rule 101(D) STL RPE.

119 Rule 65(E) SCSL RPE. However, note that this has been interpreted as only requiring the defendant to show that 'the Trial Chamber may have erred in making the impugned decision': *Sesay* SCSL-04-15-T (Decision on Confidential Motion Seeking Disclosure of Documentation Relating to the Motion for the Recruitment of Child Soldiers, 28 July 2004) para 10.

One early sign was the order, on application by the Prosecutor, for the release of four suspects who had spent three years in custody in Lebanon.[120] However, that decision concerned persons who were held by the domestic jurisdiction, not under an arrest warrant issued by the Tribunal itself, and their release was not 'provisional' but rather ordered on the basis that there was insufficient evidence.

3.3.3 Special Court for Sierra Leone

The SCSL provisions are modelled on those of the ICTR, except that it uses the traditionally Anglo-Saxon term 'bail', and employ the same criteria.[121] Additionally, there is power to detain wherever 'otherwise necessary for the conduct of the investigation'.[122] This has included where release would pose a threat to public order,[123] or based on concerns for the safety of the accused.[124] As at the ICTY and ICTR, there is a procedural requirement that the receiving State be heard, but their submissions are not decisive.[125] The burden of proof lies with the defendant.[126]

Unlike other internationalized jurisdictions, which require periodic review of detention, only one application may be made 'unless there has been a material change in circumstances'.[127] There is provision for the posting of bail in the traditionally Anglo-Saxon sense,[128] but this has never been utilized.

4. LEGAL CRITERIA IN DETAIL

As explored above, two standard criteria govern the grant of provisional release – the risk of flight, and the dangers upon release: to victims, to witnesses, or the danger of reoffending generally. Those criteria, variously formulated, broadly reflect the jurisprudence of the ECtHR and inform the rules of most domestic jurisdictions.[129] With slight variations, these elements comprise the broadly accepted formula that is applied at each of the international tribunals.

---

[120] *El Sayed* CH/PTJ/2009/06 (Order Regarding the Detention of Persons Detained in Lebanon, 29 April 2009).

[121] Rule 40bis(B) SCSL RPE.

[122] Rule 40bis(B) SCSL RPE; see also Rule 65(B).

[123] See *Sesay* SCSL-04-15-AR65 (Decision Appeal against Refusal of Bail, 14 December 2004) para 36.

[124] *Sesay* SCSL-04-15-PT (Decision on the Motion for Bail, 23 February 2004) para 44.

[125] *Kallon* SCSL-04-15-PT (Decision on the Motion for Bail, 24 February 2004) paras 36–39; *Sesay* SCSL-04-15-PT (Decision on Application for Provisional Release, 31 March 2004) para 42.

[126] *Sesay* SCSL-04-15-PT (Decision on Application for Provisional Release, 31 March 2004) para 37.

[127] Rule 65(C) SCSL RPE.

[128] Rule 65(D) SCSL RPE.

[129] Art. 5(3) ECHR.

4.1 Risk of Flight

No accused has ever absconded while on provisional release from any UN assisted international tribunal.[130] Yet, the risk that the flight of the accused will prevent the continuation of the trial has been the foremost consideration in provisional release applications before the international tribunals.[131] At the ICC, for example, Bemba Gombo was routinely refused release due to the risk of flight, notwithstanding the provision of State guarantees.[132] The international tribunals are not alone in this regard: in one domestic case involving the detention of a Nazi Staffelführer accused of the murder of 148 Jews at a concentration camp, the European Commission of Human Rights rejected an objection to the detention of the defendant for nearly seven years between arrest and conviction on the basis that this was the only means of ensuring his presence at trial.[133]

There are a number of factors that may be considered significant in assessing the risk of flight. First is the gravity of charges and the weight of the expected sentence. The extremely serious nature of the crimes has frequently been raised to justify detention at the *ad hoc* Tribunals,[134] ECCC, ICC,[135] and SCSL[136] on the basis that it may increase the incentive to flee.[137] At times this logical link has been tenuously maintained: at the ICTR, for example, some applications have been dismissed having regard to the seriousness of the allegations, even where the Chamber was explicitly satisfied that

---

[130] There have however been incidents of non-compliance with conditions (*Prlić et al* IT-04-74-T (Decision on Motion for Provisional Release, 24 November 2011) para 28) and fugitives from the Bosnian hybrid tribunal: see 'The Search for Dušan Janković' (Balkan Investigative Reporting Network, 22 December 2010) <http://www.bim.ba/en/250/10/31414/> accessed 14 June 2015. Note also Vojislav Šešelj's overt statements that he would not return from Serbia, leading to the revocation of his provisional release in *Šešelj* IT-03-67 (Decision on Prosecution Appeal against the Decision on the Prosecution Motion to Revoke the Provisional Release of the Accused, 30 March 2015).

[131] See for example the summary of the most pertinent factors, each of which appears to relate to the risk of flight, in *Sainović and Ojdanić* IT-99-37-PT (Decision on Applications of Provisional Release, 26 June 2002) para 6.

[132] *Bemba Gombo* ICC-01/05-01/08-1088 (Decision on the Review of Detention, 17 December 2010) paras 14–16; *Bemba Gombo* ICC-01/05-01/08-1565) (Decision on Application of Provisional Release, 27 June 2011) paras 55–61; *Bemba Gombo* ICC-01/05-01/08 (Decision on the Accused's Application for Provisional Release, 27 September 2011) paras 21–26.

[133] *Rosenbaum v Federal Republic of Germany* App no 3376/67 (ECtHR, 4 February 1969) YB12 250, 282; cf. *Jentzsch v Federal Republic of Germany* App no 2604/65 (ECtHR, 5 May 1971) YB 14 218, 238.

[134] See eg *Limaj* IT-03-66-AR65 (Decision on Request for Provisional Release, 31 October 2003) para 30; *Aleksovski* IT-94-14/1 (23 January 1998) 3; *Duch* 001/18-07-2007/ECCC (15 June 2009) para 24.

[135] See eg *Bemba Gombo* ICC-01/05-01/08-1088 (Decision on the Review of Detention, 17 December 2010) para 36; *Lubanga* ICC-01/04-01/06 (Decision on Request for Interim Release, 18 October 2006) 3.

[136] See for example *Sesay* SCSL-04-15-PT (Decision on Request for Provisional Release, 31 March 2004) para 40.

[137] *Simić* IT-95-9-A 21 (Decision on Motion for Provisional Release, October 2004) para 15.

there is no risk of flight.[138] Several Chambers at the ICTY have accepted these matters cannot by themselves form a sound basis for pre-conviction detention.[139] That reflects the position that has been taken at the ECtHR.[140] The ICC Appeals Chamber has reaffirmed that position.[141]

Second, the tribunals have considered procedural developments and the quality of the evidence in refusing provisional release to an accused.[142] Other procedural developments considered to heighten the risk of flight have included the dismissal of a defence challenge to jurisdiction,[143] and, at the *ad hoc* Tribunals, the close of the Prosecution case. This appears to have been on the basis that by that point the applicant's chances of acquittal have been diminished by an accumulation of evidence rising high enough to withstand a no-case submission (whether actually made or not).

Third, the extent of an accused's ties to the country where the accused is being detained may affect his likelihood of flight.[144] As observed by the ICC,[145] the ECCC,[146] the ICTR,[147] and the ICTY,[148] defendants before the international tribunals frequently have contacts abroad and the means to escape.[149] Such considerations are less relevant for defendants who are confined by illness, age or other impairment.[150] Tribunals have almost invariably denied release until that impairment is so advanced that the defendant

---

[138] Such was the case even where the defendant had been acquitted on four of five counts, and a retrial ordered on the remaining count: *Muvunyi* ICTR-00-55-AR65 (Decision on the Defence Motion for Provisional Release, 29 January 2009) para 5; *Muvunyi* ICTR-00-55-AR65 (Decision on the Defence Motion for Provisional Release, 3 April 2009) para 17.

[139] *Stanišić and Simatović* IT-03-69-AR65.2 (Decision on Prosecution's Appeal against Decision on Provisional Release, 3 December 2004) para 15; *Prlić* IT-04-74-PT (Order on Provisional Release, 30 July 2004) para 20; *Haradinaj et al* IT-04-84-PT (Order on Provisional Release, 6 June 2005) para 29; *Ljubičić* IT-00-41-PT (Decision on Second Application for Provisional Release, 26 July 2005) para 30.

[140] *Letellier v France* App no 12369/86 (ECtHR, 26 June 1991) para 43; *Smirnova v Russia* App no 46133/99 and 48183/99 (ECtHR, 24 July 2003) para 60.

[141] *Lubanga* 01/04-01/06 (OA 7) (Judgment, 13 February 2007) para 136.

[142] See eg *Halilović* IT-01-48-T (Decision on Motion for Provisional Release, 21 April 2005) 3–4.

[143] *Bemba Gombo* ICC-01/05-01/08-1088 (Decision on the Review of Detention, 17 December 2010) para 32.

[144] This has been recognized as a basis for detention at the ECtHR also: see for example *Stögmuller v Austria* App no 1602/62 (ECtHR, 10 November 1969) para 15; *W v Switzerland* App no 14379/88 (ECtHR, 26 January 1993) para 33.

[145] *Bemba Gombo* ICC-01/05-01/08-1088 (Decision on the Review of Detention, 17 December 2010) para 40; *Lubanga* 01/04-01/06 (OA 7) (Judgment, 13 February 2007) para 136.

[146] *Chea et al* 002/19-09-2007/ECCC (16 February 2011) paras 39–41.

[147] *Haxiu* IT-04-84-R77.5 (Decision on Provisional Release, 23 May 2008) para 7.

[148] *Sainović and Ojdanić* IT-99-37-AR65 30 (Decision on Defence Motion for Provisional Release, October 2002) para 9; *Stanišić* IT-04-79-AR65.1 (Decision on Prosecution's Interlocutory Appeal, 17 October 2005) paras 17–18.

[149] Consider for example the cases of Mladić and Karadžić: C. Supernor, 'International Bounty Hunters for War Criminals: Privatising the Enforcement of Justice' (2001) 50 *Air Force Law Review* 215, 215.

[150] This approach is consistent with that taken at the ECtHR: see for example *Matznetter v Austria* App no 2178/64 (ECtHR 10 November 1969) Series A No 10 para 11 and per Zekia J at para 40.

is unfit to stand trial,[151] and in the case of Ieng Thirith at the ECCC, not even that level of impairment was sufficient to warrant release.[152]

Fourth, is the extent of cooperation of an accused with the Prosecutor,[153] and in particular, the circumstances of their surrender.[154] Several defendants have appeared voluntarily at the ICC, including all six Kenyan accused, whom the Chamber did not feel was necessary to detain.[155] Three accused in the Situation in Sudan have also been allowed to remain at liberty prior to their trial following their appearances in The Hague.[156] The Pre-Trial Chamber subsequently declined to confirm the charges against one of those accused.[157] There is also an increasing frequency of voluntary surrender at the *ad hoc* Tribunals,[158] and the circumstances in which defendants came before the tribunal have been weighed in favour of those who surrendered voluntarily and against those who evaded arrest.[159] However, voluntary surrender has not necessarily guaranteed entitlement to provisional release,[160] nor has a demonstrated record of adherence

---

[151] At the ICTY, see *Đukić* IT-96-20-T (Decision on Request for Provisional Release, 24 April 1996) 2; *Brđanin et al* IT-99-36-T (Decision on Motion for Provisional Release, 20 September 2002) paras 32–33.

[152] She was detained for a further nine months 'to determine whether there is a prospect that the Accused will regain her fitness': *Ieng Thirith* 002/19-09-2007/ECCC (13 December 2011).

[153] See for example *Stanišić and Simatović* IT-03-69 (Decision on Stanišić's Urgent Motion for Provisional Release), para 9; cf. the provisional release of Volislav Šešelj, despite a long history of contempt, in *Šešelj* IT-03-67 (Order on the Provisional Release of the Accused *Proprio Motu*, 6 November 2014), which was revoked by the Appeals Chamber five months later: see above, n 130.

[154] See for example *Muvunyi* ICTR-00-55-AR65 (Decision on Defence Motion for Reconsideration of Decision Denying Provisional Release, 3 April 2009) para 15. At the ECtHR, see *W v Switzerland* App no 14379/88 (ECtHR, 26 January 1993) para 33; *Chraidi v Germany* App no 14379/88 (ECtHR 26 October 2006) para 40; *Stögmuller v Austria* App no 1602/62 (ECtHR, 10 November 1969) para 15 (voluntary surrender, a history of compliance with conditions of release and return for trial).

[155] See *Muthaura, Kenyatta and Ali* ICC-01/09-02/11 (Decision on Prosecutor's Application for Summonses to Appear, 8 March 2011) para 55.

[156] *Abu Garda* ICC-02/05-02/09 (Registration in the Record of the Power of Attorney, 7 May 2009); *Banda and Jerbo* ICC-02/05-03/09 (Summonses to Appear, 27 August 2009).

[157] *Abu Garda* ICC-02/05-02/09-243 (Decision on the Confirmation of Charges, 8 February 2010).

[158] *Brđanin et al* IT-99-36-PT (Decision on Motion for Provisional Release, 25 July 2000) para 17; *Nshogoza* ICTR-07-91-PT (Decision on Preliminary Challenges, 17 December 2008) para 12.

[159] *Mrđa* IT-02-59-PT (Decision on Second Motion for Provisional Release, 15 April 2002) para 34; *Ljubičić* IT-00-41-PT (Decision on Second Motion for Provisional Release, 26 July 2005) para 31; *Nahimana* ICTR-99-52-T (Decision on the Defence Motion for the Release or Alternatively Provisional Release, 5 September 2002) para 10; *Muhimana* ICTR-95-1-B-1 (Decision on Provisional Release, 1 October 2002) para 7.

[160] *Nshogoza* ICTR-07-91-PT (Decision on the Defence Motion for Provisional Release, 17 December 2008) paras 12–13.

to release conditions and punctual return for trial.[161] By contrast, an accused with a history of absconding is unlikely to secure provisional release.[162] Also relevant is the accused's conduct in detention, in court and willingness to be interviewed.[163] However, this principle does not extend to penalizing an accused for remaining silent during a prosecution interview,[164] which would conflict with the right against self-incrimination.[165] It therefore appears that an accused will have the benefit of being cooperative in interviews for the purposes of a provisional release application even if not all questions were answered.[166]

Fifth, in practical terms provisional release has not been seriously considered during trial proceedings. At least one Trial Chamber at the ICTY has elevated this practice to a legal principle, observing that the language 'will appear for trial' in Rule 65(B) 'ma[kes] it clear that the application of the Rule is confined to the provisional release of an accused whose trial has not yet begun'.[167] Others have reached the conclusion at the level of the prescribed criteria, stating that 'it would be inappropriate to grant provisional release during trial because, inter alia, release could disrupt the remaining course of the trial'.[168] By extension, the fact that an accused's trial is soon to commence has also been cited as a ground against provisional release.[169]

Finally, the limitations of international tribunals in their coercive abilities to rearrest and their typical dependence on the cooperation of States have been cited as important considerations in determining applications for provisional release.[170] This is especially problematic, for example, at the ICC in light of recurring tensions with the African

[161] *Prlić et al* IT-04-74-AR65.5 (Decision on Appeal against Provisional Release, 11 March 2008) para 19; cf. where a 'pattern of disregard for the Tribunal's orders': *Nshogoza* ICTR-07-91-PT (Decision on Defence Motion for Provisional Release, 17 November 2008) para 20.

[162] *Gotovina* IT-06-90-AR65.1 (Decision on Provisional Release, 17 January 2008) para 18.

[163] *Josipović* IT-95-16-T (Decision on Provisional Release, 6 May 1999) 2; *Čermak* IT-06-90-T (Decision on Appeal against 12 March Decision, 18 July 2008) para 19; *Krajišnik* IT-00-39&40-T (Decision on Provisional Release, 8 October 2001) para 21; *Čermak and Markač* IT-03-73-AR65.1 (Decision on the Defence Motion for Provisional Release, 2 December 2004) para 23; *Stanišić and Simatović* IT-03-69-T (Decision on the Urgent Defence Motion for Provisional Release, 31 March 2010) para 23.

[164] *Brahimaj* IT-04-84-AR65.2 (Decision on Interlocutory Appeal against Provisional Release, 9 March 2006) para 18; cf *Brahimaj* IT-04-84-PT (Decision on Interlocutory Appeal against Provisional Release, 3 November 2005) 6.

[165] For recognition of the principle at the ICTY, see *Stanišić* IT-04-79-AR65.1 (Decision on Interlocutory Appeal against Provisional Release, 17 October 2005) para 24.

[166] *Simatović* IT-03-69-AR-65.1 (Decision on the Defence Motion for Provisional Release, 3 December 2004) para 9.

[167] *Milutinović et al* IT-05-87-AR65.2 (Expedited Appeal against Decision on Defence Motion for Provisional Release, 14 December 2006) para 9 (referring to and reversing Impugned Decision para 4).

[168] *Krajišnik and Plavšić* IT-00-39 and 40-PT (Decision on Application for Provisional Release, 8 October 2001) paras 10, 14.

[169] *Ndindabahizi* ICTR-2001-71-I (Judgment, 15 July 2004) 3; *Muvunyi* ICTR-2000-55A-AR65 (Decision on Provisional Release, 20 May 2009) para 8.

[170] *Barayagwiza* ICTR-97-19 (Decision on Provisional Release, 3 November 1999) para 42; *Tolimir et al* IT-04-74-PT (Decision on Provisional Release, 19 July 2005) para 8.

Union,[171] in Cambodia given the ECCC international contingent's continuing conflict with the country's former Khmer Rouge-dominated government,[172] and at the ICTY, where detainees are typically released to their own countries, over which the Tribunal has little control.[173] This problem is aggravated by the fact that the States from which alleged war criminals tend to come may have unstable political climates.[174]

Guarantees from the receiving State have come to be regarded as practically essential – although not, as the ICTR emphasized, a determinative prerequisite.[175] They are given far greater weight than any undertakings or patterns of behaviour of the accused themselves.[176] The quality of such undertakings and the practical and administrative limitations of the guarantor must also be considered,[177] including the official capacity of the guarantor within the State to provide the guarantee.[178] In the *Bemba Gombo* case, for example, despite the 'significant undertaking' of the receiving State to closely monitor and restrict the accused, 'the Chamber [wa]s not persuaded that it mitigate[d] the risks identified'.[179] Due to the volatile situation in the Balkans, the ICTY was reluctant to rely on guarantees from Croatia until 1999[180] and Serbia until 2001.[181]

---

171 See eg D. Akande, 'The African Union takes on the ICC Again: Are African States Really Turning from the ICC?' (EJIL Talk, 26 July 2011) <http://www.ejiltalk.org/the-african-union-takes-on-the-icc-again/> accessed 6 June 2015.

172 S. Heder, 'A Review of the Negotiations Leading to the Establishment of the Personal Jurisdiction of the Extraordinary Chambers in the Courts of Cambodia' (Cambodia Tribunal Review, 1 August 2011) <http://www.cambodiatribunal.org/blog/2011/08/review-negotiations-leading-establishment-personal-jurisdiction-extraordinary-chambers> accessed 6 June 2015.

173 *Delalić* IT-96-21-T (Decision on Motion for Provisional Release, 25 September 1996) para 20.

174 *Prlić* IT-04-74-AR65.8 (Decision on Provisional Release, 25 April 2008) para 16; cf. *Stanišić and Simatović* IT-03-69-PT (Decision on Provisional Release, 26 May 2008) para 45.

175 *Nsengimana* ICTR-01-69-AR65 (Decision on Interlocutory Appeal, 23 August 2005) 3; *Ngirumpatse* ICTR-99-44-AR65 (Decision on Provisional Release, 7 April 2009) para 13.

176 See for example *Milutinović* IT-99-37-PT (Decision on Motion for Provisional Release, 14 April 2005) para 8; *Sainović* IT-99-37-PT (Decision on Motion for Provisional Release, 14 April 2005) para 12.

177 See *Sesay* SCSL-04-15-PT (Decision on Defence Application for Leave, 31 March 2004) para 43; *Limaj et al* IT-03-66-AR65 (Decision on Request for Provisional Release, 31 October 2003) para 25; *Seselj* IT-03-67-PT (Decision on Motion for Provisional Release, 23 July 2004) para 7.

178 *Rukundo* ICTR-2001-70-I (Decision on Provisional Release, 15 July 2004) para 17; *Nsengimana* ICTR-01-69-I (Decision on Provisional Release, 11 July 2005) para 18.

179 *Bemba Gombo* ICC-01/05-01/08 (Decision on Application for Judicial Review, 27 September 2011) para 36.

180 *Čerkez* IT-95-14/2-T 14 (Decision on Provisional Release, 23 September 1999) 2; *Čermak* IT-06-90-T (Decision on Motion for Provisional Release, 2 December 2008) para 11; cf *Blaskić* IT-95-14-T (Order Denying a Motion for Provisional Release, 20 December 1996) 5.

181 *Plavšić* IT-00-39&40-T (Application of Pardon, 5 September 2001) 3; *Milutinović* IT-99-37-PT (Decision on Motion for Provisional Release, 14 April 2005) paras 21-23; cf *Krajišnik* IT-00-39&40-T (Decision on Motion for Provisional Release, 8 October 2001) para 10; *Drljača and Kovačević* IT-07-24-PT (Decision on Defence Motion for Provisional Release, 20 January 1998) para 27.

Likewise, at the ICTR, where such guarantees cannot be obtained, personal undertakings, including residing in a country that provides no guarantees of its own, have been insufficient to secure release.[182]

4.2 Danger to Witnesses and Victims and Risk of Reoffending

The second primary consideration in provisional release applications is the danger of what an accused might do while at liberty. This encompasses the danger of the commission of further offences, or of interference with victims, witnesses or evidence.

4.2.1 Danger of reoffending

Those detained by international tribunals are generally less likely than domestic criminals to reoffend once the relevant conflict is over and the political situation has been stabilized. Often they were not the direct perpetrators of the crimes. Nonetheless, this consideration may retain some relevance where there is a concern that the accused might reengage in political or paramilitary affairs that may precipitate such crimes. This is most pertinent in cases brought before a tribunal when the relevant conflict has not yet finished.[183]

There should be a distinction drawn between preventing further crimes and interfering in domestic politics. On the one hand, the removal of destabilizing individuals may aid a politically volatile region to regain peace and security. On the other, political intervention is not the object of detention on remand. In the *Haradinaj* case, for example, it was considered that the prohibition on participation in political activity as a condition for provisional release was an undue restriction on his freedom of speech,[184] although one judge cautioned that his release on such terms 'could be perceived as a de facto re-instatement of the Accused'.[185] The six accused in the Situation in Kenya, three of whom were ministers, surrendered themselves to the ICC on summonses which required them, inter alia, to abstain from interfering with witnesses, but contained no restriction on political activity;[186] two of them contested presidential elections in 2013 and one was elected.[187]

---

[182] *Bicamumpaka* ICTR-99-50-T (Decision on Defence Motion for Provisional Release, 25 July 2001) para 3; *Rukundo* ICTR-2001-70-I (Decision on Defence Motion for Provisional Release, 18 August 2003) para 22; *Muhimana* ICTR-95-1-B-1 (Decision on Provisional Release, 1 October 2002) para 7.

[183] The ICTY, for example, was established by SCRes 827 on 25 May 1993, whereas the Dayton Peace Agreement was not signed until 14 December 1995. At the ICC, the risk of the commission of further crimes has been expressly retained as a consideration: Art. 58(1)(b)(iii) ICCSt.

[184] *Haradinaj et al* IT-04-84-PT (Decision on Defence Motion for Provisional Release, 12 October 2005).

[185] Ibid., per Agius J (dissenting in part) 6.

[186] *Muthaura, Kenyatta and Ali* ICC-01/09-02/11 (Decision on Prosecutor's Application for Summonses to Appear, 8 March 2011).

[187] See 'Kenya Supreme Court upholds Uhuru Kenyatta election win' (BBC News, 30 March 2013) <http://www.bbc.co.uk/news/world-africa-21979298> accessed 12 June 2015.

4.2.2 Danger to witnesses

Detention may also be justified by concerns that an accused might endanger (potential) witnesses or interfere with complex investigations.[188] In the *Bemba Gombo* case, for example, the ICC gave substantial weight to incidents of witness intimidation in refusing release.[189]

Witness intimidation has been a recurring problem at the *ad hoc* Tribunals.[190] In the *Haradinaj* trial, the intimidation created 'significant difficulties in securing the testimony of a large number of witnesses [who] cited fear as a prominent reason for not wishing to appear before the Trial Chamber to give evidence'.[191] Haradinaj was acquitted,[192] but a partial retrial was ordered on the basis of the intimidation of witnesses.[193] At the ICTR, a Hutu woman and her husband and seven children were killed after testifying against Akayesu.[194] At least ten witnesses were killed in 1996 before they had a chance to testify, and another 11 were killed on account of one person's choice to answer questions for ICTR investigators.[195] At the ICC, the Chamber has heard *ex parte* of '[s]everal incidents (...) since July 2011 in which threats [were] allegedly (...) made against prosecution witnesses and their families in connection with their testimony at the Court'.[196]

At the ICTY, earlier cases had found that the risk of intimidation increases as the trial proceeds and the previously confidential identities of witnesses are revealed.[197] A similar position was stated in early decisions at the ICC.[198] However, this logic was criticized in later years with the observation that mere knowledge of witness identities without more cannot properly found an inference regarding the risk to their safety should the accused be released.[199] That is especially true where the evidence suggests

---

[188] See for example *Chea et al* 002/19-09-2007/ECCC (Interlocutory Decision on the Applicable Law, 16 February 2011) para 59. This is consistent with observations of the ECtHR: *W v Switzerland* App no 14379/88 (ECtHR, 26 January 1993) para 35; *Wemhoff v Germany* App no 2122/64 (ECtHR, 27 June 1968) para 14.

[189] *Bemba Gombo* ICC-01/05-01/08-1565 (Decision on Application on Provisional Release, 16 August 2011) para 63; *Bemba Gombo* ICC-01/05-01/08 27 (Decision on Application for Judicial Review, September 2011) paras 29–33.

[190] For examples, see A. Trotter, 'Witness Intimidation at the ad hoc Tribunals: Balancing the Need for Protection against the Rights of the Accused' (2012) 44 *George Washington International Law Review* 521.

[191] *Haradinaj et al* IT-04-84-T (Judgment, 3 April 2008) para 6.

[192] Ibid., para 502.

[193] *Haradinaj et al* IT-04-84-A (Judgment, 19 July 2010) para 40.

[194] C. Walsh, 'Witness Protection, Gender and the ICTR: A report prepared as a result of investigations in Rwanda in June and July 1997' (ICTR 1997) para 1.

[195] Ibid., paras 1–3.

[196] *Bemba Gombo* ICC-01/05-01/08 (Decision on Application for Judicial Review, 27 September 2011) para 29.

[197] *Blaskić* IT-95-14-T (Decision on Provisional Release, 25 April 1996) 5; *Kupreškić et al* IT-95-16-PT (Order on Motion for Provisional Release, 15 December 1997) para 16; *Kvočka* IT-98-30/01-PT (Decision on Motion for Provisional Release, 2 February 2000) 3.

[198] *Lubanga* ICC-01/04-01/06 (Decision on Application for Interim Release, 18 October 2006) 3.

[199] *Brđanin* IT-99-36-PT (Decision on Provisional Release, 25 July 2000) para 19; *Talić* IT-99-36-PT (Decision on Provisional Release, 28 March 2003) para 34.

that there has been no such interference despite an opportunity to do so.[200] In addition to the past conduct of the accused in relation to witnesses (if any),[201] other relevant factors may include any stated intention of the accused to prejudice or obstruct the trial,[202] the effectiveness or any breach of protective measures afforded to witnesses,[203] the proximity of witnesses to the proposed location of release,[204] or the volatility of the political situation in that location.[205]

4.2.3 Danger to the public

In some cases, the risk of danger caused by the release of the accused has been cast in broader terms as an issue of 'public order'.[206] This consideration has been adopted at the SCSL,[207] and ECCC.[208] Its relevance at those two tribunals is considered to be increased by the fact that the seat of the tribunal is in the same country where the offences are alleged to have been committed.[209] However, an early suggestion at the ICTY that the release of the accused might of itself affect the willingness of witnesses to testify[210] has since been rejected as overly general and failing to account for the particular circumstances of the defendant.[211] Nonetheless, it has continued to receive

---

200 *Stanišić and Simatović* IT-03-69-AR65.4 (Decision on Defence Motion for Provisional Release, 26 June 2008) para 55.

201 See for example *Brahimaj* IT-04-86bis-PT (Decision on Defence Motion for Provisional Release, 10 September 2010) para 27.

202 Consider the case of *Šešelj* IT-03-67-PT (Decision on Defence Motion for Provisional Release, 23 July 2008) para 8; *Šešelj* IT-03-67-R77.3 (Judgment, 31 October 2011) paras 49–65; *Šešelj* IT-03-67-R77.4 (Initial Appearance, 6 July 2011) T. 1–3.

203 As was the case in *Bemba Gombo* ICC-01/05-01/08 (Decision on Defence Application on Provisional Release, 27 September 2011) para 30.

204 *Boškoski* IT-04-92-AR65.2 (Decision on Ljube Boškoski's Interlocutory Appeal on Provisional Release, 28 September 2005) paras 19–20; cf *Čerkez* IT-95-14/2-T (Decision on Defence Motion for Provisional Release, 14 September 1999) 3; *Stanišić* IT-03-69-PT (Decision on Defence Motion for Provisional Release, 19 July 2005) para 18.

205 *Brahimaj et al* IT-04-84-PT (Decision on Defence Motion for Provisional Release, 3 November 2005) 6.

206 That concept as a basis for refusing bail finds its origins in the French legal system and has been accepted with some qualification by the ECtHR: *Letellier v France* App no 12369/86 (ECtHR, 26 June 1991) paras 38–39, 51; cf *Romanova v Russia* App no 23215/02 (ECtHR, 10 November 2011) para 132; *Kemmache v France (no 1 and 2)* App no 12325/86&14992/89 (ECtHR, 27 November 1991) para 52; *Tomasi v France* App no 12850/87 (ECtHR, 27 August 1992) para 91.

207 *Fofana* SCSL-04-14-T (Decision on Motion for Provisional Release, 11 March 2005) para 31.

208 See eg *Ieng Thirith* 002/19-09-2007/ECCC (9 July 2008) para 72; *Chea et al* 002/19-09-2007/ECCC (20 March 2008) paras 74–76.

209 See for example *Sesay* SCSL-04-15-PT (Decision on Defence Application for Leave, 31 March 2004) paras 42–43.

210 *Blaskić* IT-95-14-T (Decision on Motion of Defence on Provisional Release, 25 April 1996) 5; *Kunarac* IT-96-23-PT (Decision on Provisional Release, 11 November 1999) para 7.

211 *Brđanin* IT-99-36-PT (Decision on Motion for Provisional Release, 25 July 2000) para 20.

some limited support from separate and dissenting opinions.[212] The proposition has not found favour at the ICC.[213]

4.2.4 Danger to victims' rights

In its broadest form, the 'danger to victims' criterion has been characterized as the offence to victims' rights generally, rather than any specific concern for their safety. Civil parties at the ICC have argued that to release an alleged war criminal is to trivialize the inhumanity of the crimes,[214] and to 'cultivate a sense of impunity on the part of perpetrators'.[215] Likewise, at the *ad hoc* Tribunals, this analysis was employed to support the requirement to demonstrate 'compelling humanitarian reasons' after the close of the prosecution case, because a 'perception that persons accused of international crimes are released, for a prolonged period of time (...) could have a prejudicial effect on victims'.[216] The ICC Appeals Chamber allowed the participation of 47 anonymous victims in the prosecutor's ultimately successful appeal against the provisional release of Bemba Gombo.[217] By contrast, the participation of victims in Duch's application for release at the ECCC was denied.[218]

Although there is a trend towards giving victims a greater role in international criminal proceedings due to the nature of the charged crimes and the dual punitive and restorative role of international criminal trials, this line of reasoning has been criticized as departing too far from the central purpose of detention on remand – to secure the proper administration of the trial – and yielding to the demands of victims at the expense of criminal process and the presumption of innocence.[219] In some cases, the submission has been put more bluntly still as an issue of public perception, although such arguments have not found traction.[220]

---

212 See eg *Halilović* IT-01-48-T (Decision on Motion for Provisional Release, 1 September 2005; its only acceptance is in separate or dissenting opinions such as Separate Opinion of Judge Shahabudeen in *Sainović and Ojdanić* IT-99-37-AR65 (Decision on Provisional Release, 30 October 2002) para 17; *Prlić et al* IT-04-74-AR65.6 (Decision on Provisional Release, 23 April 2008) per Schomburg J (dissenting) para 10.

213 *Bemba Gombo* ICC-01/05-01/08-1565 (Defence Urgent Motion for Provisional Release, 16 August 2011) paras 35–36; *Lubanga* ICC-01/04-01/06-1418 (Decision on Release, 2 July 2008) para 21.

214 *Lubanga* ICC-01/04-01/06-1487 (Decision on the Appeal against Provisional Release, 21 October 2008) para 28.

215 Ibid., Dissenting Opinion of Judge Pikis para 9.

216 *Petković et al* IT-04-74-AR65.7 (Decision on Motion for Provisional Release, 21 April 2008) para 17.

217 *Bemba Gombo* ICC-01/05-01/08-566 (Decision on Legal Assistance, 20 October 2009) para 17; see also *Lubanga* 01/04-01/06 (OA 7) (Decision on the Appeal against Provisional Release, 13 February 2007) para 54.

218 *Duch* 001/18-07-2007/ECCC (Written Record of Proceedings Trial Chamber, 6 April 2009) 3–4.

219 See generally L. Henderson, 'The Wrongs of Victims' Rights' (1985) 37 *Stanford Law Review* 937, 986.

220 See eg submissions of the Prosecution in *Stanišić* IT-08-91-T 18 (Decision Granting Provisional Release, November 2011) para 7.

4.3 Other Requirements

In addition to the two core considerations set out above, there have been controversial developments in the provisional release formula at the *ad hoc* Tribunals that deserve particular mention.

First, the RPE as originally enacted allowed release 'only in exceptional circumstances'.[221] That requirement was removed by unanimous vote at the ICTY in November 1999. The equivalent rule was not amended at the ICTR until May 2003.[222] The implication was a strong presumption against provisional release.[223] The effect was to confine provisional release to cases in which 'very precise and specific reasons presented themselves which leant strongly in favour of release'.[224] One factor considered relevant was the duration of the detention of the accused,[225] although it never founded a successful application despite considerable delays in the trial process.[226]

In practical terms, release was confined to cases of serious or terminal illness of the accused[227] or a close family member.[228] An accused seeking provisional release based on their own illness would be called on to demonstrate a lack of adequate treatment locally.[229] If on the basis of the illness of a family member, the gravity of their condition was closely scrutinized.[230] Despite numerous applications, only four met that threshold at the ICTY, and none at the ICTR. Shortly after the standard was removed, the same Chamber granted two accused whose applications had been previously

[221] Rule 65(B) ICTY RPE (Original version, 11 February 1994).

[222] This was despite submissions to the contrary in various cases: see for example *Bagosora et al* ICTR-98-41-T (Decision on Motion for Provisional Release, 12 July 2002) para 22; *Kanyabashi* ICTR-96-15-T (Decision on Motion for Provisional Release, 21 February 2001) paras 4–5; *Ndayambaje* ICTR-98-42-T (Decision on Motion for Provisional Release, 21 October 2002) para 20; *Sagahutu* ICTR-00-56-T (Decision on Appeal Against Provisional Release, 25 September 2002) para 47; *Sagahutu* ICTR-00-56-I (Decision on Defence Motion for Provisional Release, 26 March 2003) 5.

[223] See for example *Blaskić* IT-95-14-T (Order Denying a Motion for Provisional Release, 20 December 1996) 4; *Drljača and Kovačević* IT-07-24-PT (Decision on Provisional Release, 20 January 1998) para 6; *Aleksovski* IT-95-14/1-PT (Decision Denying a Request for Provisional Release, 23 January 1998) 4.

[224] *Ademi* IT-01-46-PT (Order on Motion for Provisional Release, 20 February 2002) para 13.

[225] *Delalić et al* IT-96-21-T (Decision on Motion for Provisional Release, 25 September 1996) para 21.

[226] See for example *Kordić and Čerkez* IT-95-14/2-PT (Decision Rejecting the Application to Withdraw the Indictment and Order for Provisional Release, 22 March 1999) 4.

[227] *Đukic* IT-96-20-T (Decision on Provisional Release on Humanitarian Grounds, 24 April 1996); *Simić et al* IT-95-9-PT (Decision on Application for Provisional Release, 26 March 1998).

[228] *Josipović* IT-95-16-T (Decision on Motion for Provisional Release, 6 May 1999); *Čerkez* IT-95-14/2-T (Decision on Motion for Provisional Release, 14 September 1999).

[229] *Drljača and Kovačević* IT-07-24-PT (Decision on Provisional Release, 20 January 1998) para 14; *Kunarac* IT-96-23-PT (Decision on Provisional Release, 11 November 1999) para 8.

[230] See for example *Kupreškić et al* IT-95-16-T (Order on Application for Provisional Release, 30 July 1999) 2–3; *Kupreškić et al* IT-95-16-T (Decision on the Motions of Provisional Release, 13 September 1999) 3.

denied,[231] although that trend was not true for all cases.[232] Several decisions that followed emphasized that the change fell short of creating a presumption in favour of release.[233] It remains a minority view that the effect of the repeal was 'to bring the Rule in line with modern international human rights law that detention shall not be the general rule'.[234]

Second, in April 2008 the *ad hoc* Tribunals' common Appeal Chamber implied into the rule a requirement that any application for provisional release brought after the close of the Prosecution case be supported by 'serious and sufficiently compelling humanitarian reasons'.[235] The justification for the implied requirement was that the rejection of a no-case submission at the end of the prosecution case constituted a confirmation that 'that a reasonable trier of fact could make a finding beyond any reasonable doubt that the accused is guilty'; therefore a Trial Chamber must thereafter take a more conservative approach towards release.[236] Some decisions reasoned that detainees would, after this point, be more likely to abscond.[237] However, the standard was taken to apply equally in cases where no no-case submission had been made.[238]

'Compelling humanitarian reasons' appear to have been much the same in scope as 'exceptional circumstances', including the 'need to visit a seriously ill family member in the hospital'.[239] For this reason the former was seen by many as the effective re-enactment of the latter.[240] Further, it appears that compelling humanitarian grounds

---

[231] The requests were presented on 19 January 1999 and denied on 15 February 1999; decision denying vacated and matter remanded on procedural grounds on 28 July 1999; amendment of rule 65(B) at plenary session in November 1999, entering into force on 6 December 1999: *Kvočka* IT-98-30-PT (Decision on Motion for Provisional Release, 2 February 2000).

[232] *Kupreškić et al* IT-95-16-T (Decision on Motion for Provisional Release, 20 December 1999) para 3.

[233] *Kvočka* IT-98-30-PT (Decision on Motion for Provisional Release, 2 February 2000) 4; *Brđanin* IT-99-36-PT (Decision on Motion for Provisional Release, 25 July 2000) para 12; *Krajišnik* IT-00-39&40-T (Decision on Motion for Provisional Release, 8 October 2001) para 12. See also the observations of the ICTR to that effect: *Nahimana* ICTR-99-52-T (Decision on Motion for Release or Alternatively Provisional Release, 5 September 2002) para 11; *Muhimana* ICTR-95-1-B-1 (Decision on Motion for Provisional Release, 1 October 2002) para 5.

[234] *Krajišnik and Plavšić* IT-00-39&40-T (Decision on Notice of Motion for Provisional Release, 8 October 2001) per Robinson J (dissenting) paras 2, 16.

[235] *Petković* IT-04-74-AR65.7 (Decision on Appeal against Provisional Release, 21 April 2008) para 17.

[236] Ibid.

[237] See the explanation to this effect in *Prlić et al* IT-04-74-AR65.5 (Decision on Appeal against Provisional Release, 11 March 2008) para 20.

[238] *Petković* IT-04-74-T (Decision on Provisional Release, 31 March 2008) 3 (successfully appealed by Prosecution in *Petković* IT-04-74-AR65.7 (Decision on Appeal against Provisional Release, 21 April 2008)).

[239] *Petković* IT-04-74-AR65.7 (Decision on Appeal against Provisional Release, 21 April 2008) para 17; see also to similar effect *Petković* IT-04-74-T (Decision on Provisional Release, 31 March 2008) 7; *Čorić* IT-04-74-T (Decision on Motion for Provisional Release, 2 December 2008) para 34.

[240] *Petković* IT-04-74-AR65.7 (Decision on Appeal against Provisional Release, 21 April 2008) per Guney J (dissenting) para 4.

could not be achieved by a combination of reasons.[241] The implied standard was met with overt judicial[242] and academic opposition.[243] In 2011 the criterion was reduced from a pre-requisite to an *ex gratia* consideration by a majority of judges at an extraordinary plenary session on 20 October 2011.[244] However, this criterion retains a discernible impact: for example the provisional release of Goran Hadžić was not ordered until five judges of the Appeals Chamber intervened, six months after he collapsed in court and was unable to take part in proceedings due to terminal brain cancer.[245]

5. COMPARISON WITH DOMESTIC JURISDICTIONS AND INTERNATIONAL STANDARDS

The ICCPR stipulates clearly that '[i]t shall not be the general rule that persons awaiting trial shall be detained in custody'.[246] Under ECtHR jurisprudence detention may initially be justified by a reasonable suspicion that the person arrested has committed an offence.[247] However, 'the persistence of suspicion does not suffice to justify, after a certain lapse of time, the prolongation of the detention'.[248] In such cases detention may be continued 'only if there are specific indications of a genuine requirement of public interest which, notwithstanding the presumption of innocence, outweigh the rule of respect for individual liberty'.[249] The purpose of any detention prior to final judgment must be to protect the public and the interests of justice, not to anticipate the sentence and impose a pre-emptive punishment.[250] As put by one Trial

---

241 *Pusić* IT-04-74-AR65.6 (Decision on Appeal against Provisional Release, 23 April 2008) per Schomburg J (dissenting) para 16.

242 Eg *Stanišić* IT-08-91-AR65.2 (Decision on Appeal against Decision on Provisional Release, 29 August 2011) per Güney J para 1; *Stanišić* IT-08-91-AR65.1 (Decision on Provisional Release, 11 May 2011) per Robinson J; *Miletić* IT-05-88 (Decision on Motion for Provisional Release, 15 October 2009) per Prost J; *Gvero* IT-05-88 (Decision on Motion for Provisional Release, 17 December 2009) per Agius J.

243 For more detail, see A. Trotter, 'Innocence, Liberty and Provisional Release at the ICTY: a Post-Mortem of "Compelling Humanitarian Grounds" in Context' (2012) 12 *Human Rights Law Review* 353.

244 The rule entered into force seven days after the amendment was passed, on 28 October 2011: Rules 6(D) and 65(B) ICTY RPE (Rev. 46, 20 October 2011). See also *Stanišić and Župljanin* IT-08-91-T (Decision Granting Request for Provisional Release, 18 November 2011) para 14.

245 *Hadžić* IT-04-75 (Decision on Urgent Motion for Provisional Release Filed on 28 April 2015, 21 May 2015); but see *Hadžić* IT-04-75 (Consolidated Decision on the Continuation of Proceedings, 26 October 2015).

246 Art. 9(3) ICCPR; see also UN General Assembly, Report of the 3rd Committee of the General Assembly (UN Doc A/4045, YB 1958) HR 205 para 56.

247 Art. 5(1)(c) ECHR; *W v Switzerland* App no 14379/88 (ECtHR, 26 January 1993) para 30.

248 *Stögmuller v Austria* App no 1602/62 (ECtHR, 10 November 1969) para 4.

249 *W v Switzerland* App no 14379/88 (ECtHR, 26 January 1993) para 30.

250 *Letellier v France* App no 12369/86 (ECtHR, 26 June 1991) para 51.

Chamber, a determination on this basis would require the Chamber 'to weigh the evidence adduced by the Prosecution against that of the Accused, and this is a task reserved for the Chamber's final assessment of all the evidence at the conclusion of the trial'.[251]

There is a special duty of diligence where the defendant is kept in detention,[252] which applies equally in complex trials for international crimes.[253] If the trial is not appropriately expedited, the detention is less likely to be reasonable, and the appropriate remedy is more likely to be release.[254] Hence, at the STL for example, there is provision for the release of an accused, with or without conditions, if a person is 'detained for an unreasonable period prior to trial due to inexcusable delay by the Prosecutor'.[255]

Many domestic courts have frequently fallen below these standards. In most jurisdictions those charged with grave crimes tend to be detained pending or during their trial. In Canada bail is not available for persons charged with genocide, crimes against humanity or war crimes.[256] In the United States the onus of proof at bail hearings is reversed in the case of certain repeat offenders.[257] In other countries a lesser standard of proof is required of the prosecution when charges are particularly serious.[258] The crimes over which the international tribunals have jurisdiction fall into that category. In addition, in some jurisdictions, the detention of a defendant may be ordered at preliminary stages based on the strength of the prosecution case against them,[259] and the constitutionality of such provisions has been judicially affirmed in both the United States[260] and Canada.[261] Some national courts have also concluded that the presumption of innocence should not be given such broad application as to factor in interlocutory matters.[262]

---

[251] This statement was made in the context of denying a request for provisional release on the basis that the evidence against the accused had weakened: *Pavković* IT-05-87-T (Decision on Motion for Temporary Provisional Release, 7 December 2007) para 9. The defendant in question was later acquitted.

[252] *Kuibishev v Bulgaria* App no 39271/98 (ECtHR, 8 April 2004) para 70.

[253] *Jentzsch v Federal Republic of Germany* App no 2604/65 (ECtHR, 5 May 1971); *Gericke v Federal Republic of Germany* App no 2294/64 (ECtHR, 16 December 1964).

[254] *Kuibishev v Bulgaria* App no 39271/98 (ECtHR, 8 April 2004) para 70; *EMK v Bulgaria* App no 43231/98 (ECtHR, 18 January 2005) paras 124–125.

[255] Rule 101(E) STL RPE.

[256] Sections 469(c.1), 515(11) Criminal Code (Canada); ss 4(1), 6(1) Crimes Against Humanity and War Crimes Act (Canada). The same applies to several other crimes.

[257] Para 3142(e) 18 U.S.C. (2006); cf. para 3142(j).

[258] See eg s 172 Criminal Procedure Act 1981 (Norway); Art. 112(3) Code of Criminal Procedure (Germany) (interestingly, not including war crimes and crimes against humanity); Art. 148(1)(4) Code of Criminal Procedure (Montenegro).

[259] Art. 56(3) Code of Criminal Procedure (Bulgaria); Art. 112(3) Code of Criminal Procedure (Germany).

[260] Para 3142(g)(2) 18 U.S.C. in *United States v Salerno* [1987] 481 U.S. 739, 744.

[261] Para 515(10)(c) Criminal Code (Canada) R.S.C. 1985 c.C-46 in *R v Hall* [2002] 3 S.C.R. 309 para 40.

[262] This has been the position at various points in the past, for example, in Scotland (*H.M. Advocate v M'Glinchey* [1921] JC 75 cited with approval in *McLeod v Wright* [1959] J.C. 12,

On the other hand, it would not be correct to say that the international tribunals have consistently exhibited human rights credentials that domestic jurisdictions have lacked. For example, international jurisdictions typically lack the complex and specific rules setting out strict time limits, locations and the clearly defined roles of appointed officials that are often well developed in domestic jurisdictions. Another obvious example is the onus of proof in the *ad hoc* Tribunals, cast on the accused to secure their release. The ICTY, for example, has had mixed approaches to the presumption of innocence. It has from time to time relegated it to one factor for consideration in balancing the interests of the accused against those of the public.[263] In some cases, the Tribunal has preferred to make a determination according to this balancing exercise without giving it specific regard.[264] In others, it has expressly renounced its relevance to the equation, insisting 'there is no right of an accused to provisional release (…) derived from the presumption of innocence'.[265] On the other hand, other Chambers have stated that the principles of provisional release 'must be seen as emanating from or as the corollary of the principle of the presumption of innocence'.[266] In the first decision following the amendments of October 2011, Trial Chamber II returned to a recognition of the significance to provisional release applications of 'the continuing presumption of innocence afforded to the Accused at all stages of trial prior to the rendering of a final Judgment'.[267]

By way of contrast, the Canadian Supreme Court, for example, has averred that it is a 'principle of fundamental justice that the starting point for any proposed deprivation of life, liberty or security of the person of anyone charged with or suspected of an offence must be that the person is innocent'.[268] In France the close logical link is expressly recognized by the legislative provision ensuring that the default position is release.[269] Likewise, the uniform detention of defendants during their trial, even following their release during the pre-trial stages, stands at odds with the jurisprudence of the ECtHR, which makes no such distinction.[270]

The fundamental question is therefore whether a higher standard should be expected of international jurisdictions. Where domestic jurisdictions have fallen below that standard, they have been criticized by international bodies. The ECtHR has been highly critical of a statutory presumption in favour of detention for a certain class of accused

---

14) and the US (*Bell v Wolfish* [1979] 441 U.S. 520, 533; a sentiment closely followed by the enactment of draconian bail reforms approved in *United States v Salerno* [1987] 481 U.S. 739).

263 *Talić* IT-99-36-T (Decision on Motion for Provisional Release, 20 September 2002) para 14.

264 *Jokić* IT-01-42-PT (Order on Motion for Provisional Release, 20 February 2002) para 20.

265 *Perišić* IT-04-81-T (Decision on Motion for Provisional Release, 17 December 2008) para 15.

266 *Aleksovski* IT-94-14/1 (Decision on Provisional Release, 23 January 1998) 3; *Sesay* SCSL-04-15-AR65 (Decision on Appeal against Refusal of Bail, 14 December 2004) para 34.

267 *Stanišić* IT-08-91-T (Decision Granting Request for Provisional Release, 18 November 2011) para 23.

268 *R v Pearson* [1992] 3 SCR 665 para 24; see also *Stack v Boyle* [1951] 342 U.S. 1, 4.

269 Art. 137 Code of Criminal Procedure (France).

270 *Wemhoff v Germany* App no 2122/64 (ECtHR, 27 June 1968) paras 6–7; *W v Switzerland* App no 14379/88 (ECtHR, 26 January 1993) para 30.

in Bulgaria, saying that 'it was incumbent on the authorities to establish' the necessity for detention.[271] The ECtHR also found a violation of the right not to be unreasonably detained by a similar provision in relation to serious offences in the UK.[272] Likewise, the HRC has called for the reform of terrorism provisions in Australia placing a heavy burden on the accused to avoid detention.[273] Some have argued that the higher standard should be the starting point for international tribunals: that the most prominent of trials is not the place to be making concessions on human rights.[274]

Any divergences from human rights jurisprudence are often explained in terms of the exceptionality of the circumstances surrounding international tribunals.[275] It has also been argued that 'care should be taken that too great a reliance is not placed upon [the decisions of the ECtHR] as defining what is a reasonable length of pre-trial detention in an international criminal court or tribunal rather than in particular domestic jurisdictions in Europe'.[276] The crimes in question in international trials are of greater gravity. The defendants may have greater capacity to avoid capture and interfere with witnesses or evidence. The tribunals themselves have less power and fewer resources to apprehend offenders. They are often situated in Host States that refuse to allow alleged war criminals to take up residence at liberty during their trials, or local political tensions may make their release otherwise diplomatically untenable. The defendants may be notorious figures associated by the public with infamous atrocities, and their trials may come with considerable delay, and themselves take several years.

It has been suggested that this 'innate powerlessness', stronger 'punitive impulses', more difficult factual and legal tasks and higher aspirations to 'end impunity' of international courts militate in favour of lowering the bar for procedural fairness which might otherwise inhibit these pursuits.[277] The competing need for a swift trial in the interests of both defendants and victims could require a more measured approach to such aspects of procedural fairness as the right to self-representation, admissibility of evidence obtained by questionable means, or the privilege of self-incrimination.[278] Such reasoning could no doubt be extended to many other matters which prolong international criminal cases in the name of procedural fairness, including certain appellate rights, and the depth to which the finer or more procedural points of law are allowed to be litigated. It might be argued that the same logic applies to provisional release.

---

[271] *Ilijkov v Bulgaria* App no 33977/96 (26 July ECtHR, 2001) para 85.

[272] *SBC v UK* App no 39360/98 (ECtHR, 19 June 2001) para 22; see also *Caballero v UK* App no 32819/96 (ECtHR, 8 February 2000) ECHR 2000-II paras 20–21.

[273] HRC, Consideration of Reports Submitted by States Parties under Article 40 of the Covenant: Concluding observations of the HRC (Australia) (UN Doc. CCPR/C/AUS/CO/5, 7 May 2009) para 11.

[274] See arguments advanced to this effect by Fairlie (n 1) 1148.

[275] See for example *Ademi* IT-01-46-PT (Order on Motion for Provisional Release, 20 February 2002) para 12; *Ntabakuze* ICTR-98-41-A (Decision on Motion for Provisional Release, 2 September 2009) para 22.

[276] *Brđanin* IT-99-36-PT (Decision on Motion for Provisional Release, 25 July 2000) paras 26–27.

[277] M. Damaška, 'Reflections on Fairness in International Criminal Justice' (2012) 10 JICJ 611, 613.

[278] Ibid., 617–19.

On the other hand, provisional release may be segregated from this category on the basis that it is not simply a matter of procedural fairness. The question of whether a defendant is detained in custody or allowed to remain at liberty until convicted does not affect in the same way as the examples cited above the ability of the accused to contest their case. Bearing in mind that provisional release is only granted in any event where the risks of flight and interference with witnesses can be appropriately managed, it might be said that provisional release is not affected by the tension between the need for swift justice and the rights of the accused.

6. CONCLUSION

While the procedures governing provisional release differ from tribunal to tribunal according to their constitutional framework, the guiding principles are the same. In each instance, fundamentally, provisional release is to be made available where the accused's absence from the tribunal is unlikely to conflict with the need to see the trial progress without interference. In the particular case of international criminal trials, that principle is visibly constrained by the limitations on the tribunals' power to ensure the return of the accused and the political climate of the home State. The agreement between the ICC and Belgium signed in April 2014 may ameliorate this situation.[279] That agreement is the first and a significant move towards overcoming the practical difficulties that have been cited in support of more stringent standards. Its practical effect on the implementation of those standards at the ICC will be an area to be closely watched in the years to come.

However, the reluctance to grant provisional release, particularly in the case of the *ad hoc* Tribunals, appears to extend beyond those practical considerations. Such matters include the reversed onus of proof, extraneous legal standards, broad discretion to detain the accused, and reference to somewhat vague or tenuous bases for continuing detention such as the rights of victims or public order. That such a tendency is frequently coupled with reference to the gravity of the alleged crimes suggests that the strict approach to provisional release is a consequence not only of the practical limitations of the tribunals but also of a level of anxiety to ensure they are successful in their legally and diplomatically challenging pursuit of prosecuting powerful actors for serious crimes. At times that has arguably come at the expense of the strict observance of international human rights standards. The critics would suggest that among these considerations, pre-conviction detention has come to be treated more as the norm than as a 'serious departure from the rules of respect for individual liberty and of the presumption of innocence'.[280] This has created some conflict with international human rights standards.

---

[279] ICC, 'Press Release, Belgium and ICC sign agreement on interim release of detainees' (10 April 2014).

[280] *Stögmuller v Austria* App no 1602/62 (ECtHR, 10 November 1969) para 4; see eg *Ademi* IT-01-46-PT (Order on Motion for Provisional Release, 20 February 2002) para 12.

It must be recognized that the flexibility in provisional release has come a considerable way since the modern naissance of international criminal law at Nuremberg, where it was not even considered. The *ad hoc* Tribunals were the first significant courts to have been established since then, and the progress from a human rights point of view made by the ICC has been considerable, despite its political challenges. As the *ad hoc* Tribunals draw to a close, the focus must shift to the ICC to adopt a more liberal approach to provisional release that is more consistent with international human rights standards and with the presumption of innocence. In particular, that requires that the onus of proof be borne by the prosecution, and that preventative detention be imposed only where it is necessary to ensure the accused's presence at trial or to avoid an unnecessary risk of danger to the community or to particular witnesses or complainants, rather than by reference to extraneous standards of the kind discussed in this chapter. The alternative is to acknowledge that the presumption of innocence does not apply in the same manner in the context of international criminal law, where the evidence may be overwhelming or the purposes and functions of institutions are broader than the determination of individual criminal responsibility. The latter proposition is attended with some with difficulty, not least because international criminal proceedings are at particular risk of politicization, and because several defendants have been acquitted by the international tribunals.

PART II

INTERNATIONAL PENALTIES

The international criminal tribunals and courts were established to try and eventually punish the most heinous crimes known to mankind. It is difficult to imagine penalties that can be regarded as adequate responses to such crimes. It may indeed be expected that such responses are to some extent based on the international community's retributivist and deterrent purposes in establishing these international tribunals and courts (among other purposes). International human rights law, however, sets limits to the modes of punishment that are available to these institutions.

The penalties that may be imposed by international tribunals and courts are laid down in their statutes. Both under their legal frameworks and in their actual practice, imprisonment is the most important penalty. The exclusion of the death penalty from the available penalties at the international criminal tribunals and courts established since the 1990s reflects relevant developments in human rights law towards its abolition.[1]

Since criminal punishment can be defined as the institutionalized infliction of harm by a State or, in the context of international criminal justice, by an international court or tribunal, the principles of respect for human dignity and for the rule of law demand a justification for the establishment, the meting out and enforcement of penalties. In this section's first chapter (Chapter 3) Kai Ambos, aside from examining individual criminal liability and the modes of participation in supranational criminal law, explores the theoretical underpinnings of the (existence of the) world community's right to punish individual perpetrators of international crimes. Hence he addresses the question that must precede even the formulation of penalties, or of such objectives of punishment as retribution, deterrence and rehabilitation.

After this more theoretical first chapter, Chapters 4 and 5 focus on specific penalties that may be imposed by international criminal courts and tribunals. In Chapter 4, Dirk van Zyl Smit examines the penalty of imprisonment in the supranational criminal justice context. He first discusses how imprisonment became the most important sanction in supranational criminal justice and examines the critique of this supreme status of imprisonment as a criminal penalty. Van Zyl Smit further discusses the defects in both the process of determining the appropriate length of a prison sentence and the

[1] See, in more detail, W. Schabas, *The UN International Criminal Tribunals. The former Yugoslavia, Rwanda and Sierra Leone* (Cambridge University Press 2006) 546.

process of deciding upon requests for early release. He also examines the actual enforcement of imprisonment in the supranational context and discusses the limited role that rehabilitation plays in enforcing international prison sentences.

Imprisonment is the most important, but not the only penalty that may be imposed in the supranational criminal justice context. Rebecca Young, in Chapter 5, discusses fines and forfeiture in supranational criminal justice and in particular at the ICC. Fines are not listed as a possible penalty in the legal frameworks of other criminal courts and tribunals. Although the possibility of forfeiture is listed, it has not been utilized in those institutions' actual practice. Aside from setting out the ICC's legal regime that is applicable to fines and forfeiture and discussing its (non-)punitive nature, Young also critically assesses the applicable regime in light of both the cooperation of the ICC with States and procedural fairness.

3. *Ius puniendi* and individual criminal responsibility in international criminal law

Kai Ambos

1. INTRODUCTION

This chapter treats two fairly distinct, but at the same time related, topics since individual criminal responsibility is predicated on the recognition of a *ius puniendi*. The imposition of punishment is, in turn, predicated upon the determination of criminal responsibility. Thus, *ius puniendi*, responsibility and punishment are all interrelated elements of the (international) criminal justice process. The former element is a necessary, but not sufficient condition of the latter one, e.g., the *ius puniendi* is a necessary condition of responsibility and this, in turn, is a necessary condition of punishment. From a prosecution perspective, if everything goes according to plan the accused will be punished and the sentence enforced because his or her responsibility for the acts charged has been demonstrated beyond reasonable doubt.

As said at the beginning, however, this chapter will not treat the punishment element[1] but be limited to the *ius puniendi* and individual criminal responsibility. After clarifying the relevant concepts (Section 2), the chapter explores in more detail the *ius puniendi* and individual criminal responsibility in International Criminal Law ('ICL'). The former may be inferred from two limbs of a primarily collective and a primarily individualistic nature: on the one hand from the incipient supranationality of the world order (understood normatively as an order of values) and, on the other hand, from our basic human rights (human dignity) as citizens of the world society (see Section 3). As to individual criminal responsibility the chapter explains that an, at least, terminologically differentiated model of participation prevails in modern ICL. It further discusses the theoretical approaches to interpret the modes of liability in Article 25 ICCSt preferring a normative or theoretical against a merely positivist ('letter of the law') approach. Finally, the theoretical options to attribute crimes to the most responsible perpetrators are set out, i.e., joint criminal enterprise ('JCE'), indirect perpetration and command responsibility. Of course, the doctrine is difficult to reconcile with the ICCSt given its predominantly individualistic – instead of collective – conception of criminal responsibility.

---

[1] But see on international punishment and sentencing K. Ambos, *Treatise on International Criminal Law. Volume II: The Crimes and Sentencing* (Oxford University Press 2014) 267.

2. CONCEPTUAL CLARIFICATIONS: *IUS PUNIENDI* AND INDIVIDUAL CRIMINAL RESPONSIBILITY

2.1 *Ius Puniendi* (Concept and Meaning)

The question of the *ius puniendi*, i.e., the right or authority to punish, in ICL, comes down to the question of whether and how punitive power can exist at the supranational level without a sovereign supranational power to exercise this right in the first place. In other words, if the *ius puniendi* is part of the power of the State[2] how can there be such a right without a State, i.e., without a normative order to be defended by a (supranational) criminal law in the first place? I will give a – hopefully convincing – answer to this question in the third section of this chapter.

But what do we mean if we speak of ICL? Here ICL is understood in the strict sense, i.e., as the supranational law of the international core crimes (genocide, crimes against humanity, war crimes and the crime of aggression) with the respective rules of attribution (individual criminal responsibility) and the other areas of law necessary for a comprehensive ICL regime (the law of international criminal procedure, cooperation, etc.).[3] Thus, ICL *stricto sensu* (‘*Droit pénal international*’, ‘*Derecho penal internacional*’, ‘*Diritto penale internazionale*’, ‘*Völkerstrafrecht*’) comprises ‘the totality of international law norms of a penal nature which conjoin typical legal consequences of criminal law with a decisive conduct – namely the international crime – and as such can be applied directly’.[4] The idea of individual criminal responsibility and the ensuing prosecution of individuals for specific (macro-criminal) conduct[5] is derived from

[2] The ‘prima facie authority of the state to punish’ is fairly undisputed, see for a (brief) discussion with further references A. Ashworth and L. Zedner, ‘Punishment Paradigms and the Role of the Preventive State’, in Simester et al (eds), *Liberal Criminal Theory. Essays for Andreas von Hirsch* (Hart 2014) 3, 7–8.

[3] See, more broadly, for six meanings of ICL G. Schwarzenberger, ‘The Problem of an International Criminal Law’ (1950) 3 *Current Legal Problems* 263, 264–74; narrowing it down to four meanings C. Kreß, ‘International Criminal Law’, in R. Wolfrum (ed), *The Max Planck Encyclopedia of Public International Law* (Oxford University Press 2008) paras 1–14 (online edition, available at <www.mpepil.com> accessed 26 June 2015) including ICL *stricto sensu* as understood here.

[4] O. Triffterer, *Dogmatische Untersuchungen zur Entwicklung des materiellen Völkerstrafrechts seit Nürnberg* (Albert 1966) 34 (‘*Völkerstrafrecht im formellen Sinne (…) die Gesamtheit aller völkerrechtlichen Normen strafrechtlicher Natur, die an ein bestimmtes Verhalten – das internationale Verbrechen – bestimmte, typischerweise dem Strafrecht vorbehaltene Rechtsfolgen knüpfen, und die als solche unmittelbar anwendbar sind.*’ all translations from German by the author).

[5] On politically motivated macro-criminality as already an object of ICL K. Ambos, *Der Allgemeine Teil des Völkerstrafrechts* (Duncker & Humblot 2002) 50; See more recently F. Neubacher, *Kriminologische Grundlagen einer internationalen Strafgerichtsbarkeit* (Mohr Siebeck 2005) 18, 24, 30, 240–43, 479; R. Borsari, *Diritto punitivo sovranazionale come sistema* (Padova Cedam 2007) 442–4.

criminal law, while the classical (Nuremberg) offences[6] form part of (public) international law and thus the respective conduct is directly punishable under ICL (principle of direct individual criminal responsibility in public international law).[7]

Being primarily criminal law, enforced by international criminal Tribunals and the ICC, ICL fully encompasses the well-known principles of a liberal criminal justice system, in particular the principles of legality, culpability and fairness.[8] The further institutionalization of ICL with the establishment of the ICC entails the creation of a single penal system of and for the international community[9] – understood as a major group of States bound together by common values[10] – extending beyond the core areas of substantive and procedural law towards other branches of criminal law (law of sanctions, enforcement of sentences, judicial assistance etc.). This new penal system, however, represents only one – the supranational – element of the new 'International Criminal Justice System'. This system is a three-level system which gives priority to the territorial and suspect State (first level), subsidiary competence to the ICC (second level) and, lastly, third States on the basis of universal jurisdiction (third level). It may

---

[6] Cf. Art. 6 IMTSt (Agreement for the Prosecution and Punishment of the Major War Criminals of the European Axis, and Charter of the International Military Tribunal [London, 8 August 1945] 82 U.N.T.S. 279): Crimes Against Peace, War Crimes and Crimes Against Humanity.

[7] See generally G. Dahm, *Zur Problematik des Völkerstrafrechts* (Vandenhoeck & Ruprecht 1956) 14–17; more recently G. Werle, 'Die Zukunft des Völkerstrafrechts', in S Grundmann et al, *Festschrift 200 Jahre Juristische Fakultät der Humboldt-Universität zu Berlin* (De Gruyter 2010) 1219, 1225; B. Jesse, *Der Verbrechensbegriff des Römischen Statuts* (Duncker & Humblot 2009) 57.

[8] This view gains more and more ground in the international literature see D. Robinson, 'The Identity Crisis of International Criminal Law' (2008) 21 LJIL 925, 925–6, 961–2, speaking of a 'liberal system of criminal justice'; B. Sander, 'Unravelling the Confusion Concerning Successor Superior Responsibility in the ICTY Jurisprudence' (2010) 23 LJIL 105, 125.

[9] O. Triffterer, 'Universeller Menschenrechtsschutz auch durch das Völkerstrafrecht?', in, 'Die universale Geltung der Menschenrechte' (1995) Politische Studien Sonderheft 1/1995 32, 38; See also A. Zahar and G. Sluiter, *International Criminal Law* (Oxford University Press 2008) VII ('criminal law of the international community'); H-H. Jescheck, 'Schlußworte', in U. Sieber and H-J. Albrecht (eds), *Strafrecht und Kriminologie unter einem Dach* (Duncker & Humblot 2006) 152, 160; V. Reuss, *Zivilcourage als Strafzweck des Völkerstrafrechts* (Lit 2012) 54.

[10] I follow here Andreas Paulus' distinction between international community and society as explained in A. Paulus, 'International Law and International Community', in D. Armstrong (ed), *Handbook of International Law* (Routledge 2009) 44, 45 (giving 'community' a more normative meaning with a focus on 'values, beliefs and subjective feelings'); for a more profound study A. Paulus, *Die Internationale Gemeinschaft im Völkerrecht* (Beck 2001). For a similar value-based approach K.J. Fisher, *Moral Accountability and International Criminal Law* (Routledge 2012) 5–6 (referring to common liberal values but also common threats). Critic of the concept as privileging the powerful (western) States M. Koskenniemi, 'Between Impunity and Show Trials' (2002) 6 *Max Planck Yearbook of United Nations Law* 1, 10; conc. partly K.J. Fisher, *Moral Accountability and International Criminal Law* (Routledge 2012) 60–61.

be conceived as an instrument of global (judicial) governance operating through legalization and formalization.[11]

2.2 Individual Criminal Responsibility

In its most basic form, the principle of individual criminal responsibility in ICL merely states the obvious, i.e., that natural persons – as opposed to legal entities – are directly responsible for international crimes under international law. This is obvious since ICL is premised on such responsibility, although, admittedly, it needed Nuremberg and subsequent proceedings to bestow universal recognition upon this principle.[12]

Quite a different and, indeed, more complicated question is what the constituting elements of such responsibility are. Most writings on ICL concentrate on the historical development, and organizational and procedural matters relating to an international criminal court, or the specific crimes, but neglect the development and analysis of the elements of individual criminal responsibility. Only recently, in light of Article 25 ICCSt and the ensuing jurisprudence, have the technical issues received a more profound treatment in academic literature.[13] The most promising approach to refine the elements of individual criminal responsibility is to go back to the primary sources of ICL, that is, international and national war crimes jurisprudence since Nuremberg, ICL conventions, and other written sources. We will return to the modes of participation with a particular focus on the 'most responsible' perpetrators, i.e., the leadership level, in the fourth section of this chapter.

---

[11] See for a profound analysis Ch. Burchard, 'Völkerstrafrecht als global governance' (2008) 83 Die Friedens-Warte 73 (arguing that ICL means 'governing or regulating beyond the nation state' and thus serves to evaluate, correct and sanction national governance shortcomings (para 74)).

[12] See the seminal statement of the IMTN: '[E]nough has been said to show that individuals can be punished for violations of International Law. Crimes against International Law are committed by men not by abstract entities, and only by punishing individuals who commit such crimes can the provisions of International Law be enforced.' (IMT, *Trial*, xxii (1947), 447). This has been restated by Principle I of the Nuremberg Principles: 'Any person who commits an act which constitutes a crime under international law is responsible therefore and liable to punishment.' (Principles of International Law recognized in the Charter of the Nuremberg Tribunal and in the Judgment of the Tribunal, as adopted by the ILC: ILC, 'Report of the International Law Commission Covering its 2nd Session' (5 June–29 July 1950) UN Doc A/1316, in *YbILC* ii, 2 (1950) 374–8). For further, more recent references, see K. Ambos, *Treatise on International Criminal Law. Volume I: Foundations and General Part* (Oxford University Press 2013) 102–3.

[13] For a first approach, see M.C. Bassiouni, *Crimes Against Humanity* (Cambridge University Press 1999) 369. See also C.G. Tornaritis, 'The Individual', in M.C. Bassiouni (ed), *Treatise on ICL* I (Charles C. Thomas Pub Ltd 1973) 103–21; L. Sunga, *Individual Responsibility* (Martinus Nijhoff Publishers 2002); E. van Sliedregt, *Criminal Responsibility* (Asser Press 2003); E. van Sliedregt, *Criminal Responsibility* (Oxford University Press 2012); G. Werle and F. Jessberger, *Principles of International Criminal Law* (3rd edn Oxford University Press 2014) 428; G. Werle, 'Individual Criminal Responsibility in Article 25 ICCSt' (2007) 5 JICJ 953; Ambos (n 12) 120.

3. *IUS PUNIENDI* AND INTERNATIONAL CRIMINAL LAW

As I have argued elsewhere,[14] the *ius puniendi* of ICL can be inferred from two limbs of a primarily collective and a primarily individualistic nature: on the one hand from the incipient supranationality of the world order (understood normatively as an order of values) and, on the other hand, from our basic human rights (human dignity) as citizens of the world society.

3.1 The Counterfactual Collective Claim: ICL as Defence of the Incipient International Order

The international community today finds itself where the Nation-State stood when it came into existence: charged with the building-up and consolidation of a monopoly of power, i.e., at the stage of an incipient State-like order at best. Of course, Nation-States may enforce ICL by way of delegation[15] but such a power offers only a formal explanation of a supranational *ius puniendi*; it does not provide for the underlying normative reasons which would justify such a supranational authority in its own right.

A normative approach must take on those theories for which the use of criminal law is predicated upon the existence of a State-like legal order, worthy of being defended by (supranational) criminal law in the first place; in the absence of such an order the imposition of punishment is, in a nutshell, the application of brute, naturalist force.[16]

This argumentation is, however, based on a flawed premise, i.e., that the existence of law and of any legal order is predicated on the existence of a State with the respective monopoly of power. It does not take account of the whole picture since it fails to do justice to the international limb of ICL. And it takes a too narrow perspective on the fundamental issue of the validity of (international legal) norms. To begin with the latter: the validity of norms may be predicated on their real, actual existence in a given society, but validity can also be linked to the material (normative/moral) foundation of their claim of being obligatory. In this sense one can distinguish between social and material validity or, what is the same for our purpose, (factual) validity and (material) legitimacy of norms.[17] In fact, the question of legitimacy plays a fairly important role in all theories of validity of norms, being that the theories of (law as) force are the exception to the rule.[18] Indeed, even for (moderate) positivists the positive (empirically existing) law ultimately operates with a legitimacy reservation, i.e., it also requires a plausible claim of material (moral) validity.[19] In international law, the power of

---

[14] Cf. K. Ambos, 'The Ius Puniendi Issue of International Criminal Law' (2013) 33 OJLS 293. In this section I draw on this previous paper.

[15] Either by way of a treaty to an international criminal court or by way of a SCRes under Chapter VII of the UN Charter (ICTY, ICTR). See for further references Ambos, ibid., 298–9.

[16] See in particular G. Jakobs, *Norm, Person, Gesellschaft* (3rd edn, Duncker & Humblot 2008) 118.

[17] For a good summary of the debate see M. Mahlmann, *Rechtsphilosophie und Rechtstheorie* (2nd edn, Nomos 2012) 261.

[18] Ibid., 249–51 with detailed references.

[19] See e.g., H. Kelsen, *Reine Rechtslehre* (2nd edn, Deuticke 1960) 7–8, 196–7, 200–9 arguing, on the basis of his juridical theory of validity ('*juristische Geltungstheorie*'), that any

legitimacy is recognized at least since Thomas Franck's seminal study on the subject.[20] Thus, while there is a tension between validity and legitimacy, the latter is making 'room for something grander'.[21] Pluralist accounts of international law go even further and recognize – in contrast to the State-centred, top-to-bottom approach of the so-called realist, interest-based theories – different sources of international law outside the realm of State authority with 'varying degrees of impact'.[22] Ultimately, however, this undermines the law's claim to authority and there is no alternative account to replace this claim.[23]

In any case, from a broader perspective, state-centred approaches have been rightly criticized for they put 'validity' (in the sense of *Geltung* in a material-normative sense) and 'order' (*Ordnung*) on an equal footing and thus ignore the potential force of norms as per their material, normative legitimacy, independent of an enforcement order in the form of a State or otherwise. In fact, such a concept of validity/existence of norms does not only negate the possibility of law at the international level, but also quite often at the domestic level, namely with regard to those States which do not possess a fully functioning monopoly of (State) power and/or where norms do not enjoy full social recognition. This does not only concern (fully) failed States but also those with a partial collapse of their justice systems within the meaning of Article 17(3) ICCSt.[24] The criminal law of these States would then not even be accorded a normative value due to the absence of enforcement power.

More fundamentally the question arises as to whether it makes sense at all to apply the theories of validity of norms, developed with the classical Nation-State in mind, to a supranational (criminal law) order which follows different rules of organization than a Nation-State. In any event, the critics are unconcerned with the complex subtleties of the emerging international order and the ensuing judicialization of international law.[25]

norm requires objective validity to be derived from a supreme 'Basic Norm' ('*Grundnorm*') whose own legitimacy however remains unclear. H.L.A. Hart, *Concept of Law* (2nd edn, Clarendon Press 1994) 211–12, albeit missing, in line with his positivist approach, in international law a 'unifying rule of recognition specifying "sources" of law and providing general criteria for the identification of its rules', admits that international law is 'in a stage of transition towards acceptance' of generally recognized rules (236).

[20] T. Franck, *The Power of Legitimacy among Nations* (Oxford University Press 1990) 24–6.

[21] M. Koskenniemi, 'Legal Cosmopolitanism: Tom Franck's Messianic World' (2003) 35 *New York University Journal of International Law and Politics* 471, 480.

[22] See instead, of many P.S. Berman, 'A Pluralist Approach to International Law' (2007) 32 YJIL 301, 302, 307, 311–22 (discussing the 'new' New Haven school of Yale University and the different areas where pluralism operates, in particular where a disaggregation of the State can be identified).

[23] Cf. for a recent critique of Berman's approach M. Guidice, 'Global Legal Pluralism: What's Law got to do with it?' (2014) 34 OJLS 589.

[24] The provision refers in the relevant part to the 'unavailability' of the national judicial system whereby 'the State is unable to obtain the accused or the necessary evidence and testimony or otherwise unable to carry out its proceedings'.

[25] See on this judicialization and an 'international constitutional judiciary' T. Broude, 'The Constitutional Function of Contemporary International Tribunals, or Kelsen's Visions Vindicated' (2012) 4 *Goettingen Journal of International Law* 519, 528.

Neither do they inquire into the role and competence of the UNSC in the UN's system of collective security, in particular with regard to the establishment of international criminal tribunals and the enforcement of their decisions and judgments, nor do they deal with the possibility of decentralized prosecutions by Third States. Thus, they ignore that there is already an existing, albeit incipient, supranational (legal) order at work – as one expression of the institutionalization or even constitutionalization of international law[26] where community interests prevail over unilateral or bilateral state interests.[27] In fact, it is not overly idealistic to claim that the different mechanisms of criminal accountability, existing both at the national and international level, have merged into the already-mentioned international criminal justice system which may be considered either the product of a certain normative criminal law order or in and of itself amount to such an order.

3.2 The Normative Individualistic Claim: ICL as an Enforcer of Human Dignity and Fundamental Human Rights

3.2.1 The original Kantian individualistic, human dignity-based claim

The argument that there is a normative international order, based on certain values worthy of being defended by ICL, can be traced back to the Kantian idea of human dignity – notwithstanding Kant's own, rather State-oriented approach[28] – as a source of fundamental human (civil) rights which, ultimately, must be enforced by a supra- or transnational (criminal) law. Dignity is intrinsic, deontological and non-negotiable (replaceable), it is the basis of the individuality and the mutual recognition (interpersonal relationship) of the members of a society.[29] Human dignity so understood is a self-sufficient, humanist concept, which claims recognition and respect for and among human beings based on their status as persons with common peculiar characteristics (e.g., reason).[30] It accords any person a legal status for being human, independent and before the existence of community constituted as a State.

---

[26] There are, of course, different constitutionalist approaches. See already, as perhaps the most important precursor of the contemporary debate, A. Verdross, *Die Verfassung der Völkerrechtsgemeinschaft* (Springer 1926); for a modern version of this markedly legalistic position B. Fassbender, *The UN Charter as the Constitution of the International Community* (Nijhoff 2009) discussing Verdross at 28. For a comprehensive treatment of the debate T. Kleinlein, *Konstitutionalisierung im Völkerrecht* (Springer 2012) 5–97 and the special issue of (2012) 4 *Goettingen Journal of International Law* 343–647.

[27] See for a summary B. Simma, 'Universality of International Law from the Perspective of a Practitioner' (2009) 20 EJIL 265, 267–8.

[28] For Kant (international) law was predicated on the existence of a public power to enforce it, see I. Kant, 'Handschriftlicher Nachlass/Reflexionen zur Rechtsphilosphie – Ius publicum universale in genere' (c. 1772–75) in Preussische Akademie der Wissenschaften (ed), *Gesammelte Schriften* vol XIX (1st edn, De Gruyter 1934) 482; I. Kant, 'Metaphysik der Sitten' (1797) in Preussische Akademie der Wissenschaften, *Gesammelte Schriften* vol VI (1st edn, Reimer 1907) 231.

[29] Kant, 'Metaphysik der Sitten' (1797) (n 28) 462; I. Kant, 'Grundlegung zur Metaphysik der Sitten' (1785) in Preussische Akademie der Wissenschaften, *Gesammelte Schriften vol IV* (Reimer 1903) 428.

[30] Cf. Mahlmann (n 17) 309–11.

Kant's conception of human dignity is complemented by his vision of an 'eternal peace'.[31] To be 'eternal', i.e., permanent and sustainable, such a peace presupposes the fulfilment of at least two conditions: most importantly, that the States have a republican constitution guaranteeing the liberty and equality of their citizens as 'inalienable rights';[32] further, a world citizen law (*Weltbürgerrecht*) which entails the 'right of hospitality' (*Recht der Hospitalität*),[33] i.e., that each citizen must not to be treated with hostility by another State.[34] From this a two-step argument follows.[35] First, a just and thus permanent peace is predicated on the recognition and respect for the rights of citizens, i.e., in modern language, human rights. Secondly, violations of these rights have to be stigmatized as serious wrongs and punished. Also, what is important in Kant's idea of a *Weltbürgerrecht* is the recognition of a (minimum) set of rights for each person, overcoming the individual's classical mediatization within the State order and in a world order between States.

Following Kant, a series of other, in particular German, scholars have argued that the State and the international community are called upon to protect human dignity by way of criminal law.[36] Other scholars[37] employ a more cosmopolitan vision which can also be traced back to the Kantian idea of a *Weltbürgerrecht*, and to his concept of human dignity, focusing on people instead of States as subjects of the international order.[38] Human dignity is here also understood as a moral source of subjective rights of all people, of universally recognized human rights which ultimately have to be protected by a universal, interculturally recognized criminal law. It is a form of cosmopolitanism based on principles of reason with a claim of universal validity. There is a unique mixture of a concrete consideration and an abstract claim which dismisses any general relativistic cultural challenge, partly as a result of post-modern theories of legal pluralism.[39] The concrete consideration consists of the reference to concrete violations of fundamental human rights, translated into severe crimes against fundamental legal values of humanity and codified as international core crimes in Articles 5–8 ICCSt,

---

[31] I. Kant, 'Zum ewigen Frieden' (1795/96) in Preussische Akademie, *Gesammelte Schriften vol VIII* (1st edn, Reimer 1912) 383.

[32] Ibid., 350.

[33] Ibid., 357.

[34] The limitation to the right of hospitality may be explained by the historical fact that at the time of Kant's writing, visit in a foreign country was the only point of contact with a foreign sovereign power (Kleinlein (n 26) 302).

[35] Cf. K. Günther, 'Falscher Friede durch repressives Völkerstrafrecht?', in W. Beulke et al (eds), *Das Dilemma des rechtsstaatlichen Strafrechts* (Berliner Wissenschafts-Verlag 2009) 79, 83–5.

[36] See for references K. Ambos, 'Punishment without a Sovereign?' (2013) 33 OJLS 306–7 with fns 81–88.

[37] See for references ibid., 307–10 with fns 89–108.

[38] See in particular J. Rawls, *The Law of Peoples* (Harvard University Press 1999) 23 and passim.

[39] This is, in a way, the flip side of the pluralist, democratic, grassroots account discussed above: Legal pluralism is a descriptive, not normative theory; it does not provide for a hierarchy of norms but accepts all the norms and sources recognized, in principle, as equal; see Berman (n 22) 327–8.

which can hardly be approved of by any culture.[40] The abstract claim refers to the underlying moral position of the universal reach of these fundamental human rights and their punishment as international core crimes.[41] As a philosophical universalist position, it cannot be geographically restricted or culturally challenged since there is 'nothing about the way in which moral judgments are formed (…) which restricts the range of their appropriate application'.[42]

3.2.2 The individualistic claim from the State and world society perspective

Anglo-American theorists come to similar results, albeit focusing more strongly on international law considerations.[43] Some start from a State's duty to protect basic human rights and thus punish offenders. Failing to do so, a State cannot legitimately object to (international) humanitarian intervention in the form of supranational prosecutions and punishment. It loses, from a sovereignty perspective, the legitimacy to invoke the (absolute) sovereignty defence. In fact, this line of argument is based on the understanding of the international community as a community bound together by common values and the existence of an international constitutional order rooted in the same values (constitutionalization thesis), both mentioned above. A value-based international community does not only stand for 'State values' but also for 'community values' of concern to humankind as such, e.g., universal peace and the protection of fundamental human rights. As to the latter there exists a minimum, 'overlapping' consensus[44] regarding the universal normative validity of fundamental human rights.[45] As a consequence, the international community, as the holder of the international *ius puniendi,* has a right to take criminal action against the perpetrators of the international core crimes. The existence of an international legal framework in the sense of a 'constitutional order', which protects certain common values, in particular fundamental human rights, entails, as just mentioned, a limitation of classical State sovereignty (in the sense of a genuine *domaine resérvé*) in that States can no longer claim this right if they fail to protect or even actively violate fundamental human rights. In other words, the legitimacy of the exercise of State power is predicated on respect for fundamental human rights.[46] Thus, in essence, the common values recognized by both the international community and the international constitutional order limit the sovereignty of

---

[40] Islamic scholars also recognize that there is 'a sufficient degree of cultural consensus regarding (…) the protection and promotion of human rights …' (A.A. An-Na'im, 'Toward a Cross-Cultural Approach to Defining International Standards of Human Rights: The Meaning of Cultural, Inhuman, or Degrading Treatment or Punishment', in A.A. An-Na'im, *Human Rights in Cross-Cultural Perspectives* (University of Pennsylvania Press 1992) 27).

[41] The fact that States frequently fail to punish such crimes is generally due to reasons related to national power politics and less to an (open) rejection of the underlying value systems.

[42] J. Waldron, 'How to Argue for a Universal Claim' (1999) 30 *Columbia Human Rights Law Review* 305, 307, distinguishing on this basis between respectable concrete (relevant) and disrespectable general (irrelevant) relativist challenges (307–9).

[43] See for references Ambos (n 36) 310–11 with fns 109–119.

[44] In the sense of John Rawls' concept of an 'overlapping consensus of reasonable comprehensive doctrines', i.e., between different political or moral conceptions in a pluralist, liberal society (J. Rawls, *Political Liberalism* (Columbia University Press 2005) 133–4).

[45] Paulus (n 10) 254–60.

[46] Kleinlein (n 26) Chapter 7 (in particular 511–37, 613-4, 699–700, 712–13).

Unrechtsstaaten (outlaw States). Other Anglo-American authors[47] focus rather on a human rights and human dignity approach in its own right stressing the – already mentioned – cosmopolitan vision of a world society composed of citizens as subjects in their own rights with their own world citizen law.[48]

Ultimately, an approach based on the core human rights of world citizens, makes us see that a universal legal order, i.e., the order of the world society of world citizens, is possible by the force of the intrinsic value of its norms[49] 'without a central legislator and a judiciary' (Luhmann)[50] and 'without the monopoly of power of a world State and without world government' (Habermas).[51] Thus, it links human dignity/rights with the idea of a normative international order. The above-mentioned international criminal justice system, if it does not amount in itself to a proper legal order, rests on this value-based order. Its *ius puniendi* is derived from autonomous persons united in a world society: *ubi societas ibi ius puniendi.*[52] It represents a value judgment expressing the legal and moral necessity to punish macro criminal conduct.[53] Its law, ICL, can be considered a progress of civilization[54] and, in this sense, an ethical project.[55] The international crimes to be prevented and/or punished by this law concern the fundamental international values of our international order and world society; they may even amount to *ius cogens* crimes, i.e., crimes of a peremptory, non-derogable and

---

47 See for references Ambos (n 36) 311–13 with fns 120–35.

48 Focusing on national law, a similar approach is taken by the theory of 'legal republicanism' according to which the law in general and the criminal law in particular shall strengthen and promote the idea of a citizens' society with citizens' values and virtues (see for a summary of the different approaches R. Dagger, 'Republicanism and Crime', in S. Besson and J.L. Martí (eds), *Legal Republicanism. National and International Perspectives* (Oxford University Press 2009) 147, 157).

49 This intrinsic value manifests itself in the acting of different agents at different levels (Cf. Burchard (n 11) 77, 79, 81 with regard to global governance and ICL).

50 N. Luhmann, *Das Recht der Gesellschaft* (reprint, Suhrkamp 1997) 574. Of course, Luhmann's approach is premised, in line with his system theory, on (worldwide) social communication within the one single (global) social system whose subsystems are held together by certain basic values, in particular fundamental human rights, Cf. C. Mattheis, 'The System Theory of Niklas Luhmann and the Constitutionalization of the World Society' (2012) 4 *Goettingen Journal of International Law* 625, 637–8, 643, 644–5.

51 J. Habermas, 'Bestialität und Humanität' (Die Zeit, 29 April 1999) 1.

52 F. Meyer, *Strafrechtsgenese in Internationalen Organisationen* (Nomos 2012) 695, 931.

53 E. David, 'Les valeurs, politiques et objectifs du droit pénal international à l'heure de la mondialisation' (2004) 19 Nouvelles Études Pénales 157–69.

54 K. Ambos, 'International Criminal Law at the Crossroads', in C. Stahn and L. van den Herik (eds), *Future Perspectives on International Criminal Justice* (Asser Press 2010) 161, 165.

55 Insofar I agree with M. Dubber, 'Common Civility – The Culture of Alegality in ICL' (2011) 24 LJIL 923; yet, he goes too far if he argues that ICL is not law and rather an 'ethical-administrative enterprise' than a legal one. Dubber presents his critique in a grandiose, overblown rhetoric, but hardly supports it with substantial arguments, let alone with inquiries into the concrete law. In fact, Dubber is unconcerned with the realities and technicalities of current ICL, i.e., he does not speak to those who either as practitioners or academics or both apply and shape ICL.

overriding character.[56] As a consequence, a State on whose territory such crimes have been committed cannot hide behind the curtain of a post Westphalian, Grotian sovereignty concept but must make sure that those responsible are held accountable; otherwise the international community or third States (universal jurisdiction) will have to take care of them.

4. INDIVIDUAL CRIMINAL RESPONSIBILITY AND INTERNATIONAL CRIMINAL LAW

As has been said above individual criminal responsibility is predicated on the existence of an international *ius puniendi*. Of course, both topics can and indeed are mostly treated separately but strictly speaking there can be no theory of individual criminal responsibility without a theory of an international *ius puniendi*. The latter is a necessary condition of the former in that responsibility can only be reasonably established if a right (and power) to punish exists in the first place. The same goes for the punishment itself of course, i.e., there can be no (legitimate) punishment without a right to punish in the first place. Otherwise, punishment would amount to brute force – a critique which, as we have seen above, has indeed been made against international punishment – but not the consequence of a legitimate legal process. From this perspective, responsibility connects *ius puniendi* and punishment. In other words, it constitutes the interface between *ius puniendi* and punishment; it establishes the link that would otherwise be missing. However, there is a more concrete contribution of responsibility to punishment, namely that of a sentencing factor. Given that international tribunals look, among other factors, at the accused's culpability, his role and contribution in the crime,[57] i.e., his scope of responsibility, its determination has an impact on sentencing. Indeed, it is safe to say that the more nuanced a criminal justice system's approach to responsibility is the more concrete and specific a given form of responsibility finally meted out on the sentence is.

4.1 What Model of Participation Follows Modern ICL?

National legal systems can be classified with regard to modes of participation in crimes either as unitarian or as differentiated systems.[58] The unitarian model of participation is based on the 'equivalence theory', which considers every person as perpetrator/principal who contributes in a causal way to the criminal result. Unitarian systems

---

[56] See the definition in Art. 53 VCLT. It is, of course, controversial how far this *ius cogens* claim can reasonably go, i.e., whether it extends beyond the international core crimes as codified in Art. 5 ICCSt or if it even encompasses all these crimes, including for example all war crimes of Art. 8; See Ambos (n 36) 314 with fn 143.

[57] Cf. Ambos (n 1) 283.

[58] Cf. G. Fletcher, *Rethinking Criminal Law* (1978, reprinted Oxford University Press 2010) 649 and Ambos (n 5) 543–5; See also the country reports in U. Sieber and K. Cornils (eds), *Nationales Strafrecht in rechtsvergleichender Darstellung: Allgemeiner Teil* (Volume 4, Duncker & Humblot 2010) 3 and K.J. Heller and M. Dubber (eds), *The Handbook of Comparative Criminal Law* (Stanford University Press 2011) section II B 3 ii (complicity) respectively.

generally do not make any distinction between different forms of participation at the level of attribution/imputation. The criminal responsibility of each participant is established separately from the responsibility of other participants. Each participant commits his own crime and in consequence each has to be considered as a perpetrator. Yet, the different degree of contribution to the criminal result may be taken into account at the sentencing level. Unitarian systems of participation exist in common law countries and in some civil law countries, such as Denmark or Italy. Some unitarian systems, such as the Polish or Austrian systems, distinguish between different forms of participation with the view to the different functions of participants, i.e., as (main) perpetrators or mere accomplices. These systems are called 'functional' unitarian systems which, arguably,[59] would be best suited for the complex system of international criminal law.

The differentiated model of participation is characterized by a distinction between principals/perpetrators and accessories/secondary participants according to their relative contribution to the crime. Accordingly, a perpetrator only qualifies as a participant when he either commits the crime by himself (direct perpetrator), controls the commission together with others (co-perpetrator) or commits through another by means of a predominant influence (indirect perpetrator). Other parties (accessories) to crime are considered as (secondary) participants differentiating between those who encourage or induce/abet and those who merely assist or aid. Accessories can only be held liable if the principal at least attempts the (unlawful) act. Their liability is derived from that of the principal perpetrator (and, thus, accessorial). The differentiated model of participation prevails for example in France, Germany, Portugal, Spain, Switzerland, the Netherlands, Russia and Latin America.[60]

Given the fragmentation in ICL, due to the large number of different courts and codifications, there is no uniform approach with respect to the modes of participation. Broadly speaking, we can distinguish two approaches:[61] one is based on the ICCSt, another on the Statutes of the *ad hoc* Tribunals established by the UNSC, in particular the ICTY. Article 25(3) ICCSt contains different modes of participation in paragraphs (a)–(d): committing a crime individually, jointly or through another person; ordering, soliciting or inducing a crime; and aiding, abetting and otherwise assisting and contributing to a group crime. Article 7(1) ICTYSt provides criminal responsibility for planning, instigating, ordering, committing or otherwise aiding and abetting in the planning, preparation or execution of a crime. It is clear, comparing these statutory

---

[59] Cf. J. Stewart, 'Overdetermined Atrocities' (2012) 10 JICJ, 205. For profound comparative studies, see K. Hamdorf, *Beteiligungsmodelle im Strafrecht. Ein Vergleich von Teilnahme- und Einheitstätersystemen in Skandinavien, Österreich und Deutschland* (Ed. Iuscrim 2002) 43, 75, 104; B. Weißer, *Täterschaft in Europa: Ein Diskussionsvorschlag für ein Europäisches Tätermodell auf der Basis einer rechtsvergleichenden Untersuchung der Beteiligungssysteme Deutschlands, Englands, Frankreichs, Italiens und Österreichs* (Mohr Siebeck 2011).

[60] See for France and Spain, Sieber and Cornils (n 58) 77, 285; for further references see Ambos (n 5) 544 w.fn. 7; cf. also N. Jain, *Perpetrators and Accessories in International Criminal Law – Individual Modes of Responsibility for Collective Crimes* (Hart 2014) 103 (perpetration in English criminal law), 166 (perpetration in German criminal law), 155 (accessory in English criminal law), 176 (accessory in German criminal law).

[61] See Ambos (n 12) 120 with further references.

approaches, that the ICCSt overcomes the unitarian approach of the ICTYSt and replaces it, taking its wording seriously, by a more nuanced approach differentiating between different modes of participation[62] (leaving aside the controversial, but secondary question of a possible hierarchy enshrined in Article 25(3)).[63]

Of course, such a differentiated approach entails the need to search for a guiding principle or even concrete guidelines to make the necessary distinction between the different forms of participation possible.[64] Also, it is clear that both objective and subjective considerations must inform the distinction between principal and secondary participation, i.e., the correct approach is not an either/or approach but a combined one. Indeed, neither an extreme (formal) objective nor an extreme (*animus*-like) subjective theory of perpetration is compatible with Article 25(3),[65] but only a theory which

---

[62] *Lubanga* ICC-01/04-01/06-2842 (Judgment, 14 March 2012) para 976; insofar concurring *Katanga* ICC-01/04-01/07-3436 (Judgment, 7 March 2014) paras 1384, 1387; in the same vein *Lubanga* ICC-01/04-01/06-3121-Red (Judgment, 1 December 2014) para 462; *Blé Goudé* ICC-02/11-02/11-186 (Confirmation Decision, 11 December 2014) para 135. See also Ambos (n 12) 145.

[63] In favour *Lubanga* ICC-01/04-01/06-2842 (Judgment, 14 March 2012) para 996; Werle and Jessberger (n 13) 520; G. Werle, *Völkerstrafrecht* (Mohr Siebeck, 2012) 479–80; *Lubanga* ICC-01/04-01/06-2842 (Judgment, 14 March 2012) Separate Opinion of Judge Fulford para 8; *Ngudjolo* ICC-01/04-02/12-3 (Judgment, 18 December 2012) Concurring Opinion of Judge Van den Wyngaert para 22; *Katanga* ICC-01/04-01/07-3436 (Judgment, 7 March 2014) para 1386 with fn. 3185 (distinguishing between the recognition of different forms of participation in Art. 25(3) and a value and blame-based hierarchy between these forms which is to be rejected for the lack of the assignation of differing sentences: '*la distinction proposée entre la responsabilité de l'auteur du crime et celle du complice ne constitue en aucun cas une "hiérarchie de culpabilité" pas plus qu'elle n'édicte, même implicitement, une échelle des peines.*'); also J.D. Ohlin, E. van Sliedregt and T. Weigend, 'Assessing the Control Theory' (2013) 26 LJIL 725, 728, 740, 745–6; L.N. Sadat and J.M. Jolly, 'International Criminal Courts and Tribunals – Seven Canons of ICC Treaty Interpretation: Making Sense of Article's 25 Rorschach Blot' (2014) 27 LJIL 755, 758, 775, 782; summarizing the discussion about the structure of Article 25(3): C. Stahn, 'Justice Delivered or Justice Denied? The Legacy of the Katanga Judgment' (2014) 12 JICJ 809, 822. For my view see K. Ambos, 'The First Judgment of the ICC (*Prosecutor v. Lubanga*): A Comprehensive Analysis of the Legal Issues' (2012) 12 *International Criminal Law Review* 144–5.

[64] Cf. *Katanga* (n 63) para 1388 ('*indispensable de déterminer quel principe directeur permet de faire le partage entre les auteurs d'un crime et les complices*'); Cf. also *Lubanga* (n 62) paras 462–463, which distinguishes (confusing terminologically, however, 'commit' and 'perpetrate') between perpetration and accessorial responsibility, the former being more blameworthy than the latter (462), making it necessary therefore to determine the basis of this distinction (463).

[65] Cf. *Katanga* (n 63) paras 1391–1392 (convincingly arguing that, on the one hand, the possibility of an indirect perpetration [through another person] cannot be reconciled with the objective theory [assuming that perpetrator is only the person acting with 'his own hands'] and, on the other, the general applicability of the mental element provision of Art. 30 to all forms of participation goes against a pure subjective approach [leaving alone, I take the liberty to add, its artificiality and impossibility to prove]). See previously *Lubanga* ICC-01/04-01/06-803-tEN (Decision on the Confirmation of Changes, 29 January 2007) paras 326–330, 334–335; *Lubanga* (n 63) paras 919–921, 1003; *Katanga and Chui* ICC-01/04-01/07-717 (Confirmation Decision, 30 September 2008) paras 482–484; See also Ambos (n 12) 150.

combines both objective and subjective considerations. This leaves us with the control of the act theory as the only functional objective-subjective approach so far applied by the ICC.[66] In fact, the *Katanga* Trial Chamber not only acknowledged the importance of the control of the act theory, but explicitly recognized the ensuing forms of control,[67] and in particular elaborated on the *Organisationsherrschaftslehre* ('*contrôle sur l'organisation*'), giving extensive credit to its founder Claus Roxin and suggesting two criteria for its application: the nature of the organization and its effective control by the persons who employ it for the commission of crimes.[68] In the meantime, the *Lubanga* Appeal Chamber also confirmed the control over the crime theory as 'a convincing and adequate approach'[69] and it seems now settled that this theory is indeed the guiding principle to distinguish between perpetration and accessorial responsibility in ICC law.[70] The Appeal Chamber's reasoning starts by recognizing the existence (and

---

[66] Cf. *Lubanga* (n 65) paras 330–334, 342 (relying on the theory of the 'functional control over the act' [*funktionelle Tatherrschaft*]); *Lubanga* (n 62) paras 1003–1005; confirmed by *Lubanga* (n 62) paras 469, 471, 473 (requiring 'a normative assessment of the role of the accused person'); conc. *Blé Goudé* (n 62) para 135; more explicitly *Katanga* (n 63) paras 1393–1395 (arguing that this theory, being objective and subjective at the same time ['*seul critère fusionnant à la fois les composantes objectives et subjectives, pour permettre de distinguer entre les auteurs d'un crime et les complices*'], fits best to Art. 25(3) ['*le plus conforme à l'article 25*'] and makes a distinction between the different forms of participation possible ['*rendre opérationnelle la distinction entre les auteurs d'un crime et les complices*']); for this reason the Chamber retains this theory (ibid., para 1382 ['*il n'y a pas lieu de s'écarter de l'interprétation … fondée sur la théorie du contrôle sur le crime*'], para 1396 ['*entend donc retenir le critère du contrôle*']). The Chamber then applies this theory to define perpetrators ('*auteurs*') as persons '*qui ont un contrôle sur la commission dudit crime et qui ont connaissance des circonstances de fait leur permettant d'exercer ce contrôle*' (ibid., para 1396) and the indirect perpetrator ('*auteur indirect*') as ['*celui qui a* le pouvoir de décider si et comment le crime sera commis *dans la mesure où c'est lui qui en détermine la perpétration*'] [ibid., emphasis in the original, fn. omitted]) while the accomplice ('*complice*') '*n'exerce pas un tel contrôle*' (ibid). Judge Van den Wyngaert still disagrees (Minority Opinion paras 279–281) in line with her position echoed in the *Ngudjolo* (n 63) para 5 (following the separate opinion of Judge Fulford in *Lubanga* (n 63) paras 10–12) but she does not offer any principle or theory to distinguish between the forms of participation set out in Art. 25(3).

[67] *Katanga* (n 63) paras 1402–1403 ('*contrôle sur la volonté*' pursuant, inter alia, to '*contrainte*' or '*erreur*', and control pursuant to an '*appareil de pouvoir organisé*').

[68] *Katanga* (n 63) paras 1404–1416 with the development of the two criteria in para 1407. See for a summary of these groundbreaking considerations K. Ambos, 'A Workshop, A Symposium and the Katanga Trial of 7 March 2014' (2014) 12 JICJ 219, 228 with fn. 14. Against this background, the caveat that the theory of organizational control is not the only '*réponse juridique*' in interpreting Art. 25(3)(a) Alt. 3 (para 1406) appears as a mere concession to internal disagreements or discussions given Judge Van den Wyngaert's continuing rejection of this theory (n 66); summing up this rejection Jain (n 60) 94. In any case, more important is the Chamber's clarification that other forms of participation may be relevant at the level of the internal structure of the organization (para 1410). In casu the Chamber rejected the control requirement (para 1417) and convicted Katanga pursuant to Art. 25(3)(d) ICCSt (para 1643). Cf. also Stahn (n 63) 824, who holds that the *Katanga* Trial Chamber invoked a relatively high threshold for indirect perpetration than the *Lubanga* Pre-Trial Chamber.

[69] *Lubanga* (n 62) paras 469, 473.

[70] Cf. also *Blé Goudé* (n 62) para 135, quoting the *Lubanga* (n 62).

liability) of a perpetrator behind the perpetrators, even in cases where the latter 'are themselves fully criminally responsible for that crime', and requires 'a normative assessment of the relationship between the person actually carrying out the incriminated conduct and the person in the background, as well as of the latter person's relationship to the crime'.[71] The same normative assessment requires the Appeal Chamber in the case of indirect co-perpetration, since what applies to the indirect perpetration is also applicable to the indirect co-perpetration,[72] in order to distinguish co-perpetration from accessorial responsibility.[73]

Of course, there is still room for argument about how the control theory should best be understood and applied in future case law. It is by no means written in stone but flexible enough to adjust to new challenges posed by international crimes, criminal organizations and the ensuing rules of imputation. Indeed, Roxin himself always understood *Tatherrschaft* (control of the act) as an 'open concept' – more a guiding principle than a fixed rule with precise inferences.[74] I have myself challenged the traditional individualistic reading of the theory and tried to adjust it to the particularities of imputation in ICL by giving it a certain collective turn and putting the criminal enterprise, entity or organization at the centre of imputation.[75]

4.2 Letter of the Law or Theoretical Approaches in the Interpretation of Modes of Participation?

The controversial discussion about the control over the act theory at the ICC revealed fundamentally different approaches as to the method of interpretation to be used with regard to the ICCSt. While the majority view, adopting the control over the act theory with regard to Article 25, showed a general openness towards theoretical or conceptual considerations, the dissenting judges, Fulford and Van den Wyngaert, plainly rejected this theory, opting for a plain, literal reading of the Statute pursuant to Article 31(1) of

---

71 *Lubanga* (n 62) paras 458, 465 (responsibility without personal commission (own hands)).

72 Ibid., para 466 ('it is not required that a person actually carry out directly and personally the incriminated conduct in order to be a co-perpetrator. Rather, in order to determine whether a person is a co-perpetrator, a normative assessment of that person's role is required'.).

73 Ibid., para 469. This assessment should be 'primarily based on the objective criterion of the accused person's extent of contribution to the crime' (para 468). 'The contribution of a co-perpetrator must be of greater significance' than that of the accessories (para 467).

74 Cf. C. Roxin, *Täterschaft und Tatherrschaft* (8th edn, De Gruyter 2006) 122.

75 Cf. K. Ambos (n 12) 177–8 with further references in fn 666. I would therefore not consider myself 'a staunch supporter of the control theory and its (alleged) hierarchical structure' as suggested by J.D. Ohlin, E. van Sliedregt, T. Weigend, 'Assessing the Control-Theory' (2013) 26 LJIL 725, 744. There would be much to say to reply to some assertions in this (otherwise) excellent paper. I may do this at another opportunity. Here it suffices to say that I even doubt that the control theory has a 'hierarchical structure' (for this view also Judge Van den Wyngaert (n 66) para 281); in any case, this question refers exclusively to the correct interpretation of Art. 25(3) ICCSt (n 63) which is, of course, an entirely different question. In other words, one thing is the correct interpretation of Art. 25(3), another thing is the correct interpretation of the control theory. The latter requires the ability to read German or at least Spanish since the relevant literature on this theory only exists in these two languages.

the Vienna Convention on the Law of Treaties (VCLT).[76] Thus, in fact, the disagreement between the majority and the dissenters goes well beyond the mere interpretation of a definitional element of a mode of responsibility but concerns a matter of principle, namely, how much legal theory, if at all, is needed in ICL treaty interpretation, here in the law of criminal responsibility. While the majority adopts a doctrinal or normative approach, Fulford and Van den Wyngaert opt for a rather positivist or naturalist approach, at first sight from a practitioner's perspective quite reasonable, since it avoids any time-consuming and intellectually demanding inquiry into theoretical considerations. Leaving aside the question if the dissenter's rejection of the control over the act theory is convincing,[77] the issue of principle is whether legal texts, especially the ones belonging to the general part of criminal law, can be interpreted, let alone understood, by an ordinary reading. In my view, the answer is clearly negative. First of all, even Article 31(1) VCLT does not call for an isolated recourse to the 'ordinary meaning' but surrounds the ordinary approach by 'good faith' as the overarching principle of interpretation as well as 'context' and 'object and purpose' as points of reference for the ordinary meaning.[78] Secondly, Fulford and Van den Wyngaert put too much trust in the 'plain' meaning of the legal text. Law is not a natural science which can be approached in an entirely empirical-naturalistic manner. Legal statutes are riddled with highly normative terms and for this reason alone theoretical inquiries are necessary to

---

[76] Fulford Separate Opinion (n 63) paras 12 ('plain reading of Article 25(3)(a)', 'unnecessary to invoke the control of the crime theory'), 13 ('Court's approach to this issue should be rooted in the plain text of the Statute'), 16; *Ngudjolo* ICC-01/04-02/12-3 (Judgment, 18 December 2012) Concurring Opinion of Judge Van den Wyngaert paras 6, 8, 11 ('ordinary meaning'); *Katanga* ICC-01/04-01/07-3436 (Judgment, 7 March 2014) Minority Opinion of Judge Van den Wyngaert para 281 (relying on 'the ordinary meaning of the language of article 25(3) of the Statute in light of its object and purpose ...').

[77] For my view see K. Ambos, 'The First Judgement of the International Criminal Court: A Comprehensive Analysis of the Legal Issues' (2012) 12 ICLR 142–3; Ambos (n 12) 154. It suffices to say here that, while it is, of course, possible not to read the control theory into Art. 25 (3), a pure or naturalistic 'plain' reading of the text lacks the theoretical approach necessary for the imputation of the 'crime base' to the 'most responsible' who, normally, belong to the top level of the respective State or organization. Indeed, if Van den Wyngaert does not only reject the control theory, in particular *Organisationsherrschaft* (in the same vein L.N. Sadat and J.M. Jolly, 'Seven Canons of the ICC Interpretation' (2014) 27 LJIL 755, 757–8, 781), but also JCE, one fails to see how she wants to hold these top level people responsible; summing up Stahn (n 63) 822; on the persuasiveness of the control theory, favouring of a normative reading of Art. 25 (3), G. Werle and Ch. Burghardt, 'Establishing Degrees of Responsibility: Modes of Participation in Article 25 of the ICCSt', in E. van Sliedregt and S. Vasiliev (eds), *Pluralism in International Criminal Law* (Oxford University Press 2014) 301, 311, 316.; G. Werle and Ch. Burghardt, 'Täterschaft und Teilnahme im Statut des Internationalen Strafgerichtshofs', in M. Heger, B. Kelker, and E. Schramm (eds), *Festschrift für Kristian Kühl zum 70. Geburtstag* (C.H. Beck 2014) 851, 862–3. See also Ambos (n 68) 227 with fn. 11.

[78] See for a detailed analysis O. Dörr, in O. Dörr and K. Schmalenbach (eds), *Vienna Convention on the Law of Treaties. A Commentary* (Springer 2012) Article 31 para 38 (pointing to 'a single combined operation' of interpretation taking into account all factors mentioned in Article 31(1) and stressing the variety of different meaning, not least for the recourse to the normally six authentic treaty languages).

find the most plausible and reasonable meaning.[79] In sum, I do not see how complex normative legal terms such as 'commits', 'solicits' or 'assists', to name but a few, can be interpreted and distinguished without any theoretical framework or at least some guiding principle, just relying on the ordinary meaning of the respective terms.

4.3 Attributing Crimes to the Most Responsible: Theoretical Options

If ICL is to pursue the most responsible, the major criminals, the leaders, as is nowadays recognized in prosecutorial strategies,[80] one has to develop or invoke theories which allow for the attribution of the 'crime base', i.e., the crimes committed by the subordinates and executors, to these most responsible. Modern ICL offers insofar three approaches: joint criminal enterprise (JCE), indirect perpetration, in particular by way of an organisation and command responsibility. As I have explored these theories of imputation in detail elsewhere,[81] I will here only offer an explanation of their basic conceptual design.

4.3.1 Joint criminal enterprise

JCE has become part of the consolidated case law of the ICTY and ICTR since the *Tadić* Appeals Judgment of 15 July 1999. The case law distinguishes three forms. First, the *basic* form where the participants act on the basis of a 'common design' or 'common purpose' and with a common intention regarding the crimes to be committed or furthered by the JCE. Second, the systemic form, i.e., the so-called concentration camp cases where crimes are committed by members of military or administrative units such as those running concentration or detention camps on the basis of a common plan ('common purpose'). Third, the so-called extended joint enterprise where acts going

---

[79] This methodological point has recently been made by the STL in its seminal Appeals decision on the (international) crime of terrorism, most regrettably Judge Antonio Cassese's last decision (Interlocutory Decision on the Applicable Law: Terrorism, Conspiracy, Homicide, Perpetration, Cumulative Charging, STL-11-01/I/AC/R176bis, 16 February 2011) paras 19–21, 29–30, 37; see for a discussion with further references K. Ambos, 'Judicial Creativity at the Special Tribunal for Lebanon: Is there a Crime of Terrorism under International Law?' (2011) 24 LJIL 655, 657–9. About the scholarly authority as a 'residual third source' of law, see recently G.P. Fletcher, 'New Court, Old Dogmatik' (2011) 9 JICJ 179, 180 and (in greater detail) G.P. Fletcher, 'Truth in Codification' (1998) 31 *University of California Davis Law Review* 745, 746, 750. I note in passing that Judge Van den Wyngaert herself admits that Art. 25 contains 'open-textured concepts' (Minority Opinion (n 76) para 12). In the same vein now also *Lubanga* (n 62) paras 470–471, holding that 'the Appeals Chamber considers it appropriate to seek guidance from approaches developed in other jurisdictions in order to reach a coherent and persuasive interpretation of the Court's legal texts. This Court is not administrating justice in a vacuum, but, in applying the law, needs to be aware of and can relate to concepts and ideas found in domestic jurisdictions.' (referring to JCE as an example where a normative approach was used).

[80] Cf. K. Ambos and I. Stegmiller, 'Prosecuting International Crimes at the International Criminal Court: Is There a Coherent and Comprehensive Prosecution Strategy?' (2012) 58 *Crime Law Soc Change* 391–413.

[81] See only Ambos (n 12) 123 (JCE), 154 (indirect perpetration), 160 (JCE), 197 (command responsibility) with further references.

beyond the common plan or purpose are imputed to the members of the JCE because these acts constitute, in an objective and subjective sense, a 'natural and foreseeable consequence' of the realization of the plan. In particular this third form has generated criticism with regard to its compatibility with fundamental principles of criminal law.[82]

From a conceptual perspective the doctrine serves to impute certain criminal acts or results to persons on the basis of their participation in a collective ('joint') criminal enterprise. The 'criminal enterprise' is defined by a common – explicit or tacit – agreement or understanding to commit certain criminal acts for an ultimate criminal objective or goal, e.g., in the case of a genocidal enterprise, the ultimate destruction of the targeted group. Such a global or broad enterprise may consist of various smaller ('subsidiary') sub-enterprises, e.g., the running of concentration or prison camps for the members of the targeted group, the local or regionally organized persecution of members of the group, etc. The participants in the enterprise are bound together by their common will to achieve the ultimate goal by all necessary means, i.e., by the crimes that must be committed on the road to the ultimate criminal goal. The underlying rationale of a JCE, its core feature, is the combined, associated or common criminal purpose of the participants in the enterprise. The common purpose is the collective element of the JCE doctrine which links the members together and turns it into a theory of collective responsibility based on an institutional-participatory or systemic model of imputation or attribution.

4.3.2 Indirect perpetration, *Organisationsherrschaft*, indirect co-perpetration

The notion underpinning the concept of indirect perpetration (perpetration by means, perpetration through another person) is that principals to a crime are not limited to those who physically carry out the objective elements of the offence, but also reaches those who, in spite of being away from the scene of the crime, control or mastermind its commission because they decide whether, and sometimes even, how the offence will be committed. Perpetration through another person presupposes in its classical form, that the person who commits the crime ('intermediary', '*intermédiaire*', '*Tatmittler*') can be used as an instrument or tool by the indirect perpetrator ('*auteur médiat*') as the mastermind or 'man in the background' ('*Hintermann*').[83] He or she is normally an innocent agent, not responsible for the criminal act. A typical example is the case where the individual agent or instrument acts erroneously or is not culpable because he

[82] Cf. Ambos (n 12) 172, with further references; recently *Đorđević* IT-05-87/1-A (Judgment, 27 January 2014) para 906; See also Jain (n 60) 63.

[83] See generally for perpetration by means G.P. Fletcher, *Basic Concepts of Criminal Law* (Oxford University Press 1998) 197–200; H-H. Jescheck and T. Weigend, *Strafrecht. Allgemeiner Teil* (Duncker & Humblot 1996) 662 and Ambos (n 12) 154. In French criminal law the '*auteur médiat*' is not codified, but exceptionally recognized if the direct perpetrator is used as a 'simple instrument' (Cf. A.K. Czepluch, *Täterschaft und Teilnahme im französischen Strafrecht* (Duncker & Humblot 1994) 30–33). With regard to Art. 25 see also (conc.) A. Eser, 'Individual Criminal Responsibility (Article 25)', in A Cassese et al (eds), *The Rome Statute of the ICC: A Commentary vol. I* (Oxford University Press 2002) 767, 793; E. van Sliedregt, *Criminal Responsibility* (Oxford University Press 2012) 94–5.

or she is a minor or because of a mental defect. The perpetrator through another person is also considered a principal in common law.

In the field of 'macrocriminality', i.e., systematic or mass criminality organized, supported or tolerated by the State[84] or by powerful non-State actors, the direct perpetrator or executor normally performs the act with full responsibility. Thus, the question arises if the *Hintermann* ('man in the background') can also, in cases with a fully responsible direct perpetrator, be responsible as a(n) '(indirect) perpetrator behind the (direct) perpetrator' (*'Täter hinter dem Täter'*). This has, pursuant to Claus Roxin's seminal 1963 paper,[85] indeed been affirmed for cases in which the '*Hintermann*' dominates the direct perpetrators by way of a hierarchical organizational structure, i.e., where he or she dominates the commission by way of an organization ('*Organisationsherrschaft*'). So understood, *Organisationsherrschaft* is a variation or sub-group of the theory of indirect perpetration.

The key issue of this doctrine is whether the mastermind is able to exercise effective control over the (fully responsible) direct perpetrators by means of the organizational apparatus possibly created and in any case dominated by him.[86] While the 'Hintermann' will hardly be able to completely control the direct perpetrators, this lack of control may be compensated by the control of the apparatus, which produces an unlimited number of potential willing executors. In other words, although direct perpetrators acting with full criminal responsibility cannot be considered mere 'interchangeable mediators of the act' ('fungible *Tatmittler*') as such, the 'system' provides for a practically unlimited number of replacements and thereby for a high degree of flexibility as far as the personnel necessary to commit the crimes are concerned.[87] While such a concept rests on the assumption that the apparatus operates hierarchically from top to bottom and one may rightly question the applicability of this assumption to all kinds of criminal organizations, a too naturalistic or mechanical perspective distorts the highly normative basis of this theory.

As a follow up of *Organisationsherrschaft*, a system of 'organizational domination in stages' (*'stufenweise Organisationsherrschaft'*) has been developed pursuant to Dencker's theory of a '*Zurechnungsprinzip Gesamttat*'.[88] This theory advocates a concept of imputation which focuses on the criminal act or enterprise as a whole, and

---

[84] See H. Jäger, *Makrokriminalität. Studien zur Kriminologie kollektiver Gewalt* (Suhrkamp 1989).

[85] C. Roxin, 'Straftaten im Rahmen organisierter Machtapparate' (1963) 110 Goltdammer's Archiv für Strafrecht 193, 207; English translation as 'Crimes as Part of Organized Power Structures' (2011) 9 JICJ 197; See also C. Roxin, *Täterschaft und Tatherrschaft* (8th edn, de Gruyter 2006) 242, 252, 653–4.

[86] Crit. for example T. Weigend, 'Perpetration through an Organization: The Unexpected Career of a German Legal Concept' (2011) 9 JICJ 91, 92, 103 (disapproving of the concept's 'vagueness of dominance', in essence rejecting the organizational element in art. 25(3)(a) and instead militating for assessing an indirect perpetrator's control over the executor on a case-by-case basis, independent from the existence of organizational structures). Introducing a modified account of *Organisationsherrschaft*, where the focus is whether the person is 'the *Zentralgestalt* in the course of events leading up to the crimes', Jain (n 60) 141.

[87] Cf. Ambos (n 5) 594, 597–8, 614 with further references; conc. Jain (n 60) 142.

[88] F. Dencker, *Kausalität und Gesamttat* (Duncker & Humblot 1996) 116, 124, 125, 127, 138, 160, 250.

results from the modification of the system of individual attribution commonly used for cases of ordinary criminality. Its central feature is that the criminal enterprise or organization as a whole serves as the entity upon which attribution of criminal responsibility is based. Thereby, it is intended to develop a doctrine of imputation which better corresponds to the needs of ICL, i.e., to create and develop a mixed system of individual-collective responsibility. The ensuing concept of 'organizational domination in stages' takes up the distinction between main perpetrators and secondary participants (accomplices) and distinguishes three levels of participation: the first and highest level is composed of those (main) perpetrators who plan and organize the criminal events as a whole and as such belong to the leadership level ('*Führungstäter*'); at the second level we find those (still main) perpetrators of at least the mid-level of the hierarchy who exercise some form of control over a part of the organization ('*Organisationstäter*'); the third and last level consists of the physical perpetrators who merely execute the crimes ('*Ausführungstäter*') and thus may be considered, in a normative sense, as mere secondary participants (accomplices).[89]

The ICC *Katanga/Chui* Confirmation Decision introduced the – internationally novel – concept of (joint) indirect co-perpetration.[90] In fact, indirect co-perpetration constitutes a combination of individual responsibility on the basis of the theory of indirect perpetration (perpetration through another person) and mutual attribution on the basis of the theory of co-perpetration.[91] Thus, acts committed by direct perpetrators (e.g., the members of a militia) are attributed to all indirect perpetrators (e.g., the militia leaders) involved in the criminal agreement at the leadership level (between the militia leaders). Consequently, each indirect perpetrator (militia leader) is responsible for all crimes committed by the direct perpetrators (militia members) even if they belong to a group not under his direct control.[92] One may distinguish between two scenarios with a view to the number of groups or collective entities involved.[93]

---

[89] See Ambos (n 12) 177–9 with further references.

[90] *Katanga and Chui* (n 65) paras 489, 492, 519, 540, 561.

[91] It does not constitute a new (fourth) mode of attribution, but is only the result of the 'factual coincidence of two recognized forms of perpetration', Weigend (n 86) 110; See also S. Eldar, 'Indirect Co-Perpetration' (2014) 8 *Crim L and Philos* 605, 611–13. This also follows from the very explanation of the Pre-Trial Chamber speaking of a 'combination of (…) committing crimes through other persons together with the mutual attribution among the co-perpetrators …' (*Katanga and Chui* (n 65) para 492). See also H. Olásolo, *The Criminal Responsibility of Senior Political and Military Leaders as Principals to International Crimes* (Hart 2009) 307, 313–14, 316; J.L. Černič, 'Shaping the Spiderweb: Towards the Concept of Joint Commission Through Another Person under the Rome Statute and Jurisprudence of the International Criminal Court' (2011) 22 CLF 539, 558.

[92] *Katanga and Chui* (n 65) paras 548–560. See for the same approach *Bemba Gombo* ICC-01/05-01/08-14-tENG (Arrest Warrant Decision, 10 June 2008) paras 69–72. However, in *Bemba Gombo* ICC 01/05-01/08-424 (Confirmation Decision, 15 June 2009) paras 348–351 the Chamber restricted the mode of liability to simple co-perpetration. Critical, S. Manacorda and C. Meloni, 'Indirect Perpetration versus Joint Criminal Enterprise: Concurring Approaches in the Practice of International Criminal Law?' (2011) 9 JICJ 159, 174 (arguing that the concept could 'overly broaden' the thresholds of liability for perpetration and therefore would need further clarification in the upcoming case law). G. Werle and Ch. Burghardt, 'The German Federal Supreme Court (*Bundesgerichtshof*, BGH) on Indirect Perpetration – Introductory Note' (2011) 9

4.3.3 Command responsibility

Command responsibility provides for individual criminal responsibility of commanders or superiors who fail to prevent or punish crimes committed by their subordinates.[94] In contrast to the other modes of liability, command responsibility does not incriminate 'active' conduct, but establishes liability for omissions. Command responsibility can be either regarded as an additional mode of participation or a distinct crime. Whereas at the *ad hoc* Tribunals command responsibility was incorporated in the provision dealing with the modes of participation, the ICCSt has, with Article 28, created a separate provision. I will focus on this (modern) codification here.[95]

Article 28 ICCSt explicitly distinguishes between the responsibility of military commanders and those of other civilian superiors, thereby, in fact, establishing a broad 'superior responsibility'. While JCE (as well as co-perpetration) is characterized by the horizontal cooperation between the perpetrators, command responsibility necessarily presupposes an element of verticality between the commander/superior and the subordinates. However, a combined use of both doctrines seems highly useful in cases of complex criminal organizations. The same is true for the relationship between command responsibility and the above-explained doctrine of *Organisationsherrschaft*.

First and foremost, command responsibility requires the defendant to assume a position of superiority versus his or her subordinates. Superiority demands both the *de jure* position of command and the factual ability to command. Additionally, a military leader must dispose of effective command and control over his or her subordinates, a

---

JICJ 207, 210–11; G. Werle and Ch. Burghardt, 'Mittelbare Täterschaft', in R. Bloy et al (eds), *Festschrift Maiwald* (Duncker & Humblot 2010) 849, 861 correctly claim that a correct application of the 'control over the act' theory requires that only the crimes committed jointly by the different organizations (and not also those committed by one organization alone) shall be attributed to the co-perpetrators; Werle and Jessberger (n 13) 558. Welcoming the Chamber's findings and relating them to the Preamble's call against impunity ('the most serious crimes (…) must not go unpunished') Černič (n 91) 558, 565 (calling this mode 'joint commission through another person'). Against this 'radical expansion of Article 25(3)(a)' in such cases, *Chui* ICC-01/04-02/12-4 (Judgment, 18 December 2012) Concurring Opinion of Judge Van den Wyngaert paras 58–64.

[93] When various organizations collaborate, we have the scenario of indirect co-perpetration ('*mittelbare Mittäterschaft*'), just described above (n 92) and the accompanying text. If, however, there exists only one (criminal) organization led and dominated by (various) co-perpetrators acting with a common purpose we have the scenario of joint indirect perpetratorship ('*Mittäterschaft in mittelbarer Täterschaft*'); cf. Weigend (n 86) 92, 111; Werle and Burghardt (n 92) 849, 857, 863; G. Werle and Ch. Burghardt, 'Introductory Note' (2011) 9 JICJ 207, 210–11; Werle and Jessberger (n 13) 556.; cf. also Eldar (n 91) 611-3; Ambos (n 12) 157. Joint indirect perpetratorship was the case in *Al Bashir* ICC-02/05-01/09-1 (Arrest Warrant Decision, 4 March 2009) paras 209–223, charging Al Bashir as an indirect perpetrator or indirect co-perpetrator; and most recently in *Blé Goudé* (n 62) para 136 (149: 'exercised control, jointly with the other co-perpetrators, over the pro-Gbagbo forces, which were organised and hierarchical in nature and through which the crimes charged were committed'). *Blé Goudé* (n 62) Partially Dissenting Opinion of Judge Van den Wyngaert para 5, with (n 3) (holding that the 'notion [of indirect co-perpetration] is incompatible with article 25(3)(a) of the Statute').

[94] Cf. *Bemba* (n 92) para 405; *Gbagbo* ICC-02/11-01/11-656-Red (Confirmation Decision, 12 June 2014) para 262; Werle and Jessberger (n 13) 578.

[95] See on the history and theoretical considerations Ambos (n 12) 14–5, 180.

non-military (civilian) leader must show effective authority and control. A lack of administrative or operational control does not foreclose or preclude the obligation to take any other measures at the superior's disposal. In cases where subordinates no longer obey the orders of their superiors, control no longer exists and criminal liability of the superior is thus precluded. The repetition of 'effective control' in Article 28(b)(ii) demonstrates that the requirement of effective control is particularly important for non-military superiors. From this wording, it may also be inferred that the drafters wanted to limit the liability of a civilian compared to a military superior on the objective level. In this context it must be taken into consideration that, in general, control in civilian hierarchies is less strict than in military ones. A delegation of the duty of supervision does not exculpate the defendant from superior responsibility; rather this duty is converted into a duty of proper selection, which might eventually lead to responsibility for a wrongful or bad selection.

The subordinates' crimes must constitute a causal consequence or result from the superior's failure to properly supervise. Normative theories of attribution, for example, the proximate cause theory and the doctrine of risk increase, may serve to better assess and qualify the legal impact of the defendant's omissions vis-à-vis the committed crimes.[96] Finally, the superior must have failed to prevent crimes that are going to be or have yet to be committed, or he must have failed to repress (i.e., take punitive measures) crimes that already have been committed. The superior must dispose of both the legal competence and the material possibility to prevent or repress the crimes. A commander is also obligated to punish crimes which have been committed before his assumption of the command position which have become known to him.

The *mens rea* side of command responsibility, requiring either positive knowledge with respect to the crimes committed by subordinates or a 'should-have-known' element, contains some intricacies which are unique and do not arise in the context of other modes of participation. The undisputed element of positive knowledge of the subordinates' crimes, is applicable to both military and civilian leaders. The knowledge-element must be interpreted in the light of Article 30(3) ICCSt, i.e., 'awareness that a circumstance exists or a consequence will occur in the ordinary course of events'. The awareness must encompass all objective requirements set out above, particularly the effective control, and also the objective elements of the crimes. In contrast, it does not have to comprise the subjective elements of the crimes, which means that the commander does not have to possess any specific intent such as the intent to destroy in respect to the crime of genocide.

However, the second variant, the negligence standard is differently phrased for military and civilian leaders ('should have known' versus 'consciously disregarded information …'). What is clear is that the standard, introducing some sort of negligence threshold, results in negligence liability (of the commander) for intentional acts (the crimes committed intentionally by the subordinates). Given the logical inconsistency of this construction, one should regard the negligence form of command responsibility as a separate offence of 'failure of proper supervision', a crime which consequently deserves much more lenient punishment than the 'intentional' omission of preventive or punitive acts.

---

96 Cf. Ambos (n 12) 215–6.

In any case, the superior's negligence must be inferred from objective information that the superior should have been aware of the subordinates' crimes. If information, which clearly indicates the occurrence of crimes, is accessible to the commander, but he nevertheless ignores it, criminal liability ensues. This failure (to know) might either have the quality of negligence (the superior fails to perceive a risk he should have perceived), or it may amount to recklessness (the superior perceived the risk but consciously disregarded it). Indeed, the non-military standard 'consciously disregarded information that clearly indicates (...)' can be equated to the concept of 'wilful blindness', situated between positive knowledge and recklessness. While the military leader must take any information into account, the civilian leader must only pay attention to information clearly indicating the crimes. All in all, this is a reasonable distinction which, of course, will have to be further developed by the case law.

5. CONCLUSION

This chapter wanted to show that the starting point of any discussion on imposing punishment by way of international criminal tribunals is the *ius puniendi* issue, i.e., the question of whether and how an international right to punish can be explained and developed from a theoretical perspective. Only if this right exists can we legitimately argue about the contours, forms and limits of individual criminal responsibility. Responsibility itself serves as the interface between the *ius puniendi* and punishment/sentencing. The more precise the responsibility determination is the more concrete turns the impact on sentencing out to be. Of course, in discussing responsibility one must not lose sight of the 'most responsible' as the targets of international prosecution. The chapter therefore focused on those forms of responsibility which link the international crimes to the men in the background. These, in turn, deserve, as a rule, higher sentences than the mere executors or the middlemen since they bear the greatest overall responsibility.

4. Determinate and indeterminate sentences of imprisonment in international criminal justice

Dirk van Zyl Smit

1. INTRODUCTION

In contemporary international criminal justice imprisonment is the predominant sanction. Every international court and tribunal established since the ICTY in 1993 has made this explicit in its founding documentation; and every person sentenced by one of those bodies since that date has had imprisonment as their primary punishment.[1]

The pre-eminence of the sentence of imprisonment should not surprise anyone interested in penology. Since the European Enlightenment of the late eighteenth century, imprisonment has gradually established itself worldwide as the sentence best suited to dealing with most, and in many countries all, serious crimes. What is surprising is that in international criminal justice imprisonment has only achieved this position relatively recently. In order to understand the pressures to establish imprisonment also as the primary punishment in international criminal law one must understand how it came to be pre-eminent in modern penal systems.

Accordingly, this chapter begins in Section 2 with a brief outline of how imprisonment generally came to be the pre-eminent form of punishment. It also deals with early criticisms of imprisonment, which shaped its modern evolution, as well as with the more recent and fundamental scholarly critique of the hegemonic status of imprisonment as a form of punishment. This latter account provides a basis for critical reflections throughout this chapter. The chapter then focuses in Section 3 on how, when capital punishment lost its universal legitimacy as an acceptable penalty for very serious offences, imprisonment came to dominate penal discourse in the international criminal context. It explains that it did so by establishing itself as the only acceptable primary punishment for such offences.

The following part, Section 4, turns to the way in which the determination of the sentence of imprisonment has been interpreted by the *ad hoc* Tribunals that have dominated the practice of international criminal justice until recently. The chapter argues that both the imposition of imprisonment and release from it before the full term

---

[1] By 24 March 2015 the ICTY had sentenced 79 persons to terms of imprisonment and the ICTR had similarly sentenced 50 persons. The ICC had sentenced two persons. For historic figures of the ICTY up to 20 January 2015: <http://www.icty.org/sections/TheCases/KeyFiguresoftheCases> accessed 24 March 2015; for figures after 20 January 2015 see for the ICTY <http://www.icty.org/sections/TheCases/JudgementList> accessed 24 March 2015; for the ICTR <http://41.220.139.198/Cases/StatusofDetainees/tabid/202/Default.aspx> accessed 24 March 2015; for the ICC <http://www.icc-cpi.int/en_menus/icc/situations%20and%20cases/cases/Pages/cases%20index.aspx> accessed 24 March 2015.

has been served have had several shortcomings when evaluated against standards of legality and proportionality. It then turns to the still largely untested requirements for determining the sentence of imprisonment set by the ICCSt and argues that they show more respect for these particular standards. Section 5 considers the substantive requirements for the implementation of sentences of imprisonment imposed by the organs of international criminal justice. It argues that the limited focus on rehabilitation during the implementation phase has influenced not only how offenders are treated while serving their terms but also assumptions about how they should be sentenced and what they can expect to be subjected to after release.

The final part of the chapter, Section 6, questions whether the determination of the length of time convicted offenders actually serve and the implementation of sentences of imprisonment in international criminal justice have been developed sufficiently to engage fully with wider human rights standards that are supposed to protect all sentenced offenders. It concludes that there are shortcomings in this regard. Paradoxically however, the relative lack of intervention in the lives of prisoners who are the sentenced subjects of international criminal justice, may lead to their being less exposed to the power of the authorities than 'ordinary' sentenced prisoners.

2. THE LONG ROAD TO THE PRE-EMINENCE OF IMPRISONMENT IN INTERNATIONAL CRIMINAL JUSTICE

Although forms of incarceration have existed for as long as people have been able to build secure structures in which others can be detained against their will, the rise of imprisonment as a primary penalty is relatively recent. Its roots are to be found in the development of the modern administrative state, which coincided with the movement from the mid-eighteenth century onwards, towards the sentence of imprisonment becoming the primary punishment for more serious criminal offences.[2]

Enlightenment thinking recognized the essential humanity of all offenders, who should not be subject to disproportionately severe sentences and who, if they became prisoners, should not be subject to random cruelty. The former position is most closely associated with the writings of Césare Beccaria, whose book, *Dei Delitti e Delle Pene,* shaped the ideas of penal reformers of the Enlightenment.[3] Beccaria argued that, in order to deter potential offenders, prison sentences for specific offences should be spelt out in law, but that these penalties should be proportionate to the crime and be only the minimum necessary to achieve their objective. These ideals of legality, proportionality and parsimony have been associated with classical criminal law ever since the eighteenth century and remain the underpinning of modern systems of criminal law.

The rejection of random cruelties is linked to John Howard, whose book, *The State of the Prisons*, first published in 1777, exposed the appalling conditions to which prisoners were subject throughout the United Kingdom and in much of Europe, and

[2] N. Morris and D. Rothman (eds), *The Oxford History of the Prison* (Oxford University Press 1995).

[3] C. Beccaria, *Dei Delitti e Delle Pene* (1764, published as *Of Crimes and Punishments* (trans J. Grigson) (Oxford University Press 1964).

argued for better regulated and therefore less cruel treatment of prisoners.[4] After the Second World War in particular, Howard's ideals have been reinforced by the international recognition that prisoners have a range of human rights that deserve protection, including controversially a right to be given opportunities to rehabilitate themselves, so that on release they can again become full members of society.[5]

A more radical strain of modern scholarship has cast doubts on the notion that the emergence of the prison can be explained primarily in terms of the impact of the ideas of leading figures of the European Enlightenment. Particularly influential have been the original insights of the French scholar, Michel Foucault, who argued that the dramatic changes from the end of the eighteenth century onwards should be understood not as philanthropy but in terms of developments in which the 'traditional, ritual, costly, violent forms of power (…) fell into disuse and were superseded by a subtle, calculated technology of subjection'.[6]

Foucault emphasized the techniques available to the authorities in redesigned prisons from the nineteenth century onwards – what he called the 'micro-physics of power'.[7] The techniques enabled prison authorities to exercise far greater control over individuals because they focused more strongly than before on the mind or 'soul' of prisoners, rather than directly on their bodies, in order better to discipline them and change their attitudes to authority more thoroughly.

In contrast to the traditional view of prison history, which has seen the penal reforms of the late eighteenth and early nineteenth centuries and the movement towards the pre-eminence of imprisonment unequivocally as desirable forms of progress, the Foucauldian vision was deeply pessimistic. In Foucault's words: '[I]n penal justice, the prison transformed the punitive procedure into a penitentiary technique; the carceral archipelago transported this technique from the penal institution to the entire social body.'[8]

This pessimistic vision is in turn disputed by those, such as the present author, who argue that the rise of the modern prison is best understood as an interaction between different forces that shape penal practice.[9] While they accept that imprisonment does reflect the exercise of power in a particular way, the impact of this power can be ameliorated significantly by legal constraints. Close attention to principles of legality and proportionality can ensure that imprisonment is not abused by being applied too widely or for too long, while the recognition of the human rights of prisoners can

---

[4] J. Howard, *The State of the Prisons in England and Wales, with Preliminary Observations, and an Account of some Foreign Prisons and Hospitals* (Warrington 1777).

[5] D. van Zyl Smit, 'Punishment and Human Rights', in J. Simon and R. Sparks (eds), *Handbook on Punishment and Society* (Sage 2012) 395–415.

[6] M. Foucault, *Discipline and Punish: the Birth of the Prison* (Penguin 1977) 27.

[7] Ibid., 26.

[8] Ibid., 246.

[9] This approach is developed more fully in D. van Zyl Smit and S. Snacken, *Principles of European Prison Law and Policy; Penology and Human Rights* (Oxford University Press 2009). For a nuanced view of the historical evolution that places Foucault in a wider context, see M. Ignatieff, 'State, Civil Society, and Total Institutions: A Critique of Recent Social Histories of Punishment' (1981) 3 *Crime and Justice* 153–92.

reduce the harshness of the punishment and ease the transition of prisoners to again becoming full members of free society.

In the following section the somewhat belated emergence of imprisonment as the predominant form of punishment in international criminal justice is considered in the light of the broad trend towards imprisonment since the late eighteenth century.

3. THE DOMINANCE OF IMPRISONMENT IN INTERNATIONAL CRIMINAL JUSTICE

It may be that at a fundamental level it has been the power that can be exercised through the prison that has increasingly made imprisonment a highly attractive sentencing option to the proponents of international criminal justice. However, initially imprisonment battled to achieve the full recognition in international criminal justice that it enjoyed in domestic legal systems. In part this may have been because of perceived weaknesses in the enforcement of sentences of imprisonment in this sphere. After the First World War, for example, some trials were held which historians regard as forerunners of the trials of the international criminal justice system, but sentences of imprisonment imposed there were very light and not served in full.[10]

In part, however, the reason for the delayed acceptance of imprisonment was the continued attraction of punishments of the body for the particularly violent offences with which international criminal justice is called to deal. In Foucauldian terms, the punishment of the body still triumphed when it came to these offences. In particular, imprisonment still had to establish its primacy over the death penalty as the punishment for the most serious offences in the emerging field of international criminal justice. A striking illustration of the relative prominence of the death penalty is to be found in the key penal provision of the 1945 Charter of the IMTN. It did not even mention imprisonment directly, but instead provided only: 'The Tribunal shall have the right to impose upon a Defendant, on conviction, death or such other punishment as shall be determined by it to be just.'[11]

Of course, imprisonment, including life imprisonment, was a prominent part of the sentencing mix at Nuremberg and at the contemporaneous IMTFE. However, all prisoners sentenced by the latter tribunal were released after having served relatively short terms, as were the majority of those sentenced to life imprisonment by the tribunal in Nuremberg. A prominent exception was Rudolf Hess, who was sentenced to life imprisonment by the IMTN and who remained in prison until his death more than

---

[10] See for example the *Llandovery Castle* case, one of the Leipzig Trials after the First World War, where the defendants were convicted of manslaughter as a war crime and sentenced to four years' imprisonment, but escaped and never served their sentences: T. McCormack, 'From Sun Tzu to the Sixth Committee', in T. McCormack and G. Simpson (eds), *The Law of War Crimes* (Kluwer 1997) 50–51.

[11] Art. 27 IMTN Charter.

40 years later. However, it was widely recognized that the exceptionally long term he served was more the product of political expediency than carefully calculated penal policy.[12]

After the International Military Tribunals of the immediate post Second World War had completed their work, the issue of appropriate punishment for crimes against international law was not an item on the international agenda for the next 40 years. Only after the end of the Cold War, at the beginning of the 1990s, did the International Law Commission (ILC) begin to debate the issue again in the course of developing a draft Code of Crimes against the Peace and Security of Mankind.[13] By then the somewhat mixed success of imprisonment as a punishment for these crimes had faded and the ILC was able to look at the whole issue of imprisonment afresh within a very different climate.

From a narrowly penological perspective perhaps the most prominent feature of this changed climate was that by the 1990s at the national level the pendulum had swung very strongly against the death penalty. Many countries had abolished the death sentence or were in the process of abolishing it. Where it had been abolished, it had universally been replaced by a sentence of imprisonment, often, but not universally, by a sentence of imprisonment for life. For this reason alone it could be expected that imprisonment would become the dominant penalty in international criminal justice too.

There were also deeper ideological changes, which not only informed the swing away from the death sentence but which would have an impact on the form that imprisonment would take in international criminal justice. One such change was that in the four decades from the early 1950s onwards, a coherent body of international human rights law with implications for sentencing was beginning to emerge. Questions began to be asked about its implications for punishment in general and for imprisonment in particular. In 1948 the UDHR had provided that no one should be subjected to torture, or to cruel, inhuman and degrading forms of punishment.[14] This prohibition was reflected in the 1950s and 1960s in regional human rights standards. It was reinforced by a myriad of national constitutions that followed recent international law,[15] as well as the much older constitutional restrictions on cruel and unusual punishments.[16] These provisions provided the constitutional bedrock for the prisoners' rights movement that flourished in the USA and elsewhere as prisoners haltingly came to be recognized as

---

[12] N. Goda, *Tales from Spandau: Nazi Criminals and the Cold War* (Cambridge University Press 2007).

[13] W. Schabas, 'War Crimes, Crimes against Humanity and the Death Penalty' (1997) 60 *Albany Law Review* 733, 742–3.

[14] Art. 5 UDHR (GARes 217A (III), 10 December 1948) 3 UN GAOR Supp (No. 11A) 71, UN Doc A/810, 7 (1948).

[15] M.C. Bassiouni, 'Human Rights in the Context of Criminal Justice: Identifying International Procedural Protections and the Equivalent Protection in National Constitutions' (1993) 3 *Duke Journal of Comparative and International Law* 263.

[16] In the English Bill of Rights of 1689 and the Eighth Amendment to the US Constitution a century later.

citizens with fundamental legal rights.[17] Rights to human dignity and to due process are key elements of international human rights law, with particular implications for penal law. These relate directly to the interpretation of the prohibition on cruel, inhuman and degrading punishments. This prohibition has long been interpreted as comprising two complementary elements: a prohibition on punishments that are inherently incompatible with the standard and a prohibition against all punishments that 'by their excessive length or severity' are grossly disproportionate to the seriousness of the offence.[18] While the death penalty fell afoul of the first prohibition, the second prohibition, which of course is directly applicable to imprisonment, had to be considered too.

The debate in the ILC reflected the human rights-inspired changes in attitudes. From the outset there was agreement that the principle of legality inherent in the new emphasis on proportionate punishment required any penal provision in a Code of Crimes against the Peace and Security of Mankind to go further than the Charter used in Nuremberg in specifying penalties. The first attempt in 1990 to draft a clause on penalties for the proposed Code included a provision that related to the death penalty, but it was soon clear that there would not be a consensus in favour of it.[19] The draft put forward in 1991 dropped the death penalty entirely and proposed simply: 'Any defendant found guilty of any of the crimes defined in this Code shall be sentenced to life imprisonment. If there are extenuating circumstances, the defendant shall be sentenced to imprisonment for a term of 10 to 20 years.'[20]

The ILC may have addressed the need for specificity of punishment and the move away from the death penalty, but were the Commissioners mindful of the need to test the penalties that were to be allowed against the standards of international human rights law? More specifically, was adequate attention paid to these standards in respect of the sentence of life imprisonment, the most severe sentence that could be imposed, in the various proposals that refined the ideas put forward in 1991? There can be no doubt that at an early stage in the debate about which punishments should be allowed, the various experts involved recognized that life imprisonment was potentially problematic.[21] The debate was so vigorous that at the end of it the Special Rapporteur of the ILC amended the draft penal clause and proposed various options from which life imprisonment could be omitted completely. The substance of this debate is of considerable interest, for it is a rare example of arguments for and against life imprisonment being developed systematically in the context of international law.

---

17 For the wider context of this movement in the USA, see J.B. Jacobs, *New perspectives on Prison and Imprisonment* (Cornell University Press 1983) Chapter 1 'Macrosociology and Imprisonment' 17–32.

18 *Weems v United States* 217 US 349 [1909] 371. The implications of proportionality in this context are explored more fully in D. van Zyl Smit and A. Ashworth, 'Disproportionate Sentences as Human Rights Violations' (2004) 67 *Modern Law Review* 541–60.

19 *Summary Record of the 2157th Meeting* (1990) 1 Yearbook of the International Law Commission (UN Doc A/CN.4/SER.A/1990) 51.

20 *Ninth Report on the Draft Code of Crimes against the Peace and Security of Mankind* (1991) 2(1) Yearbook of the International Law Commission 37-44 UN Doc A/CN.4/435 and Add 1 para 29.

21 See (n 19) 50.

A feature of the debate was that a considerable number of Commissioners declared their principled opposition to life imprisonment. Particularly prominent were the views of several Commissioners from Latin America. For example:

> Life imprisonment did not seem to be compatible with the Latin American legal system. The criterion adopted in the ACHR, for instance, was that penalties should not only be correctional in nature but should also rehabilitate the convicted person so that he could resume his place in society. A more realistic penalty would be imprisonment for a minimum of 10 years and a maximum of 25 years, which was the longest term of imprisonment in many Latin American countries.[22]

This passage highlights two recurring themes in the opposition to life imprisonment at the international level. The first objection is that it is not a competent penalty for even the most serious crimes in the domestic law of some States.[23] Secondly, the claim is that it undermines the human rights of offenders by denying them the opportunity to rehabilitate themselves so that they could later live in society as free citizens.[24]

Supporters of life imprisonment among the Commissioners who were opposed to the death penalty based their advocacy on three primary arguments: the need for an appropriately retributive punishment; general deterrence; and the incapacitation of offenders. The first two of these were given expression by the Commissioner from Panama, who argued that: 'Crimes against the peace and security of mankind called above all for the adoption of exemplary penalties which reflected the feeling of condemnation that such acts aroused in the international community and which also had a deterrent effect.'[25]

Of particular interest is that this Commissioner relied on human rights norms not only for his rejection of the death penalty but also for his support for life imprisonment in the face of opposition to it from other Commissioners from Latin America. The latter penalty was required 'in order to prevent [barbarous crimes] from being committed again and to protect human rights and fundamental freedoms'.[26] He noted that the international instruments, which made national statutes of limitation inapplicable to war crimes and crimes against humanity and which denied their perpetrators rights of asylum, were based on the same criteria of protecting human rights. Implicit in this argument is the idea that the exceptionally serious crimes that were involved here required life imprisonment as the exemplary penalty, even where it may be opposed for 'ordinary' crimes. In his words: 'Any potential criminal [contemplating crimes against

22 Commissioner Tuleda from Peru: *Summary Record of the 2212th Meeting* (1991) 1 Yearbook of the International Law Commission 34 UN Doc A/CN.4/SER.A/1991 para 4. See also the comments of Commissioner Barboza from Argentina: Ibid., para 20; and the comments of Commissioner Rodriques from Brazil: Ibid., 12 para 21.

23 Commissioner Njenga from Kenya: *Summary Record of the 2210th Meeting* (1991) 1 Yearbook of the International Law Commission 26 UN Doc A/CN.4/SER.A/1991 para 47.

24 Commissioner Graefrath from the German Democratic Republic *Summary Record of the 2208th Meeting* (1991) 1 Yearbook of the International Law Commission 10 UN Doc A/CN.4/SER.A/1991 para 10.

25 *Summary Record of the 2213th Meeting* (1991) 1 Yearbook of the International Law Commission 43 UN Doc A/CN.4/SER.A/1991 para 14.

26 Ibid., 42 para 12.

the peace and security of mankind] should realise that, while he might not actually have to suffer the death penalty, he would none the less be outlawed from society.'[27]

The case for life imprisonment as an instrument of incapacitation was put by Commissioner Arangio-Ruiz from Italy who argued that the death penalty was 'plainly out of the question'.[28] However, for pragmatic reasons he would be:

> less hesitant than some other members' about life imprisonment (...) [H]e would find it difficult to contemplate the release, even after 20, 25 or 30 years, of a dictator of the type common around 1930, who had been guilty of aggression, genocide and other crimes of similar magnitude, or even the release of a major drug trafficker. Such people could not just be returned to society, as the English had soon realised in the 100 days following Napoleon Bonaparte's exile on the island of Elba. It was a question of fitting the punishment not only to the crime but also to the gravity of the danger, and of preventing a recurrence at all costs.[29]

In addition to those Commissioners who supported life imprisonment in principle, a number of Commissioners supported life imprisonment only with provision for a sufficient degree of flexibility in the imposition and implementation of the sentence. The draft made life imprisonment the sentence imposed as a matter of course, in the absence of extenuating circumstances. Some Commissioners expressed the view that it did not allow the sentencing body sufficient freedom to choose between life imprisonment and a fixed term[30] and that it did not provide clearly for the release of a person sentenced to life imprisonment when continued enforcement could no longer be justified.[31]

Although the 1991 debate of the ILC did not resolve the issue of whether life imprisonment should be adopted as a penalty, it reveals the extent to which the Commissioners felt it necessary to consider human rights principles when arguing both for and against life imprisonment. The opponents of this form of punishment relied on these principles directly. Even the supporters mentioned human rights, both the rights of victims that the life sentence would protect or vindicate and, at a different level, the rights of offenders that could and should be guarded in a system that imposed and implemented life sentences appropriately. In all, the debate went a long way towards confirming that if the international community wished to take international human rights seriously it could not simply assume that life imprisonment did not raise issues of human rights principles.

The focus on life imprisonment should not lead us to overlook a key point of consensus. All the Commissioners agreed that imprisonment was the appropriate punishment for crimes against the peace and security of mankind. There was some discussion about having harsher forms of imprisonment, such as imprisonment with

---

27 Ibid., 43 para 14.

28 (n 23) para 32.

29 Ibid., para 36.

30 Commissioner Ogiso from Japan, ibid., para 25.

31 *Summary Record of the 2209th Meeting* (1991) 1 Yearbook of the International Law Commission 18 UN Doc A/CN.4/SER.A/1991 para 29.

hard labour,[32] but this idea did not find favour. Its defeat signalled that what the Commissioners had in mind was a modern form of imprisonment in which loss of liberty per se was the punishment and further pains were not to be added deliberately by the manner of enforcement.

The somewhat leisurely deliberations of the ILC were overtaken by events in Yugoslavia and Rwanda. When in 1993 and 1994 the Security Council decided to establish *ad hoc* International Tribunals to try individual offenders for crimes against humanity committed in those countries, it was directly confronted by the lack of a developed penal framework at the international level.

As with the Nuremberg Charter, the penal provisions of the Statutes that the UNSC adopted for the two Tribunals are very brief. Article 24 (1) ICTYSt provides: 'The penalty imposed by the Trial Chamber shall be limited to imprisonment. In determining the terms of imprisonment, the Trial Chamber shall have recourse to the general practice regarding prison sentences in the courts of the former Yugoslavia.'

Two further key articles deal with the enforcement of sentences[33] and with pardon and commutation,[34] respectively. These three short provisions, which are repeated in substantially identical terms in the ICTRSt,[35] reveal some important developments in penal policy since Nuremberg. One is that the death penalty should not be imposed. The second is that imprisonment had now been recognized as the primary sentence in international criminal justice. The third was that there should be a mechanism in place to create legal certainty and to avoid the charge of retrospective legislation in the sphere of punishment: the mechanism put forward here was that the determination of its term should be linked to an existing penal system.[36] And finally the *ad hoc* Tribunal should play a key role in the release of sentenced prisoners.

With the wisdom of hindsight it is clear that the exclusion of the death sentence in the charters for the *ad hoc* Tribunals of the 1990s was an important station on the road to the abolition of capital punishment as a form of punishment that could operate at the international level.[37] Hindsight too supports its corollary, that with these two Charters imprisonment had triumphed: it was now the dominant sentence in international criminal justice. This was further underlined by the adoption of imprisonment as the only punishment that could be imposed in the other 'mixed' tribunals which the UN played a part in creating on varying legal bases to try crimes against international law

---

32 *Summary Records of the 2240th Meeting* (1991) 1 Yearbook of the International Law Commission 8 UN Doc A/CN.4/SER.A/1991 paras 29, 31, 41.

33 Art. 27 ICTYSt.

34 Art. 28 ICTYSt.

35 Art. 23 ICTRSt (penalties), Art. 26 ICTRSt (enforcement of sentences) and Art. 27 ICTRSt (commutation of sentences).

36 H. Corell, 'Nuremberg and the Development of an International Criminal Law' (1995) 149 *Military Law Review* 87, 93–5.

37 The UNSC was prepared to alienate the government of Rwanda, which had initially called for the establishment of an *ad hoc* International Tribunal, but in the end formally opposed it and refused to co-operate with it, on the grounds that offenders convicted by the national courts of Rwanda would face the death penalty while those convicted by the Tribunal of arguably more serious crimes would not: P. Akvahan, 'The International Criminal Tribunal for Rwanda: The Politics and Pragmatics of Punishment' (1996) 90 *American Journal of International Law* 501.

in post-conflict situations, jointly with local judges: the SCSL (2002), and the hybrid tribunals in Kosovo (1999), East Timor (1999) and Cambodia (2003).[38]

In international criminal justice too, imprisonment has now achieved the position of dominance that in the eighteenth century Beccaria had advocated for it as a potentially proportionate punishment and that in the twentieth century Foucault feared as an instrument of human repression. What remains to be seen is whether it has been possible to develop the sentence of imprisonment in international criminal justice in ways that would enable it to meet Beccaria's ideal of proportionality, while counteracting the Foucauldian nightmare of total control.

4. DETERMINING THE APPROPRIATE SENTENCE OF IMPRISONMENT

Consideration of whether a sentence of imprisonment is appropriate requires in the first instance consideration of how long it will be. This in turn requires an analysis of both the imposition of prison terms and of the release from them, for the actual length of the time served is determined too by the early release from prison of such sentenced offenders.

4.1 The Sentencing Frameworks of the *ad hoc* Tribunals

Once the ICTY and the ICTR began imposing sentences of imprisonment it soon became clear that the ideals of classical criminal law – legal certainty, proportionality and parsimony in the imposition of sentence – were not being met by requiring the *ad hoc* Tribunals to have recourse to the general practice regarding prison sentences in the former Yugoslavia and Rwanda respectively. Although the Tribunals followed the injunction to 'have recourse' to the specified national sentencing practice in every case, this was largely an empty formality. Neither Tribunal found much of value on which to rely in the national sentencing jurisprudence to which they were referred.[39]

The ICTY, moreover, directly ignored an important limit on sentencing discretion in the law of the former Yugoslavia, which had allowed only for maximum fixed-term sentences of less than 30 years or death sentences. The Tribunal determined[40] that it could impose life sentences, even though there had been no provision for them in the Yugoslavian sentencing law or guidelines for determining the length of prison

---

[38] W. Schabas, *The UN International Criminal Tribunals: The former Yugoslavia, Rwanda and Sierra Leone* (Cambridge University Press 2006) 3–4.

[39] More fully, see D. van Zyl Smit, 'Punishment and Human Rights in International Criminal Justice' (2002) 2 *Human Rights Law Review* 1–17; S. Beresford, 'Unshackling the Paper Tiger – The Sentencing Practices of the ad hoc International Tribunals for the Former Yugoslavia and Rwanda' (2001) 1 *International Criminal Law Review* 33–90; J. Meernik and K. King, 'The Sentencing Determinants of the International Criminal Tribunal for the Former Yugoslavia: An Empirical and Doctrinal Analysis' (2003) 16 *Leiden Journal of International Law* 717–50.

[40] By adding to its own RPE, Rule 101(A), which specifically allows the imposition of life sentences.

sentences.[41] Its justification for doing this was that, in the absence of the death penalty, a life sentence was necessary to mark the heinousness of the crimes over which it had jurisdiction.[42] Moreover it has made it clear that it does not regard general international human rights provisions, such as Articles 7 and 10 ICCPR, as prohibiting life imprisonment.[43]

Once it had taken that step, the ICTY had no compunction about imposing sentences of more than 30 years, where a life sentence was not deemed to be necessary but a harsher punishment than 30 years was regarded as appropriate. The ICTR too departed freely from the admittedly limited guidance that could be found in the sentencing legislation and jurisprudence of Rwanda. The result is that in the jurisprudence of the *ad hoc* Tribunals there is effectively no maximum to the length of determinate sentences that can be imposed. Maximum sentences have exceeded 40 years,[44] and in the case of the SCSL, which has no provision for life imprisonment,[45] they have exceeded 50 years.[46]

Have the Tribunals been able, by developing their own sentencing jurisprudence, to provide a sufficient degree of predictability and certainty about the length of prison terms that they would impose? This is a question about sentencing jurisprudence and therefore more properly addressed in Chapter 6. However, from the point of view of the structure within which the imposition of sentences of imprisonment operates the answer must be negative. It is true that sentences of imprisonment imposed by the two *ad hoc* Tribunals can and have been reconsidered on appeal, something which could not be done by the post Second World War International Military Tribunals. However, the guidance given on sentencing by both Trial and Appellate Chambers has not created clear structures. Attempts to create a hierarchy of crimes in international criminal law[47]

---

[41] This issue did not arise in the case of ICTR as the law in Rwanda made provision for both sentences of death and of life imprisonment.

[42] In *Jelisić* IT-95-10-A (Judgment, 5 July 2001) para 100, the Appellate Chamber specifically noted that 'it falls within the Trial Chamber's discretion to impose life imprisonment', although at that stage the ICTY had not done so.

[43] *Stakić* IT-97-24-A (Judgment, 22 March 2006) para 395; *Popović and others* IT-95-10-A (Judgment, 5 July 2001) para 100.

[44] The Appeals Chamber of the ICTR imposed a sentence of 40 years in *Nchamihigo* ICTR-2001-63-A (Judgment, 18 March 2010); and one of 45 years in *Kajelijeli* ICTR 98-44-A (Judgment, 23 May 2005). The Appeals Chamber of the ICTY imposed a sentence of 40 years of imprisonment in *Jelisić* (note 42) and the same sentence of 45 years in *Stakić* (ibid).

[45] The reason for not allowing for the option of life imprisonment in the SCSLSt is not clear: Schabas (n 38) 549.

[46] The Special Court for Sierra Leone imposed a sentence of 52 years on appeal in *Sesay* SCSL-04-15-A (Judgment, 26 October 2009). A 50-year sentence was affirmed on appeal by the same Court in *Taylor* SCSL-03-01-A (Judgment, 26 September 2013).

[47] R. May and M. Wierda, 'Is there a Hierarchy of Crimes in International Law', in L.C. Vordah et al (eds), *Man's Inhumanity to Man: Essays on International Law in Honour of Antonio Cassese* (Kluwer 2003) 511–32.

have been dismissed, as have attempts to introduce sentencing guidelines.[48] In sum, imprisonment is being imposed by these Tribunals within a framework that allows such wide judicial discretion that there must be doubts whether it meets the minimum requirements of legal certainty.[49]

4.2 The Release Frameworks of the *ad hoc* Tribunals

Penologists have long recognized that the sentence of imprisonment cannot be fully understood without also looking at procedures for release. In practice it is these procedures which determine whether the sentence actually served is proportionate – that is, proportionate not only to the crime, but also to other penological objectives which the sentence was intended to serve. Could early release serve this complex function in the case of the *ad hoc* Tribunals?

On their face the provisions of the Statutes in this regard are unhelpful. Article 28 ICTYSt and Article 27 ICTRSt stipulate that if in terms of the law of the State in which a convicted person is imprisoned, such person is eligible for 'commutation or pardon' the State must inform the Tribunal. Only then will the President of the Tribunal, in consultation with the judges, decide whether to release the person concerned 'on the basis of the interests of justice and the general principles of law'.[50] This vague standard gives little guidance on the criteria to be applied in the decision on release.

This provision is seriously flawed in other ways too. The major difficulty is that the trigger lies in the national laws of States. These laws may vary greatly and result in the same sentence being implemented for different periods depending on where it is served. The ICTY tried to overcome this by issuing a Practice Direction[51] and by using model agreements with the States that undertook to incarcerate sentenced prisoners,[52] in terms of which European States were assumed to require two-thirds of a sentence to be served prior to the consideration of executive release. These agreements were then enforced by the President of the ICTY.

As both the ICTY and the ICTR complete their work this role has been taken over by the UN MICT.[53] It seems to operate in a fairly rigid and bureaucratic way and to have adopted the same standards that had previously been used by the ICTY and also

---

48 A. Danner, 'Constructing a Hierarchy of Crimes in International Criminal Law Sentencing' (2001) 87 *Virginia Law Review* 415; D.B. Pickard, 'Proposed Sentencing Guidelines for the International Criminal Court' (1997) 20 *Loyola LA International & Comparative Law Journal* 123.

49 S. Szoke-Burke, 'Avoiding Belittlement of Human Suffering: A Retributivist Critique of ICTR Sentencing Practices' (2012) 10 *Journal of International Criminal Justice* 561. For a less critical view, see B. Holá, C. Bijleveld and A. Smeulers, 'Consistency of International Sentencing: ICTY and ICTR Case Study' (2012) 9 *European Journal of Criminology* 539–52.

50 Art. 28 ICTYSt.

51 ICTY Practice Direction on the Procedure for the determination of Applications for Pardon, Commutation of Sentence, and Early Release of Persons convicted by the International Tribunal (IT/146/Rev.2, 1 September 2009).

52 D. Tolbert and A. Rydberg, 'Enforcement of Sentences', in R. May et al (eds), *Essays on ICTY Procedure and Evidence in Honour of Gabrielle Kirk McDonald* (Kluwer 2001) 533–43.

53 <http://www.unmict.org/en/about> accessed 17 August 2014. On the policy of equality across the Tribunal, see *Bisengimana* MICT-12-07 (Decision of the President on Early Release,

applied them to the release of prisoners sentenced by the ICTR, which previously had had stricter standards.[54] While this new release regime may have the advantage of consistency, it is unlikely that it will be flexible enough to compensate for weaknesses in the initial process of imposing sentences or for the imperfectly developed release system.

The problem of clarity about when and how release should be considered is much worse in the case of life sentences. No logical assumptions can be made about what is two-thirds of a human life. Most countries, in Europe and elsewhere, have a specified minimum period after which an offender sentenced to life imprisonment must be considered for release, but these periods vary widely.[55] In addition, in some countries some persons sentenced to life imprisonment for particularly heinous offences are not considered for release at all.[56] At the other extreme, certain countries have no provision for life sentences in their national legislation. They will therefore not have provided procedures in their national legislation, which could be applied in considering the release of persons serving their life sentences in such countries.[57]

The sentencing jurisprudence of the Tribunals has not improved this situation. The ICTR, which has imposed the most life sentences,[58] has referred in its jurisprudence

---

11 December 2012); *Serushago* MICT·12·28·ES (Decision of the President on Early Release, 12 December 2012).

[54] For further details, see R. Mulgrew, 'Releasing International Prisoners', in M. Herzog-Evans (ed), *Offender Release and Supervision: The Role of Courts and the Use of Discretion* (Wolf Legal Publishers, 2014) 21–52.

[55] For example, 15 years in Germany (s. 57a of the German Penal Code), 25 years in Russia (s. 79.5 of the Russian Criminal Code), and 35 years in Argentina (s. 13 of Argentinian Criminal Code).

[56] For example, s. 269(4) of the 2003 Criminal Justice Act, allows the trial judge to impose sentences of life imprisonment with whole life orders in England and Wales; and in the Australian jurisdiction of New South Wales, s. 19A of its Crimes Act 1900 establishes that someone who commits the crime of murder can only be released if they are granted mercy – thus excluding any release on parole.

[57] A pragmatic way of avoiding this difficulty has been found in the case of Spain, where until recently the maximum sentence allowed by national law was 30 years. The agreement with Spain specifies that it will only accept prisoners who have been sentenced to fixed terms of less than 30 years: see ICTY Press Release, The Hague, 11 December 2001.

[58] The ICTR's Trial Chamber has imposed 20 sentences of life imprisonment, of which 13 have been reaffirmed by the Appeals Chamber: *Akayesu* ICTR-96-4-T (Judgment, 2 October 1998) and ICTR-96-4-A (Judgment, 1 July 2001); *Gatete* ICTR-2000-61-T (Judgment, 31 March 2011) and ICTR-00-61-A (Judgment, 9 October 2012); *Hategekimana* ICTR-00-55B-T (Judgment, 6 December 2010) and ICTR-00-558-A (Judgment, 8 May 2012); *Kambanda* ICTR 97-23-S (Judgment, 4 September 1998) and ICTR 97-23-A (Judgment, 19 October 2000); *Kamuhanda* ICTR-99-54A-T (Judgment, 22 January 2004) and ICTR-99-54A-A (Judgment, 19 September 2005); *Karera* ICTR-01-74-T (Judgment, 7 December 2007) and ICTR-01-74-A (Judgment, 2 February 2009); *Kayishema* ICTR-95-1-T (Judgment, 21 May 1999) and ICTR-95-1-A (Judgment, 1 June 2001); *Muhimana* ICTR- 95-1B-T (Judgment, 28 April 2005) and ICTR-95-1B-A (Judgment, 21 May 2007); *Musema* ICTR-96-13-A (Judgment, 27 January 2000) and ICTR-96-13-A (Judgment, 16 November 2001); *Ndindabahizi* ICTR-2001-71-I (Judgment, 5 July 2004) and ICTR-01-71-A (Judgment, 16 January 2007); *Niyitegeka* ICTR-96-14-T (Judgment, 16 May 2003) and ICTR-96-14-A (Judgment, 9 July 2004); *Renzaho* ICTR-97-31-T

both to sentences of life imprisonment and to sentences of imprisonment for the remainder of the offender's life. On the face of it the implication seems to be that the former sentence is reducible and the latter is not. Scholarly writing has demonstrated that there is no real basis for this distinction.[59] In more recent decisions the usage is remarkably inconsistent, with Trial and Appellate Chambers of the ICTR using different formulations to refer to the same sentence in the same case.[60]

In any event, there must be serious doubt whether a sentence of imprisonment from which an offender has no prospect of release meets the minimum standards of international human rights law. Certainly, European human rights law has been developed to the point that failure to provide a prisoner serving a life sentence with a reasonable prospect of being considered for release and, at the time of sentence, with an indication of what form such consideration will take, is regarded as inhuman and degrading. Such a failure would thus breach the prohibition on torture and inhuman or degrading treatment or punishment in Article 3 ECHR.[61]

Sentencing judges appear to have no clear idea of the practical implications of the life sentences they impose. This was illustrated by the case of *Bagosora*[62] in which the Appellate Chamber of the ICTR decided by a majority of three to two to replace an earlier sentence of life imprisonment with a fixed term of 35 years. The dissenting judges referred scathingly to this change as a 'monumental reduction' in harshness of the sentence.[63] This makes one think that that the dissenting judges believed that a

---

(Judgment, 14 July 2009) and ICTR-97-31-A (Judgment, 1 April 2011); *Rutaganda* ICTR-96-3-T (Judgment, 6 December 1999) and ICTR-96-3-A (Judgment, 26 May 2003). In addition, the Appeals Chamber of the ICTR has increased to life imprisonment two fixed-term sentences imposed by the Trial Chamber in *Gacumbitsi* ICTR-2001-64-A (Judgment, 7 July 2006) and *Seromba* ICTR-2001-66-A (Judgment, 12 March 2008).

The Trial Chamber of the ICTY has imposed five sentences of life imprisonment, of which one has been reaffirmed by the Appeals Chamber: *Lukić* IT-98-32/1-T (Judgment, 20 July 2012) and IT-98-32/1-A (Judgment, 4 December 2012). As for the rest, three are still pending appeal (*Tolimir* IT-05-88/2-T (Judgment, 12 December 2012); *Beara* IT-02-58-T (Judgment, 10 June 2010); and *Popović* IT-02-57-T (Judgment, 10 June 2010)), and one has been lowered to 40 years (*Stakić* IT-97-24-T (Judgment, 31 July 2003) and IT-97-24-A (Judgment, 22 March 2006)). Besides, the Appeals Chamber of the ICTY has increased to life imprisonment a sentence of 20 years imposed by the Trial Chamber: *Galić* IT-98-29-T (Judgment, 5 December 2003) and IT-98-29-A (Judgment, 30 November 2006).

59 E. Gumboh, 'The Penalty of Life Imprisonment under International Criminal Law' (2011) 11 *African Human Rights Law Journal* 75–92.

60 For example, in *Clément Kayishema and Obed Ruzindana* ICTR-95-1-T (Judgment, 21 May 1999), the Trial Chamber sentenced Kayishema to 'imprisonment for the remainder of his life'. Later on, the Appeals Chamber ICTR-95-1-A (Judgment, 1 June 2001) 'affirmed the sentence of life imprisonment imposed'. Similarly, in *Tharcisse Renzaho* ICTR-97-31-T (Judgment, 14 July 2009) the Trial Chamber uses the expression 'life imprisonment', whereas the Appeals Chamber ICTR-97-31-A (Judgment, 1 April 2011) 'affirms Renzaho's sentence of imprisonment for the remainder of his life'.

61 *Kafkaris v Cyprus* App no 21906/04 (ECtHR, 12 February 2008) 2009 49 EHRR 35 paras 68–76, in which the international and European law on this point is collected. Affirmed in *Vinter and others v UK* App nos 66069/09, 130/10 and 3896/10 (ECtHR, 9 July 2013).

62 *Bagosora and Nsengiyumva* ICTR-98-41-A (Judgment, 14 December 2011).

63 Ibid., joint dissenting opinion of Judges Pocar and Liu 270 para 1.

35-year sentence would in practice be much shorter than a life sentence. However, given that Bagosora's 35-year sentence will entitle him to consideration for release after having served two-thirds, at best,[64] that is, 23 years and four months, is the period before a person sentenced to life imprisonment by the ICTR will be considered for release likely to be much longer? The dissenting judges do not address this question.

The ICTY has not fared better in creating legal certainty in this respect. In the case of *Stakić*[65] the Trial Chamber imposed a life sentence for the first time and at the same time tried to create some legal certainty by ruling that a court in the country in which the convicted person would serve his sentence should consider his release after 20 years. The Appellate Chamber rejected this ruling addressed at another court as beyond the powers of the ICTY and replaced the life sentence with imprisonment for 40 years.[66] Although the Appellate Chamber may have been technically correct in its rejection of the 20-year period before reconsideration of the life sentence would be mandatory, it did not explain why it considered a 40-year sentence, which implies a minimum term of 26 years and eight months (two-thirds of the full sentence), to be a lesser term than a life sentence.

Since the *Stakić* case the ICTY has imposed life sentences,[67] but it has not given a clear indication of what they mean. The ICTY, like the ICTR, has used the terms 'life imprisonment' and 'imprisonment for the remainder of the convicted person's life' interchangeably.[68] This left open the possibility that in the case of life sentences, unlike fixed term sentences, where the two-thirds rule applies, there would be no uniform minimum period after which early release will be considered automatically. In all, it was dubious whether the release processes of the *ad hoc* Tribunals, particularly those relating to life sentences, would ensure the predictability and proportionality of the sentences of imprisonment that they impose.

In June 2015, in the case of *Galić*[69] the President of the MICT, Judge Meron, sought to cut the Gordian knot of uncertainty about release from life sentences imposed by the ICTY and the ICTR. He did so by deciding that from now on all persons sentenced to

---

[64] The ICTR did not routinely release sentenced prisoners early. It only did so in a few instances of significant cooperation with the prosecution: Mulgrew (n 54). However, the MICT is now in control and it will consider for release at the two-thirds point: ibid.

[65] *Stakić* (n 58).

[66] *Stakić* IT-97-24-A (Judgment, 22 March 2006).

[67] See, for example, *Galić* IT-98-29-A (Judgment, 30 November 2006); *Popović, Beara and others* IT-05-88-T (Judgment, 10 June 2010); *Zdravko Tolimir* IT-05-88/2-T (Judgment, 12 December 2012); *Lukić and Lukić* IT-98-32/1-A (Judgment, 4 December 2012).

[68] For example, in *Lukić and Lukić* IT-98-32/1-T (Judgment, 20 July 2009) the Trial Chamber sentenced Milan Lukić to 'imprisonment for the remainder of his life'; whereas the Appellate Chamber IT-98-32/1-A (Judgment, 4 December 2012) 'affirms Milan Lukić's sentence of life imprisonment'. Similarly, in *Popović, Beara and others* (n 67) the ICTY sentences both Vujadin Popović and Ljubisa Beara to 'life imprisonment'. However, in the same decision the ICTY had previously referred to the Rules of the Chamber, stressing the fact that they provide the possibility of imposing a sentence including 'the remainder of the convicted person's life' (para 2228). J. Mujuzi, 'Is There a Need for the ICTY to Clarify the Difference(s) between Life Imprisonment and Imprisonment for the Remainder of the Offender's Life – The *Galić* and *Lukić* Decisions' (2010) 10 *International Criminal Law Review* 855.

[69] *Galić* MICT-14-83 (Decision on Early Release, 23 June 2015).

life imprisonment by these two Tribunals would normally be considered for release after having served 30 years. Only if other factors, such as substantial co-operation with the prosecution or the wider interests of justice, were present would the President of the MICT not focus on the position of similarly situated prisoners. In such cases release could take place before 30 years had elapsed.

This decision has the advantage of clarity in terms of the minimum 30-year period that would normally apply, even if the State in which the prisoner was serving his sentence would have allowed release at a much earlier stage.[70] It also ensures consistency in the consideration of release of similarly situated prisoners, no matter how their life sentences were formulated by the sentencing tribunal. In addition, the decision makes clear that all life sentenced prisoners should have a prospect of release. In so doing, it brings the international law explicitly into line with the 2013 decision of the Grand Chamber of the ECtHR in *Vinter and others v United Kingdom*,[71] that the human dignity of all prisoners requires recognition of the possibility that they may be rehabilitated during their sentences. If this happens, they should be released once they have been adequately punished, as the balance of the penological justifications for their continued detention would have changed over time.

Notwithstanding these strengths, it must be recognized that the decision of the MICT in *Galić* is an extraordinary example of judicial legislation, as there is nothing in the Statutes of the Tribunals, or the rules and directions issued by the Tribunals or by the MICT, that specifies a 30-year minimum period. What the President has done is to focus on the fact that the maximum fixed term imposed by the ICTR has hitherto been 45 years. He has then argued that the term normally served by someone sentenced to life imprisonment should not be less than two-thirds of that, i.e. 30 years. This 30-year normal minimum term is higher than the 25-year minimum provided by the ICCSt[72] and the same term recommended by the Grand Chamber of the ECtHR in *Vinter*.[73] It is also higher than the minimum terms set in the majority of European States.[74] The very fact that the President could come to a different, harsher, conclusion than these persuasive, if not binding, authorities illustrates just how wide his discretion is, and how inadequate the provisions of the original Statutes of the ICTY and ICTR were in establishing a clear release procedure.

4.3 The ICC

Most of the substance of what may be regarded as the contemporary use of imprisonment as a penalty imposed in the international penal system has hitherto been provided by the *ad hoc* Tribunals and, to a lesser extent, by the mixed courts of Sierra Leone and Cambodia. However, the ICC may be expected to play a more dominant role

---

70 In Galić's case the German authorities recommended release, primarily on the ground that he had been rehabilitated, after he had served 15 years, the standard minimum period that applies in that jurisdiction.

71 *Vinter* (n 61) above.

72 See text Art. 110(3) ICCSt.

73 (n 61 above) para 120.

74 D. van Zyl Smit, 'Outlawing Irreducible Life Sentences – Europe on the brink?' (2010) 23 *Federal Sentencing Reporter* 39–48.

and also influence the development of the penalties in international criminal justice generally. In developing the Rome Statute, which established the ICC,[75] the international community had the advantage of being able to draw on the experience with the *ad hoc* Tribunals, which were then beginning their work. In the debate on appropriate penalties for offences to be tried before the ICC a prominent place for imprisonment was not controversial. However, as had been the case when the ICL discussed its proposals in the early 1990s, there was again much debate about what the maximum determinate sentences of imprisonment should be and about life imprisonment.[76] Some States were still opposed to life imprisonment in principle, and wanted clearly defined fixed-term sentences. Other states, which would have preferred the death penalty, would only accept a penal provision if it included life imprisonment with a relatively long minimum period before release could be considered. In the end a compromise was accepted which made provision for life imprisonment with a long minimum term, but restricted its use.[77]

The solution that was finally agreed is reflected in Article 77 of the ICCSt on 'Applicable penalties'.[78] It confirms imprisonment as the penalty that the Court may impose for the infringements of International Criminal Law covered in the Statute: although the Court may order a fine or forfeiture as further penalties,[79] these may only be imposed in addition to imprisonment.

The terms of imprisonment that the ICC may impose are delineated as follows:

(a) Imprisonment for a specified number of years, which may not exceed a maximum of 30 years; or
(b) A term of life imprisonment when justified by the extreme gravity of the crime and the individual circumstances of the convicted person.[80]

Moreover, when a person has been convicted of more than one crime, the ICC must pronounce a sentence for each crime and a joint sentence specifying the total period of imprisonment.[81] This avoids the less rigorous practice of the ICTY and the ICTR, which could impose a single global sentence without specifying how the individual offences contributed to it. The joint sentence that the ICC may impose is limited too; it may not exceed 30 years or, in particularly grave cases, life imprisonment.

---

[75] The Rome Statute (ICCSt) adopted on 17 July 1998 and came in to force on 1 July 2002.

[76] See (n 19).

[77] See the observer's notes by R.E. Fife on Article 77 in O. Triffterer, *Commentary on the Rome Statute of the International Criminal Court* (2nd ed Beck, Hart, Nomos 2008) 1419–37.

[78] *See* in general W. Schabas, *The International Criminal Court: a commentary on the Rome Statute* (Oxford University Press 2010) 891–7.

[79] Art. 77(2) ICCSt.

[80] Art. 77(1) ICCSt. A further power to impose sentence is vested by r. 146 ICC RPE in the Presidency of the Court to impose imprisonment for the 'wilful non-payment' of fines. The creation of this power by the rules rather than in the Statute itself has been rightly criticized as an infringement of the principle of legal certainty: R. Mulgrew, *Towards the Development of the International Penal System* (Cambridge University Press 2013) 16–17.

[81] Art. 78(3) ICCSt.

In addition, imprisonment imposed by the ICC is specifically made subject to the provision in Article 110 ICCSt relating to the reduction of sentence. Only the Court itself can reduce sentences and it must do so by reviewing the sentence after the sentenced person has served two-thirds, or 25 years in the case of a life sentence.[82]

Taken together these provisions create a much more rigorous formal framework for the imposition of both determinate and indeterminate sentences of imprisonment than did the Statutes of the ICTY and the ICTR. The length of determinate sentences is clearly restricted to 30 years, thus largely eliminating the possibility of sentences that are so long that they become life sentences in practice.

The life sentence too is constrained in interesting ways. Its use is limited by specific sentencing criteria, the requirements that the crime must be extremely grave and that the individual circumstances of the convicted person must justify its use. This formulation was apparently inserted to bridge the gap between those who wanted a life sentence as the ultimate penalty and those who were totally opposed to its introduction.[83] Its effect, however, is to establish a fixed term of imprisonment as a norm and the life sentence as an exceptionally heavy penalty that will have to be justified in specific cases. This contributes both to certainty about, and proportionality in, the use of this penalty. Moreover, before a life sentence can be imposed, the ICC RPE require that at least one of the aggravating factors that it lists must be present.[84] The absence of such aggravating circumstances was used by the ICC in the *Lubanga* case to limit the consideration of sentence to a fixed term of imprisonment.[85]

Further legal clarity is added by the release provisions. Linking them specifically to sentences that may be imposed signals up front that the determination of the actual term of imprisonment to be served depends not only on the initial sentencing decision of the court, but also on its decision on release. This too contributes to legal certainty.

The same effect is achieved by bringing the release decision fully back to the ICC and not requiring the States where the prisoner is serving the sentence to have to initiate the process. The consideration of early release after two-thirds is now guaranteed in the Statute rather than indirectly as in the case of the *ad hoc* Tribunals by agreements with enforcing States. This is particularly important in the case of life sentences where the clear provision for review after 25 years removes much uncertainty; 25 years is a long minimum period, but given the extremely serious nature of the crimes that the ICC tries and the restrictions in its Statute on the use of life imprisonment even for such crimes, its length is probably justifiable. It is notable that the release procedures of the ICC, in the sense of judicial review after a fixed period of 25 years, have been endorsed by the Grand Chamber of the ECtHR as an example to which national systems should aspire.[86] In the *Lubanga* case[87] the ICC referred in passing to a 'whole life sentence'. However, it cannot literally mean that the Court could order that for the whole of a prisoner's life the sentence cannot be reconsidered,

---

82 Art. 110(3) ICCSt.
83 Fife (n 77).
84 Rule 145 ICC RPE.
85 *Lubanga* ICC-01/04-01 (Judgment, 10 July 2012) para 96.
86 *Vinter* (n 61) para 96.
87 *Lubanga* (n 85) para 96.

as the ICCSt makes the review of all life sentences automatic. These words are an unfortunate rhetorical flourish and nothing more should be read into them.

As in the case of the *ad hoc* Tribunals, whether sentences imposed by the ICC will actually be predictable and proportionate will depend not only on the legal framework within which they are imposed but also on the development by the courts of clear and routinely followed principles of sentencing. The ICC has not heard sufficient cases for one to draw any conclusions on whether it will develop such a framework. However, what one can conclude is that the ICC's formal framework for the imposition of sentences and early release from them has much greater potential than that of the *ad hoc* Tribunals for producing outcomes that meet the requirements of legality and proportionality.[88] This applies both to the length of determinate prison sentences and to the appropriateness of life imprisonment. It also applies to the eventual determination of how long prisoners serving both determinate and life sentences should actually serve before being released.

5. THE SUBSTANCE OF THE SENTENCE OF IMPRISONMENT

Finally, no discussion of sentences of imprisonment in international criminal justice will be complete without some consideration of what such sentences should, and actually do, entail for the prisoners subjected to them. Human rights lawyers in particular should take this issue seriously, as it reveals whether the penitentiary techniques used to exercise power over prisoners, which so concerned Foucault, are restricted at the international level, in theory and in practice, by legal constraints. Part of the answer to this question is contained in other chapters of this volume that deal in detail with international standards governing the deprivation of liberty and the oversight of international imprisonment (see Part VI) as well as the complex relationship between international tribunals and courts that impose sentences of imprisonment and the national states that enforce them (Chapter 10). Here I propose to limit my comments to the rules and principles governing the substance of imprisonment, which guide judges in modern international courts and tribunals when making decisions related directly to the sentence of imprisonment.

In regard to the content of the sentence of imprisonment it is noteworthy that the ICTY in its first sentencing judgment, the *Erdomović* case,[89] dealt comprehensively with the treatment of prisoners and held that 'the penalty imposed as well as the enforcement of such penalty must always conform to the minimum principles of humanity and dignity which constitute the inspiration for the international standards governing the protection of the rights of convicted persons'.[90] It then went on to refer

[88] For a more critical view, see D. Scalia, 'Long-Term Sentences in International Criminal Law. Do They Meet the Standards Set Out by the European Court of Human Rights?' (2011) 9 *Journal of International Criminal Justice* 669–87.

[89] *Erdomović* IT-96-22-T (Judgment, 29 November 1996).

[90] Ibid., para 74, internal references omitted. The Trial Chamber based its right to supervise how persons it had convicted were treated on Article 27 ICTYSt and Rule 104 ICTY RPE.

to a number of international instruments on human rights generally, and the rights of prisoners in particular, before concluding that:

> [t]he significance of these principles resides in the fact that a person who has been convicted of a criminal act is not automatically stripped of all his rights. The Basic Principles for the Treatment of Prisoners state that 'except for those limitations that are demonstrably necessitated by the fact of incarceration, all prisoners shall retain the human rights and fundamental freedoms set out in the Universal Declaration of Human Rights' (...) [T]he Trial Chamber considers that the penalty imposed on persons declared guilty of serious violations of humanitarian law must not be aggravated by the conditions of its enforcement.[91]

This passage is of considerable significance because it subjects the implementation of the prison sentences of prisoners who are held in national prisons to the same set of international instruments that were used to structure the regimes that are followed at the detention units at the headquarters of the Tribunals. Whether this is true in practice is of course much more difficult to determine.

Most of the prisoners' rights recognized by the Tribunals in this way are negative or defensive rights not to be ill-treated in any way. The question is whether international prisoners also have positive rights, such as a right to 'rehabilitation'. This is controversial; for many penologists have pointed out that a policy of rehabilitating prisoners can be repressive. Indeed, Foucault's critique of modern penological techniques is based in part on the idea that they can be used by prison authorities to impose additional burdens on prisoners. Such burdens can range from compulsory treatment programmes, through to invasive surgery and can also include an element of unfettered discretion where 'experts' decide on prisoners' release by determining whether they have been 'rehabilitated'.

However, recognizing prisoners' right to social rehabilitation or resocialization may also have a positive implication for them in that they may use it as a basis to claim opportunities to improve themselves and most importantly a right to be considered for release. The right to social rehabilitation has been recognized as an element of human dignity and is increasingly used by international human rights courts in a way that can work to the advantage of prisoners, both while they are in prison and when their release is being considered. Thus, for example, the Grand Chamber of the ECtHR based its conclusions that prisoners should be allowed access to artificial insemination in appropriate circumstances,[92] and that even prisoners sentenced to whole life terms of imprisonment have a right to be considered for release,[93] on a positive right to opportunities for rehabilitation.

Thus far prisoners' positive right to rehabilitation has played a relatively small role in both the determination and implementation of prison sentences in international criminal justice.[94] Considerations of rehabilitation do not play a clear role at the imposition

---

[91] Ibid.

[92] *Dickson v UK* App no 44362/04 (ECtHR, 4 December 2007) para 28.

[93] *Vinter* (n 61) para 119.

[94] See in general G. Vermeulen and E. Dewree, *Offender Reintegration and Rehabilitation as a Component of International Criminal Justice? Execution of Sentences at the Level of*

stage.[95] It is also notable that there is no mechanism to ensure that the early release of prisoners be subject to conditions designed to assist their rehabilitation.

In the somewhat mechanistic release procedures of the *ad hoc* Tribunals, concerns about resocialization have also played a relatively minor role. In the future the situation will be somewhat different where the ICC is concerned. Although its Statute does not mention rehabilitation or resocialization at all, it is a consideration introduced indirectly into the release process. When the Court considers early release of sentenced prisoners, after two-thirds, or 25 years in the case of those sentenced to life imprisonment, it may reduce their sentences if it finds that they have co-operated with the ICC in its investigations and prosecutions, or assisted it in enforcing its judgments, or if there are other factors present among a list in the ICC RPE.[96] Included in this latter list of criteria is the sentenced person's 'prospect of resocialisation and successful resettlement'.[97]

This single reference to resocialization should be seen in context. It is clear from the Statute that, also in release matters, the primary concern of the ICC is to use imprisonment as an instrument to combat the offences specified in its Statute, rather than to manipulate the consciousness of individual offenders. Even in the secondary list, other criteria, for example whether the 'early release of the sentenced person would give rise to significant social instability',[98] apparently enjoy equal weight to the resocialization of the sentenced person.

6. CONCLUSION

On reviewing the penal framework that has operated since the early 1990s, when imprisonment became the predominant sentence in international criminal justice, it is clear that it has considerable shortcomings. Not enough was done initially in the Statutes of the ICTY and the ICTR, as well as the other hybrid courts and tribunals modelled on them, to ensure legality and proportionality in the imposition of prison sentences or release from them. In the course of applying these statutes the meaning of some of their provisions did become clearer. However, with the sentence of life imprisonment in particular grave uncertainties about when it should be imposed and when persons serving life sentences should be considered for release have remained unresolved.

The ICCSt holds out the promise of developing international criminal justice in the direction of more legal certainty. It could result in sentences of imprisonment both becoming more predictable and not excessively long. Its regime for life imprisonment

---

International Tribunals and Courts: Moving Beyond the Mere Protection of Procedural Rights and Minimal Fundamental Interests? (Maklu 2014).

[95] S. D'Ascoli, *Sentencing in International Criminal Law* (Hart 2011) 138–9; J. Nemitz, 'The Law of Sentencing in International Criminal Law: The Purposes of Sentencing and the Applicable Method for the Determination of the Sentence' (2001) *Yearbook of International Humanitarian Law* 87, 94; more critical: Schabas (n 38) 559.

[96] Art. 110(4) ICCSt.

[97] Rule 223 ICC RPE: Criteria for review concerning reduction of sentence.

[98] Rule 223(c) ICC RPE.

has the potential for ensuring that it is only imposed when strictly necessary and that release from it is fairly and timely considered.

It is still too early to say whether the ICC will deliver what it promises in respect of sentences of imprisonment. Nevertheless, the overall trajectory of developments in international criminal justice allows for some optimism that it will eventually satisfy the ideals of legal certainty, proportionality and parsimony, first articulated by Beccaria and still key elements in the classical conception of criminal law.

It is more difficult to judge the success of the developing legal framework governing imprisonment in international criminal justice as a response to the more radical Foucauldian critique. To the extent that international criminal justice is moving toward legality and proportionality in the imposition of prison sentences, these are a significant legal protection that may also negate some of the problems Foucault foresaw.

Similarly, the ICCSt in particular introduces an element of due process into the consideration of release. This should reduce the scope for the unfettered exercise of power that Foucault rightly feared in the implementation of sentences of imprisonment. The gradual development of a framework for recognising and protecting the rights of prisoners held within the international criminal justice system and the recognition by international tribunals and courts of their obligation to enforce these rights is also a positive antidote to the Foucauldian dystopia of the increasing use of punitive penitentiary techniques.

International criminal justice clearly places less emphasis on social rehabilitation and resocialization than many modern national criminal justice systems. From a Foucauldian perspective this may be both positive and negative. Positively, it may mean less interference with the 'minds' of sentenced prisoners convicted by international tribunals and courts. And the absence of the possibility of 'parole',[99] on conditions allegedly designed to assist the person who is given early release, may be seen as the absence of the power to control that Foucault saw modern penal systems exercising beyond the initial prison sentence over individuals who have returned to 'free' society.

Ironically, the relative absence of concern for social rehabilitation and the re-integration of released prisoners may also mean that sentenced persons in the international system find it harder to claim the rights that social democratic penal theory sees as flowing from prisoners' rights to resocialization. This may change if the social rehabilitation and reintegration of international prisoners is given more prominence in the future. The future imposition and the implementation of both determinate and indeterminate sentences of imprisonment in international criminal justice are likely to be shaped by whether the call for more active intervention is interpreted as giving additional powers to the (international) sentencers and prison authorities or additional enforceable rights to the prisoners.

---

[99] A partial exception to this general rule is the belated introduction of a possibility of conditional early release for offenders convicted by the SCSL (see T.A. Doherty and S.A. Fisher, 'Enforcement of sentences and oversight of prisoners convicted by the Special Court for Sierra Leone', Chapter 15 in this volume). However, the situation in Sierra Leone is different because the Special Court operated in a way that embedded it more closely in the national criminal justice system than was the case with the ICTY or the ICTR.

5. Fines and forfeiture in international criminal justice

Rebecca Young[*]

1. INTRODUCTION

While imprisonment is undoubtedly the principal form of punishment within the international penal system a comprehensive examination of such system must consider the available supplementary sanctions of fines and forfeiture.[1] A fine is a financial penalty of a fixed amount that must be paid by a sentenced person. Forfeiture refers to permanently depriving a sentenced person of certain proceeds, property or assets.[2] Although fines and forfeiture are only ever likely to play a minor and subsidiary role, their close consideration is warranted as they raise issues lying at the heart of international criminal justice, such as ensuring fairness to accused persons (an obligation which should not end upon conviction) and the necessity of international cooperation.

After first outlining the statutory regimes and fledgling practice of other international criminal jurisdictions, this chapter will focus on the regime for fines and forfeiture established by the ICC. Following a brief review of the relevant *travaux préparatoires* of the ICCSt in this regard, this chapter will set out in detail the key features of the ICC's regime for fines and forfeiture, considering the issue of whether fines and forfeiture are regarded as punitive in nature in view of the Rome Statute's ambiguity in this regard. The chapter will highlight the gaps and errors which remain in the ICC's regime and critically assess its use of fines and forfeiture in its sentencing practice to date.

---

* The author is grateful to Hirad Abtahi and Scarlet Kim for their comments on an earlier draft of this chapter. All views expressed, as well as any errors and omissions, are the author's own.

1 See R. Mulgrew, *Towards the Development of the International Penal System* (Cambridge University Press 2013) 17.

2 Art. 77(2)(b) ICCSt; See also the definition of 'confiscation' in Art. 1(f) of the UN Convention against Illicit Traffic in Narcotic Drugs and Psychotropic Substances 1988. This chapter understands forfeiture generally as a permanent deprivation of proceeds, property or assets, without being concerned by the technical question of the potential different forms of forfeiture (eg restitution). Accordingly, this chapter reproduces the language used by each relevant statutory instrument (eg deprivation, restitution, confiscation, forfeiture, recovery) without assigning a specific technical meaning to each term, regarding these terms as broadly interchangeable for present purposes. This approach is consistent with that of international criminal tribunals themselves which have not assigned unique technical meanings to the various terms which might be employed to refer to the taking of proceeds, property or assets.

This chapter will then focus on the operationalization of fines and forfeiture at the ICC, considering two key issues: enforcement and fairness. It will first consider the challenges of transforming the ICC's statutory regime for fines and forfeiture into an operational one, examining the relationship between the ICC and enforcement at the national level. Then, it will consider fundamental concerns as to procedural fairness and respect for human rights within the fines and forfeiture regime by examining the controversial notion that a term of imprisonment may be extended for the non-payment of a fine.

2. FINES AND FORFEITURE BEFORE INTERNATIONAL CRIMINAL COURTS AND TRIBUNALS

This section will outline the use of fines and forfeiture in the legislative texts and practice of various international (and internationalized) criminal jurisdictions other than the ICC, explaining that their use is highly underdeveloped. It will demonstrate that fines against convicted persons do not feature explicitly in any of the relevant governing texts. While forfeiture powers do exist, they have not been utilized. Further, as to their nature, forfeiture powers are usually expressed in a manner which does not regard them as part of the punitive regime.

The International Military Tribunals in Nuremberg (IMTN) and the Far East (IMTFE) possessed broad sanctioning powers. Article 27 of the Charter of the IMTN empowered the Tribunal 'to impose upon a Defendant, on conviction, death or such other punishment as shall be determined by it to be just', not expressly permitting, but also not excluding, the possibility of financial penalties. It is arguable, however, that the juxtaposition of 'death' and 'such other punishment' could indicate that even the latter was intended to cover the most serious forms of punishment, such as imprisonment.

Article 28 of the Charter of the IMTN further provided that '[i]n addition to any punishment imposed by it, the Tribunal shall have the right to deprive the convicted person of any stolen property and order its delivery to the Control Council for Germany'. Such deprivation of property is clearly regarded by the Charter as an addition to punishment, rather than being considered an integral component of the punishment as such. Article 16 of the Charter of the IMTFE contained a broad sanctioning power in practically identical terms to Article 27 of the Charter of the IMTN, although there was no equivalent forfeiture provision. No deprivation of property or financial punishment was ever imposed by either tribunal.[3]

The ICTY and ICTR (*ad hoc* Tribunals) provide for a narrower scope of penalties. Article 24(1) of the ICTYSt mandates that '[t]he penalty imposed by the Trial Chamber

---

[3] W. Schabas, *The International Criminal Court: A Commentary on the Rome Statute* (Oxford University Press 2010) 896; R.E. Fife, 'Article 77: Applicable Penalties', in O. Triffterer (ed), *Commentary on the Rome Statute of the International Criminal Court* (2nd edn, C.H. Beck 2008) 1425; C. Kress and G. Sluiter, 'Fines and Forfeiture Orders', in A. Cassese, P. Gaeta and J.R.W.D. Jones (eds), *The Rome Statute of the International Criminal Court: A Commentary* (Oxford University Press 2002) 1823.

shall be limited to imprisonment'. Accordingly, there is no provision for fines.[4] The ICTYSt does, however, provide that 'the Trial Chambers may order the return of any property and proceeds acquired by criminal conduct, including by means of duress, to their rightful owners'.[5] The same is provided for by the ICTRSt.[6]

The issue of the restitution of property has not been closely considered by the *ad hoc* Tribunals. In the case of *Milošević et al*, the ICTY ordered the provisional freezing of assets of the accused,[7] however, this did not occur in the context of penalties. In seeking the indictment against the accused, the Prosecutor argued that an order freezing assets could be undertaken for two purposes: first, in order to grant restitution of property after conviction, pursuant to Rule 105 of the RPE; and second, in order to prevent accused persons still at large from using their assets in order to evade arrest or putting their assets beyond the reach of the Tribunal.[8] The ICTY emphasized the second of these reasons, ordering '[t]hat all States Members of the United Nations make inquiries to discover whether the accused (or any of them) have assets located in their territory and, if so, adopt provisional measures to freeze such assets, without prejudice to the rights of third parties, until the accused are taken into custody'.[9] This appears to indicate that the purpose of this provisional freezing of assets related largely to ensuring the Tribunal's capacity to arrest the accused persons, as States were only required to conduct such freezing until the suspects were in custody.

At the ICTR the only references to restitution in the context of Rule 105 of the RPE relate to two applications by a Non-Governmental Organization to appear as *amicus curiae*.[10] In the first of these two applications the Tribunal noted that the indictment against the accused contained no charge of unlawful taking of property and that, moreover, the application had not demonstrated that the applicant could assist the Tribunal.[11] In the second case the ICTR specified that '[a]s Rule 105 envisions a special hearing on restitution which only takes place after a Judgment of conviction specifically includes findings on the unlawful taking of property', the application was ill-timed.[12] In conclusion, the *ad hoc* Tribunals do not provide for fines as a sanction against a convicted person and have not exercised their powers in relation to the return of property and proceeds acquired by criminal conduct.

---

4 It is noted, however, that the legislative texts of the *ad hoc* Tribunals provide for fines in the limited context of contempt of court, see r. 77(G) ICTY RPE; rr. 46(A), 77(G) ICTR RPE. This chapter will not consider these limited instances as they are not relevant to the role of fines and forfeiture at the penal stage of the international criminal justice system.

5 Art. 24(3) ICTYSt.

6 Art. 23 ICTRSt; In addition, r. 105, of both the ICTY RPE and ICTR RPE, provides further information as to the procedural steps to be undertaken by a Trial Chamber in relation to the restitution of property.

7 *Milošević et al* IT-99-37 (Decision on the Review of Indictment and Application for Consequential Orders, 24 May 1999).

8 Ibid., para 27.

9 Ibid., para 29.

10 *Musema* ICTR-96-13-T (Decision on an Application by African Concern for Leave to Appear as Amicus Curiae, 17 March 1999); *Bagosora et al* ICTR-98-41-T (Decision on Amicus Curiae Request by African Concern, 23 March 2004).

11 *Musema*, ibid., paras 10–11, 13–14.

12 *Bagosora et al* (n 10) para 9.

The SCSLSt contains no reference to fines. Article 19(3) thereof provides that '[i]n addition to imprisonment, the Trial Chamber may order the forfeiture of the property, proceeds and any assets acquired unlawfully or by criminal conduct, and their return to their rightful owner or to the State of Sierra Leone'.[13] As this Statute does not expressly state that imprisonment is the only punishment available, it is unclear whether such forfeiture is envisaged as an additional punishment to imprisonment or simply as an addition which is not inherently punitive in nature. However, there appears to be no obvious reason to interpret this lack of clarity as an intention to take a position on the punitive nature of forfeiture which radically differs from that which had been taken by the IMTN and the *ad hoc* Tribunals. Indeed, the language of '[i]n addition to imprisonment' is similar to the language of Article 28 of the Charter of the IMTN, '[i]n addition to any punishment imposed', further suggesting that the SCSL's understanding of the nature of forfeiture was intended to be consistent with that of its predecessors and that, while not being expressly stated, it is imprisonment which is envisaged as the available penalty.

The SCSL has considered only the issue of the provisional freezing of assets of accused persons with a view to recovery upon any eventual conviction.[14] The relevant decision referred to the complex issues surrounding the freezing of assets belonging to persons presumed innocent, while recognizing the pragmatic need to do so in certain circumstances.[15] The decision emphasized that even where the request for targeting property occurred in a post-conviction context, the key requirement is a connection to its unlawful acquisition or it being a result of criminal conduct.[16] As a result, the SCSL considered that:

> [T]he proper test to be applied in determining whether or not to grant an application by the police or the Prosecution to freeze assets in the bank account of a person charged with crime pending trial is whether there is clear and convincing evidence that the targeted assets have a nexus with criminal conduct or were otherwise illegally acquired. What is 'clear and convincing evidence' depends on the particular facts and circumstances of each case. The targeted property must be specifically identifiable as a product of criminality or illegality. Neither probable cause nor mere suspicion or speculation will suffice.[17]

The SCSL then considered that this standard had not been satisfied, describing the prosecution's request as 'tenuous and highly speculative'.[18]

Turning to the Extraordinary Chambers in the Courts of Cambodia (ECCC), its establishing law makes no reference to fines. Chapter XI, entitled 'Penalties', specifies first, in Article 38, that '[a]ll penalties shall be limited to imprisonment', prior to going on to indicate in Article 39, that, inter alia, '[i]n addition to imprisonment, the Extraordinary Chamber of the trial court may order the confiscation of personal

---

[13] Rules 88(B) and 104 SCSL RPE further specify the operation of this provision.

[14] *Norman et al* SCSL-04-14-PT (Norman – Decision on *inter partes* motion by Prosecution to freeze the account of the accused Sam Hinga Norman at Union Trust Bank (SL) Ltd or at any other bank in Sierra Leone, 19 April 2004).

[15] Ibid., paras 5–6.

[16] Ibid., para 11.

[17] Ibid., para 13.

[18] Ibid., para 15.

property, money, and real property acquired unlawfully or by criminal conduct. The confiscated property shall be returned to the State'. Thus, like the IMTN and the *ad hoc* Tribunals, such confiscation is not conceptualized as a penalty since the only such penalty available is imprisonment. In addition to the confiscation of property, the Internal Rules of the ECCC also provide for a system of collective and moral reparations.[19]

Finally, the STLSt does not provide for either fines or the confiscation of property or assets in connection with punishment or sentencing, but provides for compensation for victims to be pursued through domestic proceedings.[20]

To conclude this examination of fines and forfeiture in international criminal bodies other than the ICC, the relevant founding documents of such bodies do not expressly provide for fines. Although the IMTN and IMTFE do not expressly exclude the possibility that a fine could be imposed as an 'other punishment', no such fine was ever imposed. The IMTN also provided that a convicted person could be deprived of stolen property, although this was specified as an addition to, and not part of, the punishment. Similarly, both the *ad hoc* Tribunals and the ECCC specify that imprisonment is the only penalty available, thus both precluding the possibility of fines and ensuring that their respective provisions for the return or confiscation of criminally acquired property are conceptualized as beyond the scope of punishment. While the SCSL does not specifically limit punishment to imprisonment, it also does not expressly provide for fines and uses a forfeiture regime extremely similar to that of the *ad hoc* Tribunals, thus likely indicating an intention to function consistently with those other bodies. None of the above bodies have applied the provisions governing the restitution of criminally acquired property at the post-conviction stage. Accordingly, the ICC regime was developed against this background of a paucity of practice concerning the role of fines and forfeiture in international criminal justice.

3. THE ICC'S SYSTEM OF FINES AND FORFEITURE

This section will briefly outline certain key elements of the drafting history of the ICCSt on fines and forfeiture, before considering the key theoretical issue of whether fines and forfeiture are treated as punitive in nature. It will then outline the key statutory provisions relating to fines and forfeiture, before briefly addressing the relationship between these elements and the Trust Fund for Victims (TFV).

3.1 Drafting History

The relevant *travaux préparatoires* of the ICCSt are readily accessible[21] and their insight as to the approach of States Parties to fines and forfeiture has been well

---

19 Rule 23*quinquies* ECCC IR.

20 Art. 25 STLSt.

21 See eg M.C. Bassiouni, *The Legislative History of the International Criminal Court Vol 2* (Transnational Publishers 2005) 552–67.

documented elsewhere.[22] Thus, this section outlines only a number of salient features by way of introduction to the eventual provisions of the Rome Statute.

The International Law Commission's 1994 Draft Statute for an International Criminal Court proposed the penalties of imprisonment and fines, indicating that one or more of these penalties could be imposed. This draft did not regard fines as only supplementary, nor did it contain any reference to forfeiture. It is explained in the commentary to then Article 47 that although earlier ILC drafts had provided for forfeiture it was ultimately removed due to perceived difficulties with matters relating to stolen property being addressed by the ICC, preferring to leave this to national jurisdictions.[23]

In the course of the work of the 1996 Preparatory Committee much of which involved the compilation of a large range of different options and alternatives, the notion of forfeiture was re-introduced under the guise of the confiscation of objects used in criminal conduct or of objects or profits obtained by criminal conduct.[24] There was also a proposal which simply listed both 'pecuniary sanctions' and 'seizure of instruments and objects of the crime' as possible penalties.[25]

By the time of the 1998 Preparatory Committee, both fines and 'reparations' were listed as potential penalties, although the issue of whether a fine should only be imposed in association with a sentence of imprisonment had been highlighted, as had the issue of whether reparations to victims should be appropriately addressed under the rubric of penalties.[26]

Throughout the drafting process, a number of key concerns were expressed by States Parties. There was concern over the appropriateness of fines as a penalty in view of the extremely grave nature of the crimes in question,[27] a concern which appears to have been resolved through the subsidiary status of fines. There was further discussion concerning the appropriateness of including the confiscation of the instrumentalities of crimes (ie the property and assets used in the perpetration of the crime), in particular as the nature of the crimes rendered it possible that such instrumentalities could include State property which might be subject to immunity.[28] The eventual scheme for forfeiture was thus designed to avoid these significant practical and legal concerns.[29]

Issues related to the enforcement of fines and forfeiture also dominated discussion. There was divided opinion as to whether the enforcement of fines and forfeiture orders should be conducted directly by the ICC or whether this would be a matter for national

---

[22] See Fife (n 3) 1425–6; Schabas (n 3) 891–4; Kress and Sluiter (n 3) 182–67; R.E. Fife, 'Penalties', in R.S. Lee (ed), *The International Criminal Court: Elements of Crimes and Rules of Procedure and Evidence* (Transnational Publishers 2001) 563–72.

[23] *Yearbook of the International Law Commission 1994* (Vol. II Part Two) UN Doc. A/49/10 60.

[24] See Bassiouni (n 21) 565.

[25] Ibid., 562.

[26] Ibid., 553–4.

[27] See Fife (n 3) 1425; Schabas (n 3) 896.

[28] See Fife (n 3) 1426; C. Kress, 'Penalties, Enforcement and Cooperation in the International Criminal Court Statute (Parts VII, IX, X)' (1998) 6 *European Journal of Crime, Criminal Law and Criminal Justice* 442, 445.

[29] See Fife (n 3) 1425; Schabas (n 3) 1426.

authorities.[30] A further divisive issue was sanctions for non-payment, including the potential sanction of imprisonment.[31] This latter issue proved so contentious that at the time of the drafting of the RPE certain delegates maintained that no power to impose the sanction of imprisonment for non-payment could be derived from the Rome Statute.[32] This issue will be further discussed in detail below, as it remains one of the key issues in the enforcement of fines and forfeiture orders.

Following the adoption of the ICCSt on 17 July 1998, the final form of Article 77 introduced a regime of applicable penalties more comprehensive than that of any other international criminal body. The first paragraph specifies that a convicted person can face the penalty of imprisonment, either for life or for a specified number of years not exceeding 30. The second paragraph further indicates that the ICC may order a fine and/or '[a] forfeiture of proceeds, property and assets derived directly from that crime, without prejudice to the rights of *bona fide* third parties'. A number of fundamental elements are immediately evident from the chapeau of the second paragraph of Article 77. First, neither a fine nor a forfeiture measure can be imposed in the absence of a sentence of imprisonment as these are additional to imprisonment. Further, the language of 'may' highlights the discretionary nature of these powers. Article 77 leaves the elucidation of further detail to the ICC's subsidiary texts.

3.2 The Punitive Nature of Fines and Forfeiture

The fact that Article 77 is entitled 'Applicable penalties' and then lists three possible actions – imprisonment, fines or forfeiture – appears to indicate that both fines and forfeiture are regarded as falling within the rubric of penalties. On the other hand, the inclusion of the words 'in addition' in paragraph 2, a term which echoes the language of earlier bodies such as the IMTN, introduces some ambiguity. It could be argued that despite all three potential actions against a convicted person being placed under the broad heading of 'penalties', the words 'in addition' indicate that fines and forfeiture are of a different nature. Alternatively, the words 'in addition' could simply express the notion that these are supplementary punishments to be imposed together with imprisonment.

Some clarity is offered in relation to fines by Rule 145(1)(a) of the RPE, which refers to 'the totality of any sentence of imprisonment and fine', and thus clarifies that a 'sentence' may include a fine, positing fines clearly within the punitive regime. It is less clear in relation to forfeiture. Rule 145, which is titled 'Determination of sentence', does not refer to forfeiture at all, thus implying that it is not considered to be part of the sentence. This could reflect a view that forfeiture may not constitute a penalty, but rather a mechanism to ensure that convicted persons do not profit from the proceeds of their crimes.[33] On the other hand it remains that Rule 147 detailing the procedure to be followed for the issuance of forfeiture orders is contained within Chapter 7 of the RPE

---

30 See W. Schabas, 'Article 109: Enforcement of fines and forfeiture measures' in O. Triffterer (n 3) 1678–80.

31 See Fife (n 3) 1425; Schabas (n 3) 1429–30.

32 Kress and Sluiter (n 3) 1828; Fife (n 22) 568–70.

33 See Kress (n 28) 443; Fife (n 3) 1425–6.

entitled 'Penalties'. Thus, the reference to 'any sentence of imprisonment and fine' in Rule 145(1)(a) appears to strongly indicate that a fine, unlike a forfeiture, is punitive.

There is also a need for caution in placing too much weight on structural elements, such as the discussion of forfeiture under the heading of 'Penalties' in Chapter 7. As forfeiture can only be imposed in the event of imprisonment, it is clearly closely inter-related therewith, thus it appears natural to place the section on forfeiture under the heading of 'Penalties' regardless of whether it is formally conceptualized to be of the same punitive character as imprisonment and fines. This view that forfeiture is not punitive would also be consistent with the contemporary and historical precedents which existed at the time of the drafting of the Rome Statute, as discussed in the previous section.

The view that fines and forfeiture are conceptually different is also supported by their different treatment at the level of enforcement. While it is specified that the non-payment of a fine can result in an increased period of imprisonment (see extensive discussion of this issue below), there is no prescription as to how the ICC is to address a failure to enforce a forfeiture order.[34] This distinction further indicates that the better view is that fines are understood to be more punitive in nature than forfeiture orders.

Forfeiture thus appears to perform a largely corrective, rather than punitive role, coming into play when a set of preconditions are satisfied (eg a term of imprisonment has been imposed after conviction for an international crime and there exists property, proceeds or assets derived directly or indirectly from this crime). This view also satisfies the underlying concern that the practically oriented process of ensuring the return of illegally obtained gains is different in nature from the punishment itself.

Whilst it is clear that there remains scope for differences of opinion on this issue, the most important point at this stage is that the ICC clearly provides for both fines and forfeiture as part of the post-conviction stage of proceedings, establishing detailed regimes for the issuance and enforcement of both of these 'beyond imprisonment' elements. This chapter will now outline pertinent details of Article 77(2)'s treatment of both fines and forfeiture.

3.3 Fines

As Article 77(2)(a) provides that fines may be imposed under criteria to be established in the RPE, the parameters for the imposition of fines are set out in detail in Rule 146,[35] the first paragraph of which narrows the scope for the use of fines as a potential penalty. The clear provision in Article 77 that fines are a subsidiary penalty is reinforced by the requirement that in order to determine whether to order a fine and the amount, 'the Court shall consider whether imprisonment is a sufficient penalty'. The ICC is also required to give due consideration to the financial capacity of the convicted person, including the effect of any forfeiture orders or reparations. This paragraph also

[34] Other than ongoing monitoring, see reg. 117 ICC ROC.

[35] In addition, Article 78 ICCSt sets out the factors the court must take into account during the determination of a sentence. Although, on its face, it appears to be most relevant to the determination of a sentence of imprisonment, it remains technically applicable also to the penalty of a fine.

introduces an additional element to the ICC's determination of fines: 'whether and to what degree the crime was motivated by personal financial gain'. Rule 146(2) specifies that fines must be set at an appropriate level, although no fixed minimum or maximum amounts are established, as some States advocated during drafting,[36] and as occurs in the applicable legal texts of the *ad hoc* Tribunals in relation to contempt of court. Rather, a maximum ceiling is set which is subjective to each convicted person's individual financial situation, namely that '[u]nder no circumstances may the total amount exceed 75 per cent of the value of the convicted person's identifiable assets, liquid or realizable, and property, after deduction of an appropriate amount that would satisfy the financial needs of the convicted person and his or her dependants'.[37]

This immediately calls to mind the practice of the ICC (and indeed of the *ad hoc* Tribunals) concerning the calculation of indigency in respect of entitlements to legal assistance paid by the Court, which is similarly based on a presumption of the need to ensure the satisfaction of the financial needs of a suspect or accused person and his or her dependants.[38] In practice, it is possible that the approach used by the ICC in indigency calculation could be adopted when assessing the appropriate amount of fines. Indeed, given that the system for the calculation of indigence is well established and has been the subject of extensive review and consultation, it is highly advisable that it be adapted to this new context which rests similarly on the basic principle of ensuring financial capacity in view of the needs of dependants. This would mean that the assessment of the financial needs of a convicted person might allow for the exclusion of certain assets and property from the pool available to be subjected to fines, such as a family home, furnishings, certain motor vehicles and an amount to cover the living expenses of dependants.[39] It should be noted that the vast majority of accused persons before the ICC have been determined fully or partially indigent for the purpose of their entitlement to legal assistance paid by the ICC. If the ICC's experience to date is indicative, it would be rare that a convicted person would have considerable financial assets available after his or her own needs and the needs of his or her dependants have been addressed. This, together with the strict criteria for the imposition of fines discussed above, further indicate that the imposition of fines is likely to be an extraordinary occurrence.

---

[36] On the advocacy by certain States for such specification of maximum and minimum amounts see, Schabas (n 3) 892–4; Fife (n 22) 566.

[37] Rule 146(2) ICC RPE.

[38] See ICC-ASP/6/INF.1 (Report on the principles and criteria for the determination of indigence for the purposes of legal aid (pursuant to paragraph 116 of the Report of the Committee on Budget and Finance of 13 August 2004), 31 May 2007) para 9; See also ICC-ASP/10/4 (Report of the Court regarding the desirability of absolute thresholds for the purposes of indigence calculation, 17 June 2011); ICC-ASP/12/3 (Registry's single policy document on the Court's legal aid system, 4 June 2013). The Court's system for the calculation of indigency has also been subject to judicial review by the Presidency in ICC-RoC85-01/08-4-Anx (Decision on the 'Request for Review of the Registrar's Decision of 25 August 2008 on the Application for Legal Assistance Paid by the Court', 25 February 2009).

[39] ICC-ASP/6/INF.1 ibid., paras 12–18.

Rule 146 goes on to discuss the modalities of the imposition of a fine, allowing for the possibility of payment by lump sum, instalments or as a system of daily fines.[40] The rule then considers one of the most contentious aspects of the regime, the consequences of non-payment. In the event of 'wilful non-payment', the Presidency may, either *proprio motu* or acting upon a request of the Prosecutor, after having ensured that all available enforcement measures have been exhausted, extend the term of imprisonment by up to five years or one-quarter of the term imposed, whichever is the least.[41] Any such extension is not allowed to result in a total period of imprisonment of more than 30 years. The ramifications of this aspect of the regime for fines is comprehensively explored as a key issue below.

3.4 Forfeiture

Turning to forfeiture, Article 77(2)(b) applies to the forfeiture of proceeds, property and assets derived directly or indirectly from the crime of which a person has been convicted, specifying that this is to be without prejudice to the rights of *bona fide* third parties. This protection of *bona fide* third parties is a key feature of the ICC's forfeiture regime.[42] Such protection has no equivalent before the *ad hoc* Tribunals. Indeed Rule 105(B) of the RPE of the ICTY and ICTR specify that property may potentially be seized from such third parties. It is not immediately apparent from the face of Article 77 whether it is the ICC itself or the State enforcing a forfeiture order, which must assess such potential prejudice. Article 109(1) of the ICCSt gives a clear role to national authorities in that States shall give effect to fines or forfeitures ordered by the ICC 'without prejudice to the rights of *bona fide* third parties, and in accordance with the procedure of their national law'. The same article also provides that '[i]f a State Party is unable to give effect to an order for forfeiture, it shall take measures to recover the value of the proceeds, property or assets ordered by the Court to be forfeited, without prejudice to the rights of *bona fide* third parties', thus appearing to indicate that if a State is unable to give effect to an order for forfeiture, possibly due, inter alia, to the *bona fide* rights of third parties, it may take alternative measures.[43] Yet, if Article 77 is read together with Rule 147, it seems to require that the ICC itself also consider the

---

[40] For discussion of the intention behind this latter option see R.E. Fife, 'Penalties', in Lee (n 22), 568. Daily fines are part of the domestic criminal law of a number of States Parties to the ICCSt, see eg art. 46 Criminal Code of Bosnia and Herzegovina; Art. 51 Criminal Code (Croatia); Para 44 Penal Code (Estonia); Art. 1 of Chapter 2(a) Penal Code of Finland; Art. 40 Criminal Code (Germany); Art. 51 Criminal Code (Hungary); Art. 40 Criminal Code of the Republic of Montenegro; Art. 33 Penal Code (Poland); Art. 49 Criminal Code (Serbia); Art. 47 Criminal Code of the Republic of Slovenia; Art. 50 Criminal Code (Spain); Art. 34 Swiss Criminal Code; Art. 38 Criminal Code (The Former Yugoslav Republic of Macedonia); Art. 75 *Código Penal de Timor-Leste*. All of the domestic legislation discussed in this chapter has been accessed as English language versions as recorded in the National Implementing Legislation Database in the ICC's Legal Tools project: available online at <http://www.legal-tools.org/en/go-to-database/national-implementing-legislation-database/> accessed 12 June 2015.

[41] Rule 146(5) ICC RPE.

[42] C. McCarthy, *Reparations and Victims Support in the International Criminal Court* (Cambridge University Press 2012) 202–9.

[43] See Kress and Sluiter (n 3) 1829–30.

rights of such third parties. Rule 147 requires that a Chamber give notice to any *bona fide* third parties which it has identified as having an interest in the relevant property and enables the third party to submit relevant evidence which the Chamber must take into account in issuing any forfeiture order. This strongly indicates that the ICC itself will conduct an initial assessment of the interests of *bona fide* third parties and that States would only have such a role to the extent that their national law requires or to the extent that the ICC has not been able to identify a *bona fide* third party.

Another key feature of Article 77(2)(b) is the reference to proceeds, property and assets derived 'directly or indirectly' from the crime. As the case law of the ICTR and SCSL previously indicated, other jurisdictions require a direct link between the property and the crime for which a person has been convicted. The ICC's broad formulation is intended to minimize the evidentiary burden in conducting its assessment of the extent to which a convicted person has benefited from his or her crime.[44]

3.5 Trust Fund for Victims

Finally, in order to complete this detailed outline of the ICC's regime for fines and forfeiture, it should briefly be noted that Article 79 of the ICCSt establishes a trust fund for the benefit of victims of crimes within the jurisdiction of the ICC and the families of such victims. The Statute permits money and property collected by the ICC through fines and forfeiture to be transferred to the TFV. This power is permissive, rather than mandatory. Rule 148 provides that, prior to making any such order for transfer, a Chamber must receive written or oral observations from the TFV. This permissive nature of the power is further reinforced by Rule 221 which empowers the Presidency to take decisions on the disposition or allocation of property or assets realized through enforcement orders of the ICC, although it is to do this in consultation with appropriate parties such as the Prosecutor, the sentenced person, victims, the State of enforcement or the TFV. It is likely that, in practice, a considerable degree of deference will be accorded by both the Chamber and the Presidency to the expert views of the TFV.[45] Further, while not being part of the penal regime, it is worth noting that a convicted person may, in addition to the above, be ordered to pay direct compensation to victims as part of the procedure concerning reparations to victim.[46]

[44] See Fife (n 3) 1430; for further discussion of the potential application of the notion of property, proceeds and assets 'directly or indirectly derived' see McCarthy (n 42) 199–202.

[45] For more information on the TFV, including its role more broadly than in the context of receipt of fines and forfeiture, see H. Abtahi and S.A. Koh, 'The Emerging Enforcement Practice of the International Criminal Court' (2012) 45 *Cornell International Law Journal* 1, 17–21.

[46] Art. 75(2) ICCSt, r. 98(1) ICC RPE. See also r. 98(1) which provides that '[i]ndividual awards for reparations shall be made directly against a convicted person'.

4. THE ICC'S SENTENCING PRACTICE IN RESPECT OF FINES AND FORFEITURE

Having outlined the key features of the scheme for fines and forfeiture at the ICC, this section will consider the application of the scheme in the ICC's sentencing practice. The first case in which the ICC issued a sentencing decision was the case of *Thomas Lubanga Dyilo*.[47] In this case, a group of victims requested that a fine be imposed, the proceeds of which would be transferred to the TFV.[48] The lack of detail in the request renders its evaluation difficult, however, a number of key elements were observed by the victims. The group of victims submitted that the amount of any fine should be fixed in relation to the harm and prejudice caused by the sentenced person.[49] The victims' observations also noted that while the amount of a fine cannot exceed 75 per cent of realisable assets, the Trial Chamber ought to make an estimation based on the assets which could be reasonably presumed to be at the disposal of the sentenced person.[50] In addition, the victims also requested forfeiture, referring to the economically lucrative nature of the conflict in Ituri.[51] The victims' observations referred to the potential recovery of military goods in which the militia group controlled by the sentenced person likely invested.[52]

The Trial Chamber dismissed these requests very briefly, determining only that '[p]ursuant to Article 77(2) of the Statute and Rule 146(1) of the Rules, the Chamber considers it inappropriate to impose a fine in addition to the prison term, given the financial situation of Mr. Lubanga. Despite extensive enquiries by the ICC, no relevant funds have been identified'.[53] The Trial Chamber's summary of the victims' arguments in the previous paragraphs appears to indicate that the Trial Chamber considered this response to address the requests for both a fine and forfeiture.

The Trial Chamber's reason for not considering either a fine or forfeiture was simply the lack of assets of the sentenced person. The Chamber did not refer to the fact that it had no evidence before it as to the extent to which the crime was motivated by personal financial gain. Rule 146(1) mandates that the ICC must consider this factor, together with financial capacity, making it difficult to understand why the Trial Chamber felt it appropriate to stop its assessment at financial capacity.[54] While it is arguable that a

---

47 *Lubanga*, ICC-01/04-01/06-2901 (Decision on Sentence pursuant to Article 76 of the Statute, 10 July 2012).

48 *Lubanga*, ICC-01/04-01/06-2880 (*Observations sur la peine pour le groupe de victimes* V01, 14 May 2012) para 8.

49 Ibid., para 9.

50 Ibid., para 10.

51 Ibid., paras 11–12; Ituri is the region of the Democratic Republic of the Congo with which this case is concerned.

52 Ibid., para 13.

53 *Lubanga* (n 47) para 106.

54 The relevant Appeal Judgment in the case does not directly address any issues concerning fines and forfeiture, *Lubanga* ICC-01/04-01/06-3122 (Judgment on the appeals of the Prosecutor and Mr Thomas Lubanga Dyilo against the 'Decision on Sentence pursuant to Article 76 of the Statute', 1 December 2014). It does, however, emphasize, albeit in the different context of assessing r. 145(1)(b), that the mandatory language of 'shall' means that a failure to consider a

complete lack of financial capacity to pay any fine may render it impracticable to go beyond this, it remains that the criteria established in Rule 146(1) refer to cumulative elements which must be considered: whether imprisonment is sufficient, due consideration of financial capacity and degree of motivation by financial gain. Noting the mandatory language introducing each of these elements, the Chamber appears to have given inappropriate primacy to financial capacity, an approach which is further unjustified given that Rule 146(1) only required 'due consideration' of such capacity, clearly not granting it any decisive role.

The Trial Chamber also appears to have focused its response on fines. To the extent that it intended to respond to the request for forfeiture, the Trial Chamber's finding appears inadequate in that the financial capacity of an accused is not relevant in the context of forfeiture – any proceeds, property or assets derived directly or indirectly from a crime should be returned regardless of a sentenced person's financial situation. The Trial Chamber could have more clearly indicated that there is no scope for forfeiture in these circumstances because no proceeds, property or assets appropriate for such forfeiture (ie related directly or indirectly to the crime) had been identified.

To date, the only other case in which the ICC has issued a sentencing decision is the *Katanga* case.[55] Once again, the treatment of Article 77(2) is extremely brief. As in the previous case, the Chamber's ultimate rationale in imposing a sentence of imprisonment only is the absence of financial capacity.[56] Once again, the distinction between fines and forfeiture is blurred. The opening sentence of the relevant paragraph on this issue indicates that it will address both fines and forfeiture,[57] however, it inaccurately implies that Rule 146 addresses the modalities for the implementation of both of these, whereas this rule concerns only fines. Further, the remainder of the Chamber's analysis appears to address only fines, concluding, for example, that '*[e]n l'absence d'éléments d'appréciation suffisants, la Chambre ne prononcera pas de peine d'amende*'.[58] In addition, a consultation of the document submitted to the Trial Chamber by the Registry[59] includes an extract of correspondence from the Chamber which appears to indicate that the Chamber requested information from the Registry concerning fines only.[60] Thus, it appears that despite the reference to '*la confiscation des biens et avoirs*

listed mandatory factor could amount to a legal error (para 42). Such general finding could also be relevant to the interpretation of the language 'shall' in r. 146(1). This finding must, however, be read in its context, with the Appeals Chamber later clarifying that the requirement to consider all mandatory factors does not necessarily demand that the Trial Chamber indicate which specific evidence it has relied upon in relation to each mandatory factor (paras 69–70).

55 *Katanga* ICC-01/04-01/07-3484 (*Décision relative à la peine (article 76 du Statut)*, 23 May 2014).

56 Ibid., para 169.

57 Ibid., '*Aux termes de l'article 77-2 du Statut, la Cour peut ajouter une amende et/au ordonner la confiscation des biens et avoirs tirés directement ou indirectement du crime et la règle 146 définit les modalités du prononcé de telles peines*'.

58 Ibid.

59 Unlike in the *Lubanga* case, there does not appear to have been any request for fines and/or forfeiture submitted by victims to the Chamber.

60 The Registry indicates that the email from the Chamber requested the following information: '*si Germain Katanga peut être considéré comme solvable et se voir éventuellement infliger une peine d'amende (article 77 du Statut et Règle 146 du Règlement*', *Katanga*

tires directment ou indirectment du crime' in the opening sentence, the Chamber addresses only the possibility of fines, rather than forfeiture. The same criticisms outlined above thus seem equally applicable to this decision. For the purpose of imposing a fine, the Chamber's analysis begins and ends at the convicted person's lack of assets and insolvency, with no consideration of whether the crimes were financially motivated. Moreover, the possibility of forfeiture does not appear to have been considered at all or, if the Chamber's assessment is intended to also address forfeiture, it is again done in terms of a lack of financial capacity without making clear that what really motivates the decision is the lack of assets directly or indirectly related to the crime.

In conclusion, the ICC's early forays into fines and forfeiture give a misleading impression. The ICC has thus far failed to consider the compulsory criterion of the extent of motivation by financial gain, giving a false impression of the importance of financial capacity, which should be treated as a significant, but not sole, factor. Further, by framing the request for forfeiture under the guise of a lack of relevant funds, the impression could be given that forfeiture may not be ordered where a sentenced person lacks financial capacity. A more careful and less cursory approach, addressing the possibility of each of a fine and forfeiture separately, could be advised in future sentencing decisions.

5. ANTICIPATED OPERATIONAL ISSUES

As the ICC's caseload continues to increase and it moves closer towards the sentencing stage in a number of cases, there are certain operational issues which can be foreseen. This section will now analyse two of these, namely cooperation with States and international organizations, and the controversial issue of the extension of a term of imprisonment for the non-payment of a fine.

5.1 Cooperation in Enforcing Fines and Forfeiture

As has already been briefly indicated, fines and forfeiture are also closely related to the provisions of the ICCSt concerning cooperation and enforcement. Part 9 of the Statute, concerning 'International Cooperation and Judicial Assistance', is based on the obligation of States Parties to cooperate fully with the ICC.[61] Article 109 requires States to enforce the fine and forfeiture orders made by the ICC, although deference is given to national law in determining the modalities of such enforcement. In addition to more widely known forms of cooperation, such as the arrest and surrender of persons, other forms of cooperation are provided for, including Article 93(1)(k), which provides that:

ICC-01/04-01/07-3453 (*Observations du Greffe relatives à la solvabilité, l'indemnisation des victimes et au comportement en détention de Germain Katanga*, 4 April 2014). As only an extract of the Chamber's correspondence is provided it cannot, however, be determined for certain whether the Chamber's request for information was limited to fines.

[61] Art. 86 ICCSt.

> States Parties shall, in accordance with the provisions of this Part and under procedures of national law, comply with requests by the Court to provide the following assistance in relation to investigations or prosecutions (…) [t]he identification, tracing and freezing or seizure of proceeds, property and assets and instrumentalities of crimes for the purpose of eventual forfeiture, without prejudice to the rights of *bona fide* third parties.

Interestingly, it appears that although this provision clearly states that requests for cooperation must be sought for the purpose of eventual forfeiture, in practice, it may have been used for other purposes. For example, it appears from the records of the Assembly of States Parties (ASP) that Article 93(1)(k) has been used to identify the assets of persons for the purpose of the calculation of indigence in the context of the entitlement to legal assistance paid by the ICC.[62]

By way of brief aside, the reference in Article 93(1)(k) to 'instrumentalities of crimes' is problematic. As the ICC does not have any power to make orders in respect of the instrumentalities of crimes, there would appear to be no reason for the provisional seizure of such for the purpose of eventual forfeiture. As the rationale for the eventual exclusion of such power related to the risk of the ICC being asked to seize property subject to State immunity, such concern applies equally to the notion of a provisional seizure. An abbreviated compilation of proposals by the Working Group on International Cooperation and Judicial Assistance dated 25 November 1997, identifies this provision as being derived from Article 5(2) of the UN Convention against Illicit Traffic in Narcotic Drugs and Psychotropic Substances 1988.[63] That Working Group later attached a footnote to the provision indicating that '[t]he issue of whether the Court is to be vested with such powers is being considered by the Working Group on Penalties'.[64] Similar language, containing a warning linking this provision to the eventual form of the provision on penalties, persisted in the work of the 1998 Preparatory Committee,[65] as well as during the early stages of the Rome Conference itself.[66] Yet, by 13 July 1998, this warning disappeared from the text without further explanation.[67] It thus seems that the reference to instrumentalities of crimes survived in Article 93 of the ICCSt purely due to an oversight during the drafting process.

Turning to operational issues, it might first be briefly noted that cooperation in order to ensure the successful functioning of the ICC's regime for fines and forfeiture is not solely the domain of States. A practical issue in relation to the enforcement of fines and forfeiture relates to the fact that persons suspected, accused or sentenced before the ICC may also be the subject of individual financial sanctions by the UN Security Council.[68] While such mechanisms are unlikely to ultimately prevent the enforcement

---

[62] ICC-ASP/10/4 (Report of the Court regarding the desirability of absolute thresholds for the purposes of indigence calculation, 17 June 2011) para 5.

[63] A/AC.249/1997/WG.5/CRP.1/Add.3, 25 November 1997 2.

[64] A/AC.249/1997/WG.5/CRP.2/Add.2, 11 December 1997 2.

[65] A/AC.249/1998/CRP.15, 1 April 1998 14.

[66] A/CONF.183/C.1/WGIC/L.15, 6 July 1998 3.

[67] A/CONF.183/C.1/L.68, 13 July 1998.

[68] Pursuant to SCRes 1596 (2005) and SCRes 2078 (2012) relating to the Democratic Republic of the Congo, the following individuals who either are or have been in the custody of the Court or are or have been subject to an arrest warrant, are all subject to a freezing of their

of fines and forfeiture, they are likely to cause practical difficulties in the interim. When the ICC transmits a request for the enforcement of fines and forfeiture to a State Party, that State Party might also be under a conflicting obligation pursuant to the relevant Security Council Resolution to maintain the freezing of all assets of the sentenced person. Accordingly, in practice, it is likely that close coordination and communication between the UN, the ICC and the enforcing State will be necessary in order to prevent these types of procedural barriers interfering with the efficient enforcement of fines and forfeiture.[69]

Turning to enforcement issues involving States, of the 122 States Parties to the Rome Statute,[70] only 26 have in place national implementing legislation which specifically provides for cooperation with the ICC in respect of the enforcement of fines and forfeiture,[71] with these provisions often also covering cooperation in respect of reparations. A further 26 have either domestic laws governing fines and forfeiture or mutual assistance legislation which enables them to enforce acts of foreign courts,[72] although it is not entirely clear whether such legislative mechanisms will be practically useful in the event of requests for enforcement from the ICC.

Of the national legislation which provides for the enforcement of fines and forfeiture of the ICC, several are extremely brief. For example, the relevant Finnish law simply

---

funds, financial assets and economic resources: Germain Katanga, Thomas Lubanga Dyilo, Callixte Mbarushimana, Sylvestre Mudacumura, Mathieu Ngudjolo Chui and Bosco Ntaganda, see S/Res/1596 (2005) para 15 and UNSC Sanctions Committee, 'List of Individuals and Entities subject to the Measures Imposed by Paragraphs 13 and 15 of SCRes 1596 (2005), as Renewed by Paragraph 3 of SCRes 2078 (2012)', Last updated on 12 April 2013 <http://www.un.org/sc/committees/1533/pdf/1533_list.pdf> accessed 6 November 2013. Similarly, in relation to the situation in Libya, the 'funds, other financial assets and economic resources' (S/Res/1970 (2011) para 17), directly or indirectly controlled by both Saif Al-Islam Gaddafi and Abdullah Al-Senussi remain frozen (see Security Council Committee Established Pursuant to SCRes 1970 (2011) Concerning Libya, 'List of Individuals Subject to the Measures Imposed by Paragraph 15 of Resolution 1970 (2011) (the Travel Ban) and/or Paragraph 17 of Resolution 1970 (2011) or Paragraph 19 of Resolution 1973 (2011) (the Assets Freeze)'), last updated on 29 July 2013 <http://www.un.org/sc/committees/1970/pdf/List%20of%20Individuals%20and%20Entities.pdf> accessed 6 November 2013. Further, in respect of Côte d'Ivoire, the assets of both Laurent Gbagbo and Simone Gbagbo have been directly frozen by the Security Council (See S/Res/1572 (2004) para 11; S/Res/1975 (2011) Annex I).

[69] In this respect, it is noted that, Art. 15(1) of the Negotiated Relationship Agreement between the ICC and the UN, together with Art. 87(6) of the ICCSt likely provide a sufficient legal basis to ensure that cooperation for the purpose of such enforcement can occur.

[70] As of 4 November 2013.

[71] Australia, Austria, Belgium, Canada, Denmark, Finland, France, Georgia, Germany, Ireland, Kenya, Liechtenstein, Malta, Mauritius, The Netherlands, New Zealand, Norway, Samoa, Serbia, Slovenia, South Africa, Sweden, Switzerland, Trinidad and Tobago, Uganda and the United Kingdom; Based on the legislation available in the National Implementing Legislation Database as of 4 November 2013.

[72] Albania, Azerbaijan, Bangladesh, Bosnia and Herzegovina, Bulgaria, Croatia, Estonia, Guyana, Hungary, Latvia, Lithuania, Moldova, Mongolia, Montenegro, Namibia, The Philippines, Poland, Portugal, Romania, Sierra Leone, Slovakia, Spain, Tajikistan, Tanzania, The Former Yugoslav Republic of Macedonia and Timor-Leste; Based on the legislation available in the National Implementing Legislation Database as of 4 November 2013.

provides that '[t]he enforcement of fines and reparations to victims ordered by the International Criminal Court shall take place in Finland as requested by the Court'.[73] Those instances of national implementing legislation which are more comprehensive typically perform a number of key functions: allocating domestic institutional responsibility; setting out the legal procedures to be followed domestically, often including a mechanism for placing the ICC's request before a domestic judicial body; and detailing how such requests interact with other relevant national legislation.[74] It is also commonplace for such legislation to set out a number of basic factors which must be verified by the responsible domestic authority, such as verifying that the sentenced person has relevant property/assets within the jurisdiction and that the judgment and sentence against such person have become final. This section will now outline some of the more interesting aspects of national legislation, considering first a number of legal issues before moving on to more practical concerns.

5.2 Legal Issues

Diverse legal issues may arise in enforcing fines and/or forfeiture orders within States, including the consistency of extensions of imprisonment for the non-payment of a fine with national law, cost recovery for enforcement measures and the potential inter-relationship with bankruptcy proceedings.

The Danish implementing legislation specifies that '[i]n this country, penalty of a fine, which has been determined by the International Criminal Court, cannot be replaced by penalty of imprisonment'.[75] This is particularly interesting as Denmark is one of only a handful of countries with which the ICC has an in-force Agreement on

---

[73] Art. 9 Act on the Implementation of the provisions of a legislative nature of the ICCSt and on the application of the Statute No 1284/2000 (Finland); the relevant Norwegian law is similar, although contains some further guidance, see Act No 65 of 15 June 2001 relating to the implementation of the ICCSt of 17 July 1998 in Norwegian law para. 11; Art. 12(a) ICC Act (Malta).

[74] See Pt. 10 ICC Act 2002 (Cth) (Australia); Federal Law no 135: Cooperation with the ICC (Austria); Art. 40 Act of 29 March 2004 on Cooperation with the ICC and the International Criminal Tribunals (Belgium); Art. 9.2 Mutual Legal Assistance in Criminal Matters Act R.S., 1985, c.30 (4th Supp) (Canada); Para 3 Act No 342/2001 on the ICC (Denmark); Code of Criminal Procedure: *Loi relative à la cooperation avec la Cour pénale internationale* N. 2002-268 *du 26 février* 2002 (France); Arts 3, 45 Law of Georgia on Cooperation between the ICC and Georgia (Georgia); Law on Cooperation with the ICC (Germany); Pt. 4 ICC Act 2006 (Ireland); The International Crimes Act 2008 (Kenya); Liechtenstein Law of 20 October 2004 on Cooperation with the ICC and other International Tribunals; Pt. VI ICC Act 2011 (Mauritius); Arts 73–81 ICC Implementation Act 2002 (The Netherlands); International Crimes and ICC Act 2000 (New Zealand); Art. 95 ICC Act 2007 No 26 (Samoa); Art. 33 Law on cooperation with the ICC (Serbia); Art. 25 Cooperation between the Republic of Slovenia and the ICC Act 2002; Arts 25–26 Implementation of the ICCSt (Act No 27 of 2002) (South Africa); Arts 24, 25, 28 Cooperation with the ICC Act N.2002.329 (Sweden); Federal Law on Cooperation with the ICC (Switzerland); The ICC Act 2006 (Trinidad and Tobago); The ICC Act 2010 (Uganda); s. 49 ICC Act 2001 (United Kingdom); s. 26 ICC (Scotland) Act 2001.

[75] Para 3(4) Act No 342/2001 on the ICC (Denmark).

the Enforcement of Sentences.[76] This provision of Danish law is thus a matter which may be relevant to the Presidency when taking its decision to designate the State of enforcement.[77] For example, the Presidency might, if a sentenced person has been sentenced to a fine, elect another State of enforcement in order to avoid any potential problems. Alternatively, even if the sentence of a person subject to a fine is enforced in Denmark, the Presidency should remain aware that an extension for non-payment could likely lead Denmark to claim that it is impossible to enforce this new part of the sentence, pursuant to Article 17 of the Agreement between Denmark and the ICC. Thus, the ICC would likely have to arrange a transfer to a new enforcing State in relation to the period of any extension of imprisonment for non-payment.

This example sheds light on potential broader issues concerning enforcement and the potential extension of terms of imprisonment for non-payment, for example, the possibility of an extension rendering the length of an overall term of imprisonment illegal or unconstitutional under domestic law. The ICCSt specifies that 'the sentence of imprisonment shall be binding on the States Parties, which shall in no case modify it'.[78] There is some ambiguity here in that a decision to extend a period of imprisonment for non-payment of a fine may not technically be 'the sentence of imprisonment' which appears to refer more naturally to the term of imprisonment originally imposed in accordance with Article 77(1). Arguably, there is greater clarity in Article 110(1) of the ICCSt which provides that '[t]he State of enforcement shall not release the person before the expiry of the sentence pronounced by the Court'. This language appears broader, with the 'sentence pronounced by the Court' liable to include both the term of imprisonment and any penalty of fine, therefore potentially including any extension of the term of imprisonment relating to the latter which has been pronounced by the ICC through the Presidency. Further, Rule 220 of the RPE also specifies that a sentence of a fine cannot be modified by national authorities. A broad interpretation of this could be that penalties (including imprisonment) derived from the sentence of fine similarly cannot be modified. Further, the ICC's enforcement agreements specify broadly that the enforcing State 'shall not release the person before expiry of the sentence pronounced by the Court'[79] or similar, thus encompassing the broader notion of sentence which does not appear to be necessarily limited only to the original sentence of imprisonment. Given that a State would appear not to be entitled to ignore any increased term of imprisonment relating to non-payment, it is likely that any issues such extension could

---

[76] Agreement between the Kingdom of Denmark and the ICC on the Enforcement of Sentences of the ICC, ICC-PRES/12-02-12, entry into force 5 July 2012. In addition, as of 15 November 2013, agreements concerning the enforcement of sentences were in force between the Court and Mali, Serbia, Finland, Belgium, the United Kingdom and Austria. For a detailed exposition of these agreements see Abtahi and Koh (n 45).

[77] For further information on the procedure for the designation of a State of enforcement see Mulgrew (n 1) 39–45.

[78] Art. 105(1) ICCSt.

[79] See Art. 12(2) Agreement between the Kingdom of Denmark and the ICC on the Enforcement of Sentences of the ICC (ICC-PRES/12-02-12), entry into force 5 July 2012; Art. 11(2) Agreement between the ICC and the Government of the Republic of Finland on the Enforcement of Sentences of the ICC (ICC-PRES/07-01-11), entry into force 24 April 2011.

create in terms of domestic legality will most likely be resolved through the designation of a new State of enforcement.

Interestingly, the ICC's enforcement agreement with Mali contains a provision specifying that '*[l]a Présidence doit solliciter l'accord du Mali aux fins de l'allongement de la période d'emprisonnement*'.[80] No equivalent provision appears in any of the ICC's other enforcement agreements. This might indicate that Mali is particularly concerned by the potential for the extension of a term of imprisonment. When read in context, however, this provision is unlikely to alter the situation described above. In effect, if Mali is unable to offer its agreement, the ICC will be effectively forced to seek alternative enforcement arrangements in order to ensure that it fulfils its obligation to retain control over the sentence.

A number of States make provision for the recovery of costs associated with the enforcement of fines and forfeiture, with such legislation providing that the State will transfer recovered funds to the ICC 'less any expenses incurred with the execution of such sentence or order'.[81] Such allowance for cost recovery by the State to whom a request has been addressed appears to violate the requirement under Article 109(3) to transfer proceeds to the ICC and the requirement in Rule 220 not to modify imposed sentences. As enforcement of fines and forfeiture orders is one of the cooperative responsibilities assumed by the States Parties in establishing the Rome Statute, it seems inappropriate for such States to seek cost recovery in respect of complying with international obligations imposed on them by the Rome Statute.[82] Further, noting that such money or property transferred to the ICC will most likely be designated for distribution to individual victims or through the trust fund for victims, it seems undesirable that enforcing States be permitted to reduce the funds available to such eventual recipients through cost recovery. In sum, the legality of any provision for cost recovery in implementing legislation seems questionable. Further, in practical terms, the costs of such enforcement to a State are likely to be relatively minimal when compared to the costs of enforcing other obligations imposed upon States Parties by the ICCSt (for example, the cost of the arrest and surrender of persons).

The Irish legislation addresses a further potentially significant issue: the relationship between requests for the enforcement from the ICC and proceedings for bankruptcy, with realizable property which is the subject of an ICC order being excluded from the property of the bankrupt.[83] It is foreseeable that a sentenced person whose property is being targeted through a forfeiture order of the ICC may seek the protection of domestic bankruptcy provisions, thus it is surprising that the Irish implementing legislation is the only one that addresses this scenario directly.

---

80 Art. 6(3) *Accord entre la Cour pénale international et le Gouvernement de la République du Mali concernant l'exécution des peines prononcées par la Cour* (ICC-PRES/11-01-12), entry into force 13 January 2012.

81 Art. 36(4) ICC Act 2011 (Mauritius); Art. 26(2). The same is effectively provided for by Implementation of the ICCSt (Act No 27 of 2002) (South Africa).

82 In this respect, it is noted that the Agreements on the Enforcement of Sentences entered into between the Court and individual States Parties specify that the State is to cover the ordinary costs of such enforcement.

83 See eg Art. 44 ICC Act 2006 (Ireland).

5.3 Practical Issues

There remain further issues which may commonly arise in relation to the practical enforcement of fines and forfeiture which have not been considered in the implementing legislation. For example, certain national legislation requires that the sentenced person appear before the domestic court which is addressing the application for enforcement.[84] As, however, it is highly likely that the State in which the sentence of imprisonment is being enforced is not the same State which is enforcing the fines or forfeiture, there may be a range of practical difficulties in ensuring such physical presence. In reality, close coordination between the two States and the ICC is likely to be necessary in order to ensure that the requirements of national legislation can be complied with and it is foreseeable that a number of issues will arise in this regard, such as who is to bear the costs associated with the transfer of a sentenced person to be present in another State for the purpose of domestic proceedings on the enforcement of fines and forfeiture. A similar cost-related practical issue is whether a sentenced person is entitled to legal aid in respect of national proceedings related to enforcement, with the only national implementing legislation to refer even to 'the possibility of obtaining legal aid'[85] being that of the Netherlands.

This brief survey of national implementing legislation highlights that many practical issues are likely to arise related to the fact that Article 109 gives deference to the national legal system in relation to implementation of the ICC's enforcement orders concerning fines and forfeiture. Given that the vast majority of States Parties have no such implementing legislation at all, thus requiring all enforcement issues to be resolved on a case-by-case basis, it seems that many challenges lie ahead in guaranteeing the smooth operation of the enforcement process. Nonetheless, this review of the implementing legislation which does exist highlights some key issues for which the ICC should prepare, such as ensuring the presence of sentenced persons, legal aid, the possible unwillingness and/or incapacity of some States to enforce any extensions of imprisonment related to the non-payment of fines and issues concerning cost recovery.

5.4 Imprisonment for the Non-Payment of a Fine

By way of background, the Regulations of the Court establish an enforcement unit within the Presidency to assist in the exercise of the functions related to the enforcement of fines, forfeiture orders and reparation orders.[86] For this purpose, the Presidency, with the assistance of the Registry, is to make the necessary arrangements for tasks such as receiving the payment of fines, receiving the relevant property or proceeds of sale, accounting for interest gained on monies received and ensuring the transfer of money to the trust fund for victims.[87] The Presidency is also able to conduct

---

84 Art. 74(1) ICC Implementation Act 2002 (The Netherlands).

85 Art. 75 ICC Implementation Act 2002 (The Netherlands).

86 Reg 113 ICC ROC; for an outline of such functions, see rr. 217, 219–220 ICC RPE.

87 Reg. 116 ICC ROC.

ongoing monitoring of the financial situation of a sentenced person, even after the completion of a sentence of imprisonment.[88]

The Regulations of the Court thus ensure a system of dual responsibility in which the relevant Chamber (usually the Trial Chamber, although it may also be the Appeals Chamber) takes decisions concerning the imposition of fines and forfeiture orders, while the Presidency implements them through its enforcement unit. One responsibility of the Presidency relates to the potential extension of a term of imprisonment for the non-payment of a fine under Rule 146(5). It thus appears somewhat anomalous that it is the Presidency, rather than the Chamber, which is assigned this task. On one hand, the Presidency, having been closely involved in the implementation of the fine, is familiar with the enforcement methods which have been pursued, and may be best placed to see these issues through to their conclusion. On the other hand, the imposition of a penalty as serious as imprisonment should be regarded as more than just a procedural step and the appearance of fairness would be aided if any decision concerning imprisonment occurred before a Chamber.

This is not to suggest, of course, that the Presidency is ill-suited or incapable of taking such decisions. The Presidency, like a Trial Chamber, consists of three judges of the ICC,[89] all of whom continue to sit in their respective divisions of the Court. The Presidency thus has the necessary judicial experience to make such determinations and it is specified in Rule 146(6) that the Presidency shall sit *in camera* for such determinations and obtain the views of the sentenced person and the prosecutor, with the sentenced person having the right to be assisted by counsel. Thus, certain procedural rights of the sentenced person are safeguarded, as is fitting in respect of the potential imposition of such serious penalties. This is the only situation in which the Presidency is required to exercise its powers *in camera*, although it is by no means the only example of the Presidency exercising judicial power.[90]

The power granted to the Presidency in Rule 146(5) to increase a sentence of imprisonment in the case of the non-payment of a fine has long been one of the most controversial aspects of the ICC's regime. The International Covenant on Civil and Political Rights[91] (ICCPR) provides at Article 11 that '[n]o one shall be imprisoned merely on the ground of inability to fulfil a contractual obligation', with a possible interpretation of this being that imprisonment for debt is itself a human rights violation.[92] In view of the requirement in Article 21(3) of the Statute that the application of law by the ICC 'must be consistent with internationally recognized human rights', it might be said that the possibility of imprisonment for the non-payment of a fine may, at minimum, raise questions concerning the consistency of this provision with human rights law.

---

[88] Reg. 117 ICC ROC.

[89] Art. 38 ICCSt.

[90] On the exercise of judicial powers by the Presidency in the form of judicial review, see H. Abtahi, O. Ogwuma and R. Young, 'The Judicial Powers of the Presidency of the International Criminal Court: Safeguards for the Protection of Human Rights' (2013) 12 *The Law and Practice of International Courts and Tribunals* 281.

[91] (1976) 999 UNTS 171.

[92] Schabas (n 3) 896.

Yet, it is by no means evident that international human rights law prohibits the substitution of a fine for imprisonment. Article 11 of the ICCPR relates to a narrow category of imprisonment for the inability to fulfil a contractual obligation, which is different in nature from imprisonment for failure to satisfy a financial penalty. Thus, it is only taking a broad interpretation of Article 11 with a view to progressively extending the scope of this provision that the claim can be made that Rule 146(5) violates international human rights standards.

Further, several arguments could be made in defence of Rule 146(5)'s apparently careful inclusion of imprisonment for non-payment as a last resort. At a normative level, it should be recalled that the money collected from fines is likely to be allocated to the trust fund for victims which aims to benefit the victims of crimes within the ICC's jurisdiction,[93] thus a robust enforcement mechanism in the event of the non-payment of fines serves the purpose not only of ensuring that a sentenced person serves his or her full punishment, but that victims' interests are served, an aim entirely in keeping with the ICC's progressive approach to victims' participation at the various stages of its proceedings.[94]

In addition, it does not appear tenable to maintain that the absence of reference to the punishment of imprisonment for the non-payment of a fine in the ICCSt, renders Rule 146(5) illegal because any applicable penalties must have an explicit statutory basis. Article 77(2)(a) specifies that the penalty of a fine will be further elucidated in the RPE. While it is true that, technically, it specifies that the 'criteria' for fines are to be elucidated, it would be a very narrow reading which understood the reference to 'criteria' as prohibiting other related matters from being addressed in the RPE. Even in the absence of the specific reference to the RPE in Article 77(2)(a), it is common practice that aspects not specifically addressed in the ICCSt are further developed and detailed in the subsidiary texts.

Further, even if one accepts the view that Rule 146(5) is unusual in that it goes somewhat beyond a mere elucidation, the fact remains that the RPE have been adopted by the requisite two-thirds majority of the ASP.[95] Read in conjunction with the requirement that '[t]he Rules of Procedure and Evidence (...) shall be consistent with the Statute',[96] this indicates that the requisite majority of States Parties consider that Rule 146(5) is not inconsistent with the ICCSt and the rule's formal legality is thus established. Essentially, given that Rule 146(5) is clear and validly established, there is no scope for the ICC itself to reject its application. Any desire to revisit its content would ultimately have to be found within the ASP.[97]

---

[93] Art. 79 ICCSt.

[94] See Art. 75, ICCSt; for further detail on victims at the ICC see McCarthy (n 42); T.M. Funk, *Victims' Rights and Advocacy at the International Criminal Court* (Oxford University Press 2010).

[95] Art. 51(1) ICCSt.

[96] Art. 51(4) ICCSt.

[97] Art. 51 ICCSt. Although, of course, an absolute majority of judges or the Prosecutor could also propose an amendment to the RPE, any such amendment would have to be adopted by a two-thirds majority of the ASP prior to entry into force, thus necessitating the willingness of the latter.

Further, the ICC regime makes clear that fines are regarded as punitive in nature, as is imprisonment (see discussion above). It could thus be argued that, although, of course, imprisonment involves a more serious encroachment upon an individual's rights than a fine, there remains no inherent illogic in substituting one type of penalty for another, following a sitting *in camera* to hear the views of the sentenced person (in other words, at least this situation does not fall into the trap of imposing a penalty in response to a failure to satisfy a non-punitive order, as it would, for example, if the extension of imprisonment were authorised in response to a failure to comply with a forfeiture order). Further, the requirement in Rule 146(7) that the ICC 'shall warn the convicted person that failure to pay the fine in accordance with the conditions (…) may result in an extension of the period of imprisonment' ensures that a sentenced person is fully forewarned of the potential consequences of non-payment, thus satisfying fundamental requirements of legality.

In sum, while the mechanism of imprisonment for the non-payment of fines may be inconsistent with a broad desire for the ICC to be a standard-setter in the field of human rights in the criminal justice context, it is not obvious that Rule 146(5) is clearly invalid or violates human rights standards. Thus, unless steps are taken to pursue its amendment, it is evident that the provision must be applied by the ICC as it stands. Thus, at minimum, a certain pragmatic solace might be sought in the reality that the likelihood of this provision being used is very small. Not only is the exercise of the power to extend a term of imprisonment completely discretionary, the possibility of such further imprisonment depends on 'continued wilful non-payment' and specifies that it is to be a 'last resort'. The use of such overtly cautious language appears to strongly suggest that where a sentenced person has cooperated with the ICC but, ultimately, remains financially unable to pay the full amount of the fine (eg due to unanticipated changes to his or her financial situation or the needs of dependants), such instances could not be reasonably characterized as 'wilful non-payment'. Given that a fine should have been imposed in the first place by reference to the convicted person's financial capacity and need to support dependants, the situation of non-payment due to a lack of financial capacity should be very rare. Yet, despite the unlikelihood of a situation of non-payment arising, the language of 'wilful' appears to have been introduced to provide yet a further safeguard for the sentenced person. In view of the many levels of safeguards designed to ensure that fines are imposed within financial means, together with the granting of reasonable periods within which they are to be paid,[98] it is likely to be extremely rare that the Presidency will be asked to exercise its power under Rule 146(5).

In the event that Rule 146(5) is eventually invoked, it is worth noting that a further challenge at an operational level will be implementing the sanction for non-payment, particularly that of determining the period of extension. The only guidance provided in Rule 146(5) itself is that 'the amount of the fine, imposed and paid' will be relevant. It will be interesting to see if the Presidency seeks to take guidance from the types of sentences used in domestic legal systems. The provision in Rule 146 allowing for the potential extension of imprisonment of up to five years for non-payment of a fine appears to be quite a harsh punishment when compared to the domestic legislation of

---

[98] Rules 146(3)–146(4) ICC RPE.

those States Parties to the ICCSt which do allow for imprisonment in relation to failure to pay a fine and which specify in such legislation the maximum term of such imprisonment. Some States Parties specify that the maximum duration of such period of imprisonment must be no more than six months.[99] In Timor Leste, the maximum duration of such imprisonment is eight months ie two-thirds of the maximum period allowed for the imposition of daily fines which is 360 days.[100] A number of States Parties specify one year as the maximum possible prison term for the non-payment of a fine.[101] Others allow for two[102] or three years at most.[103] Very few States Parties allow for a term of imprisonment of up to five years in respect of the non-payment of a fine.[104] Further, there are States Parties which allow for unpaid fines to be satisfied through community service.[105] It is also noted that in the practice of a number of States Parties, the period of imprisonment in the event of non-payment is set at the same time as the fine itself is imposed, rather than being assessed at the time of actual non-payment.[106] Given that the key criteria in determining the period of extension is the amount of the fine, there is no impediment to determining such an extension period together with the fine and such an approach would have the advantage of enabling a sentenced person to know more precisely in advance the consequences of non-payment. In view of the fact that many States Parties simply do not allow for any extension of imprisonment in the event of a non-payment of a fine, the maximum period of extension of five years allowed under Rule 146 appears to be somewhat out of touch with certain domestic practice of States Parties in this area. It is arguable that this disparity should influence the Presidency's careful use of its discretion when it comes to setting actual periods of extension in any concrete case.

There remain a number of further characteristics of Rule 146 which could result in legitimate concerns in relation to the application of this provision to sentenced persons. Rule 146 empowers the Presidency to extend sentences of imprisonment, yet there is no provision for the appeal of such decisions, a situation which raises the question of whether a sentenced person is being denied procedural fairness. Part 8 of the Rome Statute, governing 'Appeals and Revision' provides for appeals against decisions of acquittal or conviction or against sentence,[107] yet the provision permitting appeals on sentences is 'on the ground of disproportion between the crime and sentence'.[108] This

---

99 Art. 28 The General Civil Penal Code (Norway); Art. 87(1) Criminal Code of the Republic of Slovenia; Art. 38a(2) Criminal Code (The Former Yugoslav Republic of Macedonia).

100 Arts. 75–76 *Código Penal de Timor-Leste*.

101 See Art. 12(3) Criminal Law (Offences) Act (Guyana); Art. 39(6) Criminal Code of the Republic of Montenegro; Art. 51 Criminal Code (Serbia); Art. 53 Criminal Code (Spain); Arts. 35-36 Swiss Criminal Code.

102 Art. 29(d) Code of Criminal Law (Tanzania).

103 Art. 47.3 Criminal Code of Mongolia.

104 Art. 41(6) The Criminal Law (Latvia); Art. 57(3) Criminal Code (Slovakia).

105 See eg Art. 64(5) Criminal Code of the Republic of Moldova; Art. 69 The Criminal Code (Romania); Art. 51 Criminal Code (Serbia); Art. 53 Criminal Code (Spain).

106 Art. 57(3) Criminal Code (Slovakia); Art. 28 The General Civil Penal Code (Norway).

107 Art. 81 ICCSt.

108 Art. 81(2)(a) ICCSt.

makes it clear that this form of appeal has no relevance to the increase of a sentence for reason of non-payment of a fine. While it could be argued that an extension of a term of imprisonment could interfere with the overall proportionality of the total duration of imprisonment vis-à-vis the crime committed, thus an appeal against an extension of imprisonment for non-payment could be subsumed under the category of an appeal against sentence, this is by no means clear. It could be argued to the contrary that because the 'sentence' handed down in accordance with Article 78 of the ICCSt does not include any subsequent extension for non-payment, the latter simply does not fall into the scope of this appeal power regardless of any issues of disproportionality which might later arise. It is evidently desirable that there be greater clarity on this issue and that a sentenced person know in advance whether or not a right exists under Article 81 to appeal a decision extending imprisonment.

Further, Article 82 of the Rome Statute, governing other types of appeals, does not give the Appeals Chamber the capacity to review these decisions. In particular, it seems unlikely that a decision extending a sentence for non-payment of a fine could be convincingly analogized to 'a decision granting or denying release of the person being investigated or prosecuted',[109] because a person who has been found guilty and sentenced is clearly no longer such a person. Moreover, there seems little scope for the Presidency itself to send an issue before the Appeals Chamber, using Article 82(1)(d),[110] because the Presidency is not empowered to make such referrals and such appeals must relate to issues affecting the outcome of the trial.

In sum, there appears to be little scope for the Presidency's decision to extend an imprisonment to be subject to appeal. While this likely reflects a belief that the penalty originally imposed by the Chamber (including the fine) has been subject to extensive possible appeals and the subsequent possibility of imprisonment for non-payment is to be imposed in very limited circumstances of which a sentenced person has been fully forewarned, such situation appears somewhat ill at ease with the otherwise extensive safeguards for procedural fairness built into the ICCSt system. Further, although the situation provided for in the legal texts is consistent with the range of other important judicial decisions entrusted to the Presidency which are not subject to appeal,[111] the nature of the consequence of prolonged imprisonment is sufficiently serious that this particular power of the Presidency could have been treated differently. Accordingly, this provision places a heavy burden on the Presidency to make infallible decisions.

There may, however, be more scope for the ICC itself to take action in respect of clarifying the issue of access to the Appeals Chamber. Whereas the fact of imprisonment for non-payment is clearly provided for in Rule 146(5) of the RPE, the above discussion indicates that the existence of appeals in respect of such decisions is unclear

---

[109] Art 82(1)(b) ICCSt.

[110] Article 82(1)(d) provides that:

> [e]ither party may appeal any of the following decisions in accordance with the Rules of Procedure and Evidence (…) [a] decision that involves an issue that would significantly affect the fair and expeditious conduct of the proceedings or the outcome of the trial, and for which, in the opinion of the Pre-Trial or Trial Chamber, an immediate resolution by the Appeals Chamber may materially advance the proceedings.

[111] Abtahi, Ogwuma and Young (n 90) 283.

and has not been specifically addressed. Article 51(3) of the ICCSt provides that 'in urgent cases where the Rules do not provide for a specific situation before the Court, the judges may, by a two-thirds majority, draw up provisional Rules to be applied until adopted, amended or rejected at the next ordinary or special session of the Assembly of States Parties'. It is arguable that the narrower issue of access to the Appeals Chamber in respect of these decisions could be regarded as a lacuna justifying recourse to this provision, thus there is scope for the judges of the ICC themselves to take the initiative in seeking to ensure the availability of an appeal for these important decisions, although any such initiative would be temporary in nature, with the ultimate decision-making power in this regard remaining with the ASP.

A further human rights issue concerns whether sentenced persons are entitled to legal assistance paid by the ICC in relation to the proceedings before the Presidency concerning an extension of sentence. Rule 146(6) provides that '[t]he sentenced person shall have the right to be assisted by counsel', but this does not resolve the issue of financial assistance in relation to such counsel. Article 67(1)(d) of the ICCSt provides for a right 'to have legal assistance assigned by the Court in any case where the interests of justice so require, and without payment if the accused lacks sufficient means to pay for it', yet such right is granted in the context of the 'determination of any charge'. When such charges have been determined, it is by no means clear that the enumerated rights of the accused set out in Article 67 remain applicable. The Regulations of the Court do not offer any further clarity in this respect, providing that '[l]egal assistance paid by the Court shall cover all costs reasonably necessary as determined by the Registrar for an effective and efficient defence',[112] with the current situation again not clearly falling within the scope of 'defence'. The various reports which have been considered by the ASP on the subject of legal aid have not directly considered the eligibility of a sentenced person to paid legal assistance at this stage,[113] although the description of the 'Appeals Phase' for legal aid purposes as lasting '[f]rom transfer of dossier of the case to Appeals Chamber till decision of Appeals Chamber' seems to create an impression that there is no further access to legal aid beyond this point.[114] Although it may simply be that the ICC has not yet considered its policy approach to legal aid following the judgment on appeal, it must be noted that there are

---

[112] Reg. 83(1) ICC ROC.

[113] See ICC-ASP/12/3 (Registry's single policy document on the Court's legal aid system, 4 June 2013); ICC-ASP/9/9 (Updated Report of the Court on legal aid: Legal and financial aspects of funding victims' legal representation before the Court, the comparison between internal and external counsel, 30 July 2010); ICC-ASP/8/3 (Interim report of the Court on legal aid: Legal and financial aspects for funding victims' legal representation before the Court, 6 May 2009); ICC-ASP/8/4 (Interim report of the Court on legal aid: Alternative models for assessment of indigence, 6 May 2009); ICC-ASP/7/12 (Interim report on different legal aid mechanisms before international criminal jurisdictions, 19 August 2008); ICC-ASP/6/4 (Report on the operation of the Court's legal aid system and proposals for its amendment, 31 May 2007); ICC-ASP/3/16 (Report to the Assembly of States Parties on options for ensuring adequate defence counsel for accused persons, 17 August 2004).

[114] ICC-ASP/8/4 (Interim report of the Court on legal aid: Alternative models for assessment of indigence, 6 May 2009); ICC-ASP/7/12 (Interim report on different legal aid mechanisms before international criminal jurisdictions, 19 August 2008) 16; See also ICC-ASP/6/4 (Report on the operation of the Court's legal aid system and proposals for its amendment, 31 May 2007)

a range of matters arising beyond such a point which will be of significance to sentenced persons. In addition to the extension of sentences, a sentenced person is entitled to present his or her views to the ICC in a range of situations, including in relation to the designation of the State of enforcement,[115] in the event of a request for extradition in relation to other offences[116] and in proceedings concerning the reduction of sentences.[117] It is arguable that it is in the interests of justice that where the ICC's legislative texts provide a right, here, the right to be assisted by counsel, there is also an accompanying obligation to ensure that such a right is meaningful, in this case, through providing access to legal aid for the purposes of hearings on the extensions of sentences for non-payment.[118]

In sum, it appears that certain aspects of Rule 146 risk denying sentenced persons procedural fairness, the right to paid legal assistance and knowledge of the extent of the extensions of sentence which could be imposed for non-payment. The Presidency, as the body of the ICC empowered to address all matters related to such enforcement, will have a significant role to play in ensuring that the potential risks outlined above are properly addressed and ameliorated. While, of course, it is impossible for any body to completely ameliorate certain failures of the statutory regime, such as the inclusion of the sanction of imprisonment in circumstances of non-payment or the failure to clearly provide for appeal, it is arguable that the Presidency is one of the best-placed bodies within the ICC to assume these significant responsibilities. Its mandate in respect of judicial review of decisions of the Registrar means that it is experienced in the assessment of human rights considerations and, unlike Chambers, which focus largely on the right to a fair trial, the work of the Presidency has focused more broadly on various rights of persons suspected and accused before the ICC, particularly their human rights in the context of detention. The Presidency may thus be able to aid in addressing some of the inherent potential unfairness which appears to exist in the statutory texts, for example, through a cautious approach to setting periods of imprisonment, through ensuring that the legal aid scheme is accessible to sentenced persons at this stage of proceedings and in potentially taking the lead to encourage temporary amendments which may be made by the Judges, such as ensuring that access to the Appeals Chamber is available in respect of decisions to extend a sentence for non-payment.

16, which appears to indicate in its graphical representation that the handing down of the Judgment on appeal constitutes the final stage in the legal aid process.

[115] Art. 103(2) ICCSt.

[116] Art. 108 ICCSt.

[117] Art. 110 ICCSt.

[118] On the ensuring of meaningful rights before the ICC, see ICC-RoR217-02/08-8 (Decision on 'Mr Mathieu Ngudjolo's Complaint Under Regulation 221(1) of the Regulations of the Registry Against the Registrar's Decision of 18 November 2008', 10 March 2009) para 31.

6. CONCLUSION

Ultimately, the various issues outlined above indicate that the role of fines and forfeiture in international criminal justice is very much an instance of 'watch this space'. Further, since many of the key prospective issues relate not to the ordering of fines and forfeiture by the ICC, but to the more long-term enforcement thereof in cooperation with relevant actors, it is obvious that such observation will be necessary for many years before any clear answers to the issues raised in this chapter will begin to emerge. Although this unique regime requires operational development, the significance of the current lack of clarity in respect of certain aspects should not be over-estimated, given that fines and forfeiture remain supplementary to the primary punishment of imprisonment. Further, the stringent conditions for the imposition of fines and forfeiture and the reality that the majority of persons appearing before the ICC have been classified as indigent, indicates that, despite this comprehensive new regime, fines and forfeiture are likely to be imposed in very few cases.

PART III

INTERNATIONAL SENTENCING

Sentencing refers to the stage of the criminal process in which the appropriate punishment is determined and meted out. The question, however, immediately arises as to whether it is at all feasible to arrive at an *appropriate* sentence for atrocity crimes. If, for example, life sentences imposed by international criminal tribunals and courts were really to be proportionate to the inherent gravity of the crime, what would that say about life sentences meted out in domestic jurisdictions? And further, in the words of the Israeli Supreme Court in the *Eichmann* case: '[e]ven as there is no word in human speech to describe deeds such as the deeds of the appellant, so there is no punishment under human law sufficiently grave to match the appellant's guilt'.[1] Moreover, such sentencing objectives as retribution and deterrence may easily clash with human rights considerations of proportionate punishment and the prospect of reintegration into society, especially in the international criminal justice context.[2]

In Chapter 6, Silvia D'Ascoli sets out the sentencing law and practice of international criminal courts and tribunals. She first describes the applicable law and explains the procedure of meting out punishment. Next, she discusses international sentencing jurisprudence, focusing on a number of specific aspects of sentencing law including purposes in international sentencing, the effect of modes of liability in sentencing and sentencing criteria such as the gravity of the crime and mitigating and aggravating circumstances.

Annika Jones, in Chapter 7, points to the international sentencing judges' broad discretionary powers. Statutes and RPE only provide some starting points that may be used by judges to determine the appropriate sentence in a specific case. But it has been largely up to sentencing judges themselves to determine the sentencing principles, rationales and the criteria that must be taken into account in sentencing. Apart from the risks this vagueness and paucity of sentencing norms entail for the legal position of international accused persons, this also means that international sentencing judges are left largely in the dark. It therefore comes as no surprise that judges have sought inspiration from other judicial bodies' sentencing jurisprudence. Jones examines the practice of judicial cross-referencing in international sentencing. In Chapter 7's first

---

[1] Cited in A.M. Danner, 'Constructing a Hierarchy of Crimes in International Law Sentencing' (2001) 87 *Virginia Law Review Association* 418.

[2] See D. Abels, 'Commentary', in A. Klip and G. Sluiter (eds), *Annotated Leading Cases of International Criminal Tribunals. Volume XIV* (Intersentia 2008) 875–91.

substantive part, Jones sets out the views of the different tribunals and courts on the relevance of other bodies' jurisprudence, examines the frequency of judicial cross-referencing as well as the issues on which international sentencing judges tend to seek inspiration from other judicial bodies. She further analyses the manner in which judicial cross-referencing is being utilized by international sentencing judges. In Chapter 7's second substantive part, Jones explores the significance and implications of judicial cross-referencing in international sentencing.

6. International sentencing: law and practice

*Silvia D'Ascoli**

1. INTRODUCTION

This chapter focuses on international sentencing and discusses, in particular, the law and practice on sentencing of the UN *ad hoc* Tribunals ICTY and ICTR, the ICC and the SCSL. 'Sentencing' here refers to the process of meting out punishment and determining an appropriate sanction when individual criminal responsibility is ascertained, including the criteria for the individualization of the penalty. 'International sentencing', more specifically, refers to the process of meting out punishment by international courts and tribunals.

Sentencing should be regarded as one of the most important parts of the adjudication process. A sentence plays a fundamental role for the convicted person, the victim(s), the general public (considering the impact of the judgment upon society) and for the judges, as a judgment represents the concluding stage of the proceedings and thus their final outcome. International sentencing, in particular, acquires an important additional function: to underscore the existence of international justice. In fact, it serves the purpose of demonstrating the seriousness with which the international community regards violations of its laws, condemns transgressions and metes out penalties for the commission of crimes of international concern.

Despite its importance, what is surprising about international sentencing, especially when compared to national sentencing, is the lack of a defined set of norms and principles guiding the determination of penalties in international criminal law. In fact, international sentencing has thus far not been regulated by strict norms, rules or principles, or significant guidelines. Furthermore, at least until the UN *ad hoc* Tribunals began operating, there was very little jurisprudential precedent to assist international courts in sentencing and, for a long time, the Nuremberg and Tokyo Military Tribunals ('IMTs') represented the only two precedents with regard to the determination of penalties by international tribunals.[1] However, sentencing provisions in the Nuremberg Charter were characterized by extreme vagueness,[2] and the jurisprudence of the IMTs, as well as that of the national military tribunals established after the Second World War, was not very enlightening with regard to the principles and rules applied to sentencing.

* The views expressed in this chapter are those of the author alone and do not necessarily reflect the views of the Mechanism for International Criminal Tribunals or the United Nations in general.

[1] For an introduction to international sentencing, see W. Schabas, 'International Sentencing: From Leipzig (1923) to Arusha (1996)', in M.C. Bassiouni, *International Criminal Law. Vol III* (2nd edn, Trans-national Publishers 1999) 171–93.

[2] See Arts 27–29 Nuremberg Charter.

With regard to the 'law of sentencing' of the four international courts that will be analysed in this chapter, that is the UN *ad hoc* Tribunals, the SCSL and the ICC, neither their Statutes nor their RPE provide any specific ranges of penalty for the crimes falling under the jurisdiction of these courts. It is only provided that the primary penalty to be imposed is imprisonment.[3] The Statutes do not rank the crimes by severity and, in theory, available penalties are the same – namely, a maximum term of life imprisonment[4] – for all the international crimes (war crimes, crimes against humanity, genocide) within the jurisdiction of these courts. With regard to the circumstances to be taken into account in sentencing, the Statutes of the *ad hoc* Tribunals, SCSL and ICC only provide for some factors to be considered in the process of sentencing.[5] International judges thus have quite broad discretion in meting out penalties, much greater than is normal in the determination of sentences at the national level. Furthermore, if we look at the sentencing practice of international courts, these courts did not always develop harmonized guidelines either, which is not only unfortunate, considering that these courts are substantially called on to apply the same international humanitarian law, but also problematic for a number of reasons. In fact, the risks linked to the lack of a strong sentencing regime or sentencing guidelines are numerous: inconsistencies in sentencing between similar cases; different interpretations of the same sentencing factors; lack of uniformity, proportionality,[6] and thus fairness, in international sentencing, as well as of a uniform sentencing policy for international justice.

In discussing the law and practice on sentencing of the *ad hoc* Tribunals, the ICC and the SCSL, this chapter is divided into two main parts. Section 2 addresses the relevant provisions on sentencing in the Statutes and RPE of the four international courts, focusing on the applicable penalties and the process of determination of sentences. Section 3 offers an overview of the jurisprudence of the four international

---

[3] See Art. 24 ICTYSt; Art. 23 ICTRSt; Art. 19 SCSLSt; and Art. 77 ICCSt. See also Section 2.1 (Applicable Penalties) below for more details.

[4] Life imprisonment is not a penalty applicable by the SCSL, whose Statute and RPE only provide for the possibility of imposing 'imprisonment for a specified number of years'. See Art. 19(1) SCSLSt and Rule 101(A) SCSL RPE.

[5] See Section 2.2 below.

[6] The principle of proportionality of penalties is a general principle of criminal law common to national legal systems as well as to the law and practice of international criminal tribunals. The requirement that penalties must not be disproportionate also derives from international human rights standards. This significant principle is meant to ensure two important elements: first, that the punishment does not exceed the gravity of the offence (thus the principle would impose restraints on excessive or arbitrary penalties); second, that a minimum level of punishment be guaranteed and imposed upon the accused (thus the principle would ensure that the final sentence takes into account the concrete seriousness of the offence and the gravity of the crime). The principle of proportionality is regarded as a key sentencing principle by the doctrine. See eg: A. Von Hirsch, 'Proportionality in the Philosophy of Punishment' (1992) 16 *Crime and Justice* 55–98; E. Ellis, *The Principle of Proportionality in the Laws of Europe* (Hart Publishing 1999); A. Ashworth and D. van Zyl Smit, 'Disproportionate Sentences as Human Rights Violation' (2004) 67(4) *The Modern Law Review* 541–60; A. Von Hirsch and A. Ashworth, *Proportionate Sentencing* (Oxford University Press 2005).

courts on diverse issues of sentencing, including for example purposes of punishment, gravity of the offence and application of aggravating and mitigating circumstances.

2. LAW: THE RELEVANT PROVISIONS FOR INTERNATIONAL SENTENCING

This first part on the 'law of sentencing' presents the normative provisions that can be found in the Statutes and RPE of the four international criminal courts under analysis:[7] the ICTY, ICTR, ICC and SCSL. The following sub-sections focus on applicable penalties, determination of sentences and the structure of the sentencing process.

2.1 Applicable Penalties

There is a stark difference between domestic and international justice with regard to the applicable penalties for crimes. Detailed penalty ranges for each offence, often including maximum and minimum terms of imprisonment, are normally set out in domestic criminal codes. To the contrary, the Statutes of the ICTY, ICTR, SCSL and ICC provide only minimal provisions about the penalties applicable to crimes under their jurisdiction. These provisions are: Article 24 ICTYSt, Article 23 ICTRSt, Article 19 SCSLSt, and Article 77 ICCSt.

Article 24(1) ICTYSt and Article 23(1) ICTRSt prescribe that penalties imposed by Chambers of the Tribunals shall be limited to imprisonment and that, in determining the terms of imprisonment, Trial Chambers shall have recourse to the 'general practice regarding prison sentences' in the courts of the former Yugoslavia and Rwanda.[8] Article 19(1) SCSLSt takes a similar approach by simply providing that Trial Chambers shall impose 'imprisonment for a specified number of years' and that, in determining such terms of imprisonment, they shall have recourse, as appropriate, to the practice regarding prison sentences not only of Sierra Leone's national courts but also of the ICTR. This seems to be an effort on the part of the legislators to harmonize sentencing in international criminal justice. The SCSL also offers a specific provision for juvenile offenders (that is offenders between 15 and 18 years of age):[9] in the disposition of a case against juvenile offenders, the SCSL shall not impose a sentence of jail time but shall order a rehabilitation measure from those listed in Article 7(2) of its Statute.[10]

[7] There have been no substantial changes to the positive law concerning sentencing in the Statute and RPE of the UN MICT, which was established by the UNSC in December 2010 to carry out a number of essential functions of the ICTY and ICTR after the completion of their respective mandates.

[8] For a more detailed discussion of the scope of this provision and its application, see eg, W. Schabas, 'Perverse Effects of the *nulla poena* Principle: National Practice and the *ad hoc* Tribunals' (2000) 11(3) *European Journal of International Law* 521; S. D'Ascoli, *Sentencing in International Criminal Law* (Hart Publishing 2011) 115–23, 141–3.

[9] Art. 7(1) SCSLSt.

[10] For example, care guidance and supervision orders, community service orders, counseling, foster care, correctional, educational and vocational training programmes inter alia (see Art. 7(2) SCSLSt).

The Statutes of these three courts also present a provision that has never been applied in practice: the possibility for Trial Chambers to order the return of any property, proceeds or assets acquired unlawfully or by criminal conduct, including by means of duress, to their legitimate owners (or to the State of Sierra Leone, in the case of the SCSL).[11]

No other provision is devoted to penalties and no indication is to be found in the Statutes or RPE of ICTY, ICTR and SCSL concerning the *quantum* of penalties: that is, no maximum length or ranges of imprisonment for the crimes falling under their jurisdiction; no differentiation (in gravity and terms of imprisonment) between the various crimes; no indication of which crimes are to be punished with life imprisonment; and no provisions on minimum sentences. Thus for genocide, crimes against humanity and war crimes, penalties are in theory all equal, consisting of a sentence of imprisonment for a certain number of years, up to and including life imprisonment.[12]

Applicable penalties are also determined only in general terms in the ICCSt. The basic penalty to be imposed by the ICC pursuant to Article 77 of its Statute is imprisonment, up to and including life imprisonment. Rather than setting out specific sentencing ranges and distinguishing between each specific offence, or at least between categories of offences, Article 77 only provides for two 'ranges' of imprisonment, namely imprisonment for a specific number of years not exceeding 30 years, and life imprisonment when justified by the extreme gravity of the crime and the individual circumstances of the convicted person.[13] Further, the ICCSt also allows the Court to impose a fine, but only 'in addition to imprisonment' and not as an alternative to it.[14]

2.2 Determination of the Sentence

The provisions devoted to the criteria for the determination of the sentence are equally very minimal in the Statutes and RPE of the four courts under analysis.

In this respect, the Statutes of the ICTY, ICTR and SCSL contain an identical provision by which, in imposing sentences, Trial Chambers 'should take into account

---

[11] See paras 3 of Art. 24 (ICTY), 23 (ICTR) and 19 (SCSL). See also Rule 105 ICTY/ICTR RPE; Rule 104 SCSL RPE.

[12] On the issue of a hierarchy of international crimes, see: A.M. Danner, 'Constructing a Hierarchy of Crimes in International Criminal Law Sentencing' (2001) 87 *Virginia Law Review* 415–501; M. Frulli, 'Are Crimes Against Humanity More Serious Than War Crimes?' (2001) 12(2) *European Journal of International Law* 329–50; R. May and M. Wierda, 'Is there a Hierarchy of Crimes in International Law?', in L. Vohrah et al (eds), *Man's Inhumanity to Man: Essays on International Law in Honour of Antonio Cassese* (Kluwer Law International 2003) 511–32; O. Olusanya, *Sentencing War Crimes and Crimes Against Humanity under the International Criminal Tribunal for the Former Yugoslavia* (Europa Law Publishing 2005).

[13] Art. 77(1)(a) and (b) ICCSt. The 'extreme gravity of the crime' is for example evidenced by the existence of one or more aggravating circumstances, as indicated by Rule 145(3) ICC RPE. See also W. Schabas, *An Introduction to the International Criminal Court* (2nd edn, Cambridge University Press 2004) 166.

[14] Art. 77(2)(a); see also (b). Rules 146 and 147 ICC RPE further specify the criteria and modalities for fines and orders of forfeiture.

such factors as the gravity of the offence and the individual circumstances of the convicted person'.[15]

The RPE of these three courts provide slightly more detail by adding that, in determining the sentence, Trial Chambers shall also take into account any aggravating and mitigating circumstances, the general practice regarding prison sentences in the courts of the former Yugoslavia and Rwanda,[16] and the extent to which the convicted person has already served penalties imposed by national courts for the same act.[17] The list provided by the RPE should not be considered exhaustive but only intended to provide some guidance.[18]

Aggravating and mitigating circumstances are thus not at all specified or defined in the Statutes and RPE of the *ad hoc* Tribunals and SCSL. Substantial cooperation with the prosecution by the offender, before or after conviction, is the only mitigating circumstance expressly indicated by the RPE of the *ad hoc* Tribunals and SCSL.[19] Superior orders is the other mitigating circumstance mentioned by the Statutes of the *ad hoc* Tribunals and SCSL, whereby such orders do not relieve the accused of criminal responsibility 'but may be considered in mitigation of punishment'.[20] Further, the Statutes of the four courts herein analysed prescribe that the official position or capacity of any offender, even if Head of State or Government, shall not relieve such a person of criminal responsibility nor mitigate punishment.[21]

The lack of guidance about what constitutes aggravating and mitigating circumstances may create problems at the sentencing stage. In fact, given that judges are not provided with a defined or specific catalogue of the type of aggravating and mitigating circumstances to be taken into account and the weight that should be attributed to them, the risk of a different, or even conflicting, assessment, or consideration of such circumstances at the sentencing stage by different judges (and different courts) is unavoidable.

With regard to the ICC, according to Article 78(1) ICCSt, in determining the sentence the Court shall take into account the gravity of the crime and the individual circumstances of the convicted person. In accordance with the ICC RPE,[22] relevant factors to be considered in the determination of the sentence also include mitigating and aggravating circumstances. Rule 145 indicates some of these circumstances and provides some guidance for the process of determination of the sentence. For instance, a fundamental principle is that the totality of the sentence must reflect the culpability of

---

15 See Art. 24(2) ICTYSt; Art. 23(2) ICTRSt; Art. 19(2) SCSLSt.

16 This is recalled only by Rule 101(B)(iii) ICTY/ICTR RPE; the SCSL RPE do not refer to this factor again but only recall the factors provided for by Art. 19(2) SCSLSt.

17 See Rule 101(B) ICTY, ICTR and SCSL RPE.

18 In fact, Rule 101(B) ICTY, ICTR and SCSL RPE, by using the expression 'such factors as', are not meant to be exhaustive. Commentators have argued that the vagueness of the RPE constitutes a violation of the principle of legality of penalties. See S. Zappalà, *Human Rights in International Criminal Proceedings* (Oxford University Press 2003) 201.

19 See Rule 101(B)(ii) ICTY, ICTR and SCSL RPE.

20 See Art. 7(4) ICTYSt; Art. 6(4) ICTRSt; Art. 6(4) SCSLSt.

21 See Art. 7(2) ICTYSt; Art. 6(2) ICTRSt; Art. 6(2) SCSLSt, Art. 27(1) ICCSt.

22 See Rule 145 ICC RPE.

the convicted person,[23] and that all relevant factors (eg, mitigating and aggravating factors and circumstances related to the accused and the crime) must be mutually balanced.[24] The Court must also take into account the degree of participation of the convicted person in the crime(s), the circumstances of the convicted person (eg, age, education, social and economic conditions) and the crime (eg, time, manner and location), and the harm caused to the victims and their families.[25] The Court must also ensure that the sentence be proportionate to the crime.[26]

Rule 145(2)(a) provides that the Court shall take into account, as appropriate, mitigating circumstances such as factors falling short of constituting grounds for the exclusion of criminal responsibility (eg, substantially diminished mental capacity or duress) and the convicted person's conduct after the act, including any efforts by the accused to compensate the victims and any cooperation with the Court. The factors listed as mitigating have the sole purpose of providing guidance, since the Court has discretion to consider other factors besides those expressly mentioned.

Similarly, Rule 145(2)(b) indicates some of the aggravating circumstances that the Court may take into account in determining the sentence. The list includes: prior criminal convictions for crimes of a similar nature to those under the jurisdiction of the Court; abuse of power or official capacity; victimization (for example where multiple victims are concerned or where victims are particularly defenceless); and commission of the crimes with particular cruelty or for motives involving discrimination. Again, this list is not exhaustive. In fact, the clause contained in Rule 145(2)(b)(vi) adds a broad reference to 'other circumstances (…) not enumerated above' which could also be taken into consideration as additional aggravating circumstances in sentencing. These 'other circumstances' not specifically identified might be taken into account only when 'by virtue of their nature they are similar to those mentioned'.[27]

Further, Rule 145(3) recalls that life imprisonment may be imposed when justified by the extreme gravity of the crime and the individual circumstances of the convicted person. Such a case would be evidenced, for instance, by the existence of one or more aggravating circumstance. This final provision, which supposedly has the aim of helping judges in identifying cases deserving the imposition of life imprisonment, is indeed too vague to be able to effectively provide guidance in meting out penalties. Although Rule 145 constitutes an already significant step towards a more comprehensive 'theory' of circumstances of crime, if compared to the scant provisions of the *ad hoc* Tribunals and SCSL, substantial gaps still persist particularly in relation to: general principles to apply to aggravating and mitigating circumstances; criteria to evaluate them; and the relative weight (for example, *quantum* of increase or decrease of penalty) to attribute to such circumstances in sentencing.[28]

---

[23] Rule 145(1)(a) ICC RPE.

[24] Rule 145(1)(b) ICC RPE.

[25] Rule 145(1)(c) ICC RPE.

[26] Art. 81(2)(a) ICCSt.

[27] For a critique of this provision as not satisfactory in terms of certainty of the law, see Zappalà (n 18) 202; D'Ascoli (n 8) 270.

[28] For a more detailed discussion, see D'Ascoli (n 8) 188–94, 268–71.

Finally, the Statutes and RPE of the *ad hoc* Tribunals, SCSL and ICC, all provide for the well-established principle according to which any time previously spent in detention pursuant to orders of these courts (typically, detention during trial and appeal proceedings) shall be deducted from the final sentence.[29]

2.3 The Structure of the Sentencing Process

When the *ad hoc* Tribunals began their work, the structure of the final stages of the proceedings was different from the current one, as far as sentencing is concerned. The RPE of the two Tribunals originally provided for a separate hearing on sentencing issues, where evidence concerning the determination of the penalty and the sentence was to be heard. The hearing took place only after a guilty verdict.[30] Separate sentencing hearings were in fact held in the early cases of the *ad hoc* Tribunals (eg, the *Tadić* case before the ICTY and the *Akayesu* case before the ICTR). The RPE were later amended[31] to abolish the separate sentencing hearing and unify the process by anticipating the presentation of evidence on sentencing matters at the trial stage and/or the closing arguments of the parties,[32] in other words *before* the verdict on guilt or innocence. The reasons for this modification were mainly linked to the need to expedite the trial process.

In the author's view, holding a separate sentencing hearing is a more appropriate choice, given that evidence concerning sentencing matters can, in this way, be better presented and articulated to Trial Chambers.[33] Sentencing hearings better serve the need for detailed and comprehensive submissions on sentencing, aggravating and mitigating factors and other evidence specifically relevant for sentencing purposes. Similar submissions otherwise run the risk of remaining vague, very limited,[34] or even being absent during trial proceedings.[35]

---

[29] See Rule 101(C) ICTR and ICTR RPE; Rule 101(D) SCSL RPE; Art. 78(2) ICCSt.

[30] See former Rule 100 of the RPE, Revision 6, 6 October 1995: 'If a Trial Chamber finds the accused guilty of a crime, the Prosecutor and the defence may submit any relevant information that may assist the Trial Chamber in determining an appropriate sentence.'

[31] See RPE Revision 13, 10 July 1998.

[32] See current Rule 85(A)(vi) on the presentation of evidence, and Rule 86(C) on closing arguments.

[33] See also R. Henham, 'Procedural Justice and Human Rights in International Sentencing' (2004) 4 *International Criminal Law Review* 185–210, 191; M.B. Harmon and F. Gaynor, 'Ordinary Sentences for Extraordinary Crimes' (2007) 5(3) *Journal of International Criminal Justice* 683, 708; R.D. Sloane, 'Sentencing for the "Crime of Crimes": The Evolving "Common Law" of Sentencing of the International Criminal Tribunal for Rwanda' (2007) 5(3) *Journal of International Criminal Justice* 713, 734.

[34] Absent a devoted sentencing hearing, sentencing submissions at the ad hoc Tribunals have at times been given scant attention in final briefs or closing arguments. See eg, *Milutinović et al* IT-05-87-T (Prosecution's Final Trial Brief, 28 July 2008) paras 1099–1100; *Đorđević* IT-05-87/1-T (Prosecution's Public Redacted Final Trial Brief, 20 December 2011) paras 1353–1354; *Nchamihigo* ICTR-01-63-A (Appeal Judgment, 18 March 2010) para 390.

[35] Cases before the *ad hoc* Tribunals during which no sentencing submissions were made at all were not infrequent. See eg, *Karera* ICTR-01-74-A (Appeal Judgment, 2 February 2009) para 388; *Mrkšić et al* IT-95-13/1-A (Appeal Judgment, 5 May 2009) para 388; *Kalimanzira*

The possibility of a sentencing hearing is expressly regulated in the ICC system. Pursuant to Article 76, in the event of a conviction, the Trial Chamber shall decide upon the 'appropriate sentence' in a separate phase, by taking into account the evidence presented and submissions relevant to sentencing made during the trial.[36] There is the possibility of holding a distinct sentencing hearing following conviction, in order to hear any additional evidence or submissions relevant to sentencing. This hearing, which is not mandatory, may be triggered at the request of either the prosecution or the defence, or may also be initiated by the Trial Chamber on its own motion.[37]

That is, for example, how Trial Chamber I of the ICC proceeded in the *Lubanga* case, where it indicated that, in the event of a conviction, it intended to hold a separate sentencing hearing.[38] For the purposes of this hearing, the parties thus filed *ad hoc* submissions with specific arguments on the length of sentence to be imposed, the gravity of the crimes and mitigating and aggravating circumstances.[39] Further, during the sentencing hearing, the *Lubanga* defence was also granted leave to introduce additional evidence relevant to sentencing.[40]

A separate sentencing hearing was also held in the *Katanga* case, where the defence, in the closing brief, expressed its intention for such a hearing to take place in case of a conviction.[41]

Sentencing hearings, accompanied by specific sentencing submissions and briefs, are also prescribed within the SCSL system and have regularly taken place in the cases before this court.[42] In fact, Rule 100 SCSL RPE, which regulates the sentencing

---

ICTR-05-88-T (Trial Judgment, 22 June 2009) para 743; *Rukundo* ICTR-2001-70-A (Appeal Judgment, 20 October 2010) para 255.

[36] Art. 76(1) ICCSt. See also Rule 143 ICC RPE.

[37] Art. 76(2) ICCSt. The provision does not operate in case of an admission of guilt (see Art. 76(2) and Art. 65).

[38] This sentencing hearing was held on 13 June 2012. See *Lubanga* ICC-01/04-01/06-2871 (Order Fixing the Date for the Sentencing Hearing, 24 April 2012); *Lubanga* ICC-01/04-01/06-2844 (Scheduling Order Concerning Timetable for Sentencing and reparations, 14 March 2012) para 4. Additionally, the Chamber indicated that evidence relating to sentence would also be admissible during the trial, for reasons of efficiency and economy. See also *Lubanga* ICC-01/04-01/06-2901 (Decision on Sentence pursuant to Art. 76 of the Statute, 10 July 2012) para 20.

[39] *Lubanga* ICC-01/04-01/06-2881 (Prosecution's Sentence Request, 14 May 2012); ICC-01/04-01/06-2891-Red (Observations de la Défense sur la peine, 3 June 2012).

[40] Namely, to call two witnesses and introduce a new document concerning the time spent by Lubanga in detention in the DRC. See *Lubanga* ICC-01/04-01/06-2892 (Requête de la Défence sollicitant l'autorisation de présenter des éléments de preuve supplémentaires lors de l'audience sur la peine prévue le 13 juin 2012, 3 June 2012); *Lubanga* ICC-01/04-01/06-2895 (Order on the Defence request to present evidence during the sentencing hearing, 11 June 2012). See also *Lubanga* ICC-01/04-01/06-2901 (Decision on Sentence pursuant to Art. 76 of the Statute, 10 July 2012), paras 10–11.

[41] See *Katanga* ICC-01/04-01/07-3266-Corr2-Red (Second Corrigendum Defence Closing Brief, 23 April 2012) para 1333. See also *Katanga* ICC-01/04-01/07-3484 (Décision relative à la peine (Art. 76 du Statut), 23 May 2014) paras 2–3.

[42] See eg, *Fofana and Kondewa* ('CDF case') SCSL-04-14-T (Judgment on the sentencing of Moinina Fofana and Allieu Kondewa, 9 October 2007) para 9; *Brima et al* ('AFRC case') SCSL-04-16-T (Sentencing Judgment, 19 July 2007) paras 1–2; *Taylor* SCSL-03-01-T (Sentencing Judgment, 30 May 2012) paras 2, 5.

procedure, establishes that – in the event of a conviction or guilty plea – the parties should file sentencing briefs to 'submit any relevant information that may assist the Trial Chamber in determining an appropriate sentence'[43] and the Trial Chamber shall 'hear submissions of the parties at a sentencing hearing'.[44]

With regard to the pronouncement of sentences, before all four courts, the judgment must be pronounced in public and, wherever possible, in the presence of the accused;[45] the judgment shall be rendered by a majority of the judges and be accompanied or followed by a reasoned opinion in writing, including eventual separate or dissenting opinions.[46]

The *ad hoc* Tribunals, the SCSL and the ICC regulate differently the modalities linked to the pronouncement of sentences for cases where the accused is convicted of more than one crime with the same sentence. The *totality principle* is the guiding sentencing principle for cases where the accused receives cumulative convictions: the final penalty should reflect the entire criminal conduct of the offender and his overall culpability. This is accepted and recognized by both the ICTY and ICTR,[47] by the SCSL,[48] as well as the ICC.[49] What differs across these courts is whether Trial Chambers pronounce a separate sentence for each crime in addition to a joint (total) sentence or not.

For example, the current practice of *ad hoc* Tribunals in cases of multiple convictions is that the precise *quantum* of penalty (number of years of imprisonment) for each finding of guilt, that is, for each crime/count of which the accused is convicted, is not spelled out. Multiple convictions are in fact directly merged into a final and global sentence, which is supposed to reflect the total culpability of the accused.

In the initial system of the *ad hoc* Tribunals, former Rule 101(C) only prescribed that Trial Chambers would indicate whether multiple sentences were to be served consecutively or concurrently.[50] In the majority of cases, the practice was thus already that of imposing a global/total sentence with no specification of the amount of the single underlying penalties imposed for each crime/count of which the accused was found guilty. Rule 101 was then amended and the provisions of its paragraph (C) converged

---

43 Rule 100(A) SCSL RPE.

44 Rule 100(B) SCSL RPE.

45 See Rule 98*ter*(A) ICTY RPE; Rule 88(A) ICTR RPE; Rules 88(A) and 100(C) SCSL RPE; Art. 76(4) ICCSt and Rule 144(1) ICC RPE.

46 See Rule 98*ter*(C) ICTY RPE; Rule 88(C) ICTR RPE; Rule 88(C) SCSL RPE; Art. 74(3) and (5) ICCSt.

47 See Rule 87(C) ICTY and ICTR RPE. For the case-law, see eg, *Delalić et al* IT-96-21-A (Appeal Judgment, 20 February 2001) paras 429–430; *Kunarac et al* IT-96-23-T and -23/1-T (Trial Judgment, 22 February 2001) para 551; *Vasiljević* IT-98-32-T (Trial Judgment, 29 November 2002) para 266.

48 See eg, *Fofana and Kondewa* SCSL-04-14-A (Appeal Judgment, 28 May 2008) paras 546; *Brima et al* SCSL-2004-16-A (Appeal Judgment, 22 February 2008) para 322; *Sesay et al* SCSL-04-15-A (Appeal Judgment, 26 October 2009) para 1229; *Taylor* SCSL-03-01-A (Appeal Judgment, 26 September 2013) paras 662–664, 705.

49 See Rule 145(1)(a) ICC RPE.

50 Up to the version of 14 July 2000 of the RPE, Rule 101(C) stated: ' (...) The Trial Chamber shall indicate whether multiple sentences shall be served consecutively or concurrently ...'. This provision was then eliminated in Revision 19 of the RPE, 13 December 2000.

into Rule 87, paragraph (C). Rule 87 again gives discretion to Trial Chambers as to the imposition of concurrent or consecutive sentences; it also presents an interesting novelty introduced in December 2000: the obligation for judges to specify the penalty imposed for each crime/count of which the accused is found guilty, unless they decide to pronounce a single sentence.[51] In practice, judges mostly impose a single sentence for the totality of findings regarding the criminal conduct of the accused, with no specification of the single penalties for each underlying conviction.[52]

Also Rule 87(C) SCSL RPE prescribes that, when a Trial Chamber finds the accused guilty on one or more of the counts contained in the indictment, it shall also determine the penalty to be imposed in respect of each of the counts. The Chamber shall then also indicate 'whether multiple sentences shall be served consecutively or concurrently'.[53] In practice, judges at the SCSL have at times specified the single terms of imprisonment for each crime and indicated that the single sentences should run concurrently,[54] and other times – expressly following the practice of the *ad hoc* Tribunals[55] – have imposed directly single or 'global' sentences without indicating the specific penalty for each count,[56] thus contrary to what prescribed by the letter of Rule 87(C) SCSL RPE.

It is the author's view that the practice of imposing single or global terms of imprisonment without indicating the specific penalties underlying each finding of guilt omits essential sentencing details, since the specification of the actual penalty meted out in respect of each finding of guilt and of each crime is crucial to clarity, transparency and consistency in sentencing, as well as being important for the accused at the appeals' stage. In order to improve these aspects of the sentencing process, even when a single and total sentence is ultimately imposed, specific penalties should be indicated for each finding of guilt.

With regard to the ICC, when an accused is convicted of more than one crime, Article 78 of the Statute requires the Court to pronounce a separate sentence for each crime and then a joint sentence for all the convictions, specifying the total period of

---

51 See Rule 87(C):

> (…) If the Trial Chamber finds the accused guilty on one or more of the charges contained in the indictment, it shall impose a sentence in respect of each finding of guilt and indicate whether such sentences shall be served consecutively or concurrently, unless it decides to exercise its power to impose a single sentence reflecting the totality of the criminal conduct of the accused.

52 See eg, for the ICTY, *Brđanin* IT-99-36-T (Trial Judgment, 1 September 2004) paras 1152–1153; *Mrkšić et al* IT-95-13/1-T (Trial Judgment, 27 September 2007) paras 712–716; *Popović et al* IT-05-88-T (Trial Judgment, 10 June 2010) vol II 831–837 (Disposition); and for the ICTR, *Gacumbitsi* ICTR-2001-64-T (Trial Judgment, 17 June 2004) para 356; *Kalimanzira* ICTR-05-88-T (Trial Judgment, 22 June 2009) para 756.

53 See Rule 101(C) SCSL RPE.

54 See eg, *Sesay et al* SCSL-04-15-T (Sentencing Judgment, 8 April 2009) paras 18, 93–98 (Disposition); *Fofana and Kondewa* SCSL-04-14-T (Judgment on the sentencing of Moinina Fofana and Allieu Kondewa, 9 October 2007) 33–34 (Disposition).

55 See eg, *Brima et al* SCSL-04-16-T (Sentencing Judgment, 19 July 2007) para 33; *Taylor* SCSL-03-01-T (Sentencing Judgment, 30 May 2012) paras 10–11.

56 *Brima et al* SCSL-04-16-T (Sentencing Judgment, 19 July 2007) 36 (Disposition); *Taylor* SCSL-03-01-T (Sentencing Judgment, 30 May 2012) 40 (Disposition).

imprisonment.[57] The maximum sentence 'shall be no less than the highest individual sentence pronounced and shall not exceed 30 years' imprisonment or a sentence of life imprisonment'.[58] So far, in the two cases where ICC Trial Chambers have entered convictions, judges followed this rule: they first pronounced separate penalties for each of the convictions, and then a joint sentence for the total period of imprisonment.[59] In the author's view, this approach is more correct and transparent than the one adopted by Chambers of the *ad hoc* Tribunals.

3. PRACTICE: OVERVIEW OF RELEVANT CASE-LAW

Having illustrated in Section 2 the sentencing provisions contained in the Statutes and RPE of the ICTY, ICTR, ICC and SCSL, Section 3 of this chapter is devoted to 'sentencing practice' and focuses on the jurisprudence of these four international courts on diverse issues of sentencing. The analysis that follows is not intended to be exhaustive. Rather, it aims to provide the reader with an overview of the most significant decisions on critical areas of sentencing. The following issues are discussed: purposes of punishment, gravity of the offence, individual circumstances of the offender, aggravating and mitigating circumstances, and modes of liability.

3.1 Purposes of Punishment

At the outset, it should be noted that the Statutes of the *ad hoc* Tribunals, SCSL and ICC do not address the important issue of the overall purposes of punishment to be applied in sentencing.[60] We thus have to turn to the jurisprudence of these courts to learn how the purposes of punishment were assessed and interpreted.

In this respect, when looking at the practice of the *ad hoc* Tribunals, a handful of various goals were taken into account, although retribution and deterrence were deemed the primary, or most important, objectives of sentencing both by ICTY[61] and ICTR[62]

---

[57] Art. 78(3) ICCSt. See also Rule 142(2) ICC RPE.

[58] Art. 78(3) ICCSt.

[59] See *Lubanga* ICC-01/04-01/06-2901 (Decision on Sentence pursuant to Art. 76 of the Statute, 10 July 2012) paras 98–99; *Katanga* ICC-01/04-01/07-3484 (Décision relative à la peine (Art. 76 du Statut), 23 May 2014) paras 146–147.

[60] The ICCSt includes a reference to the purposes of punishment only in the Preamble (paras 3–5), which seems to encompass the purposes of retribution and general prevention within the main objectives and mission of the ICC. However, the recognition of such aims in the Preamble cannot be considered as the equivalent of a provision proposing a specific sentencing policy with regard to the purposes of punishment; one should expect to find such a provision in the body of norms of the ICCSt. However, no other provisions of the ICCSt are devoted to a prescription of the purposes to be pursued in meting out sentences within the ICC system.

[61] See eg, *Tadić* IT-94-1-T*bis*-R117 (Sentencing Judgment, 11 November 1999) paras 7–9; *Aleksovski* IT-95-14/1-A (Appeal Judgment, 24 March 2000) para 185; *Delalić et al* IT-96-21-A (Appeal Judgment, 20 February 2001) para 806; *Kunarac et al* IT-96-23-T and -23/1-T (Trial Judgment, 22 February 2001) para 838; *Deronjić* IT-02-61-S (Sentencing Judgment, 30 March 2004) para 142; *Milutinović et al* IT-05-87-T (Trial Judgment, 26 February 2009) vol III para 1144; *Popović et al* IT-05-88-T (Trial Judgment, 10 June 2010) vol II para 2128.

Chambers. Yet, despite attempts to arrive at a common definition of these purposes or their meaning in the context of international criminal trials,[63] no uniform interpretation was achieved. For example, while deterrence was at times considered the most important aim of punishment,[64] even 'over and above' the purpose of retribution,[65] conversely in other cases deterrence was deemed a factor that 'must not be accorded undue prominence in the overall assessment of the sentences to be imposed'.[66]

Similarly, while in some cases judges went so far as to affirm that – in order to achieve the objectives of retribution, deterrence and restoration of peace – Trial Chambers 'must pronounce an *exemplary penalty* both from the viewpoint of punishment and deterrence',[67] in other cases it was underlined that the call for retribution must not be understood as 'revenge' but must reflect a fair and balanced approach, so that the penalty is proportionate to the wrongdoing and thus the punishment fits the crime.[68]

With regard to other purposes, in some cases punishment was also intended to fulfil an objective of rehabilitation and reconciliation.[69] There is no uniform approach, however, to the purpose of rehabilitation by ICTY and ICTR Chambers. In some cases, rehabilitation was recognized as an important goal of sentencing,[70] in other cases it was

---

[62] See eg, *Ruggiu* ICTR-97-32-I (Judgment and Sentence, 1 June 2000) para 33; *Rugambarara* ICTR-00-59-T (Sentencing Judgment, 16 November 2007) para 11.

[63] See eg, *Blaškić* IT-95-14-A (Appeal Judgment, 29 July 2004) para 678. See also *Miodrag Jokić* IT-01-42/1-S (Sentencing Judgment, 18 March 2004) paras 31–32; *Bralo* IT-95-17-A (Judgment on Sentencing Appeal, 2 April 2007) para 81; *Kunarac et al* IT-96-23 and IT-96-23/1-A (Appeal Judgment, 12 June 2002) para 385.

[64] See eg, *Delalić et al* IT-96-21-T (Trial Judgment, 16 November 1998) para 1234; subsequently recalled by *Blaškić* IT-95-14-T (Trial Judgment, 3 March 2000) para 761.

[65] *Musema* ICTR-96-13-T (Trial Judgment, 27 January 2000) para 986.

[66] *Tadić* IT-94-1-T/IT-94-1A*bis* (Judgment in Sentencing Appeals, 26 January 2000) para 48. The *Aleksovski* Appeals Chamber concurred with this finding: *Aleksovski* IT-95-14/1-A (Appeal Judgment, 24 March 2000) para 185. Also sharing these findings: *Delalić et al* IT-96-21-A (Appeal Judgment, 20 February 2001) para 801; *Kunarac et al* IT-96-23-T and -23/1-T (Trial Judgment, 22 February 2001) para 840; *Milutinović et al* IT-05-87-T (Trial Judgment, 26 February 2009) vol 3, para 1146.

[67] *Jelisić* IT-95-10-T (Trial Judgment, 14 December 1999) para 116 (emphasis added); see also jurisprudence cited therein, footnote 170.

[68] *Orić* IT-03-68-T (Trial Judgment, 30 June 2006) para 719; *Kordić and Čerkez* IT-95-14/2-T (Trial Judgment, 26 February 2001) para 847. See also *Aleksovski* IT-95-14/1-A (Appeal Judgment, 24 March 2000) para 185.

[69] *Erdemović* IT-96-22-T (Sentencing Judgment, 29 November 1996) para 58. The importance of rehabilitation in the context of human rights violations has often been stressed. For example, Schabas connected rehabilitation to 'the need for "reconstruction and reconciliation" in the affected societies'. See W. Schabas, 'Sentencing by International Tribunals: A Human Rights Approach' (1997) 7 *Duke Journal of Comparative and International Law* 461, 503.

[70] See eg, *Delalić et al* IT-96-21-T (Trial Judgment, 16 November 1998) para 1233; *Elizaphan and Gérard Ntakirutimana* ICTR-96-10 and 96-17-T (Judgment and Sentence, 21 February 2003) para 887; *Momir Nikolić* IT-02-60/1-S (Sentencing Judgment, 2 December 2003) para 93; *Obrenović* IT-02-60/2-S (Sentencing Judgment, 10 December 2003) paras 48–49; *Češić* IT-95-10/1-S (Sentencing Judgment, 11 March 2004) paras 27–28; *Blagojević and Jokić* IT-02-60-T (Trial Judgment, 17 January 2005) paras 817, 824.

considered a goal not to be given undue weight or not to 'play a predominant role' in the decision-making process.[71] As to statutory provisions, a reference to rehabilitation is only found in Rule 125 ICTY RPE (Rule 126 ICTR RPE) on general standards for granting pardon or commutation of sentences.[72]

Respect for the rule of law, national reconciliation, restoration of peace, and protection of society are among the other objectives which were considered by some Chambers of the *ad hoc* Tribunals as being relevant in determining the appropriate sentence.[73]

The SCSL followed the jurisprudence of the *ad hoc* Tribunals and recognized retribution and deterrence as the primary objectives of punishment.[74] Retribution was interpreted to mean that the punishment must be proportionate to the guilt of the accused and the gravity of the crime.[75] Deterrence was intended as both general and individual deterrence, preventing further future criminal conduct by the offender.[76] Rehabilitation was considered an important element in sentencing, although one which is 'of greater importance in domestic jurisdictions than in International Criminal Tribunals'.[77] Some Chambers considered that, in relation to the commission of

---

[71] *Delalić et al* IT-96-21-A (Appeal Judgment, 20 February 2001) para 806; *Banović* IT-02-65/1-S (Sentencing Judgment, 28 October 2003) para 35; *Zelenović* IT-96-23/2-S (Sentencing Judgment, 4 April 2007) para 35; *Kunarac et al* IT-96-23-T and -23/1-T (Trial Judgment, 22 February 2001) para 844.

[72] Cf Rule 125:

> In determining whether pardon or commutation is appropriate, the President shall take into account, inter alia, the gravity of the crime or crimes for which the prisoner was convicted, the treatment of similarly-situated prisoners, the prisoner's demonstration of rehabilitation, as well as any substantial cooperation of the prisoner with the Prosecutor.

[73] *Delalić et al* IT-96-21-T (Trial Judgment, 16 November 1998) para 1232; *Kupreškić et al* IT-96-16-T (Trial Judgment, 14 January 2000) para 848; *Dragan Nikolić* IT-94-2-S (Sentencing Judgment, 18 December 2003) para 245; *Kamuhanda* ICTR-95-54A-T (Trial Judgment, 22 January 2004) para 753; *Blaškić* IT-95-14-A (Appeal Judgment, 29 July 2004) para 678; *Nzabirinda* ICTR-2001-77-T (Sentencing Judgment, 23 February 2007) para 49.

[74] See eg, *Fofana and Kondewa* SCSL-04-14-A (Appeal Judgment, 28 May 2008) para 532; *Brima et al* SCSL-04-16-T (Sentencing Judgment, 19 July 2007) para 14; *Fofana and Kondewa* SCSL-04-14-T (Judgment on the sentencing of Moinina Fofana and Allieu Kondewa, 9 October 2007) para 26; *Sesay et al* SCSL-04-15-T (Sentencing Judgment, 8 April 2009) para 13; *Taylor* SCSL-03-01-T (Sentencing Judgment, 30 May 2012) para 13.

[75] *Sesay et al* SCSL-04-15-T (Sentencing Judgment, 8 April 2009) para 13; *Brima et al* SCSL-04-16-T (Sentencing Judgment, 19 July 2007) para 15.

[76] *Sesay et al* SCSL-04-15-T (Sentencing Judgment, 8 April 2009) para 13; *Brima et al* SCSL-04-16-T (Sentencing Judgment, 19 July 2007) para 16; *Taylor* SCSL-03-01-T (Sentencing Judgment, 30 May 2012) para 14.

[77] *Fofana and Kondewa* SCSL-04-14-T (Judgment on the sentencing of Moinina Fofana and Allieu Kondewa, 9 October 2007) para 28; *Brima et al* SCSL-04-16-T (Sentencing Judgment, 19 July 2007) para 17; *Sesay et al* SCSL-04-15-T (Sentencing Judgment, 8 April 2009) para 16; *Taylor* SCSL-03-01-T (Sentencing Judgment, 30 May 2012) para 15.

international crimes, the punishment of the offender must also reflect 'the revulsion of the international community to such conduct, and denounce it as unacceptable'.[78]

The ICC too, in its first two Decisions on Sentence,[79] mainly referred to retribution and deterrence as the main purposes of punishment. While the *Lubanga* Chamber devoted only one very short paragraph to the purposes of punishment of retribution and deterrence at the ICC without delving into further analysis,[80] the *Katanga* Chamber devoted a few more paragraphs to the issue, concurring that the two main functions of punishment are indeed retribution and deterrence and also recalling the principle of proportionality of penalties.[81] With regard to the purpose of rehabilitation of the convicted person, according to the Chamber this should not be considered predominant in international criminal law.[82]

In sum, Chambers of the four international courts herein discussed limited themselves to general references to the purposes of punishment, without attempting to develop any consistent or systematic theory. The justifications of punishment in international criminal law thus remain vague and there seems to be no effort towards uniform systematization or thorough examination of these rationales in the context of international criminal adjudication.[83]

3.2 Gravity of the Offence

As discussed above, the 'gravity of the offence' is one of the few factors mandated by Statutes of international courts for Trial Chambers to take into account in imposing sentences.[84]

---

[78] *Sesay et al* SCSL-04-15-T (Sentencing Judgment, 8 April 2009) para 15; see also *Fofana and Kondewa* SCSL-04-14-T (Judgment on the sentencing of Moinina Fofana and Allieu Kondewa, 9 October 2007) para 30.

[79] *Lubanga* ICC-01/04-01/06-2901 (Decision on Sentence pursuant to Art. 76 of the Statute, 10 July 2012); *Katanga* ICC-01/04-01/07-3484 (Décision relative à la peine (Art. 76 du Statut), 23 May 2014).

[80] *Lubanga* ICC-01/04-01/06-2901 (Decision on Sentence pursuant to Art. 76 of the Statute, 10 July 2012) para 16.

[81] *Katanga* ICC-01/04-01/07-3484 (Décision relative à la peine (Art. 76 du Statut), 23 May 2014) paras 36–38.

[82] Ibid., para 38.

[83] Much attention has been devoted to the purposes of international criminal justice by doctrine and commentators. See eg, P. Akhavan, 'Beyond Impunity: Can International Criminal Justice Prevent Future Atrocities?' (2001) 95 *American Journal of International Law* 7–31; M.C. Bassiouni, 'Combating Impunity for International Crimes' (2000) 71 *University of Colorado Law Review* 409–22; Y. Beigbeder, *International Justice against Impunity* (Martinus Nijhoff Publishers 2005); A. Fatic, *Reconciliation via the War Crimes Tribunal?* (Ashgate 2000); M. Findlay and R. Henham, *Transforming International Criminal Justice: Retributive and Restorative Justice in the Trial Process* (Willan Publishing 2005); R. Henham, 'The Philosophical Foundations of International Sentencing' (2003) 1 *Journal of International Criminal Justice* 64–85; R. Henham, 'Developing Contextualized Rationales for Sentencing in International Criminal Trials: A Plea for Empirical Research' (2007) 5(3) *Journal of International Criminal Justice* 757–78; C.J.M. Safferling, 'The Justification of Punishment in International Criminal Law' (1999) 4 *Austrian Review of International and European Law* 126–63.

[84] See Art. 24(2) ICTYSt; Art. 23(2) ICTRSt; Art. 19(2) SCSLSt; Art. 78(1) ICCSt.

Across the four international courts analysed, the gravity of the offence has been acknowledged as a primary consideration in the determination of the sentence, and thus the litmus test to use to decide upon the most appropriate (length of) sentence.[85]

However, what renders the assessment of the 'gravity' of the offence in international criminal law more difficult than in domestic criminal law systems is the lack of a ranking or hierarchy of international crimes.

From a legal perspective, in the Statutes of international courts there is no ranking of the various crimes under their jurisdiction, and this applies equally to both the categories of international crimes (war crimes, crimes against humanity and genocide) and the underlying crimes (for example, murder as a war crime versus murder as a crime against humanity): no statutory gravity is assigned at all. By contrast, in most national systems the scale of penalties is determined in accordance with the statutory gravity of the offence.

While the ICC and the SCSL have not addressed the issue of the relative gravity of the various categories of international crimes, this discussion was part of the early jurisprudence of the *ad hoc* Tribunals, where there was, however, no uniform approach taken to the issue of hierarchy of international crimes. Chambers have either favoured a ranking of crimes and attempted a 'classification' according to their respective seriousness,[86] or opposed such a hierarchy mainly on the basis that in law there is no distinction between the seriousness of genocide, crimes against humanity and war crimes.[87] Accordingly, some Chambers argued that, rather than establishing some sort of hierarchy between the offences, the gravity of the crime should be determined by the

---

[85] See for the *ad hoc* Tribunals: *Aleksovski* IT-95-14/1-A (Appeal Judgment, 24 March 2000) para 182; *Delalić et al* IT-96-21-A (Appeal Judgment, 20 February 2001) para 731; *Blaškić* IT-95-14-A (Appeal Judgment, 29 July 2004) para 683; *Galić* IT-98-29-A (Appeal Judgment, 30 November 2006) para 442; *Mrkšić et al* IT-95-13/1-A (Appeal Judgment, 5 May 2009) para 375. For the SCSL: *Fofana and Kondewa* SCSL-04-14-T (Judgment on the sentencing of Moinina Fofana and Allieu Kondewa, 9 October 2007) para 33; *Brima et al* SCSL-04-16-T (Sentencing Judgment, 19 July 2007) para 19; *Sesay et al* SCSL-04-15-T (Sentencing Judgment, 8 April 2009) para 19; *Taylor* SCSL-03-01-T (Sentencing Judgment, 30 May 2012) para 19. For the ICC: *Lubanga* ICC-01/04-01/06-2901 (Decision on Sentence pursuant to Art. 76 of the Statute, 10 July 2012) para 36.

[86] *Tadić* IT-94-1-T (Sentencing Judgment, 14 July 1997) para 73; *Kambanda* ICTR-97-23-S (Judgment and Sentence, 4 September 1998) para 14; *Serushago* ICTR-98-39-S (Sentence, 5 February 1999) paras 13–18; *Kayishema et al* ICTR-95-1-T (Sentence, 21 May 1999) para 9; *Tadić* IT-94-1-T*bis*-R117 (Sentencing Judgment, 11 November 1999) para 28; *Tadić* IT-94-1-T/IT-94-1A*bis* (Judgment in Sentencing Appeals, 26 January 2000) Separate Opinion of Judge Cassese, paras 5–18; *Furundžija* IT-95-17/1-A (Appeal Judgment, 21 July 2000) Declaration of Judge Vohrah, paras 1–11. See also: *Blaškić* IT-95-14-T (Trial Judgment, 3 March 2000) paras 797–802.

[87] *Erdemović* IT-96-22-A (Appeal Judgment, 7 October 1997) Separate and Dissenting Opinion of Judge Li, paras 18–27; *Erdemović* IT-96-22-T*bis* (Sentencing Judgment, 5 March 1998) Separate Opinion of Judge Shahabuddeen 6–9; *Tadić* IT-94-1-T*bis*-R117 (Sentencing Judgment, 11 November 1999) Separate Opinion of Judge Robinson 2; *Tadić* IT-94-1-T/IT-94-1A*bis* (Judgment in Sentencing Appeals, 26 January 2000) para 69; *Furundžija* IT-95-17/1-A (Appeal Judgment, 21 July 2000) paras 243, 247; *Kayishema et al* ICTR-95-1-A (Appeal Judgment, 1 June 2001) para 367; *Kunarac et al* IT-96-23 and 96-23/1-A (Appeal Judgment, 12 June 2002) para 171.

intrinsic nature and seriousness of the underlying act, which reflects the accused's criminal conduct, and not by an abstract legal distinction of the offences in terms of genocide, crimes against humanity or war crimes.[88]

With regard to the existence of a hierarchy between genocide and the other international crimes, it seems that there is less disagreement. In particular, numerous judgments of the ICTR have repeatedly affirmed that genocide is the most serious crime or 'the crime of crimes',[89] also considering its *dolus specialis*.

The major dispute regarded the question of whether – all else being equal – crimes against humanity are intrinsically more serious than war crimes. At the beginning of its work, two main different positions were held in the jurisprudence of the ICTY. In the *Erdemović* case, crimes against humanity were considered to be intrinsically more serious than ordinary war crimes.[90] To the contrary, in the *Tadić* case, the majority of the Appeals Chamber found that 'there is in law no distinction between the seriousness of a crime against humanity and that of a war crime'.[91] Dissenting on the issue, in his Separate Opinion, Judge Cassese specified that although in principle no hierarchy of gravity amongst the crimes under the Statute could be outlined *a priori*, nonetheless a hierarchy of gravity with respect to each individual case should be recognized whenever *ceteris paribus* – all other circumstances being equal – the very same facts imputed to an accused person could be regarded as more serious depending on their classification. By looking at the statutory elements (*actus reus* and *mens rea*) of these crimes, crimes against humanity would possess 'an objectively greater magnitude' than war crimes.[92] This of course does not imply that crimes against humanity are always more serious offences than war crimes; there clearly exist situations in which war crimes can have an identical or an even greater seriousness. But – if every other element is equal – then crimes against humanity present a greater intrinsic gravity.

With regard to whether there is the possibility of ranking the different underlying criminal conduct within each category of international crimes, again the Statutes of international courts do not contain any distinction in 'seriousness' between the underlying offences of genocide, crimes against humanity and war crimes. The case-law of the *ad hoc* Tribunals, SCSL and ICC do not make any differentiation

---

[88] See eg, *Furundžija* IT-95-17/1-A (Appeal Judgment, 21 July 2000) paras 227, 247.

[89] See eg, *Kambanda* ICTR-97-23-S (Judgment and Sentence, 4 September 1998) para 16; *Rutaganda* ICTR-96-3-T (Judgment and Sentence, 6 December 1999) para 450; *Musema* ICTR-96-13-T (Trial Judgment, 27 January 2000) para 981; *Serushago* ICTR-98-39-S (Sentence, 5 February 1999) para 15. See also *Krstić* IT-98-33-T (Trial Judgment, 2 August 2001) para 700.

[90] *Erdemović* IT-96-22-A (Appeal Judgment, 7 October 1997). Judge Li dissented on the point that crimes against humanity can be considered as more serious than war crimes: Separate and Dissenting Opinion of Judge Li, 7 October 1997, paras 18–26; *Erdemović* IT-96-22-T*bis* (Sentencing Judgment, 5 March 1998) para 18. See also therein: Separate Opinion of Judge Shahabuddeen 6–9, expressing perplexity as to the possibility of implementing a distinction in seriousness between offences.

[91] *Tadić* IT-94-1-T/IT-94-1A*bis* (Judgment in Sentencing Appeals, 26 January 2000) para 69, Judge Cassese dissenting; the same was also upheld in the *Furundžija* case (*Furundžija* Appeal Judgment, paras 243, 247 Judge Vohrah dissenting).

[92] *Tadić* IT-94-1-T/IT-94-1A*bis* (Judgment in Sentencing Appeals, 26 January 2000) Separate Opinion of Judge Cassese, paras 6–16.

either; therefore there is no available guidance as to whether certain acts (eg, murder) should be punished more severely than others (eg, deportation).

From this brief overview, what can be observed about the 'gravity of the offence' factor is that the case-law seems to concentrate more on the gravity *in concreto*, assessing the gravity of international crimes in connection with the specific circumstances of the case and the offender, rather than on the gravity of the crimes per se *in abstracto*.

According to the case-law of the *ad hoc* Tribunals, SCSL and ICC, factors considered when assessing the 'gravity of the crime' include for example the seriousness of the underlying crimes, their nature and scale, the manner in which the crimes were committed, the circumstances of time and location, the number of victims and the degree of suffering endured by victims, and the impact of the crimes upon the victims.[93]

In evaluating the manner in which the crimes are perpetrated, Chambers consider means and methods used to commit the crimes.[94] For example, one of the aspects taken into account is the level of brutality, cruelty or sadism of the crime(s) committed, as well as the terrorising of victims.[95]

The number of victims caused by the commission of the crime(s) is often considered a significant indicator of the magnitude of the crime(s) and thus taken into account in assessing the gravity of the crimes particularly when the number of victims involved and people to whom suffering was caused is extremely high.[96] The number of victims

---

93 For the *ad hoc* Tribunals, see eg, *Delalić et al* IT-96-21-T (Trial Judgment, 16 November 1998) para 1226; *Popović et al* IT-05-88-T (Trial Judgment, 10 June 2010) vol II para 2134; *Krajišnik* IT-00-39-A (Appeal Judgment, 17 March 2009) para 779; *Krstić* IT-98-33-T (Trial Judgment, 2 August 2001) para 702; *Stakić* IT-97-24-T (Trial Judgment, 31 July 2003) para 910; *Krajišnik* IT-00-39 and 40-T (Trial Judgment, 27 September 2006) para 1148; *Milutinović et al* IT-05-87-T (Trial Judgment, 26 February 2009) vol III, para 1147. For the SCSL, see *Fofana and Kondewa* SCSL-04-14-T (Judgment on the sentencing of Moinina Fofana and Allieu Kondewa, 9 October 2007) para 33; *Brima et al* SCSL-04-16-T (Sentencing Judgment, 19 July 2007) para 19; *Sesay et al* SCSL-04-15-T (Sentencing Judgment, 8 April 2009) paras 19, 115; *Taylor* SCSL-03-01-T (Sentencing Judgment, 30 May 2012) paras 20, 74. For the ICC, see *Lubanga* ICC-01/04-01/06-2901 (Decision on Sentence pursuant to Art. 76 of the Statute, 10 July 2012) para 44.

94 *Krstić* IT-98-33-T (Trial Judgment, 2 August 2001) para 703; *Blaškić* IT-95-14-T (Trial Judgment, 3 March 2000) para 787; *Fofana and Kondewa* SCSL-04-14-T (Judgment on the sentencing of Moinina Fofana and Allieu Kondewa, 9 October 2007) para 33.

95 *Tadić* IT-94-1-T (Sentencing Judgment, 14 July 1997) para 16; *Blaškić* IT-95-14-T (Trial Judgment, 3 March 2000) para 783; *Fofana and Kondewa* SCSL-04-14-T (Judgment on the sentencing of Moinina Fofana and Allieu Kondewa, 9 October 2007) para 33; *Brima et al* SCSL-04-16-T (Sentencing Judgment, 19 July 2007) paras 40, 72, 96; *Sesay et al* SCSL-04-15-T (Sentencing Judgment, 8 April 2009) para 104; *Taylor* SCSL-03-01-T (Sentencing Judgment, 30 May 2012) para 72.

96 *Tadić* IT-94-1-T (Sentencing Judgment, 14 July 1997) para 56; *Erdemović* IT-96-22-T*bis* (Sentencing Judgment, 5 March 1998) para 15; *Kambanda* ICTR-97-23-S (Judgment and Sentence, 4 September 1998) para 42; *Galić* IT-98-29-A (Appeal Judgment, 30 November 2006) para 446; *Krajišnik* IT-00-39 and 40-T (Trial Judgment, 27 September 2006) para 1150; *Bisengimana* ICTR-00-60-T (Judgment and Sentence, 13 April 2006) para 120; *Karera* ICTR-01-74-T (Judgment and Sentence, 7 December 2007) para 579.

is also evaluated in relation to the length of time over which the crimes are perpetrated.[97]

Other elements relating to victims of crime(s) that are also taken into account in assessing the gravity of crimes are for example: the impact of the crimes upon the victims,[98] including the degree of harm, suffering and humiliation inflicted;[99] the trauma suffered and the long-term physical or psychological consequences on victims;[100] and the existence of surviving victims who continue to suffer from the consequences of crimes.[101]

In principle, when a particular factor is an element of the underlying offence or is taken into account in assessing the gravity of the offence, it cannot additionally be taken into account as an aggravating circumstance.[102] Similarly, factors that are considered to lessen the gravity of the offence cannot be taken into account as mitigating circumstances.[103]

However, since the Statutes and RPE of international courts do not exhaustively list the factors that Chambers should consider within the 'gravity of the crime' and in the context of aggravating and mitigating circumstances, Chambers have at times interchangeably considered as aggravating circumstances factors related to the gravity of the offence, or vice versa. For instance, circumstances related to the manner in which the crimes were committed are at times regarded as 'aggravating circumstances' rather than elements of the gravity of the offence. Thus, not always is the distinction between

---

[97] *Erdemović* IT-96-22-T (Sentencing Judgment, 29 November 1996) para 85; *Krajišnik* IT-00-39 and 40-T (Trial Judgment, 27 September 2006) para 1153; *Akayesu* ICTR-96-4-T (Trial Judgment, 2 September 1998) 'Sentence' para 26(iv); *Kambanda* ICTR-97-23-S (Judgment and Sentence, 4 September 1998) para 42; *Sesay et al* SCSL-04-15-T (Sentencing Judgment, 8 April 2009) para 130.

[98] *Mrkšić et al* IT-95-13/1-A (Appeal Judgment, 5 May 2009) para 408; *Krajišnik* IT-00-39-A (Appeal Judgment, 17 March 2009) para 779; *Fofana and Kondewa* SCSL-04-14-T (Judgment on the sentencing of Moinina Fofana and Allieu Kondewa, 9 October 2007) para 49.

[99] *Kayishema et al* ICTR-95-1-T (Sentence, 21 May 1999) para 16; *Krstić* IT-98-33-T (Trial Judgment, 2 August 2001) paras 702–703; *Dragan Nikolić* IT-94-2-S (Sentencing Judgment, 18 December 2003) paras 195–199; *Rajić* IT-95-12-S (Sentencing Judgment, 8 May 2006) paras 84–86; *Taylor* SCSL-03-01-T (Sentencing Judgment, 30 May 2012) para 71.

[100] *Furundžija* IT-95-17/1-T (Trial Judgment, 10 December 1998) para 287; *Jelisić* IT-95-10-T (Trial Judgment, 14 December 1999) para 132; *Blaškić* IT-95-14-T (Trial Judgment, 3 March 2000) paras 786–787; *Deronjić* IT-02-61-S (Sentencing Judgment, 30 March 2004) paras 215–218; *Martić* IT-95-11-T (Trial Judgment, 12 June 2007) para 491; *Krajišnik* IT-00-39-A (Appeal Judgment, 17 March 2009) para 779; *Brima et al* SCSL-04-16-T (Sentencing Judgment, 19 July 2007) para 46; *Fofana and Kondewa* SCSL-04-14-T (Judgment on the sentencing of Moinina Fofana and Allieu Kondewa, 9 October 2007) paras 49, 56; *Taylor* SCSL-03-01-T (Sentencing Judgment, 30 May 2012) para 71.

[101] *Vasiljević* IT-98-32-T (Trial Judgment, 29 November 2002) para 276; *Martić* IT-95-11-T (Trial Judgment, 12 June 2007) para 491; *Fofana and Kondewa* SCSL-04-14-T (Judgment on the sentencing of Moinina Fofana and Allieu Kondewa, 9 October 2007) paras 49, 56; *Taylor* SCSL-03-01-T (Sentencing Judgment, 30 May 2012) para 71.

[102] *Sesay et al* SCSL-04-15-T (Sentencing Judgment, 8 April 2009) para 24.

[103] See eg, *Fofana and Kondewa* SCSL-04-14-T (Judgment on the sentencing of Moinina Fofana and Allieu Kondewa, 9 October 2007) paras 35–36; *Sesay et al* SCSL-04-15-T (Sentencing Judgment, 8 April 2009) para 23.

factors that should be assessed within the 'gravity of the crime' and circumstances that should be considered as aggravating factors clear; this is again due to the lack of standard sentencing factors in international criminal law.

3.3 Individual Circumstances of the Convicted Person

Together with the 'gravity of the offence', the 'individual circumstances of the convicted person' is one of the other factors that – by statute – Trial Chambers should take into account in imposing sentences.[104]

Factors considered when assessing the 'individual circumstances of the convicted person' typically include the role of the accused, the degree and nature of the participation of the accused in the crime, the modalities of perpetration of crimes, and the high-level position of the offender.[105]

For example, Chambers considered whether or not the accused played an active or central role in the commission of the crimes and whether his role was 'minimal' or not.[106] Direct participation in the crimes is deemed to contribute to the seriousness of the role that the accused played.[107] Thus, 'the fact that an accused did not physically commit a crime is relevant to the determination of the appropriate sentence'.[108] However, the fact that an accused did not directly participate or order any of the crimes does not necessarily entail that he should be entitled to a lesser sentence.[109] The way modes of liability have been evaluated in the determination of the sentence will be discussed below in Section 3.5 of this chapter.

As discussed above with regard to the 'gravity of the crime', at times Chambers considered certain factors linked to the 'individual circumstances' of the offender, like the modalities or particular willingness in the commission or execution of crimes, as aggravating or mitigating circumstances. Thus again the distinction between considerations pertaining to the 'individual circumstances of the convicted person' and considerations pertaining to aggravating and mitigating factors is not always clear in the judgments of international courts. The *Taylor* Trial Chamber at the SCSL noted

---

[104] See Art. 24(2) ICTYSt; Art. 23(2) ICTRSt; Art. 19(2) SCSLSt; Art. 78(1) ICCSt.

[105] *Aleksovski* IT-95-14/1-A (Appeal Judgment, 24 March 2000) para 182; *Ruggiu* ICTR-97-32-I (Judgment and Sentence, 1 June 2000) para 48; *Fofana and Kondewa* SCSL-04-14-T (Judgment on the sentencing of Moinina Fofana and Allieu Kondewa, 9 October 2007) para 34; *Brima et al* SCSL-04-16-T (Sentencing Judgment, 19 July 2007) para 19; *Sesay et al* SCSL-04-15-T (Sentencing Judgment, 8 April 2009) paras 19–21; *Taylor* SCSL-03-01-T (Sentencing Judgment, 30 May 2012) paras 19, 21.

[106] *Dragomir Milošević* IT-98-29/1-A (Appeal Judgment, 12 November 2009) para 325; *Nchamihigo* ICTR-01-63-A (Appeal Judgment, 18 March 2010) para 400; *Sesay et al* SCSL-04-15-T (Sentencing Judgment, 8 April 2009) para 271.

[107] See eg, *Aleksovski* IT-95-14/1-A (Appeal Judgment, 24 March 2000) para 183; *Mrkšić et al* IT-95-13/1-A (Appeal Judgment, 5 May 2009) para 407; *Brima et al* SCSL-04-16-T (Sentencing Judgment, 19 July 2007) para 99.

[108] *Mrkšić et al* IT-95-13/1-A (Appeal Judgment, 5 May 2009) para 407.

[109] *Krajišnik* IT-00-39-A (Appeal Judgment, 17 March 2009) para 739.

openly that 'the individual circumstances of the convicted person can be either mitigating or aggravating'.[110]

Throughout the ICTY case-law, the fact that an accused held a high-level or leadership position within a military or civilian structure was considered a serious aggravating circumstance.[111] The ICTR meted out its highest sentences, ie, life imprisonment, to offenders holding key positions in the Rwandan genocide of 1994 and the fact that these accused had a high-level position of authority or leadership role was considered an aggravating circumstance.[112]

The SCSL also recognized an accused's leadership position to be an aggravating factor.[113] In fact, this was one of the main factors influencing the imposition of a lengthy sentence of imprisonment on Charles Taylor.[114]

The systematic, prolonged and premeditated nature of the accused's participation is another factor that Chambers considered in the assessment of the individual circumstances of the offender.[115] Again, this is also a factor that Chambers may consider when assessing aggravating circumstances more generally, including for example the temporal scope of the crimes.

3.4 Aggravating and Mitigating Factors

As discussed above, the distinction between, on the one hand, factors relevant to the gravity of the crime and the individual circumstances of the convicted person and, on the other hand, aggravating or mitigating factors is not always clear, especially considering that the Statutes and RPE of international courts do not define 'aggravating' and 'mitigating' circumstances.[116] Regardless of the characterization of these factors, it is essential that a specific circumstance is not taken into account twice, that is first as part of the gravity of the crime (or the individual circumstances of the

---

110 *Taylor* SCSL-03-01-T (Sentencing Judgment, 30 May 2012) para 22.

111 See eg, *Krstić* IT-98-33-T (Trial Judgment, 2 August 2001) para 721; *Blaškić* IT-95-14-T (Trial Judgment, 3 March 2000) paras 788–789; *Delalić et al* IT-96-21-T (Trial Judgment, 16 November 1998) paras 1242–1243; *Plavšić* IT-00-39 and 40/1-S (Sentencing Judgment, 27 February 2003) para 57; *Stakić* IT-97-24-T (Trial Judgment, 31 July 2003) paras 912–913; *Galić* IT-98-29-T (Trial Judgment, 5 December 2003) para 765, aggravating circumstance that was confirmed also in the appeal case: *Galić* IT-98-29-A (Appeal Judgment, 30 November 2006) paras 411–412.

112 *Akayesu* ICTR-96-4-T (Trial Judgment, 2 September 1998) para 36; *Kambanda* ICTR-97-23-S (Judgment and Sentence, 4 September 1998) paras 44, 61–62; *Kayishema et al* ICTR-95-1-T (Sentence, 21 May 1999) paras 14–15; *Rutaganda* ICTR-96-3-T (Judgment and Sentence, 6 December 1999) para 468; *Kamuhanda* ICTR-95-54A-T (Trial Judgment, 22 January 2004) para 764; *Karera* ICTR-01-74-T (Judgment and Sentence, 7 December 2007) para 577.

113 *Brima et al* SCSL-04-16-T (Sentencing Judgment, 19 July 2007) para 111; *Taylor* SCSL-03-01-T (Sentencing Judgment, 30 May 2012) para 29.

114 *Taylor* ibid., paras 100–103.

115 See eg, *Galić* IT-98-29-A (Appeal Judgment, 30 November 2006) para 455.

116 See Section 3.2 above.

offender), or as an element of the underlying offence, and then as an aggravating (or mitigating) circumstance.[117]

The weight to be given to aggravating and mitigating circumstances is not indicated either by the Statutes or RPE of the *ad hoc* Tribunals, SCSL and ICC; therefore, judges have discretion to attribute to such factors the mitigating or aggravating weight they deem most appropriate.[118]

With regard to the standard and burden of proof, aggravating circumstances must be proved by the prosecution beyond reasonable doubt,[119] while mitigating circumstances can be established on a balance of probabilities standard.[120]

Examples of aggravating circumstances include, inter alia: the vulnerability of the victims; the length of time during which the crime continued and/or its systematic nature;[121] the abuse of a position of authority;[122] the informed, willing or enthusiastic participation in the crime;[123] premeditation and motive;[124] the character of the accused;[125] and previous criminal record of the offender.

---

[117] See eg, *Momir Nikolić* IT-02-60/1-A (Judgment on Sentencing Appeal, 8 March 2006) paras 57–58, 61; *Brima et al* SCSL-04-16-T (Sentencing Judgment, 19 July 2007) para 23; *Sesay et al* SCSL-04-15-T (Sentencing Judgment, 8 April 2009) para 23; *Sesay et al* Appeal Judgment, paras 1234-1237; *Taylor* SCSL-03-01-T (Sentencing Judgment, 30 May 2012) para 28; *Lubanga* ICC-01/04-01/06-2901 (Decision on Sentence pursuant to Art. 76 of the Statute, 10 July 2012) para 35; *Katanga* ICC-01/04-01/07-3484 (Décision relative à la peine (Art. 76 du Statut), 23 May 2014) para 35.

[118] See eg, *Kupreškič et al* IT-95-16-A (Appeal Judgment, 23 October 2001) para 430; *Dragan Nikolić* IT-94-2-S (Sentencing Judgment, 18 December 2003) para 145.

[119] *Delalić et al* IT-96-21-A (Appeal Judgment, 20 February 2001) para 763; *Blaškić* IT-95-14-A (Appeal Judgment, 29 July 2004) para 688; *Fofana and Kondewa* SCSL-04-14-T (Judgment on the sentencing of Moinina Fofana and Allieu Kondewa, 9 October 2007) para 36; *Sesay et al* SCSL-04-15-T (Sentencing Judgment, 8 April 2009) para 24; *Taylor* SCSL-03-01-T (Sentencing Judgment, 30 May 2012) para 24; *Lubanga* ICC-01/04-01/06-2901 (Decision on Sentence pursuant to Art. 76 of the Statute, 10 July 2012) para 33; *Katanga* ICC-01/04-01/07-3484 (Décision relative à la peine (Art. 76 du Statut), 23 May 2014) paras 33–34.

[120] See *Delalić et al* IT-96-21-A (Appeal Judgment, 20 February 2001) para 763; *Dragan Nikolić* IT-94-2-S (Sentencing Judgment, 18 December 2003) para 145; *Kajelijeli* ICTR-98-44A-A (Appeal Judgment, 23 May 2005) para 294; *Fofana and Kondewa* SCSL-04-14-T (Judgment on the sentencing of Moinina Fofana and Allieu Kondewa, 9 October 2007) para 40; *Sesay et al* SCSL-04-15-T (Sentencing Judgment, 8 April 2009) para 28; *Taylor* SCSL-03-01-T (Sentencing Judgment, 30 May 2012) para 31; *Lubanga* ICC-01/04-01/06-2901 (Decision on Sentence pursuant to Art. 76 of the Statute, 10 July 2012) para 34; *Katanga* ICC-01/04-01/07-3484 (Décision relative à la peine (Art. 76 du Statut), 23 May 2014) paras 33–34.

[121] *Kunarac et al* IT-96-23 and 96-23/1-A (Appeal Judgment, 12 June 2002) para 356; *Fofana and Kondewa* SCSL-04-14-T (Judgment on the sentencing of Moinina Fofana and Allieu Kondewa, 9 October 2007) para 37.

[122] *Fofana and Kondewa* SCSL-04-14-T (Judgment on the sentencing of Moinina Fofana and Allieu Kondewa, 9 October 2007) paras 38–39; *Sesay et al* SCSL-04-15-T (Sentencing Judgment, 8 April 2009) para 26.

[123] *Jelisić* IT-95-10-A (Appeal Judgment, 5 July 2001) para 86 and *Jelisić* IT-95-10-T (Trial Judgment, 14 December 1999) paras 131, 133; *Kayishema et al* ICTR-95-1-A (Appeal Judgment, 1 June 2001) para 351; *Fofana and Kondewa* SCSL-04-14-T (Judgment on the sentencing of Moinina Fofana and Allieu Kondewa, 9 October 2007) para 37.

Examples of mitigating circumstances include, inter alia: expression of remorse by the accused;[126] the age and state of health of the accused; the character of the accused;[127] family circumstances;[128] acts of assistance or benevolent attitude towards victims of crimes;[129] the absence of prior convictions; voluntary surrender;[130] good conduct while in detention or during proceedings;[131] and substantial cooperation with the prosecution (which is a circumstance that Chambers are required to consider under their RPE).[132]

An extensive number of other individual circumstances have been considered, either as aggravating or as mitigating factors. As it is not possible to provide here a complete record of all the circumstances taken into account by international courts at the sentencing stage, only some of the most relevant aggravating and mitigating circumstances are discussed in more detail in the following pages. These circumstances are mainly taken from the jurisprudence of the *ad hoc* Tribunals and the SCSL, as the ICC has issued only two sentencing decisions so far.[133]

---

[124] *Krstić* IT-98-33-T (Trial Judgment, 2 August 2001) para 711; *Krstić* IT-98-33-A (Appeal Judgment, 19 April 2004) para 258; *Fofana and Kondewa* SCSL-04-14-T (Judgment on the sentencing of Moinina Fofana and Allieu Kondewa, 9 October 2007) para 37.

[125] *Delalić et al* IT-96-21-A (Appeal Judgment, 20 February 2001) para 788.

[126] *Brima et al* SCSL-04-16-T (Sentencing Judgment, 19 July 2007) para 25; *Fofana and Kondewa* SCSL-04-14-T (Judgment on the sentencing of Moinina Fofana and Allieu Kondewa, 9 October 2007) para 40; *Fofana and Kondewa* SCSL-04-14-A (Appeal Judgment, 28 May 2008) para 490.

[127] *Delalić et al* IT-96-21-A (Appeal Judgment, 20 February 2001) para 788; *Fofana and Kondewa* SCSL-04-14-T (Judgment on the sentencing of Moinina Fofana and Allieu Kondewa, 9 October 2007) para 40.

[128] *Brima et al* SCSL-04-16-T (Sentencing Judgment, 19 July 2007) para 25; *Fofana and Kondewa* SCSL-04-14-T (Judgment on the sentencing of Moinina Fofana and Allieu Kondewa, 9 October 2007) para 40.

[129] *Brima et al* SCSL-04-16-T (Sentencing Judgment, 19 July 2007) para 25; *Fofana and Kondewa* SCSL-04-14-T (Judgment on the sentencing of Moinina Fofana and Allieu Kondewa, 9 October 2007) para 40.

[130] *Brima et al* SCSL-04-16-T (Sentencing Judgment, 19 July 2007) para 25.

[131] *Fofana and Kondewa* SCSL-04-14-T (Judgment on the sentencing of Moinina Fofana and Allieu Kondewa, 9 October 2007) paras 40, 67.

[132] *Brima et al* SCSL-04-16-T (Sentencing Judgment, 19 July 2007) para 25; *Fofana and Kondewa* SCSL-04-14-T (Judgment on the sentencing of Moinina Fofana and Allieu Kondewa, 9 October 2007) para 40; *Taylor* SCSL-03-01-T (Sentencing Judgment, 30 May 2012) para 33.

[133] The *Lubanga* Trial Chamber did not find the existence of any aggravating circumstances and engaged in a very brief analysis of mitigating circumstances. See *Lubanga* ICC-01/04-01/06-2901 (Decision on Sentence pursuant to Art. 76 of the Statute, 10 July 2012) paras 57–81, 96 (on aggravating circumstances), 82–91 and 97 (on mitigating circumstances). The *Katanga* Trial Chamber found no aggravating circumstances but analysed more at length the mitigating circumstances submitted by the Defence. See *Katanga* ICC-01/04-01/07-3484 (Décision relative à la peine (Art. 76 du Statut), 23 May 2014) paras 75 and 144 (on aggravating circumstances), 76-90, 122–140 and 144 (on mitigating circumstances).

3.4.1 Vulnerability of victims

Besides the factors regarding victimization discussed within the gravity of the crime, other elements relating to victims of crime(s) have also been taken into account in the determination of sentences, for instance: the vulnerability of victims,[134] the age, infancy or youth of victims,[135] and the atmosphere of terror and shock caused.[136]

Chambers attribute particular weight to the special vulnerability of categories of victims such as children, the elderly, the disabled or wounded, and to specific circumstances such as victims held in confinement,[137] the position of inferiority and vulnerability of prisoners detained in inhumane conditions or at the complete mercy of their captors.[138]

On the other hand, if the accused tried to alleviate the suffering of victims, helped them or showed some kind of compassion towards victims, Chambers have considered that a factor in mitigation of the sentence.[139]

3.4.2 Abuse of authority

Abuse of authority is another aggravating circumstance consistently upheld by Chambers of the ICTY, ICTR and SCSL.[140] What Chambers considered in aggravation of the

---

[134] See eg, *Furundžija* IT-95-17/1-T (Trial Judgment, 10 December 1998) para 283; *Kvočka et al* IT-98-30/1-T (Trial Judgment, 2 November 2001) para 702; *Dragan Nikolić* IT-94-2-S (Sentencing Judgment, 18 December 2003) paras 184–185; *Martić* IT-95-11-T (Trial Judgment, 12 June 2007) para 490; *Brima et al* SCSL-04-16-T (Sentencing Judgment, 19 July 2007) para 53, 55, 87; *Taylor* SCSL-03-01-T (Sentencing Judgment, 30 May 2012) para 75.

[135] *Kunarac et al* IT-96-23-T and -23/1-T (Trial Judgment, 22 February 2001) paras 864, 874, 879, and IT-96-23 and 96-23/1-A (Appeal Judgment, 12 June 2002) paras 381, 405; *Bralo* IT-95-17-S (Sentencing Judgment, 7 December 2005) para 41.

[136] See eg, *Tadić* IT-94-1-T (Sentencing Judgment, 14 July 1997) para 56; *Delalić et al* IT-96-21-T (Trial Judgment, 16 November 1998) paras 1266, 1272, 1276; *Dragan Nikolić* IT-94-2-S (Sentencing Judgment, 18 December 2003) para 206; *Galić* IT-98-29-A (Appeal Judgment, 30 November 2006) paras 448–449, 454.

[137] *Krajišnik* IT-00-39 and 40-T (Trial Judgment, 27 September 2006) paras 1149–1150; *Krajišnik* IT-00-39-A (Appeal Judgment, 17 March 2009) para 779.

[138] *Banović* IT-02-65/1-S (Sentencing Judgment, 28 October 2003) para 50; *Krstić* IT-98-33-T (Trial Judgment, 2 August 2001) para 703; *Furundžija* IT-95-17/1-T (Trial Judgment, 10 December 1998) para 283.

[139] *Erdemović* IT-96-22-T*bis* (Sentencing Judgment, 5 March 1998) para 16(i); *Serushago* ICTR-98-39-S (Sentence, 5 February 1999) paras 38, 42; *Rutaganda* ICTR-96-3-T (Judgment and Sentence, 6 December 1999) para 470; *Kupreškić et al* IT-96-16-T (Trial Judgment, 14 January 2000) para 860; *Niyitegeka* ICTR-96-14-T (Trial Judgment, 16 May 2003) para 494; *Brđanin* IT-99-36-T (Trial Judgment, 1 September 2004) paras 1119–1120; *Serugendo* ICTR-2005-84-I (Sentencing Judgment, 12 June 2006) paras 68–69; *Krajišnik* IT-00-39 and 40-T (Trial Judgment, 27 September 2006) para 1163; *Nzabirinda* ICTR-2001-77-T (Sentencing Judgment, 23 February 2007) paras 75–77; *Strugar* IT-01-42-A (Appeal Judgment, 17 July 2008) para 366; *Ntawukulilyayo* ICTR-05-82-T (Judgment and Sentence, 3 August 2010) para 475.

[140] *Kambanda* ICTR-97-23-S (Judgment and Sentence, 4 September 1998) para 44; *Delalić et al* IT-96-21-T (Trial Judgment, 16 November 1998) para 1268; *Todorović* IT-95-9/1-S (Sentencing Judgment, 31 July 2001) para 61; *Banović* IT-02-65/1-S (Sentencing Judgment, 28 October 2003) paras 54–55; *Mrđa* IT-02-59-S (Sentencing Judgment, 31 March 2004) paras 51–54; *Serugendo* ICTR-2005-84-I (Sentencing Judgment, 12 June 2006) para 48; *Nzabirinda*

sentence was not a position of authority per se but the abuse of such authority, ie, the position coupled with the manner in which the authority was exercised.[141]

For example, in the *Ntakirutimana* case at the ICTR, in determining the sentence of Gérard Ntakirutimana, the Trial Chamber considered relevant the accused's position as a medical doctor and the fact that he abused his position by destroying lives instead of saving them.[142] Further, before the ICTR, the Trial Chamber in the *Seromba* case considered an aggravating circumstance the fact that Seromba abused his position of trust as a priest of the community where he was known and respected, thus betraying many Tutsis who had sought refuge in his church, believing they were safe.[143]

Abuse of authority can be taken into account as an aggravating factor also in the context of a conviction under command responsibility, planning or ordering the crimes, as well as aiding and abetting.[144]

3.4.3 Enthusiastic participation in the crime, premeditation and motives, cruelty and zeal

Other specific circumstances related to the offenders play a significant role in the determination of the sentence as aggravating factors.

For example, willingness in the commission or execution of the crime(s), voluntary participation in the offences,[145] as well as premeditation[146] have often been considered factors in aggravation of the penalty. Chambers pay attention also to the motives related

ICTR-2001-77-T (Sentencing Judgment, 23 February 2007) paras 61–62; *Rukundo* ICTR-2001-70-T (Trial Judgment, 27 February 2009) para 599; *Ntawukulilyayo* ICTR-05-82-T (Judgment and Sentence, 3 August 2010) para 472; *Fofana and Kondewa* SCSL-04-14-T (Judgment on the sentencing of Moinina Fofana and Allieu Kondewa, 9 October 2007) paras 59–62; *Taylor* SCSL-03-01-T (Sentencing Judgment, 30 May 2012) para 97.

[141] See eg, *Dragomir Milošević* IT-98-29/1-A (Appeal Judgment, 12 November 2009) paras 302–303.

[142] *Elizaphan and Gérard Ntakirutimana* ICTR-96-10 and 96-17-T (Judgment and Sentence, 21 February 2003) para 910.

[143] *Seromba* ICTR-2001-66-I (Trial Judgment, 13 December 2006) para 390; and *Seromba* ICTR-2001-66-A (Appeal Judgment, 12 March 2008) paras 229–230.

[144] *Dragomir Milošević* IT-98-29/1-A (Appeal Judgment, 12 November 2009) paras 302–303; *Stakić* IT-97-24-A (Appeal Judgment, 22 March 2006) para 411; *Taylor* SCSL-03-01-T (Sentencing Judgment, 30 May 2012) para 97.

[145] See eg, *Serushago* ICTR-98-39-S (Sentence, 5 February 1999) para 30; *Kayishema et al* ICTR-95-1-T (Sentence, 21 May 1999) para 13. To the contrary, see *Blagojević and Jokić* IT-02-60-T (Trial Judgment, 17 January 2005) para 849, where the Trial Chamber observed that willingness or voluntary participation in the commission of the crime(s) should be seen as part of the criminal responsibility of the accused in the element of *dolus*, therefore they should not be considered again as an aggravating circumstance. In the same sense also: *Popović et al* IT-05-88-T (Trial Judgment, 10 June 2010) vol II para 2154.

[146] *Kambanda* ICTR-97-23-S (Judgment and Sentence, 4 September 1998) para 61(B)(vi); *Serushago* ICTR-98-39-S (Sentence, 5 February 1999) para 30; *Krstić* IT-98-33-T (Trial Judgment, 2 August 2001) para 711; *Galić* IT-98-29-A (Appeal Judgment, 30 November 2006) paras 450, 455; *Lukić and Lukić* IT-98-32/1-T (Trial Judgment, 20 July 2009) paras 1063–1067.

to the commission of crimes, considering these as a factor to be evaluated in mitigation or in aggravation of the appropriate sentence.[147]

The CDF case at the SCSL presents an interesting example of how problematic the consideration of motives is for the purpose of sentencing. In its sentencing judgment, the Trial Chamber considered among the relevant mitigating circumstances for the two accused (Fofana and Kondewa) the fact that they joined the conflict in Sierra Leone to fight to restore democracy to the country.[148] The fact that the CDF forces were fighting for the democratically elected government seemed to have been accorded a substantial weight in the determination of sentences by the Trial Chamber.[149] The Appeals Chamber corrected this approach and clarified that consideration of purposes underlying the commission of a crime should not amount to allow motive as a defence.[150] It further held that: 'consideration of political motive by a court applying international humanitarian law not only contravenes, but would undermine a bedrock principle of that law'.[151] The Appeals Chamber thus increased the sentences to 15 (for Fofana) and 20 years (for Kondewa).[152]

Particular cruelty and/or sadism in the perpetration of crimes were also found to amount to aggravating factors,[153] as well as zeal in the commission of the crimes.[154]

3.4.4 Character of the accused

The 'character' evidence, comprising evaluation of aspects such as reputation, credibility, personality and social conduct of the accused, is usually intended to show that the crime committed is out of character, and on the whole it aims at providing judges with more complete information concerning the accused's life, background and characteristics.

ICTY and ICTR Chambers have often taken into consideration evidence concerning an accused's character with the interesting peculiarity that elements supporting a good

---

[147] See eg, *Delalić et al* IT-96-21-T (Trial Judgment, 16 November 1998) para 1235; *Tadić* IT-94-1-A (Appeal Judgment, 15 July 1999) para 269; *Sesay et al* SCSL-04-15-T (Sentencing Judgment, 8 April 2009) para 30.

[148] *Fofana and Kondewa* SCSL-04-14-T (Judgment on the sentencing of Moinina Fofana and Allieu Kondewa, 9 October 2007) paras 40, 82–94.

[149] Fofana and Kondewa were sentenced to a total and concurrent term of imprisonment of, respectively, six and eight years. See *Fofana and Kondewa* SCSL-04-14-T (Judgment on the sentencing of Moinina Fofana and Allieu Kondewa, 9 October 2007) 33–34.

[150] *Fofana and Kondewa* SCSL-04-14-A (Appeal Judgment, 28 May 2008) para 523.

[151] Ibid., para 531.

[152] Ibid., paras 189–194, 554–565 (Disposition).

[153] *Vasiljević* IT-98-32-T (Trial Judgment, 29 November 2002) para 279; *Todorović* IT-95-9/1-S (Sentencing Judgment, 31 July 2001) paras 63–65; *Niyitegeka* ICTR-96-14-T (Trial Judgment, 16 May 2003) para 499; *Dragan Nikolić* IT-94-2-S (Sentencing Judgment, 18 December 2003) paras 189, 213; *Češić* IT-95-10/1-S (Sentencing Judgment, 11 March 2004) para 51; *Bralo* IT-95-17-S (Sentencing Judgment, 7 December 2005) paras 32–34; *Blaškić* IT-95-14-A (Appeal Judgment, 29 July 2004) para 686.

[154] *Kvočka et al* IT-98-30/1-T (Trial Judgment, 2 November 2001) para 705; *Brđanin* IT-99-36-T (Trial Judgment, 1 September 2004) para 1109; *Popović et al* IT-05-88-T (Trial Judgment, 10 June 2010) vol II para 2159; *Karera* ICTR-01-74-T (Judgment and Sentence, 7 December 2007) para 580; *Kayishema et al* ICTR-95-1-A (Appeal Judgment, 1 June 2001) paras 351, 361; *Brima et al* SCSL-04-16-T (Sentencing Judgment, 19 July 2007) para 56.

character, a balanced personality, or evidence of a strong and high educational and professional background, have been considered sometimes as factors in mitigation of the penalty,[155] and sometimes as factors in aggravation of the penalty.[156] Other Chambers opted for a flexible approach by finding that whether factors related to the accused's character constitute aggravating or mitigating circumstances depends largely on the circumstances of each case.[157]

3.4.5 Criminal record

The fact that an offender does not have previous criminal convictions (thus being a so-called first offender) is often considered a mitigating circumstance, on the assumption that people who have never committed crimes before have better rehabilitative prospects and will respond more positively to the deterrent effect of the trial process. Being a first offender is also consistent with findings of a 'good character' prior to the offence(s); thus, the two circumstances have often been considered in conjunction. The significance of the accused's previous conduct is, however, a complex factor. Generally, it is accepted that the accused's prior criminal record can be of some influence in meting out the sentence and that an offender with a clean criminal record is entitled to a certain degree of mitigation in sentencing. However, in international sentencing, it is not entirely clear which aspects of the accused's criminal record should be regarded as relevant. Is it the absence of any previous criminal convictions at all or, more restrictively, only crimes of a similar nature to those under the jurisdiction of international courts? In most of the cases, the criminal record of the offender was taken into account as such in relation to the existence of any prior convictions, without requiring that the nature of similar convictions be of the same type or similar to that of international crimes.[158]

As seen for the 'good character' factor, the criminal record of the accused has also been evaluated in various and, at times, contrasting ways. The absence of previous criminal convictions has been considered a mitigating factor in a number of cases

---

155 See eg, *Ruggiu* ICTR-97-32-I (Judgment and Sentence, 1 June 2000) para 67; *Niyitegeka* ICTR-96-14-T (Trial Judgment, 16 May 2003) para 496; *Obrenović* IT-02-60/2-S (Sentencing Judgment, 10 December 2003) paras 130–134; *Strugar* IT-01-42-T (Trial Judgment, 31 January 2005) para 468; *Rutaganira* ICTR-95-1C-T (Judgment and Sentence, 14 March 2005) paras 122–127; *Serugendo* ICTR-2005-84-I (Sentencing Judgment, 12 June 2006) para 65; *Nzabirinda* ICTR-2001-77-T (Sentencing Judgment, 23 February 2007) para 92.

156 See eg, *Tadić* IT-94-1-T (Sentencing Judgment, 14 July 1997) para 59; *Brđanin* IT-99-36-T (Trial Judgment, 1 September 2004) para 1114; *Stakić* IT-97-24-T (Trial Judgment, 31 July 2003) para 915; but contrary: *Stakić* IT-97-24-A (Appeal Judgment, 22 March 2006) para 416.

157 *Hadžihasanović and Kubura* IT-01-47-A (Appeal Judgment, 22 April 2008) para 328 (see also paras 323–329); *Lukić and Lukić* IT-98-32/1-T (Trial Judgment, 20 July 2009) para 1056.

158 To the contrary, an ICTY Trial Chamber in the *Kunarac* case affirmed that 'propensity to commit violations of international humanitarian law, or, possible crimes relevant to such violations' can be discerned only on the basis that an offender might have a record of previous criminal conduct 'relevant to those committed during the armed conflict' since 'in practically all cases before the International Tribunal the convicted persons would be first time offenders *in relation to international crimes*'. See *Kunarac et al* IT-96-23-T and-23/1-T (Trial Judgment, 22 February 2001) para 843.

before the ICTY,[159] the ICTR[160] and the SCSL.[161] At the same time, some Chambers have either decided not to assign this factor any substantial mitigating weight[162] or to mention it but without specifying whether it should be considered relevant or not in mitigation.[163]

3.4.6 Family circumstances

The 'family situation' of the accused, particularly if married and with children, is another factor that has been given attention by Chambers of the *ad hoc* Tribunals, SCSL and ICC. In fact, this circumstance has been considered a mitigating factor in a majority of cases.[164]

Once again there are some different approaches in the jurisprudence and thus in some instances Chambers have mentioned the family status of the accused, but without indicating whether any relevance was given to such circumstance in sentencing.[165] In other cases, Chambers have given little or no mitigating weight to this factor,[166] as

---

159 *Aleksovski* IT-95-14/1-T (Trial Judgment, 25 June 1999) para 236; *Dragan Nikolić* IT-94-2-S (Sentencing Judgment, 18 December 2003) para 265; *Kordić and Čerkez* IT-95-14/2-A (Appeal Judgment, 17 December 2004) para 1090; *Mrkšić et al* IT-95-13/1-T (Trial Judgment, 27 September 2007) para 701; *Rasim Delić* IT-04-83-T (Judgment, 15 September 2008) para 585; *Milutinović et al* IT-05-87-T (Trial Judgment, 26 February 2009) vol III para 1179; *Popović et al* IT-05-88-T (Trial Judgment, 10 June 2010) vol II, para 2156.

160 *Ruggiu* ICTR-97-32-I (Judgment and Sentence, 1 June 2000) paras 59–60; *Rutaganira* ICTR-95-1C-T (Judgment and Sentence, 14 March 2005) paras 129–130; *Bisengimana* ICTR-00-60-T (Judgment and Sentence, 13 April 2006) para 165.

161 *Fofana and Kondewa* SCSL-04-14-T (Judgment on the sentencing of Moinina Fofana and Allieu Kondewa, 9 October 2007) para 68 and *Fofana and Kondewa* SCSL-04-14-A (Appeal Judgment, 28 May 2008) paras 511–512.

162 See eg, *Rajić* IT-95-12-S (Sentencing Judgment, 8 May 2006) paras 162–163; *Milan Simić* IT-95-9/2-S (Sentencing Judgment, 17 October 2002) para 108; *Brđanin* IT-99-36-T (Trial Judgment, 1 September 2004) para 1128; *Sesay et al* SCSL-04-15-T (Sentencing Judgment, 8 April 2009) para 221.

163 See eg, *Delalić et al* IT-96-21-T (Trial Judgment, 16 November 1998) paras 1256, 1270.

164 *Aleksovski* IT-95-14/1-T (Trial Judgment, 25 June 1999) para 238; *Kunarac et al* IT-96-23 and 96-23/1-A (Appeal Judgment, 12 June 2002) para 362; *Vasiljević* IT-98-32-T (Trial Judgment, 29 November 2002) para 300; *Banović* IT-02-65/1-S (Sentencing Judgment, 28 October 2003) para 82; *Brđanin* IT-99-36-T (Trial Judgment, 1 September 2004) para 1130; *Nzabirinda* ICTR-2001-77-T (Sentencing Judgment, 23 February 2007) paras 80–81; *Milutinović et al* IT-05-87-T (Trial Judgment, 26 February 2009) vol III para 1199 (for the accused Lazarević); *Bagaragaza* ICTR-05-86-S (Sentencing Judgment, 17 November 2009) para 37; *Ntawukulilyayo* ICTR-05-82-T (Judgment and Sentence, 3 August 2010) para 476; *Katanga* ICC-01/04-01/07-3484 (Décision relative à la peine (Art. 76 du Statut), 23 May 2014) paras 84–85, 88.

165 *Blaškić* IT-95-14-T (Trial Judgment, 3 March 2000) para 779.

166 *Obrenović* IT-02-60/2-S (Sentencing Judgment, 10 December 2003) para 140; *Mrđa* IT-02-59-S (Sentencing Judgment, 31 March 2004) paras 91–94; *Serugendo* ICTR-2005-84-I (Sentencing Judgment, 12 June 2006) para 67; *Zelenović* IT-96-23/2-S (Sentencing Judgment, 4 April 2007) para 55; *Nchamihigo* ICTR-01-63-T (Judgment and Sentence, 12 November 2008) paras 393–394, confirmed by *Nchamihigo* ICTR-01-63-A (Appeal Judgment, 18 March 2010) paras 389, 391; *Lukić and Lukić* IT-98-32/1-T (Trial Judgment, 20 July 2009) para 1093 (for the accused Sredoje Lukić); *Popović et al* IT-05-88-T (Trial Judgment, 10 June 2010) vol II paras

family circumstances are in theory applicable to a great number of accused and, as such, should not be given undue weight.

3.4.7 Expression of remorse

Among the other circumstances related to the offender, 'remorse' acquires particular importance and represents a significant factor in mitigation of the sentence. Remorse shown by the accused for the crime(s) committed may afford a significant degree of mitigation in sentencing, especially when it is more than a mere expression of sorrow and involves a concrete demonstration of repentance.

To accept remorse as a mitigating circumstance in the determination of the sentence, a Trial Chamber must be satisfied that remorse is genuine and sincere.[167]

In assessing the sincerity of the remorse expressed, Trial Chambers have relied upon circumstantial evidence, such as specific statements made by the accused, his subsequent behaviour (including in the courtroom), the undertaking of positive actions, apologies to victims and witnesses, as well as cooperation with the OTP.[168]

When the remorse expressed by the accused is recognized as being sincere and honest, it is generally considered as a substantial factor in mitigation of the penalty,[169] with a few exceptions.[170] To the contrary, when Trial Chambers are not satisfied that the accused had demonstrated any genuine remorse, such a factor is not taken into account nor given any mitigating relevance in sentencing.[171] The fact that an offender

2200 (for the accused Radivoje Miletić), 2225 (for the accused Vinko Pandurević); *Brima et al* SCSL-04-16-T (Sentencing Judgment, 19 July 2007) paras 119–120; *Sesay et al* SCSL-04-15-T (Sentencing Judgment, 8 April 2009) paras 230, 254; *Katanga* ICC-01/04-01/07-3484 (Décision relative à la peine (Art. 76 du Statut), 23 May 2014) para 88.

167 See eg, *Strugar* IT-01-42-A (Appeal Judgment, 17 July 2008) para 365.

168 See eg, *Milan Simić* IT-95-9/2-S (Sentencing Judgment, 17 October 2002) para 94; *Serushago* ICTR-98-39-S (Sentence, 5 February 1999) para 40.

169 See for the ICTY: *Erdemović* IT-96-22-T (Sentencing Judgment, 29 November 1996) paras 96–98; *Todorović* IT-95-9/1-S (Sentencing Judgment, 31 July 2001) paras 89–92; *Milan Simić* IT-95-9/2-S (Sentencing Judgment, 17 October 2002) para 94; *Plavšić* IT-00-39 and 40/1-S (Sentencing Judgment, 27 February 2003) paras 70–73, 110; *Banović* IT-02-65/1-S (Sentencing Judgment, 28 October 2003) paras 70–72; *Obrenović* IT-02-60/2-S (Sentencing Judgment, 10 December 2003) para 121; *Zelenović* IT-96-23/2-S (Sentencing Judgment, 4 April 2007) para 56. For the ICTR: *Serushago* ICTR-98-39-S (Sentence, 5 February 1999) paras 40–42; *Ruggiu* ICTR-97-32-I (Judgment and Sentence, 1 June 2000) paras 69–72; *Rutaganira* ICTR-95-1C-T (Judgment and Sentence, 14 March 2005) paras 156–158; *Serugendo* ICTR-2005-84-I (Sentencing Judgment, 12 June 2006) paras 63–64; *Nzabirinda* ICTR-2001-77-T (Sentencing Judgment, 23 February 2007) paras 69–70; *Bagaragaza* ICTR-05-86-S (Sentencing Judgment, 17 November 2009) para 38. It is worthy of note that in the *Musema* case, where the Trial Chamber took into account the expression of remorse and regret by the accused, the final sentence imposed was still imprisonment for life (*Musema* ICTR-96-13-T (Trial Judgment, 27 January 2000) paras 1005–1006). For the SCSL: *Sesay et al* SCSL-04-15-T (Sentencing Judgment, 8 April 2009) para 256 (for the accused Kallon).

170 See eg, *Momir Nikolić* IT-02-60/1-S (Sentencing Judgment, 2 December 2003) para 161.

171 See eg, *Jelisić* IT-95-10-T (Trial Judgment, 14 December 1999) para 127; *Vasiljević* IT-98-32-T (Trial Judgment, 29 November 2002) para 297; *Mrkšić et al* IT-95-13/1-T (Trial Judgment, 27 September 2007) para 700; *Lukić and Lukić* IT-98-32/1-T (Trial Judgment, 20 July 2009) para 1094 (for the accused Sredoje Lukić); *Nchamihigo* ICTR-01-63-T (Judgment and

did not express any remorse or regret, irrespective of whether he or she pleaded guilty, cannot be used as an aggravating factor.[172]

3.4.8 Voluntary surrender

The continuous struggle of international courts in obtaining the presence of the offenders is well known. Due to the intrinsic characteristics of international criminal adjudication and the fact that it relies heavily on State cooperation, the surrender of fugitives to international tribunals and courts is of vital importance to their proper functioning. This also explains why the voluntary surrender of offenders has had substantial relevance for the sentencing process at the ICTY and ICTR, and has thus been considered a factor in mitigation of the penalty. Trial Chambers assumed that voluntary surrender may inspire other indictees to act accordingly, and improve the effectiveness of the work of the *ad hoc* Tribunals.

The ICTY and the ICTR have considered voluntary surrender as a mitigating factor in a number of cases;[173] in the majority, surrender has also been linked to the accused's cooperation with the OTP.

Although voluntary surrender is considered a mitigating factor in a majority of cases before the *ad hoc* Tribunals, elements of ambiguity persist in this area.[174] In some cases, Chambers have mentioned the surrender of the accused without further specifying whether this circumstance is considered or not in mitigation of the sentence.[175] In

Sentence, 12 November 2008) para 392, confirmed by *Nchamihigo* ICTR-01-63-A (Appeal Judgment, 18 March 2010) paras 392–395; *Brima et al* SCSL-04-16-T (Sentencing Judgment, 19 July 2007) para 67, 139; *Sesay et al* SCSL-04-15-T (Sentencing Judgment, 8 April 2009) paras 231–232; *Taylor* SCSL-03-01-T (Sentencing Judgment, 30 May 2012) para 91.

[172] See eg, *Stakić* IT-97-24-T (Trial Judgment, 31 July 2003) para 919.

[173] *Serushago* ICTR-98-39-S (Sentence, 5 February 1999) para 34; *Kunarac et al* IT-96-23-T and -23/1-T (Trial Judgment, 22 February 2001) para 868; *Plavšić* IT-00-39 and 40/1-S (Sentencing Judgment, 27 February 2003) paras 82–84; *Miodrag Jokić* IT-01-42/1-S (Sentencing Judgment, 18 March 2004) para 73; *Blagojević and Jokić* IT-02-60-T (Trial Judgment, 17 January 2005) paras 856–857 (for the accused Dragan Jokić); *Strugar* IT-01-42-T (Trial Judgment, 31 January 2005) para 472; *Kvočka et al* IT-98-30/1-A (Appeal Judgment, 28 February 2005) para 713; *Seromba* ICTR-2001-66-A (Appeal Judgment, 12 March 2008) para 236; *Dragomir Milošević* IT-98-29/1-T (Trial Judgment, 12 December 2007) para 1003; *Rasim Delić* IT-04-83-T (Judgment, 15 September 2008) para 573; *Milutinović et al* IT-05-87-T (Trial Judgment, 26 February 2009) vol III para 1200 (for the accused Vladimir Lazarević); *Kalimanzira* ICTR-05-88-T (Trial Judgment, 22 June 2009) para 753; *Bagaragaza* ICTR-05-86-S (Sentencing Judgment, 17 November 2009) para 38; *Popović et al* IT-05-88-T (Trial Judgment, 10 June 2010) vol II paras 2202 (for the accused Radivoje Miletić), 2207 (for the accused Milan Gvero).

[174] There are a number of cases where the surrender of the accused was not considered as a mitigating factor for a number of reasons (for example because the accused surrendered several years after the initial indictment against him), see eg, *Mrkšić et al* IT-95-13/1-T (Trial Judgment, 27 September 2007) para 698 (for the accused Mile Mrkšić); *Milutinović et al* IT-05-87-T (Trial Judgment, 26 February 2009) vol III paras 1184 (for the accused Nikola Šainović), 1189 (for the accused Dragoljub Ojdanić), 1194 (for the accused Nebojsa Pavković), 1204 (for the accused Sreten Lukić).

[175] See eg, *Blaškić* IT-95-14-T (Trial Judgment, 3 March 2000) para 776.

other cases, surrender has been recognized as a mitigating factor, but only minimal weight has been attached to it.[176]

3.4.9 Cooperation with the Office of the Prosecutor

As seen above, substantial cooperation with the prosecution is the only mitigating circumstance openly mentioned by the RPE (Rule 101B(ii)) of the *ad hoc* Tribunals and SCSL, and which these courts are obliged to take into account, if appropriate.[177]

Cooperation can assume various forms, from facilitating the presentation of the Prosecutor's case,[178] to testifying and providing evidence in other cases,[179] to disclosing new information[180] or corroborating known information,[181] or also contributing to the identification of other perpetrators of crimes. The extent and quality of the information provided to the prosecution are factors to take into account when determining whether the cooperation has been substantial.[182]

Once judges ascertain that the cooperation provided is substantial, then this factor has generally been evaluated as a significant mitigating circumstance, also due to the fact that it was considered to facilitate an expeditious trial.[183]

On the other hand, when Chambers ascertain that cooperation is forthcoming reluctantly or was sporadic or not substantial, they do not consider it of any particular

---

[176] See eg, *Martić* IT-95-11-T (Trial Judgment, 12 June 2007) para 510; *Popović et al* IT-05-88-T (Trial Judgment, 10 June 2010) vol II paras 2160 (for the accused Vujadin Popović), 2168 (for the accused Ljubisa Beara), 2177 (for the accused Drago Nikolić), 2192 (for the accused Ljubomir Borovčanin), 2224 (for the accused Vinko Pandurević).

[177] This circumstance is also one of those mentioned by the Rule 145(2)(a)(ii) ICC RPE.

[178] See eg, *Milan Simić* IT-95-9/2-S (Sentencing Judgment, 17 October 2002) para 111.

[179] *Serushago* ICTR-98-39-S (Sentence, 5 February 1999) paras 31–33; *Todorović* IT-95-9/1-S (Sentencing Judgment, 31 July 2001) paras 84, 87–88; *Obrenović* IT-02-60/2-S (Sentencing Judgment, 10 December 2003) para 122; *Deronjić* IT-02-61-S (Sentencing Judgment, 30 March 2004) para 247.

[180] *Todorović* IT-95-9/1-S (Sentencing Judgment, 31 July 2001) para 87; *Serugendo* ICTR-2005-84-I (Sentencing Judgment, 12 June 2006) paras 61–62.

[181] *Deronjić* IT-02-61-S (Sentencing Judgment, 30 March 2004) para 246; *Blaškić* IT-95-14-T (Trial Judgment, 3 March 2000) para 774.

[182] See eg, *Češić* IT-95-10/1-S (Sentencing Judgment, 11 March 2004) para 62; *Deronjić* IT-02-61-S (Sentencing Judgment, 30 March 2004) para 244.

[183] *Erdemović* IT-96-22-T (Sentencing Judgment, 29 November 1996) paras 99–101 and *Erdemović* IT-96-22-T*bis* (Sentencing Judgment, 5 March 1998) para 16(iv); *Ruggiu* ICTR-97-32-I (Judgment and Sentence, 1 June 2000) paras 56–58; *Todorović* IT-95-9/1-S (Sentencing Judgment, 31 July 2001) paras 87–88; *Obrenović* IT-02-60/2-S (Sentencing Judgment, 10 December 2003) paras 128–129; *Mrđa* IT-02-59-S (Sentencing Judgment, 31 March 2004) para 74; *Serugendo* ICTR-2005-84-I (Sentencing Judgment, 12 June 2006) paras 61–62; *Zelenović* IT-96-23/2-S (Sentencing Judgment, 4 April 2007) para 52; *Milutinović et al* IT-05-87-T (Trial Judgment, 26 February 2009) vol III paras 1183 (for the accused Nikola Šainović), 1198 (for the accused Vladimir Lazarević); *Bagaragaza* ICTR-05-86-S (Sentencing Judgment, 17 November 2009) paras 39–40. 'Cooperation with the Court' was also the only mitigating circumstance that the *Lubanga* Chamber at the ICC found relevant in the circumstances of the case. In fact, the Chamber acknowledged Lubanga's 'notable cooperation with the Court', his respectful and cooperative behaviour throughout the proceedings (*Lubanga* ICC-01/04-01/06-2901 (Decision on Sentence pursuant to Art. 76 of the Statute, 10 July 2012) paras 91, 97).

mitigating value.[184] Failure to cooperate with the Prosecutor is not an aggravating circumstance and cannot be considered in aggravation of the punishment.[185]

Finally, an unusual case of cooperation is represented by the *Niyitegeka* case before the ICTR. Here the Trial Chamber gave credit to the accused 'for the extent to which his counsel cooperated with it and with the Prosecution in the efficient conduct of the trial'.[186]

3.5 Modes of Liability

With regard to modes of liability, the main problem as far as sentencing is concerned is that Statutes and RPE of international courts do not differentiate between different modes of liability for sentencing purposes. Therefore, there is no statutory distinction in gravity between direct or indirect perpetration, participation in a joint criminal enterprise, ordering or instigating, aiding and abetting or cooperation in the crime. This leaves judges again with no specific guidance to assess the seriousness of the accused's criminal conduct and liability.

To the contrary, national systems of criminal law make precise choices in terms of the criminal policy to adopt for modes of liability, thus giving indications to judges and guiding them in the decision-making process in sentencing. Some national systems assign by Statute the same degree of seriousness to all persons involved in the commission of a crime notwithstanding their role (principal, accessories, and so on); other systems differentiate between principal or direct offenders and accessories, aider and abettors or instigators, providing more lenient punishment for the latter categories.

No expressed choice or principled approach exists in international criminal law insofar as modes of liability vis-à-vis sentencing are concerned. This constitutes one of the numerous lacunae of the current system of international sentencing, with mostly negative effects on the consistency of the sentencing.

Modes of liability do influence sentencing and the length of the final penalty meted out. For instance, when considering the role and degree of participation of the offender in the crime, the different modes of liability and contributions to criminal acts come into play. It is thus interesting to see how certain modes of liability have been interpreted in sentencing in the practice of the four international courts under scrutiny.

For instance, the *Krstić* Trial Chamber at the ICTY found that 'indirect participation' of the offender to the crime(s) may mitigate a sentence, considering that 'assistance to a crime is a form of participation in a crime often considered less serious than personal participation or commission as a principal' and, depending on the circumstances, might

---

184 *Jelisić* IT-95-10-T (Trial Judgment, 14 December 1999) para 127; *Krstić* IT-98-33-T (Trial Judgment, 2 August 2001) para 716; *Vasiljević* IT-98-32-T (Trial Judgment, 29 November 2002) para 299; *Rasim Delić* IT-04-83-T (Judgment, 15 September 2008) para 577; *Milutinović et al* IT-05-87-T (Trial Judgment, 26 February 2009) vol III para 1194 (for the accused Nebojsa Pavković); *Taylor* SCSL-03-01-T (Sentencing Judgment, 30 May 2012) para 90.

185 *Plavšić* IT-00-39 and 40/1-S (Sentencing Judgment, 27 February 2003) para 64; *Banović* IT-02-65/1-S (Sentencing Judgment, 28 October 2003) para 61; *Milutinović et al* IT-05-87-T (Trial Judgment, 26 February 2009) vol III para 1150.

186 *Niyitegeka* ICTR-96-14-T (Trial Judgment, 16 May 2003) para 498.

warrant a lighter sentence than that imposed for direct commission.[187] The Appeals Chamber of the *ad hoc* Tribunals also stated that, as a general matter, 'a finding of secondary or indirect forms of participation in a joint criminal enterprise relative to others may result in the imposition of a lower sentence'.[188]

However, the fact that the offender did not directly perpetrate, order or instigate any of the crimes does not necessarily entail that the accused should be entitled to a lesser sentence, especially in the JCE context.[189] The Appeals Chamber, for instance, held that a well-established principle of gradation in sentencing is that 'leaders and planners should bear heavier criminal responsibility than those further down the scale'.[190] The particular facts of the accused's involvement must of course be assessed for each specific case.[191]

The principle that indirect forms of commission or participation in crimes may warrant lower penalties has also been recognized by the ICTR in some cases.[192] The principle would not apply to liability under Articles 7(3) ICTYSt/6(3) ICTRSt cases of command responsibility. Command responsibility consists of a failure to punish or prevent the commission of crimes by subordinates. Therefore, an accused person convicted under Articles 7(3)/6(3) could not claim in mitigation that he did not actively participate in the crime.[193] However, with regard to liability under Articles 7(3)/6(3) of the Statutes of the *ad hoc* Tribunals, the Appeals Chamber acknowledged that 'in appropriate cases, a conviction under Article 7(3) of the Statute may result in a lesser sentence as compared to that imposed in the context of an Article 7(1) conviction'.[194] There are exceptions to this principle for cases where the conduct pursuant to command responsibility extends over a significant period of time. In fact, a superior's failure over an extended period of time to prevent or punish crimes committed on an ongoing basis may be regarded as encouraging the commission of crimes and thus, from a sentencing perspective, as more serious than a single failure to prevent an isolated crime by a subordinate.[195]

Further, the Appeals Chamber of the *ad hoc* Tribunals acknowledged that aiding and abetting is a form of liability that generally results in lower sentences than liability as

---

[187] *Krstić* IT-98-33-T (Trial Judgment, 2 August 2001) para 714.

[188] *Babić* IT-03-72-A (Judgment on Sentencing Appeal, 18 July 2005) para 40, citing to *Kajelijeli* ICTR-98-44A-T (Judgment and Sentence, 1 December 2003) para 963 and *Krstić* IT-98-33-A (Appeal Judgment, 19 April 2004) para 268.

[189] *Krajišnik* IT-00-39-A (Appeal Judgment, 17 March 2009) para 739; *Momir Nikolić* IT-02-60/1-A (Judgment on Sentencing Appeal, 8 March 2006) para 56.

[190] *Kalimanzira* ICTR-05-88-A (Appeal Judgment, 20 October 2010) para 236.

[191] *Momir Nikolić* IT-02-60/1-A (Judgment on Sentencing Appeal, 8 March 2006) para 56; *Kalimanzira* ICTR-05-88-A (Appeal Judgment, 20 October 2010) paras 236–237.

[192] *Kajelijeli* ICTR-98-44A-T (Judgment and Sentence, 1 December 2003) para 963; *Nchamihigo* ICTR-01-63-T (Judgment and Sentence, 12 November 2008) para 388.

[193] See eg, *Delalić et al* IT-96-21-A (Appeal Judgment, 20 February 2001) para 737.

[194] *Dragomir Milošević* IT-98-29/1-A (Appeal Judgment, 12 November 2009) para 334. See also: *Rasim Delić* IT-04-83-T (Judgment, 15 September 2008) para 562.

[195] *Delalić et al* IT-96-21-A (Appeal Judgment, 20 February 2001) para 739; *Fofana and Kondewa* SCSL-04-14-T (Judgment on the sentencing of Moinina Fofana and Allieu Kondewa, 9 October 2007) paras 51, 58.

a co-perpetrator.[196] However, a proper assessment of the role of the accused in the commission of the crimes will ultimately depend on the specific circumstances of the case and requires consideration of the accused's knowledge and the form of assistance he provided to the principal perpetrators.[197]

Interestingly, at the SCSL, this approach was adopted by Trial Chambers[198] and then rejected by the Appeals Chamber.[199] In fact, the Trial Chamber in the *Taylor* case, which convicted Charles Taylor to 50 years' imprisonment despite convicting him 'only' as an accessory/accomplice under Article 6(1) SCSLSt on the basis of aiding and abetting and planning,[200] acknowledged that aiding and abetting as a mode of liability 'generally warrants a lesser sentence than that to be imposed for more direct forms of participation'.[201] The Trial Chamber also considered the 'unique circumstances' of Taylor's case and his leadership position as head of State in determining an appropriate sentence, factors that the chamber used to justify departure from the jurisprudence on aiding and abetting.[202] In particular, the imposition of a lengthy sentence was influenced by the official position of Taylor as head of State, which placed Taylor in a different category of offenders for the purposes of sentencing.[203] The *Taylor* Appeals Chamber, however, rejected the approach that aiding and abetting liability generally warrants a lesser sentence than other forms of criminal participation and concluded that in the Statute, Rules and customary international law, 'there is no hierarchy or distinction for sentencing purposes between forms of criminal participation'.[204]

4. CONCLUSION

Sentences meted out by international courts and tribunals are the final and public acts through which the work and efficacy of these international institutions are evaluated. It

[196] *Vasiljević* IT-98-32-A (Appeal Judgment, 25 February 2004) para 182; *Krstić* IT-98-33-A (Appeal Judgment, 19 April 2004) para 268; *Mrkšić et al* IT-95-13/1-A (Appeal Judgment, 5 May 2009) para 407; *Blagoje Simić* IT-95-9-A (Appeal Judgment, 28 November 2006) para 265.

[197] *Blagojević and Jokić* IT-02-60-A (Appeal Judgment, 9 May 2007) para 140.

[198] *Fofana and Kondewa* SCSL-04-14-T (Judgment on the sentencing of Moinina Fofana and Allieu Kondewa, 9 October 2007) para 50; *Taylor* SCSL-03-01-T (Sentencing Judgment, 30 May 2012) paras 21, 36.

[199] *Taylor* SCSL-03-01-A (Appeal Judgment, 26 September 2013) paras 666–669.

[200] *Taylor* SCSL-03-01-T (Sentencing Judgment, 30 May 2012) paras 168, 177; see also para 94. Taylor's conviction for planning was overturned on appeal with no consequences on the sentence, which was affirmed. See *Taylor* SCSL-03-01-A (Appeal Judgment, 26 September 2013) paras 574, 707 305 (Disposition).

[201] *Taylor* SCSL-03-01-T (Sentencing Judgment, 30 May 2012) para 21.

[202] Ibid. The specific/unique circumstances that the Chamber identified were: the number of ways in which Taylor aided and abetted the charged crimes (para 76); the length of time (nearly five years) over which Taylor aided and abetted those crimes (para 78); and the fact that the conflict in Sierra Leone might have ended earlier without Taylor's assistance (para 76). The Trial Chamber also rejected a number of mitigating circumstances offered by the defence (paras 87–94).

[203] Ibid., paras 100–103.

[204] *Taylor* SCSL-03-01-A (Appeal Judgment, 26 September 2013) para 670.

is thus imperative that those sentences be perceived as fair, proportionate and consistent. Proportionality, consistency and effectiveness in sentencing are only achievable if a coherent system of guiding principles is developed and applied by international courts.

One of the reasons for the existing criticism levelled against sentencing in international criminal justice is precisely the lack of clear principles or guidelines. These would contribute to the clarity, consistency and proportionality of the sentences imposed by international tribunals/courts.

While Trial Chambers are certainly entitled to discretion in sentencing, this discretion is not unlimited and must be supported by sound reasoning and thorough findings. To the contrary, the jurisprudence of international courts has often shown a superficial approach to a number of issues in sentencing, for example the purposes of punishment, aggravating and mitigating circumstances, modes of liability and the overall process of determining a sentence. This practice is clearly not laudable in terms of clarity and fairness for a number of reasons. The accused and the international community should not be left guessing 'how' and 'if' a certain factor has influenced a Trial Chamber's sentence. Further, excessive focus on judicial discretion and individualization of sentences might come at the expense of the principles of proportionality and legal certainty, to the point of questioning the fairness of sentencing in international criminal justice. Judges should thus be required to explain in detail the length of sentence associated with a specific crime, and what increase or reduction is applied as a consequence of findings of aggravating and mitigating circumstances. This approach would enhance adherence to the fair trial principles of legal certainty and proportionality. While sentences should of course be individualized to the extent possible, a consistent interpretation and application of sentencing factors across cases (and across international tribunals and courts) is essential to ensure fairness in sentencing.

7. Judicial cross-referencing in the sentencing practice of international(ized) criminal courts and tribunals

Annika Jones[*]

1. INTRODUCTION

The statutes of international(ized) criminal courts and tribunals have given judges a significant degree of discretion in determining the sentences to be imposed on individuals found guilty of the commission of international crimes.[1] Even the highly detailed ICCSt offers just 'a few laconic provisions establishing the maximum available sentence and, by and large, leaving the determination in specific cases to the judges'.[2] Judges have been left to determine, inter alia, the specific goals and objectives to be achieved through the sentencing process, the principles that govern the determination of sentences by international(ized) courts and tribunals, the full range of factors that should be taken into account in the sentencing process and the weight to be given to them.

As judges have encountered these issues they have shown a tendency to refer not only to their own previous decisions, but also to the decisions of other international(ized) and domestic criminal courts and tribunals, and to do so with considerable frequency. The tendency of judges to refer to external jurisprudence on sentencing issues can be viewed as part of a broad, and growing, interaction between various international(ized), regional and domestic courts and tribunals, both within and beyond the field of international criminal law.[3] This trend has been driven by a number of factors, including the movement of personnel between judicial institutions, new opportunities for judges and legal officers from different institutions to come into contact with one another and the increasing availability of external jurisprudence

* I am grateful to Mathilde Pavis for translation assistance in the preparation of this chapter.

[1] S. D'Ascoli, *Sentencing in International Criminal Law: The UN ad hoc Tribunals and Future Perspectives for the ICC* (Hart Publishing 2011) 1–2.

[2] W. Schabas, *An Introduction to the International Criminal Court* (4th edn, Cambridge University Press 2011) 331.

[3] On the practice of judicial cross-referencing between international courts and tribunals, see, for example, N. Miller, 'An International Jurisprudence? The Operation of "Precedent" Across International Tribunals' (2002) 15 LJIL 483, 488; C.P.R. Romano, 'Deciphering the Grammar of the International Judicial Dialogue' (2009) 41 *International Law and Politics* 755; A.Z. Borda, 'Precedent in International Criminal Courts and Tribunals' (2013) 2(2) *Cambridge Journal of International and Comparative Law* 287.

through easily accessible online databases.[4] In the context of international sentencing the practice of judicial cross-referencing between international(ized) courts and tribunals is also supported by the existence of statutory provisions that require judges to 'have recourse to' the sentencing practice of other institutions.[5] Such provisions provide not only a legal basis, but also an obligation for judges to engage in the practice of judicial cross-referencing in the course of their decision-making.

While the sentencing practice of international(ized) criminal courts and tribunals has triggered a significant amount of legal scholarship, little attention has been paid to the interaction between judicial institutions on sentencing issues. Furthermore, research into the nature and scope of interaction between various international and domestic courts and tribunals in the interpretation and application of international law has tended not to focus on the specific issue of when and how judges refer to the decisions of other judicial institutions in the course of their sentencing decisions, or the significance of the practice.

In light of the above, the purpose of this chapter is to provide an insight into the practice of judicial cross-referencing in the sentencing decisions of international criminal courts and tribunals and to consider its implications. It does so by surveying the sentencing decisions of three international(ized) criminal justice mechanisms: the SCSL, the ECCC, and the ICC.[6] These institutions have been chosen as a point of focus for the study because they have all produced sentencing decisions against the backdrop of a large, and growing, body of international case law on sentencing issues, much of which has been produced by the two *ad hoc* Tribunals, the ICTY and ICTR. Consequently, the judges of all three institutions have had considerable scope to refer to the decisions of other courts and tribunals in the course of their reasoning. For the purposes of this chapter, content analysis of the sentencing decisions of the SCSL, the ECCC and the ICC has been used to highlight patterns and trends in the reference to, and use of, external jurisprudence in international sentencing decisions, and to consider its potential implications.

It is important to note that analysis of the sentencing decisions of the SCSL, the ECCC and the ICC cannot provide a comprehensive account of the use of external jurisprudence in the sentencing of individuals for the commission of international crimes. A key reason for this is that judicial decisions only reveal the aspects of the judicial decision-making process that have been committed to paper.[7] They may not

[4] For discussion of the causes of judicial interaction, see A-M. Slaughter, 'A Typology of Transjudicial Communication' (1994) 29 *University of Richmond Law Review* 99, 129–32. See also A-M. Slaughter, 'Judicial Globalisation' (1999–2000) 40 *Virginia Journal of International Law* 1103, 1111.

[5] Art. 24(1) ICTYSt; Art. 23(1) ICTRSt; Art. 19(1) SCSLSt; Regulation 2000/15 on the Establishment of Panels with Exclusive Jurisdiction over Serious Criminal Offences, s. 10.1; Art. 24(1) STLSt.

[6] Whereas the ICC is purely international in nature, the SCSL and the ECCC can be described as 'internationalized' or 'hybrid' criminal justice mechanisms on the basis that they combine both international and domestic elements in terms of applicable law and personnel. See L. Raub, 'Positioning Hybrid Tribunals in International Criminal Justice' (2009) 41 *New York University Journal of International Law and Politics* 1013, 1016.

[7] For discussion of the limits of content analysis in this context, see Romano (n 3) 761–2.

record all instances of judicial cross-referencing that have taken place or give precise details about how external jurisprudence has been used in the course of the judicial decision-making process. Nonetheless, the analysis can offer a significant insight into the practice of judicial cross-referencing and is an important foundation for critical discussion.

The remainder of this chapter is divided into three sections. The first provides a brief overview of the methodology used for the study and the terminology that has been adopted. The second presents the results of the content analysis and highlights patterns and trends in the use of external jurisprudence that can be found in the sentencing decisions of the SCSL, the ECCC and the ICC. The final section assesses the implications of the practice of judicial cross-referencing in international sentencing decisions. The chapter concludes with a look to the future of judicial cross-referencing in the field of international sentencing and the role that the ICC may come to play as a source of jurisprudence on sentencing issues.

2. METHODOLOGY AND TERMINOLOGY

The content analysis referred to in the following section encompasses all of the sentencing decisions that have been rendered by the SCSL, the ECCC and the ICC up to the end of May 2014. This includes four decisions of the Trial Chambers of the SCSL,[8] one decision of the Trial Chamber of the ECCC,[9] and two decisions of the Trial Chambers of the ICC.[10] It also includes relevant judgments of the Appeals Chamber of the SCSL and the Supreme Court Chamber of the ECCC in which sentencing issues have been considered.[11] All relevant separate and dissenting opinions of the judges of the SCSL, ECCC and ICC have been included in the analysis. Decisions relating to the sentencing of individuals for contempt of court have not been included on the basis that such decisions do not concern the imposition of sentences for core international crimes and are not, therefore, of a similar nature to the other decisions included in the study.

The analysis used in the study is largely qualitative. However, some numerical data has been included in relation to readily quantifiable concepts, namely the frequency of reference to external jurisprudence and the range of institutions that have been referred to. For the purposes of quantifying references to the decisions of other courts and tribunals, reference to several decisions from the same institution have been treated as

---

[8] *Brima, Kamara and Kanu* SCSL-04-16 (Sentencing Judgment, 19 July 2007); *Fofana and Kondewa* SCSL-04-14-T (Judgment on the Sentencing of Moinina Fofana and Allieu Kondewa, 9 October 2007); *Sesay, Kallon and Gbao* SCSL-04-15-T (Sentencing Judgment, 8 April 2009); *Taylor* SCSL-03-01-T (Sentencing Judgment, 30 May 2012).

[9] *Duch,* 001/18-07-2007/ECCC/TC (Judgment, 26 July 2010).

[10] *Lubanga* ICC-01/04-01/06-2901 (Decision on Sentence Pursuant to Article 76 of the Statute, 10 July 2012); *Katanga* ICC-01/04-01/07-3484 (Décision Relative à la Peine (Article 76 du Statut), 23 Mai 2014).

[11] *Brima, Kamara and Kanu* SCSL-04-16-A (Judgment, 22 February 2008); *Fofana and Kondewa* SCSL-04-14-A (Judgment, 28 May 2008); *Sesay, Kallon and Gbao* SCSL-04-15-A (Judgment, 26 October 2009); *Taylor* SCSL-03-01-A (Judgment, 26 September 2013); *Duch* 001/18-07-2007/ECCC/SC (Judgment, 3 February 2012).

one citation where they concerned the same legal issue.[12] If it was unclear whether or not the matter being addressed should be treated as one issue or two separate issues, it was presumed that there were two. Where judges have addressed sentencing issues alongside other matters in the course of their decisions, the analysis has been limited to the parts of the decisions where sentencing has been considered.

Throughout the chapter, the term 'judicial cross-referencing' has been used to describe the practice of a judge in one institution referring to the decisions of a judge in another.[13] The term has been used to refer to the simple act of reference to the decision of another judicial institution without indicating the way in which the decision has been used.

3. JUDICIAL CROSS-REFERENCING IN INTERNATIONAL SENTENCING DECISIONS: INSIGHTS INTO THE EMERGING PRACTICE

The following sections highlight different aspects of the practice of judicial cross-referencing in the sentencing decisions of the SCSL, the ECCC and the ICC. The implications of the patterns and trends identified in these sections are discussed in Section 4 below.

3.1 Views on the Relevance of External Jurisprudence

On a number of occasions, judges of the SCSL, the ECCC and the ICC have discussed the significance of the practice of other courts and tribunals for their own deliberations. The case law of the SCSL and the ECCC indicates a different attitude towards reference to the decisions of the courts of the territorial State, on the one hand, and reference to the decisions of international courts and tribunals, on the other.

The judges of the SCSL and the ECCC have considered the significance of the practice of domestic courts of the territorial State in their sentencing decisions. The judges of the SCSL are in a similar position to the judges of the *ad hoc* Tribunals in that the statutes of all three institutions require their judges to 'have recourse to' the practice of the national courts of the territorial State.[14] In their sentencing decisions, the judges of the SCSL have tended to adopt a similar approach to the *ad hoc* Tribunals in finding that the statutory requirement does not impose an obligation on the Trial Chamber to conform to the practice of domestic courts, but rather to 'take into account

[12] For example, if a Chamber cited a number of decisions of the ICTY in considering whether a certain form of conduct could be considered as a mitigating factor, this would be treated as one citation of the case law of the ICTY. If the Chamber cited decisions from the ICTY to establish the goals underpinning the sentencing process and to establish whether or not certain conduct could be considered in mitigation, this would be treated as two separate citations.

[13] The term 'judicial cross-referencing' has been used in this chapter to avoid use of the loaded term 'precedent'. See discussion in Miller (n 3) 488.

[14] Art. 24(1) ICTYSt; Art. 23(1) ICTRSt; Art. 19(1) SCSLSt.

that practice as and when appropriate'.[15] In the *AFRC* case, the Trial Chamber of the SCSL concluded that it was 'not appropriate' to adopt the practice of the national courts of Sierra Leone since none of the accused had been indicted for, or convicted of, offences under Article 5 of the Statute, namely crimes under Sierra Leonean law.[16]

The judges of the ECCC have also indicated their reluctance to draw from the practice of domestic courts in Cambodia when determining the sentences that should be imposed on individuals for the commission of international crimes. In the *Duch* case, the Trial Chamber of the ECCC considered that 'the international nature of the crimes for which the Accused has been convicted, and the uncertainties and complexities evident in the evolution of Cambodian criminal law from the 1956 Penal Code onwards, rules out the direct application of Cambodian sentencing provisions'.[17] The Chamber did, however, indicate that it would 'seek guidance from' Cambodian sentencing principles and factors in determining the sentence of the accused.[18]

In the cases referred to above, the SCSL and the ECCC were only considering the significance of the practice of the domestic courts of the territorial State. The tendency of judges of the SCSL to refer to the practice of the domestic courts of other States will be discussed further in the section below.[19]

While judges of the SCSL and the ECCC have shown some reticence in following the practice of the domestic courts of the territorial State in their sentencing decisions, the Chambers of all three institutions have expressed their readiness to take into consideration the sentencing practice of other international criminal courts and tribunals when faced with gaps and ambiguities in their own legal frameworks, even where there is no statutory provision expressly requiring them to do so.

At the SCSL reference to case law of the ICTR has a statutory basis. In addition to requiring judges to have recourse to the practice of domestic courts, Article 19(1) of the SCSLSt places an obligation on judges of the SCSL to have recourse to 'the practice regarding prison sentences in the [ICTR]'. No such reference is made to the sentencing decisions of the ICTY. Nonetheless, judges of the SCSL have confirmed their readiness to 'consider' the sentencing practice of the ICTY on the basis that the provisions of the ICTYSt are 'analogous to those of the Special Court and the ICTR'.[20] In the *CDF* case, the Trial Chamber of the SCSL described the sentencing practice of both institutions as 'instructive'.[21] The approach of the Trial Chamber was, however, criticized by Justice

---

15 *Brima, Kamara and Kanu* SCSL-04-16 (Sentencing Judgment, 19 July 2007) para 32; *Taylor* SCSL-03-01-T (Sentencing Judgment, 30 May 2012) para 37.

16 *Brima, Kamara and Kanu* SCSL-04-16 (Sentencing Judgment, 19 July 2007) para 32. In the *Taylor* case, the Trial Chamber also emphasized that 'Mr Taylor was not indicted for, nor convicted of, offences under Article 5 of the SCSLSt in the Sierra Leonean law' before noting the approach of the law of Sierra Leone to the sentencing of accessories to crimes. See *Taylor* SCSL-03-01-T (Sentencing Judgment, 30 May 2012) para 37.

17 *Duch* 001/18-07-2007/ECCC/TC (Judgment, 26 July 2010) para 577.

18 Ibid., para 578.

19 See Section 3.2.

20 *Brima, Kamara and Kanu* SCSL-04-16 (Sentencing Judgment, 19 July 2007) para. 33. *Taylor* SCSL-03-01-T (Sentencing Judgment, 30 May 2012) para 36.

21 *Fofana and Kondewa* SCSL-04-14-T (Judgment on the Sentencing of Moinina Fofana and Allieu Kondewa, 9 October 2007) para 41.

Gelaga King of the Appeals Chamber on the basis that Article 19(1) of the SCSLSt does not make reference to the practice of the ICTR's sister tribunal.[22]

Judges of the ICC have also indicated that the decisions of the *ad hoc* Tribunals provide a potential source of guidance in their sentencing decisions, despite the absence of an express provision in the ICCSt requiring them to consider the decisions of other judicial institutions.[23] When discussing the relevance of external jurisprudence to the sentencing of Mr Thomas Lubanga Dyilo, the Trial Chamber of the ICC rightly noted that 'the decisions of other international courts and tribunals are not part of the directly applicable law under Article 21 of the Statute'.[24] However, it went on to acknowledge that 'the *ad hoc* tribunals are in a comparable position to the Court in the context of sentencing', indicating the potential significance of their case law as a source of guidance for the ICC.[25]

The judges of the ECCC have taken a similar approach. In the *Duch* case the Trial Chamber of the ECCC noted that it would 'seek guidance from' international, as well as Cambodian, sentencing principles in exercising its discretion in the determination of sentence.[26] On appeal the Supreme Court Chamber also explained that in the absence of 'comparable jurisprudence before Cambodian domestic courts' it had 'examined sentences of other international criminal tribunals addressing similar or comparable issues' as a source of guidance.[27]

While the judges of all three institutions have been receptive of the case law of other international criminal courts and tribunals, they have also indicated that factors might stand in the way of consistency with the approaches taken by judges working elsewhere. Judges have drawn attention, in particular, to the need to ensure that the sentences they impose reflect the individual circumstances of the case and the conduct of the accused.[28]

3.2 The Frequency of Judicial Cross-referencing and Range of Institutions Referred to

All of the decisions that have been included in this study contain instances of judicial cross-referencing. References to external jurisprudence can be found in the decisions of

---

22 *Fofana and Kondewa* SCSL-04-14-A (Judgment, 28 May 2008) Dissenting Opinion of Justice Gelaga King paras 112–113.

23 Art. 21 ICCSt, which outlines the applicable law of the ICC, only makes reference to the ICC's own prior decisions. See Art. 21(2) ICCSt ('The Court may apply principles and rules of law as interpreted in its previous decisions').

24 *Lubanga* ICC-01/04-01/06-2901 (Decision on Sentence Pursuant to Article 76 of the Statute, 10 July 2012) para 12.

25 Ibid.

26 *Duch* 001/18-07-2007/ECCC/TC (Judgment, 26 July 2010) para 578.

27 *Duch* 001/18-07-2007/ECCC/SC (Judgment, 3 February 2012) para 374. See also *Duch* 001/18-07-2007/ECCC/TC (Judgment, 26 July 2010) 578.

28 *Brima, Kamara and Kanu* SCSL-04-16 (Sentencing Judgment, 19 July 2007) para 11. *Taylor* SCSL-03-01-A (Judgment, 26 September 2013) para 705; *Duch* 001/18-07-2007/ECCC/SC (Judgment, 3 February 2012) para 374.

both trial and appeals chambers, and in separate and dissenting opinions of individual judges, as well majority decisions.

Overall, judges of the ICC have referred to the decisions of other courts and tribunals less frequently than the judges of the SCSL and the ECCC. The number of instances of judicial cross-referencing identified in the sentencing decisions of the SCSL, the ECCC and the ICC are shown in Table 7.1 below.

Table 7.1 Table showing the institutions referred to and the frequency of judicial cross-referencing

Institution	Instances of Judicial Cross-Referencing: Trial Chamber	Instances of Judicial Cross-Referencing: Appeals Chamber	Instances of Judicial Cross-Referencing: Separate Opinions	Instances of Judicial Cross-Referencing: Total	Average number of citations per decision*
SCSL	104	75	0	179	22.4
ECCC	24	31	10	55	27.5
ICC	17	0	0	17	8.5

Note: *This column shows the total number of instances of judicial cross-referencing divided by the number of sentencing decisions that have been included in the analysis for each institution.

When divided by the number of decisions included in the analysis, this suggests a frequency of judicial cross-referencing of 22.4 references per decision at the SCSL, 27.5 references per decision at the ECCC and 8.5 references per decision at the ICC.

The lower rate of reference to external jurisprudence by judges of the ICC may reflect a desire to distinguish the first permanent international criminal court from its predecessors and contemporaries. However, it may also be attributable to the attitude of individual judges towards the citation of external jurisprudence and the nature of the issues that have been raised in the sentencing decisions of the ICC to date.

Figures 7.1, 7.2 and 7.3 below indicate the range of institutions that judges have referred to in their sentencing decisions and the frequency of reference to the decisions of each institution.

The above figures indicate that judges have been more willing to refer to the decisions of other international(ized) criminal courts and tribunals than they have been to refer to other international, regional or domestic courts or tribunals. References to the case law of the *ad hoc* Tribunals are particularly frequent. This is, perhaps, unsurprising, given the large quantity of sentencing decisions that the two institutions have produced. The high frequency of reference to the decisions of the *ad hoc* Tribunals may also be influenced by the movement of judges, legal officers and other court staff from the *ad hoc* Tribunals to the institutions that form the focus of this study.

The judges of the SCSL, ECCC and the ICC have all referred to the case law of the ICTY more frequently than to that of the ICTR. This is particularly noteworthy in the context of the SCSL since the SCSLSt makes no mention of the practice of the ICTY,

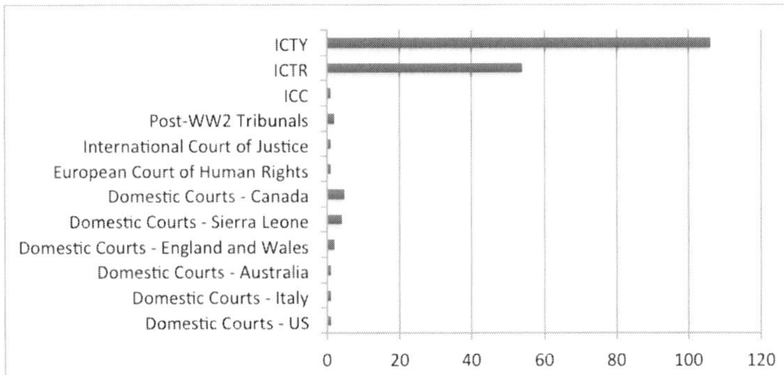

Figure 7.1 Reference to external jurisprudence in the sentencing decisions of the SCSL

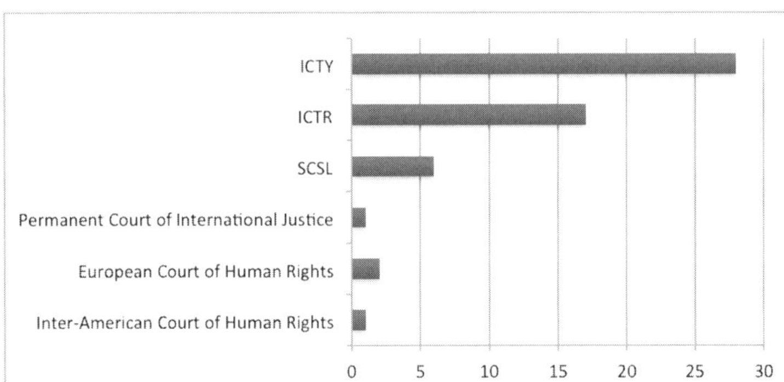

Figure 7.2 Reference to external jurisprudence in the sentencing decisions of the ECCC

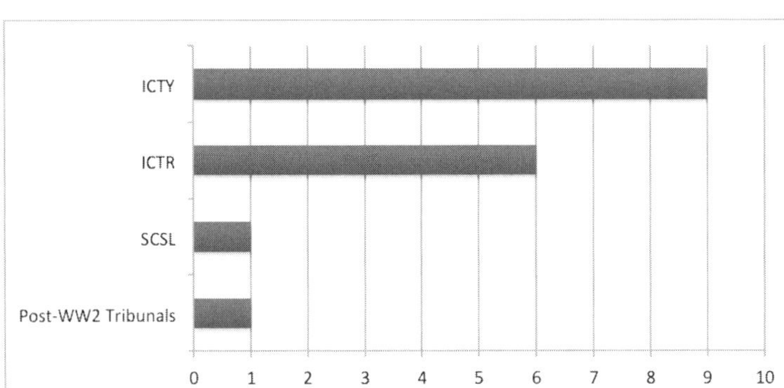

Figure 7.3 Reference to external jurisprudence in the sentencing decisions of the ICC

whereas it does require judges to have recourse to the practice of the ICTR.[29] The tendency of judges to refer more frequently to the case law of the ICTY than that of the ICTR may be explained by the number of sentencing decisions that the ICTY has produced, as well as the range of crimes that it has addressed.

Both the ICC and the ECCC have made reference to the case law of the SCSL, suggesting that the legacy of the Special Court, which has now completed its mandate and transition to a residual mechanism, may also live on in the sentencing decisions of other courts and tribunals.[30] It should, however, be noted that the reference to the case law of the SCSL by the judges of the ICC in the *Lubanga* case was made primarily for the purpose of highlighting the sentences that the SCSL had rendered for crimes under the consideration of the ICC.[31] There is no indication that the case law influenced the final decision of the Trial Chamber regarding the sentence to be imposed on the accused.

The case law of the ICC has only been referred to on one occasion in the sample of decisions studied. The infrequent reference to the case law of the ICC can be attributed, at least in part, to the fact that the ICC has only produced two sentencing decisions, both of which were rendered after the majority of decisions included in this study had been produced. The sole reference to the case law of the ICC is found in the judgment of the SCSL Appeals Chamber in the *Taylor* case.[32] In that case, the Appeals Chamber rejected the finding of the Trial Chamber that aiding and abetting generally warrants a lesser sentence than other forms of participation in international crimes.[33] In support of its approach, the Chamber made reference to the law of several domestic legal systems, including that of Sierra Leone, as well as the practice of the *ad hoc* Tribunals and post-World War II case law.[34] It also made reference to the Separate Opinion of Judge Adrian Fulford to the final judgment of the Trial Chamber in the *Lubanga* case, which noted Judge Fulford's reluctance to accept that it would 'assist the work of the Court to establish a hierarchy of seriousness that is dependent on creating rigorous distinctions between the modes of liability' contained in the ICCSt.[35]

The reference of the SCSL Appeals Chamber to the Separate Opinion of Judge Fulford highlights the importance of separate opinions and the influence that they can have on the development of international law in subsequent cases, perhaps even in other institutions. It also suggests that the practice of judicial cross-referencing is not

---

[29] Art. 19(1) SCSLSt.

[30] See *Duch* 001/18-07-2007/ECCC/TC (Judgment, 26 July 2010) paras 580, 583, 584, 587, 591. *Duch* 001/18-07-2007/ECCC/SC (Judgment, 3 February 2012) Partially Dissenting Joint Opinion of Judges Agnieszka Klonowiecka-Milart and Chandra Nihal Jayasinghe para 27. *Lubanga* ICC-01/04-01/06-2901 (Decision on Sentence Pursuant to Article 76 of the Statute, 10 July 2012) paras 12–15.

[31] *Lubanga*, ibid.

[32] *Taylor* SCSL-03-01-A (Judgment, 26 September 2013) para 666, footnote 1945.

[33] Ibid., para 666.

[34] Ibid., paras 666–669.

[35] Ibid., para 666, footnote 1945. Judge Fulford went on to say that '[w]hilst it might have been of assistance to "rank" the various modes of liability if, for instance, sentencing was strictly determined by the specific provision on which an individual's conviction is based, considerations of this kind do not apply to the ICC'.

driven only by the formal nature of the decision being referred to, but also the quality of reasoning contained within it or the conclusions that have been drawn. In the same decision, and in relation to the same point, the SCSL Appeals Chamber also made reference to the Separate Opinion of Judge David Hunt in the ICTY's *Milutinović* case in support of its reasoning.[36]

Judges of the SCSL and the ICC have shown a tendency to refer not only to recent case law within the field of international criminal law; they have also referred to post-World War II case law of the Allied Military Tribunals on several occasions. In addition to the decision of the SCSL Appeals Chamber in the *Taylor* case already discussed, reference can be found in the SCSL Appeals Chamber's decision in the *CDF* case and in the ICC's *Katanga* case.[37] On both of these occasions, the case law was used to support the proposition that while mitigating circumstances may influence the sentence imposed, they do not alter the gravity of the crime.

The SCSL is the only institution of the three that have been studied that has made reference to the decisions of domestic courts and tribunals in the course of its sentencing decisions. More often than not, where judges have referred to the decisions of domestic courts, the courts referred to are not those of a State with a clear jurisdictional link to the crimes being addressed. For example, when considering the objectives underpinning international sentencing in the *CDF* case, the Trial Chamber of the SCSL referred to and expressly adopted the definition of retribution that had been offered by Lamer J of the Supreme Court of Canada. In the same case, the Trial Chamber of the SCSL referred to a range of domestic courts when considering the applicability of the doctrine of necessity as a defence.[38] The Appeals Chamber also made reference to the decisions of the domestic courts of Australia, the UK and Canada when considering the alleged error of the Trial Chamber in holding that the sentences imposed on the accused would run concurrently.[39] Having reviewed the relevant jurisprudence, the Appeals Chamber of the SCSL concluded that 'Trial Chambers typically enjoy broad discretion to choose between concurrent and consecutive sentences'.[40]

While judges have tended to refer to other criminal justice mechanisms in the course of their decision-making, they have, on occasion, looked beyond institutions that focus on the criminal responsibility of individuals and have turned to institutions concerned primarily with the responsibility of States. The decisions included in the study contained several references to the case law of regional human rights courts. One example can be found in the *Duch* case before the ECCC: the Trial Chamber referred to the case law of the ECtHR when considering the impact of prior violations of the rights of the accused – in this case, a period of unlawful detention – on the sentence issued by

[36] Ibid.

[37] *Fofana and Kondewa* SCSL-04-14-A (Judgment, 28 May 2008) para 519. *Katanga* ICC-01/04-01/07-3484 (Décision Relative à la Peine (Article 76 du Statut), 23 Mai 2014) para 77.

[38] *Fofana and Kondewa* SCSL-04-14-T (Judgment on the Sentencing of Moinina Fofana and Allieu Kondewa, 9 October 2007) paras 73–75. The Chamber referred to the case law of Canada, the US and England and Wales.

[39] *Fofana and Kondewa* SCSL-04-14-A (Judgment, 28 May 2008) paras 456–550.

[40] Ibid., para 547.

the Trial Chamber.[41] The Chamber referred to the case law of the ECtHR to support its finding that the reduction in sentence 'must be express and measurable and based on the totality of the circumstances of the case'.[42] The case law of the I-ACtHR was also referred to by two judges of the Supreme Court Chamber of the ECCC when addressing the same issue on appeal.[43] The case law was used to establish that the period of detention had been unlawful, to reflect on the purpose of a remedy under international law and to support the finding that an appropriate remedy for excessive or unlawful detention is a reduction in sentence.[44]

Judges have also referred to general principles of law that have been developed by the International Court of Justice (ICJ) and its predecessor, the Permanent Court of International Justice (PCIJ). Reference to the case law of the PCIJ can be found in the Partially Dissenting Joint Opinion of Judges Agnieszka Klonowiecka-Milart and Chandra Nihal Kavasinghe to the Judgment of the Supreme Court Chamber of the ECCC in the *Duch* case. In their joint opinion, the two judges referred to the PCIJ's *Chorzow Factory* case when discussing the appropriate remedy to be imposed in respect of a period of unlawful detention.[45]

There was just one reference to the case law of the ICJ in the decisions included in the study. In the *Taylor* case, the Trial Chamber of the SCSL referred to the case law of the ICJ in concluding that the extraterritorial nature of the criminal acts of the accused could be taken into consideration as an aggravating factor.[46] It cited the findings of the ICJ in the *Nicaragua* case concerning the implications of State support for an organization in another State and the principles of non-intervention and the prohibition on the use of force.[47] While acknowledging that these customary provisions govern the conduct between States, the Chamber held that 'violation of [the principle of non-intervention] by a Head of State individually engaging in criminal conduct can be taken into account as an aggravating factor'.[48]

On appeal, the defence argued that the *Taylor* Trial Chamber had erred in 'erroneously apply[ing] customary international law principles of state responsibility to find that the extraterritoriality of conduct by a head of State is an aggravating factor relevant to sentencing'.[49] The Appeals Chamber found that while it was 'unnecessary for the Trial Chamber to refer to public international law in order to take into consideration the

---

41 *Duch* 001/18-07-2007/ECCC/TC (Judgment, 26 July 2010) para 625.

42 Ibid.

43 *Duch* 001/18-07-2007/ECCC/SC (Judgment, 3 February 2012) Partially Dissenting Joint Opinion of Judges Agnieszka Klonowiecka-Milart and Chandra Nihal Kayasinghe paras 14, 18, 19.

44 Ibid.

45 Ibid., para 18, citing *Chorzow Factory* Series A no 17/13 (Merits Judgment 'Claim for Indemnity', 13 September 1928) 47. The PCIJ had held that 'reparation must, as far as possible, wipe-out all consequences of the illegal act and re-establish the situation which would, in all probability, have existed if that act had not been committed'.

46 *Taylor* SCSL-03-01-T (Sentencing Judgment, 30 May 2012) para 27.

47 Ibid.

48 Ibid. Citing *Nicaragua v United States* (Merits Judgment 'Military and Paramilitary Activities in and against Nicaragua', 27 June 1986) ICJ Reports para 209.

49 *Taylor* SCSL-03-01-A (Judgment, 26 September 2013) para 680.

extraterritorial nature and consequences of Taylor's acts and conduct', these factors were 'directly related to Taylor and the gravity of his culpable conduct, justifying holding him responsible'.[50] Consequently, in the one decision where the ICJ has been cited, the relevance of its case law was called into question.

Overall, the content analysis indicates that while the judges of the SCSL, the ECCC and the ICC have tended to refer most frequently to other international(ized) criminal justice institutions, they have been willing to refer to a wider range of institutions where warranted by the issues raised in the case. References to post-World War II case law and decisions of the PCIJ suggest that the practice of judicial cross-referencing is not confined to recent cases and that judges are willing to look back to older case law that supports the arguments that they wish to make. Furthermore, references to separate opinions of judges of other courts and tribunals also indicate that the practice is driven not only by the weight or authority of the decision referred to, but also by the reasoning included in the decision or the arguments that have been put forward.

3.3 Issues Prompting Reference to External Jurisprudence

In their sentencing decisions judges have referred to the decisions of other courts and tribunals in relation to a range of legal issues. A large proportion of the instances of judicial cross-referencing contained in the sentencing decisions of the SCSL, the ECCC and the ICC concerned the aggravating and mitigating factors to be considered in the determination of sentence to be imposed on the accused. Judges frequently referred to external jurisprudence to establish what conduct could be considered in aggravation or mitigation of sentence, to determine the standard of proof that must be met in order for an aggravating or mitigating factor to be considered and in determining the weight such factors should be given.

The judges of the three institutions also made frequent reference to the decisions of other courts and tribunals in order to establish or confirm the existence of general principles to guide the sentencing process. Such general principles include the prohibition on double counting, whereby the same factor must not influence the sentence of the convicted person twice,[51] and the totality principle, according to which a Trial Chamber must impose a sentence which reflects the totality of the convicted person's culpable conduct, including the gravity of the conduct, the circumstances of the case and the form and degree of participation of the accused.[52] The discretion of the Trial Chamber to impose cumulative or consecutive sentences on individuals convicted of multiple crimes,[53] and the practice of imposing a single 'global' sentence for multiple convictions,[54] also prompted a number of references to external jurisprudence.

On several occasions judges made reference to external jurisprudence when considering the goals or objectives that underpin the sentencing process. In the *CDF* case, for

---

[50] Ibid., para 683.

[51] See, for example, *Lubanga* ICC-01/04-01/06-2901 (Decision on Sentence Pursuant to Article 76 of the Statute, 10 July 2012) para 35.

[52] See, for example, *Taylor* SCSL-03-01-A (Judgment, 26 September 2013) para 662.

[53] See, e.g., ibid., para 9.

[54] See, e.g., ibid., para 10.

example, the Appeals Chamber of the SCSL listed several goals that had been 'recognized by the ICTY as legitimate sentencing processes', including individual and general deterrence, individual and general prevention, retribution, public reprobation and stigmatisation by the international community, and rehabilitation.[55] The Chamber cited relevant case law from the ICTY in relation to each of the listed goals. In the same case, the Appeals Chamber also referred to case law of the ICTY to support its finding that '[t]he primary objectives must be retribution and deterrence'.[56] As already noted, the SCSL Trial Chamber has also referred to the definition of retribution provided by Lamer J of the Supreme Court of Canada.[57] These references reflect an assumption that there are common goals underpinning the imposition of sentences by different international(ized) criminal courts and tribunals, and that at least some of those goals are also shared with domestic criminal justice institutions.

As noted above, judges have also cited the decisions of other courts and tribunals as a point of reference when considering the length of sentence imposed on the accused. Often such comparative reflection has been prompted by the parties to the proceedings, who have cited the practice of other judicial institutions as a means of challenging the sentences imposed by the relevant trial chambers. An example of this practice can be found in the judgment of the SCSL Appeals Chamber in the *RUF* case. On appeal, one of the defendants, Augustine Gbao, argued that the sentence that had been imposed by the Trial Chamber was inconsistent with the jurisprudence of the *ad hoc* Tribunals and previous cases before the SCSL.[58]

In response to Gbao's challenge, the SCSL Appeals Chamber expressly 'endorse[d] the view of the ICTY Appeals Chamber that sentences of like individuals in like cases should be comparable'.[59] However, the Chamber went on to emphasize that the relevance of previous sentences is often limited due to differences in, among other things, 'the number, type and gravity of the crimes committed, the personal circumstances of the convicted person and the presence of mitigating and aggravating circumstances'.[60] The Appeals Chamber recognized that 'a disparity between an impugned sentence and another sentence rendered in a like case can constitute an error if the former is out of reasonable proportion with the latter'.[61] However, it found that the cases cited by Gbao were 'readily and significantly distinguished from the present

---

[55] *Fofana and Kondewa* SCSL-04-14-A (Judgment, 28 May 2008) para 532.

[56] Ibid.

[57] The Chamber adopted the definition of retribution that had been provided by Lamer J who had held that '[r]etribution, in a criminal context, by contrast [to vengeance] represents an objective, reasoned and measured determination of an appropriate punishment which properly reflects the moral culpability of the offender'. See *Fofana and Kondewa* SCSL-04-14-T (Judgment on the Sentencing of Moinina Fofana and Allieu Kondewa, 9 October 2007) para 27.

[58] *Sesay, Kallon and Gbao* SCSL-04-15-A (Judgment, 26 October 2009) para 1296. The Appeals Chamber noted that 'Gbao contends that his analysis of the sentences imposed in these cases demonstrates that his own sentence is "so disproportionate as to amount to an unprecedented and irrational act of judicial retribution"'.

[59] Ibid., para 1317.

[60] Ibid.

[61] Ibid., para 1318. According to the Chamber, while a disparity would not in itself be erroneous, it may infer that the Trial Chamber 'failed to exercise its discretion properly in applying the law on sentencing'.

case' and were not, therefore, instructive.[62] The SCSL Appeals Chamber took a similar approach in the *Taylor* case.[63]

The Supreme Court Chamber of the ECCC has adopted similar reasoning. In their appeal of the Trial Chamber's sentencing judgment, the co-prosecutors argued that the Trial Chamber had 'fail[ed] to give reasons for the Trial Chamber's decision to impose a thirty-five year sentence on Kaing Guek Eav, and ha[d] therefore determined the sentence arbitrarily without relying upon any jurisprudence from comparable cases and the relevant law cited by the Co-Prosecutor at trial'.[64] While the Supreme Court Chamber acknowledged the need to 'take into account the circumstances of individual cases and accused persons, and the risk of relying on dissimilar cases', it recognized the sentences imposed by other international criminal tribunals in relation to 'similar or comparable facts and issues' as 'a source of guidance' in revising the sentence imposed on the accused.[65]

The case law referred to above demonstrates the willingness of judges to refer to external jurisprudence not only to identify and elaborate upon principles that guide the sentencing process and the factors that judges should take into account in the course of their sentencing decisions, but also to consider the final sentences that have been imposed by other judicial institutions, even if they cannot, in practice, be followed.

3.4 The Use of External Jurisprudence in International Sentencing Decisions

The references to external jurisprudence found in the decisions of the SCSL, the ECCC and the ICC can be separated into two categories: those that are used in the reasoning of the judges and those that have more of a background, or 'scene-setting' function. An example of the latter can be found in the decision of the Trial Chamber of the ICC in the *Lubanga* case. The Trial Chamber acknowledged that 'the only convictions by an international criminal tribunal for the recruitment or use of child soldiers are from the Special Court for Sierra Leone' and summarized the decisions that had been rendered.[66] While the sentencing decisions of the SCSL may have influenced the reasoning of the judges, the Trial Chamber did not connect the decisions of the SCSL to its own reasoning or the sentence that it imposed on the accused.

Other instances of judicial cross-referencing that can be placed in the 'scene-setting' category are found in the sections of sentencing decisions that set out the arguments of the parties to the proceedings. Although these instances of judicial cross-referencing are often not immediately connected with the reasoning of the Chamber, the cases cited by

---

[62] Ibid., para 1319.

[63] The Appeals Chamber found that '[t]he totality principle requires an individualized assessment of the particular circumstances of the case. As such, any attempt to compare an accused's case with others that have already been the subject of final determination is of limited assistance in challenging a sentence'. *Taylor* SCSL-03-01-A (Judgment, 26 September 2013) para 705.

[64] *Duch* 001/18-07-2007/ECCC/SC (Judgment, 3 February 2012) para 357.

[65] Ibid., para 374.

[66] *Lubanga* ICC-01/04-01/06-2901 (Decision on Sentence Pursuant to Article 76 of the Statute, 10 July 2012) paras 12–15.

the parties are frequently returned to and discussed in greater depth in the sections of the sentencing decision that contain the deliberations of the judges.

Where judges have referred to the case law of other courts and tribunals in the course of their own deliberations, the references have generally been used to support the reasoning of the relevant Chamber. Often judges have simply supported their reasoning with a footnote containing reference to relevant external jurisprudence.[67] On some occasions, however, judges have emphasized the fact that their reasoning is consistent with the case law of other courts and tribunals in the text of their decision. In the *RUF* case, for example, having concluded that the location of an attack could be considered as part of the gravity of the offence or as an aggravating factor, the Appeals Chamber stressed that its finding was 'consistent with the case law of the Trial Chambers at the Special Court and the ICTR'.[68]

Judges have shown a tendency to cite the decisions of other courts and tribunals even where they have been able to refer to previous case law from their own institutions. In the *Taylor* case, for example, the Appeals Chamber of the SCSL referred to previous decisions of the SCSL and the ICTY in holding that sentences imposed must '[reflect] the totality of the convicted person's culpable conduct'.[69]

In some instances, judges have supported their decisions by reference to the law and practice of a range of other courts and tribunals. An example of this practice can be found in the *Duch* case before the ECCC. In its decision, the Trial Chamber discussed the permissibility of imposing a single (global) sentence on an individual convicted of several offences.[70] The Chamber reviewed the practice of the Nuremberg and Tokyo Tribunals, the *ad hoc* Tribunals and the SCSL, the ICCSt and the practice of Cambodian courts before determining that 'it may impose a single sentence that reflects the totality of the criminal conduct where an accused is convicted of multiple offences'.[71]

The tendency of judges to support their reasoning with the case law of other courts and tribunals may be motivated by a number of different factors, including the desire of judges to give their reasoning greater weight or authority, or to promote a sense of consistency in the interpretation and application of international law. It may, however, simply indicate the factors that the judges have considered, or the points of reference that judges have used, in the course of their reasoning.

On occasion, judges have indicated the weight that they have given to external jurisprudence in the course of their decisions. In a number of decisions, the case law of other courts and tribunals have been referred to as a source of 'guidance', indicating that it has influenced the reasoning of the judges, albeit to an unspecified degree. It has already been highlighted that in the *Duch* case, the Supreme Court Chamber of the ECCC considered the sentencing practice of other international criminal tribunals to

---

[67] In the *Lubanga* case, for example, having recounted the principle of double counting, the Trial Chamber of the ICC included a footnote citing case law of the ICTY which articulated the principle to which the Chamber was referring. See *Lubanga*, ibid., para 35.

[68] *Sesay, Kallon and Gbao* SCSL-04-15-A (Judgment, 26 October 2009) para 1275.

[69] *Taylor* SCSL-03-01-A (Judgment, 26 September 2013) para 662.

[70] *Duch* 001/18-07-2007/ECCC/TC (Judgment, 26 July 2010) paras 587–590.

[71] Ibid., para. 590.

offer a source of guidance in determining the final sentence to be imposed on the accused.[72] The Trial Chamber of the ECCC also referred to the case law of the ICTR as a source of 'helpful guidance' in determining the impact of a prior violation of the rights of the accused on the sentence imposed by the Trial Chamber.[73]

In some decisions, judges have expressly 'adopted' aspects of the reasoning of other courts and tribunals. The judges of the SCSL have done so on a number of occasions. In the *Taylor* case, the SCSL Trial Chamber 'adopt[ed] the jurisprudence of the ICTY and ICTR that aiding and abetting as a mode of liability generally warrants a lesser sentence than that to be imposed for more direct forms of participation'.[74] In the *RUF* case, the Appeals Chamber of the SCSL 'adopt[ed] the view of the ICTY Appeals Chamber that the fact that the aggravating circumstances "must relate to the offender himself is not to be taken as a rule that such circumstance must specifically pertain to the offender's personal characteristics (…)"'.[75] Similarly, in the *Duch* case, the Supreme Court Chamber of the ECCC 'agree[d] with and adopt[ed]' the standard that had been articulated by the ICTY Appeals Chamber regarding the standard of review that should be followed when assessing the sentence imposed by the Trial Chamber.[76]

Another example of the adoption of the reasoning of the ICTY by the SCSL can be found in the *RUF* case. When addressing the permissibility of cumulative convictions, the Appeals Chamber acknowledged that '[t]he jurisprudence on cumulative convictions has been thoroughly addressed at the international tribunals' and that '[t]he test to determine the permissibility of cumulative convictions was set out in the *Čelebići* Appeals Judgment'.[77] This case, and those considered above, indicate that a direct transfer of reasoning is taking place between different international(ized) criminal justice institutions.

In the decisions included in this study, there are a small number of instances where judges used the term 'precedent' when referring to the case law of other courts and tribunals. One example is found in the *CDF* case before the SCSL, where the Trial Chamber '[applied] the precedent' of the English case of *Dudley and Stephens* in holding that necessity could not be sustained as a defence in the case under consideration.[78] In the *Taylor* case, the Trial Chamber of the SCSL also made reference to the 'precedents' of the *ad hoc* Tribunals when responding to the submission of the defence that 'a Trial Chamber may only consider aggravating circumstances that have been pleaded in the indictment'.[79] According to the Trial Chamber, the 'precedents' of the *ad hoc* Tribunals suggested that this was not the case.[80] While the term 'precedent'

---

72 *Duch* 001/18-07-2007/ECCC/SC (Judgment, 3 February 2012) para 374. See Section 3.3 above.

73 *Duch* 001/18-07-2007/ECCC/TC (Judgment, 26 July 2010) para 625.

74 *Taylor* SCSL-03-01-T (Sentencing Judgment, 30 May 2012) para 21.

75 *Sesay, Kallon and Gbao* SCSL-04-15-A (Judgment, 26 October 2009) para 1276.

76 *Duch* 001/18-07-2007/ECCC/SC (Judgment, 3 February 2012) para 354.

77 *Sesay, Kallon and Gbao* SCSL-04-15-A (Judgment, 26 October 2009) para 1190.

78 *Fofana and Kondewa* SCSL-04-14-T (Judgment on the Sentencing of Moinina Fofana and Allieu Kondewa, 9 October 2007) para 74.

79 *Taylor* SCSL-03-01-T (Sentencing Judgment, 30 May 2012) para 30.

80 Ibid.

may be associated with the doctrine of *stare decisis*,[81] or a sense of obligation to follow prior decisions, there is no indication that judges of the SCSL considered the case law that they were referring to was in any way binding on them.

While judges have generally followed, or reasoned in accordance with, the case law cited in their decisions, there are a few occasions where judges have distinguished or departed from the decisions of other courts or tribunals. In most instances where judges have departed from external case law, they have tended to distinguish the facts of their own cases from those considered by other institutions. The decision of the Trial Chamber of the SCSL in the *CDF* case provides a good example of this practice. When considering the significance of the circumstances prevailing at the time of the atrocities as a mitigating factor, the Trial Chamber distinguished its case from previous decisions of the *ad hoc* Tribunals.[82] It reasoned as follows:

> The Chamber has taken note of some significant and enlightening precedents on sentencing principles from sister International Criminal Tribunals of the ICTY and ICTR that have been cited by the Parties. However, even though the statutorily oriented sentencing principles in those cases remain relevant in guiding and assisting us to arrive at a decision in this case, it is pertinent to note that there is an important factual and contextual difference and distinction that the Chamber would like to draw between those cases as against this one which we consider relevant and pertinent in scaling the sentences that we are about to hand down on the Accused Persons in relation to the Counts for which we have found them guilty.[83]

The Chamber went on to highlight, as the 'main distinguishing factor', the fact that the CDF/Kamajors, with which the accused were associated, was fighting for a legitimate cause, namely 'to restore the democratically elected Government of President Kabbah which had been illegally ousted through a [*Coup d'Etat*]'.[84]

In the same case, the Trial Chamber noted that while it had the discretion to impose a global sentence in relation to the crimes committed, it had decided to impose separate sentences on the basis that this would 'better [reflect] the culpability of the Accused for each offence for which they were convicted, given that distinct crimes were committed by each Accused in discrete geographical areas'.[85] The Chamber distinguished cases from the ICTY 'in which global sentences were held to be appropriate where the crimes occurred in one geographical location or where the crimes all formed part of one transaction'.[86]

Another factor that has led judges to depart from the decisions of other courts and tribunals is variation in the nature and function of different judicial institutions. An example can be found in the Separate Opinion of Judges Agnieszka Klonowiecka-Milart and Chandra Nihal Jayasinghe to the judgment of the Supreme Court Chamber in the *Duch* case. In their separate opinion, the two judges disagreed with the reasoning of the majority regarding the consequences of unlawful pre-trial detention for the

---

81 See discussion in Miller (n 3) 488.

82 *Fofana and Kondewa* SCSL-04-14-T (Judgment on the Sentencing of Moinina Fofana and Allieu Kondewa, 9 October 2007) para 82.

83 Ibid.

84 Ibid., para 83.

85 Ibid., para 97.

86 Ibid., para 97 fn 139.

sentence imposed on the accused. The majority had adopted the approach of the *ad hoc* Tribunals, which had required the existence of a link between the sentencing court and the illegality of the detention in order for a remedy to be granted.[87] Judges Klonowiecka-Milart and Jayasinghe disagreed with the majority's 'mechanistic application of the ICTY and ICTR approach', given the 'obvious differences regarding the position held by the ECCC, as compared with the ad hoc criminal tribunals, [vis-à-vis] the national systems that occasioned the violations'.[88] They reasoned as follows:

> While the responsibility of an international court for domestic conduct may be limited to explicit 'concerted action', a different analysis is required of an 'internationalized' court, which is an emanation of the state that called it into being. We propose that it is a larger principle of shared responsibility that controls the question whether a hybrid court ought to be accountable for the acts of the domestic system. The extent of a tribunal's 'shared responsibility' must be determined as a matter of fairness, taking into account the entirety of the circumstances.[89]

The judges concluded that the requirement of a link between the sentencing court and the violation should not be applied in the context of the ECCC and that the accused was entitled to a remedy for the infringement of his right to liberty, including recognition of the violation and reduction of sentence.[90]

It has already been noted that judges have tended not to expressly dispute or disagree with the reasoning of other courts and tribunals, but to refer instead to differences in the facts being considered or the institutions rendering the decisions. One exception to this can be found in the case law of the SCSL. In the *Taylor* case, the Appeals Chamber rejected the holding of the Trial Chamber that aiding and abetting generally warrants a lesser sentence than other forms of participation.[91] In its decision, the Chamber considered the case law of the *ad hoc* Tribunals that had been cited by the defence and adopted by the Trial Chamber, principally the holding of the ICTY Appeals Chamber in the *Vasiljević* case. The Appeals Chamber expressly stated that it '[did] not consider that holding persuasive', finding that '[a] number of the national laws relied on in the *Vasiljević* Appeal Judgment do not support the principle that aiding and abetting *as a form of criminal participation* warrants a lesser punishment, but only establish that an accused's minor participation in the commission of the crime may be a mitigating circumstance'.[92] The Chamber also highlighted other case law to the same effect.

The decisions cited above demonstrate that judges have been willing to depart from the case law of other courts and tribunals where justified by the facts of the particular case or the nature of the institution issuing the decision, or on the basis that they disagree with the reasoning it contains. It is clear, therefore, that the practice of judicial cross-referencing will not always lead to consistency in the decisions of different

---

[87] *Duch* 001/18-07-2007/ECCC/SC (Judgment, 3 February 2012) Partially Dissenting Joint Opinion of Judges Agnieszka Klonowiecka-Milart and Chandra Nihal Jayasinghe para 4.
[88] Ibid.
[89] Ibid., para 7.
[90] Ibid., para 20.
[91] *Taylor* SCSL-03-01-A (Judgment, 26 September 2013) para 666.
[92] Ibid., para 667 (emphasis in the original).

judicial institutions. Nonetheless, the process of distinguishing cases and explaining departures from the decisions of other courts and tribunals can be considered beneficial for reasons that will be discussed further below.

3.5 Summary

Analysis of the sentencing decisions of the SCSL, the ECCC and the ICC reveals a significant level of judicial cross-referencing. While judges have tended to refer to other international(ized) criminal tribunals most frequently, they have turned to the decisions of other courts and tribunals on a number of occasions. In most instances, the decisions of other courts and tribunals have been used to support the reasoning of the Chambers. However, judges have demonstrated a willingness to depart from external jurisprudence in response to the facts of the case, the nature of their institution or a disagreement with the reasoning of another court or tribunal. The remainder of this chapter will consider the implications of the trends that have been observed in the case law.

4. THE IMPLICATIONS OF JUDICIAL CROSS-REFERENCING IN INTERNATIONAL SENTENCING DECISIONS

The tendency of judges to refer to and use the decisions of other courts and tribunals in the course of their sentencing decisions has a number of potential implications, many of which are highly desirable. The various implications of the practice will be examined in turn in the sections below.

4.1 The Development of a Coherent Sentencing Regime

The practice of judicial cross-referencing in sentencing decisions can be considered highly beneficial insofar as it helps to support the development of a coherent body of law regulating sentencing for international crimes. The importance of a coherent sentencing regime must be considered in light of concerns about the implications of the proliferation of international courts and tribunals for the coherence of international law more generally.[93] A number of international(ized) courts and tribunals have now been created with the authority to impose sentences on individuals found guilty of the commission of international crimes. In the absence of any formal hierarchy between these international institutions, or concrete obligation for judges in one tribunal to

[93] This issue was raised by Judge Guillaume, as President of the International Court of Justice, at the Sixth Committee of the General Assembly of the UN, 27 October 2000. The issue has since been considered by the International Law Commission. See International Law Commission (finalized by M. Koskenniemi), *Fragmentation of International Law: Difficulties Arising from the Diversification and Expansion of International Law* (A/CN.4/L.682, 13 April 2006). For academic debate, see symposium in (1999) 31 *New York University Journal of International Law and Politics*; M. Koskenniemi and P. Leino, 'Fragmentation of International Law? Postmodern Anxieties' (2002) 15 LJIL 553. G. Hafner, 'Pros and Cons Ensuing from Fragmentation in International Law' (2004) 25 *Michigan Journal of International Law* 849.

follow the decisions of another, there is a risk that inconsistencies may arise in the case law of different courts and tribunals.

As in any field of international law, coherence is important insofar as it promotes the certainty and clarity of the law and, in doing so, promotes fairness and the equal treatment of its subjects.[94] The relationship between the consistency of punishment, on the one hand, and fairness and equal treatment, has been recognized by the judges of international(ized) criminal courts and tribunals in the course of their sentencing decisions.[95] In the context of international sentencing, the coherence of the law has also been understood to support the perceived legitimacy of international criminal justice as well as its ability to deter future crimes by outlining a clear standard of punishment.[96]

By referring to the decisions of other courts and tribunals in the course of their decision-making, in the manner discussed above, judges have helped to support the development of a coherent body of law on sentencing issues, both in terms of the principles and factors taken into account in the determination of sentence and the length of the sentence that is ultimately imposed on the accused. The content analysis referred to above reveals a tendency for judges to refer not only to other criminal justice institutions, but also judicial institutions which are primarily concerned with the responsibility of States, such as regional human rights courts and the ICJ. This is significant insofar as it helps to promote coherence in the interpretation and application of norms beyond the specific field of international criminal law.

Of course, reference to the practice of other courts and tribunals may not necessarily result in the adoption of a consistent approach to similar issues. The sentencing decisions of the SCSL, the ECCC and the ICC have indicated that judges may depart from external jurisprudence for a number of different reasons, including disagreement with the reasoning of the judges as well as variations in the nature and function of different judicial institutions and the particular facts and circumstances of the cases that they have addressed. Differences in the legal frameworks of judicial institutions may also prevent the development of a coherent jurisprudence on certain issues. Even where judges depart from the decisions of other courts and tribunals, the practice of referring to external jurisprudence can be considered beneficial in that it allows judges to ensure that deviations from previous decisions are not arbitrary, but based on clear reasoning.

4.2 The Quality of Decisions that Judges Produce

Even if judicial cross-referencing does not result in a consistent body of jurisprudence on sentencing issues, the practice has value insofar as it introduces new ideas into the judicial decision-making process and, in doing so, contributes to the depth of reasoning, and thus the quality, of the decisions that judges produce. At the domestic

---

[94] D'Ascoli (n 1) 199. K. Ambos, *Treaties on International Criminal Law. Volume II: The Crimes and Sentencing* (Oxford University Press 2014) 269–70.

[95] *Delalic et al* IT-96-21-A (Judgment, 20 February 2001) para 756; 'One of the fundamental elements in any rational and fair system of criminal justice is consistency in punishment. This is an important reflection of the notion of equal justice', cited in *Duch* 001/18-07-2007/ECCC/SC (Judgment, 3 February 2012) para 374.

[96] D'Ascoli (n 1) 199.

level, comparative reasoning has been understood to have a valuable function by 'expand[ing] the interpreter's horizons',[97] and by encouraging judges to approach problems 'more creatively or with greater insight'.[98] While the proliferation of international courts and tribunals has increased the risk that different institutions may interpret and apply the law in an inconsistent manner, it has also opened up new opportunities for comparative reasoning at the international level.

The incorporation of new ideas into the judicial decision-making process may enhance the quality of judicial decisions in different ways, beyond promoting coherence in the interpretation and application of the law by a variety of judicial institutions. First, judicial cross-referencing may increase the quality of judicial decisions by leading judges to adopt new and qualitatively 'better' approaches to the legal issues they have been called upon to address; approaches which have been developed, and perhaps even tried and tested, elsewhere. Secondly, even if judges do not follow the decisions of other courts and tribunals, the process of referring to, considering and rejecting approaches taken by other institutions may increase the quality of sentencing decisions by prompting greater depth of reasoning and encouraging judges to give stronger justifications for the approaches that they adopt.[99] This process could be considered just as valuable, if not more so, than the development of a coherent jurisprudence, which may be the consequence of the interaction.

4.3 The Weight and Authority of Sentencing Decisions

Another beneficial implication of the practice of judicial cross-referencing is that it could serve to increase the weight or authority of sentencing decisions by showing that the reasoning that the decisions contain is in line with existing case law, including, perhaps, that of more established judicial institutions. The tendency of judges to cite the decisions of other courts and tribunals and emphasize the consistency of their reasoning with that of other courts and tribunals may be driven, at least in part, by the desire of judges to strengthen the decisions that they produce.

The potential for reference to external jurisprudence to increase the weight or authority of sentencing decisions is, however, dependent on the way in which external jurisprudence is used. Misinterpretation of external jurisprudence could call into question the reasoning of a particular judge or chamber. In the decisions surveyed above, there have been instances where misinterpretation of external jurisprudence by the Trial Chamber, or the parties to the proceedings has been highlighted on appeal.[100] Reference to external jurisprudence might also be called into question where it leads judges to depart from their own legal frameworks or transplant rules and principles into

---

[97] A. Barak, *Purposive Interpretation in Law* (Princeton University Press 2005) 170.

[98] A-M. Slaughter, *A New World Order* (Princeton University Press 2004) 77.

[99] See discussion in W.T. Worster, 'Competition and Comity in the Fragmentation of International Law' (2008–2009) 34 *Brooklyn Journal of International Law* 119.

[100] *Duch* 001/18-07-2007/ECCC/SC (Judgment, 3 February 2012) para 395. The Supreme Court Chamber found that the Trial Chamber had 'committed an error of law in granting a remedy based on "the case law of the ICTR Appeals Chamber" which, upon deeper analysis, was misinterpreted by the Trial Chamber'. See also *Sesay, Kallon and Gbao* SCSL-04-15-A (Judgment, 26 October 2009) paras 1248–1249.

a context to which they are not suited. Provided that judges take care to avoid these risks, reference to external jurisprudence could be a useful tool for judges to strengthen their own decisions. It may be particularly useful for judges working in relatively new institutions which have not yet produced a large body of jurisprudence on sentencing issues.

4.4 The Efficiency of the Criminal Justice Process

The practice of judicial cross-referencing could also have consequences for the efficiency of the criminal justice process. While the efficiency of judicial proceedings is a key consideration in many areas of law, it is particularly important in the field of international criminal law because of the disparity that currently exists between the number of complex serious international crimes cases requiring adjudication and the capacity of judicial institutions to address them.

In some instances, the practice of judicial cross-referencing may serve to increase the efficiency of the judicial decision-making process by offering judges a starting point in their deliberations, or even a ready-made solution to the issues that they are called upon to address. Adopting principles and rules that have been developed elsewhere may simply be quicker and easier for judges than starting from scratch. However, any efficiency gain that is associated with the practice of judicial cross-referencing is likely to be lost if judges exercise due caution in their use of external jurisprudence. In order to avoid misinterpretation, judges must consider the decisions of other courts and tribunals with great care. They must also consider whether or not a transplant of rules and principles from one institution to another is appropriate, bearing in mind the context in which they are to operate. Thorough review of the decisions of a wide range of judicial institutions may, in practice, be a time-consuming, rather than a time-saving, process. Where this is the case, the benefits of judicial cross-referencing must be weighed against its negative implications for the efficiency of the criminal justice process. Arguably, any detrimental impact that the review of external jurisprudence may have for the efficiency of the criminal justice process is outweighed by the benefits of the practice that have been outlined above.

4.5 Indeterminacy

The greatest concern raised by the practice of judicial cross-referencing is its potential to introduce a degree of indeterminacy into international sentencing decisions. Concerns about the indeterminacy of sentencing decisions may arise if judges fail to provide a clear methodology for their reference to external jurisprudence and if they are seen to refer to external case law in an *ad hoc* or arbitrary manner. This is particularly likely in circumstances where judges draw directly from external case law to solve a legal issue without reference to the sources of law that they are bound to apply.[101]

[101] A. Cassese, 'The Influence of European Court of Human Rights on International Criminal Tribunals – Some Methodological Remarks', in M. Bergsmo (ed), *Human Rights and Criminal Justice for the Downtrodden: Essays in Honour of Asbjørn Eide* (Martinus Nijhoff Publishers 2003) 21.

Writing in relation to the use of regional human rights jurisprudence at the *ad hoc* Tribunals, Former President of the ICTY, Antonio Cassese, has advised against such a 'wild' approach to external jurisprudence, which, he argued, lacks both legal rigour and fairness to the accused.[102] Concern that a 'wild' approach to external case law may lead to lack of foreseeability and fairness have also been raised in the specific field of international detention.[103]

The sentencing decisions included in this study suggest that judicial cross-referencing may indeed be a source of indeterminacy in international sentencing decisions. In the decisions referred to above, judges have not tended to explain their rationale for referring to external jurisprudence, or, in most instances, their legal basis for doing so. Even where judges have expressly drawn from the decisions of other courts and tribunals, they have not explained their approach by reference to their sources of applicable law. They have not, for example, argued that the decisions that they have drawn from reflect the current state of customary international law or identify a general principle of law to be applied in the present case. The result is a sense of arbitrariness and lack of clarity as to why external case law has been cited and how it has been used. Such practice is particularly problematic in situations where judges have drawn from the decisions of regional human rights courts or domestic legal systems that have no apparent link with the accused or the crimes that have been committed.

The risk that judicial cross-referencing will increase the indeterminacy of international sentencing decisions can easily be avoided if judges provide a clear methodology for their reference to external jurisprudence and ensure that any citations that are made are explained by relevant sources of applicable law and interpretation. If judges take this approach, they can ensure that the benefits of judicial cross-referencing are realized whilst ensuring that the practice does not have a negative impact on the certainty and fairness of the sentencing process.

4.6 Summary

In sum, the practice of judicial cross-referencing can be considered largely beneficial. Provided that judges exercise due caution in their reference to external jurisprudence, the practice could boost the weight and authority of the decisions that judges produce, increase their overall quality and contribute to the coherence of international law, both within and beyond the field of international criminal law.

5. CONCLUSION

Content analysis of the sentencing decisions of the SCSL, the ECCC and the ICC has confirmed that the practice of judicial cross-referencing, which has been observed in other areas of international law, is also seen in the sentencing decisions of international(ized) criminal justice institutions. In the decisions included in this study, judges have

---

[102] Ibid.

[103] D. Abels, *Prisoners of the International Community: The Legal Position of Persons Detained at International Criminal Tribunals* (TMC Asser Press 2012) 160.

referred to a range of other courts and tribunals in relation to a number of different legal issues. The sentencing decisions of the three institutions suggest that while judges have not considered themselves bound by the case law of other judicial institutions, they have, at times, drawn heavily from it.

The tendency of judges to refer to and use the decisions of other courts and tribunals in the course of their decision-making can be viewed in a positive light. While detailed review of external case law may have negative implications for the efficiency of the criminal justice process, this disadvantage is outweighed by a number of benefits associated with the practice: benefits for the weight and authority of sentencing decisions, the quality of reasoning that they contain and the coherence of international law. The greatest concern raised by the practice of judicial cross-referencing in the decisions included in this study is that the practice will introduce indeterminacy into the field of international sentencing. Judges can avoid this risk by providing a clear methodology for their reference to external jurisprudence and by situating each reference in their sources of applicable law and interpretation. If judges take this approach, they can realize the benefits of judicial cross-referencing while ensuring that the practice does not undermine the clarity and fairness of the sentencing process.

It is important to note that many of the benefits associated with judicial cross-referencing that have been referred to in this chapter are not confined to the early years of the operation of a criminal justice institution. While judicial cross-referencing may be particularly useful for young institutions which have not developed their own body of jurisprudence on sentencing issues, the benefits of judicial cross-referencing for the coherence of international law and the quality of the decisions that judges produce will continue throughout the lifespan of each individual court or tribunal. Consequently, it is hoped that the practice that has been observed in this study will continue in the practice of the ECCC and the ICC, which remain in operation.

The sentencing decisions included in this study reveal that while judges have referred to a number of other judicial institutions in the course of their sentencing decisions, the case law of the *ad hoc* Tribunals has been referred to more frequently than that of any other judicial institution. As the work of the two *ad hoc* Tribunals comes to a close, it is probable that the ICC will become a more prominent voice in the dialogue between judicial institutions on sentencing issues. The ICC is in a powerful position to influence the development of international criminal law in future years, both within and beyond the field of international sentencing, due to its permanence and wide-ranging jurisdiction. With this in mind, it is important that the judges of the ICC continue to build upon the body of jurisprudence that has already been established by the two *ad hoc* Tribunals and strive for clarity and consistency in their own decisions. In doing so, they could play an important role in encouraging the development of a coherent body of jurisprudence on sentencing issues and realising the benefits that this might entail.

PART IV

INTERNATIONAL TRANSFERS

International sentences of imprisonment are typically enforced by cooperating States.[1] To facilitate this cooperative endeavour, the international courts must transfer convicted persons to national prison systems. In so doing, these courts delegate responsibility for enforcing international sentences of imprisonment to national authorities. To understand how these transfer mechanisms have evolved, it is important to understand the system upon which they were based.

Harmen van der Wilt notes, in Chapter 8, that the mechanism established by the ICCSt amounts in law to the transfer of the execution of judgment, a 'device that is well-known in the realm of international cooperation in criminal matters'. He therefore analyses this system in light of inter-State practice. This chapter further explores the nature of the relationship between the ICC and States under this transfer mechanism and examines the extent to which changes had to be made to the framework established by the inter-State transfer system in the international context. In this regard it compares the nature of the relationship between the parties and some of the requirements for transfers, namely dual criminality and the nationality of sentenced persons. Moreover, it analyses the impact of the ICC's system on sentenced persons, looking at both the issue of consent and the level of responsibility the ICC retains for transferees.

Though the transfer mechanism used to facilitate the enforcement of sentences places responsibility for the day-to-day implementation of international custodial sanctions with national authorities, the international court retains responsibility for both the sentence it imposes and the prisoner's welfare until the sentence has been completed and the prisoner has been released. The *ad hoc* Tribunals have also used transfers in another operational context, however, whereby responsibility for the trial, sentencing and the enforcement of any sanction imposed are transferred to national authorities.

In Chapter 9, Olympia Bekou examines the Rule 11*bis* system. Introduced by the *ad hoc* Tribunals to facilitate their completion strategies by transferring lower-level cases to national courts for trial, this system allows for 'the direct implementation of national sentencing schemes for individuals indicted at the international level'. The scheme can be differentiated from the transfer system described above as it does not involve the implementation of international sentences of imprisonment. The Rule 11*bis* transfer mechanisms is however, as Bekou notes, significant for a discussion about the

---

[1] Some sentences may in practice be served in international remand facilities.

international penal system for several reasons. First, the process created a burden-sharing partnership in the international context dealing with penal matters. Secondly, the mechanism was used to transfer persons already in the custody of the ICTY or the ICTR in The Hague and Tanzania. Thirdly, issues related to penalties, sentencing and prison regimes were raised at both the referral hearings at the international tribunals and with monitors overseeing the trial post-transfer. Finally, Rule 11*bis* transfers provide insights into the realities of implementing sentences in the prisoner's country of origin and/or the location of the conflict during which the crimes were committed. As Bekou notes, transferees, if convicted, would serve 'their sentences in prisons to which they would most likely not have been transferred, had they been convicted by the Tribunals'. In her chapter, Bekou outlines the key components of the Rule 11*bis* mechanism, explores the issues outlined above and draws attention to some of the reforms undertaken by national systems to accommodate such transfers.

8. The transfer of the execution of sentences of the International Criminal Court in light of inter-State practice[1]

Harmen van der Wilt

1. INTRODUCTION

The ICC and other international criminal tribunals have at their disposal premises for the purpose of the pre-trial detention of accused. However, for the enforcement of their sentences these international tribunals are dependent on the assistance of States. Article 103 of the ICCSt stipulates that a sentence of imprisonment shall be served in a State designated by the ICC from a list of States which have indicated to the Court their willingness to accept sentenced persons. Legally, this amounts to a transfer of execution of a (foreign) judgment, a device that is well-known in the realm of international cooperation in criminal matters. In this horizontal context such transfers are usually governed by international treaties, the most famous of them being the Convention on the Transfer of Sentenced Persons.[2] This Convention leaves States parties ample leeway to arrange the transfer of sentences and prisoners, but attaches a number of minimum requirements, like the condition that the sentenced person, the sentencing State and the administering State all agree to the transfer, that the sentenced person is a national of the administering State and that the condition of 'double criminality' is satisfied. Such conditions serve to reconcile the interests of States with those of the sentenced person.

In the vertical framework of cooperation between the ICC and States, both the sovereign interests of States involved and the position of the individual are less prevailing and, indeed, are expected to succumb to the overarching aspirations of international criminal justice. The aim of this chapter is to explore whether the current regulations on the enforcement of ICC sentences reflect the different nature of the relationship between the ICC and States. Has the existing body of law that governs inter-State transfers by and large served as a useful framework that only required small adaptations? Or has the hierarchical relationship between the ICC and States more radically pervaded the entire legal perspective? And how has this shift affected the position of the sentenced person?

[1] This chapter partially draws from and is an extension of my contribution (in Dutch) to the *Liber Amicorum* for G. de Jonge: 'Zware jongens in gevangenschap. De tenuitvoerlegging van de strafvonnissen van het Internationale Strafhof', in J. Claessen and D. de Vocht, *Humaan strafrecht* (Wolf Legal Publishers 2012) 391–407.

[2] Strasbourg, 21 March 1983, European Treaties Series No 112.

The chapter is structured as follows. Section 2 addresses the mutual rights and obligations of the sentencing and administering entities in a comparative perspective, highlighting the differences and commonalities between horizontal and vertical cooperation. Sections 3 and 4 investigate whether two strongholds of the transfer of enforcement of foreign judgments – double criminality and the nationality requirement, respectively – still apply in the vertical context. In Sections 5 and 6 the emphasis shifts to the position of the sentenced person. Section 5 explores the relevance of the consent of the sentenced person as a condition for the transfer of the execution of an ICC judgment to a particular State. And Section 6 inquires whether the ICC bears responsibility for the execution of its sentences by a State. The final topic requires some elucidation. Within the realm of inter-State relations, the cooperating States share mutual responsibility for the parts performed by each of them. While the administering State may take the fairness of the criminal trial in the sentencing State into consideration in deciding whether or not to take over the enforcement of the judgment, the sentencing State may be concerned about the way its sentence is executed. Although a refusal of the execution of a judgment rendered by the ICC on the basis of the verdict falling short of accepted fair trial standards cannot be excluded *a priori*, the chance that this will happen is merely theoretical, in view of the high procedural standards of the ICCSt. Conversely, it is more realistic that the ICC may have qualms about the quality of detention in the State of enforcement. The pertinent question is whether the Court has any powers of control over and whether it bears responsibility for the enforcement of its sanctions. The chapter concludes with some reflections on the nature of transfer of enforcement of sentences against the backdrop of the general regime of international cooperation between States and the ICC.

2. VERTICAL AND HORIZONTAL COOPERATION IN THE REALM OF TRANSFER OF ENFORCEMENT OF SENTENCES

Part 9 of the ICCSt on international cooperation and judicial assistance starts from the premise that States parties are under an obligation to cooperate with the ICC.[3] The regulation on the enforcement of prison sentences obviously departs from this principle. Not only are States parties at liberty to express in general terms their willingness to enforce the Court's sentences (Art. 102, s. 1(a)), they also have the right to refuse a particular request, in spite of their previously articulated commitment.[4] Without doubt, this more flexible attitude has been inspired by the consideration that the enforcement of prison sentences is a costly affair which may also involve political repercussions for the States.[5] Against this background, it seems wise to seek the voluntary cooperation of States. Be that as it may, the regulation on the transfer of

[3] Art. 86 ICCSt provides 'that State Parties *shall* (…) cooperate fully with the Court in its investigation and prosecution of crimes within the jurisdiction of the Court' [emphasis added].

[4] That follows *a contrario* from Art. 103(1)(c) which stipulates that a State designated in a particular case shall promptly inform the Court whether it accepts the Court's designation.

[5] On this topic, see G.A.M. Strijards, 'Art. 103', in O. Triffterer (ed), *Commentary on the Rome Statute of the International Criminal Court* (Nomos 2008) 1648–50.

sentences in the ICCSt resembles the inter-State regime, rather than reflecting the hierarchical relationship between international criminal tribunals and States.[6] After all, the Convention on the Transfer of Sentenced Persons, mentioned above, is equally predicated on the sovereign decisions and freedom of States to cooperate or not. On closer scrutiny, however, this respect for State sovereignty is slightly deceptive, because after the State has consented, the Court's will prevails. In this respect the ICCSt closely follows the practice and approach of the *ad hoc* Tribunals. Abels observes that 'in line with the other tribunals' experiences, the ICC has sought to strike a balance between the interests of the States of enforcement and the notion of primacy'.[7] And Strijards distinguishes sharply between the two chronological stages (before and after consent): 'The basic conclusion could be that, with a view to the enforcement, the Court enjoys before the statal acceptance of the sentenced person no primacy at all, and after acceptance a moderate or diffuse primacy.'[8]

The primacy of the Court comes to the fore in a number of ways. First, it is revealed in Article 105, Section 1 of the Statute, prescribing that the sentence of imprisonment shall be binding on the States parties, which shall in no case modify it. It implies that the State of enforcement is not allowed to tamper with the nature and length of the sentence by, for instance, granting early release to the convict. The ICTY has deduced the prohibition from the special legal relationship between the Tribunal and the State which acts as its agent:

> Accordingly, a State which has indicated its willingness and has been designated will execute the sentence on behalf of the International tribunal in application of international criminal law and not domestic law. Therefore, that State may not in any way, including by legislative amendment, alter the nature of the penalty so as to affect its truly international character.[9]

Secondly, the enforcement of a sentence of imprisonment shall, according to Article 106, Section 1 of the Statute, be subject to the supervision of the Court.[10] The scope of this provision is not entirely clear: does the supervision only pertain to the enforcement of the sentence or does it also cover the conditions of detention? The ICTY has clearly opted for the latter, broader interpretation: 'The International Tribunal bases its right to

[6] On the cooperation regime of the ICC as an intermediate between inter-State cooperation and cooperation between States and the *ad hoc* International Criminal Tribunals, see the excellent essay by B. Swart and G. Sluiter, 'The International Criminal Court and International Criminal Co-operation', in H.A.M. von Hebel, J.G. Lammers and J. Schukking (eds), *Reflections on the International Criminal Court; Essays in Honour of Adriaan Bos* (TMC Asser Press 1999) 91–127.

[7] D. Abels, *Prisoners of the International Community. The Legal Protection of Persons Detained at International Criminal Tribunals* (TMC Asser Press 2012) 462.

[8] Strijards (n 5) 1651.

[9] *Erdemović* IT-96-22-T (Sentencing Judgment, 29 November 1996) para 71.

[10] The supervision connotes a hierarchical relationship, compare D. Tolbert, 'The International Tribunal for the former Yugoslavia and the Enforcement of Sentences' (1998) 11 *Leiden Journal of International Law* 659: '"Supervision" generally implies a relationship in which one party has authority over the other or at least has the right to decisively intervene.'

supervise how persons it has convicted are treated on Article 27 of the Statute and Rule 104 of the Rules.'[11]

This interpretation appears to be correct in view of the fact that both Article 28 of the ICTYSt and Rule 104 of the ICTY RPE mention the 'supervision of imprisonment'. The Tribunal does not only refer to relevant treaty provisions concerning the protection of the rights of convicts, but also to the entire body of 'soft law', like the UNSMR and the Body of Principles for the Protection of All Persons under Any Form or Imprisonment. According to the Tribunal, these principles solidly sustain the legal position of convicts, offering a basic level that should in no circumstances be undercut.[12]

The regulation in the ICCSt is more ambiguous. Whereas Article 106, Section 1 only speaks of the enforcement of a sentence being subject to the supervision of the Court, Rule 211, Section 1(a) of the ICC RPE explicitly mentions the conditions of imprisonment that the sentenced person is allowed to discuss in the communications with the Court exercising its supervision task. Abels has correctly observed that a narrow interpretation of Article 106 would be hard to reconcile with the second part of the provision which stipulates that the enforcement must be consistent with widely accepted international treaty standards governing the treatment of prisoners.[13] Remarkably, Article 106, unlike previous drafts of the provision, does not explicitly refer to the UNSMR. Schabas argues that this is no big deal. Nothing would prevent the Court from following the practice of the monitoring bodies of international treaties on the protection of human rights by interpreting the provisions of the Statute in light of these Minimum Rules.[14]

The primacy of the Court vis-à-vis States is mitigated by Article 106, Section 2 of the Statute which provides that the conditions of imprisonment shall be governed by the law of the State of enforcement. A greater control by the Court over the conditions of imprisonment was not feasible, as it would imply a major incursion on State sovereignty.[15] Interestingly, the article continues by holding that such conditions shall in no case be more or less favourable than those available to prisoners convicted of similar offences in the State of enforcement. The provision cuts both ways. On the one hand, it is in line with the principle of complementarity which imposes primary responsibility for the prosecution of international crimes on States. It would be rather arbitrary and unfair if domestically and internationally tried perpetrators were to face different conditions of detention. On the other hand, the provision may restrict the

---

[11] *Erdemović* IT-96-22-T (Sentencing Judgment, 29 November 1996) para 74.

[12] *Erdemović* IT-96-22-T (Sentencing Judgment, 29 November 1996) para 74:

> The significance of these principles resides in the fact that a person who has been convicted of a criminal act is not automatically stripped of all his rights. The Basic Principles for the Treatment of Prisoners state that except for those limitations that are demonstrably necessitated by the fact of incarceration, all prisoners retain the human rights and fundamental freedoms set out in the Universal Declaration of Human Rights.

[13] Abels (n 7) 463.

[14] W. Schabas, *The International Criminal Court. A Commentary on the Rome Statute* (Oxford University Press 2010) 1082.

[15] Ibid.

sentencing and detention policy of the States, by pressuring them to improve the general penitentiary climate.[16]

How are we to judge the nature of the relationship between the Court and States in the realm of enforcement of sentences, when comparing it with the inter-State context of cooperation? There is no easy answer to that question. At first blush, the Court appears to exercise a firm grip on the enforcement of its sentences, through its powers of supervision (Art. 106, s. 1) and by way of the binding character of its sentences (Art. 105, s. 1). It would appear that the State has no other option than to accept the enforcement of the sentence 'lock, stock and barrel' and would be precluded from converting the sentence in any way.[17] The impression of ICC-dominance is countered, however, by Article 106, Section 2 which declares the law of the State of enforcement applicable to the conditions of imprisonment. This provision which pertains to the circumstances of detention does not affect the prohibition of tampering with the length of the sentence, as pronounced by the ICC, but even that interdiction may be less rigid than meets the eye. The condition that the situation of the sentenced person may not be aggravated when compared to prisoners convicted of similar offences in the State of enforcement may backfire on the ICC when that State harbours a more favourable early release regime than the ICC.[18] And while Article 110, Section 2 grants the monopoly to decide on any reduction of sentence to the Court, it is not clear whether this rule would not yield to an acceptance of a State, predicated on the very condition that it would be allowed to apply its favourable early release rules.[19] In this respect, it is telling that Article 105 subjects the stern admonition that the sentence of imprisonment shall be binding to the proviso that a State may specify conditions in accordance with Article 103.[20]

To sum up, the entire regulation of enforcement of prison sentences in Part 10 of the ICCSt is the outcome of a balancing act which typifies the relationship between the ICC and States.[21] In view of the recent sentencing judgments in *Lubanga* and *Katanga*, we will soon learn how the contest will work out in practice. Problems loom, however,

---

16 See also R.S. Clark, 'Art. 106', in O. Triffterer (ed), *Commentary on the Rome Statute of the International Criminal Court* (Nomos 2008) 1665: 'We suspect that in some cases, the levelling out that takes place will encourage an improvement of national standards as enforcement States are driven to give more attention to international standards.'

17 Both procedures are presented in the Convention on the Transfer of Sentenced Persons as possible alternatives, in Arts 10 and 11 respectively.

18 According to Art. 110 ICCSt, the Court shall review the sentence when the person has served two-thirds of the sentence, or 25 years in the case of life imprisonment, in order to determine whether it should be reduced. The provision adds that such a review shall not be conducted before that time.

19 Art. 103(1)(b) stipulates that a State may, at the time of declaring its willingness to accept sentenced persons, attach conditions to its acceptance as agreed by the Court and in accordance with this Part.

20 It should be noted, however, that Rule 200(5) ICC RPE stipulates that the bilateral agreements must be consistent with the Statute.

21 Commenting on the general cooperation regime, Swart and Sluiter (n 6) 127 observe that '(...) the need for consensus-building inevitably influenced the outcome of the negotiations. It may well have been a political necessity, therefore to accept significant differences between the system of co-operation provided for in the Statute and that of the ad hoc Tribunals'.

because some agreements do not acknowledge the Court's monopoly of decision on early release. The agreement with Denmark has copied the system that was applied in its relations with the *ad hoc* Tribunals.[22] Article 5 of this Agreement provides that Denmark will notify the Court if the sentenced person becomes eligible for early release or pardon under domestic law and it adds that, should Denmark disagree with the Court's view on the appropriateness of early release or pardon, the Court may transfer the prisoner to another State. The agreement suggests that the State of enforcement has a greater say in the release decision. Such provisions are ill-advised, if not simply flawed, because they thwart the ICC statutory system.[23]

3. DUAL CRIMINALITY

Article 3, Section 1(e) of the Convention on the Transfer of Sentenced Persons provides that a person may only be transferred for the purpose of the execution of a sentence in another State if the acts or omissions on account of which the sentence has been imposed constitute a criminal offence according to the law of the administering State or would constitute a criminal offence if committed on its territory. This provision embodies the famous dual criminality rule that imbues international cooperation in criminal matters. Several rationales sustain this rule.[24] As dual criminality guarantees symmetry in mutual performances, it connotes the idea of sovereign equality and reciprocity. Moreover, the rule safeguards States from the embarrassing situation that they would be bound to render assistance to criminal procedures in respect of conduct they do not consider criminal themselves.[25] Finally, there is a link with the *nulla poena sine lege* principle that precludes punishment without law. As extradition and the exchange of evidence do not constitute punishment, but merely assistance in criminal procedures of another State, the connection with the *nulla poena* principle is not immediately obvious. In cases of transfer of execution of sentences the link is considerably stronger, because the administering State is expected to take over a substantial part of the criminal process. States would be quite reluctant, if not precluded by their own constitutions, to imprison persons for conduct that would not constitute a criminal offence under their legal systems. It demonstrates that the interpretation and application of legal principles like the rule of dual criminality may depend on the

---

[22] Agreement between the Kingdom of Denmark and the ICC on the Enforcement of Sentences of the ICC (ICC-PRES/09-03-11, 28 May 2012).

[23] For a detailed analysis of the agreement with Denmark, see R. Mulgrew, *Towards the Development of the International Penal System* (Cambridge University Press 2013) 78–9.

[24] E. van Sliedregt, 'The Dual Criminality Requirement', in N. Keijzer and E. van Sliedregt (eds), *The European Arrest Warrant in Practice* (TMC Asser Press 2009) 52–4.

[25] As phrased by the Dutch Supreme Court in the *Pauksch* case (SC, 16 January 1973, *Netherlands Yearbook of International Law* 1974 309–10):

> that the requirement of double criminality laid down in Art. 2 of the Convention (on Extradition) is intended to avoid the imposition on the requested State of the obligation to cooperate in the maintenance of standards that are contrary to its own legal conceptions or to cooperate in cases where the requested State would not consider justified the imposition of a penal sanction.

specific form of international cooperation at hand.[26] The strong involvement of the administering State also explains why dual criminality must be assessed *in concreto* and not (only) *in abstracto*. Unlike extradition, in which the court can suffice to inquire whether the fact pattern corresponds to criminal legal provisions, in case of transfer of enforcement of foreign sentences the court of the administering State is obliged to discern whether the sentenced person could indeed have been convicted. In the latter case, the availability of justifications and excuses and the applicability of statutes of limitations are to be taken into account.[27]

Meanwhile it has become clear that the rule of dual criminality is not sacrosanct in international cooperation in criminal matters. The Framework Decision on the European Arrest Warrant identifies 32 'categories of crimes' in respect of which the executing State is required to surrender the requested person without being allowed to verify double criminality.[28] The Framework Decision on enforcement of foreign sentences has followed suit by literally copying the list of the Framework Decision on the European Arrest Warrant. This implies that a Member State would be obliged to recognize the judgment and enforce the sentence, even if the underlying conduct would not constitute a criminal offence under its national law.[29] From the perspective of consistency that makes sense. Otherwise the surrender of nationals would have to be refused in case of lack of dual criminality, because the State would not be able to enforce the foreign sentence after their return to their home country where they would be entitled to serve their sentence. Dual criminality would thus enter 'by the back door'.[30] In view of the *nulla poena* principle, however, it is problematic that someone can be detained for conduct which does not constitute an offence in the State that deprives him of his liberty.

In the vertical context, dual criminality by no means has a similar status as in the realm of inter-State relations. Neither Part 9 of the ICCSt – on general cooperation – nor Part 10 – on enforcement of sentences – mentions lack of dual criminality as a

---

[26] Compare the classic essay of Hulsman who distinguishes between primary and secondary assistance in criminal matters (*entraide judiciaire primaire et entraide judiciaire secondaire*), L.H.C. Hulsman, 'Transmission des poursuites pénales à l'état de séjour et exécution des decisions pénales étrangères', in *Le Droit Pénal International; Recueil d'Études en Hommage a Jacob Maarten van Bemmelen* (Brill 1965) 113–14.

[27] See the Council of Europe's *Explanatory Report on the Convention on the Transfer of Sentenced Persons*, Strasbourg 1983, 11: 'The condition (of dual criminality) is fulfilled if the act which gave rise to the judgment in the sentencing State would have been punishable if committed in the administering State *and if the person who performed the act could, under the law of the administering State, have had a sanction imposed on him*' [emphasis added].

[28] Provided that the crime is punishable in the issuing State by a custodial sentence or a detention order for a maximum period of at least three years. Council Framework Decision of 13 June 2002 on the European Arrest Warrant and the surrender procedures between Member States, OJ EC, L 190/1, Art. 2, s. 2.

[29] Council Framework Decision on the application of the principle of mutual recognition to judgments in criminal matters imposing custodial sentences or measures involving deprivation of liberty for the purpose of their enforcement in the European Union, Brussels 21 April 2008, 5602/08, COPEN 12, Art. 7 s. 1.

[30] See also Van Sliedregt (n 24) 63.

proper ground for refusal of cooperation.[31] The absence of dual criminality in the Rome Statute need not surprise us. After all, allowing a State to invoke a lack of dual criminality would defeat the very purpose of the Statute. The principle of complementarity requires that national States should have priority in prosecuting and trying suspects of international crimes. Failure to incorporate the elements of international crimes into domestic legislation would render those States 'unable' to genuinely carry out investigations and prosecutions. But if they would subsequently be allowed to present the lack of domestic implementation as a reason not to cooperate, they would be able to frustrate the Court and impede it from performing its default function. In the case of the transfer of execution of sentences, the fact that a State has not implemented the corresponding crimes in its legislation will prevent that State from enforcing the sentence. As the enforcement of ICC sentences is predicated on the voluntariness of the State, a State can simply inform the Court that it will decline to take over the execution of the sentence, in conformity with Article 103 ICCSt.[32]

4. TRANSFER OF ENFORCEMENT AND NATIONALITY OF THE SENTENCED PERSON

One of the major goals of transfer of enforcement of sentences is the social rehabilitation of the offender, the assumption being that he or she will have a future in his/her home country and that he/she will more easily reintegrate into society if the prison sentence is served in the home State. Legal instruments explicitly refer to this objective.[33] Against this backdrop, it makes sense that the 1983 Convention stipulates that a sentenced person can only be transferred if he/she is a national of the administering State (Art. 3, s. 1(a)). Paragraph 4 of the same provision adds that any State may by way of declaration define the term 'national' for the purpose of the Convention. The Explanatory Report elucidates that the provision enables Contracting States to extend the application of the Convention to persons other than nationals within the strict meaning of national legislation, encompassing, for instance, stateless

[31] Compare, in respect of surrender, B. Swart, 'Chapter 41: Arrest and Surrender', in A. Cassese, P. Gaeta and J.R.W.D. Jones (eds), *The Rome Statute of the International Criminal Court: A Commentary, Volume II* (Oxford University Press 2002) 1681: 'Where surrender of persons to the Court (ICC) is concerned, a State Party is not entitled to refuse cooperation on the grounds that the conduct does not constitute a criminal offence according to domestic law.'

[32] In their negotiations with international criminal tribunals, States have revealed particular preferences and choices. Finland, for example, is only prepared to execute sentences of the SCSL that have been imposed in respect of international crimes, *id est* not for crimes under Sierra Leonean law that belong to the jurisdiction of the Court (Art. 5 SCSLSt). Information derived from Mulgrew (n 23) 38.

[33] Explanatory Report on the Convention on the Transfer of Sentenced Persons (n 27) para 9 and Framework Decision (n 29) Art. 3(1): 'The purpose of this Framework Decision is to establish the rules under which a Member State, with a view to facilitating the social rehabilitation of the sentenced person, is to recognize a judgment and enforce the sentence.'

persons or citizens of other States who have established roots in the country through permanent residence.[34]

The concept of 'residency' has acquired special relevance in light of the freedom of movement within the European Union, the idea of 'European citizenship' and the repercussions on international cooperation in criminal matters. After all, the Framework Decision on the European Arrest Warrant has conferred certain rights on people being resident of, or even staying in a Member State, equalizing them with nationals. Article 5, Section 3 of the Framework Decision provides that the execution of a European Arrest Warrant in respect of a national or resident of the executing Member State may be subject to the condition that the person is returned to the executing State in order to serve there the custodial sentence or detention order passed against him in the issuing Member State. In that situation, the legal instruments of surrender and transfer of enforcement are applied consecutively. Article 4, Section 6 of the Framework Decision proposes transfer of enforcement as an alternative to surrender: a Member State is entitled to refuse the execution of a European Arrest Warrant for the purpose of the execution of a sentence if the requested person is staying in, or is a resident or national of the executing State and that State undertakes to execute the sentence or detention order itself.

In some landmark decisions, the European Court of Justice has shed light on the content of 'staying in' and 'residency'. In *Kozlowski*, the ECJ held that the interpretation of the terms 'staying' and 'resident' could not be left to the assessment of each Member State, but rather should be given an autonomous and uniform interpretation throughout the Union, 'having regard to the context of the provision and the objective pursued by the legislation in question'.[35] The Court continued by emphasizing that the ground for optional refusal of Article 4(6) of the Framework Decision in particular served the purpose of increasing the requested person's chances of reintegrating into society when the sentence expires (para 45). Next, the Court defined the terms 'resident' and 'staying' – in the light of that objective – respectively, as 'the situations in which the person (…) has either established his actual place of residence in the executing Member State or has acquired, following a stable period of presence in that State, certain connections with that State which are of a similar degree to those resulting from residence' (para 46). The Court explained that:

> in order to determine whether there are connections between the requested person and the executing State (…) it is necessary to make an overall assessment of various objective factors characterizing the situation of that person, which include, in particular, the length, nature and conditions of his presence and the family and economic connections which he has with the executing Member State.[36]

In the *Wolzenburg* case, the right of a resident to be considered on the same par as nationals for the purpose of the enforcement of foreign sentences was explicitly put into the key of the prohibition of discrimination on account of nationality (Art. 18 EC Treaty; Art. 12 EC Treaty (old)) and the freedom of movement and residence within the

---

34 Explanatory Report (n 27) para 20.
35 *Kozlowski* C-66/08 (European Court of Justice, 17 July 2008) paras 41–42.
36 Ibid., para 48.

European Union (Art. 21 EC Treaty; Art. 18 EC Treaty (old)).[37] First, the Court acknowledged that a national of a Member State who was lawfully resident in another Member State could rely on Article 12 (old) EC Treaty against national legislation which lays down the conditions under which the competent judicial authority can refuse to execute a European Arrest Warrant issued with a view to the enforcement of a custodial sentence (para 47). Next, the Court held that Article 12 did not preclude Member States from distinguishing between nationals and residents, by requiring the latter to demonstrate that they had lawfully resided for a continuous period of five years in that Member State of execution (para 54). However, the Court cautioned that States should not, in addition to a condition as to the duration of residence, make application of the ground for optional non-execution of a European Arrest Warrant subject to supplementary administrative requirements, such as possession of a residence permit of indefinite duration.[38]

The case law of the ECJ demonstrates that the Court attaches major importance to the question whether the 'resident' has developed genuine bonds with the State where he prefers to serve his prison sentence. Apparently, the Court takes the objective of social rehabilitation seriously.

In the context of vertical cooperation between the ICC and States parties nationality is far less preponderant. Article 103, Section 3(d) mentions 'nationality of the sentenced person' only as one of the parameters to be taken into account by the Court in designating a State of enforcement. Schabas notes that some States parties have indicated their preparedness to enforce sentences of the ICC only in respect of nationals or residents.[39] Moreover, he mentions a proposal to allow States which had indicated their willingness to enforce sentences to make surrender of its national to the Court dependent on the condition that the person would have the right to return to that State in order to serve any sentence imposed.[40] Obviously, the proposal reminds us of the construction in the Framework Decision on the European Arrest Warrant, as expounded above. Nonetheless, it is not difficult to understand why this proposal was not accepted. The fact that the ICC requests the surrender of a State's national in the first place implies that the Court has found its ability or willingness to investigate and prosecute international crimes wanting. There may be good reasons to suspect that such deficiencies rebound on the State's capacity to adequately enforce prison sentences. It demonstrates that ideas and practices which are tested and work in inter-State relations cannot be simply transplanted to the vertical context. But it equally makes clear that the rights and interests of the sentenced person may be at peril. This takes us to the topic of the next paragraph.

---

[37] *Wolzenburg* C-123/08 (European Court of Justice, 6 October 2009).

[38] Ibid., para 53.

[39] Schabas (n 14) 1071. Nationals: Andorra, Liechtenstein, Lithuania, Slovakia, Switzerland. Residents: Liechtenstein, Slovakia, Switzerland. However, these countries have no agreements with the ICC. Sweden had attempted to include a nationality or residence clause in its agreement with the ICTY, but removed it after the ICTY had ended negotiations with Switzerland that had also insisted on incorporating this condition. See Mulgrew (n 23) 38.

[40] Schabas (n 14) 1071.

5. THE CONSENT OF THE SENTENCED PERSON

In view of the fact that one of the major goals of transfer of execution of foreign judgments is the rehabilitation of the offender, it makes sense to make any transfer dependent on his or her personal consent.[41] Hence, Article 3, Section 1(d) of the 1983 Convention requires the consent of the sentenced person or of his/her legal representative. The 2008 Framework Decision even reinforces the position of the sentenced person by granting him the formal right to request the competent authorities of the issuing State to initiate a procedure, conducive to the transfer of enforcement of the sentence. Such requests shall however not create an obligation for the issuing State to forward the judgment and the certificate to another State.[42]

In the ICCSt, the interests of the sentenced person are far less pronounced. Article 103, Section 3 mentions 'the views of the sentenced person' as one of the factors to be taken into account by the Court in designating an appropriate State of enforcement. Rule 203 of the ICC RPE elaborates on the procedure. The Presidency informs the sentenced person that it is addressing the designation of a State of enforcement and invites him to express his views, in writing or orally. The sentenced person has the right to be assisted by an interpreter, but apparently not by counsel.[43] The views of the sentenced person on the preferable State of enforcement are only one of the factors controlling the designation of the State; it is thus obvious that such designation does not require his consent. Such a requirement would indeed be far-fetched and self-defeating, as the situation is rather different from the inter-State context. After all, in that case any refusal of consent would imply that the sentenced person has to serve his sentence in the administering State. Such a natural alternative is not available in the vertical context, which means that the sentenced person might have the power to thwart any enforcement of his sentence. For several reasons, it would be practically impossible for sentenced persons to insist that they can serve their ICC imposed sentence in their home country. First of all, only eight States have concluded agreements with the ICC, indicating their willingness to enforce the Court's sentences.[44] Moreover, enforcement of sentences in turbulent States, still recovering from armed conflict and rife with political tensions may simply not be a realistic option. This has been acknowledged by the ICTY in *Erdemović*:

> The Trial Chamber shares the view of the Secretary-General that the sentences should be served outside the territory of the former Yugoslavia (S/25704, para 121). It believes that because of the situation prevailing in the region, it would not be possible to ensure the security of the convicted person or the full respect of a decision of the International Tribunal in that regard.[45]

---

[41] The Explanatory Report to the 1983 Convention (n 27) explicitly makes the connection in para 23: '[The condition of consent] is rooted in the convention's primary purpose to facilitate the rehabilitation of offenders: transferring a prisoner without his consent would be counter-productive in terms of rehabilitation.'

[42] 2008 Framework Decision (n 28) Art. 4 s. 5.

[43] Schabas (n 14) 1072.

[44] To wit, Austria, Belgium, Colombia, Denmark, Finland, Mali, Serbia and the UK.

[45] *Erdemović* IT-96-22-T (Sentencing Judgment, 29 November 1996) para 70.

Nonetheless, the Chamber expressed understanding of and concern for the predicament of the sentenced person in the very same Judgment:

> In addition, because persons found guilty will be obliged to serve their sentences in institutions which are often far from their places of origin, the Trial Chamber takes note of the inevitable isolation into which they will have been placed. Moreover, cultural and linguistic differences will distinguish them from the other detainees. The situation is all the more true in cases of convicted persons who have co-operated with the Prosecutor because it is not unreasonable to assume that they will also be excluded from the very group to which they should normally belong.[46]

Such considerations perfectly reflect the quandaries and dilemmas involved in the designation of the 'most appropriate' State. Obviously, the sentenced person has no right of choice, a privilege that is not recognized in the horizontal context either, at least not as a human right.[47] However, the European Court of Human Rights has acknowledged that in exceptional cases the right to family life may be at stake, in particular when alternative options are available:

> [T]he detention of a person at a distance from his family which renders any visit very difficult, if not impossible, may in exceptional circumstances constitute an interference with his family life, the possibility for members of the family to visit a prisoner being an essential factor for the maintenance of family life.[48]

It would be reasonable to assume that the State must make an effort to allow the sentenced person to serve his sentence in the surroundings of his family. Such an obligation might even require that the State would be under a duty to enable a transfer of the enforcement of the sentence to the home country, whenever that option is available. Although the ICC is formally not bound by the ECHR, that principle would be equally valid for the Court. The European Commissioner for Human Rights has confirmed this by, in respect of detained persons of the Court, stressing the connection between social rehabilitation as a penal goal and the obligation to enable the sentenced person to keep in touch with family and friends.[49] In view of these principles and case law, the Court should seriously take the interests of the sentenced person into account. Such concern should not only be a guide line in the choice of the most appropriate State of enforcement, but the Court must also during the detention make efforts to further contacts between the sentenced person and his family. Moreover, both the choice of the State of enforcement and the penitentiary regime should be informed by

---

[46] Ibid., para 75.

[47] This has been confirmed by the ECtHR, *Plepi et al v Albania and Greece* App nos 11546/05, 33285/05 and 33285/05 (ECtHR, 4 May 2010) (Decision on Admissibility) para 2: 'the Convention does not grant prisoners the right to choose the place of detention and the separation and distance from the prisoner's family are inevitable consequences of his detention'.

[48] *Selmani v Switzerland* App no 70258/01 (ECtHR, 28 June 2001) (decision on admissibility) para 1.

[49] Council of Europe, Opinion of the Commissioner for Human Rights regarding family visits to persons deprived of their liberty, CommDH (16 June 2008) 15 para 13; quoted by Abels (n 7) 449.

the aim of reintegration. Resocialization and reintegration are low on the list of priorities of international criminal tribunals. International prisoners are doubly ostracized, as they serve long sentences in foreign countries. However, Rule 61 of the UNSMR provides that 'the treatment of prisoners should emphasize not their exclusion from the community, but their continuing part in it'. Reintegration is no doubt a cumbersome process, that requires careful preparation during detention and that could be facilitated by a community that is sensitive to restorative justice.[50]

6. THE ICC'S POWERS OF SUPERVISION OVER AND ITS RESPONSIBILITY FOR IMPRISONMENT

In Section 2 we noticed that it is still unclear whether the Court's powers of supervision merely cover the enforcement of a sentence or must be interpreted broadly as to encompass the conditions of detention as well. We have defended the broader view and that position can arguably be sustained by referring to the practice of the *ad hoc* Tribunals and by the concept of shared responsibility which governs international cooperation in criminal matters.

Powers of supervision connote a continuous scrutiny of detention conditions and imply the interference of the supervisory body when things go awry. The *ad hoc* Tribunals have demonstrated such responsibility. The ICTR Trial Chamber in the *Serugendo* judgment expressed its concern over the plight of the sentenced person by holding that:

> [I]t is clear that Serugendo is not in a position to serve a sentence under normal prison conditions. He has recently been diagnosed with a terminal illness, has very fragile health and a poor prognosis. The Tribunal *must continue* to ensure that he receives adequate medical treatment, including hospitalization to the extent needed.[51]

One may expect the ICC to follow the example of its predecessors by displaying a similar sense of permanent responsibility.

The concept of shared responsibility in the context of international cooperation in criminal matters has taken shape in the case law of the ECtHR. In the landmark *Soering* decision the ECtHR acknowledged that a State party could incur responsibility by extraditing a person to a State where he would run a real risk of being exposed to torture, or cruel, inhuman and degrading treatment.[52] Moreover, the Court did not exclude that 'an issue might exceptionally be raised under Article 6 by an extradition decision in circumstances where the fugitive has suffered or risks suffering a flagrant denial of a fair trial in the requesting country'.[53] The *Soering* case was innovative, because the Court acknowledged for the first time that States could incur responsibility for prospective violations which occurred outside their territory. The decision served as

---

[50] On reintegration of international prisoners, see Mulgrew (n 23) 230–32.

[51] *Serugendo* ICTR-2005-84-I-T/I (Judgment and Sentence, 12 June 2006) para 94 [emphasis added].

[52] *Soering v United Kingdom* App no 14038/88 (ECtHR, 7 July 1990) Series A No 161.

[53] Ibid., para 113.

an outstanding precedent for a rich jurisprudence on extradition and human rights.[54] However, the *Soering* case concerned an extradition within the inter-State context. In order to ascertain whether the principles expressed in *Soering* have any bearing on the responsibility of the ICC for the detention conditions in the State of enforcement, we should make two leaps. First, we have to ascertain whether the human rights considerations in horizontal cooperation also govern the vertical relations between international courts and States, or at least serve as a normative framework for their actions. Next, we must inquire whether States – and *mutatis mutandis* international criminal courts – assume similar responsibilities for human rights violations in the sentencing State as, apparently, in the case of extradition.

The first issue came to the fore in the *Naletilić* decision of the ECtHR, in which the applicant challenged his transfer to the ICTY, contending among others that the Tribunal could not be qualified as an independent and impartial court established by law, which is required by Article 6, Section 1 of the ECHR. The Court rejected the complaint:

> The Court recalls that exceptionally an issue might be raised under Article 6 of the Convention by an extradition decision in circumstances where the applicant risks suffering a flagrant denial of a fair trial. However, it is not an act in the nature of an extradition which is at stake here, as the applicant seems to think. Involved here is the surrender to an international court which, in view of the content of its Statute and RPE, offers all the necessary guarantees including those of impartiality and independence. Accordingly, no issue arises under Article 6, para 1 in this respect.[55]

It is not immediately clear how this passage should be interpreted.[56] On the one hand one could argue that the Court puts the ICTY to the test of Article 6 and concludes that it meets the requirements of an independent and impartial tribunal. This would imply that in exceptional circumstances surrender to the Tribunal should be refused if it were to transpire that the fundamental rights of the requested person would not be respected.[57] On the other hand, it may just be that the ECtHR took the quality of justice delivered by the Tribunal for granted, leaving States no discretion to refuse surrender at all. In that case, the *Soering* case law would not govern the international cooperation between international criminal tribunals and States.

While the distinction is subtle and relevant in cases where States are expected to cooperate with international tribunals' conducting criminal trials, it is of less concern in the reversed situation, when international tribunals assist States in criminal law

---

[54] See, among other decisions, *Mamatkulov and Askarov v Turkey* App nos 46827/00 and 4695/99 (ECtHR, 4 February 2005); *Al-Moayad v Germany* App no 35865/03 (ECtHR, 20 February 2007); *Saadi v Italy* App no 37201/06 (ECtHR, 27 February 2008). Compare also H. van der Wilt, 'On the Hierarchy between Extradition and Human Rights', in E. de Wet and J. Vidmar (eds), *Hierarchy in International Law; The Place of Human Rights* (Oxford University Press 2012) 148–75.

[55] *Naletilić v Croatia* App no 51891/99 (ECtHR, 4 May 2000).

[56] See the perceptive annotation to this case by C. Buisman in *NJCM-Bulletin* 26(1) (2001) 50.

[57] Buisman, ibid., mentions the example of a terminally ill suspect whose surrender would constitute inhuman treatment in the sense of Art. 3 ECHR.

enforcement. After all, in the former case States are typically confronted with a conflict of obligations which can be resolved by postulating the priority of either respect for human rights or the duty to surrender. International criminal tribunals do not face similar legal constraints. The observance of human rights is an integral part of the application and interpretation of law by the ICC, as Article 21 of the Statute makes abundantly clear. And while there may be tensions between forensic truth finding and human rights, the *ad hoc* Tribunals have acknowledged that, although they are not formally bound by regional or international conventions on human rights, the provisions of these conventions are general principles of international law or constitute evidence of international custom. As such they are part and parcel of the law to be applied by the Tribunals.[58] Moreover, international criminal tribunals are generally not under an obligation to cooperate with States. In other words, they are not confronted in the same sense as States with a conflict of legal obligations. Their predicament derives rather from practical necessities, requiring them to seek the assistance of States for an adequate performance of their functions. The relevant issue concerns the limits of their dedication to human rights. Are international criminal tribunals and the ICC co-responsible for (grave) violations of human rights of sentenced persons during their detention in the State to which they transferred for the enforcement of a sentence?[59] Here again a comparison of the inter-State practice in the realm of international cooperation may shed light on this interesting question.

The ECtHR has addressed the (shared) responsibility of States in the context of the transfer of prisoners on several occasions. In the *Drozd and Janousek* case the applicants asserted that the denial of a fair trial during criminal proceedings in Andorra should be attributed to France which had taken over the execution of the sentence, due to the insufficient detention facilities in Andorra.[60] The Court rejected the complaint, but accepted the theoretical chance that France could have incurred responsibility in case of a flagrant denial of justice:

> As the Convention does not require the Contracting Parties to impose its standards on third States or territories, France was not obliged to verify whether the proceedings which resulted in the conviction were compatible with all the requirements of Article 6 of the Convention. To require such a review of the manner in which a court not bound by the Convention had

[58] *Barayagwiza* ICTR-97-19-AR72 (Decision, 3 November 1999) para 40. The Appeals Chamber of the Special Court for Sierra Leone confirmed that the Court's proceedings 'must be in tune with international human rights instruments', *Norman et al* SCSL-2004-14/16-AR72E (Decision on Constitutionality and Lack of Jurisdiction, 13 March 2004) para 55. On this topic see L. Gradoni, 'The Human Rights Dimension of International Criminal Procedure', in G. Sluiter et al, *International Criminal Procedure; Principles and Rules* (Oxford University Press 2013) 74–95.

[59] The attack on Radislav Krstić in 2010 by three armed men in Wakefield prison in the UK, in revenge for the massacre of Muslims in Srebrenica, an event for which General Krstić had been held criminally responsible as aider and abettor by the ICTY, provides a good example. While the three men faced trial in the UK and Krstić was moved to another prison in the UK, the ICTY insisted on his return to the UNDU. Whereas for all practical purposes this was the wisest thing to do, it did not offer the international prisoner a remedy for the violation of his rights, as Mulgrew (n 23) 187 correctly observes.

[60] *Drozd and Janousek v France* App no 12747/87 (ECtHR, 26 June 1992) Series A no 240.

> applied the principles enshrined in Article 6 would also thwart the current trend towards strengthening international cooperation in the administration of justice, a trend which is in principle in the interests of the persons concerned. The contracting States are, however, obliged to refuse their cooperation if it emerges that the conviction is the result of a flagrant denial of justice (see mutatis mutandis the *Soering v the United Kingdom* judgment of 7 July 1989).[61]

This balancing act serves a certain logic. Precisely because a principled rejection of a previous trial falling short of accepted standards of justice would damage the interests of the sentenced person, it makes sense to put the threshold as high as possible. It begs the question, though, what should be understood by a 'flagrant denial of justice'. In *Othman (Abu Qatada) v the United Kingdom* – a case of expulsion to Jordan – the ECtHR has neatly summarized its findings and opinions on the issue. First, the Court more generally found that the concept would entail a breach of the principles of a fair trial guaranteed by Article 6 'so fundamental as to amount to a nullification or the destruction of the very essence of the right guaranteed by that Article'.[62] Next, the Court, referring to other case law, identified a number of situations which could amount to such a 'flagrant denial of justice'.[63] On the basis of the *Drozd and Janousek* case, we have to assume that only such blatant violations of fair trial rights would also trigger the responsibility of a State that would subsequently take over the enforcement of the sentence. Apparently, the threshold is sufficiently high to preclude the Court from taking awkward decisions.[64]

Remarkably, all these cases concern the potential responsibility of the administering State on account of preceding serious fair trial rights in the sentencing State. To my knowledge the Court has never pronounced on the reverse situation, eliciting the legal issue whether the sentencing State could, after having transferred the enforcement of its sentence, still be held responsible for ensuing maltreatment during detention in the administering State. Taking the philosophy expressed in *Soering* as point of departure, there would in my view be no reason to doubt this. After all, it would be strange if a State could be held responsible for flagrant violations of human rights after having extradited someone, but would get away with it, if it would expose a sentenced person to abuse or even torture by transferring that person to another State where he or she is

---

[61] Ibid., para 110.

[62] *Othman (Abu Qatada) v United Kingdom* App no 8130/09 (ECtHR, 17 January 2012) 'EHRC' 2012/64 note by Den Heijer para 260.

[63] *Othman (Abu Qatada) v United Kingdom* App no 8130/09 (ECtHR, 17 January 2012) para 259:

> These have included: conviction in absentia with no possibility subsequently to obtain a fresh determination of the merits of the charge; a trial which is summary in nature and conducted with a total disregard for the rights of the defence; detention without any access to an independent and impartial tribunal to have the legality of the detention reviewed; deliberate and systematic refusal of access to a lawyer, especially for an individual detained in a foreign country.

[64] To my knowledge, the Court has never held an administering State responsible on account of enforcing a sentence that was produced in a trial that lacked the elementary features of fairness, see, for instance, *Willcox and Hurford v United Kingdom* App nos 43759/10 and 43771/12 (ECtHR, 8 January 2003) 'EHRC' 2013/155 note by Van der Wilt.

to serve his/her sentence.[65] The involvement of the sentencing State is arguably even larger, as the enforcement of the sanction is an integral part of the entire criminal process that started in the sentencing State. If we accept that the sentencing State can be held responsible for grave maltreatment in the administering State, we should equally be prepared to endorse such a responsibility for international criminal tribunals and the ICC.

7. TRANSFER OF ENFORCEMENT BY THE ICC: SOME FINAL REFLECTIONS

This chapter has attempted to draw some parallels between the transfer of the execution of foreign judgments between States and transfer of enforcement of a sentence by the ICC. It soon becomes apparent that the context in which the ICC operates accounts for some conspicuous legal and practical differences. On the one hand, the hierarchical relationship between ICC and States obviates time-tested legal devices like dual criminality and the nationality of the sentenced person as prerequisites for transfer. On the other hand, the ICC has no choice other than to rely on States, a circumstance that limits the options. Unlike the inter-State context, there does not exist a 'natural alternative' – imprisonment in the sentencing State – and only a few Member States have expressed their willingness to enforce an ICC sentence in the first place.

The net result of these forces is that the position of the sentenced person may be at peril. He or she runs the risk of being sent to a State that is largely unknown and unfamiliar. The sentenced person can hardly wield influence over the choice of a State of enforcement and international criminal courts and tribunals, while not entirely oblivious to their responsibility for the fate of the sentenced person, have no legal obligations carved in stone in this respect. The prospects of rehabilitation are slight for prisoners who have no or few cultural, emotional and linguistic ties with the place where they must serve their sentence. The ambiguity of international tribunals as regards their lasting responsibility for sentenced persons can perhaps be attributed to their general posture towards rehabilitation as a sentencing goal in case of international crimes. In the *Čelibići* appeal judgment the Appeals Chamber, alluding to the (very) serious nature of the crimes being prosecuted, explicitly held that rehabilitation 'cannot play a predominant role in the decision-making process of a Trial Chamber of the Tribunal', adding that 'although rehabilitation (…) should be considered as a relevant factor, it is not one which should be given undue weight'.[66] In *Kunarac* the Trial Chamber avowed that it fully supported rehabilitative programmes, but denied that rehabilitation was a significant sentencing objective for the Tribunal. National rehabilitative programmes were the business of the States in which convicted persons would

[65] In a similar vein, H. Sanders, *De tenuitvoerlegging van buitenlandse strafvonnissen* (Intersentia 2004) 243 who observes that it would be a lot easier to determine the responsibility of the sentencing State for maltreatment of a prisoner in the administering State than in the mirror situation (the responsibility of the administering State for denial of fair trial in the sentencing State).

[66] *Delalić et al ('Čelebići case')* IT-96-21-A (Appeal Judgment, 20 February 2001) para 806.

have to serve their sentence, and were not of concern to the International Tribunal.[67] The subtle shift in emphasis is telling. Whereas the Appeals Chamber in *Čelibići* questioned the overall relevance of rehabilitation as a sentencing objective in the case of international crimes, the Trial Chamber in *Kunarac* acknowledged its importance but tried to shirk its responsibility for its success. Admittedly, the ICTY has incidentally stressed the relevance of rehabilitation, but predominantly as a factor in mitigation of sentence, not as a cause of permanent concern.[68]

One of the main lines of argument in this chapter has been that international criminal tribunals in general and the ICC in particular bear co-responsibility for the enforcement of its sentences, both as to the choice of State and as to the lasting supervision of detention conditions. In his captivating study on the Nazi interns of Spandau prison in Berlin, Norman Goda has advocated a prescient court that carefully considers the future effects of its judgment:

> Spandau thus became a macabre symbol for the Nazi past but also for the following problem. The discussion concerning war criminals and the place in the memory of the past is not national but international. And becomes most contentious not during the trial but afterward. The years and even decades of punishment must thus receive the same careful thought from the advocates of international justice as do the months of trial. Otherwise, the punishment can erode some of the foundations on which the trial itself was built.[69]

Whereas Goda primarily alluded to the political repercussions which had insufficiently been foreseen, the argument can probably be generalized. International criminal tribunals and the ICC should, when passing judgment, anticipate the enforcement of the sentence and remain to a certain extent responsible for the execution of the sanction. They cannot permit themselves the luxury of closing the books and shutting their eyes after having rendered judgment. That may sound a far-reaching responsibility, but we should not forget that international criminal justice makes heavy demands on its representatives.

[67] *Kunarac et al* IT-97-23-T and IT-96-23/1-T (Judgment, 22 February 2001) para 844.

[68] *Obrenović* IT-02-60/2-S (Sentencing Judgment, 10 December 2003) paras 143–146.

[69] N.J. Goda, *Tales from Spandau; Nazi Criminals and the Cold War* (Cambridge University Press 2007) 17.

9. Rule 11*bis*: exploring the penal aspects of transferring cases to national courts by the *ad hoc* Tribunals

Olympia Bekou

1. INTRODUCTION

Rule 11*bis*, found in the RPE of both the ICTY and ICTR[1] came into existence at the time the term 'completion strategy'[2] entered the international criminal law vernacular. Prompted by the Tribunals' finite resources in terms of both time and financial means, the Rule was seen as a way of processing more cases and was introduced alongside other structural reforms.[3] The application of the Rule meant that a number of indictees in the Tribunals' custody were transferred to national courts for trial. If convicted these individuals served their sentences in prisons to which they would most likely not have been transferred, had they been convicted by the Tribunals. The Secretary General's report that accompanied the creation of the ICTY had excluded the possibility of serving sentences in the former Yugoslavia, owing to the 'nature of the crimes in question and the international character of the tribunal'.[4] In the ICTR, despite the fact that a similar restriction did not exist, no prisoners had been transferred to Rwanda to serve their sentences prior to the 11*bis* referrals.[5] The creation of the MICT in

[1] Rule 11*bis* was adopted in 1997 and was amended four times in 2002. Note, however, that the wording in the ICTR RPE is different to that of the ICTY RPE.

[2] See SCRes 1503 (28 August 2003) and SCRes 1534 (26 March 2004). For an analysis of the completion strategy see: D. Raab, 'Evaluating the ICTY and Its Completion Strategy; Efforts to Achieve Accountability for War Crimes and their Tribunals' (2005) 3 *Journal of International Criminal Justice* 82; D.A. Mundis, 'The Judicial Effects of the "Completion Strategies" on the Ad Hoc International Criminal Tribunals' (2005) 99 *American Journal of International Law* 142; D.A. Mundis, 'Completing the Mandates of the Ad Hoc International Criminal Tribunals: Lessons from the Nuremberg Process?' (2005) 28 *Fordham International Law Journal* 591; L.D. Johnson, 'Closing an International Criminal Tribunal while Maintaining International Human Rights Standards and Excluding Impunity' (2005) 99 *American Journal of International Law* 158.

[3] See the amendment to Rules 98*bis* and 73(D), the introduction of the Court system, the increased communication between the Association of Defence Counsel and the Tribunal as well as the Special War Crimes Chamber in Bosnia and Herzegovina, training of local judges and 11*bis* referrals. See 12th annual report of the ICTY to the General Assembly of 17 August 2005 A/60/267-S/2005/532, paras 7–10.

[4] Report of the Secretary-General pursuant to paragraph 2 of SCRes 808 (3 May 1993) para 121.

[5] MICT, 'Enforcement of Sentences' <http://www.unmict.org/en/about/enforcement-of-sentences> accessed 22 July 2015.

December 2010[6] put the *ad hoc* Tribunals firmly on the road to permanently closing their doors. Since 1 July 2012 for the ICTR and 1 July 2013 for the ICTY respectively, responsibility for oversight of prisoners who spend their sentences in national courts as a result of Rule 11*bis* proceedings as well as referrals has been transferred to the MICT.[7]

Rule 11*bis* has only been used to refer 13 indictments originating at the ICTY[8] and 10 at the ICTR.[9] It is unlikely to expect that the MICT will refer more cases to national courts. Rather, its functions in this area are likely to be overseeing ICTR referrals.[10] The relatively low number of cases transferred to national courts pursuant to Rule 11*bis* may lead some to question the impact or indeed significance of the Rule. However, its significance lies in the fact that for the first time, national courts were directly involved in a burden-sharing partnership whereby they were required to take over from the international level, including with regard to penal matters. This chapter focuses on some of the constituting elements of Rule 11*bis* and aims to explore the effect of this process, which has resulted in the direct implementation of national sentencing schemes for individuals indicted at the international level. Furthermore, the chapter highlights some of the issues relating to penalties, including the quality of prisons and reforms undertaken at the national level to accommodate 11*bis* transfers.

2. THE PURPOSE OF RULE 11*BIS*

Both the ICTY and the ICTR, as Article 9 ICTYSt and Article 8 ICTRSt respectively indicate, were vested with concurrent jurisdiction with national courts. Therefore, enhancing the capacity of national legal orders could, and perhaps should, have been

---

[6] SCRes 1966 Adopted by the UNSC at its 6463rd meeting on 22 December 2010.

[7] Ibid., para 11; Arts. 1(3), 4, 6(1) MICTSt.

[8] The following indictments have been referred: Radovan Stanković, Gojko Janković, Željko Mejakić, Momčilo Gruban, Dušan Fuštar, Duško Knežević, Mirolad Trbić, Pasko Ljubičić, Mitar Rassević, Savo Todović (Bosnia and Herzegovina), Rahim Ademi, Mirko Norac (Croatia) and Vladimir Kovacević (Serbia). For analysis, see O. Bekou, 'Rule 11*bis*: An Examination of the Process of Referrals to National Courts in ICTY Jurisprudence' (2009) 33 *Fordham International Law Journal* 723; S. Somers, 'Rule 11*bis* of the International Criminal Tribunal for the Former Yugoslavia: Referral of Indictments to National Courts' (2007) 30 *Boston College International & Comparative Law Review* 175.

[9] The following indictments have been transferred: Laurent Bucyibaruta, Wenceslas Munyeshyaka (France), Fulgence Kayishema, Bernard Munyagishari, Phénéas Munyarugarama, Aloys Ndimbati, Ladislas Ntaganzwa, Charles Ryandikayo, Charles Sikubwabo and Jean Uwinkindi (Rwanda). For an analysis of the decisions taken by the ICTR under the Rule 11*bis* procedure, see N. Palmer, 'Transfer or Transformation? A Review of the Rule 11*bis* Decisions of the International Criminal Tribunal for Rwanda' (2012) 20 *African Journal of International and Comparative Law* 1.

[10] See, eg, C. Denis, 'Critical Overview of the "Residual Functions" of the Mechanism and its Date of Commencement (Including Transitional Arrangements)' (2011) 9 *Journal of International Criminal Justice* 819, 828.

key to the Tribunals' operations from the start.[11] However, Rule 11*bis* was guided purely by the need for expediency at a time when 'Tribunal fatigue'[12] had set in and the need for a completion strategy became more pressing. Consequently, the shift of some of the Tribunals' case-law and detainees from the international to the national level became possible.

Easing some of the Tribunals' workload was not the only purpose of Rule 11*bis*. Seen from the perspective of building capacity, application of the Rule saw complex cases involving serious international crimes being dealt with at the national level and highlighted the range of actions already taken by national jurisdictions. For example, in the former Yugoslavia the 'Outreach Programme'[13] or the 'Rules of the Road' initiative,[14] despite their limited success,[15] paved the way for the adoption of Rule 11*bis* and a greater responsibility for national criminal justice systems in detaining and imprisoning high level suspects.

The role of States in Rule 11*bis* referral hearings was limited to representations as regards whether the accused would receive a fair trial before the national courts under consideration for referral and that the death penalty would not be imposed. However, once a referral was upheld, although the Tribunals retained an oversight role, the trial itself was conducted exclusively before national courts, which had sole responsibility for determining the innocence or guilt of the accused, as well as responsibility for the administration of sentences and their enforcement.

---

[11] Rule 11*bis* has been particularly helpful in rehabilitating and improving national judicial systems in the SFRY, particularly in the development of the State Court of Bosnia and Herzegovina, to which the bulk of referrals have occurred, but also by encouraging the flow of evidence and other materials from an international to a national level, encouraging development of these legal systems to a point where the Tribunal is no longer necessary. See D. Tolbert and A. Kontic, 'The International Criminal Tribunal for the former Yugoslavia: Transitional Justice, the Transfer of Cases to National Courts, and Lessons for the ICC', in C. Stahn and G. Sluiter (eds), *The Emerging Practice of the International Criminal Court* (Martinus Nijhoff 2009) 136–7.

[12] S.D. Roper and L.A. Barria, *Designing Criminal Tribunals: Sovereignty and International Concerns in the Protection of Human Rights* (Ashgate 2006) 71–2.

[13] For an analysis see L.C. Vohrah, and J. Cina, 'The Outreach Programme', in R. May et al (eds), *Essays on ICTY Procedure and Evidence in Honour of Gabrielle Kirk McDonald* 547 (Kluwer 2001) 547.

[14] The parties to the Dayton Agreement agreed in Rome on 18 February 1996 that 'persons other than those already indicted by the Tribunal may be arrested and detained for serious violations of international humanitarian law only pursuant to a previously issued order, warrant of indictment that had been reviewed and deemed consistent with international legal standards by the Tribunal', Sixth Annual ICTY Report, A/54/187-S/1999/846, para 135. See also G.T. Blewitt, 'The International Criminal Tribunals for the Former Yugoslavia and Rwanda', in M. Lattimer and P. Sands (eds), *Justice for Crimes Against Humanity* 150–51 (Hart 2003).

[15] D. Tolbert, 'The International Criminal Tribunal for the Former Yugoslavia: Unforeseen Successes and Foreseeable Shortcomings' (2002) 26 *Fletcher Forum of World Affairs* 7, 14–15.

3. OVERVIEW OF RULE 11*BIS*

The body in charge of referrals at the ICTY was the Referral Bench. This *quasi*-chamber within the Tribunal, especially appointed by the Tribunal's President, was entrusted with the determination as to whether an indictment was suitable for referral. Consisting of three judges, the Chamber could order referrals either on its own accord, or following a request by the Prosecutor.[16] The Referral Bench was akin to a Chamber as it, too, consisted of three judges whose functions were governed by the Statute and the RPE.[17] However, unlike a Chamber, there were no three fixed judges assigned to it, but membership of the Bench was at the discretion of the Tribunal's President, on account of the cases to be heard. By contrast, at the ICTR, a Trial Chamber was designated to handle referrals. At both Tribunals, the assigned judges did not decide the cases in their substance. Rather, their function was to rule on whether certain indictments merited transfer to national courts. Once transferred, the cases were tried and sentences passed without their involvement.

It may be that the Bench/Chamber had discretion as to whether or not to order a referral, as evidenced by the presence of the verb 'may'[18] and the evaluation of referral decisions lay solely on whether this discretion had been exercised correctly by the Bench/Chamber, in light of the criteria set out in Rule 11*bis*,[19] but this does not mean that their decisions were purely administrative. The Tribunal sought to establish whether to send an indictment back to national courts rather than continue with the trial internationally. The selection of a suitable forum for trial is an important judicial function, not least because the selected court is then called upon to pass and enforce appropriate sentences, upon conviction. The equivalent in the ICC regime would be the determination on complementarity, and the Pre-Trial Chamber's decision on whether the case would remain for trial before a national court or it would be tried in The Hague.[20] In that sense, Rule 11*bis* is the reverse process of the complementarity model at the ICC.[21]

---

16 Rule 11*bis*(B) ICTY RPE.

17 See also Rule 11*bis*(H) ICTY RPE which equates the Bench with a Chamber in terms of its powers and obligation to follow procedures under the RPE, 'insofar as applicable'.

18 Rule 11*bis*(B) ICTY/ICTR RPE. *Mejakić et al* IT-02-65-AR11*bis*.1 (Decision on Joint Defence Appeal Against Decision on Referral Under Rule 11*bis*, 7 April 2006) para 10.

19 Ibid.

20 See Art. 18 ICCSt. See also M.H. Arsanjani, 'Reflections on the Jurisdiction and Trigger Mechanism of the International Criminal Court', in H. von Hebel, J.G. Lammers and J. Schukking, *Reflections on the International Criminal Court, Essays in Honour of Adriaan Bos* (TMC Asser Press 1999) 70–71.

21 On primacy and complementarity in the context of Rule 11*bis*, see M.M. El Zeidy, 'From Primacy to Complementarity and Backwards: (Re)-Visiting Rule 11*bis* of the Ad Hoc Tribunals' (2008) 57 *International and Comparative Law Quarterly* 403.

4. THE IMPORTANCE OF THE REFERRAL PROCESS FOR PENAL MATTERS

Before examining the specific penal matters that arise as a result of the Rule 11*bis* process, it is important to examine the types of cases that were deemed suitable for such referrals. Should the cases have been deemed unsuitable, they would have ultimately been subject to different sentencing and enforcement regimes altogether following trial at the international level. There are two types of cases examined for referral: those that were investigated to greater or lesser extent by the Prosecutor but did not result in an indictment[22] and those that, despite having been investigated and indictments against named individuals being issued by the Tribunals, were subsequently referred to national courts for trial. This chapter examines this latter category, as it involves the transfer of individuals already in custody at the Tribunals.

Rule 11*bis* outlines a series of criteria that need to be met prior to transferring an indictment to the national level. Gravity is the most important one at the ICTY. For the indictment to be received by an appropriate State, the accused must fall under the lower or intermediate categories in terms of crimes and responsibility. A notable difference between the Rule 11*bis* regime at the ICTY and that which is available at the ICTR is that the ICTY Referral Bench is directed to 'consider the gravity of the crimes charged and the level of responsibility of the accused' pursuant to Rule 11*bis*(C). The ICTR Trial Chamber is subject to no such obligation to consider gravity or responsibility. Besides gravity, the substantive law[23] likely to be applied at the national level, as well as issues pertaining to the type and appropriateness of sentences available (i.e. the death penalty), the quality of prisons and fair trial standards, are also examined.

4.1 Gravity

Within Rule 11*bis* ICTY RPE, gravity – outlined in Rule 11*bis*(C) – is key to the decision to refer (or not to refer) an indictment to national courts for trial. As such, it has been the subject of much disagreement between defence and prosecution, each supporting their respective standpoints. Most of the indictees in Rule 11*bis* hearings preferred to be tried internationally, rather than have their cases transferred to national courts. They consistently maintained that they did not fall within the lower/middle level indictee categories at the heart of the referrals. This approach is not surprising given the

---

[22] For the preparation of the indictment see Art. 18 ICTYSt. In the context of referrals, see also ICTY Press Release, CT/MO/1008 (29 September 2006).

[23] See generally ICTY (with UNICRI), *Manual of Developed Practices* (UNICRI Publisher 2009) 168–70.

lower sentences imposed by international criminal tribunals,[24] coupled also with a sense of distrust of national courts.[25]

In applying Rule 11*bis*, the Bench sought to refer indictments which were 'not *ipso facto* incompatible with referrals'.[26] If the alleged crimes were not of such gravity so as to *demand*[27] trial internationally, they would be equally suitable for trial by either the Tribunal or national courts.[28] This gravity threshold should be considered in light of the Bench's approach to concurrent jurisdiction. Rule 11*bis* is therefore viewed as a means of choosing amongst 'alternative' jurisdictions. This, in turn, does not mean that the indictments which have been chosen for referral should not have been prepared at the Tribunal. In other words, they were of sufficient gravity to warrant an investigation at the international level and therefore differ from those investigations that were not serious enough to even be investigated by the Tribunal or were investigated but did not result in an indictment issued internationally. However, the level of gravity of the referral cases was not enough to keep either the indictment or the accused persons in The Hague.

4.2 Applicable Substantive Law

As the purpose of the referral hearing was to examine the suitability of an indictment for referral, the Bench did not possess the authority required to decide in any binding way on the law (including the sentence) that would be applied at the national level,

[24] The picture at the ICTR was different, at least at the beginning of its operation, where a number of high level accused were transferred to the Tribunal. This is primarily down to the fact that it did not have recourse to the death penalty, unlike the Rwandan national courts. See eg, the arrest of Prime Minister Jean Kambanda and seven high level officials in 1997 <http://www.unictr.org/en/news/initial-appearance-jean-kambanda-former-prime-minister-rwanda> accessed 22 July 2015.

[25] These objections were put forward mainly by Bosnian Serbs whose indictments were referred to the Bosnian State Court. It is doubtful whether they would have had the same reaction had referrals to Serbian courts taken place. This may be seen from the written motions of Radovan Stanković during his trial in Bosnia. They all make reference to 'Jamahiriya Bosnia and Herzegovina' the 'so called Court of Bosnia and Herzegovina'. It may not be that these indictees placed any trust in the ICTY, but they definitely objected to being tried by Bosnian authorities. Cf. Norac and Ademi, who are perceived by a great number of Croats as national heroes, and who did not object to the referral. See *Ademi and Norac* IT-04-78-PT (Decision for Referral to the Authorities of the Republic of Croatia Pursuant to Rule 11*bis*, Referral Chamber, 14 September 2005) para 20.

[26] See inter alia, *Stanković* IT-96-23/2-PT (Decision on Referral of case under Rule 11*bis*, 17 May 2005) para 8 fn 14 and *Janković* IT-96-23/2-PT (Decision on Referral of Case under Rule 11*bis*, 22 July 2005) para 20.

[27] See Prosecutorial submissions in the *Rasević and Todović* IT-97-25/1-PT (Decision on Referral of Case Under Rule 11*bis*, 8 July 2005) para 18; similarly in *Stanković* IT-96-23/2-PT (Decision on Referral of case under Rule 11*bis*, 17 May 2005) para 15.

[28] The Tribunal acknowledges that certain cases are better placed before an international forum whereas others 'would also be suitable for prosecution before a competent national court'. The case is therefore suitable for trial either by the Tribunal or national courts. *Milošević* IT-98-29/1-PT (Decision on Referral of Case Pursuant to Rule 11*bis*, 8 July 2005) para 18.

post-referral.[29] It was the courts of the State to which the indictment would be transferred that alone possessed such authority. Although the Bench has repeatedly rebutted any implication that it is obliged to determine the applicable substantive law,[30] it has nevertheless considered the law that would potentially apply to each of the cases it has examined. However, no reference to the RPE has been made with regard to this point.

An examination of substantive (including procedural) law is therefore warranted. Under Rule 11*bis*(B) ICTY RPE and 11*bis*(C) ICTR RPE, the Referral Bench/Chamber needed to satisfy itself that the accused would receive a fair trial and that the death penalty would not be imposed. Such a determination cannot be made *in abstracto*. If, in order to meet these two criteria, a limited discussion of applicable law is necessary, the Referral Bench/Chamber can and should examine all available options. However, their findings are limited, and by no means binding on the State that accepts the referral. The lack of adequate legislation would have hampered or, arguably, would have precluded acceptance of the indictment. An examination of the applicable legal framework has been important when the Prosecutor has sought a referral under Rule 11*bis*. For example, the ICTR Trial Chamber undertook an examination of the applicable substantive law in France when the Prosecutor sought the transfer of the indictment of Laurent Bucyibaruta thereto.[31] Moreover, given that Rule 11*bis* does not contain criteria that could help the Bench/Chamber reach a decision on capability, and despite the fact that this is not explicitly provided for in Rule 11*bis*(A)(i) and (ii), an examination of substantive law should not be precluded. In such a case, the Bench/Chamber would have to provide arguments in favour of a referral to a particular State, which would mean essentially undertaking an examination of the suitability of the forum.

The Bench/Chamber also needed to satisfy itself that an adequate legal framework was in place to try the accused, who, if found guilty, would receive appropriate punishment.[32] This determination therefore guided which aspects of substantive law needed to be examined. These were, in effect, limited and did not go into submissions from either the Prosecutor or the defence. Hence, the 'apparent position' on substantive

---

[29] *Stanković* IT-96-23/2-PT (Decision on Referral of case under Rule 11*bis*, 17 May 2005) para 32; *Rasević and Todović* IT-97-25/1-PT (Decision on Referral of Case Under Rule 11*bis*, 8 July 2005) para 34; *Mejakić et al* IT-02-65-AR11*bis*.1 (Decision on Joint Defence Appeal Against Decision on Referral Under Rule 11*bis*, 7 April 2006) para 43; *Janković* IT-96-23/2-PT (Decision on Referral of Case under Rule 11*bis*, 22 July 2005) para 27; *Ademi and Norac* IT-04-78-PT (Decision for Referral to the Authorities of the Republic of Croatia Pursuant to Rule 11*bis*, Referral Chamber, 14 September 2005) para 32; *Ljubičić* IT-00-41-PT (Decision to Refer the Case to Bosnia and Herzegovina pursuant to Rule 11*bis*, 12 April 2006) para 31; *Mejakić et al* IT-02-65-AR11*bis*.1 (Decision on Joint Defence Appeal Against Decision on Referral Under Rule 11*bis*, 7 April 2006) para 45.

[30] See fourth ground of appeal in *Mejakić et al* IT-02-65-AR11*bis*.1 (Decision on Joint Defence Appeal Against Decision on Referral Under Rule 11*bis*, 7 April 2006) para 46, and the Bench's response in para 48.

[31] See *Bucyibaruta* ICTR-2005-85-I (Decision on Prosecutor's Request for Referral of Laurent Bucybaruta's Indictment to France, 20 November 2007) paras 8–17.

[32] *Mejakić et al* IT-02-65-AR11*bis*.1 (Decision on Joint Defence Appeal Against Decision on Referral Under Rule 11*bis*, 7 April 2006) para 46.

law was put forward in the Bench/Chamber's determination on whether to proceed with the referral.[33] It should be said, however, that the Bench/Chamber has neither clarified what it considered to be the apparent position, nor how it made this determination.

In essence, it should be remembered that national courts have sole responsibility to determine the applicable substantive law. As such, the Bench/Chamber remained constrained in their approach, as they would not want to be seen as encroaching on what is essentially a domestic function. However, the mere exposition of the law that the Bench/Chamber undertook may not be enough to provide any useful guidance to the national courts receiving the indictment, but on the other hand, it served the quest for expediency sought by the completion strategy. Anything more would have been beyond the remit of Rule 11*bis* and would have placed a disproportionate burden on the Tribunals. A detailed examination of applicable substantive law after the referral of the indictment would be beyond the scope of this chapter, but some potential problems that national courts may face will be briefly examined.

4.3 Fair Trial

Fair trial is an important consideration of any criminal justice process. Ensuring that the accused receives a fair trial is also key to the ICTY and ICTR Statutes, where the right to a fair trial is guaranteed through the adherence to international standards.[34] It is therefore not surprising that Rule 11*bis*(B) ICTY RPE and Rule 11*bis*(C) ICTR RPE also cover fair trials.[35] However, unlike the rest of the elements of the Rule, the Bench/Chamber, at the time of the referral hearing, does not and, in fact, cannot have an insight as to whether the specific indictee will receive a fair trial post-referral. Despite the fact that fair trial cannot be determined in the abstract, the Bench/Chamber was asked to make a finding involving a process that happened after it was no longer seized of the case. As a result, the Bench/Chamber could only hypothesise and,

---

33 *Stanković* IT-96-23/2-PT (Decision on Referral of case under Rule 11*bis*, 17 May 2005) para 36; *Mejakić et al* IT-02-65-AR11*bis*.1 (Decision on Joint Defence Appeal Against Decision on Referral Under Rule 11*bis*, 7 April 2006) para 48; *Janković* IT-96-23/2-PT (Decision on Referral of Case under Rule 11*bis*, 22 July 2005) para 32; *Ademi and Norac* IT-04-78-PT (Decision for Referral to the Authorities of the Republic of Croatia Pursuant to Rule 11*bis*, Referral Chamber, 14 September 2005) para 38; *Ljubičić* IT-00-41-PT (Decision to Refer the Case to Bosnia and Herzegovina pursuant to Rule 11*bis*, 12 April 2006) para 32.

34 See Art. 21 ICTYSt; Art. 20 ICTRSt; Art. 14 ICCPR; Art. 6 ECHR.

35 Rule 11*bis*(B) ICTY RPE. The Bench needs to be satisfied that the accused 'will' get a fair trial. In the *Stanković Appeal*, the appellant queried the wording used by the Referral Bench, which had found that the accused 'should' have a fair trial and the Chamber concurred that this was imprecise but held that 'should' in this instance meant 'will'. *Stanković* IT-96-23/2-PT (Decision on Referral of case under Rule 11*bis*, 17 May 2005) paras 27–28. In the *Ademi and Norac* case, the Bench explained that the fair trial condition in 11*bis* proceedings requires fairness not only with regard to the accused, but also towards all interested parties, which includes the victims and the international community, as fair trial entails a policy consideration for the Bench when considering referral. *Ademi and Norac* IT-04-78-PT (Decision for Referral to the Authorities of the Republic of Croatia Pursuant to Rule 11*bis*, Referral Chamber, 14 September 2005) para 53.

inevitably, limit its examination on the adequacy of the legal framework of the State considered for referral to guarantee a fair trial.[36]

In ICTY jurisprudence, both the Bench and the Appeals Chamber have addressed the main concerns raised by the individuals at the heart of the referral hearing in some detail. These cover numerous issues, such as the composition of the Court,[37] questions relating to trial without undue delay, the right to counsel of the accused's own choosing, adequate time and facilities for the preparation of a defence, the right to attend trial and examine witnesses, as well as witness availability and protection.[38]

When making a determination as to whether the accused will receive a fair trial in the State concerned, the ICTR has departed somewhat from the jurisprudence of the ICTY. In the *Mejakić Appeal*, the ICTY Appeals Chamber found that the Referral Bench is mandated only to satisfy itself that the applicable laws 'provide an adequate basis to ensure compliance with the requirement for a fair trial'.[39] If the framework was in place, there was no further need to explore the actual practice. The approach taken at the ICTR was markedly different. The ICTR has held that a Chamber ought to look beyond the legislative framework to 'examples of the practices of (…) courts',[40] thus requiring proof of the situation in practice. One consequence of this approach is that the ICTR – in determining whether an accused is likely to receive a fair trial – has taken into consideration the experiences of defence counsel in the receiving State and *amici curiae* briefs, including on the conditions of detention, in addition to the applicable legal framework.[41]

It has been said already that an inquiry by the Bench into the applicable law, determines, at best, the adequacy of the forum through a limited examination of the existence of legislation. However, in cases of referral to a State where new or untested legislation is in place, it is doubtful that such an examination would be able to

---

[36] The Bench has therefore in each case reviewed the applicable constitutional provisions but also the provisions in the Criminal Procedure Codes as well as membership to international treaties, such as the ECHR. See for instance *Stanković* IT-96-23/2-PT (Decision on Referral of case under Rule 11*bis*, 17 May 2005) para 55; *Rasević and Todović* IT-97-25/1-PT (Decision on Referral of Case Under Rule 11*bis*, 8 July 2005) para 83; *Janković* IT-96-23/2-PT (Decision on Referral of Case under Rule 11*bis*, 22 July 2005) para 62; *Mejakić et al* IT-02-65-AR11*bis*.1 (Decision on Joint Defence Appeal Against Decision on Referral Under Rule 11*bis*, 7 April 2006) para 68; *Lukić and Lukić* IT-98-32/1-PT (Decision on Referral of Case pursuant to Rule 11*bis*, 5 April 2007) paras 69–74.

[37] *Mejakić et al* IT-02-65-AR11*bis*.1 (Decision on Joint Defence Appeal Against Decision on Referral Under Rule 11*bis*, 7 April 2006) paras 83–86 where the Defence base their arguments on the lack of impartiality and independence of the State Court in BiH based on the criteria on the election of judges, the composition of the court, and the provisions on disqualification.

[38] For an overview of these issues see *Lukić and Lukić* IT-98-32/1-PT (Decision on Referral of Case pursuant to Rule 11*bis*, 5 April 2007) paras 76–97.

[39] *Mejakić et al* IT-02-65-AR11*bis*.1 (Decision on Joint Defence Appeal Against Decision on Referral Under Rule 11*bis*, 7 April 2006) para 69.

[40] *Hategekimana* ICTR-00-55B-R11*bis*-T (Decision on the Prosecutor's Request for Referral to the Republic of Rwanda, 19 June 2008) para 35.

[41] See *Munyakazi* ICTR-1997-36-I (Filing of Prosecutor's Written Submissions and Exhibit pursuant to the Directions of the Referral Chamber during the Oral Hearing of 24 April 2008, 25 April 2008) 5. For a critical view of the ICTR approach, see Palmer (n 9) 10.

guarantee a fair trial. This was the case with the former Yugoslavia for instance, where the legal system was criticised by both the OSCE and civil society.[42] For Rwanda, the more hands-on approach has led to improvements in penal matters, which will be examined next.

4.4 Sentencing Issues, Quality of Prisons and the Importance of Monitoring

Besides the fair trial issues examined above, the presence of the death penalty in the jurisdiction considered for referral, would act as a bar to transfer. This Rule 11*bis* requirement was of greater relevance at the time of the first adoption of the Rule, but ceased to be of practical relevance when the death penalty was abolished in the former Yugoslavia and Rwanda.[43] Of course, cases have also been referred to third States, eg, France, where the death penalty was equally not available. With the imminent completion of the Tribunals' work, the possibility of considering referrals to States that still have the death penalty is non-existent, not least because of the construction of Rule 11*bis*.

Following the abolition of the death penalty in Rwanda, an ambiguity remained with regard to the issue of 'life imprisonment with special provisions'. This, in essence, meant prolonged incarceration in isolation and was common to all three appeal decisions that refused transfer to Rwanda.[44] Indeed, the issue of isolation was deliberated to a significant extent in the ICTR Rule 11*bis* referral hearings, where the Appeals Chamber expressed concern about the potential application – contrary to international standards – of the penalty of life imprisonment in isolation in Rwanda.[45] In 2008 – and with the approval of the Appeals Chamber – Rwanda passed legislation

---

[42] See for an assessment of Serbian courts before the creation of the war crimes court, M.S. Ellis, 'Coming to Terms with its Past – Serbia's New Court for the Prosecution of War Crimes' (2004) 22 *Berkeley Journal of International Law* 165, 168. Regarding issues of legitimacy of Serbian criminal courts see B. Hall, 'Using Hybrid Tribunals as Trivias: Furthering the Goals of Post-Conflict Justice while Transferring Cases from the ICTY to Serbia's Domestic War Crimes Tribunal' (2005) 13 *Michigan State Journal of International Law* 39, 50–53. See also, generally, K. Zoglin, 'The Future of War Crimes Prosecutions in the former Yugoslavia: Accountability or Junk Justice?' (2005) 27 *Human Rights Quarterly* 41, 44–72.

[43] All States of the former Yugoslavia have ratified Protocol No 13 to the European Convention on Human Rights, concerning the abolition of the death penalty in all circumstances, 3 May 2003, ETS 187 <http://conventions.coe.int/Treaty/Commun/ChercheSig.asp?NT=187&CM=1&DF=&CL=ENG> accessed 25 June 2015. Rwanda abolished the death penalty in 2007. See Rwanda: Organic Law No 31/2007 of 2007 Relating to the Abolition of the Death Penalty [Rwanda], 25 July 2007 <http://www.refworld.org/docid/46bada1c2.html> accessed 1 July 2015.

[44] See N. Palmer, *Courts in Conflict: Interpreting the Layers of Justice in Post-Genocide Rwanda* (Oxford University Press 2015) 79.

[45] See *Munyakazi* ICTR-97-36-R11*bis* (Decision on the Prosecution's Appeal against Decision on Referral under Rule 11*bis*, 8 October 2008) paras 8–21; *Kanyarukiga* ICTR-2002-78-R11*bis* (Decision on the Prosecution's Appeal against Decision on Referral under Rule 11*bis*, 8 October 2008) paras 6–17; *Hategekimana* ICTR-00-55B-R11*bis* (Decision on the Prosecution's Appeal against Decision on Referral under Rule 11*bis*, 4 December 2008) paras 31–38.

clarifying that the penalty of solitary confinement would no longer apply to cases transferred under Rule 11*bis*.[46]

Staying on the issue of sentences, a quite separate, yet important, issue involves the possibility that the individual whose indictment has been referred to a national court for trial may receive, if convicted, a much higher sentence compared to the one that an international criminal tribunal would be likely to pass. Gojko Janković was sentenced to 34 years of imprisonment following the referral of his indictment for trial before the Bosnian War Crimes Chamber, a sentence which is quite high for the ICTY.[47] For a brief comparison, the different sentencing spans employed by the ICTY and the Serbian courts in the context of the cases arising out of the crimes committed in Vukovar, Croatia are of interest. The ICTY Trial Chamber acquitted Miroslav Radić, and sentenced the commander of the Serbian forces Mile Mrkšić, who was responsible for the murder of 200 people in Ovcara near Vukovar, to 20 years' imprisonment. Veselin Sljivancanin, another high-profile Serbian military officer who took part in the Vukovar battle was sentenced to five years' imprisonment. The Serbian court, for the same crime of murder of 200 civilians in Ovcara, sentenced eight people to 20 years' imprisonment and three to 15 years, including those who were part of the shooting squad. However, this is not an issue of concern to the *ad hoc* Tribunals or indeed the Bench/Chamber and, as such, cannot form part of the referral hearing.

In contrast to its apparent willingness to comment upon conditions of imprisonment, to be examined shortly, having transferred an indictment to the national courts, the ICTY has been reluctant to remark upon the national sentencing practice adopted post-referral, despite indications that the sentences imposed by domestic courts have caused concern to both the Prosecutor and the OSCE. For example, in its Final Progress Report in the *Rašević* case, which was prepared following the OSCE Monitoring Report, the Prosecutor shared the view given by the OSCE that, although commenting on the reduction of the sentence imposed on *Rašević* by the national court, he was not prepared to question its 'appropriateness'.[48] A similar approach was adopted by the Prosecutor in respect of the sentence awarded to Radovan Stanković by the BiH court.[49]

Provided that the sentence imposed at the national level is commensurate to the crime committed and in line with other cases involving similar offences, concerns over fair trial with regard to this particular point should not arise. International criminal

---

[46] Organic Law No 66/2008 of 21 November 2008 modifying and complementing Organic Law No 31/2007 of 25/07/2007 relating to the abolition of the death penalty, Official Gazette of the Republic of Rwanda, 1 December 2008. Although this law was in draft form at the time, the Appeals Chamber found that 'should this new law enter into force in its current form, the ambiguity as to the applicable punishment for transfer cases (…) would be resolved'. See *Hategekimana* ICTR-00-55B-R11*bis* (Decision on the Prosecution's Appeal against Decision on Referral under Rule 11*bis*, 4 December 2008) para 38.

[47] See BBC News, 'Bosnian Serb Jailed for 34 Years' <http://news.bbc.co.uk/1/hi/world/europe/6369483.stm> accessed 25 June 2015.

[48] *Rašević and Todović* IT-97-25/1-PT (Prosecutor's Final Progress Report, 20 April 2009) para 8.

[49] See *Stanković* IT-96-23/2-PT (Prosecutor's Seventh Progress Report, 27 June 2007) para 10.

tribunals generally impose lower sentences compared to national courts.[50] When the lower gravity of the indictments chosen for referral is the main issue for the referral itself, it is certainly paradoxical to think that the individual whose case has been transferred to national courts may end up serving a longer sentence than another accused whose trial continued internationally. However, it does not and should not affect the decision to refer.

The quality of prisons also remains of relevance. Despite the various initiatives that have been aimed at improving prison conditions, the issue was dealt with very succinctly in the jurisprudence.[51] However, on 25 May 2007, Radovan Stanković escaped from the police van transferring him to Sarajevo for dental treatment at a local hospital. He was the first indictee to have been transferred under Rule 11*bis* by the ICTY to Bosnia and Herzegovina for trial by a national court.[52] While Stanković is not the first prisoner to escape, his actions sparked debate as to the suitability of national courts to deal with cases originating at the ICTY, as well as the security of the prisons in which Rule 11*bis* individuals are held.

In this respect, it is important to acknowledge the significance of monitoring. Rule 11*bis*(D)(iv) enables the Prosecutor to send observers to monitor the proceedings before the national court the indictment is referred to.[53] The discretionary nature of this Rule[54] means that the Prosecutor is not under a firm obligation and may choose not to undertake any monitoring whatsoever. Monitoring was envisaged as a mechanism enabling observers in domestic trials to oversee the proceedings and report back to the *ad hoc* Tribunals, allowing the Office of the Prosecutor (OTP) to request the revocation of the referral, a process envisaged by Rule 11*bis*(F).[55] Due to the time limits in operation with regard to the completion of the Tribunals' work, it is unrealistic to expect that any cases will be deferred back to the ICTY or the ICTR in practice. Therefore, the effect of monitoring can only be pre-emptive. States wishing to avoid having the case removed from their national courts and deferred to the international

[50] See, generally, J.D. Ohlin, 'Towards a Unique Theory of International Sentencing', in G. Sluiter and S. Vasiliev (eds), *International Criminal Procedure: Towards a Coherent Body of Law* (Cameron May 2009).

[51] The CPT has been strongly involved in monitoring prison conditions in the States of the former Yugoslavia; for reports regarding these countries, see <http://www.cpt.coe.int/en/states.htm> accessed 25 June 2015. Cf. R. Mulgrew, *Towards the Development of the International Penal System* (Cambridge University Press 2013) 161–7.

[52] See Press Release JP/MOW/1126e, 14 November 2006.

[53] *Manual of Developed Practices* (n 23) 170–71.

[54] Note use of verb 'may' in Rule 11*bis*(D)(iv). Despite this element of discretion, in practice the Referral Bench has always imposed this extra level of scrutiny from the OTP on a referred indictment: Tolbert and Kontic (n 11) 154.

[55] Note that revocation will be done under the deferral provisions, so this is prior to the conclusion of the national trial. Even though this is not mentioned in Rule 11*bis*(F), it would be obvious that had the ICTY wanted to try a person post-conclusion of his trial before the national court, it would have to invoke the exception to the *non bis in idem* provision found in Art. 10 ICTYSt.

level for trial are more likely to abide by international standards.[56] The success of this process is dependent on the quality of the observers and the efficacy of the reporting system.

In most instances, this monitoring task is not undertaken by the OTP directly but, in the case of the ICTY, has been entrusted to the OSCE.[57] This 'outsourcing' is well within the Prosecutor's powers and given the significant experience the OSCE possesses in this field, the outcome of the monitoring process should be far superior compared to monitoring undertaken in house.[58] At the ICTR, in addition to OTP monitoring, the Registrar is empowered to send observers on behalf of the Chamber, who review detention conditions by meeting with the accused and the responsible authorities, among other issues, during their regular monitoring missions.[59] Monitors report their findings to the President of the MICT through the Registrar.[60]

The OSCE observed in its Monitoring Report in the *Janković* case that there was 'no reason to believe that there should be any problems with the conditions of detention' at the Foča Penal Correctional Institution (PCI), to which Janković was transferred to serve his sentence.[61] This is notable progress from the Final Monitoring Report in the *Stanković* case, where the Prosecutor noted the observation of the OSCE that a secure prison needed to be built at the State level.[62] Furthermore, in the period following the escape in May 2007 and its Report on the *Janković* case, the OSCE explicitly noted that the Foča PCI had undergone 'a significant rearrangement of both management and procedures' following the escape of Stanković from the same facility.[63] The OSCE specifically observed that, as a direct consequence of the Stanković escape, those deemed responsible were dismissed, while others were under investigation by the responsible national authorities.[64] Although this was regarded as welcome progress for

---

[56] For this reason, the Referral Bench has charged the Prosecutor to monitor every referred case, allowing not just oversight of the individual case but also encouraging fair trial guarantees and diligent prosecution in any subsequent or concurrent referrals: see *Ademi and Norac* IT-04-78-PT (Decision for Referral to the Authorities of the Republic of Croatia Pursuant to Rule 11*bis*, Referral Chamber, 14 September 2005) para 57.

[57] See Permanent Council Decision No 673 'Co-operation between the Organization for Security and Co-operation in Europe and the International Criminal Tribunal for the former Yugoslavia' of 19 May 2005, 556th Plenary Meeting, PC Journal No 556, Agenda Item 1.

[58] SCRes 827 (25 May 1993) para 5 'urges States and intergovernmental and non-governmental organizations to contribute funds, equipment and services to the International Tribunal, including the offer of expert personnel'. Monitoring by the OSCE would clearly come under this provision.

[59] See *Uwinkidi* MICT-12-25 (Monitoring Report for January 2015, 26 February 2015).

[60] Rule 11*bis*(D)(iv) ICTR RPE provides as follows: 'the Prosecutor may, and if the Trial Chamber so orders, the Registrar shall, send observers to monitor the proceedings in the State concerned. The observers shall report, respectively, to the Prosecutor, or through the Registrar to the President'.

[61] *Janković* IT-96-23/2-PT (Prosecutor's Ninth Progress Report, 14 February 2008) para 8.

[62] See *Stanković* IT-96-23/2-PT (Prosecutor's Seventh Progress Report, 27 June 2007) para 16.

[63] *Janković* IT-96-23/2-PT (Prosecutor's Ninth Progress Report, 14 February 2008) para 8.

[64] Ibid Annex A.

the penal system in Bosnia-Herzegovina, the OSCE recommended in its final Monitoring Report in the *Janković* case that human resource management structures ought to be strengthened, including, inter alia, recruitment procedures, oversight mechanisms for disciplinary offences and training – notably in respect of 'security procedures, prison regime, and human rights'.[65] It can therefore be said that the escape of Radovan Stanković led to a number of positive developments for the penal sanctions system in Bosnia-Herzegovina. This said, it is acknowledged that there remains scope for further improvements in future.

In Rwanda, prison conditions were discussed at greater length before the Chamber.[66] Moreover, of the national jurisdictions to which indictments have been transferred under Rule 11*bis*, this procedure has arguably had the greatest influence on prison conditions in Rwanda.[67] For example, the Monitor in the *Munyagishari* case noted that a 'special enclosure, often also referred as the "VIP Enclosure", was built to house male detainees whose cases have been transferred from the ICTR, MICT, and national jurisdictions'.[68] It was further observed that this enclosure was separated from the rest of the prison and was served by a separate entrance.[69] A number of grievances had, however, been raised by detainees whose cases were transferred to Rwandan national courts under Rule 11*bis* – and were then sentenced to imprisonment. For example, among the grievances raised by Munyagishari were the provision of inadequate food[70] and lack of access to a telephone.[71] Although the first grievance was raised again in later reports,[72] it was noted by the ICTR Monitor that consultations had taken place between detainees and the prison cook,[73] the Prison Director and a nutritionist on this matter.[74] These meetings led to the implementation of a new menu 'with the input of detainees'.[75] After the same period of time, Munyagishari also observed that there were no problems with telephone calls at the prison.[76]

It is clear from this discussion that the Monitoring Reports not only play a role in noting grievances raised by detainees, but also in recording the response thereto by the prison authorities, who also regularly meet with the Monitor. It is arguable that, without the Rule 11*bis* monitoring process, these grievances would neither be addressed as

---

65 Ibid.

66 See, eg, *Uwinkindi* ICTR-2001-75-R11*bis* (Decision on Prosecutor's Request for Referral to the Republic of Rwanda, 28 June 2011) paras 52–60.

67 See Palmer (n 44) 108.

68 *Munyagishari* MICT-12-20 (Monitoring Report for the Munyagishari Case (July–August 2013), 16 September 2013) para 17. It is noted that Jean Uwinkindi is also imprisoned within this special enclosure. See ibid., para 29.

69 Ibid.

70 Ibid., paras 32, 97.

71 Ibid., paras 30–34.

72 See, eg, *Munyagishari* MICT-12-20 (Monitoring Report for the Munyagishari Case (October and November 2013), 19 December 2013) para 7.

73 Ibid.

74 See *Munyagishari* MICT-12-20 (Monitoring Report for the Munyagishari Case (December 2013), 17 January 2013) para 14.

75 *Munyagishari* MICT-12-20 (Monitoring Report for the *Munyagishari* Case (March 2014), 27 March 2014) para 16.

76 Ibid.

quickly nor to the same extent: the process – albeit not without fault – is therefore to be commended to this end.

5. SOME CONCLUDING REMARKS

The pressing need to conclude the work of the *ad hoc* international criminal Tribunals dictated the adoption of Rule 11*bis*, which made sending cases back to national courts possible. However, this approach would have never been adopted were it not also for a significant shift in the political attitude and the ability of the judiciaries in the former Yugoslavia and Rwanda. In addition to its clear impact upon sentencing laws and prison conditions, Rule 11*bis* referrals served as a means of demonstrating that prosecution of core international crimes and enforcement of sentences can also happen at the national level. It may be that the recent emphasis placed on national courts is primarily due to the fact that the Tribunals are fast approaching the end of their lives. Nevertheless, they also demonstrate a marked improvement to the situation on the ground. Indeed, wide-ranging infrastructural improvements accompanied legislative reform in Rwanda. These included the development of a new Witness Protection Unit within the judiciary, the construction of internationally compliant detention facilities and increased capacity for delivering testimony by video-link from Rwanda.[77]

Referrals, encouraged by the completion strategy, belatedly rectify the non-engagement of national legal orders in most part with the Tribunals' work. Although concurrent jurisdiction has always played a key role in the ICTY and ICTR Statutes, the real shift came with the need to complete more cases prior to the termination of their functions. Concurrent jurisdiction was therefore reinterpreted to accommodate referrals of indictments to national courts.

Rule 11*bis* should not be heralded as a great success, however. For example, simply referring all (but two) cases to the War Crimes Chamber of the State Court of Bosnia and Herzegovina, which does not have the resources of the ICTY,[78] merely shifts the burden away from The Hague, but does not necessarily do justice for the accused nor the victims. This fact was well known to the Tribunals, prior to referrals being ordered.

Rule 11*bis* should also be seen as an opportunity for countries affected by mass violence to prove to the international community that they can exercise jurisdiction showcasing their new-found confidence in their own abilities and national procedures for sentencing. Moreover, it could be seen as the beginning of a process to try yet more cases than those referred by the *ad hoc* Tribunals. The improvement in sentencing practices and the conditions of detention might also benefit international criminal justice as a whole, as it can serve as an important precedent regarding the interplay between national institutions and an international criminal court.

---

[77] See ICTR OTP, *Complementarity in Action: Lessons Learned from the ICTR Prosecutor's Referral of International Criminal Cases to National Jurisdictions for Trial* (10 February 2015).

[78] For information on the resources available, see Court of Bosnia & Herzegovina, 'Statistics – 31/10/2012' <http://www.sudbih.gov.ba/?opcija=statistike&jezik=e> accessed 22 July 2015.

PART V

INTERNATIONAL IMPRISONMENT

The previous sections have demonstrated the fact that despite the preference for the sanction of imprisonment, and the often lengthy terms of imprisonment that are imposed, international criminal courts do not have access to an international prison. Accordingly, they must rely on cooperating States to enforce the sentences they hand down. This section examines this enforcement system from legal, practical, theoretical and penological perspectives.

Göran Sluiter's Chapter 10 sets the context for the section by describing the nature of, and legal basis for, State cooperation in this context. While 'it is a truism that international criminal tribunals cannot function without cooperation from States', he notes that the 'enforcement of sentences is a vital component of any criminal justice system'. In his chapter, Sluiter looks at the types of international sanctions that require State cooperation for their implementation and the consequences of the form of the sanction for the organisation of such cooperation. In particular, he explores whether States are obliged to cooperate in relation to the enforcement of fines imposed for administration of justice offences. The majority of the chapter focuses, however, on key components of the legal framework governing voluntary cooperation, including the designation procedure and the duty on States to respect both the rights of detained persons and the length of the term imposed by the international court.

Denis Abels' Chapter 11 adopts a more theoretical approach. In addition to looking at whether and how the goals adopted by national penal systems could be adapted for the international context, Abels also asks whether the broader objectives of the international criminal justice system have a role to play in the penal regimes of the international criminal courts. In this regard, he questions whether the objectives of international enforcement and the objectives of international criminal justice are 'ontologically connected' and asks if they should be aligned. The chapter also seeks to answer the question of 'whether, and if so, to what extent a systemic approach to the identification of objectives of international punishment is appropriate'? In other words, should the socio-political (and often conflicting) goals of international criminal justice inform the objectives governing the implementation of custodial sanctions?

The section ends with an empirically informed discussion of issues related to a particular goal for enforcement – rehabilitation. In Chapter 12, Barbora Holá and Joris van Wijk illustrate the realities involved in implementing international sentences in national prisons with reference to examples and scenarios. Noting the lack of consensus about what the term means or how it should be achieved, the chapter outlines the evolution of rehabilitative theory in domestic law and practice. This chapter then provides a comprehensive analysis of the treatment of the concept at the sentencing, enforcement and release stages of international criminal justice process.

10. State cooperation in the enforcement of sentences

Göran Sluiter

1. INTRODUCTION

It is a truism that international criminal tribunals cannot function without cooperation from States. This cooperation has many different dimensions and is subject to legal regimes that may vary per tribunal, per State and per form of cooperation.

State cooperation is also required to execute sentences that are imposed by international criminal tribunals. It is a dimension of cooperation and the functioning of international criminal tribunals that does not receive a great deal of attention.[1] This is understandable in the sense that holding international criminal trials does not appear directly dependent upon the regulation of enforcement of sentences; the trial can start and go on, even if there could be uncertainties in respect of the enforcement of sentences. That said, enforcement of sentences is a vital component of any criminal justice system; the authority and credibility of the international criminal justice system are ultimately also dependent on the adequate and fair organization of State cooperation in the enforcement of sentences.

The present chapter addresses the question whether cooperation of States in the enforcement of sentences is fair and adequate in the law and practice of international criminal tribunals. A comprehensive answer to this question is not possible in a book chapter. I will therefore have to be selective and concentrate on a number of essential elements of the aforementioned question. Before I move to some vital aspects of State cooperation in the enforcement of sentences, it is first essential to offer some observations on the types of sentences in international criminal justice and the consequences thereof for organizing State cooperation (Section 2). As to the essential elements of State cooperation in the enforcement of sentences of imprisonment, they will be treated in the following order: cooperation in accepting a convicted person (Section 3), cooperation in respecting the rights of the detained person (Section 4), and cooperation in respecting the duration of the sentence (Section 5). A separate section deals with cooperation in the enforcement of sentences other than imprisonment (Section 6). The chapter ends with some concluding observations (Section 7).

The present chapter concentrates on cooperation in the enforcement of sentences imposed by contemporary international criminal tribunals. Within that category there is in principle no attention for enforcement of sentences imposed by internationalized

[1] The literature has however been growing slightly over the years. For elaborate studies see, among others; C. Kress and G. Sluiter, 'Enforcement', in A. Cassese et al (eds), *The Rome Statute of the International Criminal Court – A Commentary* (Oxford University Press 2002) 1723–810; and in a broad manner dealing with execution of sentences: G. Vermeulen and E. de Wree, *Offender Reintegration and Rehabilitation as a Component of International Criminal Justice?* (Maklu 2014).

criminal tribunals, as these sentences tend to be executed by one State only, the justice system of which the internationalized court can be considered to be embedded in;[2] or there is not yet any practice in the enforcement of sentences.[3] It thus does not raise, at least not yet, issues of State cooperation in the enforcement of sentences. An interesting exception is the SCSL, which has sentences being enforced in Rwanda and the UK, and which will be included in the present chapter. Therefore, the focus will be on the ICTY, ICTR, their successor, the MICT, the SCSL (together also referred to as the *ad hoc* Tribunals),[4] and the ICC.

2. TYPES OF SENTENCES AND THE ORGANIZATION OF STATE COOPERATION

It is not possible to analyse State cooperation in the enforcement of sentences imposed by international criminal tribunals without some attention being paid to the types of sentences that are available and the inherent consequences thereof for cooperation.

First, as far as subject matter jurisdiction of international criminal tribunals is concerned, one needs to be aware that they may not only convict for the most serious crimes, also referred to as core crimes. They can also convict for a category of procedural crimes, so-called ‘offences against the administration of justice’, which includes, among others, contempt of court, interference with witnesses or false testimony.[5] At the ICC, it is in addition possible to impose a fine for misconduct, as referred to in Article 71 ICCSt. This may not be regarded as a punitive sanction, but as an ‘administrative measure’. Be this as it may, also for this ‘administrative measure’ the cooperation of States may be required to have it enforced.

The inclusion of less serious crimes in the practice of international criminal tribunals has an impact on sentences, and thus enforcement; it may mean that the imposition of fines occurs more frequently than anticipated by the drafters.

But since the international criminal tribunals are first and foremost about meting out punishment in respect of core crimes, it is not surprising that imprisonment ranks as the first available form of punishment. This brings us to the types of sentences – or rather categories of punishment – for which cooperation needs to be available. It seems that among the drafters of statutes of international criminal tribunals there has not been much thought beyond the obvious punishment, namely imprisonment. The ICTY and ICTR limited *penalties* to imprisonment; in addition to imprisonment, their Trial Chambers may, as a *measure* following conviction, order the return of any property and proceeds acquired by criminal conduct to their rightful owners.[6] This return of property

[2] This is the case with the ECCC and Special Panel for Serious Crimes (SPSC).

[3] This is the situation with the STL.

[4] In respect of the law of the *ad hoc* Tribunals, when there is only reference to the law of the ICTY in this chapter it implies that the law of the ICTR and SCSL contain highly similar, as good as identical, legal arrangements.

[5] Rules 77 and 91 ICTY RPE penalize contempt of court and false testimony, respectively; Art. 70 ICCSt penalizes a smaller group of offences against the administration of justice.

[6] Art. 24(3) ICTYSt.

raises many questions as to how it relates to penalties and – not in the least – how it should be enforced via State cooperation. In the practice of the *ad hoc* Tribunals, it has remained a dead letter.[7]

It makes sense that at the ICC the drafters sought to expand the category of available penalties, with (a) fines and (b) forfeiture of proceeds, property and assets derived directly or indirectly from that crime. Forfeiture is part of the provision on penalties in the ICCSt, Article 77, but one may wonder if it can be qualified as such. In addition to penalties, or measures under the heading of 'penalties', the ICC can also in case of conviction order reparation to victims.[8]

The question is whether the available penalties – or measures or orders following a conviction – are properly matched in the organization of State cooperation. For each penalty – or measures following a conviction – one has to anticipate their execution. Or in other words: penalties and measures following a conviction have little credibility or authority without adequate cooperation in their enforcement. This is the more so since it has never been envisaged in the international criminal justice system that penalties would be directly enforced by the international community, for example in the form of a 'UN prison'.[9]

The various contemporary international criminal tribunals have opted for a system in which State cooperation in the enforcement of sentences of imprisonment is of a voluntary nature.[10] At the heart of this choice lies the simple fact that a sentence of imprisonment can be enforced in any State, making it unnecessary to impose obligations more widely. Moreover, it was anticipated that there would be a sufficient number of 'volunteers' among States to receive an anticipated modest number of convicted persons. Matters are different in respect of fines, forfeiture orders and measures following a conviction, such as reparation orders. In relation to these penalties and measures a system of voluntary cooperation would not suffice. To have forfeiture orders effectively enforced, for example, not any State's cooperation would suffice, but the cooperation of the State where the convicted person's assets can be located is particularly needed. As a result, State cooperation in relation to these types of penalties and measures has developed into being obligatory.[11] Yet, it remains to be

---

[7] In the *Milošević* case, Judge Hunt of the ICTY Trial Chamber ordered the freezing of assets of the suspect. It follows from the decision that the prosecution requested the freezing of the assets with a view to enforce upon a possible conviction the order for return of property as provided in Art. 24(3) ICTYSt. Judge Hunt, however, granted the application with reference only to the assumption that freezing of assets would facilitate the arrest of the suspect: *Milošević* IT-02-54 (Decision on Review of Indictments and Application for Consequential Orders, 24 May 1999) paras 26–29.

[8] See Art. 75 ICCSt. See on victims reparations, C. McCarthy, 'The International Criminal Court's regime of victim redress: non-punitive responses to crimes under the Rome Statute', Chapter 17 in this volume.

[9] Establishing an international prison has been advocated, however, by Margaret Penrose (M.M. Penrose, 'Lest we fail: the importance of enforcement of international criminal law' (1999) 15 *American University International Law Review* 390). See M.M. Penrose, 'Creating an international prison', Chapter 18 in this volume.

[10] Art. 27 ICTYSt; Art. 103 (1)(a) ICCSt.

[11] Compare Art. 109 ICCSt.

seen – and to be addressed in Section 6 – whether this regulation of obligatory cooperation has been done in a satisfactory manner.

Cooperation in the enforcement of sentences has to strike a balance between an obligation of result, i.e. enforcing the sentence, on the one hand, and on the other hand, the rights of convicted persons and – in case of enforcing fines and forfeiture orders – the rights of third parties. In practice this means, for example, respecting the duration of a sentence of imprisonment, but also allowing for early release with a view to the reintegration of the convicted person into society. It may also mean that a forfeiture order may not be enforced if this would infringe the bona fide rights of third parties. It is worth pointing out that international criminal justice does not fully operate on the basis of (mutual) recognition of sentences and a corresponding system of direct enforcement.[12] The execution of sentences is not completely transferred to States by international criminal tribunals, as they continue to exercise substantive supervision in respect of both the duration of the sentence and the treatment of the detained person. In the context of the European Union, however, cooperation in the execution of sentences has, since 2008, been based on mutual trust and mutual recognition.[13] The result is that EU members are obliged to recognize a judgment of another EU member and are also obliged to directly enforce the imposed penalties. It may be worth considering the EU model of cooperation in the execution of sentences – just like in the execution of arrest warrants – as a point of reference for organizing State cooperation with international criminal tribunals in the future. The consequences of a model of mutual, or at least direct, recognition of sentences for international criminal tribunals is that they will lose control over the execution of the sentence, but this is justified by a high degree of confidence in the State which is executing the sentence. It furthermore carries with it the advantage that it will save international criminal tribunals resources, as they no longer would have any role to play in the execution of sentences after their transfer.

3. COOPERATION IN ACCEPTING A CONVICTED PERSON FOR THE PURPOSES OF ENFORCEMENT OF A SENTENCE OF IMPRISONMENT

The contemporary international criminal tribunals – the ICTY, ICTR and ICC – all provide for voluntary cooperation in accepting a person for the purpose of enforcing a sentence of imprisonment.[14] The ICCSt provides for a safety net in case voluntary

---

[12] See in more detail on the legal status of an ICC sentence and how this relates to national enforcement, G.A.M. Strijards, 'Article 103', in O. Triffterer (ed), *Commentary on the Rome Statute of the International Criminal Court* (Verlag C.H. Beck 2008) 1648–54.

[13] Compare Council Framework Decision 2008/909/JHA of 27 November 2008 on the application of the principle of mutual recognition to judgments in criminal matters imposing custodial sentences or measures involving deprivation of liberty for the purpose of their enforcement in the European Union.

[14] See (n 1).

assistance cannot be obtained; in that scenario, the Netherlands is obliged to execute the sentence of imprisonment.[15]

In his report accompanying the creation of the ICTY, the UN Secretary-General ruled out the possibility of having sentences enforced in the States of the former Yugoslavia and refers to the task of finding States which are prepared to execute sentences of imprisonment on a voluntary basis:

> 121. The Secretary-General is of the view that, given the nature of the crimes in question and the international character of the tribunal, the enforcement of sentences should take place outside the territory of the former Yugoslavia. States should be encouraged to declare their readiness to carry out the enforcement of prison sentences in accordance with their domestic laws and procedures, under the supervision of the International Tribunal.
>
> 122. The Security Council would make appropriate arrangements to obtain from States an indication of their willingness to accept convicted persons. This information would be communicated to the Registrar, who would prepare a list of States in which the enforcement of sentences would be carried out.[16]

In relation to the ICTR, enforcement in the State concerned, Rwanda, was not ruled out – it was even explicitly provided for: 'Imprisonment shall be served in Rwanda or any of the States on a list of States which have indicated to the Security Council their willingness to accept convicted persons, as designated by the International Tribunal for Rwanda.'[17]

Yet, in practice it was considered that other States were better suited for purposes of enforcement, on account of the risks convicted persons may incur in Rwanda.[18] Vermeulen and De Wree have brought to our attention the fact that Rwanda has consistently objected to ICTR prisoners having their sentences executed elsewhere, which has put quite some strain on the procedure designating a State of enforcement.[19]

The internationalized criminal tribunals provide for enforcement of sentences of imprisonment in the State in relation to which the tribunal/court exercises jurisdiction.[20] The STL is an exception in this regard. It has followed the approach adopted by the ICTY, meaning that enforcement will take place in a State with which an enforcement agreement has been concluded. In contrast to the ICTY model, however, the State where the crimes have been committed, Lebanon, has not been explicitly excluded as a

---

15 Art. 103(4) ICCSt.

16 Report of the Secretary-General pursuant to Para 2 of SCRes 808 (3 May 1993) UN Doc S/25704 (1993) paras 121, 122.

17 Art. 26 ICTRSt.

18 See for detailed account and analysis, D. Abels, *Prisoners of the International Community. The Legal Position of Persons Detained at International Criminal Tribunals* (TMC Asser Press 2012) 478–88.

19 Vermeulen and De Wree (n 1) 81–5.

20 See for ECCC Rule 113(1) ECCC IR, implying execution of the sentence in Cambodia: '1. The enforcement of a sentence shall be made at the initiative of the Co-Prosecutors.' For the SPSC in East Timor the national enforcement follows from the UNTAET Regulations, especially Regulation 2000/11 on the Organization of Courts in East Timor; Reg. 13 Regulation 2000/11 which deals with supervision of sentences of imprisonment.

possible place for enforcement of a sentence.[21] The SCSL provides for enforcement of sentences in Sierra Leone, but if circumstances so require sentences may be enforced in a State which has concluded an enforcement agreement with the ICTY and ICTR and which is willing to extend application of such an agreement to a person convicted by the SCSL.[22]

The ICTY, ICTR and SCSL have negotiated a substantive number of enforcement agreements.[23] These agreements do not oblige States to accept a convicted person,[24] but serve as an additional legal framework governing the transfer of sentenced persons to States which are in principle agreeable to accepting one or more convicted persons. The agreements can be seen as the *trait-d'union* between the applicable law of the relevant international criminal tribunal and the domestic law of States that allow for enforcement of sentences of imprisonment. They have a uniform set-up and contain a strong supervisory role for the sentencing international criminal tribunal. It is even possible – and has occurred in practice – that enforcement of the sentence in the receiving State is terminated and the sentenced person is returned to temporary custody at an international criminal tribunal, with a view to being transferred to another State to serve the remainder of their sentence.[25]

In the subsequent sections, the duty to respect the duration of the sentence and to respect human rights will be addressed. The process of finding a State for enforcement of the sentence is only in part a legal matter. It can be dissected in two stages. First, States need to be found which are in principle available to accept convicted persons. Second, after conviction, there is a procedure in which a State needs to be selected among the available States.

The first obvious task for each international criminal tribunal is to secure a sufficient number of States which are available to enforce sentences of imprisonment. While beggars cannot be choosers, there are a number of criteria that guide international criminal tribunals in the selection of States for the conclusion of enforcement agreements. There must, first of all, be confidence in the State being able to enforce the sentence and to respect the sentence's duration. Moreover, the State concerned must be in a position to respect the rights of the detained person. It remains uncertain to which degree other factors have played a role in the choice of States for the conclusion of enforcement agreements.[26] In this regard one can think of the availability of a

---

[21] Art. 29(1) STLSt reads as follows: 'Imprisonment shall be served in a State designated by the President of the Special Tribunal from a list of States that have indicated their willingness to accept persons convicted by the Tribunal.'

[22] See Art. 22(1) SCSLSt.

[23] The website of the ICTY mentions 16 enforcement agreements and five *ad hoc* agreements with Germany; the websites of the ICTR and SCSL respectively mention eight enforcement agreements concerning the ICTR and two involving the SCSL.

[24] See e.g. Art. 2(4) of the Agreement between UN and Mali concerning the ICTR.

[25] See the *Krstić* case discussed further below.

[26] Vermeulen and De Wree (n 1) 81: 'Moreover, it is very difficult to discover the policy behind the practice of international transfer of convicted persons by the *ad hoc* Tribunals.'

reintegration programme for a convicted person or the distance to the State where family members can be expected to live, with a view to not practically denying family visits.[27]

The reality is that the majority of enforcement agreements have been concluded with European States; this also applies to the ICC, which will be discussed below. Only in respect of sentences imposed by the ICTR and SCSL have a smaller number of African states been found prepared to conclude enforcement agreements with the relevant institutions.[28] It follows from the foregoing that the overwhelming majority of UN members have not concluded agreements for the execution of sentences of imprisonment. The overriding factor appears to be to ensure some degree of proximity to the Tribunal/Court which has imposed the sentence and the place of residence of family members; thus, European countries are a logical choice for the enforcement of ICTY sentences. However, it must also be noted that a number of ICTR and SCSL convicts – coming from Africa – have been sent to West-European countries to serve their sentences of imprisonment. It thus remains uncertain on what basis States are selected and targeted by international criminal tribunals for the conclusion of enforcement agreements. The literature makes mention of the fact that especially for the ICTR it has been quite difficult to find a sufficient number of States which are willing to accept convicted persons.[29]

The ICC has concluded to date eight enforcement agreements, with Colombia, Serbia, Denmark, Belgium, Mali, Finland, the UK and Austria. More agreements are to be concluded in the future. The number appears at least for now sufficient to ensure enforcement of sentences of imprisonment without having to resort to the residual function of the host State, as provided for in Article 103(4) ICCSt. The content of these agreements are of course modelled on the law of the ICC. Yet, the essential features are as good as identical to the ICTY and ICTR enforcement agreements, which means they contain strict obligations for the enforcing State to respect the rights of the detained person[30] and the duration of the sentence,[31] and a strong supervisory role for the Court to have these obligations enforced.[32]

The designation of a State for the enforcement of sentences entails an internal procedure for all of the contemporary international criminal tribunals. This procedure is governed by practice directions (ICTY and ICTR) or the RPE. It is as such not a matter of State cooperation and has been discussed and analysed in detail elsewhere.[33] It is clear that this designation procedure – including the element of taking into account the views of the convicted person and matters such as equitable distribution – gains in strength and importance when there are more States of enforcement to choose from.

[27] Vermeulen and De Wree adopt the view however that there is very little attention to the position of the convicted person in the course of the designation procedure – Vermeulen and De Wree, ibid.

[28] These States are Senegal, Rwanda, Swaziland, Benin and Mali.

[29] See Abels (n 18) 480–81.

[30] See, e.g. Arts 6, 7 of the Enforcement Agreement between the ICC and Finland.

[31] See, e.g. ibid., Art. 11.

[32] See, e.g. ibid., Arts 13, 14.

[33] See, among other, Abels (n 18) 464–500.

In respect of the enforcement of sentences of imprisonment the two core issues of cooperation concern the rights of the detained person and respect for the duration of the sentence. Both matters will be addressed in the two following sections.

4. COOPERATION IN RESPECTING THE RIGHTS OF DETAINEES DURING THE ENFORCEMENT OF A SENTENCE OF IMPRISONMENT

Contrary to the situation of transferring the execution of sentences between States, the international criminal tribunals retain responsibility over the protection of the rights of the convicted and detained person. As was already mentioned, this is not self-evident. The international criminal tribunals could have opted for a system in which the transfer of the execution of the sentence of imprisonment to a State ends every responsibility for the fate of the convicted person. Such a position could have been based on the degree of trust in the receiving State. The latter would then be fully responsible for the protection of the rights of the detained person, as a result of which the detained person would only have recourse to national avenues for review.

The ICTYSt, however, stands in the way of such full transfer, as Article 27 provides: 'Such imprisonment shall be in accordance with the applicable law of the State concerned, subject to the supervision of the International Tribunal.'

The reference to supervision of the ICTY appears to imply continuing responsibility for the protection of the rights of the detained person, although on the basis of the text alone one could also argue that the supervisory role is of a more restricted nature and concerns only the imprisonment as such, especially its duration. The Secretary-General, in his report accompanying the creation of the ICTY, did not mention the rights of the detained person or any supervisory role the ICTY should play in that area; his observations were in this regard limited to the issue of pardon and commutation of sentence.[34] Yet, it follows from the first enforcement agreement that was concluded with Italy in 1997 that the ICTY saw an important task for itself in ensuring that the rights of the detained person were adequately protected during enforcement at the national level. It did so in two ways.

First, the ICTY obliges the enforcing State to ensure that conditions of imprisonment will be compatible with the UNSMR, the UNBOP and the UNBP.[35]

Second, this obligation to protect the rights of detained persons is followed by an obligation to allow inspections of detention facilities by the ICRC[36] (or in later agreements by the CPT[37]). In addition, the ICTY may at any time decide to terminate the enforcement of the sentence and order the transfer of the convicted person to

---

[34] See Report of the Secretary-General (n 16) para 123.

[35] See Art. 3(5) of the Enforcement Agreement with Italy.

[36] See ibid., Art. 6(1).

[37] See Art. 6(1) of the Enforcement Agreement with Albania. See on inspection of international imprisonment: S. Snacken and N. Kiefer, 'Oversight of international imprisonment: the Committee for the Prevention of Torture', Chapter 14 in this volume.

another State or the ICTY.[38] Although it is not explicitly spelled out, it is clear that enforcement may be terminated in case of (serious) violations of the rights of the detained person.

The strong obligations on States to respect the rights of the detained person in the context of the ICTY have been followed in the ICCSt. Article 106 ICCSt provides as follows:

1. The enforcement of a sentence of imprisonment shall be subject to the supervision of the Court and shall be consistent with widely accepted international treaty standards governing treatment of prisoners.
2. The conditions of imprisonment shall be governed by the law of the State of enforcement and shall be consistent with widely accepted international treaty standards governing treatment of prisoners; in no case shall such conditions be more or less favourable than those available to prisoners convicted of similar offences in the State of enforcement.
3. Communications between a sentenced person and the Court shall be unimpeded and confidential.

One would expect 'international treaty standards governing treatment of prisoners' to require further specification in enforcement agreements and the case law of the Court. But this is generally not the case; the enforcement agreements involving Finland, Serbia, Denmark, Austria, Belgium and Mali merely repeat the yardstick set out in Article 106(1) ICCSt. An interesting variation is the agreement with the UK, in which the standard set out in Article 106(1) ICCSt is said to include obligations under the ECHR. One would assume that 'widely accepted international treaty standards governing treatment of prisoners' would include the instruments to which reference is made in the enforcement agreements concerning the ICTY and ICTR, but there is no basis for this in either the enforcement agreements or the law and practice of the Court. The uncertainty therefore subsists whether the reference to treaty standards in Article 106 – and enforcement agreements – would include non-treaty law standards such as the UNSMR. Clark adopts the view that these standards should be considered to be assimilated in general human rights treaty provisions.[39] Moreover, a convicted person could seek to improve his/her protection under Article 106 by having the Court apply additional sources (being not in a treaty) of protection pursuant to Article 21 ICCSt. Article 21 refers to rules and principles of international law more broadly (Art. 21 (1)(b)), and, importantly, to internationally recognized human rights (Art. 21(3)). It is, however, uncertain whether the difference in reference to human rights law between Article 21(3) and Article 106(1) – with the latter provision being restricted to treaty standards – will be resolved in favour of applicability of non-treaty law standards such as the UNSMR. Not only may the content of Article 106(1), in its ordinary meaning, take precedence and rule out the applicability of other sources of human rights law than treaty standards; the additional problem, one of continuing debate, is also that

---

38 See Art. 9(2) of the Enforcement Agreement with Italy.

39 R.S. Clark, 'Article 106', in Triffterer (n 12) 1664.

international standards related to detention may fall short of amounting to obligations under international law and could be – in part – disregarded on that basis.

The reference in Article 106 to supervision by the Court and the right to unimpeded and confidential communication between a sentenced person and the Court give reason to assume that there will be avenues for the detained person to have his rights directly protected by the Court; if need be, termination of enforcement in a certain State is a possibility, which is provided for in Article 104 ICCSt, as further implemented in Rules 209 and 210 ICC RPE.

All in all, the regimes of the *ad hoc* Tribunals and possibly the ICC impose strong obligations on enforcing States in terms of protecting prisoners' rights. One may wonder whether this is realistic. A substantive number of States may not be able to live up to all of the international standards in this area. In this regard, it must be borne in mind that the instruments to which reference is made in the ICTY/ICTR enforcement agreements – and which might also be the standards as meant by Article 106 ICCSt – are not treaties binding States; it is also doubtful whether these standards are part and parcel of customary international law.[40] It may also result in questionable unequal treatment between national prisoners and prisoners convicted by an international criminal tribunal. In certain African States it was even deemed necessary to build new and separate prisons for ICTR and SCSL convicts.

Be this as it may, it would also be painful if international criminal tribunals would ignore standards that are developed at the international level. By explicitly making the imprisonment conditional upon these standards, the international criminal tribunals make an important contribution to taking these standards seriously.[41]

It would be interesting to see how until this day the international criminal tribunals have respected in practice the rights of convicted persons serving their sentence of imprisonment in a State. This practice, as far as enforcement at the national level is concerned, is at present limited to the ICTY, ICTR and SCSL convicts. No person convicted by the ICC (at the time of writing Lubanga and Katanga) has yet been transferred to a State for the enforcement of his sentence.

There is only very limited jurisprudence on the protection of prisoners' rights. Complaints to the ICTY or ICTR about the treatment of detained persons are confidential; it is thus unknown to the present author how many communications dealing with prisoners' rights have been submitted directly to the ICTY or ICTR. It is as a result also unknown how the ICTY or ICTR generally respond to such communications and if, for example, they have developed certain requirements of admissibility. One could imagine, for example, that complaints about alleged violations of the rights of a detained person are only admissible in cases where available national complaint mechanisms have been exhausted.

There is one case that has generated publicly available case law that concerns the enforcement of sentences of imprisonment: Krstić in the UK. His situation has also

---

40 In more detail on this matter, see Abels, who argues, among other things, that some of the norms laid down in the UNSMR reflect customary international law (Abels (n 18) 30–44, especially 33).

41 For additional reasons to apply 'soft law' to treatment of persons convicted by international criminal tribunals, see Abels (n 18) 763–4.

been reported in the press.[42] Krstić was attacked and injured in the UK prison where he had been serving his sentence since 2004. On 4 October 2011 the President of the ICTY ordered in a confidential decision the transfer of Krstić to the UNDU pending the designation of another State for the enforcement of the sentence. On 19 July 2013 the President of the ICTY (or rather the MICT) ordered that Krstić serve the remainder of his sentence in Poland.[43]

Unfortunately, there are no publicly available decisions or filings which deal with the grounds for termination of enforcement of Krstić's sentence in the UK. From the perspective of the obligations incumbent upon States to protect the rights of detained persons, the essential question of course is whether the treatment of Krstić in the UK had in some way been inconsistent with international standards on prisoners' rights and whether on that basis the ICTY deemed it necessary to terminate enforcement of the sentence in the UK. It follows from the enforcement agreements that the ICTY may terminate execution of the sentence in a given State, without specified grounds being required. In other words, there is no basis to assume that Krstić's rights were not properly respected. Attacks on inmates are, regrettably, not uncommon and can be very difficult to prevent. It may thus very well be that Krstić's transfer to Poland is based on other considerations, such as maximizing his personal security.

In addition to the Krstić case it is worth paying attention to the endeavours of Charles Taylor to have the enforcement of his sentence in the UK terminated and to be transferred to Rwanda. On 25 June 2014 Charles Taylor, sentenced to 50 years' imprisonment by the SCSL, applied to the SCSL to have the enforcement of his sentence in the UK terminated and to be transferred to Rwanda. On 30 January 2015, the SCSL Trial Chamber denied that application.[44] Taylor submitted that his human rights and his rights as a detained person were violated on account of his detention in the UK, especially his right to family life. It was also argued that the UK would be unwilling or unable to keep Mr. Taylor in a secure setting that conforms with international standards of detention.[45] In respect of the key matter, Taylor's inability to receive visits from his family, the Trial Chamber ruled that such inability was not due to an interference with Article 8 ECHR by the UK, but was purely due to his family's failure to comply with visa requirements.[46]

There is, also in light of the available jurisprudence, no basis to question the willingness and ability of States to comply with the obligation imposed on them to ensure that imprisonment is consistent with international standards related to detained persons. That said, further research, including interviews with persons who are at present serving their ICTY/ICTR sentence, or have already done so, will be necessary to verify this assumption of compliance. In particular, it would be worthwhile knowing

---

[42] 'Brutal revenge: In a high-security British jail, a Serbian warlord has his throat slashed by three Muslim inmates' (*Daily Mail*, 8 May 2010).

[43] *Krstić* MICT-13-46-ES.1/IT-98-33-ES (Order Designating the State in which Radislav Krstić is to Serve the Remainder of His Sentence, 19 July 2013).

[44] *Taylor* SCSL-03-01-ES (Decision on Public with Public and Confidential Annexes Charles Ghankay Taylor's Motion for Termination of Enforcement of Sentence in the United Kingdom and for Transfer to Rwanda, 30 January 2015).

[45] Ibid., para 3.

[46] Ibid., para 90.

whether, and if so under what circumstances and in which ways, detained persons can call upon international criminal tribunals to exercise their supervisory function in respect of protecting the rights of detainees.

5. EARLY RELEASE? COOPERATION IN RESPECTING THE DURATION OF A SENTENCE OF IMPRISONMENT

The second vital element of State cooperation in the enforcement of sentences of imprisonment concerns respect for the duration of the sentence. Obviously, creators of international criminal tribunals want judgments to be recognized and wish to avoid, for example, a situation whereby a sentence is either reduced or increased by a State without authorization or proper procedure.

5.1 The Law of the *ad hoc* Tribunals and the ICC – Divergence in Approaches

The ICTYSt sets out the following procedure:

> If, pursuant to the applicable law of the State in which the convicted person is imprisoned, he or she is eligible for pardon or commutation of sentence, the State concerned shall notify the International Tribunal accordingly. The President of the International Tribunal, in consultation with the judges, shall decide the matter on the basis of the interests of justice and the general principles of law.[47]

The approach at the ICC differs, as follows from Article 110 ICCSt:

1 The State of enforcement shall not release the person before expiry of the sentence pronounced by the Court.
2. The Court alone shall have the right to decide any reduction of sentence, and shall rule on the matter after having heard the person.
3. When the person has served two thirds of the sentence, or 25 years in the case of life imprisonment, the Court shall review the sentence to determine whether it should be reduced. Such a review shall not be conducted before that time.
4. In its review under paragraph 3, the Court may reduce the sentence if it finds that one or more of the following factors are present:
   (a) The early and continuing willingness of the person to cooperate with the Court in its investigations and prosecutions;
   (b) The voluntary assistance of the person in enabling the enforcement of the judgments and orders of the Court in other cases, and in particular providing assistance in locating assets subject to orders of fine, forfeiture or reparation which may be used for the benefit of victims; or
   (c) Other factors establishing a clear and significant change of circumstances sufficient to justify the reduction of sentence, as provided in the Rules of Procedure and Evidence.

---

[47] Art. 28 ICTYSt. Rules 123–125 ICTY RPE further regulate the matter.

5. If the Court determines in its initial review under paragraph 3 that it is not appropriate to reduce the sentence, it shall thereafter review the question of reduction of sentence at such intervals and applying such criteria as provided for in the Rules of Procedure and Evidence.[48]

The essential difference between the ICTY/ICTR and the ICC is whether or not the starting point for 'early release' lies in the *lex loci* or in the law of the court that has imposed the sentence. The drafters of the ICTY and ICTR Statutes have on paper opted for an approach in which a detained person needs to be eligible for early release in the enforcing State before a decision to that end can possibly be taken by the ICTY or ICTR. This carries with it the disadvantage that the national approaches towards early release become decisive; as these approaches may diverge there is the risk of inequality in the treatment of convicted persons. Moreover, especially in the early cases of the ICTY, it defies the demands of legal certainty and the interests of justice that judges have to impose sentences without knowing what percentage of that sentence will eventually be executed in practice.

Conversely, at the ICC both the moment and conditions for early release have been codified in the Statute, and national law does not play a role anymore in this determination. It creates legal certainty about early release and equality among prisoners serving sentences in different States. The downside is that States may be less willing to accept convicted persons because of rigid obligations which may conflict with domestic rules applicable to early release. It remains to be seen in the future practice of the Court to what degree this will be a problem.

The law of the ICTY/ICTR and ICC only appears to deal with early release or in the terminology used by their respective statutes, pardon and commutation of sentence (ICTY/ICTR) and the reduction of sentence (ICC). This substantially affects the execution of the sentence. Matters such as leave from prison, participation in special programmes outside the prison walls are not regulated in the Statutes but have been addressed in enforcement agreements (ICTY/ICTR)[49] or RPE (ICC).[50]

One may wonder whether this will be an important point of debate in practice between the supervisory court/tribunal and the enforcing State. In this respect it must be borne in mind that certain penitentiary programmes tend to be reserved for nationals or persons residing in the State where they serve their sentence, because they are related to that person's reintegration into society. Thus, such programmes are not likely to be accessible to persons convicted by international criminal tribunals who come from other countries than the State of enforcement.

---

[48] Rules 223 and 224 ICC RPE contain further regulatory provisions.

[49] See, e.g. Art. 3(4) of the enforcement agreement with Belgium: 'The Requested State shall notify the International Tribunal if the convicted person is granted a sentence enforcement method other than early release, or if this method is revoked or suspended.'

[50] See Rule 211(2) ICC RPE:

> When a sentenced person is eligible for a prison programme or benefit available under the domestic law of the State of enforcement which may entail some activity outside the prison facility, the State of enforcement shall communicate that fact to the Presidency, together with any relevant information or observation, to enable the Court to exercise its supervisory function.

When we look at the various enforcement agreements related to the ICTY and ICTR one notices in each and every one of these agreements that the enforcing State shall be bound by the duration of the sentence. This was mentioned earlier. However, for certain States it may not be possible to enforce sentences of a certain duration, especially sentences of life imprisonment. There is also an important human rights dimension to this matter. The ECtHR has ruled that the enforcement of a sentence of life imprisonment without the possibility of early release may amount to a violation of Article 3 ECHR.[51] This is case law that should guide international criminal tribunals in their sentencing practice, but it also means that at least European States may not be able to enforce imposed life sentences without possibility of release.[52]

The conclusion of enforcement agreements opens up the possibility for States refusing to enforce sentences which are incompatible with the demands of the ECHR and even national law. Article 3(2) of the enforcement agreement with Spain, for example, provides that it will only consider enforcement of ICTY sentences where the duration does not exceed the highest maximum under Spanish law. Although this clarifies the cooperation framework for enforcement of sentences between Spain and the ICTY, it was not strictly necessary to put it in the enforcement agreement. As already mentioned, States that have concluded enforcement agreements with international criminal tribunals are not obliged to accept any particular convicted person.

5.2 The Increasing Practice in Early Release – Bridging the Gap Between the *ad hoc* Tribunals and the ICC

There is increasing case law dealing with applications for early release; this does not yet concern the ICC. These rulings, as far as they are publicly available, give interesting insights into the *ad hoc* Tribunals' practice and the role of States in cooperating with the tribunals.

At the outset, it is important to point out that there are special Practice Directions at the ICTY, ICTR (and MICT) and SCSL which govern the procedure for early release.[53] The Practice Directions provide for a procedure, in accordance with due process. One notices that contrary to what could have been inferred from the Statute, the MICT

---

51 See *Vinter and others v UK* App nos 66069/09, 130/10 and 3896/10 (ECtHR, 9 July 2013); however, for possibly nuancing *Vinter*, and taking a step backwards, see *Hutchinson v UK* App no 57592/08 (ECtHR, 3 February 2015).

52 See on the problem of life sentences in international criminal justice: D. Van Zyl Smit, 'Determinate and indeterminate sentences of imprisonment in international criminal justice', Chapter 4 in this volume.

53 ICTY: Procedure for the Determination of Applications for Pardon, Commutation of Sentence, and Early Release of Persons Convicted by the International Tribunal; ICTR: ICTR Practice Direction On The Procedure For The Determination Of Applications For Pardon, Commutation Of Sentence, And Early Release Of Persons Convicted By The International Criminal Tribunal for Rwanda. Both have been replaced by the MICT Practice Direction: The Practice Direction on the Procedure for the Determination of Applications for Pardon, Commutation of Sentence and Early Release of Persons Convicted by the ICTR, the ICTY or the Mechanism. SCSL (and RSCSL): Practice Direction on the Conditional Early Release of Persons Convicted by the Special Court for Sierra Leone.

Practice Direction does not only allow for notification of eligibility for early release through the enforcing State; it also enables a convicted person to directly petition the President for early release if he or she believes he or she is eligible.[54] Under the Practice Direction it no longer seems to be a requirement that the convicted person is eligible for early release under the national law of the enforcing State. Moreover, the eligibility for early release under national law is not even mentioned as a relevant factor for deciding on applications for early release, as set out in Rule 151 of the MICT RPE:

> In determining whether pardon, commutation of sentence, or early release is appropriate, the President shall take into account, inter alia, the gravity of the crime or crimes for which the prisoner was convicted, the treatment of similarly-situated prisoners, the prisoner's demonstration of rehabilitation, as well as any substantial cooperation of the prisoner with the Prosecutor.

The practice of the ICTY, ICTR and MICT has thus increasingly developed in the direction of the approach adopted by the ICC in Article 110 MICTSt, in which early release is exclusively a matter for the international criminal tribunal. The role of the State is reduced to informing the President of eligibility for early release under national law; the enforcing State is furthermore reminded of the fact that the President's decision not to allow early release is binding, even if this would be inconsistent with national law.[55]

In their practice, the ICTY and ICTR are keen to maximize equal treatment among convicted persons, but for a long time this was only among persons convicted by the same tribunal. Since 2003 persons convicted by the ICTY have been consistently regarded eligible for early release upon completion of two-thirds of their sentences.[56] By contrast, the practice for ICTR convicted persons since 2011 is that they are eligible upon completion of three-quarters of their sentences.[57] In a ruling of 11 December 2012, concerning an application for early release coming from Bisengimana, the President of the successor to the ICTY and ICTR, the MICT, decided this disparity in treatment should come to an end. As of that day ICTR convicts would also benefit from the two-thirds eligibility threshold.[58] It was made clear, however, that the two-thirds mark is in essence an admissibility threshold, and the relevant factors set out in Rule 151 MICT RPE could still result in denial of early release applications.[59] In other words, there is no right to early release upon completion of two-thirds of one's sentence.

It has been wise to apply the two-thirds mark for both ICTY and ICTR convicts. It is also consistent with the two-thirds threshold applicable at the ICC and SCSL. It is

---

54 Arts 2 and 3 MICT Practice Direction.

55 See Art. 11 MICT Practice Direction.

56 See the summary of the ICTY early release practice in *Bisengimana* MICT-12-07 (Decision of the President on Early Release of Paul Bisengimana and on Motion to File a Public Redacted Application, 11 December 2012).

57 See ibid., para 18.

58 Ibid., para 20: 'Although the two-thirds practice originates from the ICTY, I believe that fundamental fairness and justice are best served if the ICTY practice applies uniformly to the entire prisoner population to be ultimately supervised by the Mechanism.'

59 Ibid., para 19.

worth paying attention to the SCSL as far as its law and practice towards early release is concerned.[60] Its Practice Direction on this matter differs considerably from those related to the ICTY and ICTR.

First, the SCSL Practice Direction sets out clearly the eligibility threshold, placing it at two-thirds of completion of the sentence.[61] Second, the convicted person carries the burden of having satisfied a number of conditions, including that he is not a danger to the community and that he has made a positive contribution to peace and reconciliation in Sierra Leone.[62] Third, under the SCSL scheme, early release is only of a conditional nature; the Practice Direction contains provisions on review of the conditions and consequences in case of violations. A long list of conditions is attached as Annex C to the Practice Direction. Fourth, the procedure is far more complex, involving significant input from the Registrar and other relevant actors on a wide range of issues concerning both the convicted person's conduct during enforcement, as well as his reintegration into society, possible risks for victims and witnesses, etc.[63] In light of the extended and more complex Practice Direction it cannot come as a surprise that the SCSL Decisions on applications for conditional early release are more substantive and address more issues. Yet, the more demanding procedures have not made conditional early release impossible; it has been granted to Fofana.[64] It has also been granted to Senessie.[65]

In terms of State cooperation, the requirement of compliance with certain conditions may create an additional burden on the State to which the convicted person is conditionally released. That State must, for example, allow a Monitoring Authority to be present on its territory to supervise compliance with the decisions. Although there is no legal basis for any duty to cooperate in ensuring compliance with release conditions, the State of release has until now been restricted to Sierra Leone which may be expected to cooperate with release conditions also on a voluntary basis. However, the more elaborate approach adopted by the SCSL towards early release, including the applicability of conditions, would legally not be possible or would perhaps be too complex in the context of international criminal tribunals which deal with a wider variety of States of enforcement and release.[66]

In sum, on the matter of State cooperation on the duration of the sentence, it can be said that this has proved to be quite unproblematic in practice. The practice of the *ad hoc* Tribunals has evolved to a system in which they unilaterally decide on early

---

60 On the supervision of enforcement of SCSL sentences, especially regarding its duration, see T. Doherty and S.A. Fisher, 'Enforcement of sentences and oversight of prisoners convicted by the Special Court for Sierra Leone', Chapter 15 in this volume.

61 Art. 2(A) Practice Direction on the Conditional Early Release of Persons Convicted by the SCSL.

62 Ibid., Art. 2(B) and (C).

63 Compare ibid., Art. 5.

64 *Fofana* SCSL-04-14-ES-836 (Decision of the President on Application for Conditional Early Release, 11 August 2014).

65 *Senessie* SCSL-11-01-ES-035 (Decision of the President on Application for Conditional Early Release, 4 June 2014).

66 Also for the SCSL there may be a more complex situation if the time should come that Charles Taylor applied, and would possibly be eligible, for early release, not in Sierra Leone, but in Liberia.

release, upon application by the convicted person. I know of no situation where an enforcing State has not complied with either a decision granting early release or a decision denying early release. It is to be noted that early release granted by the ICTY and ICTR and MICT is not subject to any conditions. The SCSL approach considerably differs in this regard. While the imposition of certain conditions may be desirable for a number of reasons, it would legally be complex, if not impossible, to oblige States to cooperate in having such conditions effectively enforced. For example, the law of the *ad hoc* Tribunals and the ICC does not appear to allow for re-arrest in the case of non-compliance with possible conditions attached to early release. Moreover, receiving States would not be under any legal obligation to comply with this form of arrest warrant.

Yet, there should be serious reflection on developing a system of conditional early release that should not be overly complex and burdensome. But, especially in cases of such serious matters as harassing or intimidating key witnesses once released, there should be grounds for re-arrest and for having the convicted person serve the remainder of their sentence. This possibility alone would hopefully have a deterrent effect and contribute to the continuing protection of vulnerable witnesses.

6. THE BLACK BOX IN ENFORCEMENT – COOPERATION IN THE ENFORCEMENT OF SENTENCES OTHER THAN IMPRISONMENT

It has already been mentioned that the Statutes of the *ad hoc* Tribunals do not provide for sentences other than imprisonment. But Trial Chambers may order the return of any property and proceeds acquired by criminal conduct, including by means of duress, to their rightful owners, as provided for in Article 24(3) ICTYSt. This possibility has never been applied in practice and needs no further discussion.

The RPE allow for the imposition of sentences other than imprisonment, such as fines, for the crimes of perjury and contempt of court.[67] There is a rather elaborate Rule, 77bis, which deals with the payment of fines and even allows for the conversion of the fine into a term of imprisonment in the case of failure to pay. Fines have been imposed at the ICTY in the contempt convictions of Florence Hartmann, Haxhiu, Jović, Margetić, Marijacić, Rebić, and Vujin.

What matters in the context of this chapter is whether States have any role in cooperating in the enforcement of fines imposed by the *ad hoc* Tribunals for contempt of court or perjury. There is no basis in the law of the *ad hoc* Tribunals to request State cooperation in the enforcement of fines, let alone that States would have any obligation to that end. If fines are to be converted into sentences of imprisonment, as provided for by Rule 77bis(C), it could be argued that the ordinary cooperation regime related to imprisonment for core crimes applies. It is true that neither the Statute nor the enforcement agreements explicitly rule out the enforcement of imprisonment ensuing from converted fines. Yet, the cooperation related to imprisonment was clearly destined

---

[67] Compare Rule 77(G)–(H) and Rule 91 ICTY RPE.

to apply to core crimes only and one has difficulty seeing how States would be ready to cooperate in the enforcement of these particular types of imprisonment. There is certainly no precedent, nor will there ever be in my opinion in the context of the *ad hoc* Tribunals. But maybe all imposed fines have been paid voluntarily and there is no need to consider avenues of enforcement.[68]

It is clear that the ICC has paid slightly more attention to the matter of enforcement of sentences other than imprisonment. The key provision in the Statute reads as follows:

> Enforcement of fines and forfeiture measures
>
> 1. States Parties shall give effect to fines or forfeitures ordered by the Court under Part 7, without prejudice to the rights of bona fide third parties, and in accordance with the procedure of their national law.
> 2. If a State Party is unable to give effect to an order for forfeiture, it shall take measures to recover the value of the proceeds, property or assets ordered by the Court to be forfeited, without prejudice to the rights of bona fide third parties.
> 3. Property, or the proceeds of the sale of real property or, where appropriate, the sale of other property, which is obtained by a State Party as a result of its enforcement of a judgement of the Court shall be transferred to the Court.[69]

The Rules of Procedure contain a number of additional provisions on this matter, which tend to focus on forfeiture and reparation orders.[70]

The most important element of Article 109 is undeniably the obligation for States parties to give effect to fines or forfeitures ordered by the Court under Part 7. This obligation also exists in respect of reparation orders pursuant to Article 75(5) of the Statute. The obligation to cooperate is however not absolute. States may lawfully refuse cooperation if execution of the Court's orders would prejudice the rights of bona fide third parties.[71]

It also needs to be borne in mind that States are obliged to recover value from proceeds, property or assets as ordered by the Court if they are unable to give effect to a forfeiture order.

Whereas there is some attention (including the imposition of obligations on States) in respect of forfeiture orders, this is not the case with the enforcement of fines. States are obliged to give effect to fines, but it is not specified how they should do this. It is impossible to recover a fine through forfeiture as this is restricted under Article 77(2)(b) to proceeds, property and assets derived directly or indirectly from the crime. The law of the ICC furthermore does not provide for substitution of the fine by imprisonment in case of non-payment, as is possible under the law of the ICTY (Rule

---

[68] The case information available on the ICTY website does not mention whether or not fines imposed have been fully paid. The first fine imposed was on former counsel of Tadić, Milan Vujin. The fine was imposed in Dutch guilder (15 000) and was confirmed on 2001.

[69] On fines and forfeitures as penalties see R. Young, 'Fines and forfeitures in international criminal justice', Chapter 5 in this volume.

[70] Compare Rules 217–222.

[71] In the literature it has been debated whether the rights of third parties under national law, such as the fiscal service, should always enjoy priority over forfeiture for the benefit of victims. See W. Schabas, 'Article 109', in Triffterer (n 12) 1680.

77bis (C) ICTY RPE).[72] In cases where a person is sentenced to imprisonment and a fine, non-payment of the fine can lead to the extension of the duration of the sentence of imprisonment.[73]

Conceptually, the fine is very different from the forfeiture order when it comes to State cooperation. Cooperation in forfeiture is essential and rightfully receives attention in the law of the ICC. However, a fine carries with it an obligation for payment by the sentenced person; one can wonder whether there needs to be a general obligation for States to give effect to it. In the case of non-payment, it is for the Court to take further measures, which may include forfeiture of assets, but then this should be the focus of the cooperation obligation.

There is not yet any case law on the practical application of Article 109 or Article 75(5) ICCSt, as no fines have been imposed and no forfeiture and reparation orders involving State cooperation have been issued. Yet, there is some interesting practice and case law related to the essential phase preceding forfeiture. As is the case in national criminal justice systems, there is significant interest in ensuring that the assets of a suspect can be traced and frozen at an early stage, to make sure that possible later forfeiture orders can indeed be effectively executed. To that end, Article 93(1)(k) ICCSt obliges States Parties to comply with requests providing assistance in '[t]he identification, tracing and freezing or seizure of proceeds, property and assets and instrumentalities of crimes for the purpose of eventual forfeiture, without prejudice to the rights of bona fide third parties'. The regime of Part 9, including applicable grounds of refusal, is fully applicable to this provision. In the *Bemba* case, Portugal gave effect to a request pursuant to Article 93(1)(k) in 2008, freezing the assets of Mr. Bemba in that country.[74] The Chamber then ordered that a monthly sum was transferred from the frozen assets to Mr. Bemba with a view to meeting the obligations towards his family and to pay his defence team.[75] Strictly speaking, this order would not be in keeping with the purposes of freezing assets, which according to Article 93(1)(k) can only be done for 'eventual forfeiture', which is still a matter to be decided upon by the Court.

It seems that there are two important issues to be dealt with in the future cooperation practice of the Court in relation to fines, forfeiture orders and reparation orders.

First, Article 109 is an isolated provision in the regime of Part 10. Part 10 deals predominantly with the enforcement of sentences of imprisonment, in respect of which

---

72 Interestingly, conversion of a fine into imprisonment has been provided for in case of the less serious 'offences against the administration of justice'; see Rule 166(5) ICTY RPE. One may wonder, however, whether this rule is in keeping with the Statute as imprisonment is not provided for as a sentence under Art. 70 ICTYSt and appears restricted to the situation provided for in Art. 77 ICTYSt.

73 See Rule 146(5) ICC RPE.

74 It follows from litigation, especially the repeated Bemba Gombo defence attempts to lift freezing of assets, that on 27 May 2008 the Chamber issued a request for cooperation addressed to the Republic of Portugal to identify, trace, freeze and seize any property and assets of Mr. Jean-Pierre Bemba Gombo located on its territory, subject to the rights of bona fide third parties. This request was executed by the competent authorities of the Republic of Portugal. See *Bemba Gombo* ICC-01/05-01/08 (Decision on the Defence's Application for Lifting the Seizure of Assets and Request for Cooperation to the Competent Authorities of Portugal, 10 October 2008).

75 Ibid.

cooperation is voluntary (with the exception of the situation covered by Article 103(4)). Yet, Article 109 imposes strong cooperation obligations on States in respect of other sentences and measures. This would fit better in Part 9, which also contains cooperation obligations, similar to those in Article 109. Part 9 also sets out a number of obligations of result, such as arresting a suspect or collecting evidence. The question arises whether some of the general rules and principles, including grounds of refusal, contained in Part 9 would on the basis of this conceptual similarity also be applicable (be it by analogy) to requests for cooperation pursuant to Article 109. This matter has not yet been resolved.

Second, at present the Court is traversing a period of activity in regard to Article 70 cases.[76] At the time of writing, these cases have not yet been finalized. It may be anticipated that a fine would be a very useful and common sentence for less serious offences against the administration of justice.[77] It needs also to be mentioned that a fine can be imposed for misconduct pursuant to Article 71.[78] One notices, however, that the fines imposed under Articles 70 and 71 are not within the regime of Articles 77 and 109. Rule 167 of the ICC RPE enables the Court to request the assistance of States in relation to Article 70 crimes, but on a voluntary basis and limited to forms of cooperation set out in Part 9. The need for possible State cooperation in the enforcement of fines has thus been totally overlooked in relation to offences against the administration of justice and misconduct.

7. CONCLUSION

The cooperation of States in the enforcement of sentences, a matter usually dealt with at the end of an often very long international criminal trial, is still a matter that could receive more attention. There is increasing practice in international criminal justice in the enforcement of sentences, and the role of State cooperation therein; the ICTY, ICTR and SCSL especially have enforced, and are enforcing, a substantial number of sentences and, by and large, the issue of State cooperation appears, so far, to be relatively unproblematic.

The starting point is that the issues for enforcing States to consider are quite simplified by restricting sentences – for the ICTY, ICTR and SCSL by law and for the ICC possibly in practice – to imprisonment only. In respect of imprisonment, cooperation is voluntary for States. While this carries with it the risk that not enough States will be prepared to accept convicted persons, the advantage is that those States that do so will cooperate in good faith and can be expected to comply with the high standards of international criminal tribunals in respect of supervision of the sentence of imprisonment. The negotiation process, culminating in the conclusion of enforcement agreements, ensures that a match is achieved between the demands of the international criminal tribunal and the laws and interests of receiving States.

---

[76] In the *Bemba* case, five individuals have been prosecuted for Art. 70 ICCSt offences (Offences against the administration of justice); in the Kenya case one person.

[77] See Rule 166 ICC RPE providing further details in relation to imposition of a fine.

[78] See Art. 71 ICCSt and Rule 171(4) ICC RPE.

This context of voluntary cooperation has led to relatively high standards and corresponding cooperation obligations for States which have concluded enforcement agreements and which have accepted convicted persons. States have to meet high standards regarding the rights of detained persons and have to fully respect the duration of the sentence imposed and to comply with decisions of the relevant tribunal or court related to early release. As the ultimate remedy in cases of cooperation problems, the tribunal or court is always empowered to terminate the enforcement of a sentence of imprisonment in a certain State. In the practice of the *ad hoc* Tribunals, this has happened to my knowledge only once. In that situation, Krstić and the UK, it seems that termination was not based on any failure on the part of the UK to live up to its cooperation obligations.

State cooperation in the enforcement of sentences of imprisonment is thus essentially unproblematic. Compared with cooperation in the arrest and surrender of suspects and the collection of evidence, this is a positive determination. This can be easily explained by the combined fact that (a) the enforcement of sentences is handled by a relatively small, but highly cooperative, group of States; and (b) in the enforcement of sentences of imprisonment there are for States no important interests at stake, contrary to, for example, the arrest of Heads of States (Bashir) or the collection of sensitive information (military documents).

Although one can thus be positive as far as the enforcement of sentences of imprisonment are concerned, there is definitely room for improvement. One may wonder whether in the longer run it would be worthwhile organising cooperation in the enforcement of sentences of imprisonment along the lines of a different model, namely that of full recognition, as applied in the EU context, without a supervisory role for the court. Another matter worth addressing in the future is the issue of early release, especially whether it would be feasible to attach conditions to this, as has been the case with the SCSL. However, if this is ever to be seriously discussed it is important to realize and anticipate the consequences for cooperation. It is only worthwhile imposing conditions on early release if they can be effectively enforced, including such matters as allowing for the re-arrest and detention of the convicted person in the case of a breach of conditions.

One has to be more reserved as far as the enforcement of sentences other than imprisonment is concerned. There is not yet any State practice in terms of cooperating in the enforcement of such sentences as fines, or measures taken upon conviction such as forfeiture and reparation orders. The reason is that this matter is restricted to the ICC, which does not have any practice in this area yet.

It may seem positive for the effective enforcement of fines that there are obligations in relation to cooperation for all ICC States Parties. However, the nature and scope of the required cooperation, including the question of possible applicable grounds of refusal, should have been better addressed in the law of the ICC. An additional shortcoming of the current ICC cooperation regime in this area is that there is no duty for States to cooperate in the enforcement of fines in the situation where they are most likely to be imposed: conviction for offences against the administration of justice and misconduct (Articles 70 and 71 ICCSt).

11. Limiting the objectives of the enforcement of international punishment

Denis Abels

1. INTRODUCTION

International criminal justice is an ambitious undertaking. This is due to high expectations on the part of different stakeholders. The international criminal tribunals are generally expected to serve such 'grand' goals as promoting or maintaining peace and security, historiography, upholding and advancing the rule of law, fostering or contributing to reconciliation and giving a voice to victims of mass atrocity. The sentencing judges of international criminal tribunals and courts have added to those objectives the classic aims of punishment, i.e., retribution and prevention (the latter through deterrence, incapacitation and, to a much lesser extent, rehabilitation), which they appear to import from the domestic context.

The aim of this chapter is to lay the basis for an inquiry into the objectives of the enforcement of international punishment. Prison law is an area that is already characterized by having many, sometimes competing objectives: resocialization or rehabilitation, normalization and a rights-based approach may clash with security, order and safety considerations. This chapter addresses the issue of whether the larger objectives of international criminal justice should also play a direct role in the tribunals' penal regimes for the enforcement of the tribunals' sentencing judgments.

In the same way that it is often assumed that the objectives of international criminal procedure can only be fully understood by linking them to the goals of international criminal justice[1] and that the latter provide a basis for analysing the efficiency of the trial process, it is often assumed that the objectives of international enforcement and the objectives of international criminal justice (and those of its different components, including the sentencing stage), are ontologically connected and must be aligned. This 'systemic' way of thinking presumes that the different components (establishment and 'legislation', sentencing and execution) of international criminal justice are subject to the same objectives that govern international criminal justice as a whole. It also presumes that the different components of international criminal justice are hierarchically connected on the basis of sequence: since sentencing precedes and ultimately constitutes the justifying basis for acts of enforcement, objectives of enforcement must be aligned to the objectives of sentencing.

According to Swart, '[w]here tensions between the means and ends of international criminal justice are revealed, the question arises of how to solve them. Different options may then present themselves: adjusting the means to the ends, adjusting the

[1] J.D. Ohlin, 'A Meta-Theory of International Criminal Procedure: Vindicating the Rule of Law' (2009) 14 *UCLA Journal of International Law Foreign Affairs* 77, 83.

ends to the means, or a combination of both'.[2] However, this line of thinking is ultimately based on the idea that the courts' effectiveness can be assessed on the basis of the achievement of some pre-set objectives.[3] If, for example, reconciliation is one of the ultimate objectives of international criminal justice, while international imprisonment finds its justification in retributive sentencing and is directed towards normalization and, perhaps, rehabilitation, does this imply that these prison regimes require adaptation?

The identification of the objectives of international enforcement requires, in the first place, that the aforementioned systemic assumptions be verified or falsified, which is the purpose of this chapter. It is necessary to ascertain whether the objectives governing international criminal justice as a whole and the objectives of sentencing should govern international enforcement. In other words, it needs to be ascertained whether, and if so, to what extent, a systemic approach to the identification of objectives of international punishment is appropriate. After all, it may be argued that such socio-political goals,[4] which have been proclaimed at the macro level, should only govern the enforcement of sentences at the micro level, i.e., in respect of each convicted person, to a limited extent.[5] Only after this question has been answered can one start identifying such objectives, which is beyond the scope of this chapter. The purpose of this chapter, it should be recalled, is to lay the basis for an inquiry into such objectives. In doing so, I will argue for a modest approach towards applying socio-political goals to the tribunals' penal regimes.

A final (though by no means insignificant) point that needs to be raised here concerns the nature of the 'objectives' referred to in this chapter. The objectives of international criminal justice as set by either the tribunals' mandate givers or internal constituencies on the macro level can be regarded as the tribunals' official objectives.[6] They may to some extent be compared to the principles of international criminal law in the sense that both are often vaguely defined and open-ended (i.e., they can never be completely concretized).[7] Unlike legal principles, these socio-political objectives may conflict inter-se,[8] which may necessitate designating a hierarchy among them or fixing

---

[2] B. Swart, 'Damaška and the Faces of International Criminal Justice' (2008) 6 *Journal of International Criminal Justice* 87, 100.

[3] There are countless other factors which may have an impact on (the perceptive of) effectiveness. Shany identifies such factors as judgment compliance, usage rates, impact on State conduct. Y. Shany, 'Assessing the Effectiveness of International Courts: A Goal-based Approach' (2012) 106 *American Journal of International Law* 225, 227. See also Vasiliev, who defines effectiveness as 'the interplay and tension between the considerations related to the *goals* of the tribunals and those relating to efficiency'; S. Vasiliev, *International Criminal Trials. A Normative Theory* (diss, Oxford University Press 2014) 163.

[4] Vasiliev (n 3) 163.

[5] Swart (n 2) 101.

[6] Shany (n 3) 231.

[7] Ibid.

[8] C. Stahn, 'Between "Faith" and "Facts": By What Standards Should we Assess International Criminal Justice?' (2012) 25 *Leiden Journal of International Law* 251, 259; M. Damaška, 'What is the Point of International Criminal Justice' (2008) 83 *Chicago-Kent Law Review* 329, 331–4. Damaška points for example to the possible tension between stopping an

their relative weight in order to render them operative.[9] These official objectives are also the tribunals' ultimate ends, as opposed to objectives that are 'strategic or intermediate in nature' which may therefore more easily be altered.[10] The official objectives must, according to Shany, be distinguished from operative objectives into which the formal objectives may be translated over time in the tribunals' discharge of functions and which 'reflect the specific policies that the organization actually prioritizes'.[11] According to him, '[t]he general nature of some abstract goals renders them imprecise and leaves considerable interpretive discretion as to translating such goals into concrete judicial policies and operative or intermediate judicial goals'.[12]

2. THE OBJECTIVES OF INTERNATIONAL CRIMINAL JUSTICE AND INTERNATIONAL SENTENCING

As stated above, the question that this chapter seeks to answer is whether from this wide array of ultimate and sentencing objectives any conclusions may be drawn as to the shape that the enforcement of sentences in international criminal justice must take. Mulgrew appears to answer this question in the affirmative where she argues that '[i]n addition to an individualistic rehabilitation focus, international sentences of imprisonment should also be applied in a manner that achieves the wider goals of the international criminal justice system and meets the expectations of the stakeholders of the international penal process'.[13] Goals such as reconciliation and the maintenance of peace should, according to her, be actively pursued when enforcing international prison sentences. She rightly points to the ICC's release criteria, which take into account reconciliatory attempts undertaken by convicted persons towards victims, and argues that this logically demands a similar focus during the enforcement of sentences. Other scholars have argued that the tribunals' ultimate objectives are simply too ambitious and that some of them should either be scaled down or even abandoned.[14]

---

ongoing conflict and bringing perpetrators to justice, between individualizing criminal responsibility and historiography or between respecting the accused's procedural rights and giving a voice to victims. For an opposing view, see S. Vasiliev, 'General Rules and Principles of International Criminal Procedure: Definition, Legal Nature, and Identification', in G. Sluiter and S. Vasiliev (eds), *International Criminal Procedure – Towards a Coherent Body of Law* (Cameron May/CMP Publishing Ltd 2009) 53.

9 Shany (n 3) 233. Damaška (n 8) 339.

10 Shany (n 3) 232.

11 Ibid., 231.

12 Ibid., 233.

13 R. Mulgrew, *Towards the Development of the International Penal System* (Cambridge University Press 2013) 215. See, in a similar vein but not specifically with respect to the enforcement phase, J. Sarkin, 'Enhancing the Legitimacy, Status, and Role of the International Criminal Court Globally by using Transitional Justice and Restorative Justice Strategies' (2011–12) 6 *Interdisciplinary Journal of Human Rights Law* 83. Sarkin even argues (at 86) that '[i]f prevention were to become a central objective and steps were taken to operationalize it, the ICC could have a dramatic effect on the frequency of massive human rights abuses'.

14 Damaška (n 8) 329–65.

The objectives of international criminal justice can be found in the international tribunals' and courts' Statutes' preambles, resolutions, other official documents and the tribunals' case law. Various scholars have identified the following as the ultimate goals of international criminal justice: 'reprobation and stigmatization of the offender by the international community', 'the reassurance that the international legal system is implemented and enforced', 'providing satisfaction to the victims', 'to change a culture of impunity', 'to contribute to the restoration and maintenance of (international) peace and security', 'to provide an accurate historical record of events that make it more difficult for offenders and others to negate history', 'to promote a process of reconciliation in the region where international crimes have been committed'[15] and 'to re-establish the rule of law'.[16] Some of these objectives are probably less obviously relevant to the enforcement phase, such as creating a historical record,[17] which seems to be more appropriately applied to the trial phase (insofar as this is possible and/or desirable).[18] Similarly, the goal of norm strengthening is arguably better served in the context of sentencing.

As noted by Stahn, the selection and application of the socio-political goals is not uncontroversial. Some scholars doubt whether extra-judicial goals can be legitimately pursued by criminal justice. Others acknowledge that domestic criminal justice objectives may need to be adjusted in the international context and that broader socio-political goals might be accorded some importance, perhaps as secondary goals.[19] Ohlin takes the more conservative view in relation to the question whether the ultimate aim of restoring and maintaining international peace and security ought to play a role in international criminal trials in light of the 'sanctity and autonomy' of the judicial process.[20] Nevertheless, in his view there is no cause for concern, since the criminal trial operates at different levels: the level of institutional design – at which it may operate to restore peace and security – and the internal level of adjudication (i.e., the micro level), where it 'operates autonomously to determine individual culpability'.[21] A similar argument is made in this chapter in relation to the phase of enforcement.

---

[15] Swart (n 2) 100. See, also, Damaška (n 8) 331. See also: the list provided by Ohlin: Ohlin (n 1) 85–90; and Vasiliev (n 3) 164–71.

[16] Swart (n 2) 100. See also C.J.M. Safferling, 'Can Criminal Prosecution be the Answer to Massive Human Rights Violations?' (2004) 5 *German Law Journal* 1469, 1475. See, in particular, Ohlin, who pleads for a rule of law-based understanding of international criminal *procedure*, wherein 'international criminal procedure is also valued for its intrinsic, not instrumental, functions', i.e., vindicating the rule of law. Ohlin (n 1) 77–120.

[17] I would argue that such truth-finding/historiography would qualify perhaps as desired side-effects of transitional justice, also during the enforcement stage, but not as objectives of enforcement to be pursued in their own right. Trial and truth finding have been completed at that stage and I would argue that the principle of *lites finiri oportet* would require the authorities to refrain from interfering with individuals.

[18] Damaška (n 8) 339 note 15.

[19] Stahn (n 8) 259.

[20] Ohlin (n 1) 90.

[21] According to him, '[a]dvocates for the autonomy of the criminal law may be correct when they insist that considerations of the former should not infect the operations of the latter'. Ohlin (n 1) 90.

The international sentencing objectives can be found in the tribunals' case law and are largely based on the classic domestic aims of punishment, i.e., retribution and prevention (the latter through general and special deterrence, incapacitation and rehabilitation). Retribution is regarded as the primary aim of sentencing,[22] and must, according to the tribunals, be understood as public reprobation and stigmatization by the international community.[23] Punishment expresses the international community's condemnation of a criminal act and its perpetrator.[24] In the *Aleksovski* case, the Appeals Chamber stated that retribution is not to be understood as fulfilling a desire for revenge but as 'duly expressing the outrage of the international community at these crimes' and that sentences rendered by the ICTY 'should make plain the condemnation of the international community of the behaviour in question and show that "the international community was not ready to tolerate serious violations of international humanitarian law and human rights"'.[25] Similarly, Nuremberg Prosecutor Robert H. Jackson argued that:

> The satisfaction of instincts of revenge and retribution for the sake of retribution are obviously the least sound basis of punishment. If punishment is to lead to progress, it must be carried out in a manner which world opinion will regard as progressive and as consistent with the fundamental morality of the Allied case.[26]

In the *Stakić* case the Appeals Chamber held that during sentencing, purposes other than retribution and deterrence, such as rehabilitation, should be taken into account but not accorded undue weight.[27] At the same time, however, most sentencing chambers are of the view that deterrence should not be accorded too much weight.[28] The idea that the gravity of punishment to be imposed on a specific person should not be dictated by the aim of deterring others from committing similar crimes in the future, which is affirmed

---

22 R. Henham, 'The Philosophical Foundations of International Sentencing' (2003) 1 *Journal of International Criminal Justice* 69. See D. van Zyl Smit, 'Punishment and Human Rights in International Criminal Justice' (2002) 2 *Human Rights Law Review* 1, 10 and the case law cited there: *Aleksovski* IT-95-14/1-A (Judgment, 24 March 2000) para 182; *Delalić et al* IT-96-21-T (Judgment, 16 November 1998) para 1225; *Kupreškić* IT-95-16-T (Judgment, 14 January 2000) para 852.

23 *Blaškić* IT-95-14-A (Judgment, 29 July 2004) para 678.

24 *Jokić* IT-01-42/1-S (Sentencing Judgment, 18 March 2004) paras 31, 32; *Blaškić* IT-95-14-A (Judgment, 29 July 2004) para 678; *Bralo* IT-95-17-A (Judgment on Sentencing Appeal, 2 April 2007) para 81; *Kunarac et al* IT-96-23 and IT-96-23/1-A (Judgment, 12 June 2002) para 385.

25 *Aleksovski* IT-95-14/1-A (Judgment, 24 March 2000) para 185; see also *Kordić and Čerkez* IT-95-14/2-A (Judgment, 17 December 2004) para 1075 stating that 'retribution should not be misunderstood as a way of expressing revenge or vengeance'.

26 W. Schabas, 'Sentencing by International Tribunals: A Human Rights Approach' (1997) 7 *Duke Journal of Comparative and International Law* 461, 500.

27 *Stakić* IT-97-24-A (Judgment, 22 March 2006) para 402, citing *Delalić et al* IT-96-21-A (Judgment, 20 February 2001) para 806.

28 *Aleksovski* IT-95-14/1-A (Judgment, 24 March 2000) para 185; *Delalić et al* IT-96-21-A (Judgment, 20 February 2001) paras 801–803; *Kordić and Čerkez* IT-95-14/2-A (Judgment, 17 December 2004) para 1078; *Nikolić* IT-94-2-A (Judgment on Sentencing Appeal, 4 February 2005) para 46.

in the tribunals' case law,[29] can be traced back to the Kantian notion that persons must be treated as ends in themselves, rather than means to achieve certain ends. Deterrence further suffers from the serious deficit that it has not been proved to actually work.[30] The premise on which deterrence is based, i.e., an individual weighing the pros and cons before committing a crime, is often inaccurate or simply untrue.[31] This certainly seems to be the case in the context of mass atrocity crimes where, in Safferling's words, perpetrators are 'overcast with ideology, fanaticism or religious fundamentalism, and who conceive themselves to be over and above the law anyhow' and system criminality, which is characterized by a State or State-like entity facilitating or encouraging such acts.[32] While just as in the domestic context special prevention through incapacitation or rehabilitation may be expected to have some positive effect on preventing recidivism, it is highly speculative to assume the same in respect of general deterrence.[33]

Where reference has been made to deterrence as a sentencing rationale, the tribunals' judges have acknowledged that the general deterrent effect is merely assumed and formulated a rather limited working definition of general deterrence: 'with regard to general deterrence, imposing a punishment serves to strengthen the legal order in which the type of conduct involved is defined as criminal and to reassure society of the effectiveness of its penal provisions'.[34] It has been held that, although 'in adopting resolution 827, the Security Council established the International Tribunal with the stated purpose of bringing to justice persons responsible for serious violations of international humanitarian law in the former Yugoslavia, thereby deterring future violations and contributing to the re-establishment of peace and security in the region',[35] 'the Trial Chamber's duty remains to tailor the penalty to fit the individual circumstances of the accused and the gravity of the crime'.[36]

Rehabilitation (in sentencing, *not* as an enforcement rationale) has been defined by the ICTY Appeals Chamber as 'reintegrating the guilty accused into society'.[37] Some accused have argued on appeal that the Trial Chamber had erred in not taking into

---

29 *Krajisnik* IT-00-39-T (Judgment, 27 September 2006) para 1137. Cited by Swart in Swart (n 2) 103.

30 Safferling (n 16) 1483.

31 Damaška (n 8) 344. There appear to be some exceptions, i.e., specific categories and types of crimes and offenders in relation to which the portrayal of the offender as a *homo economicus* may be less problematic.

32 Safferling (n 16) 169–73.

33 Vasiliev (n 3) 176.

34 *Blaškić* IT-95-14-A (Judgment, 29 July 2004) para 678.

35 *Delalić et al* IT-96-21-A (Judgment, 20 February 2001) para 800, citing with emphasis para 72 of *Tadić* IT-94-1-AR72 (Decision on the Defence Motion for Interlocutory Appeal on Jurisdiction, 2 October 1995). It is noted that deterrence is used here in its role as a general justifying aim for the establishment of the ICTY, not in answering the question of how severely to punish in a concrete case.

36 *Delalić et al* IT-96-21-A (Judgment, 20 February 2001) para 717; *Nikolić* IT-94-2-A (Judgment on Sentencing Appeal, 4 February 2005) para 46.

37 *Delalić et al* T-96-21-A (Judgment, 20 February 2001) para 805; *Kordić and Čerkez* IT-95-14/2-A (Judgment, 17 December 2004) para 1079.

consideration rehabilitation as a sentencing purpose in their case.[38] However, in *Čelebići* the Appeals Chamber held that rehabilitation usually has a role to play:

> when younger, or less educated, members of society are found guilty of offences. It therefore becomes necessary to re-integrate them into society so that they can become useful members of it and enable them to lead normal and productive lives upon their release from imprisonment. The age of the accused, his circumstances, his ability to be rehabilitated and availability of facilities in the confinement facility can, and should, be relevant considerations in this respect.[39]

The Appeals Chamber pointed to the serious nature of the crimes dealt with by the international tribunal, thereby arguing that these cases are not comparable to national criminal cases and held that, therefore, rehabilitation cannot 'play a predominant role in the decision-making process of a Trial Chamber of the Tribunal' and 'cannot be given undue weight'.[40] The question is, of course, what the scope is of the latter remark. In this regard the tribunals have on the one hand reiterated that retribution and deterrence must be considered the main purposes in international sentencing,[41] while on the other expressing their 'support for rehabilitative programmes in which the accused may participate while serving his sentence',[42] thereby acknowledging the distinction between sentencing rationales and objectives of enforcement.

As correctly observed by Swart, the tribunals have the tendency to equate the ultimate objectives of international criminal justice with the aforementioned sentencing objectives imported from the domestic context. In the case of *Nikolić*, for example, it was held that the aim of the Chamber was to come as close as possible to justice for both victims and their relatives and the accused, with justice being 'of paramount

---

[38] See, for example, *Delalić et al* IT-96-21-A (Judgment, 20 February 2001) para 804.

[39] Ibid., para 805, citing Trial Judgment para 1233.

[40] *Delalić et al* IT-96-21-A (Judgment, 20 February 2001) para 806; *Kordić and Čerkez* IT-95-14/2-A (Judgment, 17 December 2004) para 1079; *Deronjić* IT-02-61-A (Judgment on Sentencing Appeal, 20 July 2005) para 136. See in this regard also *Stakić* IT-97-24-A (Judgment, 22 March 2006) para 371 in which the appellant argued that the Trial Chamber erred in refusing to hear the evidence of an expert criminologist or psychiatrist which would have been relevant to sentencing as it related to his propensity to commit crimes. The appellant had claimed that such evidence was essential to his case and would have led to a lesser sentence. The Appeals Chamber held that a Trial Chamber has the discretion to determine which experts it wants to hear depending on the circumstances of the case before it. It was stated in the *Blaškić* case that in light of the gravity of many of the crimes, the weight of rehabilitative considerations may be limited in some cases, see *Blaškić* IT-95-14-T (Judgment, 3 March 2000) para 782.

[41] *Furundžija* IT-95-17/1-A (Judgment, 21 July 2000) para 291; *Deronjić* IT-02-61-A (Judgment on Sentencing Appeal, 20 July 2005) para 136. See also *Kordić and Čerkez* IT-95-14/2-A (Judgment, 17 December 2004) para 1079 where it was stated that '[i]t would violate the principle of proportionality and endanger the pursuit of other sentencing purposes if rehabilitative considerations were given undue prominence in the sentencing process'.

[42] *Furundžija* IT-95-17/1-A (Judgment, 21 July 2000) para 291. See also *Erdemović* IT-96-22-T*bis*, (Sentencing Judgment, 5 March 1998) para 16; *Kupreškić* IT-95-16-T (Judgment, 14 January 2000) para 849.

importance for the restoration and maintenance of peace'.[43] Retribution is equated with public reprobation, norm strengthening and stigmatization, and is seen as acknowledgement of the harm done to victims, while the different modes of prevention are considered to strengthen the legal order.[44]

More convincing, however, is the argument adduced by Vasiliev, that it is dangerous to transpose the socio-political goals to the sentencing phase, since '[i]nordinate attention to institutional objectives when determining an individual sentence may result in a failure to hand down the sentence faithfully reflecting the person's level of culpability, gravity, nature and circumstances of the crime, and the relevant individual circumstances'.[45] This chapter argues that transposing ultimate goals to the enforcement stage presents similar risks. Further, the tribunals' line of reasoning does not constitute an argument for explicitly aligning the tribunals' penal regimes to the ultimate goals, since it suggests that sentencing objectives and objectives of punishment originating in the domestic context are perfectly capable of achieving the tribunals' ultimate, socio-political goals. Without any empirical proof, this must of course be regarded as nothing more than simply wishful thinking. The tribunals' reasoning also appears to assume that there is a need for aligning the objectives of the different stages or aspects of international criminal justice with its ultimate ends. The next section discusses whether there is any need for alignment in the first place.

3. THE NEED FOR ALIGNMENT OF OBJECTIVES OF INTERNATIONAL ENFORCEMENT WITH THOSE OF INTERNATIONAL CRIMINAL JUSTICE AND INTERNATIONAL SENTENCING

3.1 A Systemic Approach Towards International Criminal Justice

The (interrelated) questions that are central to this section are whether the objectives that are said to govern international criminal justice as a whole must govern all its distinct components and whether the objectives directing a certain stage must also be taken into account in the subsequent stage. It may appear that, in order for international criminal justice to be (at least potentially) effective and credible, both questions must be answered in the affirmative. As Wright puts it: 'if criminal justice is to fulfil its function of crime control, then a transformation must occur which will create a rational, well-integrated system in which a common set of goals can be pursued through a compatible set of strategies and techniques'.[46] This line of thinking is largely built on the premise that all the different parts or stages of international criminal justice

---

43 *Nikolić* IT-02-60/1-S, (Sentencing Judgment, 2 December 2003) para 4. The Appeals Chamber endorsed this view, see *Bralo* IT-95-17-A (Judgment on Sentencing Appeal, 2 April 2007) para 82 footnote 350.

44 Swart (n 2) 104.

45 Vasiliev (n 3) 169.

46 K.N. Wright, 'The Desirability of Goal Conflict within the Criminal Justice System' (1981) 9 *Journal of Criminal Justice* 209, 209.

should be governed in a systemic manner, by the same teleological principles. However, many scholars have questioned whether criminal justice can be understood in this way. Some even doubt whether, in light of 'the lack of integration among institutions and the within-institution differences that exist (…) across different locales', there is such a thing as a criminal justice system.[47] According to Duffee, '[i]n fact, applying the word "system" to criminal justice agencies and processes may be itself a good example of wishful thinking',[48] because one rarely encounters penal systems which are well integrated and coordinated and of which the different agencies strive towards the same goals.[49]

Often the term system is used in a purely descriptive manner, without any substantive reference.[50] It is likely that when legal scholars refer to the criminal justice system they are using the term in this way; they simply wish to refer to the various agents and institutions involved in criminal justice as a collective entity. In this regard, Duffee observes that the notion of the criminal justice system has political and popular origins and is not a scientific term.[51]

Systems theory is difficult to define due to the wide variety of ways in which the term 'system' is used.[52] Nonetheless, a common and essential element appears to be 'the interaction of different units toward a common goal'.[53] As such, the depiction of criminal justice as a system necessarily means that the different branches of criminal justice are seen as interrelated and as striving towards (a) common goal(s). It is precisely this argument that constitutes the most often heard critique with regards to criminal justice.[54] Duffee states that:

> police, judicial, and penal agencies – even those operating in the same locality under the same law – often have such contradictory objectives, and such independent sets of constraints, that it becomes very hard to imagine that the primary determinates of criminal justice agency action are the actions and needs of other criminal justice agencies.[55]

Some scholars have characterized the components of criminal justice 'as being non cooperative and even hostile toward one another'.[56] Scholars who disagree with this characterization have come up with common goals such as justice and efficiency.[57]

---

[47] T.J. Bernard, E.A. Paoline III and P. Pare, 'General Systems Theory and Criminal Justice' (2005) 33 *Journal of Criminal Justice* 203, 203. See also L. DeWolf, 'Criminal Justice as Defense and Restoration of Community: Our "Non-System" of Criminal Justice' (1976–77) 7 *Cumberland Law Review* 393.

[48] D.E. Duffee, *Explaining Criminal Justice. Community Theory and Criminal Justice Reform* (Oelgeschlager, Gunn & Hain Publishers 1980) 3.

[49] Ibid., 102.

[50] Bernard, Paoline and Pare (n 47) 203.

[51] Duffee (n 48) 2.

[52] Bernard, Paoline and Pare (n 47) 203, 204.

[53] Ibid., 204.

[54] Ibid., 205; Wright (n 46) 210.

[55] D.E. Duffee, *Explaining Criminal Justice* (2nd edn, Prospect Heights 1990) cited Bernard, Paoline and Pare (n 47) 205.

[56] Wright (n 46) 210.

[57] Bernard, Paoline and Pare (n 47) 205.

System may also assume the meaning, as listed in the *Oxford Dictionary*, of 'a set of things working together as parts of a mechanism or an interconnecting network'. An example would be the digestive system, or organ systems. The emphasis here is placed not so much on the teleological but on the organic or operational aspect: the functioning of the whole depends on the cooperation of the parts. Criminal justice may perhaps be analysed and characterized in this way and on that basis be identified as a system. The focus then is on the contributions of the various stages and agents of criminal justice to the system's eventual output (a successful product is something else than the pursuit of common goals). The fact that it is quite likely for the police, prosecution, judiciary and corrections to pursue different goals in handling concrete cases does not mean that they are not contributing to the output of criminal justice. The output of the distinct components and stages may differ, while each 'output' may consist of both qualitative (normative) and quantitative elements. For example, the successful product of the trial stage may be a reliable finding of fact and guilt. The successful product of the sentencing stage may be the punishment of persons found guilty of committing an offence. And the successful product of the enforcement stage may be the execution of a sentence in such a way as to prepare the convicted person as well as possible for a crime-free life in society. The qualitative and quantitative elements cannot be completely separated in a criminal justice system governed by the rule of law in a democratic society, which aims at punishing only the truly guilty. However, the output of the criminal justice system as a whole, the system's successful product, is more difficult to define, especially because finalized products may leave the system at different stages.[58]

Such an organic system of criminal justice then is a very loose, fragmentary complex and its output may perhaps only be defined as delivering justice, which may mean different things to different people(s) (whereby such differentiation may be amplified in the international context).[59] What is more, such an organically understood system says very little about the effect of ultimate objectives[60] or of objectives governing the sentencing stage or the execution stage. It certainly does not prescribe that the same objectives must govern all the different components; it would only do so if this was the only means to secure the system's output. The normative elements of the output of enforcement may, for example, include successful reintegration into society and the mitigation of the damaging effects of imprisonment. Such an output would necessarily have consequences for the sentencing stage, in the sense that it would preclude sentencing chambers from imposing harsh sentences that are not based on respect for the autonomy of the accused. And it works the other way as well. Applying retribution to the sentencing stage calls for the respectful treatment of prisoners. This is not so much based on the *jus tallionis*, 'an eye for an eye' understanding of retribution, but more on the contemporary just deserts understanding of retribution, which lies at the

[58] Vasiliev (n 3) 168.

[59] Vasiliev formulates international criminal justice's overarching goal as 'ensuring accountability and closing the impunity gap for international crimes by delivering justice to the accused, victims and society'. Vasiliev, ibid.

[60] H.L.A. Hart, *Punishment and Responsibility. Essays in the Philosophy of Law* (2nd edn, Oxford University Press 2008).

heart of the tribunals' sentencing practice. To censure a person means that she is being treated as an autonomous being who can be held responsible, someone who is believed to be able to alter her ways. It would be difficult to see how this could be combined with harsh, disrespectful punishment at the enforcement stage.[61]

Another point is that a systemic approach to retooling an organization in order to maximize or alter outputs is best used in organizations that have no specific interest in the kind of operations they employ to reach such outputs.[62] The international criminal justice apparatus, however, does have such interests: international penitentiary operations are to a large extent dictated by human rights standards and penal principles. Further, striving for a monolithic system to overcome fragmentation in criminal justice must perhaps be considered naïve. Wright argues that the conflict of goals within criminal justice is actually desirable.[63] He distinguishes between simple and complex systems stating that '[i]n a simple system, goals can be specified, tasks to accomplish those goals can be undertaken, and progress can be monitored so that the system is self-regulating. These activities are possible because the internal and external environments of the system are relatively stable'.[64] It is this type of monolithic, non-fragmentary system that proponents of the idea of criminal justice as a system usually have in mind, while criminal justice, if it can be regarded as a system at all, may only be devised as a complex system. Such a complex system does:

> not exist in stable environments, but rather finds itself in a complex and rapidly changing, or turbulent environment which produces unpredictable changes within the system itself. (…) Because the environment is turbulent, and thus drastically and dynamically affecting the system, it is simply impossible to identify and specify a set of goals and to bring about some change to remodel the system.[65]

Rather, the variety of goals, spread over the various components of criminal justice, may be regarded as something positive, since it enables the institutions to represent and protect different societal interests and needs.[66] Fragmentation and lack of integration within criminal justice are, according to that view, desirable. Wright even states that '[i]f it is assumed that the political culture and public interests vary from area to area, then the seemingly fragmented system of justice may serve to fulfil those diverse interests'.[67] With respect to international criminal justice, this latter remark may constitute an argument for enforcement as close as possible to the former conflict

---

[61] See R.L. Lippke, *Rethinking Imprisonment* (Oxford University Press 2007).
[62] Duffee (n 48) 100.
[63] Wright (n 46) 210.
[64] Ibid., 211.
[65] Ibid.
[66] See also M. Klamberg, 'What are the Objectives of International Criminal Procedure? – Reflections on the Fragmentation of a Legal Regime' (2010) 79 *Nordic Journal of International Law* 279, 280, 285.
[67] Wright (n 46) 213.

region, or for establishing an international prison with regional prison facilities, as advocated by Penrose.[68]

3.2 The Relative Autonomy of the Objectives Directing the Enforcement Stage

In his work 'Punishment and Responsibility', Hart argued that in order to arrive at a morally acceptable account of punishment, one must acknowledge that the question as to the justification of punishment requires consideration on different levels and involves different questions. According to him:

> in our inherited ways of talking about punishment there is some persistent drive towards an over-simplification of multiple issues which require separate consideration (...) What is needed is the realization that different principles (each of which may in a sense be called a 'justification') are relevant at different points in any morally acceptable account of punishment. What we should look for are answers to a number of different questions such as: What justifies the general practice of punishment? To whom may punishment be applied? How severely may we punish?[69]

According to this view, the general justifying aims, the rationales and objectives as provided by the mandate givers of international criminal justice do not necessarily explain or prescribe certain practices in concrete cases in its different components and stages. In a similar vein, back in 1975, Jonkers argued that for a proper understanding of penal purposes, a distinction must be made between the levels of legislation, application (by which he meant sentencing) and execution.[70] According to him, however, these levels are not strictly separated. The level of execution refers to that of application, which, in turn, refers to that of legislation. The 'lower' level should always take into account the aims governing the 'higher' level(s). Nonetheless, Jonkers recognized that, when enforcing a sentence, besides the task of deprivation of liberty which is prescribed by the level of application, those implementing the sentence also have a task independent from the foregoing stages. Since execution may take many forms, he argues, there are policy choices to make.[71] Jonkers' notion that a distinction must be made between the different stages or levels of the criminal justice process when examining the objectives of punishment remains highly relevant. The validity of his line of reasoning has been affirmed by later developments. Jonkers' theory dates from a time when certain contemporary penal notions were not yet widely accepted, i.e., the notions that men are sent to prison as punishment, not for punishment,[72] or

---

68 For the latter, see M.M. Penrose, 'Spandau Revisited: The Question of Detention for International War Crimes' (1999–2000) 16 *New York Law School Journal of Human Rights* 553, 585. See also M.M. Penrose, 'Creating an international prison', Chapter 18 in this volume.

69 Hart (n 60) 3.

70 W.H.A. Jonkers, 'De strafrechtelijke straf: inhoud, grondslag, doeleinden', in Y. Buruma (ed), *100 Jaar Strafrecht. Klassieke teksten van de twintigste eeuw* (Amsterdam University Press 1999) 163–76.

71 Ibid., 174.

72 A. Paterson, as cited in F.W. Bleichrodt and P.C. Vegter, *Sanctierecht* (Kluwer 2013) 93.

Freiheitsstrafe soll eine 'Beschränkung der Freiheit, nichts anderes' sein[73] and that sentenced persons retain their fundamental rights. The acceptance of those ideas enhances the autonomy of the enforcement stage in relation to the other components of criminal justice.

Indeed, it has been argued that the execution phase does not so much look back at the sentencing phase, or at the acts and purposes of the legislature, but is rather forward looking, thereby assuming a character that is in important respects different from the earlier stages of the criminal process. Van Zyl Smit and Snacken argue that a relative autonomy exists between the principles and purposes that guide sentencing judges and those that govern the enforcement stage. Aims that may govern sentencing, like retribution or prevention, are mainly translated into the duration of the sentence imposed and into the mode of punishment (deprivation of liberty, community service, fines, etc.). Such aims do not necessarily tell the executing authority how he or she should enforce the sentence imposed. For this reason they speak of the relative autonomy of prison law.[74] This relative autonomy essentially means that the execution stage has its own goals, largely independent from aims directing the other components. The judicial verdict does not permit any other infringements on the rights of convicted persons apart from the deprivation of liberty. Feest and Lesting, writing about German penal law, argue in this regard that '*[i]m Vollzug der Freiheitsstrafe treten an die Stelle der Strafzwecke die Aufgaben des Vollzuges*' and '*[n]ach der zutreffenden herrschenden Meinung ist daher die Berücksichtigung der Strafzwecke wie Schuldausgleich, Schuldschwere, Sühne, Generalprävention oder Verteidigung der Rechtsordnung im Strafvollzug nicht zulässig*'.[75]

Other than the separation of powers doctrine,[76] there may be other reasons for recognizing that the enforcement stage is largely governed by its own rationales. According to van Zyl Smit and Snacken, the relative autonomy is primarily caused by differences in time and purpose.[77] They argue that, at the moment of sentencing, the judge, at that singular moment, 'publicly expresses the censure of a particular offence with due regard to the responsibility and guilt of the offender'.[78] This sentencing moment is essentially backward looking. Of course, the judge may take into account the accused person's future when determining the mode and duration of the sentence, but the main focus is on the crime and the guilt of the accused.[79] The enforcement

---

[73] 'Prison sentences should only entail deprivation of liberty' (author's own translation), J. Feest and W. Lesting, *StVollzG Kommentar zum Strafvollzugsgesetz (AK-StVollzG)* (Carl Heymanns Verlag 2012) 18.

[74] D. van Zyl Smit and S. Snacken, *Principles of European Prison Law and Policy* (Oxford University Press 2009) 76.

[75] 'In enforcing prison sentences, the tasks of enforcement supersede the objectives of punishment' and 'according to the prevailing view, considerations relevant to objectives of punishment such as settlement of guilt, gravity of guilt, atonement, general prevention or safeguarding the rule of law are not acceptable in the stage of enforcement' (author's own translation). Feest and Lesting (n 73) 18–19.

[76] Van Zyl Smit and Snacken (n 74) 77.

[77] Ibid., 79.

[78] Ibid.

[79] Ibid.

stage, however, does not consist of one single moment, but consists of a longer period of time during which the convicted person is deprived of his liberty. And since most of these persons will someday return to society, the prison regime must necessarily be directed to the future, to a life after release (that is a crime-free life).[80]

The notion that sentenced persons retain their fundamental rights gained more and more acceptance from the 1960s onwards. It found expression in Article 10, Paragraph 1 of the ICCPR, which demands that prisoners be treated with respect for the dignity inherent to their person. As argued by van Zyl Smit, since respect for human dignity is the cornerstone, the essence of all human rights,[81] Article 10, Paragraph 1, allows for a holistic interpretation of the applicability of human rights in the prison context. Respect for human dignity of imprisoned persons implies that all their fundamental rights must be respected.[82] Although this may seem self-evident nowadays, it was not until the third quarter of the twentieth century. Until 1975, the ECtHR, for example, made use of the inherent limitations doctrine. According to that doctrine, deprivation of liberty automatically allows for infringements of other rights. In the *Golder* case, the Court rejected the inherent limitations doctrine and assessed the impugned domestic restrictions on the right to correspondence against the limitations clause of Article 8(2) ECHR.[83] Since then, the Court has repeatedly affirmed that confined persons continue to enjoy all the fundamental rights and freedoms guaranteed under the Convention save for the right to liberty.[84] This view has not only been promulgated by the ECtHR, but also by the HRC and the I-ACtHR and other human rights supervisory bodies.[85] In the case of *Fongum Gorji-Dinka v Cameroon*, for instance, the HRC stated that 'persons deprived of their liberty may not be subjected to any hardship or constraint other than that resulting from the deprivation of liberty and that they must be treated in accordance with, inter alia, the Standard Minimum Rules for the Treatment of Prisoners (1957)'.[86] Another ground for acknowledging the relative autonomy of the stage of

---

80 Ibid.

81 As held by the ICTY Trial Chamber in the *Furundžija* judgment:

> [t]he essence of the whole corpus of international humanitarian law as well as human rights law lies in the protection of the human dignity of every person, whatever his or her gender. The general principle of respect for human dignity is the basic underpinning and indeed the very *raison d'être* of international humanitarian law and human rights law; indeed in modern times it has become of such paramount importance as to permeate the whole body of international law.

Furundžija IT-95-17/1-T (Judgment, 10 December 1998) para 183.

82 D. van Zyl Smit, 'International Imprisonment' (2005) 54 *International Criminal Law Quarterly* 357, 362; van Zyl Smit (n 22) 5.

83 *Golder v United Kingdom* App no 4451/70 (ECtHR, 21 February 1975).

84 See, e.g., *Ciorap v Moldova* App no 12066/0219 (ECtHR, June 2007) para 107; *Hirst v United Kingdom (No 2)* App no 74025/01 (ECtHR, 6 October 2005) para 69.

85 See Rule 2 EPR, Art. 1 of the Kampala Declaration on Prison Conditions in Africa, Principle 5 UNBP, and *López-Álvarez v Honduras* (I-ACtHR, 1 February 2006) Series C No 141 IHRL 1525 para 104.

86 HRC, *Fongum Gorji-Dinka v Cameroon* Communication 1134/2002 UN Doc CCPR/C/83/D/1134/2002, views of 17 March 2005 para 5.2. See, in a similar vein, HRC, *Salem Saad Ali Bashasha v The Libyan Arab Jamahiriya* Communication 1776/2008 UN Doc CCPR/C/100/D/1776/2008, views of 2 November 2010 para 7.7; HRC, *Munguwambuto Kabwe Peter Mwamba*

enforcement lies in the fact that international human rights standards prescribe that the primary aim of penitentiary systems is to rehabilitate the prisoner. Rehabilitation may play a limited role at the legislative and sentencing stages. At the legislative stage it instructs the legislature to create sanctioning norms that enable the judges to take into account the accused's future, including a life after release. At the sentencing stage, it instructs the judges to individualize punishment (although this is also demanded by retribution) when determining the mode and the duration of punishment and to take into account the perpetrator's chances of successful reintegration. At the enforcement stage, however, rehabilitation may be regarded as the primary, human-rights based principle, interacting with such policy rationales as maintaining order and security inside the institution.

The relative autonomy of the objectives governing the enforcement stage is augmented in the international criminal justice context as a result of the jurisdictional fragmentation that characterizes the international enforcement of sentences. International sentences are executed in domestic prisons under domestic prison regimes. The penal regimes of these enforcement States must conform to human rights minimum standards, but such regimes do not have a particular international character and, therefore, do not provide enforcement with a specific, international quality. As such, objectives of international criminal justice and international sentencing, at least in theory, find expression in the duration (and perhaps in the future if the ICC decides to actually impose fines, the form) of the punishment, but not in the modalities of the enforcement regimes.

In conclusion, the relative autonomy of the objectives governing the enforcement stage from those that direct other components or criminal justice as a whole must be acknowledged. International criminal justice is not a simple system in which goals can be easily specified and accomplished. The aims of sentencing largely find expression in the mode and duration of the punishment imposed. The retributive foundation of the imposed punishment (as argued by Jonkers, the foundational principle of punishment is retribution, in the (limited) sense that the evil (all punishment can be regarded as additive evil) imposed by the sentencing authority finds its basis in and looks back at the crime and guilt of the offender)[87] finds expression in the deprivation of liberty. This deprivation of liberty necessarily has consequences for other rights and means that the convicted person is cut off from wider society (at least to the extent permitted by human rights law and as far as reconcilable with the objectives of normalization and resocialization). The latter aspect may resonate with Erich Fromm's theory that the leitmotiv in human suffering is man being conscious of himself being separated from other men, i.e., of his essential isolation, which creates a lifelong longing, or endeavour

v Zambia Communication 1520/2006 UN Doc CCPR/C/98/D/1520/2006, views of 10 March 2010 para 6.4; HRC, *Abdelhamid Benhadj v Algeria* Communication 1173/2003 UN Doc CCPR/C/90/D/1173/2003, views of 20 July 2007 para 8.5; HRC, *Bradley McCallum v South Africa* Communication 1818/2008 UN Doc CCPR/C/100/D/1818/2008, views of 2 November 2010 para 6.8; HRC, *Sid Ahmed Aber v Algeria* Communication 1439/2005 UN Doc CCPR/C/90/D/1439/2005, views of 16 August 2007 para 7.7; HRC, *Abdelhakim Wanis El Abani (El Ouerfeli) v The Libyan Arab Jamahiriya* Communication 1640/2007 UN Doc CCPR/C/99/D/1640/2007, views of 14 September 2010 para 7.7.

[87] Jonkers (n 70) 166–7.

to transcend or dissolve that isolation.[88] It may be precisely this dissociative aspect, which is inherent to imprisonment, that largely echoes the retributive objective.[89] Any additional harm or discomfort neither finds a basis or justification in the sentencing judgment, nor in the general aims of criminal justice.

3.3 Causality and Other Major Weaknesses of Alignment Theories

A serious problem with aligning the objectives of the enforcement stage of international criminal justice with those of the sentencing stage lies in the fact that it is extremely difficult, if not impossible, to establish any causal links between the courts' operations and the achievement of their ultimate, socio-political objectives at the domestic or regional level.[90] According to Vasiliev, '[t]he grounds underpinning most of the claims about the peace-making and reconciliatory effects of the tribunals – distinct from arguments based in morality – remain contentious'.[91] According to him, the problem lies in the over-deterministic link that is being drawn between the functions of criminal procedure and the socio-political goals.[92] In a similar vein, Stahn argues with regards to international criminal justice as a whole that 'there remains a fundamental tension between "faith" (i.e., belief in the value and worthiness of the project) and "facts" (i.e., actual and demonstrable record)'.[93] Stahn is right when he argues that a lack of facts does not necessarily undermine a faith-based approach. I am not arguing that in the absence of a clear causal connection between penal regimes and the achievement of socio-political goals, no reconciliatory efforts should be made at all. As Stahn argues, the limitations of factual assessments must be acknowledged and 'one of the most important virtues of international criminal justice may actually lie in the fact that it upholds normative values and idealism'.[94]

Nevertheless, knowing that it is unclear what actually works in penology warrants caution when implementing changes to penal regimes, especially where such changes may have consequences for the convicted persons' autonomy, respect for which, as we have seen above, is mandatory in light of the retributive foundation of international punishment. The problems with causality are at least threefold. First, the content of the ultimate objectives is imprecise. As was stated in this chapter's introduction, the ultimate ends are often vaguely formulated and open-ended, which may give 'rise to conflicting interpretations of their meaning'.[95] Such a lack of clarity may also be the

---

[88] E. Fromm, *Liefhebben. Een kunst, een kunde* (Bijleveld 2010) 20-21; E. Fromm, *Een kwestie van hebben of zijn. Naar een nieuwe levensoriëntatie in de consumptiemaatschappij* (Bijleveld 2014) 149.

[89] Compare S. Snacken and N. Kiefer, 'Oversight of international imprisonment: the Committee for the Prevention of Torture', Chapter 14 in this volume.

[90] As stated by Shany, 'even if one finds broad support for the proposition that certain effects are indeed desirable, delineating the causal relationship between judicial performance and State conduct may remain difficult'. Shany (n 3) 228.

[91] Vasiliev (n 3) 177.

[92] Ibid., 187.

[93] Stahn (n 8) 254.

[94] Ibid., 257.

[95] Shany (n 3) 233.

result of opposing political views during the identification and drafting of the objectives and may be due to the complexities of the situation that gave rise to the tribunals' establishment.[96] The definition of the different objectives' content may largely depend on the viewpoint of the different stakeholders.[97] Second, as Shany notes, the 'public goods that [the ultimate objectives] generate, such as justice, peace and legal certainty, are hard to quantify (by contrast, private organizations typically generate quantifiable profits or losses'.[98] Stahn is keen to remind us that the assessment of the achievement of socio-political objectives largely comes down to a normative assessment.[99] In this regard, it is important to reflect on the point raised by Swart that a distinction must be made between the different levels of the tribunals' operations: the macro and the micro level.[100] Whether the tribunals achieve the objectives of international criminal justice at the macro level depends on the views of the different stakeholders – victims, international organizations, mandate providers, the general public and States. Because of this multiplicity of stakeholders, such views may easily vary.[101] They are largely based on confidence and trust and will depend on such considerations as whether suspects can be apprehended, whether perpetrators of international crimes are held accountable and, more generally, on the perception of the tribunals' effectiveness. Third, the achievements of international courts are to an important extent dependent on their external environment.[102] Vasiliev adds to the aforementioned problems relating to causality the point that:

> the socio-political goals of international criminal justice are so remote from and neutral to the mechanics of the legal process that it strains imagination to try to draw a direct link. The objectives of restoring peace and reaffirming international law norms are under-determinative when it comes to defining procedural arrangements. This is where the major weakness of the theories asserting a direct interaction between the legal process and institutional goals comes to the surface. The problem is that they collapse the two dimensions of criminal justice: the micro-level perspective focusing on the individual cases and consequences of specific proceedings, on the one hand, and the political macro-dimension of the longer term and broad social consequences of the life of the tribunal, on the other hand.[103]

He argues that 'empirically or even theoretically there is neither an evident link nor necessarily alignment between the micro- and macro-outcomes of the judicial process' and that the relationship between processes and goals is complex.[104] I am of the

---

[96] Ibid., 233–4.

[97] Vasiliev (n 3) 171.

[98] Shany (n 3) 239. As argued by Stahn, 'it is evident that not all goals of international criminal justice can be fully quantified or translated into concrete indicators and measurable outcomes'. Stahn (n 8) 264.

[99] Stahn (n 8) 265.

[100] Swart (n 2) 101.

[101] Shany (n 3) 240.

[102] Ibid., 239. Shany argues (at 228) that 'since measuring effects may fail to capture the actual organizational features or dynamics leading to those effects, such measures may provide a limited understanding of those aspects of international courts in need of reform'.

[103] Vasiliev (n 3) 188.

[104] Ibid., 189.

opinion that the same applies in respect of enforcement of prison sentences imposed by the tribunals. Altering penal regimes in order for them to contribute to socio-political goals on the basis of mere feasibility, i.e., without any empirical proof or detailed theory which indicates how exactly such adapted regimes would contribute to the political objectives and the likelihood that there would be any such effect, is a highly speculative undertaking that may waste resources and put a strain on the convicted persons' autonomy resulting in bitterness and resentment. Instead, penal regimes should be governed by goals prescribed by international minimum standards, as dictated by the tribunals' own legal frameworks and human rights norms, and which have proven to prevent as much harm as possible to the persons subjected to such regimes. One might start thinking about aligning penal regimes with ultimate goals only if this can be combined with full respect for and implementation of international penal standards. But achieving the ultimate goals should be considered no more than a desired side effect.[105]

According to Shany[106] and Duffee, systemic analysis in criminal legal research tends to neglect the relationships that criminal justice has with the environmental context and other subsystems.[107] Duffee warns that bringing about changes to existing criminal justice apparatus requires: (i) clear conceptions of the existing structure; (ii) 'accuracy or some demonstrable feasibility about the nature of the future system'; and (iii) 'a reasonable connection between the two through planned guidance, control, or intervention'.[108] In the absence of clear conceptions, there are no solid arguments for revising the tribunals' penal regimes in order for them to be better able to contribute to, for example, reconciliation or restoring and maintaining peace.

The only argument one can adduce in favour of building in peace-building or reconciliatory mechanisms into the tribunals' enforcement operations appears to be that of feasibility. For example, tribunals that lack any programmes specifically aimed at outreach are, in the words of Shany, 'unlikely to facilitate the changes in public opinion necessary to realize [their] reconciliation mandate'.[109] However, this argument is not very convincing. Although it may sound logical with regard to outreach programmes, it appears a little far-fetched to argue that the same is also true for tribunals whose penal regimes do not contain, for example, any reconciliatory programmes. It may be more plausible to argue that an objective such as promoting and maintaining peace and security may be one of the macro-level, longer-term contributions of international criminal justice, even if specific programmes aimed at such objectives are not part of penal regimes, but where enforcement finds its basis in the classic (domestic) objectives of punishment. As Sarkin argues in respect of transitional and victim-oriented restorative justice objectives, '[t]he retributive justice component certainly serves these needs as it seeks accountability for those responsible for past human rights violations through criminal trials'.[110] Swart arrives at a similar conclusion on the basis of an analysis of the tribunals' interpretation of domestic sentencing objectives where he states that in

105 Ibid., 190.

106 Shany (n 3) 239.

107 Duffee (n 48) 6.

108 Ibid., 78.

109 Shany (n 3) 239.

110 Sarkin (n 13) 89.

the tribunals' case law 'reconciliation also seems to be a potential effect of punishment rather than a goal that is pursued in its own right'.[111]

Duffee also raises the point that the environment in which criminal justice operates does not allow it to work effectively towards deterrence or other penal goals because the public it serves is too differentiated, holding too many different viewpoints and not being equally able to express or define its desires and needs. He says that '[i]nstead, criminal justice operations, based upon the faulty assumption that integration exists, can actually increase the divisions among various groups and limit the chances of deriving mutually acceptable standards of how persons should act toward each other'.[112] This argument seems to apply *a fortiori* to the international context, where (in the case of the ICC) a single court located in The Hague tries to deliver justice in respect of multiple former conflict regions and victim communities in other parts of the world. And as to the risk that criminal justice operations may even increase divisions among community groups, Duffee explains – with great relevance to system criminality and mass atrocity – that an instrumental approach to criminal justice may start from the premise that delinquency is based on personal characteristics of the individual perpetrator and his or her own choices rather than on, for example, social infrastructure. He warns that this may divert attention from the group's or society's responsibility to that of the individual.[113] Stahn warns in particular against attributing too great a role to reconciliation in international criminal justice. Besides the fact that any effect of the tribunals' operations on reconciliation is difficult to measure, he explains that such operations may lead to even deeper divisions and that arguing for a greater role for reconciliation is based on the wrong premise: reconciliation would presuppose that each party to the (former) conflict is willing to reflect on its own share of responsibility, while there is no guarantee this will indeed take place.[114] Furthermore, as was stated in the introduction, the lack of a hierarchy between the tribunals' ultimate ends makes it difficult, if not impossible, to realize them, since they may conflict inter-se. Where tensions arise, it is not clear which objective should be accorded prominence. Besides a lack of hierarchy, another difficulty is that the mandates themselves, and therefore also objectives, or their weight, may vary per tribunal and may alter over time.[115] This may lead to ambiguity of objectives.[116]

Damaška searched for one leading objective in international criminal justice but had to conclude that there was no such primary objective.[117] As a consequence, the socio-political objectives hardly provide any guidance as to enforcement on the micro level. The only objectives that must be directly pursued by the tribunals on the micro level are those dictated by contemporary penal standards and human rights law. So if there is any clarity as to the proper objectives of international punishment, then it is to be primarily found in the human rights standards that are applicable to the tribunals'

---

111 Swart (n 2) 104.

112 Duffee (n 48) 102.

113 Ibid., 115. See also M. Drumbl, *Atrocity, Punishment and International Law* (Cambridge University Press 2007) 23–45.

114 Stahn (n 8) 278.

115 Klamberg (n 66) 285; Stahn (n 8) 260; Vasiliev (n 3) 172.

116 Shany (n 3) 234.

117 Damaška (n 8) 329–65.

penal regimes.[118] As argued before, achieving the socio-political objectives may be seen as no more than a desired side effect of such a legitimate undertaking.

Eventually, the question must be answered whether it is appropriate to use individual cases of punishment in order to achieve the broader socio-political objectives, where this would entail what may be regarded as more paternalistic penal regimes, i.e., regimes in which respect for the autonomy of the convicted person is no longer the primary concern. Such regimes may, for example, oblige convicted persons to participate in reconciliatory programmes in order for them to, inter alia, become eligible for early release programmes and furloughs. Vasiliev warns in this respect that:

> [s]ubmitting considerations of fair retribution and individualized punishment to utilitarian objectives means nothing else than using an individual defendant as a mere object for achieving the desired socio-political results, whereas under retribution the dignity of an individual must always be upheld in the act of punishment. The view of punishment as a means to an end conflicts with the categorical imperative which underlies retributive penal accounts.[119]

3.4 Weaknesses in Alignment Practice

Indeed, since international punishment ultimately finds its basis and legitimacy in retributive sentencing, it must be ensured that respect for the autonomy and dignity of the convicted person remains the primary concern at the enforcement stage when pursuing penal objectives dictated by human rights law such as social rehabilitation and normalization. The main argument of this chapter is that the achievement of the tribunals' ultimate objectives may be seen as no more than a desired side effect of such a legitimate endeavour and not something to pursue in its own right. This also applies to penal decisions which do not concern the enforcement regimes, but rather the duration of retributive-based punishment. It may, in this respect, be doubted whether all of the early-release criteria employed by the ICC[120] and, even more so, the criteria employed by the RSCSL to determine whether or not to grant conditional release[121] pay sufficient respect to the convicted person's autonomy. Although early release sees to the duration of the sentence and is therefore only indirectly related to prison regimes, some of the criteria employed cannot but also have an effect on the content of international enforcement regimes.

3.4.1 ICC

Some of the ICC's release criteria are in line with the sentencing rationale of prevention of crime and, more specifically, rehabilitation, i.e., the criteria that focus on the convicted person's chances of a successful reintegration into society and on the

---

[118] See G. Sluiter, 'State cooperation in the enforcement of sentences', Chapter 10 in this volume.

[119] Vasiliev (n 3) 170.

[120] Art. 110 ICCSt in conjunction with Rule 223 ICC RPE. See A. Trotter, 'Provisional release from international remand detention', Chapter 2 in this volume.

[121] See T.A. Doherty and S.A. Fisher, 'Enforcement of sentences and oversight of prisoners convicted by the Special Court for Sierra Leone', Chapter 15 in this volume.

effect of release on social stability.[122] Other criteria reflect the principle of individualization in sentencing by demanding that attention be paid to individual circumstances such as age and health.[123] More problematic from the viewpoint of sentencing rationales, however, appear to be the criteria listed in Rule 223(d), which requires that attention is paid to significant action taken by the sentenced person for the benefit of the victims, and Rule 223(a), stating that regard must be had to the conduct of the sentenced person while in detention, i.e., whether it shows a genuine dissociation from his or her crime. Although such behaviour may perhaps be taken into account as demonstrating genuine remorse and therefore better chances for the sentenced person's successful reintegration into society, as such, the ICC's sentencing rationales do not include improving the sentenced person's relationships with victims or bringing about a psychological shift or changing the sentenced person's attitude towards his delinquent behaviour. Rather, these criteria appear to be based on the macro-level goal of reconciliation. This would imply that a rationale alien to the determination of the duration of the sentence is being introduced for the first time at the early release stage. An early release decision based on this rationale may therefore intrude upon the sentencing judges' will and undermine the legitimacy of either the early release that is granted or the continued enforcement of the sentence. Furthermore, it does not show much respect for the sentenced person's autonomy to, by adopting such criteria for early release, exert pressure on him or her to reach out to victims, or to demand from him or her a change of perspective upon past behaviour. Moreover, one does not need be a die-hard cynic to doubt the veracity of such reconciliatory or pacifying behaviour while in prison, where this may be rewarded by a grant of early release. Socio-political objectives as well as respect for the autonomy of convicted persons would, arguably, be much better served without such criteria.

3.4.2 (R)SCSL

The President of the SCSL in 2013 issued a Practice Direction on the Conditional Early Release of Persons Convicted by the SCSL (hereafter: Practice Direction). A convicted person becomes eligible for early release upon having served two-thirds of the sentence. He or she must also meet certain other criteria listed in the Practice Direction. The convicted person must, inter alia, demonstrate the successful completion of any remedial, educational, moral, spiritual or other programme to which he was referred within the prison.[124] It is also listed that the convicted person must provide proof that he has made a positive contribution to peace and reconciliation in the region such as public acknowledgement of guilt, public support for peace projects, public apology to victims, or victim restitution.[125] As it was argued above in relation to the ICC early release criteria, it appears that a rationale alien to those underlining the original determination of punishment is being introduced at the stage of early release, which entails the risk that the legitimacy of the continued punishment or of early release is being undermined. Besides, requesting from the convicted person – as a condition for

---

[122] Rule 223 (b), (c), (d) ICC RPE.
[123] Rule 223(e) ICC RPE.
[124] Art. 2(B)(i) of the Practice Direction.
[125] Art. 2(C)(iii) of the Practice Direction.

early release – a public apology to victims, an acknowledgement of guilt or a positive contribution to reconciliation, appears difficult to reconcile with a liberal penal regime which takes as a starting point the dignity and autonomy of the convicted person.

4. CONCLUSION

The international criminal justice 'system' as it stands today clearly suffers from a systemic deficiency due to being spread over a myriad of jurisdictions: sentences, which must be enforced in accordance with international standards are being executed in a (potentially) large number of States that apply their own domestic penitentiary legislation. While it may already be difficult to argue that domestic criminal justice operates in a systemic way towards specified goals, one may safely say that there is no such thing as an integrated international criminal justice system. It is decentralized, fragmented and pursues inconsistent goals.[126] Although the idea that '[p]enological goals should be based on the social objectives of the criminal justice system and penal processes should promote the development of both its subjects and the society it serves'[127] is a commendable one, I would call for a 'modest' or 'moderate' approach towards pursuing macro-level objectives in international criminal justice. In this chapter, such a modest approach is advocated with respect to the pursuit of socio-political objectives in international punishment.

Admittedly, socio-political pursuits cannot but have some impact on international criminal justice. However, as stated in the introduction where I compared the tribunals' ultimate objectives to legal principles, the socio-political goals do not generate direct effect on the content of penal regimes in an all-or-nothing fashion. They can to some extent be compared to principles. They function as tools of reflection and critique and can lead to 'no more than a partial realization'.[128] They are being applied in, and as part of, a particular legal context by professional practitioners who are positioned in the sociological roles they fulfil.[129] They are applied more indirectly and, when applied, do not lead to concrete results.[130] From the relatively high level of abstraction on which they operate, they merely offer 'peremptory guidance' to practitioners in their interpretational activities and decision-making. Their high degree of abstraction, inconclusiveness (their application does not lead to concrete results) and open-endedness (they can never be fully concretized) enable principles to be relevant in different situations

[126] Compare T.J. Bernard and R.S. Engel, 'Conceptualizing Criminal Justice Theory' (2001) 18 *Justice Quarterly* 1, 3.

[127] Mulgrew (n 13) 215.

[128] See, in more detail, D. Abels, *Prisoners of the International Community. The Legal Position of Persons Detained by International Criminal Tribunals* (TMC Asser Press 2012) Chapter 4; A.A.G. Peters, *Het rechtskarakter van het strafrecht* (Kluwer 1972) 14.

[129] R. Foqué and A.C. 't Hart, 'Grondslagen ter discussie', in G.C.G.J. van Roermund, M.S. Groenhuijsen, W.J. Witteveen (eds), *Symposium strafrecht. Vervolg van een grondslagendebat* (Gouda Quint 1993) 393.

[130] P. Scholten, 'Rechtsbeginselen', in *Mededeelingen der Nederlandsche Akademie van Wetenschappen*, Afdeeling Letterkunde Deel 80 Serie B No 6 (2nd edn, Noord-Hollandsche Uitgevers Maatschappij 1941) 270.

and contexts and still 'apply' fully. As said, the same may be said of the tribunals' socio-political objectives.

Aside from the fact that their characteristics prohibit them from having an all-or-nothing effect on concrete situations of enforcement, in light of both the difficulties inherent in identifying any causal link between the tribunals' operations at the enforcement stage and the achievement of their socio-political objectives, and the risks that the implementation of socio-political objectives in the enforcement stage may entail for the autonomy of convicted persons, it would be wise to opt for a modest approach. As argued by Vasiliev in relation to international criminal procedure, the tribunals' officials should not actively try to promote the ultimate objectives, but should only ensure that their penal regimes are not inconsistent with or undermine those objectives.[131]

The issue this chapter addressed was whether the socio-political goals of international criminal justice should play a direct role in international enforcement regimes. Indeed, before one starts revising the current penal regimes and pursuing socio-political objectives, first the question must be answered whether an integrated international criminal justice system of which the different parts work towards the same goals is conceivable and, if so, whether such objectives ought to be aspired to in the enforcement phase at all.

Outreach programmes and the trial phase may perhaps be more apt to roll out peace-building, victim-oriented restorative and reconciliatory strategies than the execution phase. International punishment must not be overloaded with expectations and aims. Reconciliation, peace building and related objectives can be met, more safely and fruitfully, by other components of international criminal justice, or by other, non-legal mechanisms and activities,[132] such as economic support to the former conflict region[133] and transitional justice programmes.[134] It should be recalled here that punishment is but one answer to international crimes (and, arguably, a very limited one at that).

Ohlin suggests yet another way of seeing things, which is that, instead of considering international *procedure* as instrumental, i.e., as being directed towards achieving the socio-political goals provided by mandate givers, one may conceive it as constituting 'an end in itself', where it vindicates the rule of law in situations which oftentimes 'involve the systematic breakdown of the Rule of Law'.[135] In other words, international criminal procedure is more than its social functions, it has an intrinsic moral value.

Although Ohlin's argument is specifically directed at the trial stage, the same may to a certain extent be said for enforcement. In the enforcement context, the rule of law is also vindicated in relation to a situation where it was absent, where wrongdoers were

---

131 Vasiliev (n 3) 195–6.

132 Damaška (n 8) 329–65.

133 Safferling (n 16) 1487.

134 For the relation between transitional justice and international trials see, inter alia, J. Doak, 'The Therapeutic Dimension of Transitional Justice: Emotional Repair and Victim Satisfaction in International Trials and Truth Commissions' (2011) 11 *International Criminal Law Review* 263, 264 and L.E. Fletcher and H.M. Weinstein, 'Violence and Social Repair: Rethinking the Contribution of Justice to Reconciliation' (2002) 24 *Human Rights Quarterly* 573.

135 Ohlin (n 1) 77–120.

not being held accountable, but where they and their actions were being facilitated by and approved of by a State's infrastructure. In such a State, the penal system is not governed by the rule of law; prisoners are not protected by the minimum standards of decency that characterize imprisonment in a civilized society. International penal law, with its high levels of protection and respect for international penal principles and standards, is the antithesis to such a State of terror where fear and total dependency reign. Let that be the real worth of international punishment: showing the former conflict region and the convicted persons how communities that respect the rule of law treat their most unpopular and vulnerable members.

12. Rehabilitating international prisoners

Barbora Holá and Joris van Wijk

1. INTRODUCTION

In December 2010 Veselin Šljivančanin, a former Montenegrin Major in the Yugoslav People's Army, was sentenced to ten years' imprisonment by the ICTY. He was convicted of torture as a war crime for his involvement in the mistreatment of hundreds of prisoners of war at the Ovcara farm near Vukovar, Croatia. Six months later, he was granted early release. When in detention,[1] the ICTY President reasoned, Šljivančanin behaved well, regularly assisted in library work, maintained good relations with his family and expressed 'sympathy for the victims of the conflict in the former Yugoslavia'.[2] Although he did 'not express remorse for his own crimes', the President considered his level of rehabilitation sufficient to pardon the rest of his prison term.[3] After returning to Belgrade, Serbia, Šljivančanin received a heroic welcome, wrote a book on his unfair treatment by the ICTY and regularly frequented television shows, claiming that he does not regret his acts in Vukovar.[4]

Whereas international criminal tribunals aim to rehabilitate perpetrators of international crimes and cite rehabilitation in their case-law as one of the sentencing goals and a criterion for early release, in reality this ulterior aspiration seems to be devoid of any meaningful conceptualization, clear objectives and consistent implementation. As of 1 May 2015 the vast majority of international prisoners convicted and already released at the ICTY, ICTR and the SCSL were at the time of being released considered sufficiently rehabilitated. Consequently, the Presidents of these tribunals pardoned a part of their original sentence and set them free (57 out of 66 already released individuals were released early). Oftentimes, the Presidents assess the prisoners' rehabilitation by referring to their 'good behaviour in prison'. While serving their sentence, the prisoners are typically never asked to reflect on their crimes, while they, like Šljivančanin, might after their release continue to justify the acts for which they were condemned.[5]

---

[1] At the international criminal tribunals, the time spent in pre-trial and trial detention is credited against a final sentence. Due to the often lengthy proceedings, some convicts thus serve their entire sentence in pre-trial and trial detention.

[2] *Šljivančanin* IT-95-13/1-ES (Decision of President on Early Release, 5 July 2011) paras 26–27.

[3] Ibid.

[4] Interview with Radio Televizija Serbia (22 November 2012) <http://www.rts.rs/page/stories/sr/story/125/Društvo/1216416/Šljivančanin%3A+Išao+bih+u+Vukovar.html> accessed 10 June 2015. See also Veselin Šljivančanin, *Branio Sam Istinu* (Novosti 2012).

[5] See inter alia testimony of Vidoje Blagojević in *Mladić* IT-09-92 (Transcript of hearings, 23 April 2015) 1–3.

Drawing on previous research,[6] this chapter presents an empirical analysis of the international criminal tribunals' approach to rehabilitation and discusses the key problems of the current practice. First, the concept of rehabilitation, as it has been evolving in the context of domestic criminal justice systems and criminological and penological research, will be outlined. Then we turn to international criminal justice and argue that rehabilitation is a relevant consideration at three important stages of the international criminal proceedings. During sentencing, judges emphasize it as a relevant sentencing principle to take into account. Second, it influences (to a varying extent) the conditions of incarceration of international prisoners following their conviction at the international criminal tribunals. Finally, demonstration of rehabilitation is one of the conditions for sentence commutation and early release. As such, rehabilitation can thus be observed as a goal of international sentencing as well as a goal of incarcerating international prisoners. As our research indicates, however, international criminal tribunals in reality do not take a principled or coherent approach towards rehabilitation. We conclude that the promise of international prisoners' rehabilitation should either be abandoned or, alternatively, that much more research and resources are needed in order to develop and implement a sound rehabilitation model for perpetrators of international crimes.

2. WHAT IS REHABILITATION?

Rehabilitation is a notion that implies change. What kind of change, how it should be achieved and in what contexts remain, however, the subject of discussions on penal rehabilitation. Theory and practice related to offenders' rehabilitation have a long history, going back at least to the eighteenth century.[7] Since then, rehabilitation as a penological concept has undergone continuing transformations depending on the prevalent academic, social and political discourse and conditions. In the nineteenth century, rehabilitation-related activities were largely performed by voluntary organizations and charities (such as churches) trying to help 'sinners' to reform.[8] Rehabilitation efforts were deemed successful if prisoners were transformed into a 'respectable, self-supporting citizen making [their] way in the world' and the justification for rehabilitation was the offenders' spiritual welfare and ultimately, their salvation; offenders' souls were saved for God.[9] In the twentieth century States started

---

[6] J. Kelder, B. Holá and J. van Wijk, 'Rehabilitation and Early Release of Perpetrators of International Crimes: A Case Study of the ICTY and ICTR' (2014) 14 *International Criminal Law Review* 1177; B. Holá, J. van Wijk, 'Life after Conviction at International Criminal Tribunals: An Empirical Overview' (2014) 12 *Journal of International Criminal Justice* 109; B. Holá, J. van Wijk, J. Kelder, 'Rehabilitating Enemies of Mankind', in N. Hayashi and C.M. Baillet (eds), *Legitimacy and Effectiveness of International Criminal Tribunals* (Cambridge University Press, forthcoming).

[7] G. Robinson and I. Crow, *Offender Rehabilitation, Theory, Research and Practice* (SAGE Publications 2013) 1.

[8] P. Raynor and G. Robinson, 'Why Help Offenders? Arguments for Rehabilitation as a Penal Strategy' (2009) 1 *European Journal of Probation* 3, 5.

[9] Ibid., 6.

to take over as key agents in rehabilitating offenders. Spiritual rehabilitation was thus replaced by a more secular conceptualization of rehabilitation. A successful outcome of offender rehabilitation was no longer a redeemed sinner but a good citizen characterized by 'competence, character and usefulness' in the service of common societal goals and interests.[10] Rehabilitation was thus meant to serve the interests of society as a whole, maximizing the number of decent and useful community members. This utilitarian justification for rehabilitation manifested itself in the so-called scientific or medical model of rehabilitation.[11] Consequently, in the period after the Second World War, rehabilitation was considered to be a form of 'treatment' for offenders. Rehabilitation models focused on their deficiencies and the offenders constituted passive subjects of rehabilitative interventions. With the growing emphasis on liberal human rights, this 'instrumental use of human beings for the achievement of greater good' attracted heavy criticism.[12] In response, rehabilitation was increasingly regarded to be a right of the offender as a moral agent. Eventually, this transformed into a State obligation to mitigate damage done by punishments, including imprisonment.[13] Currently, rehabilitation is generally not conceived to merely be a form of 'treatment', but rather a learning model. Offenders are recognized as moral actors and assisted in acquiring skills and resources for making choices that would better serve both their own interests and the interests of others (such as victims and society as a whole, in the name of increased public safety). This learning model rests on the assumption that behaviours are learned responses that could be unlearned and rehabilitation serves as re-education of the 'poorly' socialized.[14]

Currently, discussions about rehabilitation are dominated by two main competing models: Risks-Needs-Responsivity model (RNR model) (or the so-called 'risk-based' or 'What works?' approaches) and Good Lives model (or the so-called 'strengths-based' or 'desistance-based' approaches).[15] Both models, their underlying principles and implementation in practice have been developed on the basis of extensive empirical criminological research into causes of criminal behaviour and extensive evaluations of rehabilitative interventions. The RNR model is based on targetting the criminogenic needs of an offender, such as a history of anti-social behaviour, impulsiveness, aggressiveness, anti-social cognitions or poor attachment to community or criminal friends. The intensity of treatment depends on the level of risk and interventions are delivered in ways that are likely to be responsive to the individuals' circumstances and characteristics.[16] More intensive rehabilitation interventions should be aimed at high-risk offenders and programmes should target their specific criminogenic needs with the

---

[10] Ibid.

[11] F. McNeill, 'Four Forms of "Offender" Rehabilitation: Towards an Interdisciplinary Perspective' (2012) 17 *Legal and Criminological Psychology* 18, 23.

[12] Raynor and Robinson (n 8) 10.

[13] Ibid., 12; Indeed, the right to rehabilitation has by now been stressed in various international hard and soft law instruments, see Section 3.2.

[14] McNeill (n 11) 23.

[15] Ibid., 18.

[16] D.L.L. Polaschek, 'An Appraisal of the Risk–Need–Responsivity (RNR) Model of Offender Rehabilitation and its Application in Correctional Treatment' (2012) 17 *Legal and Criminological Psychology* 1, 10.

objective to 'reduce maladaptive behaviour, eliminate distorted beliefs, remove problematic desires and modify offence supportive emotions and attitudes'.[17] The Good Lives model, on the other hand, claims to adopt a more positive perspective: it aims to equip offenders with the abilities to secure primary human goods (such as knowledge, autonomy, friendship, social recognition or happiness) in socially acceptable and personally meaningful ways.[18] It aims to empower offenders to take control of their lives and make more pro-social choices by helping them to learn necessary skills such as listening, critical and creative thinking, problem-solving and self-management and self-control.[19] The model emphasizes offenders' motivations and recognizes the importance of giving them (positive) reasons to change.

In addition to the two main rehabilitation models, offender rehabilitation practices are increasingly implementing principles stemming from the idea of the so-called 'social rehabilitation' (based, among others, on restorative justice principles focusing on relational dimension of rehabilitation).[20] Social rehabilitation puts relatively more weight on social relationships in the preparation of prisoners for their return to society: rehabilitation is not limited to the individual and his readiness to reintegrate but it should also attempt to rebuild social relationships, without which reintegration is inconceivable. By involving other stakeholders – such as victims, supporters of offenders and supporters of victims or members of wider communities – such programmes seek to encourage offenders to accept responsibility for their actions and reintegrate them peacefully into their communities.[21]

What is obvious from this brief history is that offender rehabilitation can be described and understood in many ways. They all share the objective to decrease the chance of reoffending, but differ with respect to their emphasis on other, broader goals such as salvation of human souls and moral reform of an offender, healing of damaged relationships and mediation between offenders and victims, or a greater sense of safety and security in the everyday life of communities. Given the lack of theoretical consensus, it is not surprising that rehabilitation interventions have taken diverse forms and shapes around the globe and include activities such as cognitive-behavioural and skill development programmes, mental health care, drug dependence treatment, education and job training, psychological counselling or victim-offender mediation.[22] Usually such interventions are informed by criminological theory and empirical research on causes of deviant behaviour and effectiveness of various interventions.[23] In

---

17 T. Ward and M. Brown, 'The Good Lives Model and Conceptual Issues in Offender Rehabilitation' (2004) 10 *Psychology, Crime and Law* 243, 245.

18 Robinson and Crow (n 7) 102.

19 Raynor and Robinson (n 8) 12.

20 Robinson and Crow (n 7) 141. Social rehabilitation as an umbrella term encompasses the approaches that focus on prisoner's place in society, access to social resources and return to citizenship and focuses on such dimensions as housing, employment, social support, etc. See also Robinson and Crow (n 7) 124–38.

21 Ibid., 152.

22 UNODC, *Introductory Handbook on the Prevention of Recidivism and the Social Reintegration of Offenders*, Criminal Justice Handbook Series (UN 2012) 32.

23 It, however, should be noted that the theoretical and empirical research and its practical manifestations in this domain are constantly evolving. It is a dynamic field of practice with

general, rehabilitative interventions are tailored to specific types of offenders and based on an individual assessment of the relevant type of intervention, which is most likely to be beneficial to the individual offender (and eventually his/her community depending on a type and objectives of the rehabilitation intervention at hand).[24]

3. REHABILITATION OF INTERNATIONAL PRISONERS – NOBLE ASPIRATIONS AND BITTERSWEET REALITY?

The previous section showed that rehabilitation, as a penological concept, is difficult to grasp and still lacks a generally accepted operative definition. It is, so to say, one of those concepts, which 'lies in the eye of the beholder'. It varies over time and place in meaning and conceptualization. As a result, States have implemented and promoted varying rehabilitation programmes and interventions, based on different goals and with a varying level of success. Despite the lack of consensus on 'what works' in domestic jurisdictions, international criminal courts and tribunals readily adopted a language of rehabilitation. In practice, rehabilitation has become a consideration at three important stages of international criminal proceedings. During sentencing, it serves as a general principle informing judges on what factors to take into account as relevant in determining sentence severity. Second, it influences to a varying extent the incarceration of international prisoners during their imprisonment following conviction. Finally, demonstration of rehabilitation is one of the conditions for commutation of international sentences and early release. As such, rehabilitation can thus be seen as both a goal of international sentencing and a goal of incarceration of international prisoners. However, in the next section we will argue that the noble aspirations to rehabilitate international prisoners are in practice lacking any coherent conceptual underpinning and clearly defined objectives. Besides, due to the decentralized enforcement of international sentences in domestic prisons, the practice of rehabilitating international prisoners is scattered and deficient and the evaluation of rehabilitation of international prisoners by the Tribunals' Presidents is erratic.

3.1 Rehabilitation as a Goal of International Sentencing

The ICTYSt, ICTRSt and SCSLSt and RPE are silent on the goals of punishment. Yet, in case-law, rehabilitation has emerged as one of the goals of international sentencing cited by judges.[25] The sentencing judgments of the ICTY and ICTR mention rehabilitation as a principle of sentencing in approximately 55 per cent of cases, while SCSL

---

constant changes, evaluation and reevaluation. It should also be noted that a link between academic research and the practice of rehabilitation should not be taken for granted (ideally that should be the case) and as with any other criminal justice policies, practical measures implemented in the field of offender rehabilitation are influenced also by many other considerations, such as resource availability, public demands, etc.

[24] Robinson and Crow (n 7) 89.

[25] B. Holá, *International Sentencing, 'A Game of Russian Roulette' or Consistent Practice?* (Uitgeverij BOXPress 2012) 31, 34.

judges refer to rehabilitation in all the SCSL's judgments.[26] In the majority of cases, however, it is emphasized that rehabilitation should not be given undue weight given the 'seriousness of the committed crimes'.[27] Rehabilitation as a sentencing goal is thus only a secondary consideration in determining the severity of a sentence. The primary goals of international sentencing are, according to judges, retribution and deterrence.[28] The relevance of rehabilitation at sentence determinations at the international criminal tribunals is, however, demonstrated by the fact that in virtually all cases (even when rehabilitation is not explicitly mentioned as a sentencing goal), judges refer to personal circumstances of an accused. As mitigating factors they consider, for instance, the defendant's character (prior to the conflict), lack of criminal record, rehabilitative potential, family circumstances, or expression of remorse.[29]

During the determination of sentences, rehabilitation thus constitutes one of the general sentencing principles, which should serve as a clue as to why a certain individual receives a lower or more severe punishment. However, international judges hardly ever elucidate on what they mean by rehabilitation and in what way it could or should affect sentence severity. Only in very few cases judges embark upon a very limited discussion – amounting to a maximum of two paragraphs – of what the rehabilitation of international criminals means. These restricted accounts, however, differ per case depending on whether a defendant pleaded guilty (in such cases rehabilitation is usually emphasized and elaborated upon), and also arguably on the bench composition and the background of the judges. According to this case-law, rehabilitation is a process of change and reflection[30] aimed largely at reducing the risk of recidivism,[31] promoting the reintegration of an offender into society[32] and at allowing perpetrators to live normal and useful lives following their release.[33] The SCSL judges similarly state that rehabilitation 'means the restoration of the convicted person to a state of physical, mental and moral health through treatment and education'.[34] It seems that judges consider the rehabilitation of war criminals and

---

[26] This data is based on K. Smith, 'Rehabilitation as a Sentencing Goal in International Criminal Justice' (2014) Working Paper for When Justice is Done Project, available at <http://www.whenjusticeisdone.org/articles/memos/Rehabilitation_KathieSmith.pdf> accessed 10 June 2015.

[27] Cf. *Milutinović et al* IT-05-87 (Judgment, 26 February 2009) para 1146; *Deronjić* IT-02-61 (Appeals Judgment, 20 July 2005) para 136. In a handful of cases, however, judges seem to ascribe more importance to rehabilitation. Cf. *Jokić* IT-01-42/1 (Judgment, 18 March 2004) para 36; *Obrenović* IT-02-60/2 (Judgment, 10 December 2003) para 53.

[28] Cf. *Milutinović* (n 27) para 1144; *Lukić and Lukić* IT-98-32-1-T (Judgment, 29 July 2009) para 1049.

[29] See Holá (n 25) 66–72 for an overview of mitigating factors accepted by the ICTY and ICTR judges.

[30] *Blagojević and Jokić* IT-02-60-T (Judgment, 17 January 2005) para 824; *Babić* IT-03-72-S (Judgment, 29 June 2004) para 46; *Mrđa* IT-02-59-S (Judgment, 31 March 2004) para 18.

[31] *Blagojević and Jokić* IT-02-60-T (Judgment, 17 January 2005) para 824; *Kupreškić et al* IT-95-16-T (Judgment, 14 January 2000) para 849.

[32] *Rutaganira* ICTR-95-1C-T (Judgment and Sentence, 14 March 2005) para 113; *Obrenović* IT-02-60/2-S (Sentencing Judgment, 10 December 2003) para 53.

[33] *Mucić et al* IT-96-21-Tbis-R117 (Judgment, 9 October 2001) para 1233.

[34] *Sesay et al* SCSL-04-15-T (Judgment, 2 March 2009) para 16.

génocidaires to be no different from the rehabilitation of conventional offenders. It is a process of change, possibly a restoration of 'the state' before the atrocities took place aiming at either reformation of the offender (implying that by participating in atrocities, the offender's mental, physical and moral health might have changed) or solely prevention of further offending or his/her successful reintegration. The mitigating factors that are accepted by judges in individual cases, such as good behaviour in detention, family circumstances, prior good character or no criminal record, seem to confirm this rather conventional interpretation of rehabilitation.

3.2 Rehabilitation as a Principle Governing Enforcement of International Sentences

The tribunals rely on a decentralized network of States to enforce their sentences. States enter into sentence enforcement agreements with a tribunal and agree to accept international prisoners and enforce international sentences on an *ad hoc* basis. The conditions of imprisonment of international convicts are thus subject to national laws of an enforcement State, but should be in line with minimum international standards regarding the treatment of prisoners.[35] These standards set out obligations and recommendations for penitentiary systems to provide for some basic minimum rehabilitation. For example, Article 10(3) ICCPR provides that 'the penitentiary system shall comprise treatment of prisoners, the essential aim of which shall be their reformation and social rehabilitation'.[36] Over time, many recommendations regarding the role of rehabilitation during incarceration have been developed under the auspices of the UN and the Council of Europe. Rules 60–81 of the UNSMR emphasize the need for the rehabilitation of prisoners, list different types of rehabilitative programmes/treatments and put emphasis on the prisoners' (gradual) integration in society.[37] The European Prison Rules also stress the importance of rehabilitation for sentenced prisoners, the importance of an individual sentence plan for each prisoner including his/her participation in education, work and other activities with the ultimate aim of facilitating reintegration into society.[38]

The minimum international standards constitute general guidelines and recommendations to be implemented by individual enforcement States in their penal systems. International prisoners are currently incarcerated across 14 European States (mainly ICTY prisoners) and three African countries (the vast majority of the ICTR and SCSL prisoners). Not only between African and European prison systems, but also across different European States, a significant variation in the implementation of rehabilitation activities exists. The sentence execution and sentence planning of international prisoners depends on the relative importance assigned to rehabilitation by the enforcement

---

35 Holá and Van Wijk (n 6) 118.

36 ICCPR (19 December 1966) U.N.T.S. 171, 16 (entered into force 23 March 1976).

37 UNSMR (1955). Adopted by the First UN Congress on the Prevention of Crime and the Treatment of Offenders, held at Geneva in 1955, and approved by the Economic and Social Council by its resolutions 663 C (XXIV) of 31 July 1957 and 2076 (LXII) of 13 May 1977.

38 Recommendation of the Committee of Ministers to Member States on the European Prison Rules Council of Europe: Committee of Ministers (11 January 2006) Rec(2006)2, Rule 6, 103 and following.

State[39] as well as the available resources and penal culture. Norway, for example, exemplifies what is referred to as Scandinavian 'exceptionalism' in penal policies and a lot of national resources and efforts are dedicated to the rehabilitation and reintegration of prisoners.[40] On the other hand, countries such as Italy or France are characterized by predominantly retributive penal system with less focus on rehabilitation.[41] Consequently, international prisoners are subjected to very different prison conditions with varying emphasis placed on rehabilitation and a large variety of rehabilitative interventions or a complete lack thereof (such as in African countries enforcing international sentences). From publicly available sources it is impossible to identify what programmes and interventions international prisoners actually take part in.

The imprisonment conditions of international prisoners are subject to supervision by the tribunals, which periodically monitor the prisons where their convicts are incarcerated.[42] This supervisory role, however, is rather passive. There have been no initiatives to advise or guide the enforcement States regarding rehabilitation processes of international prisoners, what is expected of them and how they could develop and apply rehabilitative interventions to international prisoners. As a Norwegian prison representative conferred: 'The ICTY never directly or via the Ministry instructed us to work on rehabilitation.'[43] Since international prisoners often form only a negligible part of a prison population (especially in European prisons, where no country hosts more than six international prisoners), no specific programmes tailored to the needs of international prisoners are developed and implemented in the enforcement countries.[44] Even in Norway, a country known for its rehabilitative penal policies,[45] the representative of a small Norwegian prison where two international prisoners were incarcerated stated

---

[39] R. Mulgrew, 'On the Enforcement of Sentences Imposed by International Courts' (2009) 7 *Journal of International Criminal Justice* 373; D. van Zyl Smit, 'International Imprisonment' (2005) 54 *International and Comparative Law Quarterly* 357; R. Culp, 'Enforcement and Monitoring of Sentences in the Modern War Crimes Process: Equal Treatment before the Law?' (2011) *Human Rights Seminar Series* 1.

[40] J. Pratt, 'Scandinavian Exceptionalism in an Era of Penal Excess' (2007) 48 *British Journal of Criminology* 119. It should be noted, however, that it has more recently been discussed whether these resource-intensive rehabilitation policies should also be available for foreign nationals in Norwegian prisons who are to leave Norway after serving their sentence.

[41] Holá and Van Wijk (n 6) 119.

[42] Art. 27 ICTYSt; Art. 26. ICTRSt; Art. 22 SCSLSt.

[43] Interview with a representative of a Norwegian prison (Norway, 24 July 2013) (all interview transcripts are on file with the authors).

[44] Interviews held with a representative of the French Prison and Probation Service (20 May 2013), representatives of Norwegian prisons (14 June 2013; 2 July 2013); supported in interviews with a representative of the Correctional Services Department of the Norwegian Ministry of Justice (11 June 2013), a representative of the national security unit of the Swedish prison and probation Unit (18 June 2013); and confirmed again in email conversations with a representative of the Danish Prison and Probation Service, (16 and 17 May 2013); and by a lawyer at the Judicial Unit of the Finnish Criminal Sanctions Agency (5 August 2013).

[45] S. D'Ascoli, *Sentencing in International Criminal Law: The UN Ad Hoc Tribunals and the Future Perspectives for the ICC* (Hart Publishing 2011) 63; A.M. van Kalmhout, I. Durnescu, 'European Probation Service System. A Comparative Overview', in A.M. van Kalmhout and I. Durnescu (eds), *Probation in Europe* (Wolf Legal Publishers 2008) 1–49.

that the prison staff never really talked with the inmates about the crimes they committed:

> It felt (…) unpleasant (…) it was so terrible (…) I felt I couldn't ask him (…) in a way to protect myself (…) it was so strange to us, such terrible things had been done (…) For normal crimes we had programs. Programs like 'breaking drug abuse' or 'breaking violence' (…) But what competence do we have to deal with them? We are only simple prison officers, knowing about life in [the place where the prison is located]. We are not educated in these matters.[46]

Also in Mali, Benin and Rwanda, where ICTR and SCSL convicts are concentrated in separate wings, there are no indications that special rehabilitation activities are offered to international prisoners.

Consequently, there are no programmes developed specifically for international prisoners, who are, if at all, offered conventional rehabilitation programmes developed for common prisoners convicted by domestic courts for ordinary crimes. Irrespective of the question whether such interventions are suitable for international prisoners at all (for further discussion see Section 4), practical obstacles remain. Language barriers, cultural differences and difficulties in maintaining contact with family, potentially hinder meaningful participation of international prisoners in such rehabilitation programmes. These impediments resemble problems faced by conventional foreign prisoners incarcerated outside their home countries.[47] In addition, explorative interviews with prison authorities in several enforcement countries indicate that within respective inmate populations the international prisoners sometimes have a '*status aparte*' of being a foreign war criminal or *génocidaire* and this at times affects the prisoners' participation in social life in prison or in rehabilitation programmes.[48] A further complicating consequence of serving a sentence in a faraway country is that international prisoners are almost always repatriated to their countries of origin after serving their sentence. That means that they are not to be integrated into the society of the country where a prison is located. Many rehabilitation programmes, however, are based on the gradual reintegration of prisoners into society by means of halfway houses or short-term trips to family members or their communities. Since international prisoners are generally expected to leave the enforcement country after their release, they do not participate in these progressive reintegration efforts.

---

[46] Interview with a representative of a Norwegian prison (Norway, 24 July 2013).

[47] Van Kalmhout et al conclude that language barriers cause problems such as difficulties in understanding prison regulations, inability to participate in work or education programmes or problems in communicating with other prisoners, prison staff or the outside world. Serving a sentence in a foreign country typically has a negative impact on the ability of prisoners to reintegrate into society as they become socially isolated in prison. See A. van Kalmhout et al, *Foreigners in European Prisons* (Wolf Legal Publishers 2013) 21–37.

[48] Interviews with representatives of Norwegian prisons (14 June 2013; 2 July 2013); Interview with a legal adviser of one of the international prisoners (27 May 2013); Confirmed in email conversations with a representative of the Danish Prison and Probation Service (16 and 17 May 2013) and a lawyer at the Judicial Unit of the Finnish Criminal Sanctions Agency (5 August 2013).

From the outset, many practical obstacles to the rehabilitation of international prisoners in a decentralized enforcement system exist. Countries have never been instructed on how to rehabilitate international prisoners and what is expected of them. And since international prisoners form only a negligible part of a prison population and will in practice rarely be reintegrated into the society of an enforcement country and therefore do not pose any 'risks', countries are reluctant to invest their resources in developing tailored rehabilitation programmes for international prisoners.

3.3 Rehabilitation as a Criterion of Early Release

The final stage of the international criminal proceedings, in which rehabilitation comes to the fore, is the early release procedure. Despite the fact that the incarceration of international prisoners is usually decentralized, the Presidents of the tribunals act as the ultimate authority to decide on an early release of international prisoners and the level of rehabilitation forms one of the conditions thereof. Since the ICTY and ICTR adopted a very different approach to early release procedure compared to the SCSL, these tribunals are discussed separately.

3.3.1 ICTY and ICTR

According to Rule 125/126 of the ICTY/ICTR RPE the President, when deciding on early release, is to consider four factors: (i) the gravity of crime; (ii) the treatment of similarly situated prisoners; (iii) demonstration of rehabilitation; and (iv) cooperation with the prosecutor; and any other relevant information.[49] Rehabilitation of international prisoners thus seems to be part of the aim of incarcerating international prisoners and a sufficient level of rehabilitation is to be evaluated by the President of the tribunals as one of the conditions for early release. One would assume that unless a prisoner demonstrates at least some level of rehabilitation, he/she would not qualify for early release. However, it is not clear what 'a sufficiently rehabilitated war criminal or *génocidaire*' should look – or looks – like. The law and policy papers of the tribunals[50] do not provide any guidance in this respect and as demonstrated above, there is no uniform approach across the enforcement countries. Therefore, in order to see how rehabilitation is interpreted as a criterion of early release and what the profile of a rehabilitated war criminal is, one needs to analyse early release decisions issued by the Presidents of the tribunals.

Similar to sentence determinations, the ICTY and ICTR early release decisions are usually short and dedicate very limited attention to rehabilitation. In general, there is a lack of consistency and coherence in evaluating rehabilitation of international

---

[49] Rule 151 RPE of the MICT, which took over the supervision of the enforcement of sentences of ICTY and ICTR, is identical. Rule 124 SCSL RPE states that the President decides on early release on the basis of the interests of justice and the general principles of law.

[50] Cf. Practice Direction on the Procedure for the Determination of Applications for Pardon, Commutation of Sentence and Early Release of Persons Convicted by the International Tribunal, ICTY (IT/146/Rev.3, 16 September 2010); Practice Direction on the Conditional Early Release of Persons Convicted by the SCSL (1 October 2013).

prisoners.[51] An analysis of all the early release decisions issued by the ICTY, ICTR and MICT Presidents up till 1 May 2015 identified 16 different factors that are considered relevant for the determination of a prisoner's demonstration of rehabilitation.[52] These are, however, certainly not all equally important, nor considered systematically or consistently in each decision. The tribunals' interpretation of rehabilitation in early release decisions is by no means straightforward and instead of using a clear definition and a set of pre-determined and well thought-through assessment criteria, the President relies on a seemingly coincidental *ad hoc* list of factors that are deemed to demonstrate a prisoner's rehabilitation. Despite this, it is possible to roughly categorize these factors into four broad groups: (i) the convict's period in prison and his/her behaviour during incarceration; (ii) his/her future perspectives; (iii) his/her reflection on crimes; and (iv) his/her personal characteristics.

The majority of early release decisions discuss various factors related to the period in prison as demonstrating prisoner's rehabilitation. In the vast majority of early release decisions 'conduct in prison' is cited as a relevant factor for evaluating a prisoner's rehabilitation. In these instances the President uses expressions such as 'exemplary behaviour',[53] 'good conduct',[54] or 'a model prisoner'.[55] In some decisions, good behaviour in prison was the only indicator of rehabilitation.[56] Other factors that relate to the period in prison are the extent to which the prisoner interacted with fellow inmates,[57] participated in training or rehabilitation programmes,[58] tried to learn the

---

[51] G. Vermeulen and E. Dewree, *Offender Reintegration and Rehabilitation as a Component of International Criminal Justice?* (Maklu-Publishers 2014) 67.

[52] The following discussion and data are largely based on Kelder, Holá and Van Wijk (n 6).

[53] See eg *Bisengimana* MICT-12-07 (ICTR-00-60) (Decision of President on Early Release, 11 December 2012) para 26; *Krnojelac* IT-97-25-ES (Public Redacted Version of the 9 July 2009 Decision of the President on Pardon or Commutation of Sentence, 9 July 2009) para 20; or *Radić* IT-98-30/1-ES (Decision of President on Application for Pardon or Commutation of Sentence, 23 April 2010) para 18.

[54] See eg, *Bala* IT-03-66-ES (Decision on Application for Sentence Remission, 15 October 2010) para 20; *Tadić* IT-95-9 (Decision of the President on the Application for Pardon or Commutation of Sentence, 3 November 2004) para 4; *Tarčulovski* IT-04-82-ES (Decision of President on Early Release, 8 April 2013) para 21.

[55] *Krajišnik* IT-00-39-ES (Decision of President on Early Release, 2 July 2013) para 24.

[56] *Blagojević* IT-02-60-ES (Decision of the President on Early Release, 3 February 2012) para 22; *Obrenović* IT-02-60/2-ES (Public Redacted Version of Decision of President of Early Release, 21 September 2011) para 21; *Muvunyi* ICTR-00-055A-T (Decision on Application for Early Release, 6 March 2012) para 6.

[57] See eg, *Bagaragaza* ICTR-05-86-S (Decision on the Early Release, 24 October 2011) para 12; *Krajišnik* (n 55) para 26; *Tadić* (n 54) para 6; *Tarčulovski* (n 54) para 21.

[58] See eg, *Radić* IT-98-30/1-ES (Decision of President on Application for Pardon or Commutation of Sentence, 9 January 2013) para 23; *Šljivančanin* (n 2) para 23; *Serushago* MICT-12-28-ES (Public Redacted Version of Decision of the President on the Early Release, 13 December 2012) para 21.

local language,[59] was deemed to have 'changed for the better',[60] got promoted to or behaved well in a (more) lenient prison regime,[61] and demonstrated a positive attitude towards other nationalities.[62]

The second group of factors relates to the future perspectives of the prisoner. In this respect the most important factor is whether prisoners have, or claim to have, good family relations. In that case they are regarded to be more likely to return to a stable family and lead a normal (crime free) life.[63] The prospects of future reintegration can further be demonstrated by a prisoner's relationship with his/her home country[64] or his/her career perspectives.[65] Finally, the explicitly expressed intention not to reoffend in the future by a prisoner has also been considered as demonstrating rehabilitation in a few decisions.[66]

---

59 See eg, *Bala* (n 54) para 24; *Stakić* IT-97-24-ES (Decision of President on Early Release, 15 July 2011) para 34.

60 This assessment is sometimes based on the prisoner's own claims, see *Kovač* IT-96-23 and 23/1-ES (Public and Redacted Version of the 27 March 2013 Decision of President on Early Release, 3 July 2013) para 22; *Landžo* IT- 96-21-ES (Public Redacted Order of the President on Commutation of Sentence, 13 April 2006) para 7. In other cases the criteria for this Statement are unclear, see: *Erdemović* IT-96-22-ES (Order Issuing a Public Redacted Version of Decision of the President on Early Release, 13 August 1999); *Josipović* IT-95-16-ES (Decision on the Application of Pardon or Commutation of Sentence, 30 January 2006) para 10. In *Decision of President on Early Release of Blagoje Simić* it is noted that discussion over the years has caused him to feel regret for his crimes (IT-95-9-ES, 25 February 2011) para 23.

61 In these decisions it is for instance argued that a prisoner was transferred to a more lenient prison regime as a result of good behaviour and 'rehabilitation', or it was suggested that good behaviour in a more lenient prison regime indicates that the international prisoner will behave well upon release as well. See for example: *Josipović*, ibid para 11; *Krajišnik* IT-00-39-ES (Decision of the President on Early Release, 8 November 2012) para 32; or *Tarčulovski* (n 57) para 22.

62 *Tadić* (n 54) para 5; *Tarčulovski* (n 57) para 20; *Todorović* IT-95-9/1-ES (Decision of the President on the Application for Pardon or Commutation of Sentence, 22 June 2005) para 9.

63 Eg, *Bisengimana* (n 53) para 25; *Šljivančanin* (n 2) para 25; *Rugambarara* ICTR-00-59 (Decision on the Early Release Request, 8 February 2012) para 14.

64 For positive perspective of rehabilitation in this regard, see for instance *Krajišnik* (n 61) para 31; *Simić* (n 60) para 25; or *Tadić* (n 54) para 5. For negative perspective, see for example: *Landžo* (n 60) or *Zelenović* IT-96-23/2-ES (Decision of President on Early Release, 30 November 2012) para 19. For the ICTR, the relation between the prisoner and his or her home country was considered once. This was discussed superficially in *Bisengimana*, ibid., para 26. It is remarkable that this relationship is not mentioned more often, as returning to the home country is in practice most problematic for those convicted by the ICTR. They generally cannot go back to Rwanda for security reasons and other countries are generally unwilling to accept them either. See J. van Wijk, 'When International Justice Collides with Principles of International Protection; Assessing the Consequences of ICC Witnesses Seeking Asylum, Defendants Being Acquitted and Convicted Being Released' (2013) 26 *Leiden Journal of International Law* 173.

65 Cf. *Banović* IT-02-65/1-ES (Decision of the President on Commutation of Sentence, 3 September 2008) para 13; *Erdemović* (n 60); *Kovač* (n 60) para 24; *Krajišnik* IT-00-39-ES (Decision of President on Early Release, 26 July 2010) para 21.

66 See eg *Erdemović*, ibid; *Kolunžija* IT-95-8-S (Order of the President on the Early Release, 5 December 2001); *Kovač*, ibid., para 22.

Additionally, the tribunals pay attention to the question how the prisoner reflects upon his or her crimes. Compared to the above two categories, however, these considerations do not figure in the early release decisions so frequently. In this regard, the President seems to distinguish between acceptance of responsibility and showing remorse. In the majority of the cases where the President considers reflection of a prisoner on his/her crimes, the prisoner was considered to have reflected upon his or her deeds and had either accepted responsibility, shown remorse or both.[67] It is, however, certainly not given that the reflection on crimes, acceptance of responsibility or eventual expression of remorse are indispensable pre-requisites for demonstrating rehabilitation. In some decisions these are not discussed at all or the President notes that the prisoner has not taken in the meaning of his crimes and does not accept any responsibility, without, however, any negative repercussions for the assessment of his rehabilitation.[68]

Finally, the tribunals, to a much lesser extent, consider personal characteristics of a prisoner, such as mental health (psychiatric illness or absence thereof),[69] personality traits,[70] conduct prior to the perpetration of crimes[71] and age.[72]

Although the Presidents do not use a clear definition of rehabilitation, the above suggests that to certain extent rehabilitation in the ICTY and ICTR early release decisions is interpreted in a rather systematic way. Consequently, 'a sufficiently rehabilitated war criminal or *génocidaire*' according to the ICTY and ICTR President is a person who behaves well in prison, participates in language courses, works in the kitchen or garden, has (or claims to have) at least some idea about his/her future after release (eg, a job), and plans to return to his/her family after being released. Whether or not he/she upon release actually has access to housing or a job and whether or not he/she actually has seen his family in years is not so important. In principle, he/she does not necessarily have to reflect on his crimes and his/her participation in atrocities. What is, however, very important is that he/she has served two-thirds of his/her original sentence.[73]

---

[67] See eg *Aleksovski* IT-95-14/1 (Order of the President for the Early Release, 14 November 2001); *Tadić* (n 54) para 5; *Erdemović* (n 60).

[68] Cf. *Radić* IT-98-30/l-ES (Decision of President on Application for Pardon or Commutation of Sentence, 23 April 2010) para 21; *Martinović* IT-98-34-ES (Decision of the President on Early Release, 16 December 2011) paras 21, 22.

[69] Cf. *Tarčulovski* (n 57) para 20; *Vasiljević* IT-98-32-ES (Public Redacted Version of Decision of President on Application for Pardon or Commutation of Sentence, 12 March 2010) para 21; or *Žigić* IT-98-30/1-ES (Decision of President on Early Release, 8 November 2010) para 18.

[70] Eg, *Gvero* IT-05-88-ES (Decision of President on Early Release, 28 June 2010) para 14; *Martinović* IT-98-34-ES (Decision of the President on Early Release, 16 December 2011) para 20; *Todorović* (n 62).

[71] See eg, *Rugambarara* (n 63) para 15; *Serushago* (n 58); *Tadić* (n 54) para 5.

[72] Two decisions explicitly mention age as an important factor for rehabilitation. *Erdemović* (n 60); *Imanishimwe* ICTR-99-46-S (Decision on Application for Early Release, 30 August 2007) while it is explicitly considered irrelevant elsewhere such as *Krajišnik* (n 65) para 21; *Radić* IT-98-30/1-ES (Decision of President on Application for Pardon or Commutation of Sentence, 23 April 2010) para 19.

[73] Holá and Van Wijk (n 6) 124.

3.3.2 SCSL

At the SCSL, neither the Statute, nor the RPE mentions demonstration of rehabilitation as a consideration for early release. However, the Practice Direction on Conditional Early Release explicitly lists rehabilitation among the goals to be served by the early release of SCSL prisoners.[74] The eligibility of an individual for early release at the SCSL is to be evaluated not only by considering a variety of individual-related factors,[75] but, as opposed to the ICTY and ICTR, the Practice Direction also explicitly requires examination of the prisoner's attitude towards his crimes and towards their impact on society and requires the prisoner to at least attempt to make amends in one way or another.[76] The Practice Direction in other words sets much more detailed requirements for early release, while the assessment of rehabilitation also explicitly includes an evaluation of prisoner's reflection on crimes and his contribution to peace and reconciliation in Sierra Leone.

So far, the SCSL President has issued only one decision on conditional early release in the case of Monina Fofana.[77] The factors relevant to the assessment of Fofana's rehabilitation discussed in the decision resemble the factors identified above in the early release practice at the ICTY and ICTR. The President notes that the Rwandan prison authorities have characterized Fofana as 'appropriate and respectful'[78] and 'peaceful and well-disciplined'[79] and described him as an 'exemplary prisoner'.[80] The President is also informed that 'Fofana [willingly and enthusiastically] participated in remedial, educational, moral, spiritual or other programmes to which he was referred'[81] and 'acknowledged and expressed remorse for the crimes for which he was convicted'.[82] This language literally copies the language of the Practice Direction and there is no further information provided on what type of programmes Fofana actually took part in, how these contributed to his rehabilitation and in what form and when he

---

[74] Preamble of the Practice Direction on the Conditional Early Release of Persons Convicted by the SCSL (1 October 2013).

[75] Resembling the factors that emerged in the ICTY and ICTR early release decision-making practice, these are, for example, behaviour in prison, his/her participation in any 'remedial, educational, moral and spiritual or other' programmes offered in prison, or any future prospects.

[76] For example, an applicant for early release should demonstrate that he or she has made a positive contribution to peace and reconciliation in Sierra Leone and the region, such as acknowledgement of guilt, public support for peace projects, public apology for victims, or victim restitution. Art 2(C)(iii) of the Practice Direction on the Conditional Early Release of Persons Convicted by the SCSL.

[77] *Fofana* SCSL-04-14-ES (Public Decision of the President on Application for Conditional Early Release, 11 August 2014).

[78] Ibid., para 37.

[79] Ibid., para 38.

[80] Ibid., para 41.

[81] Ibid., paras 38, 42.

[82] Ibid., paras 38, 42. In this respect it is interesting to note, that one of the judges consulted to assess Fofana's eligibility for early release 'expressed serious reservations against his early release mainly because Fofana has not, at any stage, acknowledged his own responsibility and the leadership role he played in the conflict' (para 18).

expressed remorse and acknowledged his crimes.[83] It is also not discussed how all of this amounts to 'a positive contribution to peace and reconciliation in Sierra Leone'. After weighing all the other required factors (such as gravity of his crimes, views of community he is going to be released to and views of witnesses and victims), the President granted Fofana early release, but only upon the condition that Fofana would stay incarcerated for another six months pending some additional training to make him '[understand] the [serious] nature of the crimes for which he was convicted (...); [understand] that what may be a legitimate cause does not justify the use of illegal means; and that he acknowledges his own responsibility and the leadership role he played in the armed conflict in Sierra Leone'.[84] This, indeed, is a rather puzzling line of argument. While the President at first praised Fofana's 'willing and enthusiastic participation' in the available programmes offered in prison, he somehow – without further motivation – believes it pertinent to let the prisoner stay incarcerated for another six months. Apparently some sort of additional training is to make up for the apparent omission to address Fofana's outlook on his crimes and his role during the Sierra Leonean conflict.[85]

From a rehabilitation perspective, it is also relevant that in contrast to the ICTY and ICTR, the SCSL adopted a system of conditional early release and monitoring of its released prisoners. Not only is more emphasis and scrutiny dedicated to prisoner's reintegration and post-release plans, also the future effects of his release on the community where he is going to reside are taken into account.[86] As a prerequisite for early release, a SCSL prisoner has to adhere to multiple conditions stipulated in the so-called Conditional Early Release Agreement (CERA), which is concluded between the prisoner and the SCSL. If he violates any of the conditions, he might be re-incarcerated for the remainder of his original sentence. The conditions set out in the pro forma CERA annexed to the Practice Direction range from rather strict requirements (such as obligatory residence at a designated place; intensive contact with the monitoring authority (in case of Fofana twice a month); prohibition of consumption of alcohol or possession of weapons) to very broadly formulated stipulations such as a requirement to 'pledge not to commit any offence and not to incite and promote crime

[83] According to our information – based on an interview with a prison officer in Mpanga prison (12 March 2013) – no specific rehabilitation programmes are available to international prisoners, except for courses in computer skills.

[84] *Fofana* (n 77) para 47.

[85] Apparently, the additional six-month training successfully addressed Fofana's outlook on his deeds, Fofana was released on 6 March 2015 and escorted to the village of Bo in Sierra Leone. Prior to his release, he publicly apologised to 'victims of war' and asked for their forgiveness: 'I am sorry for what happened and I want them to accept me back into their community as their brother. Thinking back, I know what happened and I feel sorry about it, and I am asking for their forgiveness.' See Residual Special Court for Sierra Leone, 'CDF Convict Moinina Fofana Returned to Bo', Press Release 16 March 2015. Apparently this statement, or other information not publicly available, convinced the President that Fofana by March 2015 understood that his crimes were serious violations of IHL, that they were not justified by a legitimate cause and that he acknowledged his responsibility and leadership role.

[86] A prisoner applying for early release has to provide information regarding his proposed address of residence after release, reasons why the proposed area of residence is suitable for his resettlement and how he will be supported financially. Art 5(B) SCSL Practice Direction (n 74).

or behave in a way which undermines public peace and security'; or an expectation 'to conduct himself honourably and peacefully in the community' and a prohibition to 'engage in secret meetings intended to plan civil unrest or join local politics'.[87]

Consequently, the post-release monitoring systems at the ICTY/ICTR and the SCSL are diametrically different. At the ICTY and ICTR, early release, in practice, amounts to an executive pardon or clemency (as known in domestic criminal justice systems), where a prisoner is released before serving his full sentence with no conditions attached and no monitoring system in place.[88] At the SCSL, early release resembles a parole decision, wherein conditions are set and monitoring (parole) authorities are asked to supervise a released prisoner. Each has its own flaws. On the one hand, releasing international prisoners early without any follow-up conditions and assistance to further their reintegration after a prolonged period of incarceration – as is the case at ICTY and ICTR – is certainly not ideal from a rehabilitation perspective. The SCSL system at least sets conditions the released individual needs to observe, but it remains questionable whether the set conditions are relevant and proportionate and to what extent monitoring these at the same time broad but also extremely detailed conditions is actually feasible.

In the tribunals' practice, the level of rehabilitation has hardly ever barred early release and the majority of released individuals have been considered to be sufficiently rehabilitated.[89] This overwhelming success in rehabilitating perpetrators of international crimes is indeed remarkable. In how many domestic penal systems do we have almost a 100 per cent success rate in rehabilitating perpetrators of ordinary crimes? We have argued elsewhere[90] that this surprisingly high success rate of rehabilitating international prisoners could be explained by at least four considerations: (i) a very uncritical attitude of the President towards information submitted by national prison authorities and international prisoners themselves, which serve as the basis for the President's decision on early release; (ii) the absence of any systematic psychological assessment of international prisoners prior and during their incarceration and before determination of their eligibility for early release; (iii) the lack of a monitoring system at the ICTY and ICTR to actually ascertain whether international prisoners are indeed leading crime-and-problem-free post-release lives; and finally, (iv) a theoretical claim that perpetrators of international crimes are usually socially well-adjusted, law-obedient

---

[87] *Fofana* (n 77) para 49.

[88] J.H. Choi, 'Early Release in International Criminal Law' (2014) 123 *Yale Law Journal* 1784.

[89] To our knowledge only in one case at the ICTY (except the RSCSL and Fofana's six-month additional training) the level of rehabilitation (which was deemed 'neutral' by the President) led to a postponement of early release. See *Radić* IT-98-30/1-ES (Decision of President on Application for Pardon or Commutation of Sentence, 9 January 2013). In all other cases (six in total) in which the President considered evidence of rehabilitation to be insufficient, it was also considered to be a 'neutral factor'. In these cases, however, this did not hinder early release. This means that apart from Radić, all other most responsible perpetrators of the most atrocious crimes committed in the former Yugoslavia and Rwanda have been found sufficiently rehabilitated to be granted early release by the time they had served two-thirds of their sentence. For more elaborate discussion see Kelder, Holá and Van Wijk (n 6) 1192.

[90] Kelder, Holá and Van Wijk (n 6).

individuals who committed their crimes under very exceptional circumstances during periods of social upheaval and conflict and, as the argument goes, constitute a fundamentally different type of offender with a very low risk of re-offending in peaceful circumstances.

4. DIFFERENT TYPE OF PERPETRATOR, DIFFERENT TYPE OF CRIMES, DIFFERENT TYPE OF REHABILITATION?

The previous section demonstrated that despite the practice of releasing almost all international prisoners early 'under the pretense' of their sufficient rehabilitation, the underlying line of argumentation at the international criminal tribunals is highly misleading. There is no clear conceptualization of what the rehabilitation of international prisoners is, what the objectives of rehabilitative efforts are, what interventions are necessary to try to achieve these objectives and how to assess whether someone is indeed rehabilitated. Since the concept of rehabilitation implies a process of change to achieve a specific well-defined objective, it is difficult to discern from the current practice what change 'rehabilitated' perpetrators of international crimes actually undergo and what aims are to be achieved by the international criminal tribunals when it comes to rehabilitation.

In this respect, it is highly relevant whether the tribunals' rehabilitation objective aims solely to prevent reoffending or to (also) achieve other and broader (societal) goals reflecting the specific context of international crimes. International crimes such as war crimes, crimes against humanity and genocide are characterized by their large-scale systematic nature. What distinguishes perpetrators of a murder or rape as an international crime from a murder or rape as an ordinary crime is the specific political, ideological and societal context, in which international crimes are committed. Such atrocious acts are usually perpetrated within a period of social upheaval, identity-based conflicts or wars. They are often politically motivated and considered necessary means in the quest for political power and often justified in the name of achieving higher goals such as State security, justice or survival of one's own group.[91] These crimes are thus often committed in the circumstances of inter-group violence between antagonized communities, which used to live peacefully before the period of atrocities and are often expected to resume their peaceful co-existence afterwards. All these considerations are relevant for reconceptualization of rehabilitation of international prisoners and its practical implications.

If the sole aim of rehabilitating international prisoners is (international) crime prevention, then, according to the existing scholarship on perpetrators of international crimes, there seem to be very limited chances for these individuals to re-offend under peaceful circumstances. As Choi stated:

---

[91] Cf. J.E. Waller, 'The Ordinariness of Extraordinary Evil: the Making of Perpetrators of Collective Violence', in A. Smeulers (ed), *Collective Violence and International Criminal Justice, An Interdisciplinary Approach* (Intersentia 2010) 19; A. Alvarez, *Governments, Citizens, and Genocide: A Comparative and Interdisciplinary Approach* (Indiana University Press 2001).

> The prototypical international defendant is a former high-ranking political leader, often very old, who has been removed from power and stands virtually no chance of regaining it. Even with regard to rank-and-file international criminals, the conditions that initially motivated and permitted their crimes have almost always disappeared by the time of their trial. (…) The rehabilitation of international convicts therefore does not affect public safety. Between their inability to regain their former power, increased international scrutiny that accompanies criminal conviction, and changed political circumstances, it is difficult to imagine recidivism in international criminal law.[92]

However, what if the circumstances have not (radically) changed and perpetrators are released back to a conflict-torn country? It is not unimaginable that Lubanga, who was 47 years old when the ICC convicted him to 14 years' imprisonment in 2012, upon release resumes his position as a military commander in the Democratic Republic of Congo, possibly still recruiting and training child soldiers while continuing to justify his crimes in the name of achieving some higher societal aims. And even if this proposition might be a bit far-fetched and a released international prisoner returns to a peaceful post-conflict country, we simply do not know whether indeed the extraordinary circumstances, under which he committed atrocities, were the main determinants of his criminal behaviour, how he was influenced by his participation in international crimes and what behaviour we can expect after his release.

In contrast to research on perpetrators of ordinary crimes, criminological research on the causes of criminal behaviour of perpetrators of international crimes and their motivations is in its inception. A majority of scholars seem to explain behaviour of perpetrators of international crimes by the already referred to 'extraordinary circumstances thesis': during periods of societal upheaval and atrocities, a social and moral normative order, based on norms prohibiting inflicting harm on other human beings, becomes reversed and people are socialized into considering violence (against a targeted group) as a necessary and legitimate means to achieve their goals.[93] Under such circumstances, many otherwise law-obedient and under normal circumstances well-socialized individuals become involved in atrocities and commit horrendous deeds.[94] Perpetrators of international crimes are according to this line of reasoning generally believed to 'differ' from perpetrators of ordinary crimes, who are deviant and poorly socialized.[95] Though perhaps convincing, these claims remain theoretical and lack any solid empirical validation. We simply do not know whether after the conflict is over and the period of transition starts, all individuals who were often involved in

---

[92] Choi (n 88) 1811.

[93] Cf. H.C. Kelman and V.L. Hamilton, *Crimes of Obedience: Toward a Social Psychology of Authority and Responsibility* (Yale University Press 1989).

[94] Cf. Waller (n 91); M.A. Drumbl, *Atrocity, Punishment and International Law* (Cambridge University Press 2007); A. Smeulers, 'Perpetrators of International Crimes: Towards a Typology', in A. Smeulers and R. Havemen (eds), *Supranational Criminology: Towards a Criminology of International Crimes* (Intersentia 2008).

[95] Smeulers, ibid; Drumbl, ibid; F. Neubacher, 'How Can It Happen that Horendous State Crimes are Perpetrated? An Overview of Criminological Theories' (2006) 4 *Journal of International Criminal Justice* 787. See also the audit of the UNDU, which concluded that ICTY detainees 'are characterized by a lack of a sense of criminal identity, relatively high average age [and] substantial resources' (The Independent Audit of the UNDU, 4 May 2006, para 2.3).

horrendous atrocities, resume their peaceful crime-free lives. Similarly, we do not know how many of them actually led peaceful crime-free lives before the period of atrocities.[96] Smeulers, among others, offered a comprehensive typology of perpetrators of international crimes derived from a review of existing literature, case-law and (auto-) biographies of various perpetrators of international crimes.[97] She distinguishes 11 types of perpetrators based on their behaviour prior to a conflict period, position and behaviour during the conflict and their main motivations to commit crimes. The Smeulers' typology not only reflects the different roles, ranks and motives of perpetrators of international crimes but also aims to distinguish between perpetrators who create a social setting in which crimes are committed (and are therefore influential in the reversal of social and moral norms, ie, leaders) and those who 'merely' accept the social setting and as a consequence thereof get involved in international crimes (i.e. followers).[98] The Smeulers' typology constitutes the most comprehensive theoretical account in this respect to date, and could serve as a potential starting point for further research into the etiology of international crimes, the behaviour of perpetrators and the future development of possible rehabilitation initiatives. The typology is, however, still very general, the presented archetypes are to an extent overlapping, and similar to other studies in this field, it lacks empirical validation. While it serves as a starting point for academic discussions about the nature of atrocity crimes, it falls short of being a practical instrument that could be used for developing tailored rehabilitation programmes. Consequently, when it comes to etiological research pertaining to international crimes and its potential relevance for developing a suitable rehabilitation model, we are left with largely theoretical accounts of why individuals commit international crimes and what the causes of this type of behaviour are. In order to understand this behaviour and eventually come up with suitable assessment tools, rehabilitation programmes and interventions, much more research is needed.

In addition, given the large-scale character, societal impact and political context in which international crimes are committed, one could argue that limiting the objective of rehabilitating international prisoners to decreasing the chance of reoffending is a restrictive conceptualization of rehabilitation. Currently, many of the released international prisoners return to post-conflict, relatively peaceful societies, in which they

---

[96] There are scholars arguing that criminal acts during conflict periods are often committed by already 'rogue' elements in society such as released prisoners and criminals: J. Mueller, 'The Banality of Ethnic War' (2000) 25 *International Security* 42. These accounts should be compared to scholars who promote the 'ordinary individuals under extraordinary circumstances' paradigm such as Smeulers or Drumbl (n 94). The limited existing empirical research seems to confirm the latter theories. Cf. S. Strauss, *The Order of Genocide, Race Power and War in Rwanda* (Cornell University Press 2006); P. Verwimp, 'An Economic Profile of Peasant Perpetrators of Genocide: Micro-level Evidence from Rwanda' (2005) 77 *Journal of Development Economics* 297.

[97] For other typologies cf. D.K. Gupta, *Path to Collective Madness – A Study in Social Order and Political Pathology* (Praeger 2001); M. Mann, *The Dark Side of Democracy: Explaining Ethnic Cleansing* (Cambridge University Press 2005); R. Crelinsten, 'In Their Own Words; The World of the Torturer', in R.D. Crelinsten and A.P. Schmid (eds), *The Politics of Pain – Torturers and Their Masters* (COMT 1993).

[98] A. Smeulers and B. Holá, 'ICTY and the Culpability of Different Types of Perpetrators of International Crimes', in A. Smeulers (ed), *Collective Violence and International Criminal Justice. An Interdisciplinary Approach* (Intersentia 2010) 203.

had often organized and incited atrocities as influential public figures prior to and during the respective conflicts. Anecdotal empirical evidence shows that after release they often come back home to a hero's welcome by their supporters, continue to justify their former deeds and do not dismiss the past atrocities and divisive policies they stood for during the conflict.[99] It does not need much imagination to foresee that such behaviour could be detrimental to the process of healing the broken social relationships between former adversaries and the reconstruction of post-conflict societies. In order to consider a perpetrator of international crimes rehabilitated, should we not require him/her to reflect on his/her crime and distance himself/herself from (often extremist) ideologies that were used to justify the crimes? If the goals of rehabilitation are broadened to incorporate notions of an offender's 'moral reform' and social rehabilitation (in its broadest sense), such inter-related aspects of reflection on one's own past deeds and individual and societal reconciliation after a conflict become also relevant. In order to try to promote these broader rehabilitation goals, one could draw inspiration from the existing rehabilitation interventions developed for conventional offenders.

Currently, a variety of cognitive behavioural programmes that 'seek to engage offenders not just as active subjects but as moral actors with the capacity both to re-evaluate the past (anti-social) choices and to make superior, pro-social choices in the future'[100] is implemented around the globe to rehabilitate conventional prisoners. At face value, one can identify no reason why similar interventions would not be apposite for international prisoners and other perpetrators of international crimes. These various offending behaviour programmes take as a point of departure that the offender has done wrong and encourage offenders to denunciate past acts, think ethically and develop victim empathy. Such interventions evolve around themes of personal responsibility, choice and recognition of moral implications of those choices.[101] In particular cases of perpetrators of international crimes, insights and lessons learned from existing de-radicalization programmes developed for rehabilitating extremist offenders and terrorists could serve as an inspiration. These interventions typically focus on the ideological and political association of extremist offenders with a higher cause.[102] In addition, given the societal dimension of international crimes and the need for post-conflict reconciliation, offending behaviour programmes could be complemented with restorative approaches by including victims and members of victims' and offender groups. As such restorative approaches could further add to individual-focused cognitive behavioural programmes to encourage reflection on crimes, awareness of their impact on others and eventual acknowledgement of wrongdoing by seeking to rebuild relationships among the main stakeholders in the crimes.[103] Such community-focused rehabilitation initiatives would not solely be offender-focused endeavours but also take into account the offender's role and position in community during the crimes and their

---

[99] Holá and Van Wijk (n 6) 130.

[100] Robinson and Crow (n 7) 121.

[101] Ibid.

[102] Cf. Policy Report by International Centre for the Study of Radicalisation and Political Violence, 'Prisons and Terrorism, Radicalisation and De-radicalisation in 15 Countries' (ICSR 2010).

[103] Robinson and Crow (n 7) 140.

aftermath, incorporate views of other stakeholders and confront the offender with the impact of his crimes. Although inspirational, we do acknowledge that such initiatives might – because of the character of international crimes, their impact on victims and societies, and the scattered enforcement of international sentences – prove to be extremely difficult to develop and implement in actual practice.

There are obviously still many questions to be explored and much more theoretical and empirical research is needed when it comes to the development of rehabilitation models for international prisoners. It is, however, reassuring that we do not have to 'reinvent the wheel' from scratch and valuable inspiration could be drawn from domestic penal policies and rehabilitation research relating to ordinary offenders and existing prison-based disengagement and de-radicalization programmes. In this respect, Ward and Maruna argue that any proper offender rehabilitation model should combine four levels:

> [a] clear and explicit account of (1) the general principles underlying rehabilitation (epistemological, ethical and normative); of (2) its objectives; of (3) its etiological assumptions (which by explaining the causes of the offending behaviour will also guide understanding of the objectives); and of (4) the intervention implications (the 'how to' element that guides effective interventions).[104]

In order to develop such a model for international prisoners, the specific character of international crimes, their perpetrators and the international criminal justice system needs to be sufficiently explored, evaluated and factored in.

5. CONCLUSION

Mark Drumbl in his pivotal work on punishment in international criminal law rightfully observed that 'the sanction imposed on extraordinary international criminals largely remains little more than an afterthought to the closure purportedly obtained by the conviction'.[105] Indeed, it seems that sentencing and its enforcement have never been given much attention in the practice of international criminal justice. This chapter demonstrated that rehabilitation of international prisoners is no exception and provided an empirical overview of existing practice in relation to the rehabilitation of international prisoners. It argued that rehabilitation is an important consideration in three stages of international criminal justice: (i) sentence determination; (ii) enforcement of international sentences; and (iii) commutation of international sentences. In all three stages, however, the reality of rehabilitating international prisoners is largely problematic.

In their sentencing judgments international judges hardly ever define what they understand rehabilitation of perpetrators of international crimes to be and how it affects sentence severity in individual cases. Countries enforcing international sentences have never been instructed on how to rehabilitate international prisoners and what is

[104] T. Ward, and S. Maruna, *Rehabilitation* (Routledge 2007) cited in McNeill (n 11) 4.
[105] Drumbl (n 94) 11.

expected of them. Nor have the Presidents of the tribunals, when deciding on early release, adopted a principled approach towards rehabilitation. In general, factors similar to considerations examined in domestic criminal justice systems to assess offender rehabilitation (such as history of anti-social behaviour or attachment to family) are assumed by the President to demonstrate rehabilitation of ‘extraordinary’ international prisoners. However, such practice could largely miss the point, since international prisoners, their rehabilitation needs and rehabilitation objectives might very much differ compared to ordinary offenders.

The ICC has adopted an enforcement system which largely resembles that of the ICTY and ICTR (Articles 103–107 ICCSt). Although the ICC RPE do not specifically refer to rehabilitation as such, the criteria for reviewing a reduction of sentence in many aspects strongly relate to rehabilitation.[106] It remains to be seen how the ICC will in practice deal with the question of who to release early, whether or not to impose any conditions and, if so, how to organize a monitoring system.

Given the largely erratic practice and unsubstantiated claims related to the rehabilitation of international prisoners thus far, it is imperative that much more research is promoted and resources are devoted to develop, implement and evaluate a sound rehabilitation model for perpetrators of international crimes. If this is not possible, the empty promise of international prisoners’ rehabilitation should be abandoned.

---

[106] These criteria are: (a) The conduct of the sentenced person while in detention, which shows a genuine dissociation from his or her crime; (b) The prospect of the resocialization and successful resettlement of the sentenced person; (c) Whether the early release of the sentenced person would give rise to significant social instability; (d) Any significant action taken by the sentenced person for the benefit of the victims as well as any impact on the victims and their families as a result of the early release; and (e) Individual circumstances of the sentenced person, including a worsening State of physical or mental health or advanced age (Art. 110 and Rule 223).

PART VI

INTERNATIONAL STANDARDS, OVERSIGHT AND SUPERVISION

In Sections I and V of this Handbook we have already seen that the establishment of international criminal tribunals and courts made it necessary to draw up regulations governing international remand detention and international imprisonment. The drafters of those regulations did not have to start from scratch, though, because they could draw from penal standards that had been developed in the context of the UN and the Council of Europe. Many questions remained to be answered, though, as regards applicable law and standards.

A distinction must be made in this regard between, on the one hand, detention at international tribunals and courts and, on the other, imprisonment in an enforcing State on behalf of an international tribunal or court. As to detention at international tribunals and courts, questions arise as to whether these institutions are bound by human rights standards that bind the States parties, or that were endorsed or even promulgated by the same organization that established the tribunal concerned. Another matter that has arisen is whether existing international penal standards (minimum norms) and human rights standards that were written with the domestic context in mind should be applied to the context of international tribunals and courts. Another point of discussion is whether the tribunals' and courts' detention regulations should be truly international in nature, or whether they may legitimately reflect the tribunal's or court's host State's, or the conflict region's penal mores. As to enforcement of international imprisonment in a domestic prison, questions arise as to who (tribunal/court or State) carries the ultimate responsibility for the treatment of the convicted persons and the consequences thereof on enforcement regimes, the standards that must govern supervision by international courts and tribunals and the standards that govern the release of convicted persons.

Lorna McGregor, in Chapter 13, discusses the law applicable to international detention and imprisonment and critically assesses the relationship between, on the one hand, the law of international criminal tribunals and courts (thereby focusing on the ICC) and, on the other, international human rights law. She examines this latter question in respect of the distinct issues of treatment of detainees in the custodial State, length of pre-trial detention, provisional release from and treatment of detainees at international tribunals and courts, and the treatment of international prisoners in States of enforcement.

The question as to which standards apply to the treatment of international prisoners is directly relevant to the supervision of the enforcement of international sentences by such organizations as the ICRC and the CPT. In their chapter, Sonja Snacken and Nik Kiefer examine supervision by the CPT. They first discuss the nature of the tripartite relationship between an international tribunal or court, the enforcing State and the CPT. Next, they describe the objectives of the CPT, its principles and its modus operandi. After examining the standards (developed and) applied by the CPT, the chapter explores the effectiveness of the CPT model of monitoring.

In Chapter 15, Teresa Anne Doherty and Shireen Avis Fisher examine the RSCSL's prisoner oversight responsibilities and, more specifically, the standards governing conditional early release from prison sentences imposed by the SCSL. First, they discuss the relationship between the enforcing State and the (R)SCSL on this issue and the question as to what triggers eligibility for early release. Next, the chapter sets out the values that should guide early release from imprisonment (at the RSCSL) and examines the variety of release schemes that the drafters of the RSCSL's release scheme could choose from. In the last sections, the authors focus on the actual release scheme that was opted for by the RSCSL, discussing applicable substantive conditions and the procedural framework, as well as relevant case law.

13. International penal law: aligned with or autonomous from international human rights law?

*Lorna McGregor**

1. INTRODUCTION

International criminal law (ICL) and international human rights law (IHRL) are closely connected. The two sub-branches of public international law overlap in substance as international crimes can also be characterised as serious human rights violations.[1] They can therefore work in parallel to provide a more complete system of accountability with ICL addressing individual responsibility[2] and IHRL addressing the responsibility of the State over the same set of crimes.[3] Treaties such as the Rome Statute (ICCSt) establishing the ICC explicitly acknowledge the relationship between ICL and IHRL in requiring that the 'application and interpretation' of the ICCSt, Elements of Crime and RPE are 'consistent with internationally recognized human rights'.[4]

The establishment of *ad hoc* international criminal tribunals such as the ICTY and the ICTR, the permanent ICC and increased accountability at the national level have enabled a richer development of ICL. When the *ad hoc* international criminal tribunals were first established, it was inevitable that they would be influenced by IHRL in areas such as the definition of crimes given the close relationship between the two sub-branches and the experience of IHRL in defining crimes such as torture. However, as the *ad hoc* international criminal tribunals handled more cases, they increasingly asserted autonomy from IHRL and preferenced self-citation due to what Frouville

* The author would like to thank Jonathan Porter, LLM student in International Human Rights and Humanitarian Law at the University of Essex for his extensive and excellent research assistance in preparing this chapter.

[1] R. Cryer, 'International Criminal Law and Human Rights' (2015) EJIL Talk! See also R. Cryer, 'International Criminal Law', in D. Moeckli, S. Shah and S. Sivakumaran (eds), *International Human Rights Law* (Oxford University Press 2010) 540.

[2] See K. Ambos, '*Ius puniendi* and individual criminal responsibility in international criminal law', Chapter 3 in this volume, for a more detailed discussion of this theme.

[3] Although see D. Robinson, 'The Identity Crisis of International Criminal Law' (2008) 21 *Leiden Journal of International Law* 925 (challenging a symmetrical purposive affinity between IHRL and ICL).

[4] Art. 21(3) ICCSt. Although commentators have argued that this provision is subordinate to the first two sub-clauses of Art. 21. See, for example, J. Powderly, 'The ICC Statute and the Attempted Corseting of the Interpretive Judicial Function', in C. Stahn (ed), *The Law and Practice of the International Criminal Court* (Oxford University Press 2015) 462–5; C. Staker, 'Interpretive Methodologies and the Use of Precedent in Cases before International Criminal Courts', in K. Khan, C. Buisman, C. Gosnell (eds), *Principles of Evidence in International Criminal Justice* (Oxford University Press 2010) 187.

characterises as a 'phenomenon of institutional dynamics'.[5] Frouville provides two further explanations for this shift towards autonomy. First, he argues that the principle of '*nullum crimen sine lege*' and the higher thresholds for individual criminal responsibility meant that 'some Chambers have observed that elements found in human rights law were not precise enough to be taken as a basis for the definition of a criminal offence'.[6] Second, he argues that 'there are "structural differences" between IHRL and ICL',[7] in that IHRL is focused on State responsibility and ICL on the individual through a 'penal law regime [and] [s]tructurally, this has been expressed by the fact that human rights law establishes lists of protected rights whereas international criminal law establishes lists of offences'.[8]

Notwithstanding these wider claims, one might still assume a close affinity or deference to IHRL in decisions to detain and in the treatment of accused and sentenced persons in detention as these issues go to the heart of IHRL and do not obviously raise the same structural issues. In this chapter, I examine the standards and norms governing the detention of accused and sentenced persons by the ICC primarily, although I reference other international criminal tribunals where their practice contrasts with the ICC's or where the ICC has not yet developed jurisprudence on the point. In doing so, I show that while in theory IHRL generally governs the detention and treatment of accused and sentenced persons, the position is more nuanced in particular areas. This nuance suggests that in the area of detention, ICL also asserts autonomy, with the international criminal tribunals sometimes taking a different approach to IHRL.

The ICCSt foresees three different detention scenarios depending on the stage of the investigation and prosecution. First, where the ICC has issued an arrest warrant against an individual, States parties are required to cooperate by detaining the individual until transfer to the seat of the ICC in The Hague is possible. Second, an accused and in certain situations a sentenced person may be detained at the ICC's own detention facility in The Hague. Third, sentenced persons typically serve their sentence in a prison in a State with which the ICC has a bilateral agreement. This chapter examines the relationship between ICL and IHRL through the lens of decisions to detain and treatment in detention at each of these three stages in turn.

2. DETENTION IN THE CUSTODIAL (PRE-TRIAL) STATE

The relationship between ICL and IHRL is first relevant where an accused person is detained in a State prior to transfer to The Hague. In theory, IHRL governs decisions to detain and treatment in detention. However, the ICCSt constrains the detaining State's ability to fully apply IHRL when deciding whether to detain and on interim release raising an issue of conflict of norms. By contrast, the ICCSt and the ICC have made

[5] O. de Frouville, 'The Influence of the European Court of Human Rights' Case Law on International Criminal Law of Torture and Inhuman or Degrading Treatment' (2011) 9(3) *Journal of International Criminal Justice* 633, 635.

[6] Ibid., 642.

[7] Ibid.

[8] Ibid., 643.

clear that the detaining State is exclusively responsible for treatment in detention. The ICCSt provides no mechanism for complaints of torture and other ill-treatment in the custodial State to be made to the ICC and the Court has set a particularly high threshold for claims that any ill-treatment affects the detainee's right to a fair trial as discussed in Section 2.2 below.

2.1 Decisions to Detain and Lengths of Detention

The ICCSt places clear obligations on States parties to arrest and detain accused persons once the ICC has issued a request for arrest and surrender. It requires States to 'immediately take steps to arrest the person in question' where they receive a request for (provisional) arrest.[9] The execution of the arrest warrant is likely to mean that an individual is detained in the arresting State before transfer to The Hague. Article 59(2) ICCSt requires that the State party brings the arrested person before 'the competent judicial authority in the custodial State' to determine, in accordance with the State's law, that:

(a) The warrant applies to that person;
(b) The person has been arrested in accordance with the proper process; and
(c) The person's rights have been respected.

Article 55 ICCSt prohibits the use of torture and other cruel, inhuman or degrading treatment ('other ill-treatment') and sets out a number of safeguards such as the right to counsel which apply during an investigation. Article 59(3) ICCSt also provides that the 'person arrested shall have the right to apply to the competent authority in the custodial State for interim release pending surrender'. Article 59(4) ICCSt presents interim release as an exceptional measure and provides the ICC with a means of supervision over the decision:

> In reaching a decision on any such application, the competent authority in the custodial State shall consider whether, given the gravity of the alleged crimes, there are *urgent and exceptional circumstances* to justify interim release and whether necessary safeguards exist to ensure that the custodial State can fulfil its duty to surrender the person to the Court.[10]

Article 59(5) also provides that:

> The Pre-Trial Chamber shall be notified of any request for interim release and shall make recommendations to the competent authority in the custodial State. The competent authority in the custodial State shall give full consideration to such recommendations, including any recommendations on measures to prevent the escape of the person, before rendering its decision.

---

9 Art. 59 ICCSt read together with Rule 117 ICC RPE.
10 Emphasis added.

By contrast, IHRL frames pre-trial detention as the exception to the right to liberty.[11] International human rights tribunals have interpreted the right to liberty in the pre-trial context as presumptive of pre-trial release, particularly in light of the presumption of innocence, unless strong public interest reasons exist for pre-trial detention. This presumption also reflects an acknowledgement of the connection between pre-trial detention and the risks of the commission of other human rights violations at the pre-trial stage.[12]

For example, the ECtHR has found that it is *sine que non* that pre-trial detention must be based on a reasonable suspicion that the detainee has committed a crime. However, this justification only applies to the initial detention. Continued detention beyond this period requires specific evidence that the individual would abscond; intimidate witnesses or interfere with evidence; commit another offence; or disturb public order.[13] The ECtHR has held that the authorities must also show that they have considered other measures to prevent absconding, for example, before reaching a decision to detain, underscoring that pre-trial detention is a measure of last resort.[14] Where the accused is detained, the detention must continue to be reviewed to assess whether the reasons that initially authorised the pre-trial detention continue to apply. Pre-trial detention also cannot continue indefinitely[15] and the ECtHR has found that the

---

[11] See HRC, General Comment no 35 ('Liberty and Security of Person') CCPR/C/GC/35 (16 December 2014) para 38 (noting that 'detention of persons awaiting trial shall be the exception rather than the rule (…) Courts must examine whether alternatives to pre-trial detention, such as bail, electronic bracelets or other conditions, would render detention unnecessary in the particular case'). See also ACmHPR, *Guidelines on the Conditions on Arrest, Police Custody and Pre-Trial Detention in Africa* (2014) Part I(1)(b).

[12] Open Society Justice Initiative, Ludwig Boltzmann Institute, University of Bristol Human Rights Implementation Centre, *Pre-trial Detention and Torture: Why Pre-Trial Detainees Face the Greatest Risk* (2011).

[13] *Smirnova v Russia* App nos 46133/99 and 48183/99 (ECtHR, 24 July 2003); *Nowak v Poland* App no 18390/02 (ECtHR 18 September 2007); *Kudla v Poland* App no 30210/96 (ECtHR, 26 October 2000); *McKay v United Kingdom* App no 543/03 (ECtHR, 2 October 2006).

[14] *Ibidalov v Russia* App no 5826/03 (ECtHR, 22 May 2012) para 140.

[15] However, see *Vrenčev v Serbia* App no 2361/05 (ECtHR, 23 September 2008) para 76 (on the risk of absconding and the relevance of the length of the sentence). In the Inter-American system of human rights, see Inter-American Commission on Human Rights, *Report on the Situation of Human Rights in Paraguay* (OEA/Ser.LV/II.44 doc 38 rev 1) 53 (noting that a failure to set a time-limit for the release of a detainee without charge violates his or her right); *Case of Suárez-Rosero v Ecuador* (I-ACtHR, Judgment of 12 November 1997) para 77, noting that the right to liberty:

> establishes the obligation of the State not to restrict the liberty of a detained person beyond the limits strictly necessary to ensure that he will not impede the efficient development of an investigation and that he will not evade justice; detention is, therefore, a precautionary rather than a punitive measure (…) preventive detention should not be the normal practice in relation to persons who are to stand trial.

In the African system, see *Free Legal Assistance Group and others v Zaire* Communication nos 25/89, 47/90, 56/91, 100/93 (ACmHPR, 1995) para 42; *International Pen and others v Nigeria* Communication nos 137/94, 139/94, 154/96 and 161/97 (ACmHPR, 1998) para 83.

authorities must demonstrate 'special diligence' and expedience in conducting the investigation.[16]

Accordingly, the obligations under Article 59 ICCSt create a tension with the State's general IHRL obligations. To the author's knowledge, no application for interim release in the custodial State that tests the relationship between the ICCSt's characterisation of interim release and the standards of IHRL has been brought.

2.2 Treatment of the Accused in the Custodial State

The ICCSt, the RPE and the ROC do not address the treatment of the accused in the custodial State. Rather, they focus on the State's obligations in apprehending the individual. There is no provision for monitoring the detention or a mechanism for the detained person to complain to the ICC about treatment in detention in the custodial State. There is also no mention of periodic judicial review which would afford additional means for raising complaints. Therefore, under the terms of the ICCSt, the law of the custodial State, including IHRL obligations, exclusively applies to treatment in detention. In theory, this means that any claims of torture or other ill-treatment should be made against the State within its own courts or to a regional human rights court or commission or UN treaty body (where available) if a remedy was not obtained at the national level. However, the lack of a mechanism for the individual to complain to the ICC of torture or other ill-treatment potentially leaves a significant gap in protection in practice. This is because it depends on the functioning of the national legal system. If the individual is detained by a State with strong safeguards in place including access to lawyers, to an independent medical practitioner, to a lawyer or NGO able to lodge a *habeas corpus* petition, and independent police and prison monitoring, he or she may be able to complain to the national authorities. However, where these protections are absent – which may be the case if detained in a situation country that is unable or unwilling to investigate[17] – he or she may have no recourse to a complaints mechanism at the national level.

The Statute establishing the STL also does not provide the Tribunal with supervision over treatment in detention by a custodial State prior to transfer to the STL's detention facilities.[18] However, while recognising the authority of Lebanon over the daily management of detention, the Tribunal has found that it must be able to assert some form of supervision over the detention 'in order to ensure that the detained persons have an effective remedy against any violation of their rights during their detention by the Lebanese authorities'[19] prior to transfer to the Netherlands. On this basis, the

---

In the HRC, see *M & B Hill v Spain* Communication no 526/1993 (HRC, 2 April 1997) para 12.3, noting that 'pre-trial detention should be the exception and that bail should be granted, except in situations where the likelihood exists that the accused would abscond or destroy evidence, influence witnesses or flee from the jurisdiction of the State party.' See also *Hugo van Alphen v The Netherlands* Communication no 305/1988 (HRC, 15 August 1990) para 5.8.

16 *Shabani v Switzerland* App no 29044/06 (ECtHR, 5 November 2009) para 65.

17 See Art. 17 ICCSt.

18 Art. 4(3) STLSt.

19 STL, *Order on Conditions of Detention* (CH/PRES/2009/01/rev) (21 April 2009) para 10.

Tribunal subsequently held that it was competent to rule on treatment conditions in the custodial State.[20]

To the author's knowledge, the ICC has not been faced with challenges to treatment in detention while the accused person is still in detention in the custodial State. However, once transferred to The Hague complaints have been made to the ICC about the impact of treatment in detention on the right to a fair trial. The Court has taken a four-pronged approach to such challenges.

First, it has found that in line with the principle of subsidiarity generally recognised by international courts and tribunals,[21] that 'such questions should primarily be raised and pursued before the national authorities as these are better placed than international jurisdictions to deal with such questions and, as the case may be, to provide for an adequate remedy'.[22] Thus, in the *Bemba Gombo* case, the Court noted that 'it is not a court of appeal in relation to national authorities and that its power to review questions of substance and procedure before national courts is limited'.[23] As noted above, such a requirement may raise challenges in practice where the national legal system does not provide appropriate redress or recourse to complaint mechanisms.

Second, it has found that ill-treatment, including torture, will only impact on the trial of the accused in exceptional circumstances. Thus, in both *Lubanga* and *Gbagbo*, the Court found that a 'permanent stay' of trial could only be granted in exceptional situations where 'the breach of the suspect's rights would make the fairness of the proceedings against him impossible'.[24]

Third, where an individual was already in detention, claims that he or she was tortured or subject to other ill-treatment prior to the issuance of the arrest warrant by the ICC will not impact upon the trial at the ICC. For example, in the *Lubanga* case, the DRC arrested Mr. Lubanga Dyilo pursuant to an Article 59 ICCSt order. He was transferred to The Hague the following day. Mr. Lubanga Dyilo had already been detained by the DRC for three years prior to the ICC arrest.

He alleged that he had been subject to arbitrary arrest and detention in the DRC and that the nature of the detention adversely impacted his arrest and transfer to The Hague.[25] The ICC found that, 'torture or serious mistreatment of the suspect in the process of bringing him to justice may justify the non-assumption of jurisdiction in any given case'.[26] It interpreted the right to compensation for arbitrary or illegal arrest or detention under Article 85(1) ICCSt read together with Article 21(3) ICCSt as requiring

---

[20] Ibid., paras 8–11.

[21] P. Carozza, 'Subsidiarity as a Structural Principle of International Human Rights Law' (2003) 97 *American Journal of International Law* 38.

[22] *Bemba Gombo* ICC-01/05-01/08 (Decision on Application for Interim Release, 20 August 2008) para 42.

[23] Ibid.

[24] *Gbagbo* ICC-02/11-01/11-212 (Decision on the 'Corrigendum of the challenge to the jurisdiction of the International Criminal Court on the basis of articles 12(3), 19(2), 21(3), 55 and 59 of the ICCSt filed by the Defence for President Gbagbo', 15 August 2012) para 92.

[25] *Lubanga* ICC-01/04-01/06 (OA4) (Judgment on the Appeal of Mr. Thomas Lubanga Dyilo against the 'Decision on the Defence Challenge to the Jurisdiction of the Court pursuant to Article 19(2)(a) of the Statute', 14 December 2006) para 5.

[26] Ibid., para 10.

interpretation in line with IHRL.[27] In this regard, it held that the right to fair trial 'embra[ces] the judicial process in its entirety'[28] and that 'evidence obtained in breach of internationally recognized human rights [is] inadmissible (...) [w]here fair trial becomes impossible because of the fundamental rights of the suspect or the accused by his/her accusers, it would be a contradiction to put the person on trial'.[29] However, it held that detention by the host State prior to the issuance of the arrest warrant 'could have no bearing on the issue of abuse of process in the absence of evidence tending to establish torture or serious mistreatment in connection with the arrest and surrender' of the individual to the ICC.[30] In this case, it found that no evidence had been advanced to support the allegations of torture.[31]

Fourth, where the individual claims that he or she was tortured or subjected to other ill-treatment after the issuance of the arrest warrant by the ICC, the Court will only find that it impacts upon the individual's right to a fair trial if it can be established that the torture or other ill-treatment was committed by or with the complicity of an ICC official. For example, in the *Gbagbo* case, the defence team sought a finding that the ICC did not have jurisdiction over the accused on the basis that the accused's right to a fair trial was compromised by a violation of his rights under Articles 55 and 59 ICCSt during the eight-month period for which he was detained in Côte d'Ivoire.[32] The defence argued that Mr. Gbagbo had been subjected to arbitrary arrest and detention, torture and 'conditions of detention amounting to inhuman and degrading treatment' in Côte d'Ivoire which they argued violated Articles 51(b) and (d) ICCSt.[33] The team also submitted that the Prosecutor had violated his obligations by failing to 'request that Ivorian authorities put an end to the very grave breaches of [Mr.] Gbagbo's rights'.[34] The Chamber found that the allegations that Mr. Gbagbo's rights had been violated by the custodial State could act as a challenge to the Court's jurisdiction under Article 19 ICCSt.[35] However, it found that the breach of his or her rights must be related to the process of bringing the person to justice for the crimes that form the subject-matter of the proceedings before the Court.[36] The Chamber also required that the abuse of process be attributable to the ICC meaning that the violation of 'fundamental rights' must have been committed directly or in collusion with an ICC official.[37] It held that 'when a violation of the suspect's fundamental rights, however grave, is established, but

---

[27] Ibid., para 37.
[28] Ibid., para 81.
[29] Ibid., para 82.
[30] Ibid.
[31] Ibid., para 10.
[32] *Gbagbo* (n 24) para 10.
[33] Ibid., para 68.
[34] Ibid., paras 69–70 (for more detail on the allegations).
[35] Ibid., para 88 (referencing the Appeals Chamber in *Lubanga* finding that 'abuse of process or gross violations of fundamental rights of the suspect are not identified as such grounds for which the Court may refrain from embarking on the exercise of jurisdiction').
[36] Ibid., para 92.
[37] Ibid.

demonstrates no such link with the Court, the exceptional remedy of staying the proceedings is not available'.[38]

It should be noted that the approach of the ICC, particularly the requirement of direct involvement or complicity of an ICC official, contrasts to the jurisprudence of the ICTY and ICTR which only requires the commission of a serious human rights violation to trigger intervention. For example, in the case of *Barayagwiza,* the ICTR stated that 'the abuse of process doctrine may be relied on in two distinct situations: (1) where delay has made a fair trial for the accused impossible; and (2) where in the circumstances of a particular case, proceeding with the trial of the accused would contravene the court's sense of justice.'[39] The Court also added that 'it is irrelevant which entity or entities were responsible for the alleged violations of the Appellant's rights'.[40] The ICTY referred to the *Barayagwiza* case in its *Nikolić* decision, adding that for abuse of process to apply, the rights of the accused must be 'egregiously violated'.[41] Agreeing that the entity violating the appellant's rights was not relevant, the ICTY found that the egregiousness of the violation did not meet the threshold necessary to stay the proceedings.[42] This reasoning was upheld in subsequent ICTY decisions.[43]

International human rights courts and quasi-judicial bodies have mainly dealt with cases in which the complainant argues that his or her right to a fair trial has been violated due to the use of evidence procured by torture or other ill-treatment. In this situation, a distinction between when the alleged torture or other ill-treatment occurred (whether before or after the issuance of the arrest warrant) or the author of the torture or other ill-treatment would not matter. However, the Court does not appear to be addressing this issue but rather the situation in which a person is subject to torture or other ill-treatment while detained by a State pursuant to the issuance of an arrest warrant by the ICC. Here, the ICC appears to base its analysis of the impact of the right to fair trial on whether or not the Court was directly involved or complicit in the torture or other ill-treatment. This part of the four-pronged test appears to miss an important step which is that the Court first needed to establish whether the commission of torture or other ill-treatment in and of itself violates the right to fair trial, even if any evidence procured by that torture or other ill-treatment is not used in the trial process. Only once it had answered this question would it be relevant to assess whether the identity of the actors responsible for the torture or other ill-treatment mattered to the impact of the torture or other ill-treatment on the right to fair trial. If it did (contrary to the position of the *ad hoc* tribunals), then it would be relevant to assess whether the ICC advanced the correct test for responsibility (direct involvement or complicity) or whether the fact that the State – even if it carried out the torture and other ill-treatment without the knowledge or permission of the ICC – was acting on the ICC's behalf pursuant to the

[38] Ibid., para 93.

[39] *Barayagwiza* ICTR-97-19-AR72 (Decision, 3 November 1999) para 77.

[40] Ibid., para 73.

[41] *Nikolić* IT-94-2-PT (Decision on Defence Motion Challenging the Exercise of Jurisdiction by the Tribunal, 9 October 2002) para 111.

[42] Ibid., paras 114–115.

[43] See *Karadžić* IT-95-5/18-PT (Decision on Motion to Dismiss for Abuse of Process, 12 May 2009).

arrest warrant rather than its own volition. Such analysis does not seem to have been undertaken and is therefore difficult to assess the justification for the ICC's approach, particularly given that it does not align with the approach taken by the *ad hoc* international criminal tribunals on the same issue.

Accordingly, the proposition that IHRL governs decisions to detain and treatment in detention by the custodial State pursuant to an ICC arrest warrant is not as straightforward as suggested by the ICCSt. The interaction between ICL and IHRL at this point both constrains the full application of IHRL and also fails to resolve gaps in protection while claiming the coverage of IHRL and national remedies that may not exist.

3. DETENTION AT THE ICC DETENTION CENTRE

The second point at which the relationship between IHRL and ICL is relevant is the transfer of the accused to the ICCDC in The Hague. The ICCDC forms part of a Dutch prison complex in The Hague but is managed by the ICC Registry. Most of the detainees held at the Detention Centre are at the pre-trial and trial stage although there is the possibility that the Detention Centre may hold sentenced persons if an enforcing State cannot be found or if the person has to be transferred from that enforcing State for reasons of protection. In such a situation, the sentenced person will be held in The Hague pending transfer to another State. Where another enforcing State cannot be found, the sentenced person will initially be held in the ICCDC and after six months, will be transferred to the Host State.[44]

For detentions at the ICCDC, the question arises whether the relevant IHRL applies or whether the ICC takes an autonomous approach to two issues: first, pre-trial detention including pre-trial release and standards on the length of detention; and second, the applicable law and safeguards governing treatment in detention at the ICCDC (regardless of the phase). This part of the chapter examines these issues in turn.

3.1 Interim Release and the Length of Pre-Trial Detention

At the pre-trial stage, one of the most critical issues that arises is whether the accused should be detained or whether he or she should be granted pre-trial release. As discussed in Section 2, under IHRL, detention is framed as the exception to the right to liberty. Articles 60(2) and (3) ICCSt, which deal with pre-trial detention, do not refer to IHRL or the right to liberty to which pre-trial detention is the exception. However, the ICC has confirmed that it considers pre-trial detention as the exception to the right to liberty.[45] This contrasts with the position of the ICTY and ICTR where it was argued

---

[44] See Art. 103(4) ICCSt and Art. 50(2) HQA between the ICC and the Host State, ICC-BD/04-01-09 (1 March 2008).

[45] See *Bemba Gombo* ICC-01/05-01/08-403 (Decision on Application on Interim Release, 14 April 2009) para 36; *Bemba Gombo* ICC-01/05-01/08-321 (Decision on Application for Interim Release, 16 December 2008) para 31; *Katanga* ICC-01/04-01/07-426 (Decision on the Conditions of the Pre-Trial Detention, 21 April 2008) 6; *Katanga* ICC-01/04-01/07-330

that the tribunals presumed detention rather than liberty.[46] Indeed, commentators such as Andrew Trotter (who examines pre-trial detention in greater detail in his chapter in this collection)[47] have argued that the ICTY and ICTR practice of treating pre-trial detention 'as the norm (...) falls heavily out of line with international human rights standards'.[48]

Equally, the structure of some decisions, such as the *Bemba* decision, do not evidence a detailed consideration of interim release. In this case, the accused was arrested in Belgium and applied to the ICC for interim release. The Chamber noted a range of factors that supported his continued detention. These included, 'Mr. Jean-Pierre Bemba's past and present political position, his international contacts, his financial and professional background, and the fact that he has the necessary network and financial resources, he may abscond and avoid the execution of the arrest warrant.'[49] It noted that 'many of the victims and witnesses are financially destitute and that, in the view of their place of residence, Mr. Jean-Pierre Bemba could easily locate them, and this places them at particular risk'[50] and that 'in his capacity as President, Mr. Jean-Pierre Bemba continues to exercise *de facto* and *de jure* control over this movement; that he can rely on this movement and his former soldiers to influence the witnesses in his case and that his behaviour in the past indicates that he will do so'.[51] Finally, the Chamber found that 'if a person is charged with grave crimes, the person may face a lengthy [sic] prison sentence, which in combination with other relevant facts may make the person more likely to abscond'.[52]

In the decision, the judge acknowledged the requirement of Article 21(3) ICCSt to interpret the Statute consistently with IHRL[53] and also noted that 'the right to liberty is of fundamental importance for everyone'.[54] However, the Single Judge did not frame pre-trial detention as exceptional, assess whether the reasons advanced for Mr. Bemba's continued detention met the high threshold or whether any alternatives existed. Rather, the Single Judge accepted the findings of the Chamber and denied the application for interim release. While the Single Judge did not acknowledge the approach as distinctive – and indeed, commentators have argued that the ICC's practice is 'very likely to satisfy human rights law'[55] – the risk arises that decisions on pre-trial detention are

(Decision on the Powers of the Pre-Trial Chamber to review *proprio motu* the Pre-Trial Detention, 18 March 2008) 6–7.

46 K. de Meester, K. Pitcher, R. Rastan and G. Sluiter, 'Investigation, Coercive Measures, Arrest, and Surrender', in G. Sluiter, H. Friman, S. Linton, S. Zappala and S. Vasiliev (eds), *International Criminal Procedure: Rules and Principles* (Oxford University Press 2013) 341.

47 See, A. Trotter, 'Provisional release from international remand detention', Chapter 2 in this volume.

48 A. Trotter, 'Pre-Conviction Detention in the International Criminal Tribunals' (2013) 11(2) *Journal of International Criminal Justice* 351, 354–5 (discussing the approach of the ICTY/ICTR).

49 *Bemba Gombo* (n 22) para 4.

50 Ibid., para 41.

51 Ibid., para 42.

52 Ibid., para 56.

53 Ibid., para 36.

54 Ibid., para 37.

55 De Meester et al (n 46) 341.

presented as compatible with IHRL without fully engaging with the tests and framework developed by courts or bodies such as the ECtHR or HRC. This is not to say that the ICC and an international human rights court or quasi-judicial body would not reach the same result when presented with the same facts. However, it is difficult to assess the compatibility of the ICC's approach with IHRL and whether they, in fact, use the same tests and standards, without it going through the same steps of analysis.

As international criminal tribunals have tended to reject applications for interim release,[56] the question about the length of pre-trial detention has been particularly pertinent. As noted above, the ECtHR considers the length of pre-trial detention within the ambit of a wider examination of whether grounds still exist to support continued detention and the investigation and prosecution are conducted with 'special diligence' and expediency.

Article 60(4) ICCSt defines 'unreasonableness' in the length of detention narrowly as an inexcusable delay by the Prosecutor. An inexcusable delay only requires the Court to 'consider' interim release 'with or without conditions' but does not make it mandatory. In the *Lubanga* case, for example, the Court found that 'pre-trial detention cannot be extended to an unreasonable degree' and the reasonableness of the length of detention had to be determined 'on the particular features of each case'.[57] In finding that the length of detention was not unreasonable under Article 60(4), the Court took into account a substantial body of jurisprudence from the ECtHR[58] and the I-ACt/mHR.[59] In this case, the ICC emphasised the complexity of the case with the 'vast majority of the evidence [located] (…) abroad'; 'the volume of evidence supporting the prosecution is huge'; and that 'the organs of the Court have acted swiftly and at no point were proceedings dormant'.[60]

In certain cases before the ICC, defence counsel have argued that the IHRL interpretation of length of pre-trial detention should apply. In particular, counsel have submitted that under IHRL, the length of pre-trial detention does not receive consideration in isolation but is rather connected to the decision to detain. However, the ICC has rejected this line of argument. In doing so, it has asserted that its assessment of the

---

[56] See A. Trotter (n 48); G. Boas, J.L. Bischoff, N. Reid, *International Criminal Law Practitioner Library: International Criminal Procedure* (Cambridge University Press 2011) 124, 130; See also *Brđanin and Talić* IT-99-36-T (Decision on Motion by Momir Talić for Provisional Release, 28 March 2001) paras 17–18, finding that:

> it cannot be said (…) because the applicant for provisional release must still satisfy the Trial Chamber that – to use the words of Rule 65(B) – he 'will appear for trial and, if released, will not pose a danger to any victim, witness or other person', it cannot be said that provisional release is now the rule rather than the exception.

[57] *Lubanga* ICC-01/04-01/06 (Decision on the Application for the interim release of Thomas Lubanga Dyilo, 18 October 2006) 7.

[58] Ibid., 6–7, citing decisions such as *Tomasi v France* App no 12850/87 (ECtHR, 27 August 1992) para 89; *Mansur v Turkey* App no 16026/90 (ECtHR, 8 June 1995) para 52.

[59] Ibid., 8, citing *Guy Malary v Haiti* Case no 11.335, Report no 78/02 (I-ACmHR, 27 December 2002) para 64; *Genie Lacayo v Nicaragua* (I-ACtHR, Judgment of 29 January 1997) Series C no 30 para 78.

[60] *Lubanga* (n 57) 7.

length of pre-trial detention aligns rather than contradicts IHRL without a clear explanation of how that alignment has been achieved.

For example, in the *Katanga* case, the defence team submitted that Article 60(4) ICCSt does not align with IHRL. It argued that the length of pre-trial detention cannot be separated from the grounds for pre-trial detention. Rather, the team argued that both must be analysed together and subjected to periodic judicial review.[61] The defence team submitted that the Prosecutor carries the burden of satisfying a three-part test that:

- 'There must be sufficient evidence justifying the continuation of detention';
- 'There must be a valid ground justifying the continuation of detention'; and
- 'The continuation of detention must not amount to an unreasonable period prior to trial'.[62]

The Court did not find a detention of nine months to be unreasonable, noting that in its view 'this interpretation of Article 60(2) ICCSt is consistent with the case law of the Human Rights Committee, the Inter-American Court of Human Rights and the European Court of Human Rights'.[63] However, the Chamber did not appear to engage with the defence's argument about the incompatibility of Article 60(4) with IHRL and did not elaborate on the three-part test advanced by the defence.[64] As noted above, these types of situations merit much more detailed reasoning by the ICC on how they reached their interpretation of IHRL and why it supersedes or aligns with one of the parties. Where the interpretation of IHRL is particularly contested, the Court might take a more proactive approach to seeking *amicus curiae* briefs including from other international human rights tribunals.[65]

3.2 Treatment in Detention

Finally, with the exception of Article 55 ICCSt and Rule 120 ICC RPE, neither the ICCSt nor the RPE contain specific provisions on the standards of treatment in detention. Article 55 sets out the rights of persons 'during an investigation' and includes that the person 'shall not be subjected to any form of coercion, duress or threat, to torture or to any other form of cruel, inhuman or degrading treatment or punishment'. However, Article 21, dealing with the applicable law, incorporates IHRL at three junctures. First, Article 21(1)(b) provides that 'applicable treaties and the principles and rules of international law' apply to the interpretation of the ICCSt, the Elements of Crime and the RPE. Second, Article 21(1)(c) refers to the 'general

---

[61] *Katanga* ICC-01/04-01/07-186 (Response of the Defence to the Prosecution's Observations on the Pre-Trial Detention of Mr. Germain Katanga, pursuant to the Statute and the Rules, 7 February 2008) para 16.

[62] Ibid., para 7.

[63] *Katanga* ICC-01/04-01/07-330 (Decision on the powers of the Pre-Trial Chamber to review *proprio motu* the pre-trial detention of Germain Katanga, 18 March 2008) 7.

[64] *Katanga* ICC-01/04-01/07-702 (Review of the 'Decision on the Conditions of the Pre-Trial Detention of Germain Katanga', 18 August 2008) 13.

[65] Rule 103(1) ICC RPE allow *amicus curiae* and 'other forms of submission' from a State, organisation or person, on any issue that the Chamber deems appropriate.

principles of law derived by the Court from national laws of legal systems of the world including, as appropriate, the national laws of States that would normally exercise jurisdiction over the crime' and third, Article 21(3) requires that 'the application and interpretation of law pursuant to this article must be consistent with internationally recognized human rights'. It can therefore be argued that the standards of treatment in detention as defined in IHRL apply to the interpretation of the ICCSt and RPE through Article 21. Indeed, the ICC has referred to penal standards such as the UNSMR.[66]

Beyond the main texts of the ICCSt, Elements of Crimes and RPE, Regulation 91 ICC ROC provides that:

1. All detained persons shall be treated with humanity and with respect for the inherent dignity of the human person.
2. There shall be no discrimination of detained persons on grounds of gender, age, race, colour, language, religion or belief, political or other opinion, national, ethnic or social origin, wealth, birth or other status. Measures applied under these Regulations and the Regulations of the Registry to protect the rights and special status of particular categories of detained persons shall not be deemed to be discriminatory.

However, it is the ICC ROR that deal with treatment at the ICCDC in detail. Notably, however, they do not refer to the prohibition of torture and other ill-treatment meaning that it is only set out in relation to investigations within the ICCSt. The ROR also do not refer to the prevention of and response to deaths in detention (with the exception of the regulation on the prevention of suicide) despite the centrality of this issue to detention. Unlike Article 21 ICCSt, no mention is made of the requirement to interpret the ROR in line with IHRL.[67] As Article 21(3) ICCSt only requires consistent interpretation of the ICCSt, Elements of Crime and RPE with IHRL, a question arises as to whether this provision extends to subordinate regulations. Gilbert Bitti notes that as the ROR are subject to the ROC which are subject to the RPE, it creates a 'beautiful pyramid' which potentially supports the interpretation that Article 21(3) ICCSt extends to the ROR.[68]

The lack of clear guidance on how to interpret the ROR and in particular how to give effect to their current meaning in IHRL is potentially problematic as treatment in

[66] D. Abels, *Prisoners of the International Community. The Legal Position of Persons Detained at International Criminal Tribunals* (TMC Asser Press 2012) 148.

[67] See *Lubanga* ICC-01/04-01/06-1084 (Decision on the Status before the Trial Chamber of the Evidence heard by the Pre-Trial Chamber and the Decisions of the Pre-Trial Chamber in Trial Proceedings, and the Manner in which Evidence shall be submitted, 13 December 2007) paras 33, 47; The Trial Chamber held that the ROC are subordinate to both the Statute and the RPE. The Chamber stated that 'if use of Regulation 55 conflicted with any statutory provision or one contained in the RPE, then the latter would take precedence'.

[68] G. Bitti, 'Article 21 of the Statute of the International Criminal Court and the Treatment of Sources of Law in the Jurisprudence of the ICC', in G. Sluiter and C. Stahn (eds), *The Emerging Practice of the International Criminal Court* (Brill 2009) 291.

detention reflects one of the most active and continually evolving areas of IHRL.[69] Therefore any set of international norms and standards has to be read against the current state of IHRL. The recent updating of nine areas of the UNSMR (now the Mandela Rules)[70] illustrates the point as these rules required substantial revision to incorporate the significant developments in IHRL since they were first adopted. Without a process by which the ROR are interpreted against current standards, the risk arises that the standards may become outdated or misaligned with current IHRL. This is particularly problematic as the UNSMR 2015 (Mandela Rules) are only intended to set out minimum standards. This risk is heightened as the ROR are detailed on the treatment of detainees and therefore likely to be the main operational text to which staff in the Detention Centre refer. Three areas in the Regulations illustrate the point: first, Regulation 160 ICC ROR on detained persons with disabilities; second, the Regulations dealing with segregation and solitary confinement; and third the Regulations on the use of restraints and force.

3.2.1 Detained persons with disabilities

Regulation 160 ICC ROR reflects a marked improvement on the original language of the UNSMR.[71] At the same time, the Regulation is particularly narrow in its

---

[69] See *Selmouni v France* App no 25803/94 (ECtHR, 28 July 1999) para 101 (finding that, '[h]aving regard to the fact that the Convention is a "living instrument which must be interpreted in the light of present-day conditions", the Court considers that certain acts which were classified in the past as "inhuman and degrading treatment" as opposed to "torture" could be classified differently in the future').

[70] UNSMR 2015, UN Doc E/CN.15/2015/L.6/Rev/1 (21 May 2015). See also, 2012 and 2014 Expert Group Papers of the Expert Meetings at the University of Essex on the UNSMR Review (analysis of the compatibility of the UNSMR with current international law): <http://www.essex.ac.uk/hrc/documents/practice/summary-expert-meeting-20-nov-2012.pdf and http://www.essex.ac.uk/hrc/documents/practice/second-report-of-essex-expert-group-smr-revision-19-march-2014.pdf> accessed 11 September 2015.

[71] Rules 82 and 83 UNSMR (1955) providing that:

> 82(1) Persons who are found to be insane shall not be detained in prisons and arrangements shall be made to remove them to mental institutions as soon as possible.
> (2) Prisoners who suffer from other mental diseases or abnormalities shall be observed and treated in specialized institutions under medical management.
> (3) During their stay in a prison, such prisoners shall be placed under the special supervision of a medical officer.
> (4) The medical or psychiatric service of the penal institutions shall provide for the psychiatric treatment of all other prisoners who are in need of such treatment.
>
> 83. It is desirable that steps should be taken, by arrangement with the appropriate agencies, to ensure if necessary the continuation of psychiatric treatment after release and the provision of social-psychiatric after-care.

By contrast, Rule 5(2) UNSMR 2015 provides that: 'Prison administrations shall make all reasonable accommodation and adjustments to ensure that prisoners with physical, mental or other disabilities have full and effective access to prison life on an equitable basis' and Rule 109 UNSMR 2015 provides that:

> 1. Persons who are found to be not criminally responsible, or who are later diagnosed with severe mental disabilities and/or health conditions, for whom staying in prison would mean

understanding of disabilities and the action required by the Registrar to reasonably accommodate detained persons with disabilities. Regulation 160 ICC ROR only provides that:

> The Registrar shall provide suitable accommodation to allow a detained person with disabilities to attend to his or her personal needs and to exercise his or her rights in connection with his or her trial at the Court. Such accommodation shall be of sufficient size to allow for the use of mechanical and other aids necessary in any specific case.

The word 'accommodation' therefore only appears to refer to the physical accommodation of the detained person and rights connected with his or her trial. By contrast, Article 14(2) of the UN Convention on the Rights of Persons with Disabilities provides that:

> States parties shall ensure that if persons with disabilities are deprived of their liberty through any process, they are, on an equal basis with others, entitled to guarantees in accordance with international human rights law and shall be treated in compliance with the objectives and principles of this Convention, including by provision of reasonable accommodation.

'Reasonable accommodation' in the UN Convention requires States to take 'all necessary and appropriate modification and adjustments not imposing a disproportionate or undue burden, where needed in a particular case, to ensure to persons with disabilities the enjoyment or exercise on an equal basis with others of all human rights and fundamental freedoms'. The measures required by the UN Convention on the Rights of Persons with Disabilities may therefore go much further than provided in Regulation 160.[72]

3.2.2 Segregation and solitary confinement

The second example of where the Regulations seem to fall behind recent developments in IHRL is in relation to the provisions on segregation and solitary confinement. Regulation 201 ICC ROR deals with segregation.[73] Regulations 212 and 213 ICC ROR then deal with 'isolation' and provide that:

> an exacerbation of their condition, shall not be detained in prisons, and arrangements shall be made to transfer them to mental health facilities as soon as possible.
> 2. If necessary, other prisoners with mental disabilities and/or health conditions can be observed and treated in specialized facilities under the supervision of qualified health-care professionals.
> 3. The health-care service shall provide for the psychiatric treatment of all other prisoners who are in need of such treatment.

72 See F. Megret, 'The Disabilities Convention: Human Rights of Persons with Disabilities or Disability Rights' (2008) 30 *Human Rights Quarterly* 494–516.

73

> 1. After seeking the advice of the medical officer, the Chief Custody Officer may order that a detained person be segregated from all or some of the other detained persons in order to prevent the detained person in question from creating or contributing to any potential conflict in the detention centre or to avoid danger to the detained person in question.
> 2. The Chief Custody Officer shall report to the Registrar within 24 hours of the

> [a] detained person may only be confined to an isolation cell by order of the Chief Custody Officer in order to prevent the detained person from inflicting injury on himself or herself, or on other detained persons and, in exceptional circumstances, to preserve the security and good order of the detention centre. Under no circumstances, shall isolation be used as a disciplinary measure.

International human rights bodies recognise that segregation of detainees can be used for protection purposes but in such situations 'meaningful human contact' must be maintained.[74] However, if a detained person is placed in isolation as a result of the segregation, it may become a form of solitary confinement. The UN Special Rapporteur on Torture and Other Cruel, Inhuman and Degrading Treatment has noted that there is 'no universally agreed definition' and that 'solitary confinement' is often referred to by different names, including 'segregation' or 'isolation', therefore the nature of the 'segregation' or 'isolation' is important to examine. In his report, he defines solitary confinement as 'the physical and social isolation of individuals who are confined to their cells for 22 to 24 hours a day'.[75] He characterises solitary confinement for more than 15 days as 'prolonged' solitary confinement and finds that 'prolonged' solitary confinement can constitute torture or other ill-treatment.

These definitions are now reflected in Rule 44 UNSMR 2015. Rule 45(1) UNSMR 2015 also provides that 'solitary confinement shall be used only in exceptional cases as

---

commencement of the segregation and the Registrar may revoke or vary the conditions of segregation.
3. Segregation shall not be used as a disciplinary measure.
4. No detained person may be kept in segregation for more than seven consecutive days without review. The Chief Custody Officer and the medical officer shall review all cases of segregation at least once a week and report thereon to the Registrar.
5. If the medical officer determines, after segregation is imposed, that the physical and mental health of the detained person is at risk he or she shall inform the Chief Custody Officer in writing who shall in turn report to the Registrar.
6. If further segregation is necessary, the Chief Custody Officer shall report the matter to the Registrar before the end of the seven-day period, providing the reasons for its extension. Any such extension of segregation shall not exceed seven days.
7. The Chief Custody Officer shall inform the medical officer of any incident arising during segregation. The medical officer shall provide a written evaluation as to whether the detained person continues to be physically and mentally fit for segregation.
8. In the circumstances referred to in sub-regulation 1, a detained person may ask to be segregated from all or some of the other detained persons. Upon receipt of such a request and the reason(s) for it, the Chief Custody Officer shall consult the medical officer and determine whether such segregation is acceptable and shall report the outcome to the Registrar. A request for segregation may be granted unless, in the opinion of the medical officer, such segregation would be prejudicial to the mental or physical health of the detained person.
9. A detained person subject to segregation may file a complaint in accordance with the complaints procedure set out in Section 5 of this Chapter.

[74] Interim Report of the UN Special Rapporteur of the Human Rights Council on torture and other cruel, inhuman or degrading treatment or punishment, A/66/268 (5 August 2011) para 52.

[75] Ibid., para 26. This definition is similar to the Istanbul Statement with the inclusion of 'social'.

a last resort, for as short a time as possible and subject to independent review, and only pursuant to the authorization by a competent authority. It shall not be imposed by virtue of a prisoner's sentence'.

Rule 43(1)(b) UNSMR 2015 prohibits the use of prolonged solitary confinement.

The ICC ROR do not contain a definition of segregation or isolation. Therefore, it is possible that both practices, depending on how they are implemented, could fall within the definition of solitary confinement. If this is the case, the Regulations raise a number of issues with regard to IHRL. For example, while Regulation 201(6) ICC ROR appears to place an upper limit on the use of segregation of 14 days in line with IHRL, Regulation 212 on isolation does not appear to contain a maximum period but only refers to '[e]very extension of use of the isolation cell'.[76]

The Regulations also do not reflect other developments. For example, a growing body of international bodies, as well as Rule 45(2) UNSMR 2015 (which are only supposed to reflect minimum standards), recognise that certain individuals in a position of vulnerability should never be subjected to solitary confinement. This is not reflected in Regulation 201 or 212 ICC ROR which contain no absolute prohibitions on the use of isolation/solitary confinement but under Regulation 212(3) only requires written confirmation by the medical officer that the 'detained person is physically and mentally fit for such isolation'. Rule 46 UNSMR 2015 provides that '[h]ealth-care personnel shall not have any role in the imposition of disciplinary sanctions or other restrictive measures' except for 'pay[ing] particular attention to the health of prisoners held under any form of involuntary separation' and visiting them on a daily basis which contrasts markedly from the way in which Regulation 212(3) ICC ROR is drafted. While it does not provide a role for medical officers in the decision to impose isolation, the assessment appears more proactive in assessing whether a person is 'physically and mentally fit for such isolation'.

Finally, while the Regulations do not permit isolation as a form of discipline in line with IHRL, Regulation 209 ICC ROR also permits 'temporary' segregation '[w]here the Chief Custody Officer believes it to be necessary, [he or she may segregate] the detained person who is to be charged with a disciplinary offence'. Read together with Regulation 201(3) (which prohibits segregation as a disciplinary measure), it is not clear what this provision means and what the definition of 'temporary' is.

The only case in which segregation has been raised so far is in the *Katanga* case.[77] A provisional detention regime was established for the two detainees whereby they were prohibited from exchanging case-related materials and generally prohibited from communicating 'in relation to any public or confidential aspects of their respective cases'.[78] The Prosecution subsequently proposed that the prohibition be extended to all contact between the detainees. However, the proposed segregation was rejected for failing to fall under the permissible grounds listed in Regulation 201 ICC ROR and that

---

76 Reg. 212(6) ICC ROR.

77 *Katanga and Ngudjolo* ICC-01/04-01/07-322 (Decision Revoking the Prohibition of Contact and Communication Between Germain Katanga and Mathieu-Ngudjolo Chui, 13 March 2008) 8–10.

78 *Ngudjolo* ICC-01/04-02/07-15 (Decision on the Prosecution's Urgent Application pursuant to Regulations 90, 99(2) and 101(2) of the Regulations of the Court, 7 February 2008) 5.

the segregation was not deemed to be necessary and proportionate.[79] Additionally, the Single Judge revoked the initial provisional measures prohibiting communication between the detainees based on the facts that the Prosecution's claims of potential collusion to harm witnesses and victims was without evidence and that the detainees had not violated any measures placed on them.[80]

3.2.3 Use of force and instruments of restraint

Finally, Regulation 203 ICC ROR deals with instruments of restraint. It does not permit the use of instruments of restraint as a disciplinary measure in line with IHRL[81] and limits the use of restraints to three circumstances:

(a) As a precaution against escape during transport from and to the detention centre or from and to any other place;
(b) On medical grounds, by direction and under the supervision of the medical officer; or
(c) To prevent a detained person from inflicting injury to himself or herself or to others, or to prevent serious damage to property.

Notably, Rule 47 UNSMR 2015 only permits the use of constraints on two grounds which do not include (b) above:

(a) As a precaution against escape during a transfer, provided that they are removed when the prisoner appears before a judicial or administrative authority;
(b) By order of the prison director, if other methods of control fail, in order to prevent a prisoner from injuring himself or herself or others or from damaging property; in such instances, the director shall immediately alert the physician or other qualified health-care professionals and report to the higher administrative authority.

The Regulations also do not incorporate the IHRL test on the use of restraints. They do not reflect that restraints should only be used in exceptional circumstances, meet the requirements of legality, necessity and proportionality and as a last resort where no other alternative is available.[82] The CPT has noted that restraints can amount to ill-treatment which accounts for the exceptionality of their use.[83] By contrast, Regulation 204 ICC

---

[79] *Katanga and Ngudjolo* (n 77) 9.
[80] Ibid., 14.
[81] Reg 203(1) ICC ROR.
[82] See, EPR; I-ACmHR, 'Principles and Best Practices on the Protection of Persons Deprived of Liberty in the Americas (2008); Rule 48 UNSMR 2015.
[83] Second General Report on the CPT's activities covering the period 1 January to 31 December 1991, CPT/Inf (92)3 para 53: 'Prison staff will on occasion have to use force to control violent prisoners and, exceptionally, may even need to resort to instruments of physical restraint. These are clearly high-risk situations insofar as the possible ill-treatment of prisoners is concerned, and as such call for specific safeguards'.

ROR on the use of force recognises that force should only be used as a last resort but fails to incorporate the language of legality, necessity and proportionality.[84]

4. THE TREATMENT OF SENTENCED PERSONS IN ENFORCING STATES

The final stage of detention in which the treatment of detainees arises is after the transfer of convicted persons to enforcing States to serve their sentence. Under Article 103 ICCSt, the Court designates a State in which the convicted person[85] will serve his or her prison sentence from a list of 'States which have indicated (…) their willingness to accept sentenced persons'.[86] Article 103 ICCSt lists five factors that the Court must take into account when designating the enforcing State, the second of which is the 'application of widely accepted international treaty standards governing the treatment of prisoners'.[87] Article 106(1) ICCSt also provides that 'the enforcement of a sentence of imprisonment shall be subject to the supervision of the Court and shall be consistent with widely accepted international treaty standards governing treatment of prisoners'. Article 106(2) ICCSt sets out that:

> [t]he conditions of imprisonment shall be governed by the law of the State of enforcement and shall be consistent with widely accepted international treaty standards governing the treatment of prisoners; in no case shall such conditions be more or less favourable than those available to prisoners convicted of similar offences in the State of enforcement.

Both the ICC and the enforcing State therefore have responsibilities for the treatment of sentenced persons in the host State. Abtahi and Arrigg-Koh characterise the relationship as a joint endeavour, arguing that:

> [t]his arrangement [of supervision of the enforcement of the sentence by the ICC] strikes a key balance between the carceral system within the State of enforcement and the widely accepted standards grounded in human rights treaties[88] (…) the tension at stake here – between the State's enforcement and the Court's sentence and supervision – creates a unique system for the enforcement of sentences.[89]

They note that the Court's practice has included a requirement to include a prison inspection with some States choosing the ICRC and others opting for the CPT.[90]

---

[84] See Rule 82 UNSMR 2015.

[85] See H. van der Wilt, 'The transfer of the execution of sentences of the International Criminal Court in light of inter-State practice', Chapter 8 in this volume.

[86] Art. 103(1)(a) ICCSt.

[87] Art. 103(3)(b) ICCSt.

[88] H. Abtahi and S. Arrigg-Koh, 'The Emerging Enforcement Practice of the International Criminal Court' (2012) 45 *Cornell International Law Journal* 1, 12.

[89] Ibid., 4.

[90] Ibid 13; See further S. Snacken and N. Kiefer, 'Oversight of international imprisonment: the Committee for the Prevention of Torture', Chapter 14 in this volume.

In addition to the statutory provisions, enforcing States may sign a bilateral agreement on the enforcement of the sentence with the ICC. The Presidency has prepared a model bilateral agreement although this is not publicly available.

As with other areas of the ICCSt and the RPE, the definition of 'widely accepted international treaty standards' is not elaborated on. Citing Triffterer, Abtahi and Arrigg-Koh note that the 'word "treaty" was probably inserted into the language of Article 106(1) of the Statute because the delegations at Rome shared reservations about international customary law'.[91] At the same time, they point out that States can elect to remove 'treaty' in their bilateral agreements with the Court 'in an effort to encompass soft law' which they note Finland has done.[92]

Where the sentenced person alleges that his or her human rights have been violated, he or she should have recourse to the prison complaints system, the inspection bodies and national courts in the enforcing State and to any regional or international human rights bodies over which the enforcing State has granted permission to hear individual complaints against it. As the ICC supervises the enforcement of the sentence, individuals can also challenge their detention and apply to the ICC for transfer to another State. Article 104(2) ICCSt provides that a 'sentenced person may, at any time, apply to the Court to be transferred from the State of enforcement'.

Examining the detention of sentenced persons by the SCSL in other States, Mulgrew notes that international prisoners may be vulnerable to particular issues in detention in comparison to national prisoners such as less visits, 'socio-cultural isolation due to their ethnic and linguistic backgrounds' and 'further exclusion due to the nature of their crimes and former status'. She also points out that the 'prisoners' nationality and the length of their sentences may also result in a high security classification (…) for the duration of their sentence' and they may be placed in isolation where secure units are not available.[93] Therefore, applications for transfer may be likely from sentenced persons by the ICC.

As discussed above, the ICC has taken a different approach to the interpretation of certain detention rules than the ICTY and ICTR (such as the impact of allegations of torture or other ill-treatment on the right to a fair trial). Therefore, it cannot be assumed that the ICC will follow the approach of the *ad hoc* criminal tribunals. However, the practice of both courts as well as the SCSL may be instructive.

A number of sentenced persons have used the equivalent provision to Article 104(2) ICCSt to apply for a transfer on the basis of threats from other prisoners, the use of segregation and the right to family life. In the most well-known case, Mr. Radislav Krstić was transferred from the UK to The Hague following an attack on him in prison[94] and then, on the basis of a decision made by the MICT, he was transferred to

---

91 Ibid., 12.

92 Ibid.

93 R. Mulgrew, 'On the Enforcement of Sentences Imposed by International Courts: Challenges faced by the Special Court for Sierra Leone' (2009) 7 *Journal of International Criminal Justice* 385.

94 'Radislav Krstić Wakefield jail attackers get life terms' (*BBC News*, 21 February 2011) <http://www.bbc.com/news/uk-england-bradford-west-yorkshire-12525723> accessed 11 September 2015.

Poland to serve the remainder of his sentence.[95] As the original decision to transfer Mr. Krstić from the UK to The Hague was confidential, the grounds and reasoning are not known.

Mr. Charles Taylor was sentenced by the SCSL and transferred to the UK to serve his sentence.[96] He has similarly applied for transfer from the UK to Rwanda.[97] His application for transfer heavily relies on IHRL based on two grounds. First, he argues that his right to family life is violated as IHRL 'prohibit(s) sending a prisoner unnecessarily far away from the habitual residence of family members, or otherwise creating obstacles that prevent periodic visits' which he submits the UK has done by denying visas to his wife and daughters.[98] Second, he argues that he is held in what is 'effectively (…) isolation' since the 'prison authorities believe, correctly, that Mr. Taylor is too much of a target and too vulnerable to be accommodated within the general prison population'.[99] His defence further argues that his:

> predicament arises from his status as the sole SCSL prisoner at HMP Frankland, and is a notorious and vilified figure (…) [who] will presumably continue to need to be segregated for as long as he is detained at HMP Frankland (…) for the rest of his natural life.

They argue this is inconsistent with IHRL standards requiring isolation to be exceptional and for limited periods and that prisoners should be provided with 'a wider range of activities and ensuring appropriate human contact'.[100]

The Prosecutor contested the motion on factual and legal grounds. He also argued that 'the requested transfer gives rise to serious concerns: it would increase the possibilities available to Taylor to undermine peace, security, stability and good order in Liberia and the West African sub-region', thus introducing elements unrelated to IHRL into the decision-making.[101]

The RSCSL denied the motion for transfer.[102] It found that Mr. Taylor's right to family life was not violated on factual grounds of 'his wife's failure to comply with United Kingdom visa requirements and to her ignoring the assistance offered to her to re-apply'.[103]

On segregation, the RSCSL finds that it is for the national mechanism to decide on the categorisation of a prisoner.[104] Much of the judgment on Mr. Taylor's segregation

---

[95] *Krstić* MICT-13-46-ES.1/ IIT-98-33-ES (Order Designating the State in which Radislav Krstić is to Serve the Remainder of his Sentence, 19 July 2013) 2.

[96] *Taylor* SCSL-03-01-ES (Order Designating the State in which Charles Ghankay Taylor is to Serve his Sentence, 4 October 2013) 3.

[97] *Taylor* SCSL-03-01-ES (Motion for Termination of Enforcement of Sentence in the United Kingdom and for Transfer to Rwanda, 13 June 2014).

[98] Ibid., para 2. See, also paras 19 and 21.

[99] Ibid., para 4.

[100] Ibid., para 52.

[101] *Taylor* RSCSL-03-01-ES-1436 (12387-12443) (Decision on Charles Ghankay Taylor's Motion for Termination of Enforcement of Sentence in the United Kingdom and for Transfer to Rwanda, 30 January 2015) para 14.

[102] Ibid., para 57.

[103] Ibid., para 90.

[104] Ibid., para 102.

claims is redacted. However, the Chamber appears to place some weight on Mr. Taylor's request to be segregated for his own protection. It refers to a small number of cases from the jurisprudence of the ECtHR on solitary confinement and the standards of torture and other ill-treatment generally but does not engage in a detailed analysis of the nature or impact of segregation, whether it amounts to solitary confinement, or its prospective duration as discussed in detail above. Rather, it concludes that 'Taylor is not held in conditions of sensory or relative isolation, and that no inhuman or degrading treatment has been established and that the conditions of his imprisonment accord to international standards'.[105] The way in which IHRL is engaged with in this judgment again demonstrates the risks that it is used to support a decision without a full assessment of what it requires and the current state of the law.

In other cases, applications for transfer are still pending. For example, Mr. Milan Martić applied for a transfer from Estonia on the basis that the conditions of detention did not meet those agreed in bilateral agreements with host countries and were not equivalent to those at the UNDU which he alleged was the minimum assured by the President and the Registrar at the time of transfer.[106] In particular, he argued that health care was inadequate,[107] the prison lacked any social or rehabilitation programme for long-term prisoners,[108] and that he was barred from working until 2035.[109] He argued that his right to family life was compromised due to the distance between Serbia and Estonia and the high cost of travel for his family.[110] He also complained about the size of the prison cell and the inadequate provision for showers and exercise.[111]

A similar application has been submitted by Mr. Milan Lukić requesting transfer from Estonia to The Hague on the basis of the 'hardships his family encounters when visiting him'[112] and a lack of opportunity for 'meaningful interaction with prisoners' and prison staff due to 'linguistic barriers' placing him in a '*de facto* isolation'.[113] The defence argued that 'such isolation is further increased by the unavailability of readings in languages Lukić understands and impossibility to participate in social or psychological rehabilitation programmes'.[114] Relying on ECtHR jurisprudence, the defence alleges that this constitutes ill-treatment. The prosecution has responded to this request, arguing that there is no violation of the right to family life and that the family has not applied for financial assistance.[115] A decision has not yet been issued in this case.

---

[105] Ibid para 112.

[106] Letter from the President of the MICT to Mr. Predrag Milovančević, MICT-14-82-ES (23 October 2014, annexing the original letter to the MICT).

[107] *Martić* MICT-14-82-ES/IT-95-11 (Letter to the President, 15 October 2014) paras 9, 13.

[108] Ibid., para 5.

[109] Ibid., para 8.

[110] Ibid., paras 7, 8, 13.

[111] Ibid., paras 11–12.

[112] *Lukić* MICT-13-52-ES.1 (Motion for Reconsideration and Review of Sentence of Mr. Lukić in Estonia and Transfer to The Hague, 9 March 2015) paras 7, 10.

[113] Ibid., para 13.

[114] Ibid.

[115] *Lukić* MICT-13-52-ES.1 (Prosecution Response to Milan Lukić's motion for reconsideration and review of sentence in Estonia and transfer to The Hague, 23 March 2015) paras 6, 9.

5. CONCLUSION

As noted in the introduction, the relationship between IHRL and ICL is not as symmetrical as is often assumed. Assertions of autonomy and the need for a distinctive approach in ICL arise even in the context of detention despite the well-developed and extensive international norms and standards on the legality, legitimacy and treatment in detention in IHRL including over persons alleged or sentenced for the commission of serious crimes. In some instances, parts of IHRL are disabled, particularly where a State detains a person subject to an ICC arrest warrant but cannot extend the full safeguards required by IHRL due to the terms of the ICCSt. In such situations, the legitimacy of an autonomous approach has been under-scrutinised. In other areas a distinctive approach is not always claimed or acknowledged. This raises risks of divergent approaches in IHRL and ICL which are nonetheless presented as aligned particularly where a court simply states that the test or standard at issue follows or complies with IHRL without using the same frameworks developed in IHRL or fully reasoning how such a conclusion is reached. This chapter concludes that these are areas in which the relationship between IHRL and ICL is most acute and in need of clarification and that in the future, international courts and tribunals need to carve out sufficient time to clearly identify the relevant IHRL standards and norms and either apply them in full or explain why a different approach is taken, even if it reaches the same result. Indeed, despite the presence of Article 21(3) ICCSt which encourages interaction between IHRL and ICL, scholars have pointed to a general failure to fully apply Article 21(3) in areas of intersection, of which the legality, legitimacy and treatment in detention is no exception.[116]

---

[116] Bitti (n 68); G Bitti, 'Article 21 and the Hierarchy of Sources of Law before the ICC', in C. Stahn (ed), *The Law and Practice of the International Criminal Court* (2015) 441 (arguing that 'a closer look at ICC jurisprudence leaves the impression that although Article 21(3) mandates the Court to apply all sources of law described in Article 21 in conformity with internationally recognized human rights, sometimes references to those rights are conspicuously absent from ICC decisions' and recommends that 'in order to really apply in a consistent way Article 21(3), ICC Chambers should systematically in their decisions consider the compatibility of their conclusions with internationally recognized human rights. This is not done and the result is a selective application of internationally recognized human rights'. See also, A. Zahar and G. Sluiter, *International Criminal Law: A Critical Introduction* (Oxford University Press 2007) 276 and Abels (n 66) 144–5.

14. Oversight of international imprisonment: the Committee for the Prevention of Torture

Sonja Snacken and Nik Kiefer

INTRODUCTION

This chapter looks into the tripartite relationship between international courts, enforcing States and the Committee for the Prevention of Torture (CPT) as monitoring body. It then analyses the main characteristics of the CPT's monitoring of international imprisonment in Europe. The confidential reports on visits to international prisoners have not been published yet. We hence attempt to assess the possible effectiveness of CPT monitoring in this context through criteria that have been developed outside the international penal system, i.e. its capability (competences and resources) and direct and indirect effects.

1. THE INTERNATIONAL PENAL SYSTEM

1.1 The Implementation of International Punishment

As is the case nationally, contemporary international society has armed itself against wrongdoers who violate its rules by the creation of an international criminal justice system. Its aim is to combat impunity for the worst crimes known to man by prosecuting and assessing the guilt of suspects and, where found guilty, to sentence and mete out punishment. The logical conclusion of the international criminal justice process, which is now a new social reality, thus is international punishment.[1]

The primary punishment imposed by the international criminal courts and tribunals is imprisonment.[2] The availability of appropriate means to implement such sentences is of paramount importance, as 'the enforcement of sentences constitutes the backbone of any criminal justice system which may affect its legitimacy'.[3] The obvious means required for the international criminal justice system to truly play its part and provide

[1] R. Mulgrew, *Towards the Development of the International Penal System* (Cambridge University Press 2013) 11.

[2] Ibid.

[3] M. Penrose, 'Spandau Revisited: The Question of Detention for International War Crimes' (2000) 16 *New York Law School Journal of Human Rights* 557. See in this regard also the recent Memorandum of Understanding of 26 September 2014 between the ICC and the UN Office on Drugs and Crime (UNODC) meant to facilitate the enforcement of prison sentences in accordance with international standards and norms. (Art. 1 Memorandum of Understanding between the International Criminal Court and the United Nations, on building the capacity of

justice, is hence the availability of appropriate prison capacity. There is, however, no international prison system as such.[4] The ICTY, the ICTR, the SCSL, the STL and even the ICC all rely on a decentralized network of States to implement their custodial sanctions, as they have no prisons, prison system, or system of law and rules to apply in enforcing their sentences.[5]

Moreover, for the international criminal justice system to be credible and legitimate, its sentences should not only be implementable in practice but also be in accordance with applicable human rights standards. The bilateral enforcement agreements (BEAs) almost always[6] include a provision with regard to the appointment of an inspecting authority, usually either the ICRC or the CPT. The CPT and the ICRC thus play a pivotal role as watchdogs by guaranteeing that certain minimum standards of imprisonment are respected.[7]

1.2 Bilateral Sentence Enforcement Agreements

BEAs provide the legal framework for the cooperation between the international courts and tribunals and the enforcing States.[8] This enforcement requires: (1) a declaration of willingness by a State to the UNSC (in case of cooperation with the ICTY and the SCSL) or to the ICC itself to cooperate in relation to the enforcement of its sentences;[9] (2) a designation of that State by the international court or tribunal to receive international prisoners;[10] (3) a BEA between the State and the international criminal court or tribunal; and (4) the implementation of the sentence of an individual convicted person in national detention facilities.[11] A BEA concluded with a particular State does

States to enforce, in accordance with international standards on the treatment of prisoners, sentences of imprisonment pronounced by the Court, ICC-PRES/15-02-14.)

[4] R. Mulgrew, 'On the Enforcement of Sentences Imposed by International Courts: Challenges Faced by the Special Court for Sierra Leone' (2009) 7(2) *Journal of International Criminal Justice* 396.

[5] D. Tolbert, 'The International Tribunal for the former Yugoslavia and the Enforcement of Sentences' (1998) 11 *Leiden Journal of International Law* 657.

[6] On a rare occasion, no inspecting authority has been designated, as is the case in the agreement between the ICTY and the Government of Austria. This specific agreement only mentions that 'the competent authorities of the requested State shall allow visits of the prisoner(s) by the International Tribunal, or an entity designated by it, in accordance with Art. 27 of the Statute of the International Tribunal and, subject to the Statute, with Austrian law'. In practice though, it is the ICRC who monitors the compliance of detention conditions with international human rights standards. See R. Culp, *Enforcement and Monitoring of Sentences in the Modern War Crimes Process: Equal Treatment before the Law?* <http://www.jjay.cuny.edu/Culp_MonitoringTribunalPunishment_rev_9Apr11_1_.pdf> 6-7, accessed 9 April 2011.

[7] M. Penrose, 'No Badges, No Bars: A Conspicuous Oversight in the Development of an International Criminal Court' (2003) 38 *Texas International Law Journal* 621.

[8] See Art. 27 ICTYSt, Art. 22 SCSLSt and Art. 103 ICCSt for the statutory legal basis of this cooperation.

[9] We limit ourselves here to the ICC, ICTY and SCSL because these are the only tribunals which have concluded BEAs in which the CPT has been designated as the inspecting authority regarding the detention conditions of international prisoners.

[10] Art. 27 ICTYSt; Art. 22(1) SCSLSt; Art. 103(1)(a) ICCSt.

[11] D. Abels, *Prisoners of the International Community* (TMC Asser Press 2012) 450.

not apply automatically but on a case-by-case basis, following consultations between the parties concerning a specific convicted person.[12]

The ICTYSt provides for a division of responsibilities in which the imprisonment shall be in accordance with the applicable law of the State concerned, subject to the supervision of the International Tribunal.[13] Thus, a State which has accepted a convicted person can apply its own prison regulations to the convicted person.[14] However, the ICTY Trial Chamber in the *Erdemović* case stated that it follows from the principle of primacy[15] that States that enforce the tribunal's sentences do so on behalf of the tribunal and on the basis of international criminal law instead of domestic law. For this reason, States may not in any way, including by legislative amendment, alter the nature of the penalty so as to affect its truly international character.[16] This international character consists of two elements: 'respect for the duration of the penalty and respect for international rules governing the conditions of imprisonment'.[17] Both elements therefore remain under the control of the sentencing institution.[18]

Abels notes that 'in the ICTY's subsequent practice, however, the Trial Chamber's view has been nuanced'.[19] According to the ICTY's Registry, the enforcement regime represents a balance between the principle of primacy and the need for enforcing States to conform to domestic legislation.[20] Abels feels that 'such recognition of States' interests serves as an illustration of the difficulties the tribunals face in contracting States to enforce their sentences'.[21] As a consequence, domestic authorities have been left a certain degree of flexibility in enforcing the sentences of the Tribunal, subject to the supervision of the Tribunal.[22]

In sum, this internationalized model of justice, which relies on State cooperation for the actual implementation of sentences,[23] is characterized by three principles. First, sentences are served in the State of enforcement's prison facilities, subject to that State's laws. Second, the international courts or tribunals supervise the enforcement of

---

[12] ICTY, Press Release, CC/PIO/155-E (6 February 1997) and ICTY, Press Release, CC/PIO/192-E (8 May 1997).

[13] Art. 27 ICTYSt.

[14] Tolbert (n 5) 659.

[15] The relationship between the international criminal courts and tribunals and national courts is governed by the principle of primacy of the former over the latter in cases of concurrent jurisdiction. This means that for example the ICTY or SCSL can request national courts to defer cases falling within their jurisdiction to the competence of the ICTY or the SCSL (see in this regard Art. 9(1) and (2) ICTYSt and Art. 8(1) and (2) SCSLSt). Regarding the ICC, however, the situation is different, as its jurisdiction is complementary to national criminal jurisdictions (Art. 1 ICCSt). This means that the ICC is a court of last resort which does not have primacy over national jurisdictions regarding crimes falling within the scope of its Statute.

[16] *Erdemović* IT-96-22-T (Judgment, 29 November 1996) para 71.

[17] Ibid., para 72.

[18] Abels (n 11) 452; Mulgrew (n 4) 386.

[19] Abels (n 11) 452.

[20] ICTY, Press Release, CC/PIO/155-E (6 February 1997); ICTY Press Release, CC/PIO/192-E (8 May 1997).

[21] Abels (n 11) 452.

[22] ICTY, Press Release, CC/PIO/155-E (6 February 1997).

[23] Mulgrew (n 4) 380.

the sentence. Third, the State of enforcement is bound by the sentence that the international court or tribunal imposes.[24]

The choice to rely on voluntary State cooperation for the enforcement of sentences means that all international criminal courts or tribunals are fully dependent on the goodwill of States to provide the necessary space for international prisoners to serve their sentences. Considering thus that the enforcement system is based primarily on States and their consent, it could be said that it is essentially a consensual system,[25] based on mutual consensus, readiness and willingness.[26] In consequence, the cooperation regime governing the enforcement of the tribunals' sentences, which is characterized by voluntariness, stands in stark contrast with the general relationship between the enforcement State and the international tribunal which is defined by the primacy of the international tribunal.[27]

In fact two different cooperation regimes exist between the *ad hoc* tribunals and States: a vertical cooperation regime regarding such issues as for example arrest warrants and search warrants in the framework of which the tribunals may order States to cooperate, and a horizontal cooperation regime with regard to sentence enforcement, for which the tribunal in question is entirely dependent on the goodwill of States.[28]

2. SUPERVISION OF INTERNATIONAL IMPRISONMENT: A TRIPARTITE RELATIONSHIP

2.1 The CPT as Third Party

The relationship between an international criminal court or tribunal and an enforcement State occurs with the conclusion of a BEA. These bilateral agreements govern such issues as the procedure to be followed for the transfer of a convicted person to that State, the enforcement of the sentence and the applicable rules regarding the conditions of imprisonment, issues with regard to communication, *non-bis-in-idem*, and so on. However, supervision of the enforcement of the sentence transforms this bilateral relationship into a tripartite relationship. Enforcement includes the responsibility for the wellbeing of the international prisoner, which implies that his or her conditions must be up to par with internationally recognized standards of detention. An unbiased third party is hence needed to ensure this basic requirement is being met.

Most BEAs concluded with the various international courts or tribunals have nominated the ICRC as the inspecting authority. Some agreements have designated the CPT as the responsible organization though: the agreements between the United

[24] W. Schabas, *The International Criminal Court: A Commentary on the Rome Statute* (Oxford University Press 2010) 1066.

[25] R. Mulgrew, 'The International Movement of Prisoners' (2011) 22 *Criminal Law Forum* 125.

[26] G.K. Sluiter, *International Criminal Adjudication and the Collection of Evidence: Obligations of States* (Intersentia 2002) 65.

[27] Abels (n 11) 455.

[28] Sluiter (n 26) 65, 81–2.

Kingdom (UK) and the ICC, the (R)SCSL and the ICTY; the agreements Albania, Ukraine and Portugal have concluded with the ICTY and finally the agreement with regard to Stanislav Galić concluded between Germany and the ICTY. Therefore, the ICTY/MICT,[29] the (R)SCSL and the ICC have concluded sentence enforcement agreements in which the CPT has been designated as the inspecting authority.

All these countries[30] are already party to the European Convention for the Prevention of Torture, Inhuman or Degrading Treatment or Punishment (ECPT, 1987), ratified by the 47 member States of the Council of Europe.[31] They are bound by the Convention to cooperate with the CPT and to grant access to all places of detention. Since its establishment in 1989, the CPT has become the main international actor responsible for the control of detention conditions in Europe.[32] Although the reasons for choosing the CPT over the ICRC are not officially known,[33] the choice does not seem illogical. International prisoners are held in prisons which, under the ECPT, are already subjected to the monitoring of the CPT. Cooperation of these countries with the CPT has by now become a long-standing tradition, and the CPT Standards are well known. Choosing the CPT over the ICRC also avoids the application of potentially different standards to prisoners being held in a same prison.

The CPT, therefore, only monitors international prisoners in countries that are already bound by the ECPT. This is confirmed in the 'Exchange of Letters'[34] between the ICTY and the CPT: 'the CPT agrees to assist the ICTY in the monitoring of the conditions of imprisonment and treatment of certain convicted persons serving their sentences *in the territories of the Parties to the ECPT*'.[35]

Concerning the ICC and the SCSL however, the situation is less clear-cut. The question here is if a non-member State of the Council of Europe can accept the

---

[29] The ICTY enforcement agreements will continue to operate for the MICT even after closure of the ICTY. See SCRes 1966 (22 December 2010) para 4 and Art. 25(2) MICTSt.

[30] In alphabetical order Albania, Germany, Portugal, Ukraine and the United Kingdom. See <http://www.coe.int/en/web/about-us/our-member-States> accessed 22 March 2015.

[31] CPT/Inf/C (2002) 1 [EN]; <http://www.cpt.coe.int/en/documents/ecpt.htm> accessed 22 March 2015.

[32] D. van Zyl Smit and S. Snacken, *Principles of European Prison Law and Policy. Penology and Human Rights*, (Oxford University Press 2009) 370–71; J. Murdoch, *The Treatment of Prisoners: European Standards*, (Council of Europe 2006) 50–52. More recently, the SPT and some National Preventive Mechanisms (NPM) have been established under the Optional Protocol to the UN Convention against Torture and other Cruel, Inhuman or Degrading Treatment or Punishment, adopted on 18 December 2002. Guaranteeing the coherence and mutual reinforcement of the standard setting at these different levels is an important challenge for the future of monitoring of prisons in Europe. See: Council of Europe/Association for the Prevention of Torture, *New partnerships for torture prevention in Europe. Proceedings of the Conference* (Council of Europe 6 November 2009); Council of Europe, *The CPT at 25: taking stock and moving forward* (Conference Strasbourg 2 March 2015); <http://www.cpt.coe.int/en/conferences/cpt25.htm> accessed 20 May 2015.

[33] Information received from Mr. M. Neurauter, CPT secretariat (9 April 2015).

[34] Exchange of Letters between the International Criminal Tribunal for the former Yugoslavia and the CPT concerning the monitoring of the conditions of imprisonment and treatment of certain persons convicted by the Tribunal, Appendix (no 5) to the 11th General Report (CPT/inf (2001) 16). (hereafter ICTY-CPT Exchange of Letters).

[35] ICTY-CPT Exchange of Letters, 1: our emphasis.

competence of the CPT based not on the ECPT and therefore without acceding to the ECPT, but based solely on a bilateral agreement which contains the same obligation as the ECPT, namely to allow visits by the CPT to persons deprived of their liberty. The ECPT itself does not mention or imply that the CPT does not or cannot have competence in cases where a State, which is not bound by the ECPT, voluntarily accepts a system of obligatory visits by the CPT in, for example, a BEA. Therefore, the answer seems to be quite straightforwardly yes, a non-member State of the Council of Europe can take upon itself the obligation to allow visits by the CPT. The subsequent obligation will then be based not on Article 2 ECPT but solely on the relevant article of the Sentence Enforcement Agreement.

This, however, leads us to another question: if a State which is not bound by the ECPT, signs a BEA in which it accepts the system of obligatory visits by the CPT, can this in itself constitute an expression of consent to be bound by the ECPT?

Generally speaking, two methods are available for State accession to the ECPT: (1) signature and consequent ratification[36] (open only to member States of the Council of Europe); and (2) consent by accession[37] (open only to non-member States).[38] Consequently, the possibility does exist for non-member States of the Council of Europe to accede to the ECPT.

However, in cases where a State has not acceded to the ECPT, the only legal basis for the CPT to carry out visits on the territory of that State will be the BEA itself. We assume though that, were this to be the case, the Council of Europe would sign an agreement with that State through which the work of the CPT could continue in line with the ECPT. This is illustrated by the 'Agreement between the United Nations Interim Administration Mission in Kosovo and the Council of Europe on technical arrangements related to the European Convention for the Prevention of Torture and Inhuman or Degrading Treatment or Punishment', signed on 23 August 2004,[39] through which the CPT visits places of detention in Kosovo. The agreement repeats most of the ECPT.

To conclude, the CPT monitoring in the international penal system is currently based on the ECPT. It could be extended to non-European ICC member States that have concluded BEAs with the ICC through accession to the ECPT or an arrangement similar to the Kosovo situation outlined above.

2.2 The CPT and the ICTY/MICT

A particularity of the enforcement agreements concerning sentences imposed by the ICTY is that they have been concluded between the UN acting through the ICTY and not the ICTY itself and a State. The reason being that the ICTY, unlike the ICC or the

36 Art. 18(1) ECPT.

37 Art. 18(2) ECPT.

38 See the website of the CoE Treaty Office where with regard to the ECPT it is mentioned that the ECPT is 'open for signature by the Member States and for accession by non-member States', <http://conventions.coe.int/Treaty/Commun/ChercheSig.asp?NT=126&CM=1&DF=&CL=ENG> accessed 10 July 2015.

39 <http://www.cpt.coe.int/documents/kosovo/2004-08-23-eng.htm> accessed 10 July 2015.

SCSL, is not an international organization but a subsidiary organ of the UNSC, established by SCRes based on Chapter VII of the Charter of the UN.[40] For this reason the ICTY, as a subsidiary organ of the UNSC, lacks the necessary legal personality to enter into agreements independently.[41]

This is a major difference with the agreements concluded for the enforcement of the sentences pronounced by the ICC and the SCSL, which are both international organizations in their own right.[42] The ICC is an international organization which was established by the Treaty of Rome[43] and the SCSL is a hybrid international criminal court,[44] established by a treaty[45] between the UN and the Government of Sierra Leone. Both the ICC and the SCSL, unlike the ICTY, are thus able to conclude sentence enforcement agreements in their own name.

It should also be mentioned that the MICT,[46] on 1 July 2012 and 1 July 2013 respectively, has taken over responsibility for the supervision of all sentences pronounced by the ICTR and ICTY.[47] Considering that the BEAs concluded by the ICTY and ICTR were in reality concluded by the UN, they continue to apply even after the tribunals' mandates come to an end.[48] Paragraph 4 of the Resolution establishing the MICT clarifies in this regard that 'all contracts and international agreements concluded by the United Nations in relation to the ICTY and the ICTR, and still in force as of the relevant commencement date, shall continue in force *mutatis mutandis* in relation to the Mechanism'.[49] Therefore, all previously established agreements by the ICTY and ICTR have been taken over by the MICT, including the choice of the CPT or the ICRC as the inspecting authority. Also the supervision of the enforcement of sentences now falls under the jurisdiction of the MICT and it has the power to designate enforcement States, including for persons convicted after 1 July 2013 by the ICTY.[50] It should finally be mentioned that based on paragraph 4 of the Resolution establishing the

---

40 S.R. Luder, 'The Legal Nature of the International Criminal Court and the Emergence of Supranational Elements in International Criminal Justice' (2002) 84 *International Review of the Red Cross* 79.

41 J. Crawford, *Brownlie's Principles of Public International Law* (Oxford University Press 2012) 115.

42 W. Schabas, *The UN International Criminal Tribunals* (Cambridge University Press, 2006) 587. See also Luder (n 40) 84.

43 ICCSt.

44 *Taylor* SCSL-2003-01-I (Decision on Immunity from Jurisdiction, 31 May 2004).

45 SCA.

46 The UNMICT was established by the UNSC on 22 December 2010 to carry out a number of essential functions of the ICTR and ICTY after the completion of their respective mandates. <http://unmict.org/about.html> accessed 10 February 2014.

47 SCRes 1966 (22 December 2010) para 1; Art. 25(2) Statute of the International Residual Mechanism for Criminal Tribunals (IRMCT).

48 Sluiter (n 26) 66.

49 SCRes 1966 (22 December 2010) para 4; Art. 25(2) Statute IRMCT.

50 <http://www.icty.org/sid/10276> accessed 10 July 2014. The same can also be said with regard to the ICTR: on 1 July 2012 the MICT took over responsibility for the supervision of all sentences of the ICTR. See <http://www.unmict.org/en/about/enforcement-of-sentences> accessed 10 July 2015.

MICT (see supra), the Exchange of Letters will remain in force with regard to the relationship between the CPT and the MICT after the closure of the ICTY in 2017.[51]

2.2.1 Exchange of Letters

In 1999, the ICTY asked the CPT whether it would consider accepting the task of monitoring, in certain States, the treatment of persons serving sentences imposed by the Tribunal.[52] The answer was positive and the cooperation between the CPT and the ICTY was finalized with an Exchange of Letters dated 7 November 2000. As a result, following its written approval, the CPT could be designated to monitor the conditions of detention and treatment of persons convicted by the ICTY, in a State which had agreed to accept the transfer of the prisoners concerned.[53] Up till now, the ICTY has made agreements with the CPT as inspecting authority, with the following countries: Albania, Portugal, Ukraine, the UK and Germany. Germany is a special case because the CPT's right to visit is based on an *ad hoc* agreement for one specific prisoner, namely Mr. Stanislav Galić, who is currently serving his sentence in Germany. This monitoring is performed on the basis of two legal frameworks: (1) Article 2 ECPT,[54] which stipulates that 'each Party shall permit visits, in accordance with this Convention, to any place within its jurisdiction where persons are deprived of their liberty by a public authority';[55] and (2) Article 27 ICTYSt, which contains the legal basis for the horizontal cooperation regime governing the enforcement of sentences[56] by stipulating that 'imprisonment shall be in accordance with the applicable law of the State concerned, subject to the supervision of the International Tribunal'. Furthermore, Article 27 ICTYSt should be read in conjunction with Rule 104 which clarifies further that 'all sentences of imprisonment shall be supervised by the Tribunal or a body designated by it'.[57] Following this possibility provided by the combined reading of Article 27 ICTYSt and Rule 104 ICTY RPE, the Exchange of Letters between the ICTY and the CPT indicates that the task of inspecting detention conditions has been delegated to the CPT in those cases where a BEA has been concluded in which the CPT is appointed as the inspecting authority.[58]

The Exchange of Letters was activated for the first time in the context of the BEA concluded between the UK and the ICTY in 2004. On 20 December 2004, the first transfer of a prisoner under that agreement occurred. The treatment and conditions of detention of the person concerned were monitored by the CPT during the Committee's *ad hoc* visit to the UK in July 2005.[59] Until now the CPT has visited the UK, in

---

51 <http://www.icty.org/sid/10016> accessed 20 March 2015; 23rd General Report (CPT/inf (2013) 29) para 16.

52 10th General Report (CPT/inf (2000) 13) para 13.

53 15th General Report (CPT/inf (2005) 17) paras 14–15.

54 Preamble, ICTY-CPT Exchange of Letters.

55 Art. 2 ECPT.

56 Sluiter (n 26) 65.

57 ICTY RPE.

58 Paragraph b(1) ICTY-CPT Exchange of Letters.

59 15th General Report (CPT/inf (2005) 17) para 15.

execution of the BEA, three times: in July 2005,[60] December 2007[61] and March 2010.[62] The CPT has furthermore visited both Germany and Portugal once, respectively in December 2010[63] and in May 2013.[64] Albania has not been visited as yet.

The Exchange of Letters further sets out the basic regulatory guidelines which govern this cooperation.[65] It clarifies that according to Article 7 ECPT, the CPT may organize periodic as well as *ad hoc* visits, and that 'the timing and the frequency of the visits shall be determined by the CPT with a minimum of at least one visit per year and per prison holding Convicted Persons'.[66] The BEAs themselves on the other hand only mention that 'the competent authorities shall allow the inspection of the conditions of detention and treatment of the prisoner(s) by the CPT at any time and on a periodic basis, the frequency of visits to be determined by the CPT'.[67]

Unfortunately, following the principle of confidentiality governing the work of the CPT, the visit reports are still classified, so the outcomes of the visits effectuated by the CPT in the framework of the BEAs are still unknown. However, it is clear that it is the regime specified in the BEAs which takes precedence. The CPT, as far as prisoners convicted by the ICTY are concerned, does not conduct yearly visits to those prisons where these international prisoners are detained. Regrettably, a similar comparison could not be made with regard to the ICC and the SCSL, considering that the CPT has only visited the UK once in the framework of the implementation of the BEA between the SCSL and the UK[68] and that the CPT has made no visits to date regarding persons deprived of their liberty following a verdict of the ICC.[69]

In any case, it can be deducted from the above that based on the general principle of *lex specialis derogat legi generali*,[70] the BEAs as *lex specialis* take precedence over the ECPT as *lex generalis*,[71] at least as far as the frequency of the visits by the CPT is concerned.

---

60 Ibid.

61 18th General Report (CPT/inf (2008) 25) para 17.

62 20th General Report (CPT/inf (2010) 28) para 17.

63 21st General Report (CPT/inf (2011) 28) para 9.

64 23rd General Report (CPT/inf (2013) 29) para 17.

65 It tackles such subjects as the procedure to be followed, the visits, the reports, issues of confidentiality and the costs, which are shared between the ICTY and the enforcing State.

66 ICTY-CPT Exchange of Letters, 2.

67 See e.g. Art. 6 BEA between the UN and the Republic of Albania. It should furthermore be remarked though that in Art. 6 of the BEA between the ICTY and Austria, it is stated that the frequency of the visits is to be determined by the International Tribunal.

68 The abovementioned visit took place on 18/19 November 2014. See 24th General Report (CPT/Inf (2015) 1) para 20.

69 The ICC up until now has only convicted two persons, namely Thomas Lubanga Dyilo, for his part in the war crimes committed on the territory of the Democratic Republic of Congo (DRC) in 2002 and 2003 and Germain Katanga for his part in the war crimes and crimes against humanity equally on the territory of the DRC in 2003.

70 This principle stipulates that the special rule prevails over the more general rule. See M.N. Shaw, *International Law* (Cambridge University Press 2014) 88.

71 It should be borne in mind here that 'there is no formal hierarchy of the sources of international law'. See A. Aust, *Handbook of International Law* (Cambridge University Press 2011) 6.

2.2.2 Applicable standards

Although Article 27 ICTYSt only makes mention of 'the applicable law of the State concerned'[72] in relation to detention conditions, sentences imposed by the ICTY must be enforced in accordance with not only the applicable law of the enforcing State but also internationally recognized standards of detention. The BEAs concluded by the ICTY make this abundantly clear by expressly including references to such internationally recognized standards.

Furthermore, the CPT can take into account all relevant human rights standards when assessing detention conditions, since it is not bound by the case-law or the interpretation thereof by the ECtHR. It has hence developed its own standards (aptly named 'the CPT standards')[73] for the assessment of detention conditions. This of course raises the question, in the international context here discussed, which standards the CPT applies when assessing the detention conditions of an international prisoner: the standards laid down in the national law of the enforcing State, the European standards developed by CPT itself or the international UN standards? In order to answer this question the BEAs concluded by the ICTY with the CPT as inspecting authority have to be closely examined.

The ICTY has concluded five Sentence Enforcement Agreements (with Portugal, the UK, Ukraine, Albania and Germany (with regard to Stanislav Galić)) with the CPT as inspecting authority, in which it is stipulated that the law of the enforcing State shall govern the conditions of imprisonment.[74] However, as far as the further level of detail regarding detention conditions is concerned, a greater variety in the agreements can be observed.

The Agreement with Portugal not only prescribes that the law of Portugal applies but also clarifies that 'the conditions of imprisonment shall be compatible with the UNSMR, the UNBOP and the UNBP, as well as with other relevant human rights standards'.[75]

The Agreement with the UK on the other hand only mentions that detention conditions 'shall be in accordance with relevant human rights standards'.[76] This very broad formulation, however, is not substantially different from the Agreement with Portugal. By referring to 'relevant human rights standards', it could easily be argued that the UNSMR, the UNBOP and the UNBP are applicable without having to specifically enumerate them, considering that these are obviously relevant as human rights standards regarding detention conditions. Furthermore, this formulation, as is the case for the agreement with Portugal, allows for the applicability of any text with a human rights lookout that has a bearing on conditions of imprisonment.

Another similar formulation can be found in the Agreement between the ICTY and Germany with regard to the detention of Stanislav Galić: 'detention conditions shall be in accordance with relevant human rights standards which Germany is obliged under

---

[72] Art. 27 ICTYSt; Art. 22(2) SCSLSt.

[73] <http://www.cpt.coe.int/en/documents/eng-standards.pdf> accessed 10 July 2015.

[74] For example, Art. 3(3) BEA between the UN and Portugal.

[75] Ibid.

[76] Art. 3(3) BEA between the UN and the Government of the United Kingdom of Great Britain and Northern Ireland.

international law to respect'.[77] Neither the UNSMR, nor the UNBOP or the UNBP are binding texts. They are guidelines conceived to help States safeguard certain minimum detention conditions in their national prison systems. Nevertheless, they should be considered within the context of convention and treaty documents which are binding for the States.[78] The ICCPR and the UN Convention against Torture and other Cruel, Inhuman or Degrading Treatment or Punishment (CAT) are especially important in this regard. They both apply to detention conditions and the UNSMR and the UNBOP were first conceived to help interpret and apply the international protection against cruel, inhuman and humiliating treatment or punishment.

Germany has ratified both the ICCPR and the CAT so it has made clear in the past that it does not object to the general principles found in these texts. By excluding the UNSMR, UNBOP and UNBP from the text of the Agreement, Germany seems to want to retain its freedom in how to interpret its international obligations with regard to detention conditions.

Finally, the Agreements the ICTY has concluded with Albania and Ukraine both enumerate the same texts as the Agreement with Portugal but without the addition that other relevant human rights standards also apply. However, it could easily be argued that an all-encompassing human rights regime with regard to detention conditions is applicable here as well because both Albania and Ukraine have ratified the ECHR, the ECPT and as regards Ukraine also the ICCPR and the CAT.

It is remarkable though that none of these agreements incorporate a specific reference to the CPT standards. However, taking into account that Germany, the UK, Portugal, Ukraine and Albania are all States Parties to the ECPT, the relevance of such a reference could be called into question. We should recall that the work of the CPT is based on the ECPT, which explicitly refers in its Article 3 to the principle of cooperation.[79] In addition, the CPT systematically stresses in its national reports that this principle does not only refer to granting access, but also to applying its recommendations and standards.[80] Moreover, the ECtHR has now referred to the CPT's standards and reports in more than 350 cases.[81] We can hence conclude that the CPT Standards are increasingly binding through the case-law of the ECtHR.

A final remark as far as Portugal, Albania and Ukraine are concerned. The reference in their BEAs to the UNSMR, the UNBOP and the UNBP, transforms these texts from

---

[77] Art. 2(5) Agreement between the ICTY and the Government of the Federal Republic of Germany concerning the conditions under which Mr. Stanislav Galić's prison sentence shall be enforced.

[78] UN Office on Drugs and Crime, *Notes and comments on the United Nations Standard Minimum Rules for the Treatment of Prisoners* <http://www.unodc.org/documents/justice-and-prison-reform/AGMs/Notes_and_comments-1250048-DMU_version.pdf> accessed 10 July 2015 1.

[79] Art. 3 ECPT reads as follows: 'In the application of this Convention, the Committee and the competent national authorities of the Party concerned shall co-operate with each other.'

[80] In the CPT's 24th General Report for example it is mentioned that 'the principle of co-operation between States parties to the Convention and the Committee is not limited to facilitating the task of a visiting delegation, but requires that decisive action be taken to improve the situation in light of the CPT's recommendations' (which of course are being made based on the CPT Standards). See 24th General Report (CPT/Inf (2015) 1) para 74.

[81] 22nd General Report (CPT/Inf (2012) 25) para 23.

non-binding to binding, at least in the relationship between the ICTY and Portugal, Albania and Ukraine. This raises the difficult question of justiciability and jurisdiction. Are claims based on the violation of the UNSMR, the UNBOP and the UNBP justiciable and if so, what court could hear a claim?

Additionally, seeing that three levels of standards apply with regard to these countries (national, European and international), the question could be asked what to do if these standards conflict. The CPT applies its own standards during its visits. All three countries are member States of the Council of Europe, bound by the ECPT and the ECHR. They fall under the jurisdiction of the ECtHR, which refers extensively to the CPT Standards. Moreover, with the exception of the American Correctional Association's standards on prisons, the CPT's standards are considered 'by far the most detailed custodial standards yet developed universally, regionally or nationally'.[82] They therefore can be considered to encompass the protection provided by the UNSMR, UNBOP and UNBP. The question whether violations of the three latter texts would be justiciable therefore loses importance, because complaints can be received based on alleged violations of the ECHR, which the Court interprets in light of the CPT standards anyhow.

However, in the specific case that an international prisoner would like to file a complaint based on a violation of the UNSMR, UNBOP and UNBP, there is no reason to assume that national courts would not have jurisdiction seeing that national law applies specifically to the enforcement of sentences and that the international prisoner is serving his sentence in a national prison. It can likewise be assumed that the ECtHR, as a last resort ('when all domestic procedures have been exhausted'),[83] could also exercise jurisdiction because Portugal, Albania and Ukraine are party to the ECHR; an international prisoner whose rights are violated should have the same legal recourse to justice as a national prisoner. Proof of this can be found in Article 34 ECHR which states that 'the Court may receive applications from any person (...) claiming to be the victim of a violation by one of the High Contracting Parties of the rights set forth in the Convention or the Protocols thereto'.[84] Of course, the ECtHR only has jurisdiction over 'all matters concerning the interpretation and application of the Convention and the Protocols thereto'.[85] Therefore, an alleged violation of the rights derived from the UNSMR, UNBOP and UNBP must also possibly amount to a violation of one of the rights derived from the Convention or one of its Protocols for the ECtHR to adjudicate the case.

2.3 The CPT and the (R)SCSL

First and foremost it should be mentioned that the SCSL closed its doors in 2013 and that the RSCSL, established by treaty between the UN and the Government of Sierra

---

[82] R. Morgan and M. Evans, *Combating Torture in Europe* (Council of Europe Publishing 2001) 162.

[83] Art. 35(1) ECHR.

[84] Art. 34 ECHR.

[85] Art. 32 ECHR.

Leone,[86] currently oversees the continuing legal obligations of the SCSL after its closure, including supervision of prison sentences.[87] The sentence enforcement agreements concluded by the SCSL remain in force, only the supervision thereof has been transferred to the RSCSL.[88]

2.3.1 Exchange of Letters

As was the case concerning the relationship between the ICTY/MICT and the CPT, an Exchange of Letters exists between the RSCSL and the CPT.[89] However, the text of this Exchange of Letters is not publicly available, so unfortunately we cannot comment on the specificities of the relationship between the RSCSL and the CPT.

The SCSLSt makes it clear that imprisonment shall be served in Sierra Leone and that only if this is not possible, imprisonment may be served in one of the States that have concluded a BEA with either the ICTY or ICTR.[90]

The CPT has only been designated as the inspecting authority in one sentence enforcement agreement concluded by the SCSL, namely the Agreement between the SCSL and the United Kingdom of Great Britain and Northern Ireland.[91] Article 6 of this Agreement specifies that 'the competent authorities of the United Kingdom shall allow the inspection of the conditions of detention and treatment of the prisoners, detained under this Agreement, by the CPT at any time and on a periodic basis, the frequency of visits to be determined by the CPT'.[92]

2.3.2 Applicable standards

Article 22 SCSLSt only mentions that 'conditions of imprisonment, whether in Sierra Leone or in a third State, shall be governed by the law of the State of enforcement subject to the supervision of the Special Court'.[93] Therefore, no mention is made of international standards of detention in the SCSLSt. However, the BEAs concluded by the SCSL with Finland and Rwanda do mention that the conditions of imprisonment 'shall be consistent with the widely accepted international standards governing treatment of prisoners'.[94] The Agreement with Sweden specifically enumerates the UNSMR, UNBOP and UNBP.[95] The Agreement with the United Kingdom mentions that 'the conditions of imprisonment shall be in accordance with relevant human rights

[86] Agreement between the UN and the Government of Sierra Leone on the Establishment of a RSCSL.

[87] <http://www.rscsl.org/> accessed 10 July 2015.

[88] Follows from the combined reading of Arts 1, 23 RSCSLSt.

[89] 24th General Report (CPT/Inf (2015) 1) para 20.

[90] Art. 22(1) SCSLSt.

[91] Agreement between the SCSL and the Government of the United Kingdom of Great Britain and Northern Ireland on the Enforcement of Sentences of the SCSL.

[92] Ibid, Art. 6.

[93] Art. 22 SCSLSt.

[94] Art. 3(3) Agreement between the SCSL and the Government of Finland on the Enforcement of Sentences of the SCSL; Art. 3(4) Agreement between the SCSL and the Government of the Republic of Rwanda on the Enforcement of Sentences of the SCSL.

[95] Art. 3(3) Agreement between the SCSL and the Government of Sweden on the Enforcement of Sentences of the SCSL.

standards'.[96] It can thus be concluded that persons convicted by the SCSL also enjoy the protection of internationally recognized standards of detention even though the SCSLSt contains no reference thereto.[97]

Article 3 of the Agreement between the SCSL and the UK uses the same formulation as the Agreement between the ICTY and the UK: 'the conditions of imprisonment shall be equivalent to those applicable to prisoners serving sentences under the law of the United Kingdom and shall be in accordance with relevant human rights standards'.[98] It thus seems logical that not only the UNSMR, UNBOP and UNBP, but also the CPT Standards apply. Being more detailed and based on a Convention, these would normally prevail.

2.4 The CPT and the ICC

2.4.1 Treaty-based relationship

The relationship between the ICC and the member States of the ICCSt is governed by the law of treaties and by the principle of *pacta sunt servanda*.[99] But the regime regarding the enforcement of the ICC's sentences is equally based on voluntariness, as is made clear in Article 103(1)(a) ICCSt: 'a sentence of imprisonment shall be served in a State designated by the Court from a list of States which have indicated to the Court their willingness to accept sentenced persons'.[100]

Art. 106(1) ICCSt stipulates that 'the enforcement of a sentence of imprisonment shall be subject to the supervision of the Court and shall be consistent with widely accepted international treaty standards governing the treatment of prisoners'.[101] In this regard, Regulation 113(1)(a) of the ICC ROC states that 'the Presidency shall establish an enforcement unit within the Presidency to assist it in the exercise of its functions under Part 10 of the Statute, in particular the supervision of enforcement of sentences and conditions of imprisonment'.[102]

Based on this, the ICC has concluded an Agreement with the ICRC on Visits to Persons deprived of Liberty Pursuant to the Jurisdiction of the ICC. However, neither the Official Journal of the ICC nor the annual reports of the CPT mention that such an agreement has also been concluded with the CPT. Nevertheless, one sentence enforcement agreement does identify the CPT as the relevant inspecting authority, namely the Agreement between the ICC and the UK. All other enforcement agreements[103] the ICC has concluded (except the one with Austria which designates neither the ICRC nor the

---

96 Art. 3(3) Agreement between the SCSL and the Government of the United Kingdom (n 91).

97 All Sentence Enforcement Agreements concluded by the SCSL refer in one way or another to international standards of detention governing the treatment of prisoners.

98 Art. 3 Agreement between the SCSL and the Government of the United Kingdom (n 91).

99 Sluiter (n 26) 67–8.

100 Art. 103(1)(a) ICCSt.

101 Art. 106(1) ICCSt.

102 Reg. 113(1)(a) ICC ROC.

103 Next to the ones concluded with the UK and Austria, the ICC has sentence enforcement agreements with Belgium, Finland, Serbia and Denmark. In all four agreements, the ICRC was designated the inspecting authority.

CPT) appoint the ICRC as inspecting authority. The Agreement between the ICC and the UK thus seems to be the exception to the rule. We must assume that, in the negotiations regarding the BEA between the ICC and the UK, the UK has insisted on the appointment of the CPT as inspecting authority.

2.4.2 Applicable standards

Article 106(2) ICCSt clearly states that 'conditions of imprisonment shall be governed by the law of the State of enforcement and shall be consistent with widely accepted international treaty standards governing treatment of prisoners'.[104] The explicit reference to 'treaty' standards excludes the UNSMR, the UNBP and the UNBOP. Out of the six BEAs concluded by the ICC, three[105] have copied the wording of Article 106(2) ICCSt, thereby excluding non-treaty standards. But the other three have not,[106] leading to the following result in for example the Agreement with Belgium: 'The conditions of imprisonment shall be governed by the law of Belgium and shall be consistent with widely accepted international standards governing treatment of prisoners ...'.[107] It seems therefore, that in agreements of this last kind, the applicability of non-treaty standards was considered to be sufficiently important by the enforcing State to implicitly include them in the scope of the agreement.

In addition, the BEA between the ICC and the UK contains a different, more detailed formulation than the formulations previously encountered in the framework of the Agreements concluded by the ICTY and the SCSL with the UK. Although Article 5 of the Agreement starts off in the same way by affirming that 'the conditions of imprisonment shall be equivalent to those applicable to prisoners serving sentences under the law of the United Kingdom and shall be in accordance with relevant international human rights standards governing the treatment of prisoners', it goes further by saying that these applicable human right standards specifically include 'any obligations of the United Kingdom under the Convention for the Protection of Human Rights and Fundamental Freedoms done at Rome on 4 November 1950 as it applies to the United Kingdom'.[108] The specific reference made here to the ECHR is not made in any of the other sentence enforcement agreements the ICC has concluded.[109]

The relevance of the fact that this specific Agreement explicitly refers to the ECHR can strongly be called into question considering that all agreements stipulate that 'in no case detention conditions shall be more or less favourable than those available to

---

[104] Art. 106(2) ICCSt.

[105] See the BEAs that the ICC concluded with Austria, Serbia and Denmark.

[106] See the BEAs that the ICC concluded with the UK, Finland and Belgium.

[107] Art. 6(1) Agreement between the ICC and the Government of the Kingdom of Belgium on the Enforcement of Sentences of the ICC.

[108] Art. 5 Agreement between the Government of the United Kingdom of Great Britain and Northern Ireland and the ICC on the enforcement of sentences imposed by the ICC.

[109] The specific reason for this reference to the ECHR is probably linked to the system of parliamentary sovereignty in the UK in which Parliament is the supreme legal authority. This implies that all international conventions must be incorporated into national Parliament Acts before they can be used before the national courts. The ECHR being no exception, it was codified into UK law by the Human Rights Act 1998.

prisoners convicted of similar offences in the country concerned'[110] and that almost every State (except Mali) with which the ICC has enforcement agreements is also a member State of the Council of Europe and therefore a party to the ECHR.

In addition, Article 106(2) ICCSt mentions specifically that 'conditions of imprisonment (...) shall be consistent with widely accepted international treaty standards governing treatment of prisoners'.[111] The fact that the ECHR can qualify as a 'widely accepted international treaty standard governing the treatment of prisoners' seems unquestionable, at least in Europe. Taking in mind also that the ICCSt is a treaty which the UK has signed and ratified,[112] and consequently is bound to abide by following the principle of *pacta sunt servanda*, the obligation to adhere to the ECHR with regard to the detention conditions of international prisoners, can additionally[113] be derived in the relation between the ICC and the UK from Article 106(2) ICCSt. Finally, also Article 21 ICCSt which lists the sources of law the ICC may apply, is particularly relevant in this regard seeing that the ICC's detention regime is governed by it. Particularly important regarding detained persons is Article 21's third paragraph according to which both the application and the interpretation of sources of law stipulated in Article 21's other paragraphs must be consistent with internationally recognized human rights.[114] In consequence thereby making the specific reference to the ECHR in the Agreement between the ICC and the UK from a legal point of view a matter of only symbolical importance.

3. THE INTERNATIONAL PENAL SYSTEM: THE ROLE OF THE CPT

The CPT has been designated as the inspecting body for international prisoners held in prisons in Albania, Germany, Portugal, Ukraine and the UK. All of these countries are party to and bound by the ECPT. The international prisoners are held in prisons that, under that Convention, fall under the monitoring competency of the CPT anyway. The tripartite relationship in the international penal system hence does not fundamentally alter the bilateral relationship between the CPT and the States party to the ECPT. They are still bound by the principles laid down in that Convention which determine the aim, competences and functioning of the CPT. Visits to international prisoners are integrated into the normal periodic or *ad hoc* CPT visits to those countries[115] and thus apply the

---

110 See for example Art. 6 of the Agreement between the ICC and Belgium (n 107).

111 Art. 106(2) ICCSt.

112 UN Treaty Collection <https://treaties.un.org/Pages/ViewDetails.aspx?mtdsg_no=XVIII-10&chapter=18&lang=en> accessed 22 March 2015.

113 The obligation to abide by the ECHR can of course in the first place be derived from the fact that the UK has signed and ratified the ECHR and therefore is obliged to observe the ECHR.

114 Abels (n 11) 75–6.

115 See 15th General Report (CPT/inf (2005) 17) para 15; 18th General Report (CPT/inf (2008) 25) para 17; 20th General Report (CPT/inf (2010) 28) para 17; 21st General Report (CPT/inf (2011) 28) para 9; 23rd General Report (CPT/inf (2013) 29) para 17.

same methodology and the same standards.[116] The CPT will of course pay particular attention to the specific situation of the international prisoners, which may be very different – or not – from other (foreign) prisoners. The tripartite relationship has mainly consequences for the reporting by the CPT to the international court and the principles of confidentiality and anonymity. We will hence discuss the monitoring system of the CPT with special attention to situations involving international prisoners that may deviate from the norm.

3.1 Aim and Competences

3.1.1 Visits: access to places of detention

The aim of the CPT is to examine the treatment of persons deprived of their liberty by means of visits, with a view to strengthening, if necessary, the protection of such persons from torture and from inhuman or degrading treatment or punishment (Art. 1 ECPT). Although Article 1 uses the same words, 'torture' and 'inhuman or degrading treatment or punishment', as Article 3 ECHR,[117] it was stressed from its origin that the CPT should not interfere in the interpretation of these words by the ECtHR.[118] Reality has turned out very differently though. In the absence of binding definitions by the Court or the Convention, the CPT was free to develop its own standards inductively, based on different international human rights instruments and its observations during the visits. Acting increasingly as the 'fact-finding' instrument for the ECtHR, its standards and practical findings would eventually greatly influence the case-law of the Court (see 3.5.2).

In order to fulfil its monitoring function through visits, the CPT has quasi-unlimited access to all places of deprivation of liberty (Art. 2 ECPT). Only under exceptional circumstances can a State Party request that the CPT postpone a visit to a particular place. The grounds for this postponement are enumerated exhaustively in Article 9.1 ECPT and relate to 'grounds of national defence, public safety, serious disorder in places where persons are deprived of their liberty, the medical condition of a person or that an urgent interrogation relating to a serious crime is in progress'. Even then, arrangements must be made 'to enable the Committee to exercise its functions expeditiously. Such arrangements may include the transfer to another place of any person whom the Committee proposed to visit. Until the visit takes place, the Party shall provide information to the Committee about any person concerned' (Art. 9.2).

However, Article 17.3 states that 'the Committee shall not visit places which representatives or delegates of Protecting Powers or the International Committee of the Red Cross effectively visit on a regular basis by virtue of the Geneva Conventions of 12 August 1949 and the Additional Protocols of 8 June 1977 thereto'.

---

[116] Confirmed by Mr. M. Neurauter of the CPT Secretariat (9 April 2015).

[117] Art. 3 ECHR: 'No one shall be subjected to torture or to inhuman or degrading treatment or punishment.'

[118] Art. 1 para 27 of the Explanatory Report to the European Convention for the Prevention of Torture and Inhuman or Degrading Treatment or Punishment (CPT/Inf/C (89) 1 [EN] (Part 2)).

During the visit, the State Party must provide the Committee with several facilities (Article 8.2), which will also apply in cases involving prisoners sentenced by an international court:

(a) access to its territory and the right to travel without restriction;
(b) full information on the places where persons deprived of their liberty are being held;
(c) unlimited access to any place where persons are deprived of their liberty, including the right to move inside such places without restriction;
(d) other information available to the Party which is necessary for the Committee to carry out its task. In seeking such information, the Committee shall have regard to applicable rules of national law and professional ethics.

During the fieldwork, the CPT 'may interview in private persons deprived of their liberty' (Art. 8.3) and 'may communicate freely with any person whom it believes can supply relevant information' (Art. 8.4).

We can distinguish between two types of visits: periodic visits and *ad hoc* visits.[119] Periodic visits are organized 'on an equitable basis, regard being had to the number of relevant places in each State Party.'[120] Most countries are visited periodically every four years; countries with large numbers of detainees may be visited every year, countries with very small numbers will receive fewer visits. Periodic visits usually last between ten–14 days, cover different regions of the country and several types of institutions of deprivation of liberty. *Ad hoc* visits are shorter (two to five days), more punctual (sometimes covering only one institution or problem) and often react to recent alarming information received by the Committee. Both periodic and *ad hoc* visits can include visits to prisons holding international prisoners. The CPT often returns to places already visited in order to follow up on the situation and the implementation of its recommendations.

3.1.2 Reports

After each visit, the CPT draws up a report on the facts found during the visit and formulates any recommendations, comments and requests for information it considers necessary (Art. 10.1).[121] The findings and reports are confidential and can only be published at the request or with the consent of the State Party, together with any comments of the Party concerned (Art. 11.1 and 2). Within the international penal system, a separate report is made on the situation of the international prisoner. The principle of confidentiality of this CPT report applies to the tripartite relationship. All agreements with the UK (SCSL/UK, ICTY/UK, ICC/UK) thus emphasize that the CPT

---

[119] Art. 7.1 ECPT: The Committee shall organize visits to places referred to in Art. 2. Apart from periodic visits, the Committee may organize such other visits as appear to be required in the circumstances; Explanatory Report (CPT/Inf/C (89) 1 [EN] (Part 2)) para 19: As a follow-up, the Committee may arrange for fresh visits to the places already visited. See also S. Snacken, *Prisons en Europe. Pour une pénologie critique et humaniste* (Larcier 2011) 50.

[120] Rule 29 of the Rules of Procedure (CPT/Inf/C (2008) 1) <http://www.cpt.coe.int/en/documents/rules-procedure.pdf> accessed 10 July 2015.

[121] See also Rule 38 of the Rules of Procedure (CPT/Inf/C (2008) 1).

must submit the confidential report to the Foreign and Commonwealth Office and to the President of the Special Court/International Tribunal/Presidency. Neither the CPT nor the international court can release the report without the consent of the UK Government. The Agreements between the ICTY and Portugal, Ukraine, Albania and Germany stipulate that the CPT will submit the confidential report to Portugal/Ukraine/ the requested State, which will be responsible for its forwarding to the international court. They also stipulate that the President of the International Tribunal and the country involved shall consult each other on the findings of the CPT report; the President may thereafter request the country to report to him or her any changes in the conditions of detention suggested by the CPT.

No personal data can be published without the express consent of the person concerned (Art. 11.3). This raises particular problems within the international penal system, as a prison visited by CPT will often house only one international prisoner, whose identity may be much more difficult to conceal. The difficulties posed by the requirement to protect the anonymity of the prisoner could contribute to the fact that no report on visits to international prisoners has been published yet.

Responses to the reports are expected from the Government after six months for a periodic visit (with possibly a shorter deadline of two or three months regarding recommendations or requests for information which are considered to be particularly urgent)[122] and after three months for *ad hoc* visits ('follow-up report on action taken').[123] Visits to prisoners sentenced by an international court are treated like *ad hoc* visits, even when such a visit is carried out in the context of a periodic visit.[124] An on-going dialogue is then established between the CPT and the enforcing State concerning the implementation of the recommendations.[125]

In addition to these country reports, and subject to the rules of confidentiality, the CPT publishes annual General Reports on its activities, which are transmitted to the Consultative Assembly of the Council of Europe, and made public (Art. 12). At the time of writing, 24 such General Reports (GR) have been published. They report on the visits performed during the past year, on meetings and organizational matters, and take a closer look at some of the visit reports and government responses published during that year ('Publication highlights'). Most GRs also deal with substantive matters related to particular practices or groups of detainees, thus allowing the CPT to develop its own evolutionary standards, based on its practical findings and growing insight into risk factors and best practices in the treatment of prisoners. These substantive

---

[122] Art. 8.5: If necessary, the Committee may immediately communicate observations to the competent authorities of the Party concerned.

[123] This practice has been established by the CPT within the framework of the principle of cooperation laid down in Art. 10.2: '(…) if the Party fails to co-operate or refuses to improve the situation in the light of the Committee's recommendations (…)'. See e.g. CPT first visit to the UK (CPT/Inf (91) 15) para 242.

[124] Information provided by Mr. M. Neurauter, CPT Secretariat (22 April 2015).

[125] Rule 40.1 Rules of Procedure (CPT/Inf/C (2008) 1): After transmission of the Committee's report, the Committee and the Party may hold consultations concerning in particular the implementation of any recommendations set out in the report in the spirit of the principle of cooperation set out in Article 3 of the Convention.

comments are then summarized in a booklet, The CPT Standards. The 11th, 15th, 18th, 20th, 21st and 23rd GRs deal with 'Monitoring on behalf of the ICTY'.[126]

3.2 Principles of CPT Functioning

Five principles can be described as directing the work of CPT. The first four are derived directly from the Convention.

3.2.1 Prevention

As stressed repeatedly in the Explanatory Report to the Convention, 'it is not for the Committee to perform any judicial functions; it is not its task to adjudge that violations of the relevant international instruments have been committed (...) Its task is a purely preventive one'.[127] However, while the CPT does not 'adjudge' violations in a judicial sense, 'preventing' such violations still requires proof of risk situations and practices. An important part of the work of CPT is hence to find proof of violations through a solid methodology (see 3.3.2).[128] This also explains its multidisciplinary composition, including not only lawyers and human rights experts, but also medical doctors, psychiatrists, criminologists, experts in prison matters or juvenile delinquency, etc.

3.2.2 Cooperation

Article 3 ECPT clearly states that 'in the application of this Convention, the Committee and the competent national authorities of the Party concerned shall co-operate with each other'. The principle of cooperation works both ways. States parties have to grant access and cooperate in the improvement of detention situations, the CPT has to notify the State Party of a visit and respect confidentiality.

States Parties must grant access to any place of deprivation of liberty (Art. 2 ECPT) and provide the Committee with all facilities necessary for their monitoring (information, access, private interviews and communications: Art. 8.2–8.4 ECPT). A liaison officer is appointed by the State to facilitate the organisation of the visit (Art. 15 ECPT). The liaison officer, operating under the direct authority of the responsible Ministers, intervenes whenever necessary to guarantee access to all places, documents or persons as required by the CPT.[129] A customary practice has developed within the

[126] Exchange of letters between the ICTY and the CPT, 7 and 24 November 2000: Appendix 5 of the 11th General Report (CPT/Inf (2001) 16); Agreement to monitor the situation of persons convicted by the ICTY and serving their sentences in Albania, Germany, Portugal, Ukraine and the UK: 18th GR (CPT/Inf (2008) 25) para 17; setting up of the UN Mechanism for International Criminal Tribunals; visit to a prisoner sentenced to 20 years at Monsanto Prison, Portugal, May 2013: 23rd GR (CPT/Inf (2013) 29) paras 16–18.

[127] Explanatory Report to the European Convention for the Prevention of Torture and Inhuman or Degrading Treatment or Punishment (CPT/Inf/C (89) 1 [EN] (Part 2)) paras 17, 25.

[128] Snacken (n 119) 41–3.

[129] Examples: refusing access to a police officer's drawer where instruments used for applying electroshocks to suspects were hidden: CPT first periodic visit to Greece in 1993 (CPT/Inf (94) 20) para 22; refusing access to medical files to the CPT medical doctors: CPT first periodic visit to Belgium in 1993 (CPT/Inf (94) 15) para 7.

CPT to wait for a maximum of 15 minutes to gain access to a particular place. Any delay exceeding this period is considered a violation of the principle of cooperation.[130]

For the CPT itself, cooperation implies that it must *notify* the government of the Party of its intention to carry out a visit. After such notification, it may at any time visit any place referred to in Article 2 (Art. 8.1). Questions could be raised concerning the effectiveness of inspections to places of detention if authorities are notified in advance of the visit. The CPT hence developed in its Rules of Procedure a three-stage notification procedure, allowing it to integrate the principle of cooperation with the requirements of effective monitoring:[131]

Stage 1: each year in December, the CPT publishes a provisional programme of periodic visits for the following calendar year. The countries are thus informed of the likelihood of a visit in a given year, but without further information as to the exact dates of the visit.

Stage 2: States Parties are informed of the exact dates of the visit two weeks in advance, together with a provisional list of institutions or places likely to be inspected. This list is not binding though: as the CPT has a right of access to all places of detention, it may subsequently decide to modify the above-mentioned programme in the light of circumstances (Rule 29).

Stage 3: larger institutions are usually (but not always) informed the night before the actual visit takes place. Although this may still result in last-minute attempts by local authorities to hide certain problems or transfer particular persons, the methodology of the CPT, with its emphasis on private interviews, usually allows it to reach the truth.[132]

Ad hoc visits can be decided by the CPT anytime they appear to be required by the circumstances. Often decided in cases of urgency, notification is much shorter here (one or two days).[133]

This notification procedure is not different in cases where an international prisoner is held in one of the prisons visited.

However, the principle of cooperation laid down in the Convention is not limited to steps being taken by the member States to facilitate the task of a visiting delegation. The CPT has increasingly stressed that 'it also requires that decisive action be taken to improve the situation in the light of the Committee's key recommendations'.[134] This obligation is derived from Article 10.2 ECPT:

> If the Party fails to co-operate or refuses to improve the situation in the light of the Committee's recommendations, the Committee may decide, after the Party has had an opportunity to make known its views, by a majority of two-thirds of its members to make a public statement on the matter.

---

[130] See e.g. Report on the CPT visit to Lithuania in 2008 (CPT/Inf (2009) 22) para 5.

[131] Rules 29–31, 33 of the Rules of Procedure (CPT/Inf/C (2008) 1).

[132] Snacken (n 119) 50; see e.g. last-minute attempts at cleaning filthy prison walls, granting extra showers to detainees, hiding a particular person, etc.

[133] See eg *ad hoc* visit to Mr. Öcalan as sole inmate of the Imrali prison in February 2003 (CPT/Inf (2004) 2) para 3.

[134] See, for example, CPT Lithuania periodic visit 2004 (CPT/Inf (2006) 10) para 6; CPT Belgium ad hoc visit 2012 (CPT/Inf (2012) 36) para 7.

A violation by the State Party of its duty to cooperate and improve the situation may result in a suspension by the CPT of the principle of confidentiality. This is not different for situations involving international prisoners.[135] No public statements have been issued by the CPT with regard to the situation of international prisoners.[136]

3.2.3 Confidentiality

This principle was seen in 1987 as a prerequisite to the acceptance of a binding treaty mechanism.[137] It could also have resulted in a *de facto* silencing of the CPT. However, as the randomly selected countries which were first visited by the CPT all published their visit reports, even in cases of serious criticisms,[138] moral pressure to publish the reports increased. Within a European context where human rights protection cannot officially be ignored, failure to publish (in a first period mainly by Turkey and Spain) automatically raised suspicion of gross violations. Overall, by November 2013, with 292 of the 341 reports so far drawn up having been published, the CPT can rightly refer to 'the well-established trend of States deciding to lift the veil of confidentiality and place the Committee's findings in the public domain'.[139]

We have already discussed the specificities of this principle for the international prison system under 3.1.2.

3.2.4 Impartiality

The principle of impartiality is an important aspect of the credibility of the CPT. It consists of several aspects, which are not different for the international monitoring system.

First, it relates to the composition of the Committee. The Committee consists of a number of members equal to that of the member States (Art. 4.1). Members are elected by the Committee of Ministers of the Council of Europe, from a list of names drawn up by the Bureau of the Consultative Assembly of the Council of Europe. Each national

---

[135] This would not require permission by the international court, as there is no legal basis for such a limitation (information provided by Mr. M. Neurauter, CPT Secretariat, 22 May 2015).

[136] Public Statements have been issued with regard to Turkey (gross and systematic practices of torture by police forces); the Russian Federation (situation in the Chechen Republic); Greece (detention of irregular migrants and the state of the prison system); and Bulgaria (failure to implement its recommendations concerning police and penitentiary establishments): Public Statement on Turkey, 15 December 1992 (CPT/Inf (93) 1) and 6 December 1996 (CPT/Inf (96) 34); Public Statement on Russia concerning the Chechen Republic, 10 July 2001 (CPT/Inf (2001) 15) and 13 March 2007 (CPT/Inf (2007) 17); Public Statement concerning Greece, 15 March 2011 (CPT/Inf (2011) 10); Public Statement concerning Bulgaria, 26 March 2015 (CPT/Inf (2015) 17).

[137] M. Evans and R. Morgan, *Preventing Torture: A Study of the European Convention for the Prevention of Torture and Inhuman or Degrading Treatment or Punishment* (Clarendon Press 1998) 376.

[138] Austria (CPT/Inf (91) 10); Denmark (CPT/Inf (91) 12); Sweden (CPT/Inf (92) 4); Finland (CPT/Inf (93) 8); Norway (CPT/Inf (94) 11).

[139] 23rd General Report (CPT/Inf (2013) 29) para 30. See Appendix 6 with the State-by-State table showing the current situation as regards publication of CPT visit reports. The Russian Federation, with only two out of 19 reports published, has recently also started to publish its country reports, see (CPT/Inf (2013) 1).

delegation of the Parties in the Consultative Assembly puts forward three candidates, of whom two at least shall be its nationals (Art. 5.1). However, the members should not represent the interests of their country, but 'shall be chosen from among persons of high moral character, known for their competence in the field of human rights or having professional experience in the areas covered by this Convention' (Art. 4.2), 'shall serve in their individual capacity, shall be independent and impartial and shall be available to serve the Committee effectively' (Art. 4.3). During visits, 'the Committee may, if it considers it necessary, be assisted by experts and interpreters' (Art. 7.2). The experts 'shall have particular knowledge and experience in the areas covered by the Convention and shall be bound by the same duties of independence, impartiality and availability as the members of the Committee' (Art. 14.2).

Secondly, the member elected in respect of a State to be visited is never part of the visiting delegation.[140] The member is supposed to be well acquainted with the problems faced by his country and will provide valuable information during preparation of a visit, but does not participate in the visit itself. The same principle is applicable to the experts assisting the Committee.[141]

Thirdly, impartiality must rule the methods of investigation during the visits and the drawing up of the visit reports. Findings and recommendations must be solid, convincing and well founded.

3.2.5 Effectiveness and efficiency

The principle of effectiveness is only marginally mentioned by the Convention itself, where it refers to the 'availability' of members and experts 'to serve the Committee effectively' (Art. 4.3; Art. 14.2). It is, however, an essential feature of the credibility of monitoring bodies such as the CPT, operating in complex situations and politically sensitive domains.[142] We already mentioned the notification procedure as an illustration of this principle (supra 3.2.2). It must also direct the preparation of the visits and the fact-finding methodology during visits, allowing the CPT to select places adequately and to find solid evidence of practices and problems. Given the short period of time available during a visit, this methodology should also be efficient in time and personal resources (infra 3.3.2).

3.3 CPT Visits in Practice

3.3.1 Organization of visits[143]

Due to organizational and financial constraints, visits to international prisoners by the CPT are part of its regular periodic or *ad hoc* visits.[144] The organization is hence similar. The monitoring work of the CPT focuses on material aspects, social relations

---

140 Rule 35.2 of the Rules of Procedure: 'The member of the Committee elected in respect of the State to be visited shall not be chosen as a member of the visiting delegation.'

141 Rule 36.2 of the Rules of Procedure. A visiting delegation shall not be assisted by an expert who is a national of the State to be visited.

142 Evans and Morgan (n 137) 143 and 334–82; Snacken (n 119) 48–50.

143 See also Snacken (n 119) 50–51.

144 Information received by Mr. M. Neurauter, CPT Secretariat (9 April 2015).

(inside the institution and with the outside world) and fundamental guarantees for protection against torture and inhuman or degrading treatment (not only in law but in practice). The particular situation of an international prisoner in relation to these aspects is taken into account.

Visits are prepared by the Secretariat of the CPT, seated at the Council of Europe in Strasbourg, on the basis of different sources of information: reports by national and international NGOs, reports by national inspectorates, academic publications, court judgments, media reports, complaints, etc. The Committee then selects a provisional list of institutions to be visited in a country and determines the composition of the delegation accordingly (expertise of selected members, experts and secretariat, interpreters).[145] This may include an institution holding an international sentenced prisoner. Information on the country and places to be visited are sent in advance to the members of the delegation (relevant legislation, former CPT country reports, reports by NGOs).

During the visit, the delegation can split into different subgroups, each covering different regions or types of institutions. Each subgroup should however contain at least one medical doctor. Fieldwork focuses on respect for the CPT Standards (see Section 4.4 below); evidence of problematic situations or behaviour, their causes and frequency; and positive aspects which can contribute to a better prevention of such problems.

3.3.2 Methodology

The methodology used during the visit varies with the object of the investigation and consists mainly of observations, document analysis and interviews.[146]

Visits can take place day and night and last for three–four days for larger institutions such as the prisons where sentenced international prisoners will normally be held. Members of the delegation visit all parts of the institution (cells, sanitation, kitchen, workshops, classrooms, visiting infrastructure, disciplinary unit, etc.) and personally register all aspects relating to material circumstances (space, hygiene, natural light, overcrowding) and social relationships (between detainees and with staff).

The identification of incidents of torture and physical ill-treatment requires medical examination and evidence. Other members of the delegation should however be able to recognize symptoms of torture or physical ill-treatment, so as to refer potential victims to the medical doctor of the delegation.[147]

Relevant documents to be studied are local prison population statistics (number and allocation of prisoners, activities, visits, etc.); registers on disciplinary reports, isolation or use of force; follow-up reports of inspection or complaint procedures; medical files (by the medical doctor only).

Interviews are without doubt among the major instruments for the CPT to understand the complexity of living in closed institutions. While the focus is on detainees, it may

---

[145] Rule 35.1 Rules of Procedure: '1. The members of the Committee to carry out a visit shall be chosen by the Committee (...). Due regard shall be had to the nature of the visit in question, and in particular to the type of place or places to be visited, when the composition of the delegation is determined.'

[146] Snacken (n 119) 51–4.

[147] E.g. bruises or haematomas, but also lesions resulting from specific torture techniques such as 'Palestinian hanging' or 'falaka'.

be important to include other categories of respondents: staff members, medical doctors, visitors, defence lawyers visiting their clients, etc. International prisoners will also be seen and interviewed during such a visit. Interviews of detainees are always confidential, out of hearing and sight of staff.[148] Interviews take place as much as possible individually, in order to avoid mutual influences. This is not always easy, especially in prison systems where prisoner accommodation is based on large dormitory systems, such as in Central and Eastern Europe. This could hence be the case for international prisoners held in prisons in Albania and Ukraine, but these have not been visited yet.

Outside the international penal system, the selection of respondents depends on the topic being investigated: it may be at random (e.g. general material circumstances or regime) or systematic (e.g. all recently arrived detainees; all prisoners held in isolation or disciplinary units). The selection aims at avoiding as much as possible risks of reprisals by staff. The anonymity of the respondents is guaranteed, unless explicit consent is given by the respondent (e.g. in case of a formal judicial complaint).[149] As already mentioned, the anonymity of an international prisoner is much more difficult to guarantee and the risk of reprisal in case of complaints to the CPT is hence even higher.

While the methods used aim at building trust of the respondents in the CPT's competences and expertise, it is also important not to be credulous and to 'check and double check' all the information received. Both staff members and detainees may have reasons for not telling the truth.[150]

3.4 The CPT Standards[151]

As mentioned above, the CPT has developed its own standards, based on a variety of human rights instruments and its findings in the field.[152] The standards are evolutionary and regularly updated.

---

[148] Only in exceptional circumstances, when a prisoner is considered as unpredictably violent, will interviews take place out of hearing but within visual control of staff.

[149] Art. 11.2: 'However, no personal data shall be published without the express consent of the person concerned.'

[150] See Snacken (n 119) 52–3; for concrete examples of resistance by staff (e.g. Germany (CPT/Inf (97)9 [EN] (Part 1)) para 163, or prisoners (e.g. Bulgaria (CPT/Inf (97)1 (Part 1)) para 105; Lithuania (CPT/Inf (2001)22) paras 64–65).

[151] See: CPT Standards: CPT/Inf/E (2002)1- Rev. 2015; <http://www.cpt.coe.int/en/documents/eng-standards.pdf> accessed 10 July 2015.

[152] CPT 1st General Report (CPT/Inf (91) 3) para 5:

> In carrying out its functions the CPT has the right to avail itself of legal standards contained in not only the European Convention on Human Rights but also in a number of other relevant human rights instruments (and the interpretation of them by the human rights organs concerned). At the same time, it is not bound by the case law of judicial or quasi-judicial bodies acting in the same field, but may use it as a point of departure or reference when assessing the treatment of persons deprived of their liberty in individual countries.

With regard to the international penal system, the standards relating to inhuman and degrading treatment resulting from (long-term) imprisonment or isolation, contacts with the outside world and preparation for release seem especially relevant.[153]

3.4.1 Inhuman and degrading treatment

For the CPT, inhuman and degrading treatment does not necessarily imply 'wilful' acts. Attention should hence be paid to the overall 'quality of life' of the detainees. This depends to a large extent upon the activities offered to prisoners and the general state of relations between prisoners and staff. The climate of an institution is hence important and relates to constructive as opposed to confrontational relations between prisoners and staff.[154] But relations imply communication. International prisoners held in a country in which they do not speak the language could hence be confronted with additional communication problems. We know from the situation of other foreign nationals that this may result in social isolation within the prison and more frequent disciplinary breaches and sanctions.[155]

The combination of overcrowding, lack of activities and lack of sanitation is systematically considered to amount to inhuman and degrading treatment, but overcrowding can also in itself amount to inhuman and degrading treatment.[156] Prisoners should spend at least eight hours a day outside their cells, 'engaged in purposeful activity of a varied nature', including at least one hour of outdoor exercise. Ready access to proper toilet/washing facilities should always be guaranteed.[157] Language barriers may also result in less activities being available to international prisoners.[158]

Specific risk groups for the CPT are 'vulnerable' prisoners and prisoners held in solitary confinement. The former relates to prisoners who are at higher risk of victimization by fellow prisoners, often due to their offence (e.g. sexual offences).[159] This could also apply to some prisoners detained under the international penal system, as they may have been convicted of the most serious crimes, such as genocide, mass murder and rape. This may result in segregation from other prisoners or solitary confinement for their own protection, but in a regime offering much more limited activities programmes.

Solitary confinement can, in certain circumstances, amount to inhuman and degrading treatment. It can have an extremely damaging effect on the mental, somatic and

---

153 Mainly based on the 2nd, 7th, 11th and 21st General Report.

154 CPT Standards: CPT/Inf/E (2002)1- Rev. 2015: 2nd General Report (CPT/Inf (92) 3) paras 44–45.

155 A. van Kalmthout, F. Hofstee, van der Meulen and F. Dünkel (eds), *Foreigners in European Prisons Vols 1, 2* (Wolf 2007) 7–78.

156 CPT Standards: CPT/Inf/E (2002)1- Rev. 2015: 2nd General Report (CPT/Inf (92) 3) para 46; 7th General Report (CPT/Inf (97) 10) paras 12–15; 11th General Report (CPT/Inf (2001) 16) para 28.

157 CPT Standards: CPT/Inf/E (2002)1- Rev. 2015: 2nd General Report (CPT/Inf (92) 3) paras 46–50.

158 See also for foreign nationals generally: Council of Europe Recommendation CM/Rec (2012) 12 concerning foreign prisoners.

159 CPT Standards: CPT/Inf/E (2002)1- Rev. 2015: 11th General Report (CPT/Inf (2001) 16) paras 27, 29.

social health of those concerned, enhancing the risk of suicide.[160] It can also create an opportunity for the deliberate ill-treatment of prisoners, away from the attention of other prisoners and staff. The extra restrictions involved have to be separately justified and should be imposed for as short a period as possible. The CPT follows the traditional tests enshrined in the provisions of the ECHR and developed by the case-law of the ECtHR. The simple mnemonic PLANN summarizes these tests: solitary confinement should be proportionate, lawful, accountable, necessary and non-discriminatory.[161]

In the 25 years of experience of the CPT, other risk situations are: (1) any instances of use of force by staff, which should follow the principles of subsidiarity and proportionality and allow for an immediate examination by a medical doctor; (2) high security units, where prisoners should enjoy 'a relatively relaxed regime by way of compensation for their severe custodial situation'; (3) large capacity dormitory systems, where the risk of inter-prisoner violence is often higher than in single-cell occupancy.

Whether any of these risk situations are applicable to prisoners under the international prison system is unknown, as none of the reports have been published yet.

3.4.2 Life sentences and other long-term prisoners

International prisoners may include persons who have been sentenced to very long or life sentences.[162] In the CPT experience, such prisoners are often subject to special restrictions likely to exacerbate the deleterious effects inherent in long-term imprisonment. In line with penological insights,[163] the CPT Standards therefore stress that such prisoners should have access to a wide range of purposeful activities of a varied nature (work, preferably with vocational value; education; sport; recreation/association), and should be able to exercise a degree of choice over the manner in which their time is spent, thus fostering a sense of autonomy and personal responsibility. Additional steps should be taken to lend meaning to their period of imprisonment; in particular, the provision of individualized custody plans and appropriate psycho-social support are important elements in assisting such prisoners to come to terms with their period of incarceration and, when the time comes, to prepare for release.[164]

3.4.3 The importance of contacts with the outside world

The CPT also stresses that the negative effects of institutionalization upon prisoners serving long sentences will be less pronounced, and they will be better equipped for release, if they are able effectively to maintain contact with the outside world. Such contacts are very important, especially with regard to safeguarding relationships with

---

160 See also S. Shalev, *A Sourcebook on Solitary Confinement* (2008). <http://www.solitaryconfinement.org/sourcebook> accessed 10 July 2015.

161 CPT Standards: CPT/Inf/E (2002)1- Rev. 2015: 2nd General Report (CPT/Inf (92) 3) para 56; 21st General Report (CPT/Inf (2011) 28) paras 53–64.

162 E.g. the prisoner visited in Portugal had been sentenced to 20 years.

163 See eg Van Zyl Smit and Snacken (n 32); Council of Europe Recommendation Rec (2003) 23 on the management of life-sentence and other long-term prisoners.

164 CPT Standards: CPT/Inf/E (2002)1- Rev. 2015: 11th General Report (CPT/Inf (2001) 16) para 33.

family and close friends. This includes the possibility of unsupervised conjugal or family visits.[165]

But this may of course be very difficult for international prisoners detained far away from their country of origin. The combination of language problems and distance from family may hence result in both internal and external social isolation for this particular group.

3.5 Effectiveness of CPT Monitoring

The competence of the CPT to monitor the situation of international prisoners is limited to countries that are already bound by the ECPT and the ECHR. No reports have been published yet concerning such prisoners. We can therefore only discuss in general terms the possible effectiveness of CPT monitoring of the international penal system.

Our evaluation of the work by CPT deals with two aspects: the normative aspect of its standard setting and the practical effects of its monitoring operations.

3.5.1 Standard setting

One of us has argued elsewhere that the standard setting by the CPT should be seen within the mutual reinforcement between the three main instruments of the Council of Europe for protection of persons deprived of their liberty: the case-law of the European Court of Human Rights (judicial level), the Recommendations by the Committee of Ministers (political level) and the CPT standards (monitoring level).[166] This is not different with regard to international prisoners, as all countries holding such prisoners are bound by both the ECPT and the ECHR. While the case-law of the ECtHR is still more restrictive and timid than the standards developed by the CPT and the Recommendations,[167] it has increasingly been influenced by what it considers to be the 'legal instruments' of the Council of Europe.[168]

These 'European' standards can be categorized under two main headings: striving for the recognition of prisoners as 'legal citizens'[169] and for less totalitarian or 'post-authoritarian' prison institutions.[170] Legal citizens, including prisoners, are entitled to the protection of their fundamental material rights, procedural rights and to the right to information concerning these rights. While the ECtHR limits these rights to those

165 CPT Standards: CPT/Inf/E (2002)1- Rev. 2015: 2nd General Report (CPT/Inf (92) 3) para 51; 11th General Report (CPT/Inf (2001) 16) para 33.

166 See Van Zyl Smit and Snacken (n 32); Snacken (n 119); S. Snacken, 'Les structures européennes de contrôle des administrations pénitentiaires: le rôle et l'impact du Conseil de l'Europe et du Comité de Prévention de la Torture' (2014) 38 *Déviance & Société* 4 405–23.

167 Van Zyl Smit and Snacken (n 32) Chapter 9. See especially the Recommendations Rec (2006) 2 on the European Prison Rules (EPR), Rec (2003) 23 on the management of life-sentence and other long-term prisoners and Rec (2003) 22 concerning conditional release (parole).

168 *Dickson v United Kingdom* App no 44362/04 (ECtHR, 4 December 2007) para 28.

169 See the concept of '*rechtsburger*' as developed by C. Kelk, *Nederlands detentierecht* (Gouda Quint 2000).

170 Van Zyl Smit and Snacken (n 32) Chapter 9; Snacken (n 119) Chapter 6.

protected by the ECHR and its Protocols,[171] the CPT extends this protection to the right to an adequate prison regime, to prison labour, hygiene, visits, etc. Equally, while the CPT (and the European Prison Rules)[172] advocate a right to reintegration and gradual preparation for release for all prisoners, the ECtHR only recently adapted its case-law towards the recognition of a right for all prisoners to be considered for early release.[173] The CPT has also repeatedly stressed the importance of procedural rights of complaint, effective remedies and the adequate communication of these rights.[174]

The concept of 'post-authoritarian' prison refers to standards aiming at fundamentally altering the traditional characteristics of the prison as a total institution, producing a variety of 'pains of imprisonment' and psychosocial effects which have the potential to harm the prisoners and their prospects for successful reintegration into society.[175] The CPT recognizes the diversity of risks resulting from a situation of deprivation of liberty: material conditions; a lack of adequate medical care; an impoverished prison regime; insufficient contacts with outside world; solitary confinement; searches, the use of force; and physical ill-treatment by staff or fellow prisoners have all been found to amount in some circumstances to inhuman and degrading treatment or even torture.[176]

3.5.2 Effectiveness of CPT monitoring operations

The question of the 'effectiveness' of CPT monitoring is complex.[177] Effectiveness refers to 'achieving the aims', but the aims (and the means) can be multiple. The aim of the CPT is the 'prevention of torture and inhuman or degrading treatment or punishment' in all possible situations of deprivation of liberty. The means are visits, collecting evidence on the treatment of detainees, collaboration and dialogue with the

---

[171] *Hirst v United Kingdom (No 2)* App no 74025/01 (ECtHR, 6 October 2005) para 69:

> [P]risoners in general continue to enjoy all the fundamental rights and freedoms guaranteed under the ECHR save for the right to liberty. For example, prisoners may not be ill-treated, subjected to inhuman or degrading punishment or conditions contrary to Art. 3 of the Convention; they continue to enjoy the right to respect for family life, the right to freedom of expression, the right to practise their religion, the right of effective access to a lawyer or to court for the purposes of Art. 6, the right to respect for correspondence and the right to marry. Any restrictions on these other rights require to be justified.

[172] See Basic Principle 6 EPR: 'All detention shall be managed so as to facilitate the reintegration into free society of persons who have been deprived of their liberty.'

[173] The importance of reintegration as an aim of imprisonment was recognized by the Court in several cases: *Mastromatteo v Italy* App no 37703/97 (ECtHR, 24 October 2002) para 72; *Kafkaris v Cyprus* App no 21906/04 (ECtHR, 11 April 2006); *Dickson v United Kingdom* App no 44362/04 (ECtHR, 4 December 2007) para 28. Only with *Vinter et al v United Kingdom* App nos 66069/09, 130/10 and 3896/10 (ECtHR, 9 July 2013) did the Court explicitly find whole life sentences to amount to inhuman and degrading treatment violating Art. 3 ECHR.

[174] 2nd (CPT/Inf (92) 3) and 11th General Report (CPT/Inf (2001) 16).

[175] Van Zyl Smit and Snacken (n 32) 349.

[176] Ibid., 355

[177] See S. Snacken, 'Het Europees Comité voor de Preventie van Foltering. Beter een lappendeken dan naakt in de koude nacht?' (The European Committee for the Prevention of Torture. Better a patchwork than naked in the cold night?), in K. Beyens, F. Janssens, P. Ponsaers, A. Verhage (eds), *Justitie en politie: onder controle?* Themanummer Orde van de Dag, Afl. 55 (2011) 87–94 ; Snacken (n 166) 415–17.

relevant authorities in order to tackle problems and foster good practices. Moreover, the President of the International Tribunal can increase pressure by requesting that the implementing country report to the Tribunal any changes in the conditions of detention suggested by the CPT. But how do we measure the 'effect' of these instruments on 'preventing' ill-treatment or inhuman and degrading practices? 'Prevention' is probably one of the most difficult criminological topics to assess: how do we measure what did not happen? And how do we prove the causal relationship? The CPT is only one of many actors in the field striving for a better protection of persons deprived of their liberty. How do we distinguish the impact of the CPT's work from other concurrent actions? And should we only focus on the impact for the detainees themselves, or also on politicians, the media or the public?

We cannot tackle all these issues here. We will limit ourselves to two aspects: the competences and resources required to produce effects (capability) and the variety of effects produced so far.

(a) Capability Producing monitoring effects presupposes some requirements related to the strengths and characteristics of the monitoring body. On the positive side, we would mention the large competences of access and inspection granted by the Convention; the personal resources and expertise of the CPT secretariat, consisting of 14 members and nine administrative assistants;[178] the expertise of the CPT members (and experts); the monitoring methodology and skills developed over the years, granting legitimacy and credibility to the CPT findings and reports.

Some of these positive features are also potential vulnerabilities. As the CPT stresses in its 19th General Report, 'it is of paramount importance that the Committee continues to have a highly qualified membership in terms of relevant professional expertise and empirical experience. The effectiveness of the CPT will ultimately depend on the quality of its members'.[179]

The quality of the members depends on the selection procedure applied by the national authorities in order to propose the list of three names. The CPT favours the procedure advocated by Resolution 1540 (2007) of the Parliamentary Assembly of the Council of Europe.[180] Proposals by the Parliamentary Assembly to amend the Convention in order to permit the election of CPT members by the Parliamentary Assembly were however not followed by the Committee of Ministers.[181]

---

178 See also Morgan and Evans (n 82) 26.

179 19th General Report (CPT/Inf (2009) 27) para 104.

180 Parliamentary Assembly, Resolution 1540 (2007)1 – Improving selection procedures for CPT members <http://assembly.coe.int/Main.asp?link=/Documents/AdoptedText/ta07/ERES 1540.htm> accessed 20 May 2014.

181 Committee of Ministers, Reply to Recommendation 1968 (2011) 'Strengthening torture prevention mechanisms in Europe' (Doc 12877, 21 February 2012). Another proposal concerned the automatic publication of CPT visit reports and of the responses of the Parties concerned, subject to the possibility of a State to request postponement of publication for up to six months after transmission of the visit report. <http://assembly.coe.int/ASP/Doc/XrefViewHTML. asp?FileID=13081&Language=EN> accessed 10 July 2015.

(b) Effects After 20 years of monitoring, the CPT itself wrote:

> As an assiduous reader of CPT visit reports and State responses will know, there are countless concrete examples of positive steps taken in reaction to the Committee's recommendations and observations. Safeguards against ill-treatment have been introduced or strengthened, substandard inmate accommodation has been renovated or withdrawn from service, the quality of health care for persons detained has been improved and out-of-cell activities have been enhanced. In spite of that, torture and other deliberate forms of ill-treatment of persons deprived of their liberty still exist in the Council of Europe area, and conditions of detention remain wretched in numerous establishments of various types; many published CPT reports as well as judgments of the European Court of Human Rights attest to this state of affairs.[182]

We want to distinguish six types of effects: direct and immediate; direct but long term, often in conjunction with other agencies; indirect through national courts or agencies; indirect through the ECtHR; indirect through the international tribunals; and 'symbolic' effect.

DIRECT AND IMMEDIATE The impact of the CPT's work can be direct and immediate when wholly unacceptable or individual situations are solved on the spot or soon after the visit. Examples include the withdrawal from service of 'waiting cubicles' of less than 2m[183] or decrepit disciplinary cells.[184]

DIRECT BUT LONG TERM, OFTEN IN CONJUNCTION WITH OTHER AGENCIES Certain recommendations or immediate observations concerning material circumstances or regime elements require considerable infrastructural work or longer term efforts (for an example, see the withdrawal from service of waiting cubicles in an old courthouse in Belgium).[185] They may refer to problems that have long been criticized by other agencies as well (national or international), hence complicating an assessment of the different influences.

INDIRECT THROUGH NATIONAL COURTS OR AGENCIES Published CPT reports and standards can be used by national monitoring bodies, NGOs or lawmakers and visit reports can be used by prisoners and defence lawyers in order to address problematic situations before national courts (see for example litigation before Belgian national courts to tackle gross overcrowding or the lack of psychiatric care).[186]

Cooperation between monitoring bodies at the national level, the European level (CPT) and the international level (SPT) was the object of the Conference 'New partnerships for Torture Prevention in Europe', organized by the CPT on 6 November 2009 at the occasion of its 20th anniversary. The importance of such cooperation was

---

182 19th General Report (CPT/Inf (2009) 27) para 7.

183 CPT report Latvia visit 2002 (CPT/Inf (2005) 8) para 139.

184 CPT report Belgium visit 2005 (CPT/Inf (2006) 15) para 7.

185 CPT report visit Belgium 2001 (CPT/Inf (2002) 25) para 8; Responses by the Belgian Government in 2002 (CPT/Inf (2002) 25) para 46, 2006 (CPT/Inf (2006) 15) para 36 and 2010 (CPT/Inf (2010) 24) paras 26–27.

186 See Snacken (n 177) 87–94.

stressed for exchanging information, safeguarding the coherence of the standards and guaranteeing the implementation of the standards.[187]

INDIRECT THROUGH THE ECTHR CPT standards and findings have greatly influenced the case-law of the ECtHR, especially over the last 15 years, leading to some important reversals.[188] The acceptance that inhuman and degrading treatment or punishment does not necessarily imply 'wilful acts' but can result from lack of resources or overcrowding is an important example.[189] Moreover, the CPT has increasingly become the 'fact finding' instrument for the ECtHR. By 2012, CPT visit reports or standards had been cited in up to 350 of the Court's judgments. Meetings and exchange of views between the CPT and the Court have also become an established practice.[190]

INDIRECT THROUGH THE INTERNATIONAL TRIBUNALS As already mentioned, the Presidents of the International Tribunals themselves can also increase pressure on the implementing country by requesting a report on any changes in the conditions of detention suggested by the CPT.

SYMBOLIC EFFECT Sociology of punishment studies of the last 20 years emphasize the symbolic and cultural meaning of punishment.[191] While sentencing expresses the censure of the offence and the offender through the sanction,[192] prison embodies the exclusion of the unwanted and unworthy, the undeniable cleavage between the 'good' and the 'bad' people. This is also true for international prisoners, often convicted of very serious offences against humanity. The treatment of prisoners, but also the criticisms and attempts at reform, illustrate the sensibilities and values in society. The interaction and mutual reinforcement of the European human rights instruments (CPT, ECtHR, Recommendations), their continuous emphasis on the need to protect the fundamental rights and inherent dignity of all persons, including unpopular groups such as offenders and prisoners, may be at odds with the reality in many prisons, it also nuances a purely punitive and exclusionary penal imaginary.[193]

---

[187] Council of Europe/Association for the Prevention of Torture, 'New partnerships for Torture Prevention in Europe, Proceedings of the Conference, 6 November 2009' (2010).

[188] For a more detailed overview, see Van Zyl Smit and Snacken (n 32).

[189] CPT 2nd General Report (CPT/Inf (92) 3) para 46; *Dougoz v Greece* App no 40907/98 (ECtHR, 6 March 2001).

[190] CPT 22nd General Report (CPT/Inf (2012) 25) para 23.

[191] See e.g. D. Garland, *Punishment and Modern Society. A Study in Social Theory* (University of Chicago Press 1990); D. Garland, *Culture of Control. Crime and Social Order in Contemporary Society* (Oxford University Press 2001); P. Smith, *Punishment and Culture* (University of Chicago Press 2008).

[192] A. von Hirsch, *Censure and Sanctions* (Oxford University Press 1993).

[193] A. Di Giorgi, 'State Power, Democratic Process and Human Rights: Countering the Penal Imaginary' (2010) 14(3) *Theoretical Criminology* 369.

4. CONCLUSION

International imprisonment relies on a voluntary and consensual system of sentence implementation. Sentences served in a particular State are subject to that State's laws, but are supervised by the international courts. As a result, prisoners sentenced by an international tribunal may end up in very different prison conditions. An important aspect of the choice of a particular country is whether the prison system of the enforcing State is suitable in terms of conformity with international standards. The international criminal courts therefore increasingly move away from a passive acceptance of the penal capacity provided by cooperating States and seek to conclude agreements proactively with States in the prisoners' region of origin, in order to address humanitarian concerns and to enhance the likelihood of successful reintegration. Effective monitoring of international imprisonment is part of these humanitarian concerns.

Moreover, prisoners sentenced by an international court may end up with very long sentences, which entail particular risks for inhuman and degrading treatment, enforced in a country that is difficult to reach for family, friends and services. The ever-delicate balance between censure, retribution and reintegration may be even more difficult for this category of prisoners.

Monitoring of the international penal system is performed mainly by the ICRC, but in some European countries by the CPT. The CPT develops standards based on a variety of international human rights instruments and its own findings during visits in the field. The standards are common to all the States Parties to the ECPT and involved in the implementation of international prison sentences in Europe. But international imprisonment still faces varying realities, even within Europe. Unequal treatment may hence still result from this variation.

> If consistency in the imposition of punishment is one of the fundamental elements of a fair criminal justice system, the equality of treatment of persons convicted by the same court during the implementation of those sanctions must be a fundamental element of a fair penal system. The variation in the conditions and regimes in the domestic prison systems of cooperating States inevitably results in persons convicted by the same court being treated differently. The same can be said with regard to the assessment of detention conditions.[194]

Entrusting supervision of this international prison system in European countries to the CPT has the advantage of guaranteeing the application of homogeneous standards to the countries involved.

---

[194] Mulgrew (n 1) 23.

15. Enforcement of sentences and oversight of prisoners convicted by the Special Court for Sierra Leone

Teresa Anne Doherty and Shireen Avis Fisher

1. INTRODUCTION

The SCSL is the first international tribunal to have completed its mandate and transitioned to a new institution, the RSCSL. The RSCSL has been entrusted with responsibility for meeting the Special Court's obligations to victims, witnesses and prisoners sentenced by the SCSL. Beginning in 2007 the SCSL engaged in an examination of the theoretical and practical issues raised by the possibility of early release of sentenced prisoners, and ultimately put in place a practice direction. This chapter reviews the objectives of that practice direction as well as the process it incorporates to meet those objectives, and follows the jurisprudence of the SCSL and the RSCSL in meeting its prisoner oversight responsibilities.

2. BACKGROUND

Sierra Leone, a small country on the west coast of Africa, experienced a brutal civil war from 1996 to 2002. Following the declaration of peace the Government of Sierra Leone entered into a treaty agreement with the UN to establish a special court composed of international and national judges to prosecute those who bore 'the greatest responsibility' for the war crimes, crimes against humanity and breaches of international humanitarian law perpetrated in the war. The Prosecutor preferred indictments against 14 persons. These were subsequently consolidated into three trials of the leaders of three warring groups (Revolutionary United Front or RUF, Civil Defence Front or CDF and Armed Forces Revolutionary Council or AFRC) and one individual, Charles Taylor, then President of Liberia. All the trials have been completed but there is one outstanding indictee whose whereabouts is unknown. In common with other international criminal tribunals the SCSL did not have its own prison[1] and had to enter agreements with other States to enforce its sentencing orders. But it did retain the statutory right to decide if a convicted person could have the sentence imposed commuted. The SCSL reviewed its statutory provisions and decided that a provision for conditional early release was a more appropriate method of review of sentence and one in keeping with the accepted procedure in many national jurisdictions.

[1] SCSL maintained a detention centre for remandees pending and during trial and those sentenced to short custodial sentences. It was staffed by international and national personnel.

Following the completion of the trials, the conclusion of enforcement of sentence agreements and the transfer of convicted persons to the States of enforcement the SCSL declared that it had completed its mandate. There were, however, residual functions for which the Court would continue to be responsible, notably the enforcement of protection orders for victims and witnesses and the oversight of prisoners serving sentences imposed by the SCSL. Therefore, an Agreement between the UN and the Government of Sierra Leone establishing a RSCSL was signed in July 2010.[2]

3. ISSUES OF LAW

The original provisions of the SCSLSt[3] provided at Article 23:

> If, pursuant to the applicable law of the State in which the convicted person is imprisoned, he or she is eligible for pardon or commutation of sentence, the State concerned shall notify the Special Court accordingly. There shall only be pardon or commutation of sentence if the President of the Special Court, in consultation with the judges, so decides on the basis of the interests of justice and the general principles of law.

This provision was in common with Article 27 of the ICTYSt and Article 28 of the ICTRSt but differed from Article 110 of the ICCSt which provides, inter alia, for review and reduction of sentence if criteria, specified in Article 110 are met.

The SCSL RPE Rules 123 and 124 are a recital of Article 23 divided into two parts although under Rule 123 the obligation on the State of enforcement is to notify the Registrar which, in effect, is notifying the Special Court.

The SCSLSt also provided at Article 22, inter alia, that imprisonment 'shall be served in Sierra Leone' but, if circumstances required, imprisonment could also be served in any of the States which had concluded agreements for the enforcement of sentences with the ICTR or the ICTY.[4] The provisions of Article 22(1) were not mirrored in the Statutes of the ICTY or ICTR.

---

[2] Agreement between the UN and the Government of Sierra Leone on the Establishment of a Residual Special Court for Sierra Leone.

[3] Art. 23 SCSLSt. The Statute was annexed to the SCA on 16 January 2002 (Art 2.2 SCSLSt). The Agreement was entered into pursuant to SCRes 1315 (2000). The SCSLSt has been superseded by the provisions of the RSCSLSt.

[4] The provisions were:

> (1) Imprisonment shall be served in Sierra Leone. If circumstances so require, imprisonment may also be served in any of the States which have concluded with the International Criminal Tribunal for Rwanda or the International Criminal Tribunal for the former Yugoslavia an agreement for the enforcement of sentences, and which have indicated to the Registrar of the Special Court their willingness to accept convicted persons. The Special Court may conclude similar agreements for the enforcement of sentences with other States. (2) Conditions of imprisonment, whether in Sierra Leone or in a third State, shall be governed by the law of the State of enforcement subject to the supervision of the Special Court. The State of enforcement shall be bound by the duration of the sentence, subject to article 23 of the present Statute.

All persons convicted by the Special Court were convicted under the provisions of the SCSLSt. Despite the apparent mandatory provision that convicted persons should serve sentence in Sierra Leone no person convicted by the Special Court, either for war crimes, crimes against humanity or contempt served sentence in a penal establishment of the Government of Sierra Leone. However at the time of the sentencing hearing of the first persons convicted by the SCSL, Brima, Kamara and Kanu,[5] there had been no published determination of where prisoners would serve their sentences. Hence the parties' arguments were made on the basis that the defendants might serve sentence in Sierra Leone or in another country with which the Court might enter an Enforcement of Sentences Agreement. As the Sierra Leone Prisons Act[6] provides for remission of sentence by one-third of the total sentence, calculated by the prison authorities when the prisoner is first incarcerated a question was asked by the bench about the effect of that provision on any sentence imposed. In response Prosecution Counsel referred to the Statute (Art. 23) and the provision for commutation, apparently on the premise that commutation of sentence is the same as remission.

This misunderstanding and the possible expectation[7] on the part of prisoners that they would be entitled to remission if they were incarcerated in Sierra Leone caused concern in the mind of some Judges. In the light of the enforcement agreements entered into by ICTY it was possible, as provided in the SCSL Statute,[8] that the Registrar of the SCSL might enter into enforcement agreements with Austria and Finland and/or other countries. Clearly any such agreement was within the prerogative of the Registrar and in keeping with the letter and spirit of the Statute, particularly as the ICTY and ICTR had already enforcement agreements with those States.

The possibility that convicted persons might be dispersed to serve sentence in different States and the wording of Article 23 and Rules 123 and 124 gave rise to concerns of:

1. the possible disparity of treatment that could arise if a convicted person became eligible for pardon or commutation of sentence at a time different to that of a co-defendant sentenced to the same term of imprisonment because of the applicable law of the State in which he/she was imprisoned;
2. which judges are to be consulted by the President when considering pardon or commutation; and
3. the criteria that are to be considered by the President and the judges in reaching a decision.

---

5 *Brima, Kamara and Kanu* SCSL-04-16-T (Hearing, 16 July 2007) 44–6.

6 Prisons Ordinance Act 1960 provides for remission of one-third of sentence (the law is currently under review).

7 A submission concerning entitlement to remission subsequently arose in the *Hassan Papa Bangura et al* trial, which indicated such an expectation, *Bangura, Kargbo, Kanu, Kamara* SCSL-11-02-T (Interim Decision on Application for Reconsideration of Single Judge's 5 July 2012 Decision on Release, 6 July 2012).

8 Art. 22 SCSLSt.

Disparity could arise if, for example one co-defendant was serving sentence in Finland and another co-defendant was serving sentence in the UK as Finnish legislation allows for a maximum term of incarceration of 12 years (subject to exceptions)[9] whereas the UK does not have an equivalent statutory provision.

In due course, the SCSL entered into agreements with several countries, notably Rwanda,[10] Finland,[11] Sweden[12] and the UK[13] allowing for enforcement of sentence of convicted persons in those jurisdictions. The persons convicted in three of the trials[14] are serving sentence in Rwanda and one[15] is serving sentence in the UK. Three persons convicted of contempt of court served sentence at the detention facility of the Special Court in Freetown, Sierra Leone. An agreement for enforcement of sentences had been signed with the Sierra Leone Government.[16]

4. THE LAW IN PRACTICE

The issues of how Rule 123 would be implemented, the criteria that the President might consider when deciding if 'in the interests of justice and the general principles of law' mitigated for commutation of sentence, who would be consulted and whether any conditions would be attached to an order allowing release were considered by the Judges of the SCSL and formed a part of the discussion at a Legacy Conference held in Freetown in 2007.

The Plenary of Judges resolved to appoint a Sub-Committee to consider and make recommendations on the implementation of Rules 123 and 124. The members of the Sub-Committee were Justice Shireen Avis Fisher of the Appeal Chamber, Justice Teresa Doherty of Trial Chamber II and Ms. Binta Mansaray, the Registrar.[17]

---

9 'Chapter 2(c) Imprisonment (780/2005) Section 2 of The Criminal Code of Finland – The length of imprisonment:

> 1) Imprisonment is sentenced for a fixed period or for life.
> 2) A sentence of fixed-term imprisonment is imposed for at least fourteen days and at most twelve years or, when imposing a joint sentence pursuant to Chapter 7, fifteen years.' (Finnish Ministry of Justice; <www.finlex.fi> accessed 28 June 2015.

10 The Agreement between the Special Court and the Government of Rwanda on the Enforcement of Sentences initially signed on 18 March 2009. The Agreement was subsequently amended on 16 September 2009 and 29 November 2011.

11 The Agreement between the Special Court and the Government of Finland on the Enforcement of Sentences signed on 29 June 2009.

12 The Agreement between the Special Court and the Government of Sweden on the Enforcement of Sentences signed on 15 October 2004.

13 The Agreement between the Special Court and the Government of United Kingdom on the Enforcement of Sentences signed on 10 July 2007.

14 *Brima et al* SCSL-04-16-T (Judgment, 20 June 2007); *Fofana et al* SCSL-04-14-T (Judgment, 2 August 2007); *Sesay et al* SCSL-04-15-T (Judgment, 2 March 2009).

15 *Taylor* SCSL-03-01-T (Judgment, 18 May 2012).

16 The Supplementary Agreement between the Special Court and the Government of Sierra Leone on the Enforcement of Sentences for Contempt signed on 26 March 2013.

17 Justices Fisher and Doherty are the authors of this chapter.

At the time the Sub-Committee first convened an agreement for the enforcement of sentences had been concluded with Rwanda and those persons convicted in the completed trials of the *Brima et al* case (AFRC case), the *Fofana et al* case (CDF case) and the *Sesay et al* case (RUF case) had been transferred to Mpanga Prison in Rwanda by order of the President.[18] As a result the theoretical issue of parity of treatment did not arise in the case of those convicted persons serving sentence in Rwanda. The trial of Charles Taylor was still in course of hearing. Since then, Charles Taylor has been convicted and is serving sentence in the UK.

The Sub-Committee reviewed the implementation of the equivalent provisions of Rules 123 and 124 from the ICTY and ICTR; the provisions and practice of remission in the Sierra Leone prison law and practice (as all convicted persons, at that time, were Sierra Leone citizens); the law and practice relating to early release in Rwanda and other jurisdictions; and the provisions of the UNSMR;[19] in an effort to initially determine three things:

1. The relationship between the State of Enforcement and the Court regarding whether a prisoner serving a sentence imposed by the SCSL would have that sentence pardoned or commuted;
2. The meaning of the term 'Pardon or commutation of sentence';
3. The trigger for consideration of 'pardon or commutation of sentence'.

5. QUESTIONS RAISED ABOUT EARLY RELEASE

5.1 Question 1: What is the Relationship between the State of Enforcement and the SCSL/RSCSL Regarding Authority to Grant an SCSL/RSCSL Prisoner 'Pardon or Commutation of Sentence'?

Because the SCSLSt is an 'integral part'[20] of the treaty establishing the Court ('the Agreement'), executed between the UN and the Government of Sierra Leone, it is subject to interpretation according to rules of treaty interpretation set out in Articles

---

[18] *Sesay* SCSL-04-15-ES (Order Designating State in which Issa Hassan Sesay is to Serve his Sentence, 26 October 2009); *Kallon* SCSL-04-15-ES (Order Designating State in which Morris Kallon is to Serve his Sentence, 26 October 2009); *Gbao* SCSL-04-15-ES (Order Designating State in which Augustine Gbao is to Serve his Sentence, 26 October 2009); *Brima* SCSL-04-16-ES (Order Designating State in which Alex Tamba Brima is to Serve his Sentence, 12 August 2009); *Kamara* SCSL-04-16-ES (Corrigendum, 13 August 2009); *Kanu* SCSL-04-16-ES (Corrigendum, 13 August 2009); *Fofana* SCSL-04-14-ES (Corrigendum to the Order Designating State in which Moinina Fofana is to Serve his Sentence, 24 August 2009); *Kondewa* SCSL04-14-ES (Order Designating State in which Allieu Kondewa is to serve his Sentence, 12 August 2009).

[19] Adopted by the First UN Congress on the Prevention of Crime and the Treatment of Offenders, held at Geneva in 1955, and approved by the Economic and Social Council by its resolutions 663 C (XXIV) of 31 July 1957 and 2076 (LXII) of 13 May 1977.

[20] Art. 1(2) of the Agreement reads: 'The Statute is annexed to this Agreement and forms an integral part thereof.'

31–33 of the Vienna Convention on the Law of Treaties (VCLT), now recognized under customary international law as applicable to all treaties.[21] Article 31 requires that the meaning of disputed treaty terms shall be found by determining the ordinary meaning of the term, considered in context and in light of the object and purpose of the instrument. Ordinary meaning refers to the dictionary meaning, unless a Special Meaning for the particular word or term appears to have been the intention of the parties. The context in which the meaning is to be discerned includes the entire instrument together with any relevant rules of international law.[22]

Having applied the international interpretive rules to Articles 22 and 23, read together, their ordinary meaning was clear: Notwithstanding that the prisoners once in custody of the State of enforcement are generally subject to the applicable law of that State: (1) the Special Court retains supervision over the conditions in which its prisoners are held; and (2) sentencing decisions made by the SCSL can only be adjusted by the SCSL, or its successor, the RSCSL.

Specifically, the State of enforcement may not change the original sentence imposed by the SCSL, regardless of its domestic law regarding pardon or commutation of sentence. However, the President of the Court, after consultation with the Judges, may authorize 'pardon or commutation of sentence' based on consideration of the interests of justice and general principles of law.[23] The State of enforcement is obligated to notify the President if a prisoner would be eligible for pardon or sentence commutation under domestic law. That notification may trigger the described consideration and consultation by the President, but without presidential authorization, the prisoner must remain incarcerated.

What remained unclear was the meaning of the term 'pardon or commutation of sentence', and whether the President had authority to consider 'pardon or commutation of sentence' in the absence of eligibility under the domestic law of the State of enforcement.

---

[21] R. Gardiner, *Treaty Interpretation* (Oxford International Law Library 2008) 12–19 and cases cited therein.

[22] Art. 31 VCLT reads in relevant part (emphasis added):

General Rule of Interpretation

1. A treaty shall be interpreted in good faith in accordance with *the ordinary meaning* to be given to the terms of the treaty *in their context* and in the light of its *object and purpose*.
2. The context for the purpose of the interpretation of a treaty shall comprise (…) its preamble and annexes:
(…)
3. There shall be taken into account together with the context:
(…)
(c) any *relevant rules of international law* applicable in the relations between the parties
4. A *special Meaning* shall be given to a term if it is established that the parties so intended.

[23] Art. 23 SCSLSt.

5.2 Question 2: What is the Meaning of the Term 'Pardon or Commutation of Sentence'?

The ordinary meaning of pardon is indisputable: pardon is 'an action on the part of the proper authority in a state, releasing an individual from the punishment imposed by sentence or that is due according to law' (*Oxford English Dictionary*). It results in the complete remission of the sentence, and carries the connotation of forgiveness of the penalty.

The ordinary meaning of commutation of a sentence is also clear and involves an actual change of the original sentence to a less severe sentence. The dictionary definitions support this meaning. The *Merriam-Webster* defines commutation in criminal law as – 'a change of a legal penalty or punishment to a lesser one'. Likewise, the *Cambridge Dictionary* affirms that a commutation of sentence occurs 'when a punishment is changed to one that is less severe'. *Blacks Law Dictionary* defines it as 'the executive substitution in a particular case of a less severe punishment for a more severe one that has already been judicially imposed on the defendant'. The *Oxford English Dictionary* declares that to commute is '[t]o change (a punishment, or a sentence) for (to, into) another of less severity, or a fine'.[24]

However, neither Rwanda, nor other States to which convicted persons had been sent by the ICTY and ICTR, and could be sent by the SCSL, routinely offer pardon or commutation of sentence to prisoners under their applicable national law. What they offer is some form of early release.

The term 'pardon or commutation of sentence' appears not only in Article 23 SCSLSt, but also in Article 27 ICTRSt, and Article 28 ICTYSt. None of the statutes refer to early release. The differences between pardon and commutation and the more common forms of early release found in most national legal schemes are important. Pardon results in the sentence being set aside; commutation results in the sentence being reduced; but early release has a more flexible meaning and may occur without any change to the original sentence.

Yet, notwithstanding the significant differences that exist between early release and commutation or pardon, and notwithstanding that early release is never mentioned in the Statute of either the ICTR or the ICTY, both the ICTR and the ICTY issued Practice Directions pursuant to their Rules and Statutes which were entitled 'Practice Direction on the Procedure For the Determination of Applications For Pardon, Commutation of Sentence, and Early Release ...'. One may therefore consider that pardon or commutation of sentence, as understood by these Tribunals, has a special meaning which includes early release. Article 31(4) of the VCLT provides for special

---

[24] The OED provides some examples in old English law: '1642 FULLER Holy & Prof. St. II. xvi. 111 The late custome in some places of commuting whipping into money. a1661 Worthies (1840) I. x. 42 Others ... had their deaths mercifully commuted by our magistrates into banishment. 1788 GIBBON Decl. & F. xliv. §1 (1872) V. 298 Forfeiture was sometimes commuted to a fine. 1844 H. H. WILSON Brit. India III. III. viii. 469 The [capital] sentence was commuted to imprisonment for life. 1844 Brit. Const. x. (1862) 136 The..feudal practice of commuting all punishments whatever for fines.'

meaning as an exception to ordinary meaning of a term: 'A special meaning shall be given to a term if it is established that the parties so intended.'

The parties to the Agreement establishing the SCSL, that is, the UN and the Government of Sierra Leone, expressly stated in Article 14 SCSLSt, which is 'an integral part' of the Agreement, that: 'The Rules of Procedure and Evidence of the International Criminal Tribunal for Rwanda obtaining at the time of the establishment of the SCSL shall be applicable *mutatis mutandis* to the conduct of the legal proceedings before the SCSL.'

When the parties to the Agreement intentionally repeated in Article 23 SCSLSt the language of Article 27 ICTRSt[25] and Article 28 ICTYSt,[26] and dictated in Article 14 SCSLSt that the rules implementing the SCSL Statute were to be applied *mutatis mutandis* with those of the ICTR, they incorporated the content that had been ascribed to 'pardon or commutation of sentence' by those two Tribunals. By January 2002, when the Agreement went into force, that content had a special meaning encompassing not only pardon or commutation of sentence, but also early release, a status which is flexible in application.

Subsequent relevant international law likewise supports this special meaning. Since 2002, both the ICTR and the ICTY have continued to consider forms of early release different from pardon or sentence commutation, and have either granted[27] or refused[28] it on the merits of individual cases. Both Tribunals have cited their respective statutory

---

[25] Art. 27 ICTRSt:

> Pardon or Commutation of Sentences:
>
> If, pursuant to the applicable law of the State in which the convicted person is imprisoned, he or she is eligible for pardon or commutation of sentence, the State concerned shall notify the International Tribunal for Rwanda accordingly. There shall only be pardon or commutation of sentence if the President of the International Tribunal for Rwanda, in consultation with the judges, so decides on the basis of the interests of justice and the general principles of law.

[26] Art. 28 ICTYSt:

> Pardon or commutation of sentences:
>
> If, pursuant to the applicable law of the State in which the convicted person is imprisoned, he or she is eligible for pardon or commutation of sentence, the State concerned shall notify the International Tribunal accordingly. The President of the International Tribunal, in consultation with the judges, shall decide the matter on the basis of the interests of justice and the general principles of law.

[27] See, e.g., *Jokić*, IT-01-42/1-ES (Decision of the President on Request for Early Release, 1 September 2008); *Krajišnik* IT-00-39-ES (Decision of President on Early Release of Momčilo Krajišnik, 26 July 2010); *Zarić* IT-95-9 (Order of the President on the Application for the Early Release of Simo Zarić, 21 January 2004).

[28] See, e.g, *Imanishimwe* ICTR-99-46-S (Decision on Samuel Imanishimwe's Application for Early Release, 30 August 2007); *Ruggiu* ICTR-97-32-S (Decision of the President on the Application for Early Release of Georges Ruggiu, 12 May 2005); *Rutaganira* ICTR-95-IC-T (Decision on Request for Early Release, 2 June 2006); *Rutaganira* ICTR-95-IC-AR (Decision on Appeal of a Decision of the President on Early Release, 24 August 2006); *Rutaganira* ICTR-1995-IC-R73 (Decision on the Motion for Reconsideration of the Denial of Early Release, 13 February 2008); *Serushago* ICTR-98-39-S (Decision of the President on the Application for Early Release of Omar Serushago, 12 May 2005).

articles on 'pardon or commutation of sentence' as authority for their consideration of other forms of early release.

5.3 Question 3: What Triggers Consideration of 'Pardon or Commutation of Sentence'?

Like Article 23 of the (R)SCSLSt, nothing in the Statutes of the ICTR or ICTY expressly provides for review for early release at any time other than when the Court is notified by the enforcing State of the prisoner's eligibility under domestic law. Nevertheless, both Tribunals have relied on their Statutes to authorize review for early release of prisoners even in the absence of eligibility for review in an enforcing State, in order to ensure fairness and the principle of equality.

Typical is the decision in the *Rutaganira* case where the ICTR President considered that he had the authority *proprio moto* to consider early release even though neither the Statute, Rules nor Practice Direction expressly provided it, and there was no State of enforcement:

> [The Review] is admissible even though Mr. Rutaganira's sentence is not being enforced by a designated State, and the Practice Direction of 10 May 2000 does not specify the procedure for early release in cases where convicted prisoners are serving their sentences at the Tribunal's Detention Facility, while awaiting transfer to a designated State.[29]

Similarly, the President of the ICTR, in the *Ruggiu* case, exercised his discretion in reviewing the sentence for early release of the prisoner notwithstanding the absence of notice from a State of enforcement, citing his authority under Article 27.[30] The ICTY has done likewise.[31] Both Tribunals based their authority to consider early release on their respective statutory articles which are identical to Article 23. It can be concluded that under the jurisprudence of the *ad hoc* Tribunals the authority to consider a prisoner for early release always rests in the sentencing tribunal and notice by the State of enforcement that the convicted person is eligible for early release under domestic law is not the exclusive trigger for consideration of early release.

Guided by the sentencing practices of Sierra Leone (as prescribed by Arts 14 and 19(1) SCSLSt) and the jurisprudence of the ICTR and the ICTY, as prescribed by Article 20(3) SCSLSt, and in light of the reading of Articles 22 and 23 together, it was concluded that the President, in consultation with the Judges, had the authority to review the eligibility of a person convicted by the SCSL for early release on the basis of justice and the general principles of law, regardless of whether the prisoner would have been eligible for such consideration under the domestic law of the State of enforcement. Further analysis to determine 'the interests of justice and the general

---

[29] *Rutaganira* ICTR-95-IC-T (Decision on Request for Early Release, 2 June 2006).

[30] *Ruggiu* ICTR-97-32-S (Decision on the President on the Application for Early Release of Georges Ruggiu, 12 May 2005). Likewise, *Serushago* ICTR-98-39-S (Decision of the President on the Application for Early Release of Omar Serushago, 12 May 2005).

[31] *Zarić* IT-95-9 (Order of the President on the Application for the Early Release of Simo Zarić, 21 January 2004), where the prisoner was in the UN detention unit and not in a 'State of enforcement'.

principles of law' relevant to the exercise of that authority was then undertaken. The interests of justice relevant to decisions on early release require consideration of the sentencing priorities of gravity and deterrence and the on-going priority of public safety. The general principles of law relevant to early release include equality of treatment between prisoners and individual rehabilitation.

6. GUIDING VALUES FOR EARLY RELEASE

6.1 Interests of Justice

6.1.1 Gravity and deterrence

The gravity of the offence and the need to deter others from engaging in crimes similar to those for which the person was convicted are paramount considerations in the sentencing decisions of the Special Court.[32] The length of the sentence reflects the Court's judgment that the interests of justice have been served. The sentences handed down by the SCSL for the nine persons convicted of atrocity crimes were reached and affirmed without knowledge of any early release possibilities beyond those under Articles 22 and 23, and without any knowledge by the Chambers as to where these sentences would ultimately be served, or what the applicable law on early release of the enforcing States would be.

Recognition of the gravity of the offences, an express consideration for sentence calculation under Article 19(2), is reflected in the length of the sentences imposed by the Court and the Judges' reasons for its decision in the sentencing judgments accompanying those sentences. The SCSL has made it clear in the length of its sentences and the reasoning in its judgments that crimes against humanity, war crimes against civilians and the atrocities visited upon civilians in the Sierra Leone civil war will not be tolerated by the national or the international community. The individual sentences imposed on each convicted person take into account the gravity of the conduct of that person and the punitive and deterrent response that the Court has considered necessary and appropriate to meet the interests of justice.[33] Therefore preserving the integrity of the sentence is paramount, and affirmed in Article 23. An early release programme that reduces the sentence is not acceptable.

---

[32] 'International criminal tribunals have noted that unlike the case in domestic courts, rehabilitation cannot be considered as a predominant consideration in determining a sentence, as the sentencing aims of national jurisdictions are different from the aims of international criminal tribunals', *Brima et al* SCSL-04-16T-624 (Sentencing Judgment, 19 July 2007) paras 14–17; *Deronjić* IT-02-61-A (Judgment, 20 July 2005) paras 136–137.

[33] J.C. Nemitz, 'Sentencing in International Law', in H. Fischer, A. McDonald and J. Dugard (eds), *International Humanitarian Law Yearbook 2001* (TMC Asser Press 2001) 101: '(…) starting with the International Military Tribunals and continuing with the Ad Hoc Tribunals, the ICC and the newly constituted "Special" sui generis Courts established to prosecute international crimes in Sierra Leone and East Timor, has taken a punitive approach to addressing Makrokriminalität'; M. Drumbl, 'Atrocity, Punishment and International Law', in L. May and J. Brown (eds), *Philosophy of Law: Classic and Contemporary Readings* (John Wiley & Sons 2009) 411:

Any early release programme acceptable to the Court would have to be founded on the principle that the original sentence would not be altered and premised on the Court's authority to determine the place in which the sentence was to be served and its obligation to supervise the conditions of service (Art. 22). Under any acceptable early release scheme, the convicted person would not be freed, but could be transferred to a less restrictive location in which to serve his sentence. That service would continue to be subject to the supervision of the Court under Article 22(2), and could be changed again by the Court pursuant to Article 22(1), including a return to the prison where the convicted person had served the initial portion of the sentence.

As Sierra Leone is a common law country, and a member of the British Commonwealth, a review of other Commonwealth countries' practices was undertaken. The position most aligned with that of the SCSL was articulated by the UK, in its early release (parole) scheme. If an application for early release is granted, it was a reaffirmation of the propriety of the original sentence, the imposition of which continued to be carried out.[34] As explained in the case of *R (on the application of McAlinden) v Secretary of State for Home Department*, 'M had no right to be free at the stage he was released. That was a matter of administrative discretion (…). Any issues of fact did not affect the lawfulness of his detention as that lawfulness had already been determined by the sentencing court'.[35]

6.1.2 Public safety

The 'Interests of Justice' must also take account of the safety of the public. The sentences of the SCSL aim at protecting public safety through conditions of service which make it less likely that the convicted person will reengage in atrocity crimes, pose a threat to those who were involved in their prosecutions, and undermine national reconciliation and peace efforts. Incarceration is one way to ensure public safety, although it is by no means foolproof. If conditions less restrictive than incarceration are to be considered, ensuring public safety is vital. An early release programme that jeopardizes public safety is not acceptable.

There is some scattered reference to the merits of specific deterrence in the jurisprudence of institutions that punish extraordinary international criminals. However, the focus overwhelmingly is on general deterrence, namely the notion that if one person is punished, this will reduce the likelihood that another person in that same place or somewhere else will offend in the future. As an ICTR Trial Chamber intoned, punishment 'dissuade[s] forever (…) others who may be tempted in the future to perpetrate such atrocities (…).' The UN Secretary-General has explicitly endorsed the value of the international criminal tribunals in 'deter[ring] further horrors'.

[34] *R (ex parte McAlinden) v Secretary of State for the Home Dept.* [2010] EWHC 1557 (Admin).

[35] See *R (ex parte McAlinden)* ibid., where tampering with an electronic tag prompted recall and return to prison. *R (on application of Chater) v Secretary of State* [2010] EWHC 2257, recall after allegations that he breached his conditions of early release by remaining near young children in a public library when told to leave (prisoner was convicted of sexual offences).

6.2 The General Principles of Law

The goals of pronouncing sentence differ from goals which the prisoner is expected to achieve while serving the sentence. With gravity and deterrence already addressed by the severity of the sentence imposed, and ensured by commitment to the original sentence, international law requires that in carrying out the sentence, institutions respect the general legal principles of equality of treatment of all convicted persons[36] and the rehabilitation of the prisoner.[37]

6.2.1 Equality of treatment

The practice of other international tribunals are of course relevant when considering a policy for early release for the SCSL/RSCSL convicted persons. However, as to equality of treatment of prisoners, the Special Court shared the concerns expressed by the writers of 'Sentencing and Incarceration in the Ad Hoc Tribunals' (referring to the incarceration agreements reached by the *ad hoc* Tribunals with the different States of enforcement) that:

> [a]s convicted persons are held according to the incarceration laws of the host state, these differences can make a substantial impact on the actual amount of time a convict may serve. A system has developed where the term of sentence that convicted persons will serve is dependent on the laws of the state to which a convicted person is sent.[38]

It was therefore important that criteria be developed that would apply equally to all prisoners for accessing and administering any early release programme, regardless of the State in which the prisoner was incarcerated. To that end, consistent transparent objective criteria needed to be developed.

6.2.2 Rehabilitation

Although not a goal in pronouncing sentence, under the principles of international law, rehabilitation is the primary goal promoted by the service of a sentence. Article 10(3) ICCPR states that, 'the penitentiary system shall comprise treatment of prisoners the essential aim of which shall be their reformation and social rehabilitation'. This principle is reiterated in Rule 65 UNSMR.[39] The Court endorsed this principle for practical as well as philosophical reasons.

---

[36] See also *Zarić* IT-95-9 (Order of the President on the Application for Early Release of Simo Zarić, 21 January 2004): 'Considering that the Conditions for Eligibility Regarding Early Release Applications should be applied equally.'

[37] Art. 10(3) ICCPR.

[38] I.M. Weinberg de Roca and C.M. Rassi, 'Sentencing and Incarceration in the Ad Hoc Tribunals' (2008) 44 *Stanford Journal of International Law* 1 20.

[39] Rule 65 UNSMR:

> The treatment of persons sentenced to imprisonment or a similar measure shall have as its purpose, so far as the length of the sentence permits, to establish in them the will to lead law-abiding and self-supporting lives after their release and to fit them to do so. The treatment shall be such as will encourage their self-respect and develop their sense of responsibility.

It is well understood that the availability of the means to achieve and demonstrate rehabilitation affirms the human dignity of the individual prisoner and reinforces the legitimacy of the rule of law. Because the SCSL/RSCSL is precluded from delivering life sentences, it is assumed that every prisoner will at some point complete service of his sentence and be released unconditionally. As a practical matter, release of a convicted person who has not undergone rehabilitation increases the chance that the person will continue to pose a danger to the community and to reconciliation generally, as well as to victims, witnesses, and authorities connected with the original conviction. Conversely, as SCSL convicted persons have been found to bear the greatest responsibility for the violations of international humanitarian law committed during the civil war, they could, if they affirmatively demonstrate signs of rehabilitation such as remorse and restitution, contribute positively to healing the wounds of the war and advancing reconciliation.

The UNSMR[40] reinforces the connection between public safety and rehabilitation in Rules 58 and 59:

> 58. The purpose and justification of a sentence of imprisonment or a similar measure deprivative of liberty is ultimately to protect society against crime. This end can only be achieved if the period of imprisonment is used to ensure, so far as possible, that upon his return to society the offender is not only willing but able to lead a law-abiding and self-supporting life.
>
> 59. To this end, the institution should utilize all the remedial, educational, moral, spiritual and other forces and forms of assistance which are appropriate and available, and should seek to apply them according to the individual treatment needs of the prisoners.

Because ensuring public safety is vital, rehabilitation has to take into account the nature of violations of international humanitarian law and the impact those violations have on Sierra Leone and its people. It is abundantly clear that service of a sentence within a prison does not eliminate the risk to public safety.[41] An appropriate and targeted rehabilitation programme could improve the attitude and behaviour of the convicted person while incarcerated. A hopeless prisoner is a dangerous prisoner. A conditional early release programme, if carefully constructed, could offer an important incentive for rehabilitation. As noted by the Council of Europe's Committee of Ministers Recommendation (Rec. 2003) 22:

> (…) Conditional release is one of the most effective and constructive means of preventing re-offending and promoting resettlement, providing the prisoner with planned, assisted and supervised reintegration into the community;

---

[40] Adopted by the First UN Congress on the Prevention of Crime and the Treatment of Offenders, held at Geneva in 1955, and approved by the Economic and Social Council by its resolutions 663 C (XXIV) of 31 July 1957 and 2076 (LXII) of 13 May 1977.

[41] Convicted persons Kanu and Kamara were found guilty of contempt for actions taken against protected witnesses while imprisoned in Rwanda. Kanu was convicted on the two counts of offering a bribe to a witness and of otherwise attempting to induce a witness to recant testimony given before the court. Kamara was convicted of trying to induce a witness to change his testimony, and of knowingly disclosing the identity of a protected witness. *Kanu, Kamara et al* SCSL 2011-02-T (Decision, 25 September 2012).

> (…) It should be used in ways that are adapted to individual circumstances and consistent with the principles of justice and fairness … .

It was therefore important that consideration of early release be linked to the prisoner's success in undertaking and achieving rehabilitation that is specifically geared to assuring the safety of the public through refraining from threatening or having others threaten those people associated with the prisoner's conviction, accepting responsibility for past crimes, renouncing previous violations of international law and contributing to peace, reconciliation and restitution. Therefore, any early release programme needed to require that the convicted person produce evidence that he had undertaken and accomplished rehabilitation specific to atrocity crimes and his role in their commission, before any consideration of early release be undertaken. To that end, consistent transparent subjective criteria needed to be developed.

Having in mind the identified 'principles and interests of justice', the Sub-Committee looked at the options for early release. Two options were examined: unconditional early release and conditional early release.

7. OPTIONS FOR EARLY RELEASE

7.1 Unconditional Early Release

The unconditional early release option includes three schemes, remission, amnesty, and judicial discretionary unconditional release. None of these ensure the integrity of the original sentence or the on-going safety of the public.

7.1.1 Remission

Remission involves the automatic early release of a serving prisoner after completion of a legislatively set percentage of the sentence. Remission occurs without consultation with the victims of the crime or the community into which the prisoner is to be released. It does not require the prisoner to meet any conditions following release.[42] Although remission is practised under the Sierra Leone Prisons Act of 1960, it has been rejected by the Special Court in the matter of the *Bangura* case,[43] as Article 22(2) of the SCSLSt and Section 32(1) and (2) of the Ratification Act provide that only the conditions of imprisonment shall be governed by the State of enforcement. Hence the provisions of domestic legislation allowing for remission of sentence do not apply to the sentences imposed by the SCSL.

7.1.2 Amnesty

Amnesty is the forgiveness of the crime and the immediate release of the prisoner and cessation of punishment or control. This is a political rather than a judicial decision.

[42] The period of remission may be reduced by the prison authorities if a prisoner is found guilty of a breach of internal rules or regulations.

[43] *Kanu, Kamara et al* SCSL-11-02-T (Decision on Public Urgent Motion, 7 November 2012).

There is no international political body that can grant amnesty and the SCSLSt states that the SCSL cannot recognize national amnesties for the commission of international crimes.[44]

7.1.3 Judicial Discretionary Unconditional Release (JDUR)

JDUR requires criteria to be met before release is approved, but does not require that continued release be conditioned on behaviour, nor does it provide for return to prison should the conditions not be met. At the time the Sub-Committee considered the available options, the ICTY had engaged in JDUR. Both the ICTY and ICTR had provisions in their RPE (Rule 125 and 126 respectively), which stipulated the criteria the President had to consider in deciding whether to grant early release. The ICTY and the ICTR had adopted nearly identical Rules and Practice Directions.

ICTR Rule 126 provides:

> *General Standards for Granting Pardon or Commutation*
>
> In determining whether pardon or commutation is appropriate, the President shall take into account, inter alia, the gravity of the crime or crimes for which the prisoner was convicted, the treatment of similarly-situated prisoners, the prisoner's demonstration of rehabilitation, as well as any substantial cooperation of the prisoner with the Prosecutor.

In exercising discretion under ICTY Rule 125, the President of the ICTY had ordered the release of serving prisoners convicted by the ICTY on the assessment of their behaviour while in prison and their personal mental and physical condition. The ICTY President had not imposed any post release conditions. The President of the ICTR, relying on this rule, exercised authority to review sentences for early release on the Court's own initiative, but had refused, until recently, all applications for early release based primarily on the gravity of the offence of genocide, for which the prisoners had been convicted.

7.2 Conditional Early Release

The conditional early release option includes two schemes, viz. parole and judicial discretionary conditional release. Conditional early release involves the release of the convicted person to serve part of the sentence in the community subject to his/her agreement to comply with standard and specific conditions of behaviour designed to ensure the safety of the public with provisions in place to monitor compliance with those conditions and reincarcerate the convicted person if there is a breach of those conditions or any danger to the public.

7.2.1 Parole

Parole is a national scheme allowing the convicted person to serve part of his/her sentence in a location other than a prison. Parole is triggered by criteria established by legislation or executive regulation and administered and overseen by agents of the executive branch of government. Parole requires a governmental structure absent in the

---

[44] Art. 10 SCSLSt.

international legal framework, since there are no international legislative or executive entities with equivalent authority.

7.2.2 Judicial discretionary conditional release (JDCR)

Like judicial discretionary unconditional release, JDCR requires criteria to be met before release is approved by the designated judicial authority. However, in addition, JDCR mandates compliance by the convicted person with behavioural conditions imposed by that authority after release, and includes both a mechanism whereby the person's compliance with the conditions may be monitored and a process which makes possible the return of the convicted person to incarceration by the judicial authority should the conditions be violated or unmet. This form of early release can be accomplished within the international legal framework by international judiciary, provided there is cooperation between the international judicial authority and both the State of enforcement and the State to which the convicted person may be conditionally released.

The Sub-Committee concluded that the early release option which best allowed for incorporating the relevant interests of justice and the general principles of law was judicial discretionary conditional early release. In connection with adopting this early release option, and assuring equality of treatment of convicted persons regardless of their location of incarceration and the applicable law of the State of Enforcement, the Sub-Committee recommended an amendment to Rule 124 providing that early release could occur after (and only after) two-thirds of a convicted person's sentence was served. The Plenary of Judges amended Rule 124 on 16 November 2011 to incorporate that suggestion.

The Sub-Committee was further charged with designing a conditional early release programme, consistent with the identified interests of justice and general principles of law. The Sub-Committee accepted the challenge to create a workable programme which:

- Ensured and promoted the safety of individuals, the community and the reconciliation process;
- Encouraged and rewarded rehabilitation of the individual for the specific violations of international law for which he was convicted; and
- Applied equally to all convicted persons.

8. EARLY RELEASE PROGRAMME DESIGN

Because the SCSL was the first International Tribunal to attempt to design a conditional early release programme, the SCSL Sub-Committee was obliged to look beyond the practice of the other tribunals to national programmes, and to consult with outside experts as well as principals within the Court. The Sub-Committee examined the practice in particular of countries in the Commonwealth and observed that many provided for early release or parole subject to a conditional licence, breach of which could lead to recall to custody. It also took on board the observation of the Council of Europe's Committee of Ministers that recognizes: 'That conditional release measures require the support of political leaders, administrative officials, judges, public prosecutors, advocates and the public, who therefore need a detailed explanation as to the reasons for adapting prison sentences.'[45]

The Sub-Committee recognized that the agreement and cooperation of the Government of Sierra Leone was crucial to any programme, since all but one convicted person are citizens of Sierra Leone and would likely seek to return to that country. A member of the Sub-Committee met with the Attorney General to explain the plan and seek input. The government agreed that its authorities would supervise the conditions under which convicted persons might be released to serve their on-going sentence within Sierra Leone, and cooperate in any way necessary with the reporting and violation provisions envisioned by the Court. Equally critical to creating the programme was the cooperation of the government and prison authorities of the States of enforcement. After consultation with Rwandan officials, they agreed to work with the Court to provide rehabilitation programmes within the prison individualized according to the needs of particular prisoners and furnish reports necessary for the Court to make decisions on early release.

The programme that emerged was incorporated into a Practice Direction signed into effect by the President of the SCSL on 1 October 2013.[46] In addition to the Practice Direction, form applications and form orders were created by the Sub-Committee and annexed to the Direction in an effort to simplify the process and underline the critical components that needed to be incorporated at each stage. The salient components of the programme can be highlighted.

8.1 Application for Conditional Early Release

The convicted person must undergo a two-part process. The first stage establishes eligibility for consideration for early release, and its criteria are objective. Failure to meet these criteria precludes the convicted person from proceeding to the second stage, although he is given the opportunity to reapply when he can establish that those objective criteria are met. If the first stage is successfully undertaken, the second stage, entailing collection of information and consideration by the judicial authority, commences. At both stages of the process the burden is on the convicted person to meet the objective and subjective criteria. The criteria are designed to address the identified interests of justice and principles of law: gravity and deterrence; public safety; equality of treatment; and rehabilitation.

Equality of treatment is achieved by applying the same timing, process and criteria to all convicted persons, regardless of where they might be incarcerated or the length of their sentence. The conditions, which speak to the gravity of the offence, are those which require the convicted person to acknowledge in his written application that early conditional release is not an entitlement, that his sentence will not be modified, and that he will be continuing to serve his original sentence. He must further acknowledge his understanding that, just as his conditions in prison were overseen by prison personnel

---

[45] Recommendation (Rec. 2003) 22 Preamble.

[46] See <http://www.rscsl.org/Documents/PRACTICE_DIRECTION_Conditional_Early_Release.pdf> accessed 28 June 2015.

of the State of enforcement, but supervised by the Court, his conditions while serving his sentence in the community will be monitored by a designated agency of the State of enforcement (likely Sierra Leone), and continue to be supervised by the Court. Importantly the convicted person must show in his application that he understands that his continued service of the sentence outside a prison facility is dependent on his compliance with the conditions set by the Court, and that his placement and location in the community is solely determined by the Court and can be changed from the community back to a prison should the President find that the convicted person presents a risk to the safety of any person or that he has violated any condition of his release.

Each of the criteria for early release, as well as the conditions of that release, are related in some way to public safety. Public safety in relation to those convicted of atrocity crimes means the safety not only of the public generally, but particularly the mental and physical safety of the survivors of the crimes for which the person has been found responsible, those involved with his prosecution and convictions, and the people of Sierra Leone for whom peace and reconciliation are essential to their on-going physical and psychological wellbeing. Therefore the convicted person must demonstrate that during his years in prison he not only was able to conform his conduct to the rules and regulations of the prison and refrain from any activity that posed a danger to others in the prison system, but also that he refrained from directly or indirectly interfering with witnesses, victims, and court personnel involved with his conviction, and refrained from words or actions directed at undermining the reconciliation process and the rule of law outside the prison system. The application process further requires that the convicted person acknowledge all protection orders that were issued indefinitely in his original trial, demonstrate that there are no allegations that he has violated any of these orders, and reaffirm his commitment to comply with them.

Rehabilitation, a value in its own right, is also a measure designed to protect the public. The applicant for conditional early release must be able to show that he has undertaken and successfully completed programmes within the prison system. In addition, he must demonstrate that while incarcerated he has accepted his responsibility for the crimes for which he was convicted, shown empathy for his victims, and made a positive contribution to peace and reconciliation in Sierra Leone and the region.[47]

8.2 Consideration for Conditional Early Release

Consideration for conditional early release entails the exercise of discretion by the President in consultation with the original sentencing Judges if they are available, and two other Judges if they are not. The President's discretion is circumscribed by express criteria set out in the Practice Direction, and is directed to whether conditional early release should be granted and, if so, the place and the conditions under which the convicted person should serve his on-going sentence. In reviewing the request for conditional early release, the President has the benefit of written and oral reports from

---

[47] Examples are given in the Practice Direction and include, but are not limited to, public acknowledgment of guilt, public support of a peace project, public apology to the victims, victim restitution.

the convicted person as well as other interested parties, including victims and witnesses involved in the original trial, members of the community into which the person is seeking to be released, monitors who will be responsible for supervising conditions, prison authorities in the State of enforcement and special assessments if ordered. The exercise of discretion either to grant or refuse conditional early release must be explained by the President in a reasoned decision which must address at a minimum five specific points designed to explain, among other things, how he/she has considered the safety of the public and the level of rehabilitation that has been accomplished by the convicted person. Although appeal from a decision denying the application is not possible, reapplication is. In addition, no release occurs until the Court is satisfied that the convicted person understands his conditions and agrees in writing, before witnesses, to comply with them.

8.3 Monitoring and Violation of Conditions of Early Release

Supervision in the community is the responsibility of named authorities of the State of enforcement who are obligated to report periodically to the Court. The President can in addition ask for progress reports at any time. The monitoring agency has authority to return the convicted person physically to the Court should there be reason to believe that a condition is violated or the convicted person poses a risk of harm to another person. Resolution of an allegation of violation must be fast tracked by the Court and, if found by the President after a hearing, the President has the discretion to revoke the Order for Conditional release and re-incarcerate; revoke and issue new conditions; or revoke and reinstate the original conditions.

9. IMPLEMENTATION OF THE EARLY RELEASE PROGRAMME

On 3 December 2013 the SCSL, having completed its mandate by finalizing all hearings and appeals transitioned to a residual mechanism[48] known as the RSCSL. A new statute, the RSCSLSt was promulgated. Article 23 of that Statute provided:

> 1. Imprisonment may be served in Sierra Leone or in any of the States which have concluded with the Residual Special Court for Sierra Leone an agreement for the enforcement of sentences, and which have indicated to the Registrar of the Special Court their willingness to accept convicted persons.
> 2. Conditions of imprisonment, whether in Sierra Leone or in a third State, shall be governed by the law of the State of enforcement subject to the supervision of the Special Court. The State of enforcement shall be bound by the duration of the sentence, subject to article 24 of the present Statute.
>
> (…)

Rule 124 RSCSL RPE (Pardon, commutation of sentences and early release) differed from Rule 124 above and, in keeping with the Practice Direction, provided:

---

48 See <www.rscsl.org> accessed 28 June 2015.

> There shall only be pardon or commutation of sentence or early release if the President of the RSCSL, in accordance with Article 24 RSCSLSt and in consultation with the Judges who imposed the sentence where possible, and after considering the position of the Prosecutor, which shall incorporate the interests of Prosecution witnesses and victims, as well as the convicted person individually or through counsel, so decides on the basis of the interests of justice and the general principles of law but any early release shall only occur after the prisoner has served a minimum of two-thirds of his original sentence.

As the applications for early release submitted to the President of the RSCSL were received after December 2013 those applications were subject to Rule 124 of the RSCSL RPE. An earlier application by Moinana Fofana had been ruled as premature.[49]

Since Rule 124 came into effect two convicted persons have applied for conditional early release. They were Eric Koi Senessie, who was convicted of contempt of court pursuant to Rule 77 and Moinana Fofana, who was convicted of war crimes, crimes against humanity and breaches of customary international law. Senessie had served sentence in the SCSLDF in Freetown, and on 10 May 2013, the Republic of Sierra Leone was designated as the State in which Senessie was to serve his sentence.[50] Fofana served sentence in Mpanga Prison, Rwanda.

The two convicted persons first applied for legal aid.[51] There was no provision for legal representation for applications for early release in Article 17 RSCSLSt or in Rule 45 RSCSL RPE.[52] The Sub-Committee were aware of this and had endeavoured to draft the application form to provide simple and basic information viz. name and district of the convicted person, his grounds for making the application and the period of both sentence and incarceration.

However the first applicant, Eric Koi Senessie, asked for legal assistance and it became apparent that Senessie required some assistance in completing his application. After considering his plea for legal aid and in consultation with the other Judges the President granted him legal counsel for the purpose of his application only. Following an assessment of the application and the views of the sentencing Judge, the President ruled that Senessie was eligible for consideration for early release.[53]

Thereafter in accordance with Rule 124 the President consulted with the sentencing Judge, the Prosecutor and, through the Registrar, the community in his home area

---

[49] The application was made on 21 January 2013 and is referred to in *Fofana* SCSL-04-14-ES 1264 (Public Decision on Moinina Fofana's Eligibility for Conditional Early Release, 24 April 2014).

[50] The Supplementary Agreement between the Special Court and the Government of Sierra Leone on the Enforcement of Sentences for Contempt signed on 26 March 2013.

[51] *Senessie* SCSL-11-01-ES-035 (Decision of the President on Application for Conditional Early Release, 4 June 2014) and *Fofana* SCSL-04-14-ES-1264 (Decision of the President on Application for Conditional Early Release, 11 August 2014).

[52] Rule 45 imposes a duty on the Defence Office to provide advice, assistance and representation to suspects being questioned by the RSCSL or its agents, accused persons appearing before the RSCSL and convicted persons conducting review proceedings before the RSCSL only.

[53] *Senessie* SCSL-11-01-ES-030 (Public Redacted Decision of the President on Eric Senessie's Eligibility for Conditional Early Release, 24 April 2014).

where Senessie stated that he wished to live if released early. The decision of the President[54] made clear that:

> [a] Convicted Person has no entitlement to Conditional Early Release from his or her sentence. The President merely considers, on the basis of facts supplied and the applicable law, whether it is safe and proper for the convict to serve the remaining part of the sentence other than in prison. That is why it is the convict who initiates the application for consideration for Conditional Early Release.[55]

The report of the Registrar to the President showed that interviews were conducted with relevant individuals including community activists, representatives of civil society, local government officials, traditional leaders, women's groups, youth groups, Chiefs and ordinary citizens through questionnaires, phone-in Radio programmes and Town Hall meetings. Other meetings were held in both locations with victims of the war from War Wounded and Amputee Camps and their views were recorded and a general assessment of the views collected from both locations revealed support for conditional early release being granted.[56]

The Registrar also consulted the victim/witnesses who gave evidence at the trial of Senessie. The President found that:

> [a]ll five of them expressed concerns about their security citing fears of being targeted either by Senessie himself or by members of his family if he was released. Nevertheless, the witnesses did not express opposition to the Conditional Early Release of Senessie. Those fears and security concerns were echoed by the Prosecutor who strongly submits that the interests and needs of prosecution witnesses must be a primary concern in considering whether to extend mercy to convicted persons.[57]

These submissions were made notwithstanding that Senessie was convicted of contempt rather than war crimes or crimes against humanity and reports showed that he had complied with all programmes for his rehabilitation.

The President also set out in detail the reports of the prison authorities on Senessie's behaviour while in prison and matters which the Prosecutor had referred to in her submissions.

Having comprehensively documented all of the reports and information, the President ruled:

> I find that the concerns of victims, witnesses and their families will be adequately addressed and taken into consideration if the application for Conditional Early Release is granted. I find no basis for the fear expressed by the Prosecution that the concerns of witnesses will not be adequately addressed and given priority by the Police. I have weighed the negative information against the favourable one and I am satisfied that the balance tilts towards the conclusion that Senessie has been substantially rehabilitated whilst in Prison. It is my view that he has, among other things, largely conformed to Prison directions and rules, has

---

[54] *Senessie* SCSL-11-01-ES-035 (Decision of the President on Application for Conditional Early Release, 4 June 2014).

[55] Ibid., para 15.

[56] Ibid., paras 21–22.

[57] Ibid., para 28.

> undertaken courses and work in constructive use of his time in Prison, and has not exhibited violent behaviour during his incarceration.[58]

The President concluded that, 'I find that Senessie has shown clear and convincing evidence that he will be a safe member of society and that he will comply with the terms imposed by a Conditional Early Release Agreement' and granted the application on condition that Senessie complete and execute a Conditional Early Release Agreement. No further special conditions were imposed.

After this process was completed Senessie decided he did not wish to sign a Conditional Early Release Agreement and opted to stay in detention for the short remaining period of his sentence.

The documentation relating to Fofana shows that he had originally applied for consideration for conditional release in January 2013. This was ruled as premature[59] and he reapplied on 7 March 2014. The President decided Fofana was eligible for consideration for release and directed the Registrar to compile all the information required under the Practice Direction and Fofana to file the information required of him.

Fofana was a former member of the CDF and was its National Director of War. He was charged (with others) with eight counts of war crimes and crimes against humanity. Fofana was convicted on four counts of war crimes and acquitted on four counts of crimes against humanity by a majority of Trial Chamber I of the Special Court on 2 August 2007. He was subsequently sentenced to a total term of six years' imprisonment. On appeal, Fofana's acquittal of crimes against humanity was overturned and a majority of the Appeals Chamber found him guilty on five counts and increased his sentence to a total term of 15 years.[60]

On 12 August 2009, the Republic of Rwanda was designated as the State in which Fofana was to serve sentence.[61]

The decision on that application shows that the President stressed the gravity of the crimes for which Fofana was convicted and quoted from the Appeal Chamber Decision.[62]

---

[58] Ibid., para 30.

[59] *Fofana* SCSL-04-14-ES 1264 (Public Decision on Moinina Fofana's Eligibility for Conditional Early Release, 24 April 2014).

[60] *Fofana and Kondewa* SCSL-04-14-ES 1270 (Public Redacted Decision of the President on Application for Conditional Early Release, 24 April 2014).

[61] *Fofana* SCSL-04-14-ES-8S2 (Order Designating State in Which Moinina Fofana is to Serve his Sentence, 1 August 2009).

[62] *Fofana and Kondewa* SCSL-04-14-ES 1270 (Public Redacted Decision of the President on Application for Conditional Early Release, 24 April 2014) quoting at para 15.

> Many of these crimes, as described in the Judgment, were of a very serious nature, and were committed against innocent civilians. The Chamber considers actions such as the mutilation and the targeted killing of Limba civilians and the killing and mutilation of Chief Kafala (whom the CDF Kamajors considered a collaborator) in Koribondo, to be indicative of the brutality of the offences committed by Fofana's subordinates. The Chamber also notes the gruesome murder of two women in Koribondo who had sticks inserted and forced into their genitals until they came out of their mouths. The women were then disembowelled, and while their guts were used as checkpoints, parts of their entrails were eaten.

The Judges of the Trial and Appeals Chamber were consulted. One Judge was of the view that Fofana's statements were unacceptable, some were supportive of the application but others expressed serious reservations mainly because Fofana has not, at any stage, acknowledged his own responsibility and the leadership role he played in the armed conflict. Fofana's own words were quoted. He acknowledged that he fought the rebels (RUF/SLA and the AFRC) but said that he 'honestly demonstrated my remorse during my trial and after to the Court, all of Sierra Leone and the Country at large'.

For apology, Fofana stated: 'I sincerely apologise (sic) to the victims because of my role in the Sierra Leone Civil Conflict'.[63]

There was consultation in the proposed residential area, with chiefs, traditional leaders, local government officials, religious leaders, members of civil society, leaders of women's and youth groups and members of Fofana's family as part of the submissions required under Article 6(A) of the Practice Direction. Most of the people consulted were not averse to the grant of conditional early release to Fofana if he opted to settle either in Bo City or Gbap. However the Prosecutor was opposed and voiced concerns. Her major concern related to witnesses and their families who are also members of the community. She submitted that 'the interests of justice and proper administration of justice require the provision of a sense of security and actual security to witnesses and victims as mitigation for early release' and 'the interests of the witnesses and victims should be given more weight than that of members of the community who viewed Fofana as a hero rather than a convicted war criminal who was responsible for their suffering'.[64]

The President found that most of the witnesses interviewed by the Witnesses and Victims Section on behalf of the Prosecutor requested, among other things, that the Court ensure that Fofana be strictly monitored and that regular follow ups and visitations be made to them to assure them of their safety if the application is granted. The Prosecutor proposed conditions in the event of release being granted.

Having considered the foregoing views and the reports, statements provided by prison personnel concerning Fofana's conduct while in custody, the rulings of the Trial and Appeal Chamber (particularly the principle of totality[65] enunciated by the Appeal Chamber) the President ruled:

> Upon consideration of those principles, the Statute, Rules, Practice Direction and the totality of the material placed before me, I have come to the conclusion that the application be and is hereby granted subject to service by the applicant of a further period of six (6) months from the date of this Decision, in prison custody. Within those six months, the Registrar of this court in conjunction with the Prison Authorities in Rwanda, shall conduct training for Fofana and certify that he has, as far as his level of intelligence can take him, understood the nature of the crimes for which he was convicted in that they were serious violations of International Humanitarian Law, Geneva Conventions and Crimes Against Humanity; understood that what

[63] Ibid., para 18.

[64] Ibid., paras 21, 25–26.

[65] Ibid., para 45 cites *Fofana and Kondewa* SCSL-04-14-A-829 (Judgment, 28 May 2008). The totality principle requires that 'a sentence must reflect the inherent gravity of the totality of the criminal conduct of the accused, giving due consideration to the particular circumstances of the case and to the form and degree of the participation of the accused'.

> may be a legitimate cause does not justify the use of illegal means; and that he acknowledges his own responsibility and the leadership role he played in the armed conflict in Sierra Leone.

Release was also conditional on Fofana agreeing to and complying with the standard conditions provided at Article 6(C) of the Practice Direction and the further conditions that:

- he apologise for his wrongful conduct, acknowledge his guilt and show remorse;
- neither he nor any person acting with his consent or authority shall, directly or indirectly, approach any of the witnesses in future, try to harm, intimidate or otherwise interfere with any witness in any way;
- he conduct himself honourably and peacefully in the community and not engage in secret meetings intended to plan civil unrest or join local politics, strictly observe the reporting schedules set by the Monitoring Authority and the Registrar, and
- personally report to such centre or centres as are designated, at least TWICE every month. Further regular visits are to be made by the office of the Registrar to provide assurance of security to vulnerable former witnesses.[66]

On 12 March 2015 Fofana completed the work directed by the President and, as stated in the RSCSL press release,[67] 'Fofana appeared this afternoon before RSCSL Registrar Binta Mansaray and confirmed that he understood the conditions of his release and was willing to abide by them'. Ms. Mansaray then arranged for his transport to Bo, the capital of Sierra Leone's Southern Province. Although Fofana will reside in Bo, he must still complete his sentence for his convictions for war crimes and crimes against humanity that he committed against the people of Sierra Leone, Ms. Mansaray said 'he has agreed to abide by the conditions imposed by Justice Waki'. Fofana had been ordered to acknowledge his guilt, publicly apologize, and show remorse. These conditions included requirements that Fofana cooperate with a Monitoring Authority, obey all orders of the Court, refrain from committing any crime, and to pose no threat or interfere with former witnesses, nor engage in secret meetings to plan civil unrest or join politics.

The introduction and application of the Practice Direction shows the SCSL's determination to comply with the UNSMR while considering fully the views of witnesses, victims and the community where a released convicted person will reside and the principle of totality in sentencing. The two cases completed also serve to illustrate that ultimately it is for the convicted person to agree and to comply with the conditions of any conditional early release.

---

66 Ibid., para 49.

67 'CDF Convict Moinina Fofana Granted Conditional Early Release, Will Complete His Sentence in Bo' (RSCSL Press Release, 13 March 2015).

10. SUPERVISION OF PRISONERS SERVING SENTENCES

As noted above the duties of the RSCSL are not limited to consideration of prisoners' eligibility for early release, but include the supervision of sentences of all persons convicted by the Court. Letters of complaint to the media from SCSL prisoners serving sentence in Rwanda and a 'threat' to boycott a hearing required the RSCSL to address a question which is fundamental to its concept and implementation of oversight: Is there an international prison or an international prisoner?

This question was considered by the SCSL in the *Hassan Papa Bangura et al* contempt case.[68] Two of the defendants in that matter were convicted persons serving sentence in Mpanga Prison, Rwanda and two were former AFRC colleagues then resident in Freetown. The trial was held in Freetown with video link to Kigali, Rwanda and, during the defence hearing of Kamara and Kanu, in Kigali with video link to Freetown.[69] Early in the hearing Kamara and Kanu said they were not prepared to attend the hearing because they had been moved from Mpanga prison to the Central Prison in Kigali. This had been arranged for the practical reasons that the travel from Mpanga to Kigali took a minimum of two hours each way and the two-hour time difference between Freetown and Kigali had to be accommodated in order that all the defendants hear the evidence.

Kamara and Kanu objected to the transfer to Kigali Central Prison and threatened to boycott the trial. In Kamara's words[70] he was under an international minimum standard when serving sentence and was 'never told (…) that he should go to a local prison to serve his prison term'. He 'challenged' being 'referred' to a local prison, for health reasons saying:

> I can't accept to be in that condition. I can't accept to be in that condition. Otherwise I won't attend this Court, because my health is a priority. I have a long jail term that I am going to serve. I need to protect my health. I can't be in a public place where you have many prisoners, where so many people are using one or two toilets (…) I am not sure that I can adjust to such standards.

He felt that 'this local prison, (is) adding more jail conditions to me apart' from the sentence imposed on him. Co-Accused Kanu joined with and 'buttressed' his co-accused's position saying that he 'could not adjust to such standards' and 'I do not see why they should take us to a local prison, where there are about 7,000 to 8,000 prisoners and only one toilet' (Kanu and Kamara each had their own accommodation and facilities in Mpanga).

---

[68] *Bangura, Kargbo, Kanu, Kamara* SCSL-11-02-T-691 (Decision on public with confidential annexes Prosecution motion for an investigation into contempt of the Special Court for Sierra Leone, 18 March 2011).

[69] The premises for the hearing in Kigali were given by the kind cooperation of the International Criminal Tribunal for Rwanda, the travel and other facilities by the kind cooperation of the Prison Authorities and Government of Rwanda.

[70] *Bangura, Kargbo, Kanu, Kamara* SCSL-11-02-T (Pre-Trial Conference Transcript, 16 June 2012) 42–5.

An ex tempore ruling[71] held that there is not a status of 'an international prison' and a status of 'national prison' that involve different standards of treatment. Likewise, there is not any difference between an 'international prisoner' and a person who is detained following conviction by a court of national jurisdiction, be it a high court or a magistrate's court.

Similar obiter that, '[t]he rights and restrictions applicable to persons convicted by international courts do not differ from the rights and restrictions applicable to persons convicted in national jurisdictions' was made in the matter of *Charles Ghankay Taylor*.[72] All convicted persons have an equal right to be humanely treated be they convicted of war crimes, crimes against humanity, murder or shoplifting. Being convicted by an international war crimes tribunal for breaches of the Geneva Conventions or crimes against humanity does not entitle a convicted person to accommodation superior to that of any other convicted person.

11. CONCLUSION

The SCSL and its successor the RSCSL have been confronted with interesting post-sentencing issues. The Practice Direction on Early Conditional Release will undoubtedly generate additional issues for further consideration, as its application reveals gaps and necessitates fine-tuning. As more *ad hoc* International Courts transition into residual status and the ICC generates more convictions, there is the opportunity to create a jurisprudence of post sentencing rights and obligations, an under-developed area of international criminal law. However, like all issues of first impression confronting international courts, the challenge will be to ensure that the jurisprudence advanced is principled and harmonious.

---

71 Ibid.

72 *Taylor* RSCSL-03-01-ES-1435 (Public Redacted Decision on Public with Public and Confidential Annexes Charles Ghankay Taylor's Motion for Termination of Enforcement of Sentence in the United Kingdom and for Transfer to Rwanda, 30 January 2015).

PART VII

ALTERNATIVES TO CUSTODIAL PUNISHMENT

So far, this Handbook has focused on systems used to detain and imprison persons accused of, or convicted for the commission of international crimes by international courts. There are however other mechanisms for dealing with such crimes. This section looks at other methods that can be used to address the harms caused during conflict.

In Chapter 16, Mark Drumbl questions the dominance of imprisonment as the penalty of choice for persons convicted of international crimes. His critique of this status quo, and exploration of alternative penalties, draws on indigenous, restorative and transitional perspectives. Advocating a broader understanding of sanction in such situations, he looks at ways to diversify the range of sanctions available to address atrocity crimes both within and beyond penal facilities. The chapter therefore highlights the strengths and weaknesses of supplementary or substitutory penalties, including community service, removal of civil rights, traditional cleansing ceremonies, qualified amnesties, private civil lawsuits, and the imposition of State and organisational responsibility.

Rather than look outside the current system, the next chapter in this section focuses on non-custodial means of addressing the harm caused by international crime that exist within the ICC's legal framework. In Chapter 17, Conor McCarthy examines the ICC's scheme for victim redress, drawing on recent jurisprudence and reports to discuss the mechanisms for and purposes of both the reparations system and the Trust Fund for Victims. Given its non-punitive nature, McCarthy explores the role that this scheme does (or should) play within the ICC's penal regime, and the obstacles the Court faces in discharging its mandate in relation to victim redress.

16. International punishment from 'other' perspectives

Mark A. Drumbl

1. INTRODUCTION

When it comes to punishment, international criminal courts and tribunals predominantly turn to imprisonment. While courtrooms are iconically used to prosecute suspects, jailhouses are reflexively deployed to sanction and discipline. To be sure, contemporary international criminal courts and tribunals can award restitutionary remedies (i.e. return to victims of property, proceeds, and assets acquired directly or indirectly from the convict's criminal conduct), forfeiture, and fines.[1] In practice, however, these possibilities remain spectral at best.[2] Restitution, fines, and forfeiture, moreover, can only be awarded in addition to imprisonment. Reparations are also a possibility in some instances. For example, the Trust Fund for Victims (TFV) – established by the ICCSt – has begun to support reparations projects (notably, through collective grants funded by donor States). Since this reparative approach to post-conflict justice is discussed in Chapter 17 of this book, it will not be repeated here. Notwithstanding some cause for optimism about the TFV's activities, reparative justice nonetheless remains peripheral to the implementation of international criminal law and, according to Sara Kendall, therefore remains more liminal than actual.[3]

The bottom line is that at the international level incarceration has emerged as the dominant, preferred, presumptive, and nearly exclusive penalty for persons convicted of serious international crimes.[4] International punishment means custodial sanction – this is axiomatically taken as an assured verity. Unsurprisingly, then, most of this book is given over to discussing incarceration – as it should, in light of the quasi-monopoly

---

[1] See R. Young, 'Fines and forfeiture in international criminal justice', Chapter 5 in this volume.

[2] For discussion of the historical and current neglect of the remedy of forfeiture in international criminal law generally, see M.G. Martínez, 'Forfeiture of Assets at the International Criminal Court: The Short Arm of International Criminal Justice' (2014) 12 *Journal of International Criminal Justice* 193 (arguing specifically that the ICC's legal regime regarding forfeiture is one of 'poor design and (...) excessive restrictions that produce[s] what may be termed as an amputated penalty, which is unlikely to be used in future cases' and that this stands in contrast with the recognition of the high remedial value of forfeiture among many municipal criminal justice systems).

[3] S. Kendall, 'Liminal Justice: Recasting International Criminal Law' (draft paper presented to the International Studies Association Annual Meeting, Toronto, 2014) (on file with the author).

[4] Cf. R. Mulgrew, *Towards the Development of the International Penal System* (Cambridge University Press 2013) 11 ('The primary penalty imposed by contemporary international criminal courts is imprisonment. International criminal courts now routinely impose custodial sanctions on those convicted of international crimes').

custodial sanction exerts in the law-in-practice of international institutions and the reality that imprisonment, particularly of those most responsible, seems particularly fitting for their grievous conduct. When national institutions are called upon to punish individuals convicted of genocide, crimes against humanity, and systematic war crimes, the national penological framework of the State in question governs the punishment that is meted out. Once again, incarceration emerges as the preferred modality of punishment (in part because of norm-generation at the international level), although greater diversity arises at national levels, including in some instances community service, civic consequences, and tort-based damages.

The normalization of – in fact, predilection for – custodial punishment at the international level, while understandable, also leads to an under-appreciation of the myriad alternative fashions in which penalty can be assigned to persons and entities implicated in the commission of extraordinary international crimes. This chapter therefore explores a range of penalties that present as alternatives to custodial punishment, in particular, those which are local, indigenous, restorative, or transitional in provenance. The international legal imagination largely 'others' these alternatives; it does so through its dogmatic insistence that the best way to fight impunity is to incarcerate offenders. 'Othering' protects the *status quo* and liberal legalist sensibilities. But 'othering' also occasions opportunity costs and leaves avenues unexamined. It narrows legal pluralism to questions of criminal process and the imposition of custodial punishment, rather than a richer examination of how a variety of overlapping mechanisms – legal and extra-legal – can be deployed to promote shared objectives of accountability, justice, and transition. This process of 'othering' also stunts critical reflection on what, exactly, is meant by sanction. Rather than focusing entirely on the punitive aspects of sanction, perhaps thought could be given to conceptualizing sanction elastically as redress, restoration, and denunciation. In this vein, then, sanction could be seen as promoting a panoply of other goals: compensation, reparation, reproach, the cessation of hostilities, demobilization and decommissioning, acknowledging of wrongdoing and apologizing therefore, fulfilling civic duty, rebuilding relationships, cleansing and rebirth, service to solidify the post-conflict State rather than drain resources through incarceration, and constitutional bargains to protect the interests of the oppressed through consociationalism or positive action programmes. None of these goals are obvious offshoots of international criminal law as presently conceptualized. But this does not mean that these goals cannot become compatible with international criminal law as re-imagined to instantiate a broader vision of international criminal justice.

The reformist ambitions of this chapter proceed along two tracks. First, how can greater diversification of sanction arise within the jailhouse? And, second, which forms of sanction may lie beyond the jailhouse? This chapter thereby explores how existing custodial sentences could be made more effective and then inquires whether penalties that transcend custodial punishment could fulfil valuable goals.[5] In order to be more

[5] The United Nations Standard Minimum Rules for Non-custodial Measures (the Tokyo Rules, specifically Rule 8), GA Res. 45/110 (14 December 1990), geared towards ordinary crimes committed under national criminal law, might be a helpful starting point to think about diversifying sanction in the very different context of extraordinary international crimes.

than just cosmetic, however, any such exploration must predicate itself upon a commitment to reconceive the meaning of punishment and, in this vein, take a second look at restorative, reintegrative, rehabilitative, and transitional justice objectives and methodologies. Critically interrogating the meaning and form of punishment also facilitates other objectives. For example, a move by internationalist frameworks to include penalties other than incarceration may promote the democratic legitimacy of the architecture of post-conflict justice by incorporating sanctioning mechanisms that operate at local and indigenous levels. Such a retooling would better involve the 'faces at the bottom of the well' in the formulation and operation of international legal interventions and adjudication[6] and, thereby, reflect the diversity of human experiences.[7] Pluralizing hegemonic understandings of penalty would, furthermore, permit the involvement of actors other than the most obviously guilty or responsible – for example, low-level perpetrators, mid-career administrators, corporate financiers, and civilians – whose participation in atrocity tends to be overlooked by international penal frameworks even though this participation is a condition precedent for atrocity to become truly massive in scope. In this regard, diversification of sanction offers victims a richer palette of accountability while facilitating rehabilitation and resocialization.

2. WHY PUNISH EXTRAORDINARY INTERNATIONAL CRIMINALS?

Retribution and general deterrence emerge within the practice of international criminal courts and tribunals as the two most frequently cited punishment goals.[8] Among these

---

[6] D. Bell, *Faces at the Bottom of the Well: The Persistence of Racism* (Basic Books 1992).

[7] On the need for international criminal law to protect human diversity, see S.M.H. Nouwen and W.G. Werner, 'Monopolising Global Justice: International Criminal Law as Challenge to Human Diversity' (draft paper presented to the International Studies Association Annual Meeting, Toronto, 2014) (on file with the author).

[8] *Katanga* ICC-01/04-01/07 (Décision relative à la peine (article 76 du Statut), 23 May 2014) para 38 ('[*L*]*a peine a donc deux fonctions importantes: le châtiment d'une part, c'est-à-dire l'expression de la réprobation sociale qui entoure l'acte criminal et son auteur et qui est aussi une manière de reconnaitre le préjudice et les souffrances causées aux victims; la dissuasion d'autre part, dont l'objectif est de détourner de leur project d'éventuels candidats à la perpétration de crimes similaires*.'); *Stakić* IT-97-24-A (Sentencing Judgment, 22 March 2006) 402 (stating that 'the Appeals Chamber notes that the jurisprudence of the Tribunal and the ICTR consistently points out that the two main purposes of sentencing are deterrence and retribution'); *Marqués* 09/2000 (Dili Dist. Ct. Serious Crimes Spec. Panel, Judgment, 11 December 2001) 979:

> The penalties imposed on accused persons found guilty by the Panel are intended, on the one hand, as retribution against the said accused, whose crimes must be seen to be punished (*punitur quia peccatur*). They are also intended to act as deterrence; namely, to dissuade forever, others who may be tempted in the future to perpetrate such atrocities by showing them that the international community shall not tolerate such serious violations of law and human rights (*punitur ne peccetur*).

two, however, retribution assumes a more influential declaratory role. In some instances, to be sure, international judgments fail to refer to any sentencing objectives at all.[9]

Notwithstanding the many facets of retributivist theory, one shared thread is the notion that the infliction of punishment rectifies the moral balance, in particular, when imposed through public condemnation of the criminal conduct.[10] Crudely put, the perpetrator deserves to be punished. Punishment is to be proportionate to the extent of the harm caused by the perpetrator's criminal conduct and also to the perpetrator's degree of responsibility. In international crimes, to be sure, grievous harms may be caused by persons with attenuated intent. This apparent paradox arises because of the collective nature of the violence, the deflection of authority within groups, the pressure of following orders, and the normalization of violence under rubrics of self-defence or group survival. Hence tensions may arise between these two proportionality assessments. In any event, international tribunals have emphasized that 'retribution should not be misunderstood as a way of expressing revenge or vengeance,'[11] leading to a conceptualization of retribution as the 'expression of condemnation and outrage of the international community.'[12] On this note, the moral balance is not seen as exclusive to the perpetrator and victims; the international community, as well, is victimized – hence the very notion of a crime against humanity. In sum, then, this breach of the global order – this rupture of *jus cogens* – deontologically calls out for a broader form of denunciation.

In this latter regard, retributive motivations flirt with the goals of expressivism, which presents as another penological rationale in international criminal law. The expressivist punishes to strengthen faith in the rule of law among the general public (including the aggressor community), as opposed to punishing simply because the perpetrator deserves it or will be deterred by it. Expressivism also transcends retribution and deterrence in claiming as a central goal the edification of historical narratives, the authentication of the violence through judicial text, and the public dissemination thereof.

General deterrence considers that the purpose of prosecuting and punishing those who commit mass atrocity is utilitarian in nature, that is, to dissuade others (in the same jurisdiction, elsewhere, or anywhere) from re-offending.[13] From a general deterrence perspective, punishment is inflicted because of the consequentialist effect of reducing the incidence of crime.

On occasion, judges on international criminal courts and tribunals also refer to other penological rationales, to wit, rehabilitation, incapacitation, restoration, and reconciliation. These rationales, however, are not particularly influential. Rehabilitation is among the more frequently referenced of this group of subjacent objectives, but is often

---

[9] *Rugambarara* ICTR-0059-T (Judgment, 16 November 2007).

[10] See generally H.L.A. Hart, *Punishment and Responsibility* (Clarendon Press 1968) 234–5.

[11] *Kordić and Čerkez* IT-95-14/2-A (Judgment, 17 December 2004) para 1075; *Katanga* ICC-01/04-01/07 (Sentencing Judgment, 23 May 2004) para 38.

[12] *Momir Nikolić* IT-02-60/1-S (Sentencing Judgment, 2 December 2003) para 86.

[13] Specific deterrence implies that punishing the individual offender will deter recidivism in his or her specific case. The focus of international criminal law, however, remains oriented towards general deterrence.

described as not deserving of undue weight.[14] Reconciliation, generally speaking, has not received much more than lip-service, although it arose in the 2014 *Katanga* judgment, where an ICC Trial Chamber actively recognized the convict's *post hoc* efforts to demobilize and disarm child soldiers as a mitigating factor in his eventual sentence of 12 years.[15] Restorative justice remains particularly marginal within the law-in-practice of international courts and tribunals. This neglect is somewhat perplexing insofar as retributive and restorative justice have some overlap: as Mulgrew observes, both 'share the morally intuitive foundation that an imbalance has been caused by the wrong-doing of the offender, who owes something to victims, and both attempt to restore this balance by addressing accountability through censuring reproachable behaviour and appealing to responsibility'.[16] Nonetheless, important differences also emerge between these penological ambitions. Restorative justice concerns itself with social peace, victim healing, repairing the actual harms caused, promoting dialogue, reconstructing relationships (individual and collective), navigating ongoing disputes, and reintegrating offenders, bystanders, and victims. Mulgrew observes that 'restorative communication encourages offenders to give up a passive stance in relation to responsibility and, in contrast to retributive processes, demands that a convicted person acknowledges and accepts liability for criminal acts and omissions as a non-negotiable pre-condition for dialogue'.[17] Restorative methodologies may be particularly appropriate for lower-level offenders in situations of mass atrocity. In its current instantiation, international criminal law and its trickle down effects into national socio-legal fabrics tend to ignore this important constituency. Certain transitional justice modalities operative at the national level (such as truth commissions, public inquiries, and customary cleansing ceremonies) invoke tools such as apologies, community service, unearthing the truth, qualified amnesties, re-education, and shaming – each of which may much better serve reintegrative, rehabilitative, restorative and reconciliatory goals.[18]

To be sure, one of the shortcomings of restorative justice is that it may pressure the victims to forgive the offender, or at least to accord the offender the space to repent, which may withdraw from the victim the power of moral condemnation over the offender. The ambiguity and malleability of restorative justice processes may be hurtful to victims. And yet another shortcoming is the reality that grievous international crimes may simply be too much for restorative methodologies to bear. What would restorative justice look like in the case of the destruction of an entire village? In the case of sexual torture? In the case of a soldier who amputates the hands of hundreds of civilians? Another important limitation to restorative justice, as was the case in Rwanda, is the fact that the community against which the offences were committed may not be the same community into which the perpetrator is to be reintegrated, even in the case of

---

[14] *Milutinović et al* IT-05-87-T (Judgment, 26 February 2009) para 1146.

[15] *Katanga* ICC-01/04-01/07 (Sentencing Judgment, 23 May 2004) paras 88, 115, 144.

[16] Mulgrew (n 4) 219.

[17] Ibid 225–6.

[18] To be sure, these interventions also may present a shadow side. For example, the *ingando* re-education system introduced by President Kagame's regime in Rwanda initially may have helped reform ex-*génocidaires*, but it also came to serve social control purposes and propagandize its participants into politically correct dogma leading to exclusion rather than inclusion.

the same geographic locality – many people may have been killed, left as refugees, and new people may have entered. Community may become recomposed in post-conflict spaces or, tragically, eliminated *in toto*. Notwithstanding the salience of these limitations to the restorative project, the fact remains that many international crimes do involve the kinds of conduct (theft, looting, pilfer, and related violence) that mesh with the traditional subject-matter of restorative justice. Moreover, it may well be that restorative justice methodologies have sufficient elasticity to deal with serious acts of violence when committed by compromised perpetrators, namely, those foot-soldiers acting under coercion, besmirched with propaganda, and besotted by narcotics.

In any event, whether the sentencing practice of international institutions attains its stated penological objectives remains a deeply unsettled question. There is scarce evidence, other than anecdotal, that punishing a perpetrator dissuades other perpetrators, either in the same region or elsewhere, from offending. Criminologists have established that the likelihood of getting caught is more influential than any other factor in deterring criminal conduct. Yet the likelihood of getting caught and prosecuted by an international institution in cases of atrocity crimes remains dim. A more foundational question nonetheless arises: are perpetrators of massive crimes – in particular ecological discrimination-oriented crimes such as genocide and persecution – influenced by the cost/benefit analysis central to the logic of deterrence?

In terms of retribution, can the gravity of egregious international crimes (if determined by the harms caused) ever be matched with the severity of a prison sentence? Just deserts may be implausible insofar as actually meting out such deserts suggests the abandonment of core principles of international human rights law (whether in terms of the length of sentence, or conditions of confinement, or potential use of mind-altering psychoactive drugs that trick the mind into thinking time is passing much more slowly).[19] The ICC's first two sentences, in the cases of DRC rebel leaders Thomas Lubanga and Germain Katanga, were 14 and 12 years respectively. These terms are no longer than what many offenders receive in national justice systems when convicted as ordinary criminals (including for drug crimes). The time they spent in custody awaiting their lengthy trials (and during those trials) counts as part of the sentence. Both would be eligible to apply for release following completion of two-thirds of their sentences; both did in fact apply: Lubanga's application was denied and Katanga's approved. They have been transferred to the DRC to serve out their remaining jail-time. Conditions of incarceration in comparatively posh Western prisons – where many international convicts serve their sentences – moreover may not be seen by victim communities as punishment – the defendant is carted away from the persons he or she maimed and killed, does not have to atone before the terrorized communities, and lives with a meal plan, books, and health care.

In short, the reality that custodial punishment may fall short of declared goals suggests a need to rethink both the structure of such sentences and also the centrality of incarceration to the penology of extraordinary international crimes.

---

[19] On the troubling prospect of mind-altering drugs, see F. Pasquale, 'Infinite Punishment' (blog post) (23 March 2014) <http://www.concurringopinions.com/archives/2014/03/infinite-punishment.html> accessed 3 July 2015.

The extant sentencing regime within international criminal tribunals also has been faulted for its lack of transparency, consistency, and predictability. International judges retain considerable discretion in sentencing. Judges temper their discretion through identification of aggravating/mitigating factors and criteria to consider in determining gravity. In the initial years of the work of the *ad hoc* Tribunals, sentences tended towards the erratic. Nevertheless, and on a positive note, some experts conclude that greater consistency has emerged over time, at least in the case of the identification of principles to guide gravity and individualization of sentence.[20] Barbora Holá nonetheless identifies nagging concerns regarding transparency and clarity.[21] These concerns are exacerbated by certain institutional practices (for example, the imposition of a global sentence); and also by a slippage of criteria from gravity into individualization and from the determination of elements of the criminal conduct into the determination of sentence. The slippage may lead to bootstrapping and double-counting which may in turn imperil the defendant's due process rights. Thus far, the ICC's two sentencing judgments have sought to overcome these opacity concerns, in particular, by sentencing concurrently but providing a specific sentence for each conviction, while also making clear efforts to distinguish between factors pertaining to gravity and factors pertaining to aggravation.

In conclusion, improving the quality of the regime of custodial sentences is compatible with re-theorizing the centrality of incarceration to international criminal law.

3. PLURALIZING WHAT HAPPENS IN AND AROUND JAIL

Mulgrew offers insightful suggestions as to how custodial sentences, and the concept of detention, can be modified so as to better promote restorative and rehabilitative goals. She believes that rehabilitation, resocialization, and restoration serve transitional interests and, hence, should play a more robust role within the operation of international criminal justice. One of Mulgrew's concerns is that persons convicted of serious international crimes are dispersed throughout many different national jails. The *ad hoc* international tribunals, for example, and the MICT have concluded enforcement agreements with many different States to detain convicts.[22] These placements, which she analogizes to 'warehousing',[23] offer limited opportunities for prisoners to receive

---

[20] S. D'Ascoli, *Sentencing in International Criminal Law* (Hart 2011) 259–60; B. Holá, C. Bijleveld, and A. Smeulers, 'Consistency of international sentencing: ICTY and ICTR case study' (2012) 9(5) *European Journal of Criminology* 539; K. Ambos, *Treatise on International Criminal Law Vol II* (2014) 268; B. Holá, A. Smeulers, and C. Bijleveld, 'International Sentencing Fact and Figures: Sentencing Practice at the ICTY and ICTR' (2011) 9 *Journal of International Criminal Justice* 411.

[21] B. Holá, 'Sentencing of International Crimes: Consistency of Sentencing Case Law' (2012) 4 *Amsterdam Law Forum* 3, 3.

[22] ICTY convicts have been incarcerated in Germany, Austria, Spain, Italy, Denmark, Finland, Norway, the UK, Sweden, Portugal, Estonia, and France. ICTR convicts have been incarcerated in Mali, Benin, Italy, and Sweden (nearly all in Mali and Benin, however).

[23] Mulgrew (n 4) 193.

attention tailored to the specifics of the crime in question since, according to Mulgrew, national prisons are not equipped to deal with extraordinary international criminality.[24] Mulgrew identifies an ICTY convict, sentenced, inter alia, for sex crimes, who 'was placed in a prison that had no programmes to deal with sex offences'.[25] Moreover, the present diasporic incarceration system involves interactions with a municipal corrections system that may present detainees with linguistic and cultural barriers. According to Mulgrew, 'international prisoners are often restricted in what they can do within a domestic prison system due to their nationality and the unique nature of their criminality'.[26] More foundationally, Mulgrew also observes that '[i]nternational prisoners serving their sentences in national prisons (...) may not have clear or structured sentence plans, access to offending behaviour programmes or assistance with preparation for release'.[27] She believes that thoughtful release plans, in particular, can be of considerable value in the process of individual resocialization. On this note, Mulgrew emphasizes the need to involve prisoners' families in sentence planning and preparations for release.[28] A need also arises to ameliorate post-release opportunities for international prisoners. At present, following release, these individuals 'simply disappear from the radar of the international community', and this despite the fact that their post-release experiences vary greatly *inter se*.[29]

Lessons also can be derived from national experiences. In contrast to prevailing practice within the international system, for example, Rwanda vigorously instituted alternate penalties at the national level when it came to detainees convicted through the *gacaca* system. Historically, *gacaca* is a form of local dispute resolution. It means 'justice on the grass' in Kinyarwanda. *Gacaca* was traditionally deployed to referee property disputes, small-scale violence, and conflict among neighbours. When its prisons bulged with over 100 000 suspects in the wake of the 1994 genocide, Rwanda's government began to assess how exactly to process such a large number of individuals. Approximately 10 000 persons were prosecuted in specialized criminal chambers

---

[24] Ibid., 23. Mulgrew also expresses concerns that '[t]he dispersal of international prisoners through a network of national prison systems reduced the visibility of, and dilutes the international nature of, the sanctions being imposed'.

[25] Ibid., 97. See also ibid., 98 ('Mr Kovač, who committed sex offences, was placed in a Norwegian prison that does not provide programmes which address sex offending, whereas Mr Krajišnik who did not commit sex offences was placed in a Welsh prison for sex offenders due to fears for his safety.').

[26] Ibid., 97.

[27] Ibid., 96.

[28] Ibid., 240 ('Family and community ties provide social capital and support which improve the likelihood of successful resocialization, resettlement and reintegration. Families can help released prisoners find somewhere to live and employment while also providing emotional support, advice and encouragement.').

[29] B. Holá and J. van Wijk, 'Life after Conviction at International Criminal Tribunals' (June 2014) *Supranational Criminology Newsletter* 6, 7 (noting that some 'go back to their countries of origin and return to political posts they [previously] held' and some 'return as celebrated war time heroes', while others 'just go back to their old house, cannot find a job, feel rejected (...) society and fight to make a living'). Also of salience is that some international prisoners cannot leave international detention notwithstanding being released since no country is willing to admit them.

attached to the national court system. But these prosecutions barely made a dent in the overall number of suspects. So, beginning in earnest in the mid-2000s, the government turned to *gacaca*. Traditionally *gacaca* was informal and somewhat organic. It was also starkly patriarchal. The government, however, formalized and modernized *gacaca* through national legislative enactments, mandated the election of lay judges, encouraged the participation of women, and established a detailed organizational structure.[30] This transformation yielded many benefits; along the way however it also morphed *gacaca* from a restorative system to more of a retributive system. *Gacaca* for genocide therefore departed from traditional *gacaca*.

The push to make *gacaca* look more like a criminal court than a reintegrative practice stemmed from several sources. International pressures and funding expectations constituted one such source. International lawyers and donors wished to support accountability, but preferred to do so within the context of a system that resembled criminal trials and, hence, fell within their comfort zone and meshed with international human rights understandings (though by refusing defendants the ability to have a lawyer, and assembling hearings comprised of all community members in public, the modernized *gacaca* still engendered due process concerns). The illiberal Rwandese government also seized the opportunity provided by *gacaca*. By standardizing *gacaca* and making it part of the State, rather than organically integral to the autonomy of local communities, *gacaca* consolidated State power. Most troubling, however, is that *gacaca* began to be deployed for social control purposes. Persons who criticized the government faced charges at *gacaca* hearings. Moreover, information generated by testimony at *gacaca* hearings led to large numbers of people becoming prosecuted. On the one hand, this expansion reflected the reality that participation in genocide was truly a collective project. On the other hand, many of these denunciations may have been animated by ulterior motivations. In 2012 the *gacaca* trials ended. Estimates vary wildly but it is commonly noted that approximately one million people went through the system.

The *gacaca* enacting legislation, and subsequent amendments thereto, fixed certain sentences but also adopted a detailed sentencing grid.[31] A fixed term or sentencing range was stipulated for each category of crime, and the range also was keyed to whether and when an accused may have pled guilty. Incarceration constituted the punishment in the cases of offences other than property crimes (for which reparations were the remedy). However, particularly germane to the discussion at hand is the fact that the *gacaca* legislation also diversified sanctions by introducing the possibility of community service, which was made available for certain defendants who admitted to their crimes. So, for example, the convict would serve part of the sentence in jail, part

---

[30] For details see M.A. Drumbl, *Atrocity, Punishment, and International Law* (Cambridge University Press 2007) 85–99.

[31] The sentencing regime for the Organic Law that governed proceedings in the specialized chambers also provided a mix of specified sentence and fixed sentencing ranges depending on a guilty plea (and the timing thereof) and the actual charges for which the defendant was convicted.

in community service, and part released albeit on a suspended sentence.[32] A very detailed schematic was set out in this regard. Community service was initially conceptualized as a way to promote reconciliation and managerial ends while, at a macro level, to ensure that a huge chunk of the workforce was not idling away in prison but was put to use to motor the country's post-conflict transition while also learning some practical skills.[33] Community service was thereby presented as a sentencing option that was less onerous than imprisonment (and thereby offered as an inducement to confess).

In one permutation, such service theoretically might involve the convict going directly to the victims and offering labour or donating produce as recompense for the harms that had been inflicted – in other words, working to rebuild destroyed homes and farms, to till the land, and to ameliorate public services in the region and for the people that the convict directly targeted.[34] In practice, however, this would be maddeningly complex. Some survivors would not want the perpetrator around; service relationships would be difficult to supervise, control, and manage. So the government instead began to favour broad community service projects – *travaux d'intérêt général* (TIG) – and the use of labour camps.[35] These projects involved agricultural work and building roads, houses, and infrastructure though not necessarily with specific connection to the place where the convicts had committed their crimes. It involved the convicts (also known as *tigistes*) working in groups.

Community service is not mentioned in the sentencing instruments of international institutions. This may be due to a number of factors, including the transaction costs of supervising compliance with the requirements and, to be sure, fears of indentured servitude. However, there may also be value to consider community service as a remedy, particularly in cases where the convict is willing and, perhaps, as part of an early release application. That said, reports from Rwanda also indicate that victims of the genocide may find TIG to be too lenient a sentence and too feeble in light of the gravity of the harms the convicts had inflicted.[36] Victims also have complained about feeling pressured to reconcile and accept remorse professed by defendants. *Tigistes*, on the other hand, indicate considerable support for the *gacaca* process and their service, which they perceived as central to the process of national reconciliation; that said,

---

[32] If the convict defaults on the community service commitments, then the unexpired portion of the sentence is to be served in custody.

[33] These practical skills, in theory, would assist the convict to reintegrate into society.

[34] Note that '[t]he *gacaca* law also provide[d] for restitution or repayment of looted or ransacked property, or carrying out the work required for the property to be repaired. This is distinct from community service': Drumbl (n 30) 89. The intersection of these options and the community service possibilities remains unclear; in many cases, to be sure, detainees had spent so much time in pre-trial detention that upon conviction they may simply have been released and, hence, ineligible for any community service obligations.

[35] According to the Rwandese government, at least 106 918 convicts followed the TIG programme since its initiation in 2005. See RWANDA, 'Les travaux d'intérêt general, une "punition inadequate" selon des surviants' (3 May 2010) IRIN Nouvelles et Analyses Humanitaries (on file with the author).

[36] Ibid.

interviews of *tigistes* conducted under the eye of Rwandan authorities are likely to trigger responses that are unduly supportive of the policies of the Rwandan government.[37]

The Rwandese system also attached civil consequences to criminal convictions. It did so through two separate devices: (1) civil damage awards; and (2) removal of a defendant's civic rights.

In the trials conducted at the national level in the specialized chambers, and in light of the civil law structure of Rwanda's national legal system, surviving victims and certain surviving relatives of deceased victims could file monetary damage claims as *parties civiles* to the criminal prosecution (claims also could be brought by the prosecutor on behalf of private parties). No civil damage awards could be issued if the accused had been acquitted on all charges: the awards were contingent on a criminal conviction. Although in a sense comprising another layer of punishment, *partie civile* claims pushed in a restorative and compensatory direction. In light of the impecuniousness of the defendants, however, the awards ended up largely serving only expressive or symbolic purposes.

In one judgment a Rwandese national court adopted a complex grid of damages,[38] in Rwandan francs, to attach to the kinds of losses and injuries documented:

Moral damages:

10 million Rwandan francs for the loss of a mother or a father
8 million for a child
5 million for a sibling
3 million for another close relative (e.g. uncle, aunt, nephew, niece)

Material damages:

300 000 for a cow
20 000 for a goat
2 000 for a chicken
1 000 for a rabbit
2 million for a house built out of wood and thatch
5 million for a house built out of bricks with metal doors
5 million for household articles
1 million for the harvest

Other Rwandan courts, however, valued losses differently.[39] Inconsistencies thereby arose.

---

37 'Turmoil on the Grass: Justice and Reconciliation in Rwanda' (9 September 2012) Brown Human Rights Report (document on file with the author).

38 *Nteziryayo (Emmanuel) et al* RMP 44223/S8/KA, RP 84/2/2001 (Judgment, 30 November 2001) (discussed in Drumbl (n 30) 82 from where this research is taken). While moral damages refer to harms and pain arising from the loss of certain relatives, material damages refer to goods and property that had been pillaged, stolen, or destroyed.

39 Drumbl (n 30) 82.

The size of the aggregate awards, in any event, could be substantial. One judgment resulted in an award of 144 million Rwandan francs; other judgments involved lesser sums, albeit still in the millions.[40] In the mid-2000s, when these awards were made just prior to the shutting down of the specialized chambers and their replacement (so to speak) by *gacaca* proceedings, the exchange rate for the Rwandan franc to the US dollar was about 1 to 575.[41] Hence an award of one million Rwandan francs amounted to approximately US $1 700 – a sum larger than the *per capita* annual GDP in Rwanda at the time.

Also, and perhaps most importantly, the *partie civile* claims imported considerable narrative value. The text of the Rwandese civil judgments reads very differently to the text of the criminal judgments. The civil judgments foreground the victims rather than the defendant. The storytelling is much more about the victims, the details of their suffering, and exactly what they lost.

Partie civile claims, and their effect on the tenor of national proceedings in Rwanda, depart from ICTR trials where no restitutionary claims have been heard. Ostensibly, this pluralized voice is something the ICC is trying to emulate through victim participation in the criminal proceedings and victim reparations possibilities as well. To be sure, concerns arise, notably effects on the defendant's due process rights, fears regarding judicial manageability, and gauziness regarding who can actually be granted victim status. Nonetheless, as the ICC contemplates its work to include victims, it might do well to learn from the Rwandan experience. To date at the ICC no fines or forfeitures of property have been assessed as against the two convicts owing to their indigence.

Both the *gacaca* and the proceedings in specialized chambers of national Rwandan courts also permitted as an adjunct to criminal sanction the punishment of *dégradation civique*, namely, the removal of certain civic rights. Pursuant to Article 17 of the Organic Law that governed prosecutions in the specialized chambers, these rights could be stripped permanently or temporarily. Examples of rights and privileges susceptible to being stripped were the right to vote, to be a candidate, to serve as an expert or witness in trials or to be deposed judicially other than to give simple facts, to carry arms, to serve in the armed forces, to be a police officer, and to teach in any educational institution.[42] The severity of *dégradation civique* hinged upon the gravity of the offence for which the defendant had been convicted. Deployment of *dégradation civique* might serve retributive ends in that it could differentiate among groups of offenders convicted for the same crime through a granular calibration of the proportionality of punishment and taking into account the specific characteristics of the accused. In a sense *dégradation civique* promotes lustration, namely, the purging of persons responsible for atrocity from the ranks of certain professions. *Dégradation civique*, however, clearly risks double punishment instead of substitute punishment. Another shortcoming with *dégradation civique*, as I have argued elsewhere, is that it 'is a form of shunning and stigma insofar as the perpetrator is hindered from reintegrating

---

40 Ibid., 81–3.
41 Ibid., 81.
42 Ibid., 76 (discussing case-law and Art. 66 of the Rwandese Code of Criminal Procedure).

back into the community (...) such that it is at odds with rehabilitative, reintegrative, or reconciliatory purposes'.[43]

Gacaca wound down in 2012; *gacaca* proceedings digressed from initial expectations in numerous and often disturbing ways; trials at the national level are dwindling in number; and the ICTR is in the latter stages of its completion strategy. Rwanda has transitioned from genocide, but this transition has ratcheted towards autocracy and tight control by the RPF government, which faces repeated criticism over Rwanda's meddling in transnational conflict notably in the neighbouring DRC. To some extent, then, domestic justice mechanisms were co-opted to serve ulterior purposes. These realities, however, do not mean that the potential of these mechanisms in nimbler hands should be denied or ignored. While *dégradation civique* presents a host of dangers, remedies such as community service and civil sanctions as adjuncts to or substitutes for portions of custodial sanction carry considerable potential.

4. MOVING BEYOND JAIL

So far, this chapter has discussed penalties that may supplement or replace parts of a sentence of custodial sanction. A more elastic understanding of the concept of penalty for egregious human rights abuses, however, opens the door to ruminate about sanctions that may serve as full alternatives to custodial sanction. While in each instance a retributivist may find such penalty wanting – laughable even – and a deterrence theorist may suggest that no one will be inhibited from violating human rights if there is no serious comeuppance for it, a more elastic vision of penalty for lower-level offenders could serve crucial transitional goals. This vision also recognizes the involvement of many people in atrocity rather than simply pinning blame on those ostensibly most responsible. The greatest responsibility, after all, does not mean exclusive responsibility.

Rethinking the centrality of custodial sanction to international criminal law is important because, as Nouwen and Werner posit, it is facile to conclude that other forms of justice can constantly be added to the existing presumption of punitive justice.[44] Resources and time are limited. Complementarities, as they put it, cannot be endless.[45] The response to every clash of conceptions is not always accretion. Sometimes, the status quo has to give way, to recede, and to retract. This process cannot happen without deeply interrogating the limits to that very same status quo. While individual penal accountability is richly institutionalized, other sanctioning options simply are not. This tilt places these options at considerable operational disadvantage in the process of constructing how the international community imagines or conceptualizes what justice and punishment actually mean. One goal of this chapter, then, is to recall our bias towards the courtroom and jailhouse and to remind us that this bias may not necessarily serve as a proxy for effectiveness. The response, however, should not reflexively be to institutionalize other punishment mechanisms. Rather, what

---

43 Ibid.

44 Nouwen and Werner (n 7) 19.

45 Ibid.

is proposed is to retain a space in which conceptions of punishment can ebb and flow and, hence, can continually be contested, reassessed, and debated. The solution is not to substitute one hierarchy with another, or to replace monopoly with oligopoly, but rather to promote a kaleidoscopic pluralism.

This section identifies and discusses several examples of alternative forms of punishment. Admittedly, this section proceeds diasporically. Its purpose, however, in considering these examples is to dialogue about what 'other' penalties could look like and, in this process, facilitate their appearance in conversations about accountability and justice.

4.1 *Mato Oput* and Traditional Cleansing Ceremonies

Mato oput is a community ritual among the Acholi population of Northern Uganda. *Mato oput* promotes the Acholi notion of *roco wat*, which means the restoration of harmony, in particular within communities.[46] As is well known, the Acholi community has been riven by over two decades of conflict between the government of Uganda, on the one hand, and the Lord's Resistance Army, on the other. This conflict has now abated considerably, but at its apex was debilitating and characterized by the commission of grievous human rights abuses ranging from crimes against humanity to unlawful recruitment and use of children in armed conflict.

Mato oput operates through community gathering. It serves to reintegrate ex-combatants into society, including ex-combatants reputed to have committed serial human rights abuses, and thereby promotes goals of reconciliation and stability. In the case of northern Uganda, included within this constituency are former child soldiers. Nouwen and Werner point out that, '[w]here an official aim of international criminal justice is to incapacitate and to exclude, Acholi justice ceremonies are tailored to including, focused as they are on restoring relationships within the community'.[47]

Mato oput does not lead to incarceration. It involves revival. The human rights abuser, returning from the bush, drinks the 'bitter root' (*mato oput*) and is ceremonially cleansed of the evil and reborn. Compensation for harms is to be offered. Nouwen and Werner powerfully detail how international criminal lawyers descended upon Northern Uganda to analyze *mato oput*. International lawyers – diffident and sceptical – pushed for *mato oput* to be more like international trials and to adopt core precepts of individual responsibility and punishment. Conformity with international norms was prioritized. The template of trial and jail was taken as the benchmark, from which departures had to be minimized and explained. Nouwen and Werner document that proponents of *mato oput* had to go so far as to justify, defend, and define their justice preferences in the language of international criminal law even though *mato oput* evidences a fundamentally different sensibility.[48]

While far from seamless, and often basing itself on traditions that may have atrophied, *mato oput* did serve a positive role in reintegrating ex-combatants in Uganda. What is more, the prospect of facing traditional ceremonies, and receiving an amnesty

---

[46] Ibid., 9.
[47] Ibid.
[48] Ibid., 12.

from criminal prosecution, encouraged the demobilization and decommissioning of swaths of LRA combatants. Amnesties, to be sure, are a bête noire for the international criminal lawyer. Yet, qualified amnesties, as part of a process of demobilization and decommissioning – as the next section explores – can serve the important goals of defusing conflict while promoting reconciliation and authenticating the past.

4.2 Qualified Amnesties

In their work on Darfur, Nouwen and Werner conclude that, for some of their Darfurian interlocutors, justice means the end of the war and, once peace arises, then real justice can be pursued through *judiya* (mediation among groups that leads to compensation and arrangements for future coexistence).[49] Peace negotiations, utilitarian in nature, contrast with the deontology of retributivism under which transgressions must be punished regardless of the effects thereof. International criminal law focuses on prosecuting (and ending) crime instead of focusing on ending conflict. While it is hoped that the two are coterminous, this is not always the case and in fact may not regularly be the case.[50] The amnesty is central to peace negotiations. Many conflicts have been ended by amnesty. Yet the international criminal lawyer often reflexively equates the amnesty with impunity. At times, certainly, this attribution is accurate.[51]

That said, perhaps a more sensitive assessment is possible. In this regard, the 2013 Belfast Guidelines on Amnesty and Accountability are instructive.[52] While eschewing unconditional amnesties that block investigations of human rights abuses and offer categorical pardons, the Belfast Guidelines unpack a much more granular understanding of the amnesty. According to the Guidelines, qualified amnesties that are individually determined can protect human rights; mandate combatants and offenders to engage with truth-seeking, reparative, and accountability mechanisms; require disarmament, decommissioning, and reintegration programmes (including education or public confession); and serve as a key instrument in defusing conflict and infusing reconciliation and

---

[49] Ibid., 12–13.

[50] Ibid., 13:

> When international arrest warrants in fact make the conclusion of a peace agreement more difficult and therefore in effect lead to a continuation of the conflict and crimes, the pursuit of one type of justice (the enforcement of international criminal law) may thus prevent the realization of another type (the end of a conflict and the crimes committed in the context of that conflict).

[51] Nepal is currently embroiled in debate over whether former Maoist rebels and security forces who committed gross human rights abuses should be amnestied and pardoned in support of a truth commission. Legislation has been passed to this effect. See Al-Jazeera, 'Nepal parliament passes amnesty bill' (27 April 2014) <http://www.aljazeera.com/news/asia/2014/04/nepal-parliament-passes-amnesty-bill-20144271502645838.html> accessed 3 July 2015 (reporting that UN human rights chief Navi Pillay warned that amnesties for serious abuses would 'weaken the foundation for a genuine and lasting peace in Nepal'.). Other UN officials also have sharply – and similarly – criticized the legislation.

[52] The Belfast Guidelines on Amnesty and Accountability (University of Ulster 2013).

stability.[53] The disdain expressed by international criminal law, and the institutions enforcing international criminal law, towards the amnesty may therefore simply be too generic. Amnesties may be compatible with penalty instead of intractably antithetical thereto.[54] This fine-grained analysis is all the more important in light of the continuing recourse to amnesties in practice, despite international law's admonitions. This suggests that, instead of castigating the amnesty and denying its role, it may be more helpful to channel State practice and peace negotiations towards legitimate amnesties and redirect such practice away from illegitimate amnesties. Happily, there is some indication of movement in this direction within international criminal law.[55]

4.3 Alien Tort Claims Act and Private Civil Lawsuits

Unlike the *parties civiles* claims in Rwanda, it is possible in some instances for civil damages to be issued against a human rights abuser without the need for a pre-existing or concurrent criminal conviction. The US Alien Tort Claims Act (ATCA, also known as the Alien Tort Statute (ATS)) exemplifies such a remedy. The ATCA, which dates from the First Congress in 1789, textually affords foreigners the ability to sue in US federal court, in tort, for violations of the laws of nations.[56]

The ATCA largely lay dormant for nearly two centuries until the *Filártiga* case, in which the US Court of Appeals for Second Circuit court ruled against a Paraguayan torturer on behalf of the deceased torture victim's sister (ultimately, at a subsequent

---

[53] General Principle 11 of the Belfast Guidelines lists the following as preconditions for the conferral of an amnesty:

(a) submitting individual applications;
(b) surrendering and participating in disarmament, demobilization and reintegration programmes;
(c) participating in traditional or restorative justice processes;
(d) fully disclosing personal involvement in offences, with penalties for false testimony;
(e) providing information on third party involvement with respect to offences;
(f) testifying (publicly or privately) in a truth commission, public inquiry or other truth-recovery process;
(g) testifying at the trial of those who were not granted or eligible for amnesty;
(h) surrendering assets illegitimately acquired; and
(i) contributing materially and/or symbolically to reparations. (17–18).

[54] The Belfast Guidelines posit that amnesties may in fact facilitate selective prosecution strategies.

[55] Cf *Ieng Sary* 002/19-09-2007/ECCC/TC (Decision on Preliminary Objections, 3 November 2011) para 52 (noting that amnesties for international crimes especially when unaccompanied by any form of accountability are incompatible with the goals of accountability and remedy, but also noting that certain conditional amnesties have met with widespread approval and have not been invalidated). Other examples of increased sensitivity and nuance include the approach of the ICC Office of the Prosecutor as regards the preliminary examination in Colombia and the interface with the peace process in that country.

[56] Section 1350 of Title 28 of the US Code. US courts, therefore, are required to determine whether the impugned conduct constitutes a violation of the laws of nations, which US courts have largely taken to mean customary international law.

trial, an award of $10 million – still uncollected – was awarded).[57] A wave of litigation ensued that targeted individual human rights abusers, including high-profile cases against Radovan Karadžić that helped expose the sexual violence during the Balkans conflicts at a time when these conflicts were still ongoing. Then a second wave arose in which plaintiffs, relying on aiding and abetting and accessorial modes of liability, sought to target corporate defendants for their role in human rights abuses. Claims were filed against a number of corporations engaged in natural resources extraction in the developing world. These claims were considerably more contentious (inter alia, because the damage awards could actually be collected if the corporation had assets and because of the effects on foreign investment in the developing world).

Many ATCA claims have been summarily dismissed; some survived summary judgment and led to settlement while others led to lengthy and unsuccessful proceedings; and yet some have led to monetary damage awards. To be sure, the likelihood of collecting on these awards is small. Actually recovering damages, however, often is not a central goal for many plaintiffs, for whom the process can serve important declaratory, transparency, and cathartic objectives. In my experience, victims of human rights abuses are often comfortable with ATCA claims because they feel they – rather than a public prosecutor – exercise control over the process.

In April 2013, in the *Kiobel* case, the US Supreme Court sharply reduced the scope of future ATCA claims by requiring proof of a compelling nexus with the US. Chief Justice Roberts, writing for a five-justice majority, held that the presumption against extraterritoriality applies to the ATCA. Violations of international law outside the US must touch and concern US territory with sufficient force as to displace that presumption. Justice Kennedy, and especially Justice Breyer,[58] in their separate concurrences, gestured towards slightly more generous approaches; while Justice Alito drew a line that was even more restrictive than that of Chief Justice Roberts.

Plaintiffs are filing cases to map out the precise boundaries of the ATCA, and these will be delineated over time; although the number of actionable cases likely will constrict, some will persist.[59] Civil lawsuits for gross human rights abuses in the US may migrate to State tort law or other venues. That said, nearly three decades of ATCA case-law does suggest the value of such free-standing civil claims even when undertaken extraterritorially. These claims and attendant damages embarrass, regulate, and punish. They serve a policing and monitoring function, while facilitating information gathering. These claims ensure some sort of redress, permit the cause of action to be defined by the victims (or – somewhat problematically – by public interest groups

---

[57] *Fillártiga v Pena-Irala* [1980] 630 F.2d 876.

[58] I would not invoke the presumption against extraterritoriality. (…) I would find jurisdiction under this statute where: (1) the alleged tort occurs on American soil, (2) the defendant is an American national, or (3) the defendant's conduct substantially and adversely affects an important American national interest, and that includes a distinct interest in preventing the United States from becoming a safe harbor (free of civil as well as criminal liability) for a torturer or other common enemy of mankind.

Breyer, concurring, in *Kiobel v Royal Dutch Petroleum Co* [2013] 133 S.Ct. 1659 1671.

[59] M. Drumbl, 'Extraterritorial International Criminal Law', manuscript (2016).

proceeding on behalf of the victims), and allow harms to be brought to light that might otherwise fall short of the beyond the reasonable doubt exigencies that understandably inure to criminal process. ATCA litigation also triggers vigorous conversations about corporate liability for international crimes, a concept that falls outside the remit of contemporary international courts and tribunals. Hence, and as an alternative to custodial sanction, there may be cause for international lawyers to think long and hard about a freestanding universal civil jurisdiction in cases of the commission of extraordinary international crimes.

4.4 State and Organizational Responsibility

The mainstreaming of individual culpability and custodial sanction has tended to sideline State responsibility in conversations about accountability for mass atrocity.[60] Indeed, State responsibility has a troubled history in matters of post-conflict transition. The collective guilt imposed upon Germany through the Treaty of Versailles left a sordid legacy; so much so that, in the wake of World War II, the Allies explicitly sought to prosecute individual Nazi leaders in their personal capacity. The German population, including many elements of the *Wehrmacht*, were spared and, instead, benefited from the Marshall Plan. Although the International Court of Justice (ICJ) in the *Bosnia v Serbia* litigation interpreted a breach of the Genocide Convention as dually permitting State responsibility and individual criminal responsibility, the ICJ's anaemic instantiation of remedial action against Serbia, as well as its meekness in addressing a redacted evidentiary record partly derived from the ICTY, signals many decades after Nuremberg the ongoing preference for the imprisonment of a selected few deemed to be the most blameworthy.[61]

While suspending the responsibility of the many humanizes the population, and thereby eases post-conflict transitions, this evacuation may also stand at odds with the reality of atrocity. In places like Rwanda and Cambodia, large numbers of ordinary soldiers and civilians were complicit in, and often undertook, the massacres. In the former Yugoslavia many voters supported a vociferously nationalist regime led by Slobodan Milošević.[62] White South Africans profited materially from the *apartheid*

---

[60] G. Blum, 'The Crime and Punishment of States' (2013) 38 *Yale Journal of International Law* 57, 58 ('As an alternative to State punishment, international law has channeled all punitive sanctions to individuals.').

[61] *Case Concerning the Application of the Convention on the Prevention and Punishment of the Crime of Genocide (BiH v Serbia and Montenegro)* International Court of Justice (Judgment, 27 February 2007). The ICJ held that, although Serbia was not directly responsible for committing genocide in Bosnia and Herzegovina, it was responsible for having failed to prevent genocide at Srebrenica, where 7 000 Bosnian Muslim men and boys were massacred by Bosnian Serb military forces in July 1995. Specifically, the ICJ also found Serbia responsible for breaching the Genocide Convention because of its failure to fully cooperate with the ICTY (in particular its failure to bring notorious suspects into custody). The ICJ did not award damages against Serbia. It ruled that the issuance of the judgment alone constituted satisfaction for Bosnia.

[62] Cf M. Osiel, 'The Banality of Good: Aligning Incentives Against Mass Atrocity' (2005) 105 *Columbia Law Review* 1751, 1841:

regime, which many actively supported even while keeping their distance from the brutes who tortured political dissidents on their behalf. *The Act of Killing*, Joshua Oppenheimer's poignant 2013 documentary, reveals how the mass murders of alleged Communists in Indonesia in the 1960s was undertaken by thugs who were then, and continue to be, revered by large swaths of the Indonesian populace and who remain celebrated by the three million strong Pemuda Pancasila youth paramilitary organization. States may owe duties to their citizens, but should citizens not owe duties to the State, one of which might be to endeavour to prevent the State from actualizing *jus cogens* violations or failing to prevent them?

State and collective responsibility might have become somewhat radioactive as a sanction, but perhaps this stigma is unjust. Atrocity, after all, often begins 'with the devious kindling of conflict entrepreneurs, who seek to inflame and exacerbate communal tensions'.[63] If community members ignore these efforts, or quash them while inchoate, then atrocity fails to normalize. If community members, however, partake in these efforts, then atrocity metastasizes. Community responses can nevertheless be incented or influenced, certainly in the early stages. Community members are in an advantageous position to identify, monitor, and condemn the initiatives of conflict entrepreneurs. However, because the prevailing system of punishment chooses not to reach community members and benefiting bystanders, it provides them no incentive to control the behaviour of conflict entrepreneurs.

In short, then, as Gabriella Blum notes: 'Under present international law, only individuals can "commit crimes" and be subject to criminal accountability in domestic and international tribunals. This is the case even though most international crimes committed by individuals could not have been committed outside the framework of a State or collective action.'[64]

Blum offers a nuanced analysis of how in practice international law still permits the punishment of States, albeit now only when couched within the value-neutral language of prevention.[65] Blum's work examines the reasons behind this rhetorical shift. What is clear, however, is that State punishment is disfavoured as a matter of admitted or declared international law. International lawyers become jittery and sceptical when faced with the prospect that States can be held responsible for crimes. The *épanoiussement* of international criminal law, I would add, serves a catalytic role in legitimating the rhetorical shift observed by Blum and, furthermore, in consolidating the skittishness of international lawyers toward State responsibility for *jus cogens* violations.

Could post-conflict justice reengage with collective responsibility? One possible starting point for such reengagement would be to differentiate guilt from responsibility. While a small number of people may be criminally guilty for atrocity, a much larger number of people are responsible for atrocity. How, then, to determine who bears

---

When State-sponsored mass atrocity enjoys the substantial support of a country's population, its citizens should share the costs of redressing it. This is especially true when the regime perpetrating the atrocities was relatively democratic, responsive to popular will, like Serbia during the Balkan wars.

[63] Drumbl (n 30) 202.

[64] Blum (n 60) 58–9.

[65] Ibid., 59.

responsibility? Such determinations could proceed crudely or carefully.[66] The crude way assigns responsibility to the group in whose name atrocity was undertaken independently from the conduct of the individuals – so, all Germans as responsible for the Holocaust and all Arab Sudanese as responsible for the Darfur tragedy. Crude attributions of responsibility can have harsh consequences on group members who resisted atrocity, who were victimized, or who were incapable. What about the careful way? Here, attention is paid to individual agency. Responsibility is limited to those group members who contributed to atrocity. While a presumption of responsibility can be assigned collectively to all group members, the careful approach would afford individuals an opportunity to demonstrate why their conduct during periods of atrocity should exempt them. The presumption of responsibility would in other words be rebuttable. In addition to furthering equitable outcomes, such a rebuttable process could trigger cascading conversations about who did what during times of atrocity which, in turn, could promote pedagogic and discursive goals.

The skittishness that international lawyers experience when confronted with collective responsibility may well be justified. But an underlying question persists: is it truly advantageous for this skittishness to become controlling or preemptive and, thereby, preclude investigation and conversation?

4.5 Transparency and Denunciation

Public inquiries, opening of records, and truth commissions can serve goals that arc towards sanction and punishment, notably through the power of denunciation and the sunshine of transparency. The hearings conducted by the South Africa Truth and Reconciliation Commission, notwithstanding the bargained-for amnesty, helped victims channel blame while also helping perpetrators rejoin a fundamentally changed political order. While the South Africa TRC has attracted considerable frustration and disappointment, it also eased political transition amid turbulent times. The memorialization of testimony and the advent of YouTube furthered the hearings as pedagogic devices.

Following reunification in the early 1990s, the approach taken in Germany with Stasi (the abusive East German secret police) crimes and surveillance is illustrative of the power of transparency. Rather than pursue criminal prosecutions or official inquiries, the decision was taken to permit interested members of the public access to the Stasi files. The Stasi had recruited tens of thousands of ordinary citizens in their quest to monitor over one-third of the country's population of 16 million. Ordinary citizens could suddenly learn about who was spied upon, who did the spying, who refused to spy, who was never spied upon, and whose spying resulted in the transmission of accurate or fanciful information. On this latter note, the opening of the files resulted in the public learning not only of betrayal and obsequiousness, but also of quiet acts of resistance, transgression, and tenderness among those approached to do the spying. Following their opening at the very start of 1992, nearly three million German citizens

---

[66] For further discussion, see Drumbl (n 30) 197–204.

have visited the archives containing the Stasi files.[67] While the opening of the files certainly ran the risk of vigilantism, revenge, brusque lustration, and shaming – and did lead to suicide (in the case of parliamentarian Gerhard Riege)[68] – one observer posits that on a national level these risks proved to be more apparent than real.[69] Instead, among the major outputs of the opening of the files were discussion, historical appreciation, assemblage of memory, and a search for a 'truthful understanding of the past'.[70] Relationships were ruptured and persons ostracized, to be sure; also dispelled, however, were many suspicions and the corrosive effects of fearing colleagues were informers when, in actuality, they were not. Assessments of moral guilt, which cannot be rendered by the criminal justice system, were thereby facilitated – both adroitly and gauchely – by the decision to open up these archives.[71]

5. CONCLUSION

Duties are firmly emerging – and growing – to prosecute perpetrators of serious international crimes. While the South African Constitutional Court held in the seminal *Azanian Peoples Organization* judgment that these duties did not invalidate the South African TRC (notably the invocation of the political amnesty from criminal and civil liability in exchange for full disclosure), this judgment dates from 1996.[72] The landscape has since shifted. The duty to prosecute is likely more robust and, hence, controlling. Alternatives to courtrooms and jailhouses therefore may be more compacted than before. While prima facie about heterogeneity, the Rome Statute's complementarity may in practice lead to homogeneity in terms of the kinds of institutions that are to operate in the aftermath of mass atrocity.

In any event, it remains unclear whether the duty to prosecute necessarily entails a cognate duty to incarcerate. This chapter suggests that any obligation to punish the commission of grievous human rights abuses and offer victims a remedy could – and should – be constructed more broadly. Such a move would drain the punitiveness from the international penal system by diversifying the purposes of punishment; and temper its technocratic and reductionist scientism by welcoming a myriad of bottom-up

---

[67] A. Lichtenberg, 'Germans remember 20 years' access to Stasi archives' (*Deutsche Welle*, 2 January 2012). A larger number of applications to view were made, though not all of these were granted.

[68] S. Kinzer, 'Germans Anguish Over Police Files' (*New York Times*, 19 February 1992).

[69] R. Beattie, 'The Poisoned Madeleine: Stasi Files As Evidence and History' (2009) 1:3 *Faculty of Information Quarterly* <http://fiq.ischool.utoronto.ca/index.php/fiq/article/view/15452> accessed 3 July 2015.

[70] Ibid., 3 of printout.

[71] See generally, B. Miller, *The Stasi Files Unveiled: Guilt and Compliance in a Unified Germany* (Transaction 2004).

[72] *Azanian Peoples Organisation (AZAPO) and Others v President of the Republic of South Africa and Others* (1996) (8) BCLR 1015 (CC) (South African Constitutional Court, 25 July 1996). Applicants in that case contended that South Africa was obliged by international law to prosecute those responsible for gross human rights violations and, hence, that the amnesty provisions breached international law.

sanctioning mechanisms. The end game would be for international criminal justice to concern itself with how best to respond to grievous *jus cogens* breaches in each particular case, rather than concern itself with investing in one particular response, universalizing it, and then saddling it with altitudinous goals and lofty expectations.

17. The International Criminal Court's regime of victim redress: non-punitive responses to crimes under the Rome Statute

Conor McCarthy

1. INTRODUCTION

Almost two decades since the establishment of the ICC, a great deal of uncertainty continues to surround its regime of victim redress, which comprises both a regime for Court-ordered reparations and the support provided by the Trust Fund for Victims (TFV) pursuant to the Fund's independent mandate to provide 'physical, psychological rehabilitation and/or material support' to victims.[1] Perhaps foremost among the issues which remain unresolved is the underlying role, if any, of the ICC's regime of victim redress as part of the criminal justice process established by the ICCSt. As will be seen, the Statute's regime of victim redress is not intended to have a retributivist or punitive role. Moreover, while procedures for victims to obtain redress in the context of criminal proceedings are familiar to many national legal systems, especially civil law jurisdictions which make available to victims the possibility of participating in criminal proceedings as a *partie civile* to seek reparation,[2] the proper role of such arrangements in an international criminal justice framework such as the ICC is not clear, not least given the potentially vast number of victims and the very limited resources available for redress. The present chapter therefore seeks to address two issues.[3] The chapter explores the role of the ICCSt regime of victim redress, given its non-punitive character. The chapter also seeks, non-exhaustively, to explore some of the key challenges facing the Court as it seeks to discharge its mandate for providing victim redress. Before addressing these questions, it is first necessary briefly to explain the structure and scope of the Statute's regime of victim redress.

---

1 Reg. 49 TFV Regulations (ICC-ASP/4/Res.3). See also Rule 98(5) ICC RPE.

2 For a detailed comparative survey see J. Spencer and M. Delmas-Marty, *European Criminal Procedures* (Cambridge University Press 2002). See further J. Larguier, 'The Civil Action for Damages in French Criminal Procedure' (1964) 39 *Tulane Law Review* 687; P. Campbell, 'A Comparative Study of Victim Compensation Procedures in France and the United States: A Modest Proposal' (1979) 3 *Hastings International and Comparative Law Review* 321; C. Howard, 'Compensation in French Criminal Procedure' (1958) 21 *Modern Law Review* 387, and P. Lapie, 'The *Partie Civile* in the Criminal Law of France' (1928) 10 *Journal of Comparative Legislation and International Law* 33.

3 This chapter draws on earlier work by the present author, in particular work published in *Reparations and Victim Support in the International Criminal Court* (Cambridge University Press 2012).

2. OVERVIEW OF THE ICC STATUTE'S REGIME OF VICTIM REDRESS

The creation of a regime of victim redress within the framework of the ICCSt was a novel, but controversial, feature of the Statute at the time of its creation. Agreement as to the inclusion of a regime of victim redress (and, indeed, the arrangements for victim participation more generally)[4] were matters settled at a late stage in the negotiations preceding the adoption of the ICCSt. The form ultimately taken by the Statute's regime of victim redress reflects, in part, many influences including the attitudes of States, the International Law Commission's (ILC) work on the topic and, significantly, the lobbying of NGOs, in particular the victims' lobby which played an immensely active role during, and prior to, the Rome Conference.[5] The regime of victim redress which eventually emerged at the culmination of the Rome Conference was, in consequence, not the result of some overarching 'grand design' but was rather the amalgamated result of proposals which emerged from many different quarters.[6]

Following the ILC's groundwork on a draft statute, the Preparatory Committee for the Establishment of an ICC (which provided a forum for further discussions and negotiations between States prior to the Rome Conference itself) included various options on arrangements for victim redress within its proposals, in particular at the suggestion of the French delegation to the Committee.[7] But even at the conclusion of the Preparatory Committee's work, proposals in respect of victim redress appeared only in bracketed form indicating that their inclusion was controversial for a number of delegations.[8] Certain delegations, it appears, feared that the incorporation of a power to award reparations in respect of crimes under international law may implicate the responsibility of States and may eventually be used to make reparations orders against them.[9] There was also a concern that the potentially enormous complexity of dealing with reparations in respect of crimes under international law may distract from the central purpose of the Court, namely the prosecution and punishment of those

---

[4] The ILC's Draft Statute for an ICC contained no provision for victim participation. See Draft Statute for an International Criminal Court contained in *Report of the International Law Commission on the Work of its Forty-Sixth Session* (A/49/10).

[5] For a detailed discussion of the drafting history of the Rome Statute see C. McCarthy, *Reparations and Victims Support in the International Criminal Court* (Cambridge University Press 2012) 48 *et seq*.

[6] For a detailed discussion of the negotiating history of the Rome Statute's reparations regime and the development of proposals relating to the TFV see O. Triffterer, *Commentary on the Rome Statute of the International Criminal Court: Observer's Notes, Article-by-Article* (2nd edn, Hart 2008) 1399 *et seq* (on reparations) and 1439 *et seq* (on the TFV). See also R.S. Lee (ed), *The International Criminal Court: The Making of the Rome Statute: Issues, Negotiations, Results* (Kluwer 1999) 262 *et seq* (on reparations) and 319 *et seq* (on applicable penalties).

[7] See, for example, French proposal to PrepCom regarding Article 45*bis* (the forerunner of Article 75 ICCSt), A/AC.249/1997/WG.4/DP.3.

[8] *Report of the Preparatory Committee on the Establishment of an ICC Vol II* (Compilation of Proposals) 224 para 3 A/51/22.

[9] See C. Muttukumara, 'Reparations to Victims', in R.S. Lee (ed), *The International Criminal Court: The Making of the Rome Statute: Issues, Negotiations and Results* (Kluwer 1999) 264.

responsible for heinous crimes (a concern exacerbated by the fact that many judges inevitably come from legal traditions where questions of redress rarely form an element of criminal proceedings).[10] Ultimately, consensus about the creation of a regime of victim redress emerged at a late stage, just a few days before the conclusion of the Rome Conference,[11] a consensus which resulted from the strong support by certain, influential States (most notably, France and the United Kingdom, together with some support from the United States and Japan). This was, as mentioned above, combined with the intense and highly effective lobbying efforts of a broad coalition of NGOs active in the area of victims' rights. It was all of this which culminated in the establishment of the Statute's victim redress arrangements.

In its final form, the regime provides for the possibility of redress in respect of the harm suffered by victims of crimes within the jurisdiction of the Court, including genocide,[12] crimes against humanity[13] and war crimes.[14] When the Court has jurisdiction in respect of the crime of aggression, the reparations regime and the power of the Trust Fund to provide victim support will also arise in this context. As earlier noted, the Statute's regime of victim redress encompasses two distinct elements, namely the power of the ICC to award reparations to victims of crimes within its jurisdiction and the capacity of the TFV to provide support to such victims outside the context of court-ordered reparations.[15]

The powers of the Court with regard to reparations are principally dealt with in Article 75 ICCSt. Article 75(1) empowers the Court to 'establish principles relating to reparations to, or in respect of, victims including restitution, compensation and rehabilitation'. These principles are still at a nascent stage of development. The Appeals Chamber in the *Lubanga* case has issued a decision establishing principles and procedures to be applied to reparations in that case, dealing with matters including consultation with victims, modalities of reparations, the extent of reparations to be provided to victims and well as procedural questions relating to verification and processing.[16] These principles are necessarily crafted at a broad level of abstraction.[17] In its Reparations Judgment, the Appeals Chamber made clear that these principles

---

[10] Ibid.

[11] See *Report of the Working Group on Procedural Matters* (A/CONF.183/C.1/WGPM/L.2/Add.7. A, 13 July 1998) 5; number of earlier proposals on the question of reparations were introduced in the course of the Conference by various delegations including: A/CONF.183/C.1/WGPM/L.63, 8 July 1998; A/CONF.183/C.1/WGPM/L.63/Rev.1, 11 June 1998; and (proposal by the United States delegation) A/CONF.183/C.1/WGPM/L.69, 10 July 1998.

[12] Art. 6 ICCSt.

[13] Art. 7 ICCSt.

[14] Art. 8 ICCSt.

[15] Rule 98(5) ICC RPE provides the TFV with the general power to use resources, other than those collected through fines, forfeiture or reparations, 'for the benefit of victims'. See also, Chapters I and II TFV Regulations (n 1).

[16] *Lubanga* ICC-01/04-01-06 (Judgment on the Appeals Against the Decision Establishing the Principles and Procedures to be Applied to Reparations, 3 March 2015); See also *Lubanga* ICC-01/04-01/06 (Decision Establishing the Principles and Procedures to be Applied to Reparations, 7 August 2012).

[17] The Court has not been speedy in establishing reparations principles. For its part, the Assembly of States Parties has exhorted the Court, on a number of occasions, to establish

apply regardless of whether the reparations awarded are supplemented (or provided) by the Trust Fund or are individual or collective in character.[18]

Based on such principles the Court may award reparations to victims. The Court's power to order reparations is set out in Article 75(2) which stipulates that '[t]he Court may make an order directly against a convicted person specifying appropriate reparations to, or in respect of, victims ...'. According to the Appeals Chamber, a Reparations order must contain five elements, namely (i) it must be directed against the convicted person, (ii) it must inform that person of their liability, (iii) it must specify (with reasons) the type of reparations ordered, (iv) it must identify the harm caused to the direct or indirect victims of the crimes for which the accused has been convicted and specify appropriate modalities for reparations, and (v) it must establish eligibility criteria for reparations. These criteria may encompass collective reparations to a community where that community, as a collectivity, has suffered harm as a result of the crime for which the accused has been convicted.[19] Persons who have not (individually or collectively) suffered harm from the convicted person's crime must not receive reparations (but may receive victim support), where they have been harmed by a crime under the ICCSt, other than those committed by the convicted person.

The TFV created by Article 79 ICCSt is a further crucial element of the ICCSt's regime for victim redress. Money and other property collected through fines or forfeiture may be transferred to the TFV by order of the Court.[20] In addition, the TFV may receive voluntary contributions from a range of sources including 'governments, international organizations, individuals, corporations and other entities'.[21] Resources derived from voluntary contributions to the TFV may be used to supplement resources available for Court-ordered reparations and the TFV may also play a role in the design and implementation of reparations awards.[22] In the case of *Lubanga*, the Appeals Chamber made clear that the question of the extent to which the TFV's voluntary resources are used for reparations is left to the sole discretion of the Trust Fund's Board of Directors.[23]

A further crucially important aspect of the TFV's mandate is the provision of support to victims outside the context of court-ordered reparations. Such support may be provided prior to the issuance of a reparations order by the Court against a convicted person in a given situation and may be provided to victims including those not eligible for reparations.[24] This assistance takes the form of 'physical or psychological rehabilitation and/or material support for the benefit of victims and their families'.[25] In the *Lubanga* case, the Appeals Chamber emphasized that it may be necessary for the TFV

---

principles relating to reparations 'as a priority' (See e.g. Paragraph 6 of the Resolution on 'Victims and Affected Communities, Reparations and Trust Fund for Victims', ICC-ASP/13/Res.4).

[18] *Lubanga* ICC-01/04-01-06 (Judgment (n 16)) 52.

[19] Ibid., 32, 212.

[20] Art. 79(2) ICCSt.

[21] Reg 21(a) TFV Regulations annexed to Resolution ICC-ASP/4/Res. 3 (3 December 2005).

[22] See Chapters II–V TFV Regulations.

[23] *Lubanga* ICC-01/04-01-06 (Judgment (n 16)) para 107.

[24] Reg 50 TFV Regulations.

[25] Ibid.

to consider whether to supplement a reparations award in a particular locality with programmes through its victim support mandate, to ensure that the value of reparations in a particular community is not undermined by the ineligibility of certain sections of the community for Court-ordered reparations (and the tensions which that may create).[26]

The Trust Fund undertakes a wide variety of projects as part of this mandate, often with the assistance of local partner organizations. The Fund's 2014 Progress Report (TFV 2014 Report) provides insight into the kind of concrete activities the Fund undertakes. In its reports, the TFV notes that physical rehabilitation:

> consists primarily of referrals of individuals in need of medical care to other service providers. (…) TFV partners identify victims of war crimes or crimes against humanity in accordance with TFV criteria, assess them for the types of medical and psychological treatment needed, and facilitate referrals to facilities or organizations with the necessary capacity in case of need for medical care.[27]

Similarly, psychosocial support is provided in partnership with local organizations. Programmes for counselling, especially targeting children and victims of sexual violence, have been initiated in the Democratic Republic of the Congo and Northern Uganda. It appears the TFV also undertakes other activities including micro-credit initiatives for those deprived of income or livelihood by crimes under the ICCSt as well as educational initiatives and interventions aimed at 'capacity building'.[28]

Given the negotiating history of the Statute, it is clear that the regime that eventually emerged from negotiations was the result of a confluence of different interests, agendas and concerns. Unsurprisingly therefore, it bears the hallmarks of compromise, more perhaps, than it reflects a planned, overarching scheme for redressing the human consequences of mass violence. Indeed, this is perhaps implicitly acknowledged by the fact that the drafters of the Statute have left to the Court itself the task of 'establishing' reparations' principles pursuant to Article 75(1) ICCSt, in many ways, leaving it to the Court to bring the regime to life. The Court's challenge then in its developing practice in respect of victim redress is to bring to fruition the regime and its disparate elements in a coherent and practicable way. Without doubt this will not be an easy task.

3. THE CHARACTER OF THE ICC REGIME OF VICTIM REDRESS: RETRIBUTION OR RECTIFICATION?

Although criminal justice processes, including those concerned with crimes under international law, are often justified in retributivist terms,[29] such accounts provide little

---

[26] *Lubanga* ICC-01/04-01-06 (Judgment (n 16)) para 215.

[27] TFV 2014 Report 9.

[28] TFV 2014 Report 18.

[29] Retribution can be defined as a form of criminal justice involving the infliction of punishment upon a perpetrator who is considered to be deserving of punishment. In the literature in this area a number of different theories have been put forward to explain when and why punishment may be deserved. See R. Nozick, *Philosophical Explanations* (Harvard University

by way of justification for the ICCSt's regime of victim redress. The Court's regime of victim redress is not intended to provide simply another means by which a perpetrator can be punished. This is clear from the terms of the Statute's reparations provisions, interpreted in context as well as from the negotiating history of the Statute. It is also evident from the structure and design of the reparations regime itself.

Starting with the text, the Statute expressly distinguishes the role that the reparations provisions play within the scheme of the Statute from its penalty provisions. Article 77 of the Statute, which sets out the Court's 'applicable penalties', makes no mention of reparations. In addition, Article 75 (addressing the Court's power to award reparations) is not placed in Part 7 which is concerned with 'Penalties', but is instead placed in Part 6 of the Statute, which deals with matters relating to trial proceedings. This provides a clear indication that the reparations regime is not intended to form part of the Court's punitive regime. Furthermore, from a contextual standpoint, the Court's power to impose a fine on a perpetrator exists entirely independently of the power to make a reparations order. Indeed, a reparations order may (and, in practice, normally will) be derived from resources allocated from the TFV, rather than from a perpetrator. A perpetrator may very often have little to do with a reparations order made by the Court in relation to the crimes for which he bears responsibility.

The non-punitive character of reparations is confirmed by the negotiating history of the Statute, which indicates that the decision not to treat reparations as a penalty under the Statute was a conscious decision on the part of those who negotiated it. During the Rome Conference and in the Preparatory Committee negotiations prior to the Rome Conference, France and the UK were the States most active in pursuing the inclusion of reparations provisions within the Statute. In 1997, the UK proposed a text to the Preparatory Committee which addressed reparations to victims.[30] It suggested that reparations include a 'monetary award' and that this would comprise 'a punitive element, a compensatory element or both'. In February 1998, France and the UK submitted a joint proposal to the Preparatory Committee which also included an option for a punitive reparations award.[31] The possibility of reparations representing an applicable penalty under the Statute was subsequently retained in the Draft Statute published by the Preparatory Committee immediately prior to the Rome Conference.[32] At the Conference itself, the Working Group on Penalties produced a proposal that reparations be included as a form of penalty under the Statute.[33] However, around the same time, France and the UK submitted a further proposal on reparations which did

---

Press 1981) 374–84; D. Cooper, 'Hegel's Theory of Punishment', in Z. Pelcynski (ed), *Hegel's Philosophy: Problems and Perspectives* (Cambridge University Press 1971) 151 and A. von Hirsch, 'Punishment, Penance and the State', in M. Matravers (ed), *Punishment and Political Theory* (Hart Publishing 1999) 48, 69.

[30] Proposal of the United Kingdom to the Preparatory Committee (A/AC.249/1997/WG.4/DP.13, 10 December 1997). See also Proposal of France to the Preparatory Committee (A/AC.249/1997/WG.4/DP.3, 5 December 1997).

[31] Proposal by France and the United Kingdom to the Preparatory Committee (A/AC.249/1998/WG.4/DP.19, 10 February 1998).

[32] Draft ICCSt (A/CONF.183/2/Add.1, 14 April 1998).

[33] Committee of the Whole, Rome Conference, Working Group on Penalties, Chairman's Working Paper on Article 75 (A/CONF.183/C.1/WGP/L.3, 30 June 1998).

not specify a punitive element to reparations awards.[34] Shortly thereafter, the Working Group on Penalties revised its provisions on applicable penalties and the reference to reparations was removed. A power to impose the penalty of a fine was, however, created.[35]

It must be remembered that the Statute's regime of victim redress has two elements. As regards the victim support provided by the Trust Fund, this is even further removed from notions of retribution and punishment than is the reparations regime. The Fund's victim support arrangements are funded almost exclusively through the voluntary contributions of third parties (e.g. States and some private contributions) rather than through the imposition of financial burdens upon perpetrators. Thus, although there may be cases where substantial financial burdens can be imposed upon a perpetrator, retribution, that is to say the infliction of a reparation order on a perpetrator by way of punishment does not adequately explain the role of the regime of victim redress within the institutional framework of the ICC.

Finally, it is worth noting that in its Reparations Judgment in the *Lubanga* case, the ICC Appeals Chamber,[36] endorsed the principle that 'reparations ensure that offenders account for their acts'.[37] This is right insofar as liability for reparations is imposed ultimately on the individual perpetrator convicted by the Court (in line with Article 75(2) ICCSt). This proposition should not, however, be confused with retribution, since accountability and punishment are not the same. Punishment is merely one means by which accountability can be achieved. Furthermore, the accountability principle does not provide anything close to a complete explanation for the reparations regime, since in the majority of cases (probably the vast majority) reparations will be resourced through the voluntary contributions of States and other third parties to the Trust Fund, in a manner which has some parallels to domestic social solidarity compensation schemes for victims of crime.[38] A broader understanding of the principled justification for the regime is therefore necessary (and will be explored further below).

For present purposes, however, it suffices to conclude that the *travaux* of the ICCSt, taken together with various contextual considerations, therefore confirm that the Court's regime for victim redress is not punitive or retributivist in character. Its role is not to provide simply another mechanism by which perpetrators can be punished. Thus, although the Statute's regimes for reparations and victim support exist alongside the Court's regime for the punishment of perpetrators, the regime for victim redress is separate from, rather than part of, this regime.

Given that the ICCSt's regime of victim redress is not intended to be punitive in character and is not, therefore, intended to play a role as part of the punishment and sanctioning of perpetrators, an important question arises as to the role of the ICC's

---

34 Committee of the Whole, Rome Conference, Proposal by France and the United Kingdom (A/CONF.183/C.1/WGPM/L.28, 26 June 1998).

35 Committee of the Whole, Rome Conference, Report of the Working Group on Penalties (A/CONF.183/C.1/WGP/L.14, 4 July 1998).

36 *Lubanga* ICC-01/04-01-06 (Judgment (n 16)).

37 Ibid., para 65.

38 See F. Megret, 'Justifying Compensation by the International Criminal Court's Victim's Trust Fund: Lessons from Domestic Compensation Schemes' (2010) 36 *Brooklyn Journal of International Law* 123.

regime of victim redress, as part of the criminal justice process, alongside the Court's punitive regime.

4. RELATIONSHIP BETWEEN THE ICC REGIME FOR VICTIM REDRESS AND THE COURT'S REGIME FOR THE PUNISHMENT OF PERPETRATORS

The inclusion of a rectificatory regime to deal with the harm suffered by victims as part of a criminal justice process to prosecute and punish those most responsible for crimes under international law is not a natural or obvious outworking of international criminal justice. As earlier noted, although the *partie civile* procedure is common in many civil law jurisdictions, the notion of criminal courts dealing with questions of compensation for victims is one that is alien to lawyers practising in many jurisdictions, especially those in the common law tradition. Moreover, at the international level, in contrast to the position in respect of State responsibility, individual criminal responsibility for crimes under international law has not, historically, given rise to the existence of a concomitant obligation to make reparation. As Christian Tomuschat observes:

> If the author of a [grave] crime is responsible for an act characterised by international law as unlawful, all arguments seem to favour a right for the victim or persons claiming through the victim to obtain reparation for the damage caused and a corresponding obligation to do so on behalf of the author of the crime.[39]

But as Tomuschat notes, there is no logically inevitable relationship between primary responsibility and an obligation to make reparation.[40] Despite it being long established that individuals bear criminal responsibility under international law historically no obligation has been imposed on perpetrators to provide reparation to their victims. The question arises as to whether there is a coherent role for a regime concerned with victim redress, as part of the overall framework of an international judicial institution primarily concerned with the prosecution and punishment of crimes under international law.

A key challenge faced by criminal justice processes dealing with such crimes, is that they often involve mass-scale conduct perpetrated by many individuals, at times, even involving persons who collectively comprise a substantial section of a society as a whole. This is illustrated nowhere more vividly than Rwanda where, in the years immediately following the genocide, approximately 100 000 individuals were detained and prosecuted for crimes associated with it.[41] Such was the scale of participation that the Rwandan authorities considered it necessary to establish the *Gacaca* judicial

---

[39] C. Tomuschat, 'Private Individuals', in Crawford et al (eds), *The Law of International Responsibility* (Oxford University Press 2010) 321.

[40] C. Tomuschat, *Human Rights: Between Idealism and Realism* (Oxford University Press 2008) 355.

[41] Report on the Situation of Human Rights in Rwanda Submitted by the Special Representative, Mr. Michel Moussalli, Pursuant to Resolution 1998/69 UN Doc E/CN.4/1999/33, 8 February 1999.

process, an adaptation of customary Rwandan forms of justice. But in the months following its establishment rather than providing swift closure, *Gacaca* in fact revealed an almost unimaginable level of genocidal participation, with estimates suggesting that perhaps a million individuals (in a country with a population of around seven million) were implicated in the genocide.[42]

In such situations, the investigation, prosecution and punishment of all transgressors is simply not likely to be feasible. Accountability through prosecution and punishment is inherently limited. This is almost certainly the case where national authorities are unwilling or unable to play a significant role in the prosecution of crimes under international law since the cost of trials before international tribunals is immense.[43] Moreover, even where individuals are indicted by an international court, a lack of cooperation on the part of certain States may well mean that a significant number of such persons do not in the end face prosecution and punishment. Furthermore, at the national level, in a society transitioning from conflict, the need to move beyond past events may arguably render the prosecution and imprisonment of all of those bearing a degree of criminal responsibility undesirable. In consequence, the punishment of individual perpetrators therefore provides only a limited means of administering justice in respect of crimes under international law and, in such situations, victim redress can be seen as having a role to play.

Victim redress, in particular that provided independently by the Trust Fund, can be offered to a much wider range of victims than those harmed by crimes successfully prosecuted before the ICC. Alongside the prosecution and punishment of individuals, it enables a broader approach to justice for victims of such crimes than is possible merely through retribution involving the custodial punishment of individual perpetrators. The ICC's Trust Fund will have a particularly significant role in this regard since it can provide redress to victims of crimes which are never brought before the ICC or, for that matter, any other court. The provision of redress in the form of victim support as part of a criminal justice process can ensure that, for the many victims who never see retributive justice being meted out, a significant number may at least receive some measure of justice in the form of the redress they receive and the vindication which this provides.

The sizable, often enormous, number of victims who are excluded from the benefits of the prosecution and punishment of perpetrators at the international level is not the only problem facing international criminal justice processes relying on the prosecution and punishment of individuals. Even for the victims of crimes perpetrated by

---

42 A. Meldrum, 'One Million Rwandans to Face Killing Charges in Village Courts' (*The Guardian*, 15 January 2005) <http://www.guardian.co.uk/world/2005/jan/15/rwanda.andrew meldrum> accessed 20 January 2012); J. Fierens, 'Gacaca Courts: Between Fantasy and Reality' (2005) 3 *Journal of International Criminal Justice* 896.

43 The biennial budget of the ICTY, for instance, when at full capacity, was in the region of 200–300 million USD. Around 161 individuals have been indicated by the Tribunal. The figures for the ICTR are similar, although it has tried fewer cases. See Programme Budget of the ICTY and ICTR for Biennium 2014–15 (GARes/68/256 and GARes/68/255). The budget for the ICC for the year 2015–16 is approximately €130 million, although it is presently trying many fewer cases than either the ICTY or ICTR did when operating at full capacity. See ICC Programme Budget for 2015 (ICC-ASP/13/Res.1, 17 December 2014).

individuals who are, in the end, prosecuted, such trials function far from ideally. The trial of individual high-ranking offenders[44] lacks immediacy and relevance for victims. High-level perpetrators will often be many steps removed from the harm inflicted upon the ultimate victims of their crime. In addition, the scope of a perpetrator's criminal responsibility dealt with at trial may cover a very broad factual scenario with the result that the findings contained in a Trial Chamber's judgment may bear little relation to the experience of victims individually. As Justice Robert Jackson, Chief Prosecutor for the United States at Nuremberg, put it in a letter to President Truman in June 1945: 'Our case against the Major defendants is concerned with the Nazi master plan, not with individual barbarities or perversions which occurred independently of any central plan.'[45]

While the focus on the overarching scheme of violence may be an inevitable consequence of a trial concerned with overall responsibility for a systematic campaign of violence, for the victims of the individual barbarities which comprised that campaign, the justice gained through the trial and punishment of a perpetrator may be significantly lessened, or even undermined, by the hierarchical, temporal and physical remoteness of the individual prosecuted from the atrocities for which he or she bore ultimate responsibility. This potential dislocation between the trial and punishment of a high-level perpetrator at the international level and the ultimate victims of that perpetrator may be accentuated where, as will often be the case,[46] the trial process occurs in a location geographically far removed from the locality where the crime occurred and uses procedures, processes and an institution quite different than those with which victims may be familiar.

In light of the above, it is clear that, particularly where a national legal system is unwilling or unable to prosecute, many victims – perhaps the vast majority – are unlikely to see justice in the form of retributive punishment being meted out to the perpetrators of the crimes inflicted upon them. Indeed, for some, the prosecution and punishment of one or a handful of individuals for a widespread atrocity may entirely fail to reflect the gravity of a mass atrocity and its consequences. Moreover, where trials do occur, they are likely to take place many years after atrocity occurred and relate to an overarching scheme of events of which the victims' own personal experiences and those of their family or community may comprise a miniscule component. In contrast, reparations and victim support potentially provide a more tangible and concrete form of justice and one that can readily be made manifest in the localities where victims live. Thus, to some extent, reparations and victim support provide a measure of redress for victims with an immediacy and relevance which may

---

[44] As a matter of prosecutorial policy, the ICC Prosecutor concentrates investigative resources on the prosecution of those who appear to be most responsible for crimes within the jurisdiction of the Court. See also Regs 33, 34 of the Regulations of the Office of the Prosecutor (ICC-BD/05-01-09, 23 April 2009).

[45] See R.H. Jackson, 'Report to the President from Justice Robert H. Jackson, Chief Counsel for the United States in the Prosecution of Axis War Criminals, June 7 1945' (1945) 39 *American Journal of International Law* 178.

[46] Note, however, that although Art. 3(1) ICCSt specifies that the seat of the ICC is The Hague, according to Art. 3(3) ICCSt the Court may sit elsewhere whenever this is desirable. But security and logistical problems may limit the extent to which the latter provision is used.

be lacking where an international criminal justice process relies solely on a small number of criminal trials involving the prosecution and custodial punishment of individual, high-level perpetrators.

Alongside these largely pragmatic considerations, there are principled reasons too why the use of programmes for victim redress rather than punitive measures against certain categories of perpetrator may still contribute to the purposes of criminal justice. It has long been recognized that criminal justice processes may be understood in expressivist terms.[47] Reparations arrangements, like criminal injuries compensation schemes at the national level, can be seen as part and parcel of the response to crime by the criminal justice system as broadly understood, enabling the authoritative disavowal of criminal conduct as well as the vindication of the law and the rights of victims. From a principled standpoint therefore, retribution involving the prosecution and punishment of perpetrators is not the only means by which criminal justice can be conceptualized or understood or by which societal censure and the disapproval of criminal conduct can be given expression.[48] As Joel Feinberg, one of the leading social philosophers of the twentieth century, notes '[t]o say that the physical treatment [of punishment] itself expresses condemnation is simply to say that certain forms of hard treatment have become the conventional symbol of public reprobation'.[49] Although individual punishment is the conventional means by which recognition or denunciation may be given expression there is no *a priori* reason why this must be so. A wide range of other mechanisms can also serve this purpose.[50] For its part, victim redress can provide an authoritative pronouncement that the conduct to which the victim was subjected was a specific, and particularly grave type of wrong, namely a crime under international law.[51] In this sense, the underlying rationale for the Statute's reparations and victim support regime do not serve fundamentally different purpose. Each provides a measure of vindication for victims, providing affirmation of that they were subjected to a wrong and in so doing giving expression to the denunciation of the harm they suffered.

5. THE POLITICS OF VICTIM REDRESS: THE LIMITATIONS OF RULES AND LEGAL PROCESS

Despite its non-punitive role, a coherent principled (and pragmatic) justification for the ICCSt's regime of victim redress can be found. However, the many challenges facing the regime's implementation and their potential to undermine any such role cannot be

---

[47] J. Feinberg, 'The Expressive Function of Punishment', in J. Feinberg (ed), *Doing and Deserving: Essays in the Theory of Responsibility* (Princeton University Press 1970) 95.

[48] For further consideration of role of international criminal justice and the role of reparations therein see C. McCarthy, 'Victim Redress and International Criminal Justice: Competing Paradigms or Compatible Forms of Justice?' (2012) 10 *Journal of International Criminal Justice* 351.

[49] Feinberg (n 47) 100.

[50] See further M. Drumbl, 'International punishment from "other" perspectives', Chapter 16 in this volume.

[51] For a broader exploration of the expressivist role of victim redress see McCarthy (n 48).

overlooked. Perhaps the central challenge arises from the limited resources for victim redress together with the enormous scale of the harm to be remedied. As a consequence of this tension, devising and implementing arrangements for victim redress will, at times, involve questions of a 'political', as much as a legal, character. Inevitably, decisions as to which victims receive redress, the amount of resources allocated between different groups of victims and even the modalities of forms of redress, will all be hugely complex politically.

A substantial body of principles, rules and guidance has developed in recent years on matters of remedies and reparation. Alongside the jurisprudence of the universal human rights supervisory mechanisms and regional human rights courts, principles on matters of reparation have also been espoused by claims' commissions like the UN Compensation Commission and the Eritrea-Ethiopia Claims Commission. Added to this, a body of soft law has also developed in this area, most notably in the form of the Basic Principles on the Right to Reparation adopted by the UN General Assembly in 2006.[52] For its part, Article 75(1) ICCSt provides the ICC with the power to 'establish principles relating to reparations' suited to the context of an International Criminal Court, which it will no doubt establish bearing in mind, where appropriate, the aforementioned body of rules and principles.

As earlier noted, these principles are still at a nascent stage of development. The ICC Appeals Chamber has opined on certain elements of the ICC's reparations regime in the *Lubanga* case, addressing matters including the scope and modalities of reparations, the relationship between the Trust Fund and Trial Chamber in respect of reparations awards as well as issues including the burden and standard of proof. The Appeals Chamber endorsed the view that 'victims should receive appropriate, adequate and prompt reparations' and that these could include, inter alia, restitution, compensation and rehabilitation as well as a range of other measures, for instance, those concerned with raising awareness of the Court's findings and alleviating the stigmatization of victims.[53] The detail of these matters has been left to the Trust Fund to determine (subject to the ultimate supervision of a (reconstituted) Trial Chamber). Neither the Trial Chamber nor the Appeals Chamber addressed the question of the principles by which the (very) limited resources for reparations should be prioritized as between victims or as between different forms of victimization or as between victims with different degrees of vulnerability. The Trial Chamber has left this question to the TFV, albeit that the Chamber can be seized with any contested issues which arise.[54]

Considerable caution is necessary as to the capacity of principles, rules and legal processes to resolve certain forms of dispute or problem. A danger is inherent in an overly legalized process for making decisions regarding matters of victim redress in that it can tend to obscure the reality that, in practice, questions of victim redress are often ultimately intensely political matters. Questions of victim redress often touch on more profound issues concerning how a society transitions from conflict to peace and

---

[52] Basic Principles on the Right to Reparation adopted in GARes 60/147, 21 March 2006.

[53] See *Lubanga* ICC-01/04-01-06 (Judgment (n 16)) Annex A (Order for Reparations) paras 44–48. See also *Lubanga* ICC-01/04-01/06 (Decision Establishing the Principles and Procedures to be Applied to Reparations, 7 August 2012) paras 222–241.

[54] *Lubanga* (Decision, ibid.) paras 281–288.

stability.[55] Alongside the obvious macro-level politics and pragmatics of transitional justice in the aftermath of mass violence, victim redress is also often highly politicized in other ways. Harold Lasswell, the noted American jurist and political scientist wrote of politics that it is about 'who gets what, when and how'. In other words, politics was, for Lasswell, fundamentally a process by which scarce resources of one sort or another are allocated between different individuals, groups and interests.[56]

By this definition, post-conflict victim redress, where the scale of harm is almost always going to be greater than the resources available to remedy it, is a political matter *par excellence*. The immensely limited resources available for redress, relative to the scale of harm to be remedied, mean that decisions regarding allocation and prioritization among victims or categories of harm are inevitable. Decisions must be made as regards the groups and individuals who are most deserving of redress, the forms of harm to which very limited resources should be directed and how remedial action should be administered. In all of these decisions social, inter-ethnic, gender or even class-based politics may be implicated. The capacity of rules, principles and legal processes to resolve these, at times, overtly political issues is limited.

Although, for reasons of predictability, fairness and consistency, legal principles, rules and processes can provide a useful framework for guidance in such decision-making, whether by the Trust Fund or by the Court, overreliance on legal rules can obscure the inherently political character of the judgments often involved, implicitly or explicitly, when decisions are made as to the individuals or groups to whom redress is provided and the interests that are to be prioritized as part of this. With regard to such inherently political and potentially highly charged decisions the limitations of legal rules, principles and processes must be recognized. In situations where (to say the least) not all victims can receive redress and not all forms of harm can be remedied, legal rules are of little assistance in determining matters such as the persons who are most deserving of redress or the forms of harm that are most in need of alleviation. Many different perspectives on such matters are inevitable and ultimately the resolution of these issues is as much a question of politics and policy as it is a question amenable to resolution by a framework of rights, obligations and law. For their part, judicial institutions are also not necessarily ideally suited to making determinations on such controversial policy or political questions. Nor are judges or lawyers always best placed to weigh up the competing, polycentric interests at stake. Thus, while legal principles and rules are important in ensuring consistency and fairness, in situations of limited resources, legal principles alone can do little to provide answers to questions identified in Lasswell's aphorism, that is to say, the persons to whom limited resources for redress should be allocated, how much they should receive and how redress should be provided. So on matters of victim redress legal institutions, rules and principles, at best, provide processes rather than pointing towards outcomes.

The distribution of resources will be all the more controversial in the often bitterly contested ethnic or religious politics of many post-conflict societies, not least given the selective character of prosecutions before the Court (and consequently of reparations

---

[55] See generally, P. de Greiff, 'Justice and Reparations', in P. de Greiff (ed), *The Handbook of Reparations* (Oxford University Press 2006) 451.

[56] See H. Lasswell, *Politics: Who Gets What, When, How* (Meridian Books 1958).

awards or support provided by the Trust Fund). The investigation and prosecution of crimes within the ICC's jurisdiction is necessarily selective.[57] This has implications for both victim support and reparations. As regards victim support, the Trust Fund cannot provide support in respect of a situation not under investigation by the Prosecutor; and, arguably, it cannot do so even then until at least one case from that situation has been determined to be admissible by the Court.[58] It is quite possible that, owing to limited investigative resources and to prosecutorial priorities, including those influenced by real-world political considerations, there may be situations in which crimes within the jurisdiction of the Court occur but are not formally investigated by the Prosecutor or in respect of which no cases are brought before the Court, with the result that the Trust Fund will have no power to provide victim support.

As regards Court-ordered reparations, the exercise of prosecutorial discretion is likely to have a pronounced effect with regard to selectivity. The Prosecutor has substantial power to shape proceedings before the Court, and inevitably only certain persons and certain crimes will be prosecuted. Although the decision as to who is to be prosecuted is guided by the Prosecutor's policy of prosecuting those thought to bear the greatest responsibility for crimes within the jurisdiction of the Court,[59] factors such as the availability of admissible evidence linking a particular perpetrator to specific crimes will also have a crucial bearing on who is, in the end, prosecuted and on the crimes that are charged. Thus, it is certainly not the case in any given situation that those victims who have suffered the gravest forms of harm as a result of crimes within the jurisdiction of the Court (or those with the greatest needs) will necessarily ultimately benefit from redress, even in situations where some form of reparations or victim support is provided. This has significant potential to play into inter-ethnic or other forms of societal division and will be a very real challenge in almost every situation in which some form of redress is provided.

A key question mark in respect of the ICCSt's regime of victims redress (including both the Court-ordered reparations and Trust Fund administered victim support) is how well it can navigate the politics of victim redress, avoiding the temptation for legal rules and principles to be used in a way which obscures the policy and politics of the issues at stake and, more importantly, how well the ICC and its institutions can handle the immensely complex politics of reparations. The capacity of legal processes to resolve certain forms of controversy is limited. This is certainly true in the context of post-conflict redress. Very difficult decisions will have to be made as to how resources for redress are prioritized. Which victims are to benefit? Which forms of harm or patterns of victimization are to be prioritized and which forms of harm will receive little or no redress? Questions as to the form of redress to be provided will be equally

---

57 See R. Cryer, *Prosecuting International Crimes: Selectivity and the International Criminal Law Regime* (Cambridge University Press 2005).

58 Although there is no specific rule or regulation on this issue, recall that the TFV may provide support to 'victims' under the Statute only where this would not pre-determine an issue to be decided by the Court. See Reg 50 TFV Regulations.

59 See ICC, *Paper on Some Policy Issues Before the Office of the Prosecutor* (September 2003) 3, available at <www.icc-cpi.int/Menus/ICC/Structure+of+the+Court/Office+of+the+Prosecutor/Policies+and+Strategies> accessed 29 July 2015. See also Reg 34 of the Regulations of the Office of the Prosecutor (ICC-BD/05-01-09, 23 April 2009).

controversial. It is almost inevitable that there will be controversy, even conflict, among victims as to the appropriate response to these questions. In many post-conflict societies these issues are addressed (if at all) by political rather than legal processes. Given the limited practice of the ICC to date in respect of reparations and victim support it is still too early to say whether the ICC is capable of navigating these challenges successfully.

6. CONCLUSION

The ICC's regime of victim redress is not animated by a rationale of retribution or punishment. Its primary focus is on the human consequences of crimes under international law rather than on the perpetrators of such crimes. The regime of victim redress serves a purpose conceptually distinct from the ICC's punitive regime, involving sanctions such as imprisonment and, on occasion, fines or forfeiture orders directed at perpetrators. Although the role of the regime of victim redress is conceptually distinct, this role need not be seen as being in conflict with the role of the Court.

In many cases, redress under the ICCSt, whether in the form of reparations or victim support will have little (or no) connection with an individual perpetrator. Most often, any resources for redress will likely come from voluntary contributions to the TFV, rather than from any resources derived from the perpetrators of such crimes. As Martti Koskenniemi observes, often victims 'do not so much expect punishment (though of course that is not insignificant) but rather a recognition of the fact that what they were made to suffer was "wrong", and that their moral grandeur is symbolically affirmed'.[60] The creation of a regime for victim redress offers with it the possibility of this form of symbolic affirmation and has the potential to provide a measure of justice to a much wider range of victims than is possible merely through the prosecution and punishment of individual perpetrators.

Immense practical challenges face the ICC's regime of victim redress. Resources for reparations are scarce or non-existent. Voluntary contributions to the TFV have not been especially generous.[61] Most States have contributed relatively little and many nothing at all.[62] Private contributions have been similarly lacking. The lack of resources accentuates considerably the hugely difficult problems which arise in the decisions

---

[60] See M. Koskenniemi, 'Between Impunity and Show Trials' (2002) 6 *Max Planck Yearbook of International Law* 1, 11.

[61] For the period 2012–13, the TFV received around €4.5 million in voluntary contributions and around €2.5 million in 2012. In 2013, the TFV had available funds in the region of around €7.3 million. While these sums are clearly not insignificant, they are, nevertheless, very modest in relation to scale of work falling within the TFV's mandate for reparations and victims support (see *Trust Fund for Victims financial statements for the period 1 January to 31 December 2013*, ICC-ASP/13/13, 15 August 2014).

[62] For instance, voluntary contributions in 2013 of €4.5 million came, almost exclusively, from six States (Sweden, the Netherlands, Germany, the UK, Finland and Switzerland). Very little was received from private or philanthropic contributions to the fund, despite its eligibility to receive such donations. The support is therefore financially very reliant on the continued generosity of a relatively small number of States.

which must inevitably be made about the distribution and prioritization of resources for redress, whether in the form of reparations or victim support. These questions are intensely controversial, not to say political. Ultimately the resolution of these issues is as much a question of politics and policy as it is a question amenable to resolution by a framework of rights, obligations and law. A question therefore remains as to whether the framework created for the resolution of these issues under the ICCSt is appropriate for the task at hand. In part, this will depend on how the Court itself develops its reparations regime. Time will tell.

PART VIII

DEVELOPING THE INTERNATIONAL PENAL SYSTEM

If the international penal system is conceived of as a mechanism for enforcing international sentences of imprisonment, then it is clear from the Handbook so far that it contains a significant and notable gap: there is no international prison.

In Chapter 18, Margaret Penrose addresses this structural deficiency. After a discussion of the evolution of enforcement practice to date, she highlights the inadequacies of the current system and the potential operational consequences of the omission of an internationally controlled penal facility. She concludes by calling for the creation of an international prison (system).

The international penal system requires more than structural developments however. As the international criminal justice system has matured, it has become clear that mistakes can happen. Not all indictments result in convictions. Indeed, practice to date has demonstrated that over 20 per cent of indictments have resulted in acquittals on all charges.

In the final substantive chapter (Chapter 19), Róisín Mulgrew provides a critical analysis of the compensation scheme established by Article 85(3) ICCSt. This provision goes beyond contemporary human rights law to provide access to a remedy for persons who are detained but are later acquitted (or have proceedings against them terminated). This chapter outlines the reasons for adopting this innovative provision in the international context and explains how it bridges a remedial gap in international criminal law. It proceeds to examine the statutory, regulatory and procedural limits on its use and explores the costs of suspicion in the international criminal justice context. It concludes with a recommendation to rethink the form of redress provided and the method for its delivery.

18. Creating an international prison

Margaret M. Penrose

1. INTRODUCTION: MAKING THE CASE FOR AN INTERNATIONAL PRISON

Where do individuals sentenced by an international criminal court go to serve their sentence? Currently, the answer is: 'it depends'. It depends on which international tribunal convicted the individual, which States have entered a cooperation agreement to enforce sentences with the particular tribunal, and, which State the tribunal believes is the best fit for that particular individual.[1] Because there is currently no international prison or single location to enforce the criminal sentences imposed by international tribunals, where a convict serves their sentence is a constant uncertainty.

There have been many advancements in international criminal law within the past three decades, including the development of *ad hoc* Tribunals to try those accused of war crimes or crimes against humanity.[2] The *ad hoc* Tribunals have diminished immunity for some of the world's most heinous crimes (excluding terrorism and human trafficking).[3] Ratification of the Rome Statute, which created the ICC, ensures a permanent approach to combating international crimes: individuals accused of war crimes and crimes against humanity will either be prosecuted in a court of law or ostracized.[4] This new era of accountability has resulted in the international prosecutions of high-profile defendants and former heads of State.[5] But, there remain critical

[1] See ICTY PDD, IT/137/Rev. 1 (1 September 2009); ICTR PDD (23 September 2008); SCSL PDD (10 July 2009).

[2] See ICTYSt, SCRes 827, UN SCOR, 48th Sess, 3217th mtg, UN Doc S/RES/827 (25 May 1993) (creating the ICTY, with the ICTYSt attached as an addendum to SCRes 827); ICTRSt, SCRes 955, SCRes 955, UN SCOR, 49th Sess, 3453rd mtg, S/RES/955 (8 November 1994); Creation of International Court in East Timor, SCRes 1272, UN Doc S/RES/1272 (25 October 1999); and, Recommending Creation of SCSL, SCRes 1315, 4186th mtg, UN Doc S/RES/1315 (14 August 2000).

[3] Crimes falling within the *ad hoc* and permanent ICC's jurisdiction include genocide, war crimes, crimes against humanity, and, a recent attempt to also enforce the crime of aggression. See Art. 5 ICCSt (delineating the four crimes falling within the ICC's jurisdiction). As noted in Art. 5, 'The Court shall exercise jurisdiction over the crime of aggression once a provision is adopted in accordance with articles 121 and 123 defining the crime and setting out conditions under which the Court shall exercise jurisdiction with respect to this crime.'

[4] See R. Goldstone, 'The Role of the United Nations in the Prosecution of International War Criminals' (2001) 5 *Washington University Journal of Law and Policy* 119.

[5] On 12 June 2014, the ICC confirmed that it will prosecute the former Ivory Coast President, Laurent Gbagdo, for four counts of crimes against humanity. See ICC website (12 June 2014). Another notable example was the four-year trial of former Yugoslavian President Slobodan Milošević. Milošević's trial ended without judgment as he died on 11 March 2006, in his detention cell awaiting conclusion of his lengthy trial. See IT-02-54 (ICTY Case Information Sheet Slobodan Milošević) available at <icty.org> accessed May 2015.

enforcement shortcomings in the current system.[6] The ICC is literally just a court, a building with judges, lawyers and staff, with no enforcement mechanisms to secure arrests or effectuate sentences. A mere eight States have entered sentence enforcement agreements with the ICC, none within the past three years.[7] This deficiency, while not currently posing an impediment to justice, is likely to become a problem once the ICC moves beyond a handful of convicts.[8]

The Assembly of States Parties to the ICC specifically addressed the lack of cooperating States for sentence enforcement purposes at its 13th Session in December 2014. The Bureau of Assembly of States issued a 'Report of the Bureau on Cooperation' highlighting the lack of enforcement agreements and the lack of recent commitment by States Parties to accept convicted individuals for enforcement purposes.[9] The Report noted that the ICC 'has stressed' that *ad hoc* enforcement agreements, although permissible, 'were not ideal'.[10]

Now that a permanent institution exists ready to prosecute those most deserving of international condemnation and punishment, it is strange that no corresponding permanent facility exists to house those convicted by the ICC.[11] Remarkably, little attention has been given to the important realities of a permanent criminal court – prisoners facing lengthy terms of imprisonment.[12] One cannot begin to comprehensively address international crime without addressing the full spectrum of prosecution, from arrest and pre-trial detention to incarceration, particularly when the primary penalty before international criminal tribunals remains imprisonment.[13]

We have an international criminal court, but no coexisting international prison. The maintenance of a permanent ICC requires us to assess the viability of a criminal justice

---

6 See e.g., *Kenyatta* ICC-01/09-02/11-1005 (Decision on the Withdrawal of Charges, 13 March 2015) (withdrawing charges against current, sitting head of State Kenyatta without prejudice). Kenyatta was never arrested and the Prosecutor was never able to secure sufficient evidence against Kenyatta due to lack of cooperation from Kenya.

7 Report of the Bureau on Cooperation (21 November 2014) 6.

8 To date, only two individuals have been convicted by the ICC. The first, Thomas Lubanga Dyilo, was sentenced to 14 years in prison and has already served two-thirds of his sentence in the Detention Unit at The Hague. As of July 2015, he still had not been designated to serve the remainder of his sentence in any other State. *Lubanga* ICC-01/04-01/06 A 5 (Judgment, 1 December 2014).

9 Report of the Bureau (n 7) 6.

10 Ibid., 5.

11 'ICC Holds Groundbreaking Ceremony for Permanent Premises Construction (ICC Press Release, 16 April 2013) <www.icc-cop.int> accessed July 2015. The new permanent court facility should 'leave visitors with a strong image of the Court: that of an august institution established to combat impunity by imparting justice in accordance with the rule of law'.

12 See generally R. Mulgrew, *Towards the Development of the International Penal System* (Cambridge University Press 2013); M. Penrose, 'No Badges, No Bars: A Conspicuous Oversight in the Development of an International Criminal Court' (2003) 38 *Texas International Law Journal* 621; B. Holá and J. van Wijk, 'Life after Conviction at International Criminal Tribunals: An Empirical Overview' (2014) 12 *Journal of International Justice* 109.

13 Art. 77 ICCSt (Listing the potential penalties to include '[i]mprisonment for a specified number of years', generally not to exceed 30 years except 'when justified by the extreme gravity of the crime and the individual circumstances of the convicted person').

system that fails to possess a centrally located, permanent prison capable of housing convicted war criminals and those committing crimes against humanity.[14]

Currently, all international tribunals rely on cooperating States to voluntarily agree to accept a particular convict.[15] The list of willing States has been short and regionalized. The ICC, much like the enforcement system utilized by the *ad hoc* Tribunals, continues to rely on cooperating States to help arrest those indicted and, eventually, house those convicted.[16] The lack of enforcement mechanisms have plagued the various tribunals, as numerous individuals have avoided trial simply by evading arrest while others have served the majority of their sentence in a holding cell in the Netherlands.[17] Because States' cooperation is entirely voluntary, they can reject any individual presented.[18] Thus, the ICC has no assurance that it will have an available State to enforce the sentence imposed on a convicted person.[19]

It seems unlikely that a twenty-first century international criminal justice system can successfully exist on a one-dimensional level – the maintenance of a court without corresponding police and prison enforcement mechanisms.[20] The current model is woefully incomplete, embracing the paradigm of the past, not the modern world. We have abandoned the *ad hoc* Tribunal approach, recognizing its shortcomings, and embraced the need for a permanent international criminal justice system. Why then, do we continue to use an *ad hoc*, cooperating States model to enforce penalties imposed

---

[14] See Penrose (n 12).

[15] The UNSC established the International Residual MICT to conclude the remaining tasks, including the enforcement of sentences, facing the now dormant ICTY and ICTR. See SCRes 1966 (22 December 2010) (with governing Statute appended to the end of the Resolution). The MICT began functions relating to the ICTR on 1 July 2012, and the ICTY on 1 July 2013. Art. 25 MICTSt addresses the 'Enforcement of Sentences', and Art. 26 addresses 'Pardon or Commutation of Sentences'.

Art. 25 MICT provides that '[i]mprisonment shall be served in a State designated by the Mechanism from a list of *States* with which the United Nations has agreements for this purpose. Such imprisonment shall be in accordance with the applicable law of the State concerned, subject to the supervision of the Mechanism'.

[16] See Art. 103(1) ICCSt ('A sentence of imprisonment shall be served in a State designated by the Court from a list of *States* which have indicated to the Court their willingness to accept sentenced persons').

[17] K. Hoffman, 'Some Remarks on the Enforcement of International Sentences in Light of the Galic Case at the ICTY' (2011) 10 ZIS 842 (noting that '[a]lready today, many perpetrators spend a number of years during pre-trial and trial stages in the UN prison in Scheveningen/The Hague. In case of very short prison sentences, some convicted prisoners have never been transferred to another State of enforcement').

[18] See Art. 103(1)(b), (c). See also, Holá and Van Wijk (n 12) 115 (noting the 'double-consent' process for designating a State for sentence enforcement). As Holá and Van Wijk explain, 'first a State must enter into an enforcement agreement with a tribunal and express its willingness to enforce sentences in [the] future and second, these *States* agree to accept the individual convicts on an ad hoc basis.' (Ibid).

[19] This lack of assurance for willing *States* is memorialized in the ICCSt itself. Art. 103(4) ICCSt notes that '[i]f no State is designated (…) the sentence of imprisonment shall be served in a prison facility made available by the host State'.

[20] Penrose (n 12).

by a permanent criminal court?[21] Historical deficiencies suggest the time is ripe to consider whether an international prison system is a necessary component of the nascent international criminal court system.[22]

This chapter asserts that a permanent international prison is a necessary, if not indispensable, component of any effective international criminal justice system. The chapter begins by addressing the historical approach to international sentence enforcement. Then, the chapter discusses the inadequacies of the status quo. Finally, it argues the time has come to construct a truly international prison rather than adhere to the *ad hoc* approach in dealing with international criminals and convicts.

2. THE HISTORICAL APPROACH TO INTERNATIONAL SENTENCE ENFORCEMENT: FROM NUREMBERG TO THE COOPERATING STATES MODEL

Following the UN's creation of the ICTY and, shortly thereafter, the ICTR, the international community convicted its first international war criminals since the days of Nuremberg and the Tokyo Tribunal following World War II. But, unlike the World War II courts that relied upon the Allied occupation to carry out the penalties, including both imprisonment and executions, the modern international system has no single entity tasked with overseeing the enforcement of prison sentences.[23] While the victorious Allies were able to utilize the prison facilities in Germany and Japan, the ICTY and ICTR had no such luxury.[24] Instead, they were forced to rely on cooperating States to aid in the enforcement of these Courts' criminal sentences, all of which were limited to terms of imprisonment.[25]

Likewise, while the SCSL contains a statutory preference for enforcing sentences within Sierra Leone,[26] the realities of the situation in a poverty-stricken, post-conflict nation State have precluded this from occurring.[27] So, the SCSL, much like the ICTY and ICTR 'cannot directly implement its own sanctions' due solely to the lack of a

---

[21] See e.g., H. Abtahi and S. Koh, 'The Emerging Enforcement Practice of the International Criminal Court' (2012) 45 *Cornell Law Review* 1.

[22] R. Mulgrew, 'On the Enforcement of Sentences Imposed by International Courts: Challenges faced by the SCSL' (2009) 7 *Journal of International Criminal Law* 373, 395.

[23] M. Penrose, 'Spandau Revisited: The Question of Detention for International War Criminals' (2000) 16 *New York Law School Journal on Human Rights* 553.

[24] Ibid.

[25] See Art. 27 ICTYSt; Art. 26 ICTRSt (permitting, in contrast to the ICTY, imprisonment in Rwanda 'or any of the *States* on a list of *States* which have indicated to the UNSC their willingness to accept convicted persons').

[26] Art. 22(1) SCSLSt.

[27] See Mulgrew (n 22).

functioning prison facility.[28] As a result, all SCSL convicts have been placed outside Sierra Leone to serve out their respective sentences.[29]

In contrast to the modern *ad hoc* Tribunals, the early international tribunals at Nuremberg and Tokyo had access to centralized prison space to enforce the sentences imposed. Following the World War II tribunals, that space remained in the conquered territories of Germany and Japan. However, the ICC, much like the ICTY and ICTR before it, does not possess an occupied territory and must defer to the willingness of other cooperating States to effectuate sentences. This decentralized approach to imprisonment has implications beyond mere location of prison space. The absence of a cohesive international prison system raises complications relating to family access, language difficulties and rehabilitation, thereby potentially undermining the ultimate efficacy of international justice.

While the ICTY and ICTR initially prohibited imprisonment in either Yugoslavia or Rwanda, a domestic solution was successfully used post-World War II because the occupying nations controlled the prison facilities. This practice has been adopted by one modern international tribunal;[30] the ECCC, a UN-backed domestic court tasked with investigating and prosecuting crimes relating to the Khmer Rouge regime of the 1970s, has adopted the domestic enforcement approach for its convicts.[31] Much like the World War II tribunals, the ECCC will place its inmates directly in domestic prisons which will provide far easier transitions relating to language, religion, access to counsel and visitation issues. To date, only one person, Kaing Guek Eav, has been found guilty, sentenced by the ECCC and transferred to Kandal Provincial Prison in Cambodia.[32] There is therefore little evidence of how the domestic model performs in modern society.[33] But, if the past experiences with Spandau Prison in Berlin, Germany and Sugamo Prison in Tokyo are any indication, the domestic model at least offers the benefits of a common language, a common culture and better access to family.

---

[28] Ibid.

[29] The vast majority of SCSL convicts have been sent to Mpanga Prison in Rwanda, a selection on the same continent but still 2 956 miles from Sierra Leone. The lone exception, Charles Taylor, has been sent to the UK to serve his sentence.

[30] See e.g., J. Ginn, *Sugamo Prison* (MacFarland 1992); M. Marrus, *The Nuremberg War Crimes Trial 1945–1946: A Documentary History* (St. Martin's 1997).

[31] See 'About ECCC' available <www.eccc.gov.kh> accessed 3 August 2015. The ECCC was created by Cambodian law to address crimes committed during the Khmer Rouge regime between the years 1975–79 (ibid). 'The government of Cambodia insisted that, for the sake of the Cambodian people, the trial must be held in Cambodia using Cambodian staff and judges together with foreign personnel' (ibid). Still, the ECCC utilizes a cooperative approach between national law and the UN.

[32] The Supreme Court (which functions as the Appellate Chamber) upheld the Trial Chamber's guilty verdict for crimes against humanity and grave breaches of the Geneva Convention.

[33] Two additional defendants, Nuon Chea and Khieu Samphan have both been convicted of crimes against humanity and have been sentenced by the ECCC Trial Chamber to life in prison. See <www.eccc.gov.kh> accessed 3 August 2015 (*Chea and Samphan* 002/19-09-2007/ECCC/TC (Judgment, 7 August 2014)). On 29 September 2014 notice of appeal was filed.

Perhaps recognizing the inherent limitations of a pure cooperating States model, the ICC has adopted a hybrid approach that relies primarily on willing States to house its convicts but also provides that in a given case where no State agrees to enforce the sentence imposed, the ICC's Host State, the Netherlands, will accommodate the convict in a domestic prison.[34] Because the ICC recognizes there may be some instances where a cooperating State placement is impossible to secure, its statutory design provides for this eventuality. The creation of this safety net implicitly acknowledges that the cooperating State model offers an incomplete solution and provides further evidence that a new, more permanent system should be achieved. The lack of State cooperation was further noted at the ICC Review Conference in 2010, when the option that 'imprisonment may be served in a prison facility made available in the designated State through an international or regional organization, mechanism or agency' was discussed.[35]

What remains surprising, in light of the lack of State cooperation spanning from the *ad hoc* Tribunals to the ICC, is that the international community has not pressed the need for an alternative to the status quo and has made no discernible movement toward a permanent international prison. The primary shortcoming of the cooperating States model is that only a small number of nation States participate which results in a sparse, regionalized approach to incarceration.[36] Few nation States have expressed willingness to receive international convicts from these international tribunals, with most accepting countries located in Europe and Africa.[37] The continents of Asia, Australia, and the Americas (with the exception of Colombia) have, thus far, failed to contribute prison space or facilities to enforce internationally imposed sentences.[38] Russia, too, has withheld its cooperation from the international tribunals, though several Eastern

[34] Art. 103(4) ICCSt (noting that 'if no State is designated [for enforcement of the sentence], the sentence of imprisonment shall be served in a prison facility made available by the host State').

[35] ICC Resolution on Strengthening the Enforcement of Sentences (8 June 2010). This Resolution noted its mindfulness 'of the need for broader participation of *States* in the enforcement of sentences in order to allow for such enforcement in all relevant regions and sub regions'.

[36] Mulgrew (n 22) 395 (observing that, 'with many of the difficulties relating to enforcement being attributable to the lack of support from *States*, it is perhaps time for international courts to take direct control over the implementation of their sanctions'). See also Report of the Bureau on Cooperation (21 November 2014) 6 (with the Bureau lamenting that only eight *States* have signed sentence enforcement agreements).

[37] See Holá and Van Wijk, (n 12) 113 (noting that 57 persons convicted by either the ICTY, ICTR and SCSL are serving their sentences 'in various European and African countries').

[38] Only eight countries entered bilateral agreements with the ICTR to enforce sentences: Mali (1999); Benin (1999); Swaziland (2000); France (2004); Italy (2004); Sweden (2004); Rwanda (2008); and Senegal (2010). In contrast, 16 countries entered bilateral agreements to enforce ICTY sentences, with Germany entering *ad hoc* agreements to enforce the sentence of five ICTY convicts between 2000 and 2014.

European countries have entered enforcement agreements.[39] Simply put, the majority of the world's governments and population have refused to cooperate.[40]

Thus, part of the ICC's efficacy, assuming that prosecutions and sentences become more common, will be whether there are sufficient willing nation States to house, service and rehabilitate convicted individuals.[41] At present, there have only been two convictions before the ICC, with only one conviction becoming final.[42] Because this first completed conviction took several years to accomplish, and the sentence imposed was for 14 years, there is a strong likelihood that the defendant, Thomas Lubanga Dyilo, who has already served two-thirds of his sentence, will never be sent to another State for incarceration.[43]

In over a decade of existence, with only a single final conviction, the ICC has little current need for actual prison space. But, the permanence of the ICC coupled with its ongoing investigations and prosecutions suggests that more convictions are inevitable.[44]

---

39 Sixteen countries, including Eastern European countries have entered BEA's with the ICTY. Those countries include: Italy (1997); Finland (1997); Norway (1998); Austria (1999); Sweden (1999); France (2000); Spain (2000); Denmark (2002); United Kingdom (2004); Belgium (2007); Ukraine (2007); Portugal (2007); Estonia (2008); Slovakia (2008); Poland (2008); and Albania (2008).

40 Clearly, with China, Russia and the United States refusing to offer prison space, three of the five permanent UNSC Members have opted out of cooperating with the ICC on this issue of enforcement. Further, largely populated countries like India, Brazil and Pakistan have also refused to enter sentence enforcement agreements with any of the international tribunals – *ad hoc* or permanent.

41 A consistent criticism, not without force, is that the work of the ICC has been slow and costly. As one commentator, David Davenport, noted, the ICC has been in existence for 12 years, has received approximately $1 billion in operating costs and has two convictions to date. See D. Davenport, 'International Criminal Court: 12 Years, $1 Billion, 2 Convictions' (12 March 2014) <www.forbes.com> accessed 5 August 2015. This pace does not fortify the call for any prison, much less an international prison. Rather, Davenport argues that this funding 'would be better utilized to strengthen national and regional criminal justice'.

42 The conviction of Thomas Lubanga Dyilo became final when the Appeals Chamber confirmed the verdict and 14-year sentence on 1 December 2014. The only other conviction, involving Congolese militia leader Germain Katanga, is currently on appeal. See ICC Situation and Cases (available at <www.icc-cpi.int> accessed 5 August 2015). Katanga was sentenced to 12 years' imprisonment by the Trial Chamber on 23 May 2014.

43 ICC Questions and Answers, Situation in the Democratic Republic of the Congo, *Lubanga* ICC-01/04-01/06 A 5 (Judgment, 1 December 2014) (noting that on 1 December 2014, the Appeals Chamber confirmed the Trial Chamber's 10 July 2012 decision sentencing Lugana Dyilo to 14 years' incarceration). This ICC publication notes that because Lubanga Dyilo has been in detention since 17 March 2006, he has already completed two-thirds of his sentence. Once an individual serves two-thirds of his/her sentence, the ICCSt requires a review to determine if the individual is suitable for early release. To date, no State has been selected to enforce Lubanga Dyilo's sentence.

44 Currently, the ICC reports it has 22 ongoing cases. See ICC website 'Situations and Cases' <http://www.icc-cpi.int/en_menus/icc/situations%20and%20cases/Pages/situations%20 and%20cases.aspx> accessed 5 August 2015. In addition, the ICC is investigating nine distinct situations that could yield numerous defendants. From Uganda to the recent investigation opened involving Israel's treatment of the Palestinians, there is an understanding that the ICC's judicial footprint will grow in the coming years.

And, because war crimes and crimes against humanity tend to occur in large groupings, providing several defendants at one time stemming from a given conflict, there is a likelihood that more convictions will occur in greater numbers than currently exist. At that point, when the ICC has a critical mass of sentenced individuals, will there be sufficient countries willing to accept, and bear the cost of housing, ICC convicts? The resolution of this question, coupled with the shortcomings of the status quo, strengthen the case for the creation of a truly international prison.

3. SHORTCOMINGS IN THE STATUS QUO

3.1 The Lack of Cooperating States

The ICTY, ICTR, and SCSL have ceased their official business, turning over all future activity to the MICT or, in the case of the SCSL, the RSCSL. All outstanding business, including potential future trials that would have fallen within the jurisdiction of the *ad hoc* Tribunals, has been transferred to the MICT[45] and RSCSL.[46] The most important remaining business continues to be oversight of the criminal sentences imposed by each of these *ad hoc* Tribunals, including questions of early release.[47] Accordingly, the UNSC granted powers to the MICT and RSCSL to oversee the remaining functions of the *ad hoc* Tribunals after their respective mandates expired.[48] This obligation includes designating potential enforcement States and determining questions of pardon and early release.[49] The MICT and RSCSL, just as the ICTY and ICTR before them, maintain Practice Directions to help guide these early release decisions.[50] Much like the ICTY

---

[45] The MICT began functioning for the ICTR on 1 July 2012 and the ICTY on 1 July 2013. See SCRes 1966 (22 December 2010). The MICT retains the power to implement any remaining business from the ICTY and ICTR. As the MICT indicates, '[t]he tracking, arrest and prosecution of the nine remaining fugitives still wanted for trial by the ICTR is a top priority for the MICT. As of May 2015, nine accused indicted by the ICTR (…) remain at large'. See 'About the MICT' <www.unmict.org> accessed 5 August 2015.

[46] The SCSL closed in 2013 and was replaced by the RSCSL. See 'Agreement Between the United Nations and the Government of Sierra Leone on the Establishment of a Residual Special Court for Sierra Leone' <www.rscsl.org> accessed 5 August 2015.

[47] The RSCSL projects that it may be necessary to remain in existence for the purpose of supervising prison sentences, pardons, commutations and early release for individuals convicted by the SCSL until 2055.

[48] SCRes 1966 (22 December 2010), adopted at the UNSC's 6463rd meeting. The MICT was initially put into place for a period of four years with a review scheduled every two years afterwards.

[49] See Arts 25, 26 of the MICTSt and Rules 127, 149–151 MICT RPE. See also Arts 23, 24 SCA.

[50] Practice Direction on the Procedure for Designation of the State in Which a Convicted Person is to Serve His or Her Sentence of Imprisonment (MICT 2/Rev. 1) (24 April 2014); Practice Direction on the Procedure for the Determination of Applications for Pardon, Commutation of Sentence, and Early Release of Persons Convicted by the ICTR, the ICTY or the Mechanism (MICT/3) (5 July 2012). Practice Direction on the Conditional Early Release of Persons Convicted by the SCSL (1 October 2013).

and ICTR Practice Directions, the MICT uses the domestic law of the State enforcing the sentence to trigger eligibility for early release.[51] In contrast, the RSCSL has explicitly noted in its Practice Directive that inmates are not eligible for early release prior to serving two-thirds of their sentence.[52]

As of 19 November 2014 the MICT was overseeing the enforcement of 18 sentences on behalf of the ICTY with inmates spread over 12 countries, and 29 sentences on behalf of the ICTR split between only two African countries.[53] The MICT reported that 16 ICTR convicts were serving their sentences in Mali, while 13 additional ICTR convicts were having their sentences enforced in Benin.[54] In contrast, the 18 ICTY convicts were all serving their sentences in European States including 'Austria (1), Belgium (1), Denmark (2), Estonia (3), Finland (1), France (1), Germany (3), Italy (1), Norway (1), Poland (1), Portugal (1) and Sweden (2)'.[55] Six ICTR convicts and two ICTY convicts are still being housed at the respective detention units in Arusha and The Hague, respectively.[56] All existing bilateral agreements entered into by the *ad hoc* Tribunals continue in force before the MICT.[57]

Illustrative of the ongoing limitations posed by the cooperating States model, the MICT, like each international tribunal preceding it, continues – somewhat in vain – to call on the cooperation of States to help secure additional agreements for the enforcement of sentences.[58] No new State that had not previously provided prison space for the enforcement of sentences to either the ICTY or ICTR has entered into a bilateral agreement with the MICT.[59]

---

[51] Practice Direction on the Procedure for the Determination of Applications for Pardon, Commutation of Sentence, and Early Release of Persons Convicted by the ICTR, the ICTY or the Mechanism (MICT/3) (5 July 2012). The Practice Directive section on 'Notification of Eligibility' indicates that '[u]pon the convicted person becoming eligible for pardon, commutation of sentence or early release under the law of the State in which the convicted person is serving his or her sentence (the "enforcing State"), the enforcing State shall (...) notify the Mechanism accordingly'. See also Art. 26 MICTSt.

[52] Practice Direction on the Conditional Early Release of Persons Convicted by the SCSL 4 '2. Eligibility for Consideration for Conditional Early Release.'

[53] 'Second Annual Report for the International Residual Mechanism for Criminal Tribunals' (1 August 2014) 15 para 66. But see Judge Th. Meron, 'Assessment and Progress Report of the President of the International Residual Mechanism for Criminal Tribunals' (19 November 2014) Section VII, para 44 (for the Period from 16 May to November 2014, clarifying that as of November 2014, the number of ICTY sentences being supervised is down to 18 as opposed to 21 reported in the Second Annual Report in August 2014).

[54] Meron, (ibid), Section VII, para 43.

[55] Ibid., Section VII, para 44.

[56] Ibid., Section VII, paras 43 (ICTR) and 44 (ICTY).

[57] Ibid., Section VII, para 41 (confirming that '[t]he agreements concluded by the United Nations for the two Tribunals remain in force for the Mechanism').

[58] Ibid.

[59] See generally MICT website section on Member State Agreements <www.unmict.org> accessed 5 August 2015. This tab demonstrates that only those pre-existing enforcement agreements with the ICTY and ICTR remain in effect. No new member State agreements are reported.

The lack of participating States under the cooperating States model therefore continues to be a problem.[60] Every *ad hoc* court, the MICT and now the ICC continue to call on States to aid in the enforcement of sentences, generally to little avail.[61] If States refuse to step up and accept these international prisoners, the system of international criminal justice will face a serious threat to its future endeavours. Moreover, in the Assembly of States Parties Report of the Bureau on Cooperation, the Bureau exposed the second main shortcoming to the existing model: a lack of sufficient diversity to accommodate sentence enforcement needs. The Report asserts:

> The Court would wish to have a broad range of agreements in different geographical areas and different normative regimes, so as to be ready to determine enforcements. This would allow the Court to meet the cultural and linguistic needs for sentenced persons, including for the families of the individuals concerned.[62]

Amnesty International specifically noted prior to the 13th Annual Meeting of States Parties to the Rome Statute in December 2014, the need to secure cooperating States for the enforcement of sentences remains acute.[63] In fact, Amnesty echoed the concern first reported by the Bureau of the Assembly of States Parties in its Report of the Bureau on Cooperation that only eight States have thus far entered enforcement agreements, with no new State entering into such an agreement in the past three years.[64] This dearth of cooperation has existed for each of the modern international tribunals, from the *ad hoc* Tribunals to the ICC. Simply put, reliance on the cooperating States model has proved to be a constant struggle.

3.2 Conditions, Distance, Language, Security and Cultural Distinctions

A second shortcoming in the cooperating States model is the reality that the prisons made available by the few cooperating States vary dramatically.[65] Although allocation decisions can greatly impact conditions, rehabilitation opportunities and other penal issues, these matters are largely left to the discretion of individual States. As Holá and Van Wijk observe:

> Whether an international prisoner is placed in a high security prison, protective custody, regular prison or, for example, an open prison, has great consequences for his daily life and

---

[60] Report of the Bureau (n 7) 6.

[61] Ibid. See also, MICT call for cooperation in the MICT Second Annual Report 15. President Meron reports that '[t]he Mechanism actively sought the cooperation of existing enforcement States in enforcing the sentences of the two Tribunals and continued efforts to negotiate additional agreements with States in order to increase its enforcement capacity'.

[62] Report of the Bureau (n 7) 6.

[63] Amnesty International, 'International Criminal Court: Amnesty International's Call for Pledges by States at the 13th Session of the Assembly of *States* Parties' (29 October 2014).

[64] Ibid., 3.

[65] Holá and Van Wijk (n 12) 119. Once the determination of the State of enforcement is made, generally the day-to-day details will rest 'with domestic authorities and arguably differs by State, but also by convict'.

influences the execution of his/her sentence to a considerable extent. The law of the tribunals is virtually silent regarding the type of prisons international convicts shall be sent to.[66]

The governing Statutes merely mandate conformance with basic international standards.[67] But, most germane issues are resolved locally and can vary quite dramatically from country to country and even prison to prison.[68]

One would expect that the international community would strive to provide similar imprisonment conditions to those being convicted of the same crime, or even in the same conflict. However, the status quo depends fully on the cooperation of States that are free to receive only certain individuals and, thereafter, are subject only to satisfying basic international norms, with individuals being placed in varying types of custody. Such deviations are problematic and result in some inmates' sentences carrying harsher conditions than others. Two ICTY convicts might receive the exact same sentence in terms of number of years required to be served. But, depending on the prison conditions they face, their experiences may be dramatically different.[69]

One common feature of international imprisonment, at least presently, is that nearly all international prisoners have been sent to serve their sentences in locations far from their home nations.[70] The SCSL convicts housed in Rwanda are nearly 3 000 miles from home. Even for the wealthiest individuals, opportunities to maintain relations with friends and family members imprisoned 3 000 miles away poses a choice of relocation to an unfamiliar country or constant travel which carries burdens of both time and expense.[71] As previously mentioned, the cooperating States model has resulted in 12 different European States willing to accept ICTY convicts and two African States, Mali and Benin, willing to accept ICTR convicts (roughly 2 700 miles from Rwanda). In Europe, ICTY convicts are often integrated into the local prison population and serve side-by-side with individuals convicted of domestic crimes.[72] SCSL convicts, in contrast, due largely to financial support from the Netherlands, have uniformly been placed in a special prison wing in Rwanda and are separated from domestic inmates.[73]

---

66 Ibid.

67 See e.g., Art. 106 ICCSt.

68 Holá and Van Wijk (n 12) 118–22 (differentiating between European countries like Norway, where inmates are housed in smaller facilities, usually including an individual prison cell, and Italy or France, where inmates generally face issues related to overcrowding and are housed in shared prison cells).

69 Ibid., 120 (detailing that some ICTY convicts sent to Finland have been allowed to serve their sentences in an 'open prison', described by the author as 'a facility without walls').

70 See Mulgrew (n 22) 385–6 (noting the 'very real risk that international sentences of imprisonment served in a decentralized system may be excessively isolating').

71 See J. Kelder, B. Holá, and J. van Wijk, 'Rehabilitation and Early Release of Perpetrators of International Crimes: A Case Study of the ICTY and ICTR' (2014) 14 *International Criminal Law Review* 1177, 1190 ('As it is more difficult for families to visit, convicts complain that it is difficult to maintain close contact with relatives or partners'). Special rules relating to visits have, however, been put in place for some international convicts, but like all other instances of imprisonment vary from country to country. See Holá and Van Wijk (n 12) 120–21.

72 Holá and Van Wijk (n 12) 119–20.

73 Ibid., 118. The lone SCSL exception for sentencing purposes has been Charles Taylor. His unique situation is discussed in the text more fully below.

Unlike domestic prisons, which can also be a great distance from one's village or town, the cooperating States model requires that family members traverse borders not simply miles. And, for those imprisoned on the African continent, the distances between 'home' and the prison facilities in Mali, Benin and Rwanda are close to 3 000 miles away. For some international inmates and their families, separation covering such vast distances has endangered the continuation of meaningful family relations.

Another common feature under the status quo for all of these individuals is that their sentences are being served outside their home nation, often in countries with different languages, cultures and customs. In nearly every case, it is unlikely the international convict or his or her family will speak the language of the enforcing State, which can make communicating with guards, physicians, spiritual advisers and prison staff problematic. Language shortcomings further limit an international convict's ability to participate in rehabilitation programmes, including educational opportunities or other training programmes.[74] Such linguistic issues may even impair a family's ability to familiarize itself with the prison rules, thereby limiting or hampering visitation and communications.[75] If educational classes are offered only in the enforcing State's language, which most are, the international convict may find him or herself without access to otherwise available classes.[76] The inability to communicate an inmate's basic needs on a regular basis places that individual at a serious handicap during his or her incarceration. Further, unless the prison provides individualized rules and regulations tailored to the inmate's native language, he or she may be unable to read governing policies or easily file a complaint or request services due to linguistic barriers in prison forms and policies. Even if a complaint is raised or a hearing held, unless the inmate is provided with an interpreter, he or she may be at a severe disadvantage during the proceedings, particularly in relation to domestic prisoners.

The contrast between the World War II tribunals, which housed inmates in two prisons where inmates spoke a common language, and the modern cooperating States model is stark. At Nuremberg and Tokyo, convicts remained in their home countries close to their families and lived in a culture and among a language that was familiar to them.[77] The modern system jettisoned a local confinement approach. This was due, in part, to the fact that the tribunals were a UN creation, established in nation States other than where the conflict arose and not the product of a group of conquering allies. While the Practice Directions of the international tribunals regularly state that the Registrar shall address the familial relations and linguistic skills of a particular convict, and

---

[74] Mulgrew (n 22) 389 (observing that participation in prison programmes 'requires a high degree of competency in the national language of the enforcing State'). See also Kelder, Holá, and Van Wijk (n 71) 1190 (underscoring that 'language barriers cause problems such as difficulties in understanding prison regulations, inability to participate in work or education programmes [and] problems in communicating with other prisoners, prison staff or the outside world').

[75] Mulgrew (n 22) 390 ('Though the procedures for arranging visits in enforcing States are public, relatives may not speak the languages in which the literature is published'). See also Kelder, Holá, and Van Wijk (n 71) 1190.

[76] Mulgrew (n 22) 389. See also Kelder, Holá, and Van Wijk (n 71) 1190.

[77] Mulgrew (n 22) 391. Obviously, familial relations are far easier to maintain if an individual is incarcerated in his home State.

further indicate that the President 'shall take into account the desirability of serving sentences in States within close proximity or accessibility of the relatives of the convicted person', these directions have proven to be of little benefit when only a handful of States have entered enforcement agreements with the tribunals.[78]

Exporting the internationally criminally convicted has proved no easy task. Mulgrew and others have argued that the cooperating States model exacerbates the conditions of confinement by sending the convicted war criminals to distant locations where the lack of family, friends, a common language, culture and even familiar cuisine are notably absent.[79] There is an element of isolation to these incarcerations as many international convicts are placed in foreign prisons without programmes or support systems tailored to their language, culture or circumstances.[80]

Even though international convicts receive the benefit of higher standards of imprisonment than many domestic prisoners, such protections come at the high price of distance and isolation.[81] These added protections or higher standards for incarceration based on key international human rights documents, though important, fall far short of equalizing the fact that the international convict is being housed in a location foreign to him or her in every conceivable sense of the word.[82] For example, Charles Taylor, the only SCSL convict currently held outside Africa, requested that he be imprisoned in Rwanda where other international inmates are currently being held.[83] After being sent to the UK, and denied transfer to Rwanda, Taylor complained he was being denied 'a right to family life' as his relatives were not granted visas.[84] Taylor contended that a prison sentence in Rwanda would be safer for him and less expensive for his family.[85] Finally, Taylor argued 'he was being held "effectively in isolation" because he was "too much of a target and too vulnerable" to be kept with other inmates of the Frankland prison in the northern English city of Durham' where he is being held. Taylor's final plea for an African placement was the need to be located in a prison where he shared

[78] MICT Practice Directive 2–3; ICTR Practice Directive 1–2; ICTY Practice Directive 2–3; SCSL Practice Directive 1–2.

[79] See e.g., Mulgrew (n 22) 385–6. See also Kelder, Holá, and Van Wijk (n 71) 1190.

[80] Ibid.

[81] See Kelder, Holá and Van Wijk (n 71) 1190 ('Serving a sentence in a foreign country typically has a negative impact on the ability of prisoners to reintegrate into society as they become socially isolated in prison').

A good example of this distinction is the domestic Rwandan prisoners housed in the same facility with the SCSL convicts, but living in a separate wing with different standards of living and protection. International prisons must be kept in a location where international prison standards are honoured. The same protection is not always afforded domestic inmates. See Holá and Van Wijk (n 12) 120 (discussing the special international wing of the Rwandan prison).

[82] Ibid.

[83] 'Liberia's Charles Taylor Prefers Rwandan Jail to UK' (*BBC News Africa*, 14 October 2013) (available at <www.bbc.com/news/world-africa-24520489> accessed 5 August 2015).

[84] 'Ex-Liberian President Charles Taylor to Stay in UK Prison' (*BBC News*, 25 March 2015) (available at <http://www.bbc.com/news/uk-32055482> accessed 5 August 2015). The Court found, however, that the denial of visas were due to procedural errors committed by the family.

[85] Ibid.

'a cultural affinity' with others.[86] The RSCSL denied his request.[87] Taylor's situation provides a concrete example of the cultural dimension, and shortcomings, relating to sentencing enforcement. The case of Radislav Krstić, an ICTY convict, provides an example of the security shortcomings of the status quo.[88]

3.3 Security

Beyond limited access to family, friends and familiar foods, culture and religious practices, there is evidence that security risks for these international convicts may be higher when they are dispersed among domestic inmates.[89] Radislav Krstić, an ICTY convict of Serbian heritage, suffered severe injuries after being repeatedly stabbed by three British Muslim inmates seeking revenge for Krstić's crimes against Muslims.[90] This episode, occurring within the Wakefield prison in Britain, underscores the security risk of placing international convicts within a domestic prison without physically isolating them.[91] And, as these inmates are already culturally and relationally isolated, placing international inmates in physical isolation further accentuates the inherent flaws in a 'cooperating States' model. Following the Wakefield stabbing, Krstić was transferred back to the UNDU in The Hague to await reassignment to another 'cooperating State'.[92] Krstić remained at The Hague Detention Unit for nearly two years before Poland agreed in May 2013 to receive him pursuant to a 6 December 2012 Polish Court Order.[93]

The potential security issues only compound the limitations of the cooperating State model. Not only may inmates fear being sent to a distant and unfamiliar location, there is the added fear, at least for some, that other inmates within the enforcing State will learn of their crimes and seek to inflict injurious retribution. Krstić experienced this fear and sustained injuries while housed in Britain. Charles Taylor communicated his concerns regarding this fear, though the SCSL discounted his pleas, keeping him imprisoned in Britain.[94] Interestingly, the 3 000 mile distance between England and Sierra Leone is equivalent to the distance separating Taylor's desired placement in Rwanda from Sierra Leone. But, as Taylor's request indicates, it is not merely distance

---

[86] Ibid.

[87] RSCSL Press Release, 'Taylor Application to Appeal Decision on his Motion to Transfer to Rwanda Denied' (21 May 2015) (reporting that RSCSL President, Justice Ph. Waki denied Taylor's application to appeal the January 2015 ruling entered by a special Trial Chamber to resolve the issue).

[88] 'Srebrenica General's Attackers Get Life For Revenge Stabbing in Prison' (*The Guardian*, 21 February 2011).

[89] Ibid.

[90] Ibid.

[91] Ibid.

[92] *Krstić* MICT-13-46.ES1/IT-98-33-ES (Order Designating the State in which Radislav Krstić is to Serve the Remainder of His Sentence, 19 July 2013).

[93] The *Krstić* Case Decision of the Circuit Court of Warsaw is referenced at O. Kuc, 'Krstic Case Continued' (2012) 32 *Polish Yearbook of International Law* 315. Poland entered into an Enforcement Agreement with the ICTY on 18 September 2008.

[94] RSCSL Press Release (n 87) (explaining that a special Trial Chamber appointed by RSCSL President, Justice Ph. Waki denied Taylor's motion in January 2015).

that matters, but also family relations and security. When assessing the best host country for a particular inmate, as we have seen with Krstić, issues relating to the international convict's security should be an integral part of the designation decision. But, so too should be an assessment of whether sending a particular inmate to the country of their choice for incarceration, such as Taylor's request to be sent to Rwanda with the other SCSL convicts, could raise internal or additional security concerns relating to escape or acts of violence within a host country but outside the prison walls.[95]

3.4 Rehabilitation, Release and Reintegration

A fourth shortcoming with the status quo is the uncertainty regarding early release and the absence of appropriate rehabilitation and reintegration programmes in enforcing States.[96] Because the current model relies on cooperating States and utilizes local law, in combination with tribunal consultation, for determining early release, international convicts with identical sentences may be subject to differing rules regarding early release.[97] Mulgrew notes the shortcoming with this approach, observing '[a] system that places the trigger for release eligibility with enforcing States lacks certainty and creates the potential for discrimination due to the variation between the different domestic laws'.[98]

The issue of rehabilitation, apparently relevant to the *ad hoc* Tribunals in sentencing, has largely been overlooked in international enforcement.[99] Under the status quo, international tribunals delegate rehabilitation assessments, both testing and reporting, to domestic prisons that have little experience working with those convicted of genocide, war crimes and crimes against humanity.[100] As Kelder, Holá and Van Wijk explain:

> [t]he fact that the tribunals are not actively involved in the enforcement of sentences means that the [tribunal] President relies heavily on information provided by third parties. (…) Although enforcement States have not been given any guidance on how to rehabilitate international prisoners, the President typically trusts their reports about a convicts' behaviour in prison and follows their advice in relation to the prisoner's level of rehabilitation.[101]

To delegate the imprisonment of war criminals to enforcing States whose penal policies target ordinary criminals seems incongruent with the desire to treat international convicts similarly.[102] Inconsistencies in treatment will inevitably occur.

---

[95] For a thorough and interesting explanation of how many international convicts are housed separately from domestic prisoners and kept on heightened security classification, see Mulgrew (n 22) 385–6.

[96] See Kelder, Holá and Van Wijk (n 71); Holá and Van Wijk (n 12).

[97] Art. 26 MICTSt.

[98] Mulgrew (n 12) 57.

[99] Kelder, Holá and Van Wijk (n 71) 1179 (contending rehabilitation has been 'entirely neglected by academia and practitioners alike').

[100] Ibid., 1193 (observing the tribunal 'President seems to do little to critically assess the underlying sources submitted [by enforcing States] to demonstrate prisoners' rehabilitation.').

[101] Ibid.

[102] Ibid.

Mulgrew further observes that, 'the enforcing State is under no obligation to make connections with post-release services in third States', thus limiting opportunities international convicts have for reintegration.[103] And, the basis for release hinges, at least partially, on the cooperating State's domestic structure for early release.[104] If rehabilitation entails reintegration into society, an international prison with personnel targeting the particular crimes covered – genocide, war crimes and crimes against humanity – will far better address the unique nature of such crimes and the motivations that lead otherwise ordinary individuals to commit such extraordinary acts.[105] Kelder, Holá and van Wijk assert that '[i]nternational crimes (…) are not committed by abnormal (deviant) and extraordinary people, but are instead first and foremost characterized by the fact that perpetrators commit crimes in abnormal and extraordinary circumstances'.[106] Thus, 'conventional rehabilitation programmes developed for deviant individuals aimed to reintegrate them back into society and to facilitate a crime-free life are not appropriate for international prisoners'.[107]

Without a permanent prison, and a coordinating parole or probation system, international convicts are, in the most real sense, merely warehoused in domestic prisons.[108] International inmates serve their time and, once they are scheduled for release, they are released with little to no reintegration efforts dedicated to their successful return into society.[109] There is generally no continued oversight or custodial supervision.[110] Early release, in the current international context, typically means absolute freedom. The notable exception appears to be the RSCSL's approach granting conditional release.[111] However, in some instances, early release means an inability to return home or elsewhere.[112] The individual may no longer be behind bars, but neither is he or she necessarily free to go about their pre-incarceration life.[113]

---

103 Mulgrew (n 22) 390.

104 D. van Zyl Smit, 'International Imprisonment' (2005) 54(2) *International Comparative Law Quarterly* 357, 371 (explaining '[t]he major difficulty is that the trigger lies in the national laws of States. These laws may vary greatly and result in the same sentence being implemented for different periods depending on where it is served').

105 Kelder, Holá and Van Wijk (n 71) 1196–7.

106 Ibid., 1197.

107 Ibid.

108 See e.g., Mulgrew (n 12) 390 (explaining that international convicts cannot 'avail themselves of opportunities designed to enable prisoners to look for work, to make contacts with social services and to prepare for freedom').

109 Ibid.

110 Holá and Van Wijk (n 12) 129.

111 RSCSL Practice Direction on the Conditional Early Release of Persons Convicted by the SCSL (1 October 2013).

112 Holá and Van Wijk (n 12) 129–30 (reporting on the varied outcomes international prisoners face upon release, including at least one example where an international prisoner, Erdemović, was placed in a witness protection programme and given a new identity and several others where ICTR convicts were placed in a 'safe house' in Tanzania upon their release).

113 Ibid (providing numerous examples), citing J. van Wijk, 'When International Criminal Justice Collides with Principles of International Protection: Assessing the Consequences of ICC Witnesses Seeking Asylum, Defendants Being Acquitted and Sentenced Being Released' (2013) 26 *Leiden Journal of International Law* 173.

Under most domestic prison systems, inmates scheduled for release go through a process preparing them to re-enter society, which may include graded reductions in security and increased opportunities for self-sufficiency.[114] Most domestic prison systems maintain a programmatic approach to early release, be it probation or some form of reintegration programme retaining some level of continuing oversight for the prisoner.[115] But, under the current cooperating States model where international convicts are sent to distant locations to serve their sentences, such domestic programmes are generally not available to international inmates set to leave the enforcing State.[116] As Kelder, Holá and Van Wijk observe, '[i]n contrast to the domestic jurisdictions, the practice of setting conditions upon early release – e.g., no repetition of offenses – does not exist for ICTY and ICTR convicts'.[117]

Although early release for international convicts is evaluated by assessing domestic law, and relies largely on local assessments regarding rehabilitation,[118] that same domestic law does not provide programmatic support or continuing oversight for the international convict.[119] Lacking any monitoring system for released international convicts (other than the RSCSL conditional release system),[120] 'the prisoners disappear from the tribunals' radar and are 'not of their concern'.[121] Kelder, Holá and Van Wijk provide troubling examples where failures to monitor those released by international tribunals have seemingly undermined the values of international criminal justice, with the perpetrators largely flaunting their freedom and retracting any claims of remorse.[122]

What is needed, to ensure that sentences are being uniformly served under similar conditions and that rehabilitation and reintegration are made part of the sentence enforcement process, is a permanent prison with attendant personnel, parole officers and consistent rules relating to rehabilitation and early release. If all international convicts are being sentenced for similar crimes, or at least crimes of a similar magnitude, standardized governing principles should be put into operation based on the underlying crime, independent from the nation State receiving the inmate for sentence enforcement purposes. The current *ad hoc* approach to imprisonment leads to unacceptably inconsistent approaches toward rehabilitation and early release.

Reintegration, both through graded release and continuing oversight, is a vital component of penal policy. The current model omits critical rehabilitation and reintegration structures and, thus, provides additional support for concentrating the sentence enforcement process in an international prison system.

---

114 Van Zyl Smit (n 104) 372.

115 Holá and Van Wijk (n 12) 129.

116 Ibid (describing 'Life after Release' for international convicts as a time when the 'prisoners are literally "off the radar"').

117 Kelder, Holá and Van Wijk (n 71) 1198.

118 Ibid., 1193 ('The fact that the tribunals are not actively involved in the enforcement of sentences means that the President [charged with making the final release decision] relies heavily on information provided by third parties' in the State of enforcement).

119 Ibid.

120 RSCSL Practice Direction (n 111).

121 Kelder, Holá and Van Wijk (n 71) 1198.

122 Ibid., 1199–200 (detailing the post-release behaviour of ICTY convicts, Biljana Plavšić and Veselin Šljivančanin).

4. OBSTACLES TO CREATING AN INTERNATIONAL PRISON

The creation of an international prison system, much like the creation of an international court system, presents both costs and risks. The ICC follows several *ad hoc* international tribunals and holds the promise of a more lasting solution to addressing international crimes. The work of the ICTY, ICTR, SCSL and ICC has incurred extensive financial costs and burdens.[123] And, because the work of the tribunals created long prison sentences that have outlasted the *ad hoc* Tribunals, there is the additional costs related to operation of the MICT and RSCSL.[124] Thus, the *ad hoc* Tribunals may have ceased operations, but the sentences and cases still remaining have required the creation of secondary or residual courts to slowly winnow away the remaining work still to be done.[125] The RSCSL projects that it may need to remain in operation until 2055 to finalize all its work relating to the enforcement of sentences.[126]

Judges, courtrooms and court staff are expenses that must be borne if an international court system is to function effectively. Time has provided great experience, including a demonstration of modest cooperation from nation States. From a post-World War II version of 'victor's justice' to the modern ICC, which covers nearly the entire world, international courts have evolved slowly, but deliberately. Perhaps then, as the world community considers the financial cost of erecting and maintaining a permanent international criminal court,[127] thought should be given to erecting and maintain a true, permanent prison facility for international convicts.

The first obstacle will be location. Greater consideration should be given to those countries and locations where construction might not be required from the ground up. Rather, a location in a politically stable country with a solid record regarding human rights should be selected along with an existing structure capable of providing the highest levels of service and security to international convicts. But, a complicating factor is the fact that our world is so enormous and diverse. What one country could house such distinctive populations supporting numerous languages, cultures and religions? These are troubling questions that have not yet been adequately analysed or discussed by scholars, lawyers or judges.

4.1 The Costs

Just as there have been actual costs borne by the ICTY, ICTR, SCSL and ICC, there will be actual costs borne by an international prison system, one involving building maintenance, staffing and programmatic expenditures. If the convicts of the former *ad hoc* Tribunals or the ICC are to be held in a single location, or in regional facilities overseen by a single supervising entity, a physical prison structure must either be built

---

[123] See Davenport (n 41).

[124] See MICTSt; RSCSLSt.

[125] See MICTSt.

[126] See RSCSL website <http://www.rscsl.org/RSCSL-Mandate.html> accessed 5 August 2015 (noting that as part of its *ad hoc* functions, the RSCSL 'will have the authority to manage requests for review from convicted persons and this function may extend until 2055').

[127] See ICC Press Release (n 11).

or remodelled. These costs involve real money for bricks and mortar. In addition, there will be staffing needs, from wardens, to guards, to medical and religious personnel. Building and maintaining a prison is a costly endeavour. Some country, entity or international organization – or, a combination of all of these – will need to absorb the costs associated with both constructing and running an international prison.

There are costs of outfitting the inmates, creating and printing prison rules, providing guards and prison staff capable of communicating with the inmates, medical personnel and facilities, access to psychological and psychiatric services, educational and career training, access to religious and spiritual advisors, and food services capable of feeding a variety of dietary needs, and security.

And, much like the evolution from Spandau Prison in Germany, where the Allies oversaw their convicts in a conquered country, to a system where cooperating States host international convicts, the trajectory suggests a need for consolidation – either to a single international prison unit or, perhaps, regional units existing under a single international prison umbrella. As set forth above, there are many notable shortcomings in the cooperating States model, from the obvious and consistent lack of cooperation to issues stemming from early release and lack of rehabilitation programmes. Additionally, the distance, linguistic and security concerns are already noted as issues under the status quo.

4.2 Safety and Security Issues

In addition to real financial costs, there are safety risks involved with creating an international prison. First, the risk of placing all high-level international criminals in a single location (or regional facilities) could increase security concerns for individuals displeased with tribunal outcomes or international justice. Because the ICC will be handling only those individuals whose crimes merit international attention, it can be expected that the crimes will stem, like those heard before the ICTY, ICTR and SCSL, from internal conflicts and wars with continuing unrest in the home country. Such grouped incarceration might embolden members of one of the warring factions, or others, to target an international prison or international prison employees. What country or countries would be willing to assume the risk of housing the worst of the worst, collectively, and withstand the constant security threat such inmates pose? Is the concentration of the world's most notorious international criminals in a single location a truly workable solution? While this concentration has already occurred uneventfully, at least from a security perspective, in The Hague and Tanzania, these distant locations provided some measure of security for those angry in the former Yugoslavia, Rwanda or the DRC.

On the other hand, the question of security might also be more easily answered in a single location where adequate exterior and interior security may actually provide greater protection to those convicted of the worst crimes known to humanity. If a single location could be selected, the concentration of individuals all posing a high security risk could be collectively addressed to minimize security breaches. Further, the location itself could provide heightened security protections against outside threats. From island selections to remote areas within numerous nation States, the issue of security poses both a risk and potential advantage in terms of housing war criminals and international convicts.

The security question is tied to the related issue of location. How does the international community address the risk in deciding where such an international prison, or regional prisons, should be built and maintained? Will there continue to be European and African overrepresentation? The variation of prison facilities between poorer countries and wealthier, industrialized countries is relevant from a human rights perspective. But, giving emphasis to wealthier countries could compromise certain individuals' access to family, legal counsel, religious traditions, cultural institutions and dietary requirements by placing a prison outside the realm of travel for many families. While an international prison may not resolve these location issues, at least all international convicts will be similarly disadvantaged and their families on notice of where they must travel to. And, if a single location is ultimately selected, families confronting visa requests and housing needs will face similar procedures for securing visits.

While location becomes relevant to ensuring safety, any selected location cannot be so remote that family, friends and others, like legal counsel, are prevented from visiting and maintaining relations with the inmate. If a new, truly international prison is to be constructed, efforts must be made to protect against recreating the flaws existing in the current system – such as isolation from friends and family. A centralized location, with adequate transport options (bus, rail and air) should be sought. Regardless of location, there must be efforts made to make an international prison truly transnational and capable of hosting a range of nationalities, languages, religious traditions and dietary needs.

Security is a major issue, presenting both potential risks and rewards, but other demands – particularly those exposed under the status quo – will also require attention.

5. CREATING UNIFORMITY AMONG DIVERSITY

The goal of an international prison must be to provide a standardized global response to a universal problem. An international prison will, eventually, have inmates from across the world, bringing together a cacophony of languages and cultures. The creators of an international prison will have to work diligently to ensure that no matter who is incarcerated, acceptable meals, rules and religious options are available to all. There can be no superior cultural norm – no Westernization or Easternization of treatment. There must be cultural sensitivity and, yet, common norms. This delicate balance may actually be the most daunting task facing the creation and maintenance of an international prison.

In some countries, chain gang or work requirements exist. In others, the focus of incarceration may be rehabilitation or reintegration into society as a law-abiding, even educated, citizen. But what is the penal goal of international justice? On the operational level, numerous questions arise. Will inmates receive funds to purchase items at a commissary? Will inmates be expected to work in jobs at the prison, as barbers, cooks and lawn care personnel? What standards of care, beyond the UN minimum standards, will govern? And, equally important, who will choose which norms govern? This author would delegate entirely the task of assessing both penal policies and the creation of an international prison to one entity, preferably one similar to that presented below.

The answers to these questions are still evolving. There appears to be a deep incongruity between the lengthy sentences issued by international tribunals with sentences served in unfamiliar countries and the goal of rehabilitative punishment urged by human rights documents. This chapter does not allow for a more thorough consideration of the ultimate penal policies an international prison should adopt, but does note that centralizing international convicts in a single prison will undoubtedly lead to fairer and more consistent treatment with a uniform approach to penal policy and argues for the creation of a new entity to oversee the process.

To ensure uniform treatment for all international convicts and in a move towards creating a permanent international prison, I recommend the creation of an International Prison Advisory Panel (IPAP) staffed with prison experts from a fair cross-section of the globe. The IPAP could act as an external oversight body to consider inmate issues arising from the enforcement of sentences by the current international courts and residual mechanisms. However, the IPAP should prioritize the task of creating and maintaining an international prison system. The IPAP's initial charter should enable it to establish and operate a permanent international prison (system) and to create penal policies, programmes and regimes for persons convicted of international crimes.

The IPAP should be funded by a reliable source, either the UN or the ICC. If funded by the UN, the IPAP could be located at the New York Headquarters or, in the alternative, wherever the permanent prison location is. If the ICC becomes the source of funding, the IPAP can be housed at The Hague or, again, wherever the ultimate site of the permanent prison is. While the current legal frameworks, placing supervision responsibility on the President or Presidency, do not permit complete delegation, the legal frameworks of the international courts should be amended to provide the IPAP with some role in sentence enforcement and oversight, including input regarding early and conditional release.

The purpose of the IPAP will be to ensure fair, humane and consistent treatment among internationally sentenced individuals in line with tailored international penal policy. To assist with the achievement of this objective, the IPAP should be composed of members from a range of countries that represent the different legal, penal and linguistic systems of the various regions of the world. It would be advisable to include persons who have direct experience of implementing international sentences of imprisonment. The IPAP's composition should also respect racial, gender and religious diversity. Individuals should be appointed for periods of no more than three years (to prevent the dominance of particular approaches) and the terms of members should be staggered to ensure a level of continuity.

The creation of an IPAP would ensure external oversight of international imprisonment and the continuous evolution of international penal law, policy and practice in line with international legal developments. The IPAP would be responsible for all aspects of creating and overseeing an international prison (system), from budgeting to prison inspections, to determining policies and procedures to govern the enforcement of international sentences. The IPAP could work with international courts and residual mechanisms to develop international penal policies and practices tailored to deal with persons found guilty of the commission of war crimes and crimes against humanity. These roles would mean that the IPAP would also be better placed than the current national authorities to provide reports to guide release decisions.

This chapter does not tackle that difficult question of what international penal policy should be. However, it is important that it goes beyond the current approach that appears to view international punishment as imprisonment as a term of years rather than imprisonment for a purpose. Creating and utilizing an IPAP could help properly place imprisonment in the larger context of an international criminal justice system, as opposed to merely warehousing convicted individuals, thereby improving on the current free-floating, *ad hoc* system.

6. CONCLUSION

We have a clear need to address the issue of punishment and imprisonment now that we have a permanent court.[128] And, the question of where international convicts will be housed moving forward is no longer merely a theoretical problem.[129] We have a permanent international criminal court. The time has come for a permanent prison solution. The world deserves an international criminal court that is capable of enforcing its judgments without relying on willing cooperating States. Prison, for a court whose sentencing options are primarily focused on incarceration, should have been a starting point, not an afterthought. The time is ripe for an international prison if, in fact, we are committed to international justice, not merely prosecutions. Creating an IPAP provides one vision of a potential solution.

---

[128] See Penrose (n 12).

[129] See Resolution Strengthening the Enforcement of Sentences (8 June 2010). The Resolution, while again calling on States to 'indicate to the Court their willingness to accept sentenced persons' also confirms that 'a sentence of imprisonment may be served in a prison facility made available in a designated State through an international or regional organization, mechanism or agency'.

19. The costs of suspicion: a critical analysis of the compensation scheme established by Article 85(3) of the Rome Statute

Róisín Mulgrew

1. INTRODUCTION

The ICC was established to prosecute and punish persons guilty of the most serious crimes known to mankind. To facilitate this objective, suspects are arrested and transferred to the seat of the Court and, often, remanded in detention throughout their trial. As with national criminal justice systems, international prosecutions do not necessarily result in convictions. Proceedings may be terminated for a variety of reasons and acquittals can be handed down at either first instance or on appeal. The Rome Statute (ICCSt), for the first time in international criminal law, contains a compensation scheme for arrested or convicted persons.

Article 85 ICCSt empowers the ICC to provide compensation for the deprivation of liberty in three situations: unlawful arrest or detention (Art. 85(1)), wrongful conviction (Art. 85(2)) and, in exceptional circumstances, acquittal or termination of proceedings due to a grave and manifest miscarriage of justice (Art. 85(3)). As they reflect, and indeed, virtually repeat verbatim, existing and customary human rights remedies,[1] the former two provisions are not controversial. Article 85(3), on the other hand, goes beyond contemporary human rights law.

In contrast to the ease with which delegates at the Rome Conference were willing to accept statutory provisions that reflected contemporary international treaty law,[2] there was no consensus in relation to the proposal to adopt a provision granting a power to compensate acquitted persons. Article 85(3) originated from a Japanese proposal at PrepCom to compensate persons pronounced innocent and those detained but never prosecuted.[3] The lack of agreement on this power was demonstrated by the fact that the proposed provision was entirely in square brackets.[4] States were concerned that such a power would adversely impact on prosecutorial discretion to bring proceedings, and

[1] See Arts 9(5), 14(6) ICCPR; Art. 5(5) ECHR; Art. 3 Protocol No 7 ECHR.

[2] See Y. Kim, *The International Criminal Court: A Commentary of the Rome Statute* (Wisdom House Publishing 2003) 459; S. Zappalà, 'Compensation to an Arrested or Convicted Person', in A. Cassese, P. Gaeta and J. Jones (eds), *The Rome Statute of the ICC* (Oxford University Press 2002) 1577, 1578.

[3] W. Schabas, *The International Criminal Court: A Commentary on the Rome Statute* (Oxford University Press 2010) 965.

[4] Ibid.

accordingly, if such a compensatory power was to be granted by the statute, that it should be restricted to instances of malicious prosecution.[5]

Given these concerns and the fact that there was no legal duty to provide for compensation of this kind, Article 85(3) must be welcomed as an innovative and progressive development of international (criminal) law. The decision to include a statutory power to award compensation to acquitted persons or persons against whom proceedings have been terminated can be understood in light of the particularities of the international criminal justice system and the need to bridge a remedial gap in the international legal framework. The provision does not, however, grant a right to such persons and the judicial power to grant an award is restricted by a number of statutory and regulatory fetters.

This chapter examines the scope of this new remedial power in international criminal law, analysing the reasons for its adoption, the limits on its use and the need to rethink the form and nature of the delivery of redress in this context. In other words it explores the legal, practical and personal costs of suspicion in the international criminal justice context for both suspects and the prosecuting institution.

2. REASONS FOR ADOPTING ARTICLE 85(3): THE PARTICULARITIES OF THE INTERNATIONAL CRIMINAL JUSTICE CONTEXT

In addition to the general reasons in favour of adopting a compensation scheme for victims of mistakes of the criminal justice process, there are reasons particular to the international criminal justice system that support the inclusion of this remedial power in the ICCSt. These particularities include the acquittal rate, the practice in relation to terminating proceedings, the use and impact of international remand detention and the difficulties encountered when trying to relocate acquitted persons after release from such detention.

2.1 Fallibility of the International Criminal Justice Process

If the facts and figures of the UN *ad hoc* Tribunals provide an indication of what the ICC can expect, then it is clear that a compensation scheme for acquitted accused persons is a very welcome development. At both institutions, the acquittal rate was over 20 per cent of completed cases.

The ICTY issued 161 indictments. However, as 36 indictments were withdrawn, some cases are on-going and 13 cases have been transferred to national jurisdictions – the number of completed cases is much smaller. Of the 97 completed cases to date,[6] 18 persons have been acquitted on all counts. Eleven persons were acquitted on all counts at first instance.[7] Some of these acquittals were confirmed on appeal,[8] and two

[5] Kim (n 2) 460.

[6] 31 March 2015.

[7] Dragan Papić, Zejnil Delalić, Fatmir Limaj, Isak Musliu, Sefer Halilović, Miroslav Radić, Ljube Boškoksi, Ivan Čermak, Ramush Haradinaj, Idriz Balaj.

acquittals were confirmed following a retrial ordered by the Appeals Chamber.[9] Seven persons had their convictions (and sentences ranging from two to 27 years) reversed by the Appeals Chamber.[10]

The ICTR issued 93 indictments in total. Of these, seven cases are on-going, nine fugitives remain, four persons were transferred to national jurisdictions and two persons died before the conclusion of their trial. Of the 71 finalised cases, 14 persons were acquitted on all charges and released. At first instance, six accused persons were unanimously acquitted on all counts.[11] Several unanimous first instance acquittals were confirmed on appeal,[12] although some by majority decision.[13] Some acquittals were the result of the reversal of convictions on appeal. Justin Mugenzi and Prosper Mugiraneza had their 30-year sentences overturned by a majority decision.[14] The convictions of Ndindiliyimana, Nzuwonemeye and Zigiranyirazo were unanimously reversed and a verdict of not guilty entered by the Appeals Chamber.[15]

At the ICC, of the three completed cases to date, one (Mr. Ngudjolo) has resulted in a unanimous acquittal on all counts at first instance,[16] which was affirmed by a majority decision by the Appeals Chamber.[17]

These figures reveal a high acquittal rate at international criminal courts and strengthen arguments in support of establishing a compensation scheme for acquitted persons. The provision adopted by the ICCSt is not, however, limited to instances of acquittal.

2.2 Termination of Proceedings

Article 85(3) may also be used to provide redress to persons who have been released from detention following the termination of proceedings against them because of a grave and manifest miscarriage of justice. The case-law of the *ad hoc* Tribunals provides some examples of scenarios that would potentially qualify under this heading.

---

[8] Zejnil Delalić, Fatmir Limaj, Isak Musliu, Sefer Halilović, Ljube Boškoksi.

[9] Ramush Haradinaj, Idriz Balaj.

[10] Zoran Kupreškić (10), Mirjan Kupreškić (8) and Vlatko Kupreškić (6), Naser Orić (2), Ante Gotovina (24) and Mladen Markač (18), Momčilo Perišić (27).

[11] Jean Mpambara, Hormisdas Nsengimana, Andre Rwamakuba, Gratien Kabiligi, Casimir Bizimungu, Jérôme Bicamumpaka.

[12] Emmanuel Bagambiki and André Ntagerura (Trial Chamber February 2004 – Appeal Chamber July 2006 – unanimous dismissal of Prosecutor appeal (following previous dismissal of appeal of acquittal in February 2006); *Bagilishmena* ICTR-95-1A-A (Judgment, 3 July 2002).

[13] Separate and Dissenting Opinion of Judge Mehmet Güney in *Bagilishema* ICTR-95-1A-T (Judgment, 7 June 2001) – he agreed with the majority's decision to acquit on some but not all counts.

[14] Dissenting opinion of Judge Liu Dagun – uphold TC convictions in *Mugenzi and Mugiraneza* ICTR-99-50-A (Judgment, 4 February 2013).

[15] See *Ndindiliyimana, Nzuwonemeye and Sagahutu* ICTR-00-56-A (Judgment, 11 February 2014); *Zigiranyirazo* ICTR-01-73-A (Judgment, 16 November 2009).

[16] *Chui* ICC-01/04-02/12-3-tENG (Judgment pursuant to Article 74 of the Statute, 18 December 2012).

[17] *Chui* ICC-01/04-02/12 A (Judgment on the Prosecutor's appeal against the decision of Trial Chamber II entitled 'Judgment pursuant to Article 74 of the Statute', 27 February 2015).

The majority of the 36 indictments withdrawn at the ICTY were withdrawn against indictees that were not in the custody of the Tribunal due to either their (suspected) death or the re-evaluation of prosecutorial strategy to focus on high-level perpetrators.[18] At the ICTR, the only instance where the charges were withdrawn in cases other than of persons who had deceased involved decisions to withdraw indictments to facilitate investigations and prosecutions by national authorities in Belgium.[19] Several proceedings have also been terminated at the ICC due to evidence of the death of the suspect.[20] Such cases would not fall within the scope of Article 85(3).

There were, however, some notable cases of indictments being withdrawn after indictees had spent time in international custody. At the ICTY, for example, Marinko Katava, Pero Skopljak and Ivan Šantić spent between two and three months in the UNDU following their voluntary surrender. Nenad Banović spent five months in remand custody in The Hague following his arrest. In all of these cases, the Prosecutor sought leave to withdraw the indictments due to having an insufficient evidential basis to justify or continue proceedings. In the decisions ordering their release, while the judges accepted the right of the Prosecutor to conduct investigations, they noted the emergency of such situations and warned the Prosecutor to in future 'act expeditiously on matters of such fundamental importance as the liberty of the accused'.[21] Moreover, it was in the 'interests of justice to restore (…) [their] right to liberty without delay'.[22] These situations (whereby indictees have spent time in custody before proceedings were terminated) provide examples of cases that could fall within the scope of Article 85(3).

There have also been examples of the wrong person being remanded in custody. In 1996, Goran Lajić's release from the UNDU and transfer back to Germany was ordered after the Prosecutor realised he was the wrong person.[23] Agim Murtezi spent ten days at the UNDU following his arrest by KFOR in Kosovo, before being released after the realisation that this was a case of mistaken identity.[24] These cases provide clear examples of situations that could and should fall within the scope of Article 85(3).

---

[18] See 'Order granting leave for withdrawal of charges against Nikica Janjić, Dragan Kondić, Goran Lajić, Dragomir Saponja and Nedjelko Timarac' (5 May 1998); Statement by the Prosecutor following the Withdrawal of the Charges against 14 accused, CC/PIU/314-e (OTP Press release, 8 May 1998 [Mirko Babić, Zdravko Govedarica, Gruban, Predrag Kostić, Nedeljko Paspalj, Milan Pavlić, Milutin Popović, Draženko Predojević, Zeljko Savić]. IT-95-15-I (Order authorising the withdrawal of the indictment against Zoran Marinić, 3 October 2002).

[19] Bernard Ntuyahaga (ICTR-98-40) and Leonidas Rusatira (ICTR-02-80).

[20] *Kony et al* ICC-02-04-01/05 (Decision to terminate proceedings against Raska Lukwiya, 11 July 2007) [Uganda]; *Nourain* ICC-02/05-03/09 [Sudan] terminated by TCIV on 4 October 2013; *Gaddafi* [Libya] Terminated 22 November 2011.

[21] See *Katava* IT-95-16-PT (Decision on motion by the Prosecutor for withdrawal of indictment against Marinko Katava, 19 December 1997).

[22] See *Banović* IT-95-8/1-PT (Decision on the motion of the Prosecution to withdraw the indictment against Nenad Banović, 10 April 2002).

[23] See 'Goran Lajić returned to Germany' (Press Release CC/PIO/090-E, 18 June 1996).

[24] See 'Statement on behalf of Agim Murtezi' (Press Release P.I.S/733-E, 25 February 2003); 'Agim Murtezi released following the withdrawal of the indictment against him' (Press Release CC/P.I.S/736-E, 28 February 2003).

It is important to note, however, that Article 85(3) refers to the *termination of proceedings*, and not the *withdrawal of indictments*. At the ICTY, indictments were withdrawn due to a lack of evidence without prejudice to the Prosecutor's right to bring the same or similar charges again at some point in the future if sufficient additional evidence became available.[25] This practice has been replicated at the ICC. In the *Kenyatta* case, the Prosecutor sought the withdrawal of charges due to a lack of evidence and the Trial Chamber's refusal to grant an adjournment until such time as the Kenyan Government cooperates.[26] Even in this situation, the withdrawal of charges was 'without prejudice to the possibility of bringing new charges at a later date based on the same or similar factual circumstances' on the basis of additional evidence.[27]

There have also been instances where the Pre-Trial Chamber has refused to confirm the charges against an individual without prejudice to the Prosecutor's right to request confirmation of charges at a later date if additional evidence is presented.[28]

Decisions declining to confirm or to withdraw charges (to date) have had a suspensive effect only. Moreover, this legal limbo does not seem to have a maximum permitted time frame. As proceedings are not terminated, the indictment remains open. Formalised suspicion and stigma remains, as does the potentially indefinite threat of future prosecution and detention. This approach also bars such suspects from applying for compensation under Article 85(3). This is significant given that such individuals may have spent time in international custody pending the PTC decision. For example, Mr. Mbarumshimana spent 11 months in custody at the ICCDC before being released five days after a majority decision by PTC III refusing to confirm charges against him.[29] Reliance on, and the potentially excessive length of, international remand custody are important reasons to support the adoption of Article 85(3).

2.3 The Use of International Remand Detention

The compensation scheme established by Article 85(3) aims to remedy the consequences of grave and manifest miscarriages of justice. One of the most visible consequences of such an injustice is likely to be the excessively long period of time accused persons typically spend in custody pending finalisation of the case against them. For example at the ICTY, Zejnil Delalić spend 1 000 days in custody, mostly in isolation,[30] before being acquitted on all counts at first instance (confirmed at appeal proceedings).[31] Three members of the Kupreškić family (brothers Zoran and Mirjan and cousin Vlatko) each spent four years behind bars at the UNDU (6 October/

---

25 'Indictment against Milan Zec Withdrawn' (Press Release JL/P.I.S/691e, 27 July 2002).

26 *Kenyatta* ICC-01/09-02-01 [Kenya] (Notice of withdrawal of charges against Uhuru Muigai Kenyatta, 5 December 2014) para 2.

27 Ibid., para 3.

28 *Abu Garda* ICC-02/05-02/09 [Sudan] (Decision on the Confirmation of Charges, 8 February 2010) para 236.

29 *Mbarumshimana* ICC-01/04-01/10 [DRC] (Decision on Confirmation of Charges, 16 December 2011).

30 See S. Beresford, 'Redressing the Wrongs of the International Justice System' (2002) 96(3) AJIL 628, 629.

31 *Delalić, Mucić, Delić and Landžo* IT-96-21-T (Judgment, 16 November 1998).

December 1997–23 October 2001) before being unanimously acquitted on all counts on appeal.[32] Naser Orić was sentenced to two years' imprisonment at first instance. As he had already been in custody at the UNDU for longer than the sentence imposed (three years, two months and 21 days), he was released immediately.[33] Two years later, the Appeals Chamber unanimously reversed his conviction, finding him not guilty on all counts.[34]

Likewise at the ICTR, some individuals who were unanimously acquitted on all counts at first instance had spent five,[35] seven,[36] eight,[37] 11[38] and 12 years[39] in remand detention at the UNDF. When the cases of persons who were acquitted on appeal are analysed, the situation becomes more serious. Nzuwonemeye, for example, spent nearly 14 years in custody before being acquitted on all counts on appeal.[40] His co-accused, Ndindiliyimana, had been released following sentencing at first instance as he had already served the sentence imposed (11 years). Between them they had served a quarter of a century in custody for crimes they were found not guilty of committing.[41]

This problem has continued at the ICC. Mr. Ngudjolo was detained for nearly five years (7 February 2008–21 December 2012) before his release from the ICCDC following his acquittal at first instance. Although the ICC rejected the Prosecutor's motion to have Mr. Ngudjolo detained pending the outcome of the appeal,[42] Mr. Ngudjolo was placed in administrative detention by the Host State following his release (see below).

The length of such detention, attributed to the 'long and complex trials',[43] is aggravated by the difficulties involved with getting provisional release in the international context[44] and the fact that such detention occurs in a foreign country. While there are examples of acquitted persons at the UN Tribunals who were granted

32 *Kupreškić et al* IT-95-16-A (Judgment, 23 October 2001).

33 *Orić* IT-03-68-T (Judgment, 30 June 2006) para 784.

34 *Orić* IT-03-68-A (Judgment, 3 July 2008).

35 *Mpambara* ICTR-01-65-T (Judgment, 11 September 2006).

36 *Nsengimana* ICTR-01-09-T (Judgment, 17 November 2009).

37 *Rwamakuba* ICTR-98-44C-T (Judgment, 20 September 2006).

38 *Bagosora, Kabiligi, Ntabakube, Nsengiyumva* ICTR-98-41-T (Judgment and Sentence, 18 December 2008).

39 Casimir Bizimungu, Jérôme Bicamumpaka. See *Bizimungu, Mugenzi, Bicamumpaka, Mugiraneza* ICTR-99-50-T (Judgment and Sentence, 30 September 2011).

40 See *Nzuwonemeye* ICTR-00-56-A (Motion for Compensation and Damages for Violations of the Fundamental Rights of F.X. Nzuwonemeye pursuant to SCRes 1966 (2010), MICT-13-43, 18 February 2015).

41 See *Ndindiliyimana, Nzuwonemeye, Sagahutu* ICTR-00-56-A (Judgment, 11 February 2014).

42 ICC-01/04-02/12-12 (Decision on the request of the Prosecutor of 19 December 2012 for suspensive effect, 20 December 2012).

43 *Rwamakuba* ICTR-98-44C-T (Decision on Appropriate Remedy, 31 January 2007) para 29.

44 Provisional release was almost never granted in the early years of the UN Tribunals due to the inclusion of the term 'exceptional circumstances' in Rule 65, although this did improve for ICTY prisoners in later years. See A. Trotter, 'Provisional release from international remand detention', Chapter 2 in this volume.

extensive and numerous periods of provisional release,[45] many (of these) accused persons were denied provisional release throughout their period of detention.[46]

Accused persons at the ICC can apply for release pending trial, and any decision in this regard must be reviewed every 120 days.[47] The legal procedure does not, however, address the practical and legal problem that the Host State is reluctant to facilitate the provisional release of international suspects onto its territory. The ICC has had to conclude bilateral agreements with third States to facilitate such release.[48]

The realities of the international context mean that it is foreseeable that acquitted accused persons may spend longer in detention than a convicted person at the national level. While no one would argue that such lengthy detention in a foreign country is not a serious burden to be imposed on accused persons, it has continually been upheld as lawful by international criminal courts.

While detention infringes upon the right to liberty, this right is not absolute. Detention on the basis of a reasonable suspicion is an explicitly recognised ground for liberty deprivation in human rights law.[49] International criminal procedure aims to verify that reasonable suspicion exists and thereby ensure the legality of international detention. In contrast to the procedure of the UN Tribunals, whereby an arrest warrant was issued after the judicial confirmation of an indictment,[50] a Pre-Trial Chamber of the ICC issues the arrest warrant before a hearing for the confirmation of charges.[51] An arrest warrant can be issued where there are reasonable grounds to believe the person committed crimes and if it is necessary to ensure attendance at trial, to prevent the obstruction of investigations or the commission of related crimes.[52]

Reasonable suspicion, however, only legitimises the initial detention. Continued detention requires additional justification on relevant grounds of public interest such as the prevention of the commission of further offences, flight of the accused, social disturbance or interference with the administration of justice.[53] Significantly for the purposes of this chapter, it is important to note that 'a subsequent acquittal does not render the earlier determination of a detention-justifying ground illegitimate'.[54]

---

[45] For example, following his voluntary surrender to the ICTY in March 2005, Momčilo Perišić was granted provisional release from 9 June 2005–18 September 2008, and on these subsequent occasions before his conviction by the Trial Chamber in September 2011 (22 December 2008–9 January 2009; 9–17 April 2009; 25 July 2009–4 August 2009; 9 December 2009–14 January 2010; 23 July 2010–19 August 2010).

[46] See Trotter (n 44).

[47] Art. 60(2)–(3) ICCSt.

[48] ICC and Belgium.

[49] Art. 5(1)(c) ECHR.

[50] See Arts 18(4), 19(1)–(2), 20(2) ICTYSt.; Arts 17(4), 18(2) and 19 ICTRSt.

[51] See Arts 58(1), 60(1), 61(1), (6) ICCSt.

[52] Art. 58(1) ICCSt.

[53] See *Smirnova v Russia* App nos 46133/99 and 48183/99 (ECtHR, 24 July 2003) paras 58–59; *W v Switzerland* App no 14379/88 (ECtHR, 26 January 1993) para 30; *Letellier v France* App no 12369/86 (ECtHR, 26 June 1991) paras 35, 43, 51; *Neumeister v Austria* App no 1936/63 (ECtHR, 27 June 1968) para 10; *Matznetter v Austria* App no 2178/64 (ECtHR, 10 November 1969) para 9.

[54] J. Michels, 'Compensating Acquitted Defendants for Detention before International Criminal Courts' (2010) 8 *Journal of International Criminal Justice* 407, 411.

The repeated judicial affirmations of the lawfulness of such lengthy periods of detention by international courts, however, stretches human rights' thresholds to their limits and such practice is viewed by many as a way of avoiding the need to acknowledge rights violations that would require the release of indicted or accused persons (see below).

There have been strong dissenting opinions in relation to whether acquitted accused persons' rights have been violated by lengthy detention.[55] These opinions referred, however, to fair trial rights rather than the right to liberty. Even then, the focus was on the length of time taken to render judgment following the close of argument (three years; two years and ten months), and not the overall length of proceedings (which were considered acceptable due to their complex and litigious nature). Judge Short highlighted the fact that the right to trial without delay was important, not only to serve the interests of justice, but to avoid keeping accused persons in a 'state of uncertainty as to their fate (…) [where] the Accused have been incarcerated without judgement for more than twelve years'.[56] In this particular case, the two co-accused persons, who had been sentenced to 30 years in prison, had their convictions overturned by majority decision,[57] nearly 14 years after their arrest and transfer to the ICTR.[58]

Therefore, even though human rights law recognises that detention for an unjustifiably long period renders it unlawful,[59] the international criminal courts have relied on human rights jurisprudence that has accepted the lawfulness of lengthy periods of detention by national authorities in particular cases to justify an overall policy of lengthy pre-judgment detention.

Although European penal policy explicitly warns against adopting such a policy in relation to foreign prisoners,[60] lengthy detention is likely to continue to be considered necessary for the majority of internationally accused persons for a number of reasons: the gravity of the charges against them; their perceived risk of flight or interference with witnesses or evidence; and the lack of an international police force to secure attendance at trial by re-arrest.[61]

---

55 See the Partially Dissenting Opinion of Judge Emile Francis Short, *Bizimungu, Mugenzi, Bicamumpaka, Mugiraneza* ICTR-99-50-T (Judgment and Sentence, 30 September 2011); Partially Dissenting Opinion of Judge Patrick Robinson in *Mugenzi and Mugiraneza* ICTR-99-50-A (Judgment, 4 February 2013).

56 Partially Dissenting Opinion of Judge Emile Francis Short, *Bizimungu, Mugenzi, Bicamumpaka, Mugiraneza* ICTR-99-50-T (Judgment and Sentence, 30 September 2011) para 6.

57 Dissenting opinion of Judge Liu Dagun – upheld the TC convictions in *Mugenzi and Mugiraneza* ICTR-99-50-A (Judgment, 4 February 2013).

58 *Mugenzi and Mugiraneza* ICTR-99-50-A (Judgment, 4 February 2013).

59 See *Smirnova v Russia* App nos 46133/99 and 48183/99 (ECtHR, 24 July 2003) para 62; *Wemhoff v Germany* App no 2122/64 (ECtHR, 27 June 1968) para 5.

60 See Rules 5 and 13 Committee of Ministers Recommendation CM/Rec(2012) 12 concerning foreign prisoners.

61 See *Bemba Gombo et al* ICC-01/05-01/13 OA 10 (Judgment on the Appeal of the Prosecutor Against the Decision of the PTC II of 23 January 2015 entitled 'Decision on 'Mr. Bemba's Request for provisional release', 29 May 2015); Michels (n 54) 414.

The presence of reasonable suspicion and the operational realities of the international criminal justice system are likely to 'inoculate'[62] international courts from the majority of claims for excessive detention. The judicial acceptance of the technical legality of such detention (or indeed, their refusal to acknowledge its unlawfulness) does not negate the very real and detrimental impact an international indictment and the resulting detention can have on accused persons and their families.

2.4 The Impact of International Detention

Whether the former suspect has been acquitted or had proceedings against them terminated, Article 85(3) can only be relied upon by claimants who have been detained by the ICC. Compensation under this scheme is intended to provide redress for consequences that derive from the detention associated with the grave and manifest miscarriage of justice.

Persons who fall within the scope of Article 85(3) will have lost things that 'cannot be retrieved'.[63] Acquitted accused persons have endured the loss of liberty, interference with their family life and careers, been subjected to the defamatory effects of global and public accusations of the highest form of criminality, the mental anguish of prosecution and the indignities of detention. Moreover, as Sheehy notes, the detention of an innocent person may have a more detrimental impact than the detention of a guilty person: the injustice of the incarceration inflicts greater moral harm.[64] Vlatko Kupreškić (acquitted on all counts on appeal at the ICTY) explained that, 'as far as I am concerned, four years of my life have been destroyed. My family, my mother and my businesses have been devastated'.[65] International detention not only deprives individuals of their liberty and freedom of movement; it deprives people of the fundamental aspects of human life – relationships, personal and professional fulfilment. Moreover, it imposes negative costs, such as the loss of life opportunities and exposure to increased risks of physical and mental health issues.[66]

While international detention regimes are very liberal, this does not detract from the fact that internationally accused persons are held in custody in a foreign country away from their homes and families, accused of the worst crimes known to mankind, with the uncertainty of their fate drawn out over many years. As Manns notes, 'the

62 J. Manns, 'Liberty Takings: A Framework for Compensating Pre-trial Detainees' (2005) 512 The Harvard John M. Olin Discussion Paper Series 34.

63 Justice Johnson quoted in Kimberly N. Grant, 'Ten Dollars for Twenty-Four Years: Providing Justice for Exonerees Using Victim-Oriented Mediation' (2008) 15 *Dispute Resolution Magazine* 19, 20.

64 C. Sheehy, 'Compensation for Wrongful Conviction in New Zealand' (1996–1999) 8 *Auckland University Law Review* 977, 983; K. Campbell and M. Denov, 'The Burden of Innocence: Coping with a Wrongful Imprisonment' (2004) 46(2) *Canadian Journal of Criminology and Criminal Justice* 139, 145.

65 E. Tinjak, 'Former Defendants Fight for Damages' (2011) Institute for War and Peace Reporting available online <http://iwpr.net/print/report-news/regional-report-former-defendants-fight-damages> accessed 8 August 2015.

66 See A. Grounds, 'Understanding the Effects of Wrongful Imprisonment' (2005) 32 *Crime and Justice* 1, 3.

psychological impact of the loss of liberty and degradations of imprisonment may be incalculable'.[67] Unjust detention can 'exact a heavy toll on its victims and their families'.[68] The psychological trauma can result in depression, anxiety, paranoia, drug or alcohol dependency, withdrawal and estrangement, and in serious cases, post-traumatic stress disorder and enduring personality change, that create severe mental health and adjustment problems.[69]

The impact of detention is a subjective experience and is not, necessarily, directly related to the length of such detention. For example, Marinko Katava was detained at the UNDU for two months before the case against him at the ICTY was terminated. The trauma of his detention, in what was a very security-focused regime at the time, led him to design and erect a statue in his home town, Vitez, to testify to the fundamental importance of liberty.[70]

The impact of an international indictment on an individual's reputation will vary depending on the circumstances. For example, Mr. Kenyatta was elected President of Kenya while being investigated by the ICC. Even where an individual maintains a public role, this does not mean there have not been defamatory reports and a presumption of guilt. For example, Mr. Delalić, who became a regional Minister for Justice after release, recorded over 400 news articles calling him an international criminal during his detention.[71] It seems that 'a person acquitted before an international criminal court is not an ordinary acquitted person: stigmatisation endures even after acquittal'.[72] Unfortunately, this stigmatisation has more than reputational effects. For international acquitted persons, it can have serious legal and practical consequences that can result in continued deprivations of liberty and restrictions on freedom of movement.

2.5 Relocation after Release

The process of adjusting to life after long periods of detention has practical, financial, emotional and legal dimensions. The released person may not have access to money, whether due to their assets being frozen, the cost of defence, the lack of earnings or pension, or the use of savings to support their families during their custody. Spending time in detention in a foreign country will strain family relationships. Many international detainees only receive visits once or twice a year. Even with the ICC's more

---

[67] Manns (n 62) 26.

[68] Huff cited in J. Chinn and A. Ratliff, '"I was put out the door with nothing" – Addressing the Needs of the Exonerated under a Refugee Model' (2008) 45 *California Western Law Review* 405, 416.

[69] See Grounds (n 66) 2, 3, 13, 15, 22–4, 41–2.

[70] Interview, Vitez (BiH, 6 October 2007).

[71] Written correspondence, 20 August 2008.

[72] J-P. Kilenda Kakengi Basila, 'The Case of Mathieu Ngudjolo: A Challenge for the ICC, the Host State and States Parties' (ICC-01/04-02/12-147-AnxD-tENG, 20 December 2013) 7. See also *Nzuwonemeye* ICTR-00-56-A (Motion for Compensation and Damages for Violations of the Fundamental Rights of F.X. Nzuwonemeye pursuant to SCRes 1966 (2010), MICT-13-43, 18 February 2015) paras 8, 14.

progressive and supportive approach to maintaining family relationships,[73] communications are often restricted to letters and phone calls. Moreover, forms of adaption that are functional in the prison context may be dysfunctional and counter-productive in the post-release social and family context.[74] Released persons may struggle with feelings of estrangement and loss, and find it difficult to restore previously close relationships.[75] There may also be, foreseeably, significant relational, psychological, financial and even safety consequences for family members, spouses and children in particular.[76]

Readjustment may be even more difficult in a post-conflict setting. A study of 50 former fighters released from Padema Road Prison in Freetown after proceedings against them were terminated noted that their release into a volatile post-conflict environment without support to reintegrate meant that they simply moved 'from one form of confinement to another'.[77] Jefferson explains that this continuity of confinement was created due to a lack of security, stigma and marginalisation.[78] While some of the issues (freedom of movement and assembly) in this situation were caused by a lack of paperwork demonstrating that the individuals had no case to answer,[79] physical release had not brought real freedom.[80]

The situation can become even more complicated for persons detained at the Host State of an international court. Past cases have demonstrated the long-lasting and significant impact an indictment by an international court can have on an individual. For some acquitted accused, they have returned home quietly, others to a hero's welcome. For others, the situation has not been so straightforward. Even when charges are dropped or an individual is acquitted, the international detention facility may not be able to release the individual immediately[81] due to international travel bans imposed following an indictment.[82] For some acquitted persons, the situation is much more serious than a delay in effecting release. For several persons acquitted on all charges by the ICTR, it meant moving from remand custody in an international detention facility (after pre-trial detention of seven–eight years) to custody in a safe house in the Host State.[83] The MICT has now assumed responsibility for the ICTR acquitted accused

[73] See Reg. 179(1) ICC ROR; R. Mulgrew, *Towards the Development of the International Penal System* (Cambridge University Press 2013) 113–15.

[74] Grounds (n 66) 3, 30.

[75] Ibid., 2, 33–6.

[76] Manns (n 62) 28; J. Lonergan, 'Protecting the Innocent: A Model for Comprehensive, Individualised Compensation of the Exonerated' (2008) 11 *Legislation and Public Policy* 405, 407; Grounds (n 66) 37–9.

[77] A. Jefferson, 'Traversing Sites of Confinement: Post-prison Survival in Sierra Leone' (2010) 14 *Theoretical Criminology* 387, 388.

[78] Ibid., 389, 393.

[79] Ibid., 395, 399.

[80] Ibid., 389, 403.

[81] See Rule 99(A) ICTY/ICTR RPE (subject to the power to keep in detention pending an appeal by the Prosecutor – Rule 99(B) ICTY/ICTR RPE).

[82] Interview, Paddy Craig (ICCDC CCO, 4 July 2012).

[83] See B. Henry, 'The Acquitted Accused; a Forgotten Party of the ICTR' (2005) *New England Journal of International and Comparative* Law 81, 81.

housed in Tanzania, some of whom have been seeking relocation for over eight years.[84] Unable to return to their country of origin (Rwanda) due to fears for their personal safety and the risk of persecution,[85] and without the agreement of a third State to grant them asylum,[86] they are confined to the four walls of a safe house in an unprecedented state of legal limbo. The restrictions placed on their movement and other rights mean that these acquitted persons consider the time spent in safe houses in Tanzania to be a continuation of their detention by the Tribunal.[87] These acquitted accused persons have 'no travel documents, no passports, and no official legal status (…) [and] there is nothing in the Statute or the Rules governing the status or the social reintegration of the acquitted accused'.[88]

There are both practical and legal obstacles. Without travel documents, these persons are restricted to making claims for asylum at embassies. However, as Heller explains, very few countries accept asylum claims made at their embassies.[89] Even if the acquitted accused could access the territory of a State to request asylum, Heller notes that the State could refuse the request on the basis of the original indictment. The evidential burden required for an acquittal may still mean that significant doubt remains to their guilt which entitles States to invoke Article 1F of the Refugee Convention which enables countries to deny asylum to persons if there are 'serious reasons for considering' that they have committed a war crime or crime against humanity.[90]

In regard to their liberty status, they are no longer detained by the international court, but they are not free; they cannot freely move about in the Host State and, indeed, there have been reports that the regime they are subject to in the safe house is stricter and less humane than the regime they were subject to in the UNDF.[91] They remain separated from their families and friends. Despite their acquittal, these men continue to be viewed as international pariahs and *génocidaires* who pose a threat to order and security.[92] In addition to the continuing stigma, these acquitted accused persons are 'serving time for crimes they have not committed. They are paying an unfair price for having been suspects'.[93]

Given the fact that it was foreseeable that similar issues could occur for the ICC,[94] it is disappointing that a stalemate situation arose in relation to the administrative status

---

[84] MICT Progress Report to the UNSC (16 November 2014–15 May 2015) S/2015/341 para 49.

[85] See K.J. Heller, 'What Happens to the Acquitted?' (2008) 21(3) *Leiden Journal of International Law* 663, 664–5, 668.

[86] See Henry (n 83) 85.

[87] A claim for compensation for illegal detention included the period spent in the safe house in Arusha. See *Nzuwonemeye* ICTR-00-56-A (Motion for Compensation and Damages for Violations of the Fundamental Rights of F.X. Nzuwonemeye pursuant to SCRes 1966 (2010), MICT-13-43, 18 February 2015).

[88] Henry (n 83) 84.

[89] Heller (n 85) 669.

[90] See Heller (n 85) 671, 677. (In fact, this ground was invoked by the Dutch Government to refuse asylum to Ngudjolo Chui, acquitted by the ICC – see below.)

[91] Henry (n 83) 84, 86.

[92] See Heller (n 85) 664, 668, 676.

[93] Henry (n 83) 88.

[94] Heller (n 85) 675.

of Mr. Ngudjolo at the ICC. Following his acquittal[95] and the dismissal of the Prosecutor's application for his continued detention pending the appeal,[96] Mr. Ngudjolo was released from the ICCDC. The ICC Registry had planned to house Mr. Ngudjolo in a hotel until such time as travel plans were made for him in accordance with Rule 185(1).[97] Rule 185(1) ICC RPE and Article 48(1) ICC HQA place an obligation on the ICC's Registry to make arrangements for the transfer of an acquitted person (or a person whose charges have not been confirmed) to a State that is obliged or agrees to receive the individual (or a State which has requested their extradition) and the Host State is bound to facilitate such transfers. These plans could not however be put in place until a UNSC Travel Ban pursuant to SCRes 1596 had been lifted, which required a receiving State to be found.[98] What happened instead was that Mr. Ngudjolo was arrested by Dutch police and brought to the airport to be deported back to the DRC. Mr. Ngudjolo requested that the ICC grant him protective measures under Article 68 ICCSt and his relocation to a non-African country, specifically Belgium to facilitate a request for asylum.[99] In addition, at the airport, Mr. Ngudjolo filed an application for asylum. While this prevented his immediate deportation, it resulted in his detention at an administrative detention centre for asylum seekers from the 21 December 2012 to 3 May 2013. Although he was released[100] before the Appeals Chamber could rule on his request that the ICC require the Host State to release him into the ICC's custody for the purposes of attending his appeal, the Appeals Chamber ruled that it could not have reviewed the lawfulness of this detention or ordered release as it was not the competent body.[101] In contrast to the ICTR situation, Mr. Ngudjolo was free to reside and move freely within the Host State upon his release from the retention centre.[102] It is important

---

95 ICC-01/04-02/12-3-tENG (Judgment pursuant to Art. 74 ICCSt).

96 ICC-01/04-02/12-12 (Decision on the request of the Prosecutor of 19 December 2012 for suspensive effect (AC), 20 December 2012).

97 Basila (n 72) 4.

98 See *Chui* ICC-01/04-02/12, 22 (Registry's observations pursuant to regulation 24*bis* of the Regulations of the Court on the SECOND ADDENDUM to Defence request that the Appeals Chamber order the Victims and Witnesses Unit to execute and the Host State to comply with the acquittal judgment of 18 December 2012 issued by Trial Chamber II of the International Criminal Court, February 2013) para 4.

99 ICC-O1/04-02/12-15-tENG OA (Urgent Defence Application for the international relocation of Mathieu Ngudjolo outwith the African continent and his presentation to the authorities of one of the States Parties to the ICC for the purposes of expediting his asylum application, 21 December 2012).

100 The Rechtbank Den Haag ordered his release from the alien retention centre at Schiphol Airport on the grounds that 'alien retention, whilst an asylum procedure is on-going, cannot be continuous as no exceptions to the applicable law and procedure have been demonstrated'. See 'Situation in DRC', *Chui* ICC-01/04-02/12-69-Conf-Exp (Public redacted version of Registry's update on the situation in relation to Mathieu Ngudjolo Chui, 3 June 2013) para 1.

101 See *Chui* ICC-01/04-02/12 A (Decision on Mr. Ngudjolo's request to order the Victims and Witnesses Unit to execute and the Host State to comply with the acquittal judgment of 18 December 2012 issued by Trial Chamber II of the ICC, 27 May 2013 (public redacted 12 June 2013)) para 10.

102 'Situation in DRC', *Chui* ICC-01/04-02/12-69-Conf-Exp (Public redacted version of Registry's update on the situation in relation to Mathieu Ngudjolo Chui, 3 June 2013) para 3.

to note, that the Registry was responsible for Mr. Ngudjolo (and monitoring his whereabouts) following his release from the retention centre.[103]

This state of affairs has been blamed on a legal vacuum that arose due to the operation of two concurrent jurisdictions[104] – the ICC's appellate jurisdiction and the Dutch court's administrative bench's power to rule on the right to remain in the country. Yet, it would seem that there were very clear treaty and regulatory provisions in place that set out who was responsible for Mr. Ngudjolo's relocation (Rule 185 ICC RPE; Art. 48(1) ICC HQA). The ICC Appeals Chamber acknowledged this legal framework, ruling that the pending asylum application did not 'negate the Registrar's obligation to give effect to Mr. Ngudjolo's acquittal pursuant to rule 185(1)' and instructed the Registrar to make transfer arrangements taking into account Mr. Ngudjolo's views, including as regards his security situation.[105] This would seem to reinforce the logical conclusion that the ICC's duty to relocate acquitted persons takes priority over the Host State's right to deport illegal aliens. The Registry accepted this responsibility and promised that it would do so once an appropriate place to relocate him to had been identified, and the travel ban had been lifted.[106] Interestingly, the Registry noted that should he be relocated before appeal proceedings, it would facilitate his appearance at status conferences requested by the Appeals Chamber by way of transfer or video-link.[107]

At this stage, his defence counsel asked, 'what would have happened if (...) [he] had not applied for asylum? He would have been deported irrespective of' the governing legal framework.[108] He felt that the ICC should have insisted on compliance or referred the matter to the arbitral tribunal stipulated in Article 55(2) HQA.[109] Perhaps the ICC should have done so, given that following the affirmation of his acquittal by the Appeals Chamber in February 2015, Mr. Ngudjolo was re-arrested by Dutch authorities and transferred to the airport where a flight had been scheduled to effect his deportation to the DRC. This happened without the prior knowledge of Mr. Ngudjolo or his legal representatives, and in spite of his claims to the ICC Appeals Chamber that he was unable to return to the DRC, or indeed any African nation on account of his cooperation with the ICC and his testimony incriminating a head of an African Union State, President Kabila. He stated that as he was now 'deemed a traitor' he was at risk from attack from both military and non-military groups.[110] The issue remained, again, with the Dutch immigration authorities. Mr Ngudjolo was deported to the DRC in May 2015.

---

103 Ibid., para 8; Basila (n 72) 3.

104 Basila ibid.

105 See *Chui* ICC-01/04-02/12 A (Decision on Mr. Ngudjolo's request to order the Victims and Witnesses Unit to execute and the Host State to comply with the acquittal judgment of 18 December 2012 issued by Trial Chamber II of the ICC, 27 May 2013 (public redacted 12 June 2013)) para 13.

106 'Situation in DRC', *Chui* (n 102) para 5.

107 Ibid., para 7.

108 Basila (n 72) 5.

109 Ibid., 6.

110 Appeals Chamber Transcript – ICC-01/04-02/12 – ICC-01/04-02/12-T-4-Red-ENG WT 21 October 2014 1/85 SZ A.

This event really undermined the bilateral treaty in place between the ICC and the Host State and creates a dangerous precedent for on-going cooperation in this regard. For acquitted accused persons (and the Court responsible for assisting them) it creates the danger of continued detention and uncertainty in relation to the very basic question of which country they will live in upon release. This situation is unfortunate given the existence of an explicit legal framework establishing which institution is responsible for relocating such persons. Yet the practical and political obstacle that they are released onto the territory of a Host State is unavoidable. Given these very real difficulties, the inclusion of a power to award compensation to acquitted accused persons must be welcomed.

2.6 Conclusion

Article 85(3) ICCSt is innovative and unique in the international legal arena.[111] It provides a power to grant compensation to persons who have been deprived of their liberty, despite the fact that proceedings were later terminated or they were found not guilty of all counts charged, for the first time in international law. This power is necessary in the international criminal justice system given the lengthy periods of detention faced by many accused persons pending the finalisation of their trials. In addition to its excessive length, the impact of this detention is aggravated by its implementation in a foreign country away from family and friends and the stigma attached to an international indictment. This lasting stigma can have devastating results for the individual's reputation, relationships, livelihood and, even (worryingly) their liberty and freedom of movement. The inclusion of Article 85(3) attests to the recognition of the real, lasting and complex problems faced by the individual and his or her family, and bridges a gap in the remedies that were available to international courts.

3. BRIDGING A REMEDIAL GAP

The adoption of Article 85(3) was important as it provided a statutory basis to address some of the problems outlined above, and in so doing, bridged a remedial gap in international (criminal) law. This section outlines the problems faced by international courts that do not have an explicit statutory power to grant compensation and the reluctance to grant traditional remedies demonstrated by the international judiciary.

3.1 The Consequence of a Lack of Inherent Power

While there are examples of national legislative schemes that provide compensation for the harm caused by the detention of persons who are released following an acquittal or

[111] G. Bitti, 'Compensation to an Arrest or Convicted Person', in R. Lee (ed), *The International Criminal Court: Elements of Crimes and Rules of Procedure and Evidence* (Transnational Publishers 2001) 623, 623.

termination of proceedings,[112] there was, prior to the ICCSt, no such scheme in international law.[113] Indeed, the current human rights law provisions upon which Article 85(1) and (2) are based exclude remedies in situations where the detention was lawful and the defendant was acquitted.[114] Because of this, and the receipt of requests for compensation from persons acquitted on all counts following lengthy periods of detention, the Presidents of the ICTY and ICTR wrote to the UNSC asking for amendments to the Tribunals' statutes that would facilitate such compensation.[115] As the judges of the UN Tribunals acknowledged, Article 85(3) has no equivalent in international human rights law and it is not part of customary international law.[116] That being said, these judges still felt that it would be in the interests of the Tribunals and the UN to award compensation to accused persons who are acquitted or who have proceedings against them terminated because of the 'particular circumstances' in which the Tribunals operate and the long periods of pre-trial detention faced by accused persons.

It was unfortunate that this request was not accepted. Without an explicit statutory power to grant such compensation, the judges of these institutions felt they were unable to award a remedy in these circumstances.[117] In contrast to the approach adopted where there has been a violation of an enumerated right, the judges of the ICTY and ICTR have rejected claims that they have an inherent power to grant a remedy in cases where there is no explicit underlying right, citing, inter alia, the fact that granting a remedy would go beyond their powers and create financial implications.

The *Rwamakuba* case demonstrates this dual approach and highlights the significance of the inclusion of Article 85(3). Despite spending nearly eight years in detention before being acquitted on all counts at both first instance[118] and on appeal, Mr. Rwamakuba's request for a remedy based on Article 85(3) ICCSt,[119] was denied by both the Trial and Appeals Chamber.[120] The Appeals Chamber agreed with the Trial Chamber's finding that there was no internal legal basis for such an award (either in the

---

[112] Schemes exist in Germany, Norway, Sweden, Denmark, Austria, the Netherlands, Italy and Latvia. See O. Triffterer, *Commentary on the Rome Statute of the International Criminal Court* (2nd edn, Hart Publishing and Nomos 2008) 1501; Michels (n 54) 413.

[113] See *Rwamakuba* ICTR-98-44C-A (Decision on Appeal against Decision on Appropriate Remedy, 13 September 2007) para 10.

[114] See for example HRC General Comment No 32 on Article 14 para 53.

[115] See ICTY Annual Report 2002 (A/57/379 – S/2002/985, 4 September 2002) para 28; Zappalà, (n 2) 1582.

[116] See Letter dated 19 September 2000 from the President of the ICTY addressed to the Secretary-General, Annexed to Letter dated 26 September 2000 from the Secretary-General addressed to the President of the UNSC, S/2000/904; Letter dated 26 September 2000 from the President of the ICTR addressed to the Secretary-General, Annexed to Letter dated 28 September 2000 from the Secretary-General addressed to the President of the UNSC, S/2000/925, 06/10/2000.

[117] See Ninth Annual Report ICTY (UN Doc A/578/379-S/2002/985, 4 September 2002) para 28.

[118] *Rwamakuba* ICTR 98-44C-T (Trial Judgment, 20 September 2006) Chapter IV.

[119] *Rwamakuba* ICTR-98-44C-A (Decision on Appeal against Decision on Appropriate Remedy, 13 September 2007) para 5.

[120] Ibid., para 15.

internal positive law or case-law) and it was not part of customary international law.[121] In other words, the judges could not grant compensation for lengthy detention without an explicit statutory or regulatory provision or precedent upon which to base such an award.

This can be contrasted with the practice of relying on an inherent judicial authority to award remedies in instances of violations of recognised rights. Indeed, this inherent authority was relied upon to grant Mr. Rwamakuba monetary compensation and non-monetary assistance for violations of his fair trial rights.[122] This was in spite of opposition by the Registrar who argued, inter alia, that compensation could not be awarded in the absence of a statutory provision or rule, particularly given unsuccessful attempts by the Tribunals' Presidents to have the legal framework amended to facilitate such a power.[123] The Appeals Chamber, dismissing these claims,[124] based the inherent authority to grant a remedy for violations of fair trial rights on the statutory duty to ensure a fair trial and respect for the rights of the accused (Article 19(1) ICTRSt), the need to provide an effective remedy for human rights violations (derived from ICTR and ICTY case-law and international human rights treaty law), and previous decisions noting the authority of the Tribunal to award financial compensation for human rights violations.[125] Where enumerated rights had been violated, the Appeals Chamber upheld the Trial Chamber's finding that:

> internal institutional considerations related to the execution of an order, including budgetary matters, are separate considerations from the Tribunal's authority to award an effective remedy in the form of financial compensation (…) Budgetary considerations cannot interfere with the Tribunal's authority to award financial compensation as an effective remedy for a human rights violation.[126]

Both Chambers in this case, however, rejected the argument that they had an inherent power to award a monetary remedy for wrongful prosecution. Indeed, the Appeals Chamber referred to the failed attempt by the ICTR President to seek such express powers and budgetary resources from the UNSC.[127] Without a violated enumerated right, there was no legal duty to provide an effective remedy. Without a legal duty to provide a remedy, there was no budget line to draw from.

The rejection of an inherent power to grant a remedy in such cases has resulted in claimants at other tribunals arguing for a remedy on the basis of violations of established rights. In a recent claim submitted to the MICT by an acquitted accused person, for example, while Article 85(3) was referred to, this was only to make the

---

[121] Ibid., para 10.

[122] See ibid., paras 17–18.

[123] Ibid., para 20.

[124] Ibid., para 24.

[125] Ibid., paras 22, 26.

[126] Ibid., para 30. For a contrasting view, see Judge Shahabuddeen's Partly Dissenting Opinion. He argued that judicial inherent authority could not be invoked to 'justify the acquisition of a wholly new function, more particularly one which involves the expenditure of monies provided by UN member States' (see para 5).

[127] Ibid., para 10.

point that a broader approach to compensation has been adopted within the international criminal law context. The legal basis for the claim submitted was the breach of fundamental and explicit rights (notification of charges and undue delay).[128] Moreover, the ICTR case-law outlined above was cited to support the argument that financial compensation could be paid for violations of the rights of accused persons even in the absence of an explicit statutory provision granting the judges the power to do so.

In light of the difficulties experienced at the *ad hoc* Tribunals because of the lack of both an explicit and inherent power to grant a remedy in such circumstances, Article 85(3) is a significant addition to the Rome Statute. Not only does this statutory provision provide a clear legal basis[129] for the judicial power and the funds required to implement it, the form of remedy granted, compensation, may overcome another problem encountered at the UN Tribunals. Sonia Starr calls this phenomenon 'remedial deterrence'.

3.2 A Means to Overcome Remedial Deterrence?

Without a remedial provision akin to Article 85(3), the defendant's liberty is the only compensatory currency international courts possess.[130] Convicted persons who have been detained illegally or for excessive periods due to delay can receive a sentence reduction.[131] However, prior to judgment and sentencing, the traditional remedy for violations of fair trial rights and excessive or illegal detention is release with prejudice to the Prosecutor. At the ICTR, for example, the Appeals Chamber ordered that the case against *Barayagwiza* be dropped with prejudice for the Prosecution and the accused person's immediate release because of the egregious nature of the violations of the accused's rights (detention in Cameroon and the failure to bring the accused before a judge at the ICTR for four months).[132] While release was an 'extreme measure intended as a sanction for the serious breaches of fundamental guarantees of which the Prosecution was found to be responsible',[133] the political reaction, by Rwanda in particular, resulted in the Appeals Chamber reversing its decision to order release in a controversial revision proceeding.[134] It still held however that the violations of the defendant's rights had occurred and if convicted, these would have to be taken into

---

[128] See *Nzuwonemeye* ICTR-00-56-A (Motion for Compensation and Damages for Violations of the Fundamental Rights of F.X. Nzuwonemeye pursuant to SCRes 1966 (2010), MICT-13-43, 18 February 2015).

[129] See Art. 21(1)(a) ICCSt.

[130] See S.B. Starr, 'Rethinking "Effective Remedies": Remedial Deterrence in International Courts' (2008) 83 *New York University Law Review* 693, 758.

[131] See Partially Dissenting Opinion of Judge Emile Francis Short, *Bizimungu, Mugenzi, Bicamumpaka, Mugiraneza* ICTR-99-50-T (Judgment and Sentence, 30 September 2011) para 7. Similarly, the AC ICTR compensated Juvénal Kajelijeli for the 'serious violations of the Appellant's fundamental rights during his arrest and detention in Benin and the UNDF' by reducing the sentence imposed at trial of two terms of life imprisonment and a term of 15 years' imprisonment to a single fixed term of 45 years, *Kajelijeli* ICTR-98-44A-A (Judgment, 23 May 2005) para 324.

[132] *Barayagwiza* ICTR-97-19-AR72 (Appeals Chamber, Decision, 3 November 1999).

[133] Zappalà (n 2) 1581.

[134] *Barayagwiza* (n 132).

consideration in the determination of the sentence and if acquitted, that the accused should be adequately compensated for the unjust detention.[135] As he was later convicted for inciting genocide, he was 'compensated at the penalty stage',[136] receiving a reduced sentence (32 years instead of a life sentence).[137]

A similar situation has already arisen at the ICC. The Trial Chamber in the *Lubanga* case decided to stay proceedings[138] and release[139] the accused person on the basis of the Prosecutor's non-disclosure of exculpatory evidence (and its effect on the accused's right to a fair trial), although the Appeals Chamber later overturned these decisions.[140]

Starr argues that the traditional remedies of release and retrial may go beyond the restitutionary goal of human rights law and result in a 'windfall'.[141] Given their impact on the tribunals' mandate, operational capacity and stakeholders' interests, such remedies are untenable and prohibitively costly in the international criminal justice context.[142] The practical and political constraints of a system based on State cooperation are so significant that the Tribunals 'are institutionally incapacitated from ex-post recognition of criminal procedure violations that are serious enough to require a significant remedy'.[143] Accordingly, the costs of traditional remedies are resulting in the international judiciary narrowly interpreting substantive rights, erecting procedural hurdles and imposing high evidential burdens to avoid hearing or accepting claims.[144] This approach is evident in applications for provisional release, or claims that trials have been unduly delayed.[145]

Starr argues that, in the international criminal justice context, 'an absolutist approach to the right to an effective remedy may be self-defeating' as it may result in no remedy being awarded.[146] Therefore, it is both appropriate and desirable to adopt an *interest-balancing* approach that permits departure from the requirement of full remedy in face of strong legitimate countervailing considerations related to the institutional objectives of and operational constraints faced by international courts.[147] As 'defendants' interests

---

135 Ibid., para 71.

136 Schabas (n 3) 967.

137 *Nahimana et al* ICTR-99-52-T (Judgment and Sentence, 3 December 2003) para 1107; *Nahimana et al* ICTR-99-52-A (Judgment, 28 November 2007) paras 1086–1097.

138 *Lubanga* ICC-01/04-01/06-1486 (OA13) (Judgment on the appeal of the Prosecutor against the decision of Trial Chamber I entitled 'Decision on the consequences of non-disclosure of exculpatory materials covered by Article 54(3)(e) agreements and the application to stay the prosecution of the accused, together with certain other issues raised at the Status Conference on 10 June 2008', 21 October 2008).

139 *Lubanga* ICC-01/04-01/06-1418 (Decision on the release of Thomas Lubanga Dyilo, 2 July 2008).

140 *Lubanga* ICC-01/04-01/06-1487 (OA12) (Judgement on the appeal of the Prosecutor against the decision of Trial Chamber I entitled 'Decision on the release of Thomas Lubanga Dyilo', 21 October 2008).

141 Starr (n 130) 694–5, 703.

142 Ibid., 710.

143 Ibid., 741.

144 Ibid., 695, 710.

145 Ibid., 696, 720–22.

146 Ibid., 740.

147 Ibid., 698, 739, 753.

in broad rights and remedies cannot always trump these competing considerations',[148] she argues that international judges should be able to grant less costly partial remedies. This approach is deemed preferable as it results in a remedy being granted.

If this reasoning is accepted, it could be argued that Article 85(3) represents an interest-balancing approach to remedies in the international criminal justice context. Rather than continuing the judicial fiction that violations of fair trial rights or the right to liberty are not occurring (due to the high costs of traditional remedies for such violations), Article 85(3) gives international judges the power to award compensation to acquitted accused persons to deal with the harmful consequences of excessive pre-judgment detention in international remand centres. As Trial Chamber III of the ICTR observed, the significance of the principle established by Article 85(3) 'must be understood with reference to the right of any individual to freedom, including the corresponding principle that detention should remain exceptional or, at least, limited to what is reasonable and necessary'.[149] Indeed, the normative basis for the compensation of acquitted accused persons in many domestic systems is the need to try to counteract the (exceptional) harm caused by legitimate government action resulting in detention.[150] Counteracting the negative consequences of lengthy periods of remand detention therefore appears to the implicit foundation for the remedial power granted by Article 85(3).

This approach is in line with European penal policy. The Council of Europe's Committee of Ministers has recommended that member States provide compensation to 'persons remanded in custody who are not subsequently convicted of the offence in respect of which they were so remanded'.[151] Despite recognising that a legal basis for remand may have existed, the compensation is advocated on the basis of the *non-punitive nature* of remand in custody.[152]

Michels argues that it is important to distinguish between distinct rights – the right to a speedy trial, the right not to be detained for an unjustifiably long period and any right to compensation for acquitted accused persons.[153] As he rightly states, the two former rights operate independently from findings of guilt or innocence and the remedy granted deals only with the periods that exceed what is considered a reasonable period of time.[154] He notes that the latter remedy is awarded in relation to the entire period of detention. But, Article 85(3) does not provide claimants with an entitlement to compensation. This power resulted from a fusion of the normative and principled

---

[148] Ibid., 739.

[149] *Rwamakuba* ICTR-98-44C-T (Decision on Appropriate Remedy, 31 January 2007) para 29.

[150] See Michels (n 54) 416–7.

[151] Para 34(1) Recommendation Rec(2006) 13 of the Committee of Ministers to member States on the use of remand in custody, the conditions in which it takes place and the provision of safeguards against abuse (adopted on 27 September 2006 at the 974th meeting of the Ministers' Deputies).

[152] Para 34 Explanatory Memorandum CM(2006)122 Addendum, 30 August 2006 (adopted at the 974th Meeting of the Ministers' Deputies, 27 September 2006).

[153] Michels (n 54) 412.

[154] See Partially Dissenting opinion of Judge Patrick Robinson in *Mugenzi and Mugiraneza* ICTR-99-50-A (Judgment, 4 February 2013).

foundations of the human rights protections against undue delay at trial (right to a fair trial) and excessive detention (the right to liberty). In other words, it addresses the harm caused by encroachments on these rights without the need to find an illegal act or violation of an enumerated right.

3.3 Operational Efficiency and Legitimacy

Article 85(3) does not create a right but a remedial tool to deal with the 'lawful' but worrying (and almost inevitable) consequences of international criminal justice process. Article 85(3) is necessary to empower judges to counteract the negative consequences of international indictments, prosecutions and detention. This power is not only of benefit to the applicant, but it is likely to have collateral benefits for the operational efficiency of the Court, and ultimately its legitimacy.

A compensation scheme of this type may result in caution and increased propriety in international investigations and prosecutions[155] and induce 'socially optimal'[156] levels of remand detention. Research has shown that contrary to the traditional view that it is preferable that a guilty person is found innocent than an innocent person being found guilty, this principle becomes weakened, even inverted, in situations where persons are accused of serious crimes.[157] The crimes under the ICC's jurisdiction are of the utmost gravity and have affected large, if not immeasurable numbers of victims. A scheme that urges caution in a context in which a vocal and active victim lobby demands convictions should be welcomed. Despite the initial (political) reluctance to fund compensation schemes for persons indicted for international crimes,[158] a scheme that results in a more cautious approach to prosecutions and the use of remand detention can make the international criminal justice system more cost-effective.[159]

3.4 Conclusion

While Article 85(3) may ensure greater cautiousness and propriety in the ICC's prosecutorial strategy and use of remand detention, this remedial power should not be seen as a substitute for recognising and remedying violations of enumerated rights, however costly these remedies may be for the international courts' operations and mandate fulfilment. The strong human rights protection against, and remedies for, unlawful detention on account of its excessive length and unduly delayed trials are important deterrents against the abuse of coercive power (to prosecute and detain).[160] Article 85(3) should not be used as a means to legalise or legitimise excessively

---

155 See Beresford (n 30) 635; Sheehy (n 64) 986.

156 G. Doménech-Pascual and M. Puchades-Navarro, 'Compensating Acquitted Pre-Trial Detainees' (2014) *International Review of Law and Economics* 1, 10.

157 J.W. de Keijser, E.G.M. de Lange and J.A. van Wilsem, 'Wrongful Convictions and the Blackstone Ratio: An Empirical Analysis of Public Attitudes' (2014) 16(1) *Punishment and Society* 32, 34–5, 44.

158 Bitti (n 111) 623; Beresford (n 30) 642.

159 Manns (n 62) 61.

160 See Starr (n 130) 758–9.

lengthy detention or avoiding the costs of the true remedy for such rights violations by enabling international courts to essentially pay for human rights violations.

The introduction of a judicial power to deal with the realities of international detention prior to the finalisation of proceedings is vitally important. It provides judges with an explicit power to grant a remedy in the absence of an explicit or customary international human rights obligation to do so. This explicit statutory power means that any sums awarded have a direct budgetary source. It ensures equality of treatment: convicted persons can receive compensation in the form of sentence reduction for violations of their right to liberty or a trial within a reasonable time.[161] Finally, this power recognises that the legality of detention does not detract from its detrimental impact on the individuals subject to it. The ability of ICC judges to use this power has, however, been greatly restricted by thresholds and criteria established in the Court's statute and rules.

4. ELIGIBILITY FOR COMPENSATION UNDER ARTICLE 85(3)

Article 85(3) provides the ICC judges with a power to grant compensation to 'unjustly prosecuted'[162] persons. This section outlines how this power is constrained by explicit statutory and regulatory provisions that create strict eligibility criteria.

4.1 Statutory Thresholds

Article 85(3) contains several explicit criteria which applicants for compensation must be able to demonstrate.

First, the individual must have been *released from detention* following a final decision of acquittal or a termination of proceedings. Accordingly, a person who was not remanded in custody would not be eligible for compensation.

Secondly, if the claimant has been acquitted, the acquittal must be *final*. The Prosecutor can appeal an acquittal on the grounds of a procedural, factual or legal error.[163] An acquitted person may be remanded in custody pending the outcome of the appeal, although this should only be in exceptional circumstances after consideration of a concrete risk of flight, the seriousness of the offence charged and the probability of success on appeal,[164] although any decision of this kind can be appealed.[165] If an acquittal is not appealed, it typically becomes final after 30 days.[166]

---

[161] *Duch* ECCC 001/18-07-2007 623–627, 631–633. Sentenced to 35 years in prison but only had to serve 19 – five-year reduction for illegal military detention and 11 for time already served.

[162] This term is used by the ICTY and ICTR judges in their respective letters to the UNSC.

[163] Art. 81(1) ICCSt.

[164] Art. 81(3)(c)(i) ICCSt. Both the Trial and Appeals Chamber rejected the Prosecutor's request to keep Mr. Ngudjolo Chui in detention pending the finalisation of the appeal of his acquittal.

[165] Art. 81(3)(c)(ii) ICCSt.

[166] Rule 150 ICC RPE.

Thirdly, and significantly, the release from detention must have been ordered due to the discovery of a *grave and manifest miscarriage of justice* (GMMOJ).[167] This term is not defined. The inclusion of both adjectives (grave and manifest) suggests a narrower cause of action than that created by Article 85(2) in cases of wrongful convictions.[168] This implicit requirement of a higher tier of injustice is troublesome given that the term miscarriage of justice 'connotes a failing of monumental scale'.[169]

The deliberate inclusion of a narrower cause of action could be recognition of the fact that an acquittal (or termination of proceedings) is a remedy of sorts for mistakes in criminal justice process. However, as Sheehy argues, the concept of miscarriage of justice should cover all instances whereby the criminal justice process does not work properly, with serious adverse consequences for wrongly accused persons:[170] persons acquitted following a prior conviction 'are merely further along the "continuum toward outrage", as other categories of accused may suffer many of the same burdens as those wrongly convicted'.[171]

When seeking compensation at the ICTR, Mr. Rwamakuba and his counsel argued that a GMMOJ had occurred on the basis of two distinct grounds. First, they argued that the Prosecution had relied on false and unsatisfactory evidence to arrest and prosecute him.[172] The Appeals Chamber rejected this claim, stating no evidence or convincing arguments had been produced to substantiate these allegations.[173] The second ground was based on the lengthy detention he had endured (due to failings in the collection and presentation of evidence) and the denial of his right to an expeditious trial (due to denials of requests for severance).[174] This claim was also found to be unsubstantiated.[175] Can it be inferred from this case that both grounds, if substantiated, would qualify as a GMMOJ at the ICC?

There have been instances where appeal judges have been highly critical of convictions handed down at first instance. For example, in the case of *Protais Zigiranyirazo*, a unanimous Appeals Chamber stated that serious errors made by the Trial Chamber in relation to their statement of legal principles and handling of key evidence resulted in a miscarriage of justice that invalidated the guilty verdict.[176]

---

[167] A narrower cause of action also seems to apply at the STL. The STL equivalent provision, Rule 170(D) STL RPE (added November 2010, fourth revision), does not require a grave and manifest miscarriage of justice. The only pre-condition is a final judgment of acquittal. However, this may be poor drafting as it goes on to require a serious miscarriage of justice in cases of illegal arrest or detention. This would seem incompatible with human rights law that grants an enforceable right to compensation in such instances. This threshold would seem more likely to have been intended for the former instance of final cases of acquittal.

[168] See Triffterer (n 112) 1501.

[169] P. Ewick, 'The Scale of Injustice', in C.J. Ogletree and A. Sarat (eds), *When Law Fails: Making Sense of Miscarriages of Justice* (New York University Press 2009) 303, 303.

[170] See Sheehy (n 64) 992.

[171] Ibid. (quoting from Kaiser).

[172] *Rwamakuba* ICTR-98-44C-A (Decision on Appeal against Decision on Appropriate Remedy, 13 September 2007) paras 8, 15.

[173] Ibid., para 11.

[174] Ibid., para 8.

[175] Ibid., paras 13, 15.

[176] *Zigiranyirazo* ICTR-01-73-A (Judgment, 16 November 2009) para 73.

Indeed, it held that the conviction at first instance had 'violated the most basic and fundamental principles of justice'.[177] Is this the type of decision that will be required to constitute a finding of a GMMOJ?

A further problem is caused by the statutory requirement for the grave and manifest miscarriage of justice to be demonstrated by *conclusive facts*. It is unclear what this will mean in practice.

Will the decision releasing the detainee suffice or will a separate hearing be required? Rule 173(2)(c) ICC RPE refers to notification of the decision of the Court concerning the existence of a grave and manifest miscarriage of justice. This would seem to indicate that the determination of the existence of such a fact is a duty for the Court alone. But the importance of such a finding would seem to necessitate the hearing of the views of the persons alleging the miscarriage of justice. However, the requirement of a separate hearing may result in the creation of a potentially insurmountable evidential burden on the applicant. How do you prove a 'grave and manifest' miscarriage of justice has occurred?

Further, will an acquittal based on a *majority decision* suffice?[178] This is an even more difficult question if these statutory requirements reflect an implicit preference for claims from persons who are (or at least appear to be) factually innocent (see below).

For example the majority of first instance acquittals[179] and those affirmed on appeal[180] at the ICTY were unanimous decisions. In the case of acquittals on appeal, however, there has been more discord. While the Appeals Chamber unanimously reversed the convictions of Zoran, Mirjan and Vlatko Kupreškić,[181] Judge Liu disagreed with the majority decision to reverse Momčilo Perišić's conviction (and 27-year sentence).[182] In the *Gotovina and Markač* case, the acquittal came as the result of a slim three-to-two decision.[183] In their dissenting opinions, Judge Agius and Judge Pocar were not only extremely critical of the majority's reasoning and verdict,[184] they were perplexed as to why convictions had not been entered under alternate modes of liability.[185] Judge Meron ruled out this course of action on the basis that it would be unfair to the appellants to be found guilty of crimes that were different from those they

---

177 Ibid., para 75.

178 See Art. 74(3) ICCSt.

179 Dragan Papić, Zejnil Delalić, Fatmir Limaj, Isak Musliu, Sefer Halilović, Miroslav Radić, Ljube Boškoksi, Ivan Čermak.

180 Fatmir Limaj, Sefer Halilović, Ljube Boškoksi – although see the Partially Dissenting and Separate Opinion and Declaration of Judge Schomburg, *Limaj, Bala and Musliu* IT-03-66-A (Judgment, 27 September 2007).

181 *Kupreškić, Kupreškić, Kupreškić, Josipović and Šantić* IT-96-16-A (Judgment, 23 October 2001).

182 Dissenting Opinion of Judge Liu, *Perišić* IT-04-81-A (Judgment, 28 February 2013).

183 See *Gotovina and Markač* IT-06-90-A (Judgment, 12 November 2012); J.N. Clark, 'Courting Controversy: The ICTY's Acquittal of Croatian Generals Gotovina and Markač' (2013) 11 *Journal of International Criminal Justice* 399–423.

184 See Dissenting Opinion of Judge Carmel Agius, paras 1, 91 and Dissenting Opinion of Judge Pocar, paras 2, 39. *Gotovina and Markač* ibid.

185 See Dissenting Opinion of Judge Carmel Agius, paras 71–72 and Dissenting Opinion of Judge Pocar, paras 31, 33, 36. *Gotovina and Markač* ibid.

defended against,[186] while Judge Robinson ruled it out as the fact-finding required for new convictions did not come within the appellate function.[187] These comments do not necessarily reflect a view that the appellants were considered to be factually innocent.

A similar situation arose at the ICC. Although Mr. Ngudjolo's unanimous first instance acquittal[188] was affirmed on appeal, this affirmation was also the result of a bare majority decision. While three judges affirmed the first instance decision on the basis that it had not been materially affected by a procedural, factual or legal error,[189] Judge Tarfusser and Judge Trendafilova were highly critical of the majority's review of the alleged errors made by the Trial Chamber and concluded that the acquittal should have been reversed or amended and a re-trial ordered pursuant to Article 83(2) ICCSt.[190]

Do conclusive facts of a GMMOJ exist when a minority of judges express a view that, due to the gravity of the errors made by the Trial Chamber in reaching a not guilty verdict,[191] a retrial should be ordered? At the ICTY, Judge Robinson noted that a re-trial (an exceptional measure) would not be appropriate if it would be unduly oppressive to the appellants – which would be the case if the accused had already spent long periods of time in custody[192] and a retrial would be lengthy and expensive.[193]

This view did not prevent the ICTY Appeals Chamber, by majority decision, granting the Prosecutor's appeal of an acquittal in the case of *Haradinaj, Balaj and Brahimaj* and ordering a retrial to facilitate the testimony of Prosecution witnesses.[194] Judge Robinson felt that as the case had already been extended several times on account of the Prosecutor's concerns about witness intimidation, ordering a retrial went beyond the powers of the Appeals Chamber and constituted a dangerous precedent as it prioritised the Prosecution's right to present its case over the accused's right to an expeditious trial.[195] Although TCI had unanimously acquitted Haradinaj (and ordered his release),[196] and acquitted Balaj by a majority (and ordered his transfer back to serve the sentence he was serving prior to transfer to the ICTY),[197] the Appeals Chamber ordered that they be remanded in custody pending the outcome of the retrial.[198] The new Trial

[186] Separate Opinion of Judge Meron, para 6. *Gotovina and Markač* ibid.

[187] See Separate Opinion of Judge Robinson, paras 14–16. *Gotovina and Markač* ibid.

[188] *Chui* ICC-01/04-02/12-3-tENG (Judgment pursuant to Article 74 of the Statute, 18 December 2012).

[189] *Chui* ICC-01/04-02/12 A (Judgment on the Prosecutor's appeal against the decision of Trial Chamber II entitled 'Judgment pursuant to Article 74 of the Statute', 27 February 2015) para 296.

[190] Joint Dissenting Opinion of Judge Ekaterina Trendafilova and Judge Cuno Tarfusser, *Chui* ibid., Annex A para 70.

[191] Partially Dissenting Opinion of Judge Tuzmukhamedov, *Ndindiliyimana, Nzuwonemeye, Sagahutu* ICTR-00-56-A (Judgment, 11 February 2014) para 6.

[192] By the date of the appeal in this case, Gotovina had served one-third of the sentence imposed at trial, and Markač had served half.

[193] See Separate Opinion of Judge Robinson paras 18–19, *Gotovina and Markač* (n 183).

[194] *Haradinaj, Balaj and Brahimaj* IT-04-84-A (Judgment, 19 July 2010).

[195] Partially Dissenting Opinion of Judge Robinson para 32.

[196] *Haradinaj, Balaj and Brahimaj* IT-04-84-T (Judgment, 3 April 2008) para 502.

[197] Ibid., para 503.

[198] *Haradinaj, Balaj and Brahimaj* IT-04-84-A (Judgment, 19 July 2010).

Chamber unanimously acquitted these parties on all counts contained in the retrial indictment.[199] These parties faced seven years of uncertainty in relation to their fate. Does this make it a conclusive case of a GMMOJ? Does an acquitted person who has to be returned to serve a sentence for murder qualify for compensation under a discretionary scheme?

It is clear that the statutory provision lacks clarity in relation to defining elements of the compensation scheme it establishes. Rather than add clarity, the rules that provide the detail for the operation of the scheme create further hurdles for claimants to overcome.

4.2 Regulatory Requirements

The procedure for requesting and awarding compensation is set out in Rules 173 and 174. These rules contain several requirements that may become procedural bars for applicants.

The rules establish a strict six-month time frame for applications.[200] While a short time frame can ensure potential claimants seek redress in a timely fashion, closing the claim for the ICC within a reasonable period,[201] there is a danger that it does not allow sufficient time for claimants to collate the evidence they need to substantiate their claim.[202] This is particularly true given the context: claimants will just have been released from international custody in a foreign country after a wrongful prosecution.[203] The six-month time frame, although replicated by the STL,[204] seems short when compared to national law. For example, in Bosnia-Herzegovina, acquitted persons have three years to submit a claim for compensation to the State-level Ministry of Justice.[205] The statute of limitations ranges from between one and ten years in statutory compensation schemes for wrongful conviction in the US, with an average of 2.6 years (although the Innocence Project recommends three years).[206]

Debates during the drafting of the statute show that there was a lack of clarity about what the starting point for this time frame should be.[207] The rules state that the time begins to run from the date the applicant was notified about 'the decision of the Court concerning (…) the existence of a grave and manifest miscarriage of justice under Article 85, paragraph 3'.[208] It is unclear if this rule introduces a requirement for the acquittal or decision terminating proceedings to explicitly state that there has a grave and manifest miscarriage of justice, or if, following an acquittal or termination of

---

[199] *Haradinaj, Balaj and Brahimaj* IT-04-84*bis*-T (Judgment, 29 November 2012).

[200] Rule 173(2)(c) ICC RPE.

[201] See Beresford (n 30) 645.

[202] See Lonergan (n 76) 420.

[203] See Sheehy (n 64) 997.

[204] Rule 170(D) STL RPE.

[205] See E. Mackic, 'Bosnia's Freed Indictees in Line for Big Payouts' (*Balkan Insight*, 15 March 2011) <http://www.balkaninsight.com/en/article/bosnia-s-freed-indictees-in-line-for-big-payouts> accessed 5 August 2015.

[206] R.J. Norris, 'Assessing Compensation Statutes for the Wrongly Convicted' (2011) 2 *Criminal Justice Policy Review* 1, 13.

[207] Bitti (n 111) 627–8.

[208] Rule 173(2)(c) ICC RPE.

proceedings and an indication from the acquitted person that they intend to apply for compensation, a Chamber must sit to decide if that case qualifies.

The fact that the request must be made to the Presidency in writing (Rule 173(1) ICC RPE) would support a view that the request must occur after the proceedings that resulted in the acquittal or termination of proceedings.[209] Some argue that it would be more reasonable to have deliberations on compensation decided by the same Chamber that acquits the individual or terminates proceedings, as this would speed up the decision and reduce the burden on the Court by reducing the number of 'micro-proceedings unrelated to the main object of its jurisdiction'.[210] However this expedited format is excluded by the regulatory direction that the Chamber that decides upon eligibility and compensation must be composed of judges who have not participated in any previous judgment involving the applicant.[211] Although the term 'judgment' is used in the English version, reference to the French version suggests that the drafters' intention was to preclude the involvement of judges involved in any relevant decision by the Court at any stage of proceedings.[212]

The written request must set out the grounds for the claim and state the amount of compensation sought (Rule 173(3)). An earlier requirement for applicants to submit [written] evidence substantiating the amount sought was deleted as it was considered burdensome and vague. However, it is likely that this will be required in practice by those seeking compensation under Article 85(3) as they have no right to such remedy, and so must persuade the judges that they fulfil the criteria and that their case represents a sufficiently exceptional circumstance for the judges to exercise their discretion.[213] Claims at other international courts for compensation for violations of the right to liberty or right to a speedy trial have failed or been unsuccessful in securing the amount sought[214] due to a failure to clearly set out the heads of and provide evidence to prove claims and establish causality.[215]

Finally, it seems that only the direct victim of the grave and manifest miscarriage of justice can apply for compensation. Although the rules state that 'anyone seeking compensation' can submit a request (Rule 173(1)), Article 85(3) only refers to the person who has been released from detention following a final decision of acquittal or a termination of proceedings. Relatives and heirs do not seem to have standing to make such a request, either in their own right or on behalf of their (deceased) relative. This

---

209 Zappalà (n 2) 1584.

210 Ibid., 1584–5.

211 Rule 173(1) ICC RPE. In contrast, the STL rules do not include this requirement of impartiality. See Rule 170(E) STL RPE.

212 Bitti (n 111) 627.

213 See ibid., 629.

214 For example, the ICJ ordered the Democratic Republic of the Congo to pay the Republic of Guinea less than 1 per cent of the compensation sought in the case of Ahmadou Sadio Diallo due to a lack of supporting evidence. See M. Andenas, 'Ahmadou Sadio Diallo' (2013) 107(1) *American Journal of International Law* 178, 179–81 and G. Ulfstein, 'Awarding Compensation in a Fragmented System: The Diallo Case' (2013) 4(3) *Journal of International Dispute Settlement* 477, 477, 482.

215 See D. Shelton, *Remedies in International Human Rights Law* (2nd edn, Oxford University Press 2005) 247–9, 296, 313.

restricted standing can be distinguished from the broader approach adopted in relation to applications to revise a conviction or sentence under Article 84, which can be exercised by close family members.[216] Zappalà has suggested that, in cases where the victim has died, the Prosecutor should file a request on their behalf.[217] While it is clear that the primary claimant should be the direct victim of the wrongful detention, there are no obvious reasons why close relatives and heirs should not be entitled to claim on the victim's behalf. In any case, in the event of a death, relatives should be able to pursue a submitted claim and receive any sums granted.[218] As it stands, however, it seems that claims for non-victims will be deemed inadmissible.

5. DETERMINING ELIGIBILITY CLAIMS

In addition to the strict eligibility criteria established by the statute and rules, this legal framework also imposes restrictions on the judicial discretion to award compensation. This section outlines the procedure for determining eligibility and analyses the fetters on judicial decision-making before advocating a reconsideration of this cautious approach.

5.1 Procedure

The Presidency's role in relation to implementing Article 85(3) is 'a purely administrative one (…) the Presidency has no power to reject the request and only designates a Chamber to consider the request'.[219] Bitti suggests that the use of the word 'designates'[220] means the Presidency should nominate an existing three judge Chamber (either a Pre-Trial or a Trial Chamber).[221] The designated Chamber can decide whether to hold a hearing or to determine the matter on the basis of the request and any written submissions from the Prosecutor or the applicant. Importantly, Rule 174(2) also states that a hearing must be held if so requested by either the Prosecutor or the applicant. This was added to avoid violating human rights in relation to the requirements of a fair trial.[222] The STL rules differ in this regard: while the Chamber may hear the Prosecutor's views, the rules do not give the applicant the right to be heard.[223]

The applicant is entitled to legal assistance during the procedure (whether there is a hearing or not).[224] This provision was necessary given that the statutory right to assistance (Art. 67) only extends to accused persons awaiting the determination of charges against them. What is not clear is whether or not this assistance will be provided for free. Human rights law would suggest that legal aid should be granted in

216 See Bitti (n 111) 626.
217 Zappalà (n 2) 1585.
218 See Sheehy (n 64) 997; Norris (n 206) 13.
219 Bitti (n 111) 626.
220 Rule 173(1) ICC RPE. See also Rule 170(E) STL RPE.
221 Bitti (n 111) 627.
222 Ibid., 632.
223 Rule 170(E) STL RPE.
224 Rule 173(4) ICC RPE.

such compensation claims if the applicant lacks means, it is necessary to ensure access to a court and to ensure equality of arms (especially in complex procedures). Bitti has argued that these factors would suggest that legal aid must be granted for indigent applicants claiming under Article 85(3) to ensure he or she is not placed 'at a substantial disadvantage vis-à-vis the Prosecutor'.[225]

The decision on eligibility (and any award) must be made by majority decision (Rule 174(3)). The rules do not state that this decision be made public. This is in contrast to a human rights approach to due process and statutory directions in relation to other pronouncements of Chambers of the Court.[226] This is also unfortunate given the need to remove the stigma that attaches to wrongly accused persons.

The rules also fail to state that the decision needs to be reasoned. This issue was actually debated at length during the drafting of the Statute. Unfortunately the requirement to provide reasons was deleted following a request from the Russian and Spanish delegation due to a perception that, as there was no right to such compensation, the judges should not be burdened with a requirement to set out their reasons.[227] This is disappointing from a due process perspective, and seems contrary to contemporary human rights law.[228] It is also unfortunate given that there is no practice in this regard to draw from. Moreover, human rights jurisprudence on compensation for unlawful detention and wrongful convictions has been criticised for its lack of analysis and a failure to articulate the principles governing the determination of awards.[229] The ICC should make its reasons for determining whether an individual is eligible for compensation clear. The judges should deliver reasoned decisions to ensure transparency and the development of a coherent set of principles on compensation.

Other delegates felt there was no need to include reasons for decisions, as they are final: decisions cannot be appealed.

5.2 Judicial Discretion, Exceptional Circumstances and the Consequences of Assessing Factual Innocence

In contrast to paragraphs 1 and 2 of Article 85, which incorporate existing human rights remedies and provide directly accessible rights, paragraph 3 grants a judicial power to consider claims. In addition to the criteria discussed above, this discretion is further fettered by the statutory direction that the power to grant compensation should only be exercised in *exceptional circumstances*. This not only narrows the scope of the field, but it may also require an enquiry into the factual innocence of the claimant.

Limitations are often included in compensation schemes to try to prevent persons found not guilty due to a technicality or those considered factually guilty from receiving compensation. As Sheehy points out, 'factual innocence (…) plays a central role in (…) compensation claims, restricting the right to have a claim heard, acting as

[225] Bitti (n 111) 630. This view that the rules will translate into a requirement to provide legal aid to indigent claimants is supported by Zappalà (n 2) 1583.

[226] Bitti (n 111) 633.

[227] Ibid.

[228] Ibid., 634.

[229] Shelton (n 215) 309–10.

a device for burden allocation and "gatekeeping" and determining deservedness of (…) compensation'.[230] Just as it is possible to wrongfully convict, criminal justice process may also result in wrongful acquittals.[231] Indeed, this potentiality is recognised by the ICCSt; it enables the Prosecutor to appeal an acquittal[232] and the Appeals Chamber to reverse the acquittal or order a retrial if the first instance decision was unreliable or materially affected by a procedural, factual or legal error.[233] In the context of international criminal trials in particular, there will be little support for a system that provides financial gains to persons who are considered to be factually guilty. As Beresford notes, however, 'an effective way to separate the truly innocent from those found not guilty has yet to be discovered'.[234] The statutory right to be presumed innocent results in the onus being placed on the Prosecutor to prove an accused's guilt beyond reasonable doubt.[235] Any requirement of proof of innocence from the claimant inverts this principle, reverses the burden of proof and risks undermining not only the presumption of innocence, but also the acquittal judgment itself.

The Statute states that it is for the Court to find the facts that there has been a grave and manifest miscarriage of justice. In the absence of a prior judicial determination of such facts, however, it is likely that the applicant will have to provide evidence. As Beresford notes, a claimant may not be able to prove his innocence due to factors beyond his control, such as the death of a witness.[236] In addition, as previously mentioned, the judges who decide on eligibility cannot have participated in any previous judgment regarding the applicant.[237] While it is true that 'judicial impartiality is both an essential organizing component of any legitimate judicial institution and a core right for persons brought before such an institution',[238] this requirement may result in not only another proceeding, but also another review of the facts to determine whether the prosecution and subsequent detention was indeed a grave and manifest miscarriage of justice. A requirement of proof of innocence may therefore result in a further trial during which an individual who has already 'had to fight for their acquittal (…) [having] to prove their innocence to a higher standard still'.[239]

A requirement to prove innocence could be 'disastrous for the administration of justice',[240] as it would create two classes of acquittal: 'real' acquittal when compensation is awarded, and acquittal without compensation that would be tainted with a presumption of guilt.[241] A refusal to award compensation to an acquitted person on the

[230] Sheehy (n 64) 993.
[231] See Doménech-Pascual and Puchades-Navarro (n 156) 4.
[232] Art. 81(1)(a) ICCSt.
[233] Art. 83(2) ICCSt.
[234] Beresford (n 30) 635.
[235] Art. 66 ICCSt.
[236] Beresford (n 30) 643.
[237] Rule 173(1) ICC RPE.
[238] H. Abtahi, O. Ogwuma and R. Young, 'The Composition of Judicial Benches, Disqualification and Excusal of Judges at the International Criminal Court' (2013) 11 *Journal of International Criminal Justice* 379, 380.
[239] Sheehy (n 64) 994.
[240] Beresford (n 30) 642.
[241] See Michels (n 54) 420; Sheehy (n 64) 994.

basis of continuing suspicions would have a potential defamatory effect[242] that would impose 'a reputational cost (…) [and] increased social stigma'.[243] Such a scheme creates a risk of re-victimising claimants and deterring eligible persons from applying[244] by introducing a 'de facto verdict of not proven (…) [or] probable guilt'.[245]

The ECtHR has been highly critical of requirements of this kind in national compensation schemes. In Austria, for example, claimants had to dispel suspicions in order to receive compensation, and in Norway, claimants had to show that it was probable that they did not carry out the act that formed the basis of the charge.[246] These requirements have been repeatedly criticised by the ECtHR, as a judicial determination that there is continuing suspicion as to guilt undermines the presumption of innocence protected by the Convention and violates Article 6.[247] In an attempt to bring their law in line with these findings, Austrian and Norwegian law now states that compensation cannot be refused or reduced on the basis of suspicions if the accused person has been acquitted by a final decision on the merits.[248] This jurisprudence has not, however, prevented the likelihood of guilt being a factor in judicial determinations; simply the explicit acknowledgement of the influence of this probability.[249]

National practice has demonstrated that a requirement to prove innocence often creates a higher evidential burden for those claiming compensation than is required to avoid conviction.[250] In compensation statutes in the US, the most common burden of proof is 'clear and convincing evidence'.[251] For Article 85(3), 'conclusive facts' of a grave and manifest miscarriage of justice are required. Zappalà has suggested that what will be required is not so much a determination of factual innocence but 'a more concrete judgment as to the overall justice of the outcome of the proceedings'.[252] What this means in practice, however, is not clear. Moreover, this appears to imply that a higher standard than 'on the balance of probabilities' is required. In fact, a requirement

---

242 Michels (n 54) 420.

243 Doménech-Pascual and Puchades-Navarro (n 156) 7.

244 See Michels (n 54) 421; Beresford (n 30) 643.

245 Sheehy (n 64) 993.

246 See para 2(1)(b) Austrian Compensation (Criminal Proceedings) Act 1969; Art. 444 Norwegian Code of Criminal Procedure Act 1981.

247 For example in his concurring opinion, Judge Greve noted in relation to the Norwegian law that 'the result is that a well-intended provision – that has proved valuable in a significant number of cases for which it was intended – turns out as ill-advised and not compatible with the presumption of innocence'. *O v Norway* App no 29327/95 (ECtHR, 11 February 2003). See also *Hammern v Norway* App no 30287/96 (ECtHR, 11 February 2003). For the Austrian system see *Sekanina v Austria* App no 13126/87 (ECtHR, 25 August 1993) paras 30–31; *Asan Rushiti v Austria* App no 28389/95 (ECtHR, 21 March 2000) para 31; *Lamanna v Austria* App no 28923/95 (ECtHR, 10 July 2001) para 40.

248 See Doménech-Pascual and Puchades-Navarro (n 156) 3. This article also contains a discussion of broader judicial discretion to grant or refuse compensation in other European systems (the Netherlands, Germany and Spain).

249 See Michels (n 54) 421; Doménech-Pascual and Puchades-Navarro (n 156) 3.

250 Doménech-Pascual and Puchades-Navarro (n 156) 2.

251 Only one scheme requires 'conclusive' proof. Others use the term preponderance of evidence. In some cases, only exculpatory DNA evidence was accepted. See Norris (n 206) 13.

252 Zappalà (n 2) 1577.

of conclusive facts seems more akin to a requirement to prove that a grave and manifest miscarriage of justice has occurred beyond reasonable doubt.

A due process approach would reject the imposition of such a heavy burden on claimants and insist that 'the only appropriate test is one based on the merits of the claim'.[253] Indeed some would contend that compensation should be based on a broader (legal) notion of innocence that connotes that the presumption of innocence has prevailed.[254] According to Zappalà, the very fact that a grave and manifest miscarriage of justice has been found to have occurred should constitute an exceptional circumstance, and therefore, perhaps the draftsperson uses exceptional circumstances 'more as a wish than a limitation of the scope of the rule'.[255]

5.3 Reconsidering the Restrictions on Judicial Discretion

Article 85(3) is a welcome addition to the ICCSt. It introduces the potential to grant a remedy to persons who were not previously entitled to redress under international law. However, as the ICTR judges recognised, Article 85(3) is a 'narrowly drafted provision'.[256] The contribution this compensation scheme can make to international policy and practice is limited by the inclusion of explicit and excessive restrictions. This scheme entails a number of weaknesses, including 'strict eligibility requirements, high standards of proof, numerous disqualifiers and short time limits'.[257] Moreover, the judicial discretion it grants is severely fettered by the requirement of the virtually insurmountable threshold of exceptional circumstances.[258]

As Sheehy notes, 'deciding who is eligible to claim for compensation will be a defining element of any compensation scheme'.[259] The current threshold however seems to raise the bar for eligibility too high. The legal framework currently in place creates a multitiered system to determine eligibility that considerably narrows the field of claimants that will qualify. In fact, Triffterer feels that the current thresholds will mean that 'ordinarily no compensation will be paid to persons acquitted by the Court, or against whom proceedings have been terminated before final judgment'.[260] This threshold will deter potential claimants and risks violating the presumption of innocence and undermining the integrity of the Court's judgments. Moreover, a system that operates on the basis of unreasoned decisions, that cannot be appealed, lacks transparency and fails to uphold the principle of equal treatment.[261]

To overcome these problems, the current legal framework should be revised and amended. The most important amendment would be the removal of the terms 'grave

---

[253] Sheehy (n 64) 993.

[254] Ibid., 994.

[255] Zappalà (n 2) 1583.

[256] *Rwamakuba* ICTR-98-44C-T (Decision on Appropriate Remedy, 31 January 2007) para 28.

[257] Norris (n 206) 3.

[258] The requirement of exceptional circumstances was removed in the test for provisional release at the ICTs as it had resulted in no release being granted. See Trotter (n 44).

[259] Sheehy (n 64) 992.

[260] Triffterer (n 112) 1501.

[261] See Zappalà (n 2) 1583.

and manifest' used to describe the miscarriage of justice and 'exceptional circumstances'. Both terms convey the drafters' desire to restrict the scheme.[262] However, as some delegates at the Rome Conference agreed,[263] these requirements unnecessarily restrict the judicial power to make awards. The current test imposes a burden that 'may prove insurmountable, except to applicants who were the victims of the most abhorrent cases of prosecutorial misconduct'.[264] Rather than restrict initial eligibility, a better approach is for the statutory provision to create a cause of action, leaving decisions about deservedness (based on the merits) to the judiciary. Michels has recommended a similar course of action, advocating a discretionary power to award compensation to persons released from detention following a final decision of acquittal, where it is in the interests of justice to do so.[265]

In contrast to the restrictions on eligibility found in the ICCSt, the Council of Europe has suggested that eligibility should be curtailed in situations where 'either the person remanded had, by his or her behaviour, actively contributed to the reasonableness of the suspicion that he or she had committed an offence or he or she had deliberately obstructed the investigation of an alleged offence'.[266] In other words, compensation would not be required where 'the behaviour of such persons may have had a significant influence on the decision to remand them in custody'.[267] An approach that bars claims from persons whose own (intentional or negligent) actions resulted in their detention or its prolongation can be found in national legislative schemes in Europe (Austria, Norway, Sweden and the Netherlands).[268] Caution should be used when using attribution as a bar to eligibility given the risk of pressure from prosecutors or bad legal advice.[269] Rather than act as a bar, attributability could be used to reduce the quantum of any award granted to claimants whose acts or omissions contributed to their detention.[270] The curtailment of entitlement to redress on the basis of attribution of responsibility (as with the ICC and human rights approach to wrongful convictions)[271] and reference to the legal grounds for remand detention seems more appropriate than a restriction based on political and pragmatic concerns.

5.4 Conclusion

If 'grave and manifest' and 'exceptional circumstances' are retained, these terms must be defined and concrete tests established to determine if they exist. What length of detention or degree of prosecutorial impropriety is it necessary to establish to meet

---

262 See Schabas (n 3) 965.

263 Note regarding Part 8 and Art. 81 contained in the transmittal letter from the Chairman of the Committee of the Whole to the Chairman of the Drafting Committee dated 7 July 1998 (UN Doc A/CONF.183/13(Vol.III)) 320. See Schabas (n 3) 966.

264 Beresford (n 30) 643.

265 Michels (n 54) 422.

266 Recommendation Rec(2006) 13 (n 151) para 34(2).

267 Explanatory Memorandum CM(2006)122 Addendum (n 152) para 34.

268 See Doménech-Pascual and Puchades-Navarro (n 156) 3; Michels (n 54) 421.

269 See Norris (n 206) 13; Lonergan (n 76) 417.

270 See Sheehy (n 64) 998; Michels (n 54) 422–3.

271 Art. 85(2) ICCSt; Art. 14(6) ICCPR; Art. 2, Protocol No 7 ECHR.

these thresholds? A practice direction or set of guidelines should be developed. Precise definitions and principles to govern decision-making will ensure a more transparent and fair system for adjudicating claims. The current procedure requires clarification on a number of other significant aspects. Is a determination of the likelihood of innocence required? If so, what standard of proof is required and on whom does the burden of proof lie? What constitutes 'conclusive facts'?

Without clear guidance, there is a danger that discretion will only be exercised in high-profile cases that have created a political or popular reaction. It is important that all (potential) claimants are treated equally. The present scheme is overly restrictive and does not seem to accord with the policy objectives behind its introduction – to deal with the harmful consequences of the lengthy detention that results from international prosecutions. Reliance on (guided) judicial discretion, rather than strict (but undefined) explicit criteria, to decide on eligibility will ensure the system can actually provide an effective remedy to counteract the harm caused.

6. RETHINKING REDRESS

If a claimant is deemed eligible for an award under Article 85(3), the designated Chamber must decide on the amount of compensation (if any) to award.[272] This section explores the factors considered by judges in making this decision and what compensation, as a remedy, is meant to address. It proceeds to advocate a more holistic approach to the design and delivery of remedial justice that goes beyond financial recompense.

6.1 Compensation

Compensation is a retrospective remedy that should provide damages for what has been lost as a result of the harm caused.[273] This section examines what the remedy of compensation should entail, how the quantum of awards should be determined and how awards granted can be delivered.

6.1.1 The remedy of compensation

According to the Council of Europe's Committee of Ministers, compensation to persons who are not convicted of the offence for which they are remanded in custody could cover 'loss of income, loss of opportunities and moral damage'.[274] In other words, both pecuniary and non-pecuniary damages can be sought.

Pecuniary damages would include financial recompense for lost past and future earnings and pensions, reductions in property values or property loss (taking account of

[272] Rule 175 ICC RPE.
[273] See Shelton (n 215) 291, 301.
[274] Recommendation Rec(2006) 13 (n 151) para 34(1).

inflation and the devaluation of currency), past and present pain, suffering and injury to physical and mental health, punitive fines,[275] and legal fees and expenses.[276]

Non-pecuniary damages provide for moral injury and dignity violations such as harm to reputation, fear, humiliation and mental distress; loss of enjoyment of life; loss of consortium and interference with family relationships.[277] As the intangible and subjective nature of these forms of harm can make them difficult to prove or reflect in monetary terms, such damages are often presumed.[278]

It is important to note the inclusion of the word 'any' in the Rule 175.[279] This was inserted to highlight the fact that such compensation is not a right but a discretionary power of the Chamber.[280] In other words, overcoming the eligibility thresholds will not necessarily result in an award of compensation. This suggests that a declaratory judgment could be handed down. This is doubtful for several reasons. First, there has been no violation of an enumerated right to make a declaration about. Secondly, the ECtHR's practice of refusing to award compensation for recognised violations of Article 5(5) (ruling that a declaration of violation provides just satisfaction) has received sustained criticism.[281] Judge Robinson at the ICTY has argued that the formal recognition of a violation of the right to a fair trial (undue delay) does not provide a sufficient remedy, particularly where the breach is substantial and causes claimants psychological non-pecuniary damage: financial compensation is required in such cases.[282] Finally, a decision to award no compensation to claimants who have established exceptional circumstances and the occurrence of a GMMOJ is unlikely to be considered appropriate given the objectives of the Court (ending impunity, respect for victims and human rights protection).

Compensatory damages could also be nominal (symbolic), but this too is unlikely to be appropriate under this scheme. The level of damages awarded should be proportionate to the harm caused,[283] and it is important that 'real compensation and not mere damages must be awarded'.[284] It is unclear, however, what level of awards the drafters of Article 85(3) anticipated. Zejnil Delalić (detained for over two and a half years at the UNDU) sought €255 000 in compensation for legal fees, suffering in detention, loss of

---

275 This could be an issue under Art. 85(2) if a wrongfully convicted person has paid a fine issued pursuant to Art. 77(2)(a). See R. Young, 'Fines and forfeiture in international criminal justice', Chapter 5 in this volume.

276 See Shelton (n 215) 35–6, 292, 301, 313.

277 Ibid., 292, 307.

278 Ibid., 37, 248, 317–18, 343, 368; *Ahmadou Sadio Diallo* (Republic of Guinea v Democratic Republic of the Congo) (Judgment, 19 June 2012) para 24.

279 Rule 175 ICC RPE.

280 Bitti (n 111) 636.

281 See S. Trechsel, *Human Rights in Criminal Proceedings* (Oxford University Press 2005) 496, 500; Shelton (n 215) 257.

282 See Partially Dissenting opinion of Judge Patrick Robinson in *Mugenzi and Mugiraneza* ICTR-99-50-A (Judgment, 4 February 2013) paras 6, 9, 11.

283 See *Semanza* ICTR-97-20-A (Judgment, 20 May 2005) para 125; *Rwamakuba* ICTR-98-44C-A (Decision on Appeal against Decision on Appropriate Remedy, 13 September 2007) para 27.

284 N. Jayawickrama, *The Judicial Application of Human Rights Law: National, Regional and International Jurisprudence* (Cambridge University Press 2002) 423.

earnings and the collapse of his construction business in Austria, while Vlatko Kupreskić sought a minimum of US $10 million for the harm he suffered as a result of three years in detention.[285] In a recent claim submitted to the MICT, although it was acknowledged that it was 'difficult to attach a price tag'[286] to the loss of liberty, freedoms, income, reputation and family life, the claimant sought one million US dollars.[287]

The amount of compensation awarded by regional human rights courts to applicants claiming under provisions similar to Articles 85(1) and (2) are often lower than expected[288] (although awards to applicants with successful claims of excessive delay at trial were significantly higher if the accused person was later acquitted when compared to awards granted to persons found guilty).[289] Jurisprudence reveals that this could be attributed to the fact that many claimants seeking compensation for human rights violations often fail to clearly articulate or substantiate (with evidence or legal argumentation) the heads or items of their claims.[290] Although it is not stated in the rules, it is likely that the claimant will have (and should be advised) to provide specific, itemised grounds and demonstrate with evidence that the harm claimed both occurred and was caused by (or that it was reasonably foreseeable that it would be caused by) the charges and subsequent detention by the ICC.[291] Although the burden of proof will generally fall on the claimant, it is possible for the burden to be shifted to the Prosecutor once causation has been established.

The judges, when considering the amount to award, are obliged to consider the consequences of the grave and manifest miscarriage of justice on a range of factors derived from human rights jurisprudence.[292] It seems that only the consequences of the GMMOJ for the claimant must be considered, and not the causes. Given the operational realities faced by the ICC, miscarriages of justice are likely to be attributed to structural causes rather than the acts or omissions of individuals.[293] Therefore although aggravated and punitive damages are theoretically available in addition to restitutionary damages under Article 85(3), they are unlikely.

6.1.2 Determining the quantum of an award

While the claimant may request a particular sum of compensation (Rule 173(4)), the amount (if any) to be awarded is to be determined by the designated Chamber (Rule

---

[285] See Tinjak (n 65).

[286] See *Nzuwonemeye* ICTR-00-56-A (Motion for Compensation and Damages for Violations of the Fundamental Rights of F.X. Nzuwonemeye pursuant to SCRes 1966 (2010), MICT-13-43, 18 February 2015) para 7 at 14.

[287] See ibid., para 5 at 13.

[288] Trechsel (n 281) 374.

[289] Shelton (n 215) 312.

[290] Ibid., 352; Ulfstein (n 214) 478, 483; Andenas (n 214) 179–181; Partially Dissenting opinion of Judge Patrick Robinson in *Mugenzi and Mugiraneza* ICTR-99-50-A (Judgment, 4 February 2013) para 12.

[291] See Shelton (n 215) 247–9, 296.

[292] See Trechsel (n 281) 501.

[293] See Sheehy (n 64) 990.

175). If the remedy is intended to address the consequences for the claimant on his personal, family, social and professional situation,[294] these must be assessed.

The perceived impartiality of such assessment is crucial given that it will form the basis of the official response to a grave and manifest miscarriage of justice. While the deciding judges cannot have been involved in the claimant's trial at any stage, they are still officials of the institution responsible for the harm caused. Independent input is critical in a compensation scheme that depends on discretion and that does not allow for the review of decisions. Moreover, such assessments are difficult and complex and international judges will not necessarily have the expertise required to determine the impact of the miscarriage of justice and the quantum and form of redress required to address this harm. On account of the need to ensure impartiality and the complex nature of such assessments, it is recommended that a team of independent experts be appointed to carry out this task.

In addition to taking caution in relation to arriving at a suitable and sufficient sum for any award, it is also important that the levels of any awards granted are justified. Sums awarded without reason or reference to pre-established guidelines risk being considered arbitrary and unfair.[295] Unfortunately, little guidance can be drawn from the jurisprudence of other international courts. The ICJ's discussion of the principles for determining the quantum of compensation has been criticised for being vague.[296] The ECtHR has also been criticised. Shelton notes that 'it remains hard to observe the workings of any principled decision-making'[297] and that decisions on damages are often notable for their 'lack of analysis or articulation of principles in regard to assessing damages (…) the Court never discusses the basis for the awards it makes, leaving much to speculation'.[298] The interpretation and application of the right to compensation in human rights law remains undeveloped in many respects[299] and decisions often 'do not attempt to quantify the harm [or] award precise relief'.[300] Due to the lack of practice to draw from, and the need to ensure a fair system, the ICC should adopt a practice direction or guidelines to govern such decision-making and ensure that decisions include precise and principled reasoning to ensure the development of a coherent body of jurisprudence.

6.1.3 Limiting the amount that can be awarded?

In addition to the difficulties associated with arriving at the sum to award, compensation schemes also create budgeting problems. Accordingly, some domestic systems rely on grids to set or restrict amounts that can be awarded for pecuniary damages.[301] National legislation can fix the amount that can be granted in relation to the time

---

[294] Rule 175 ICC RPE. The STL rule repeats these factors verbatim – Rule 170(E) STL RPE.

[295] Sheehy (n 64) 980.

[296] See Shelton (n 215) 293; Ulfstein (n 214) 478; *Ahmadou Sadio Diallo* (n 278).

[297] Shelton (n 215) 309.

[298] Ibid 310.

[299] R.C.A. White and C. Ovey, *Jacobs, White and Ovey, The European Convention of Human Rights* (5th edn, Oxford University Press 2010) 241.

[300] Starr (n 130) 703.

[301] Shelton (n 215) 293.

served in detention.[302] In Bosnia-Herzegovina, for example, awards have been based on a per diem rate.[303] Limits on the total amount that can be awarded, irrespective of the time actually served, are also possible.[304] Fixed amounts can make it easier for judges to decide how much to award, for the institution to budget for potential claims and for claimants to predict the level of award they should receive.[305] The idea of adopting a maximum amount for awards received support in relation to Article 85(3).[306]

However, setting such sums is difficult. They would need to be regularly reviewed and adjusted to ensure they reflect contemporary costs of living and inflation rises. Moreover, as Manns argues, while per diem or per annum rates of compensation might minimise administrative costs, they ignore the opportunity costs of detention and may result in the grant of symbolic or nominal sums that do not reflect the harm suffered by individuals.[307] What a system that uses damage schedules gains by providing a 'simple, efficient and economical resolution of claims', it loses by limiting claims to economic loss.[308]

Rather than adopt a fixed approach or limit the maximum amount that can be granted, the judges could be left to use their discretion. This would ensure that the award reflects the costs imposed on the individual claimant. This would also appear to be a fairer and fuller method of redress when considered in light of the problems of using what are necessarily arbitrary caps.[309] The wording of Rule 175 would suggest that the judges are required to undertake a subjective assessment of the impact of the miscarriage of justice on the individual claimant rather than an objective approach that seeks to standardise the amounts awarded. The grant of judicial discretion to determine what amount is appropriate in each case enables the remedy 'to reflect the real costs of pre-trial detention more comprehensively'.[310] Allowing for the recovery of all proximate or foreseeable damage can ensure a 'more complete recovery'.[311] On the other hand, reliance on wholly discretionary and individualised awards makes it 'extremely difficult to adequately budget (…) and to ensure a consistent source of funding'.[312]

A hybrid approach could be adopted that sets a floor and cap, as well as daily or yearly rates, but that also allows for additional recovery based on assessments of the opportunity costs for individuals.[313] However, this does not remove the difficulties associated with fixing rates or limits. For the ICC, it will be very difficult to set limits

---

302 See Norris (n 206) 3. For example, US Federal Law sets this limit at $50 000 per year.

303 40–70 convertible marks per day. See Mackic (n 205).

304 See Table 1 in Norris (n 206) 7; L.C. Boucher, 'Advancing the Argument in Favor of State Compensation for the Erroneously Convicted and Wrongfully Incarcerated' (2006) 56 *Catholic University Law Review* 1069, 1087; J. Costa, 'Alone in the World: The United States' Failure to Observe the International Human Right to Compensation for Wrongful Conviction' (2005) 19 *Emory International Law Review* 1615, 1639; Lonergan (n 76) 420–22.

305 Manns (n 62) 51.

306 See Bitti (n 111) 635; Zappalà (n 2) 1585.

307 Manns (n 62) 51.

308 Sheehy (n 64) 998.

309 Lonergan (n 76) 423.

310 Manns (n 62) 51.

311 Sheehy (n 64) 998.

312 Costa (n 304) 1625.

313 Manns (n 62) 52.

that reflect the standard of living relevant to all potential claimants. For example, in making a recommendation for a floor and cap for awards for violations of Article 5 ECHR, Trechsel opted for a per diem rate with a range of between €50 to €1 000. He acknowledged that this range was 'both broad and very rough' but felt it was necessary to 'enable the cost of living in the relevant states to be factored in'. Yet he also argued that the most important consideration should be that 'the compensation is substantial enough to highlight the value of personal liberty'.[314] In relation to the ICC system, Michels proposed that the amount of compensation should be fixed at a daily rate of €70. This does not seem to allow for differences in the cost of living or the varying impact the detention may have had on the individual.

What is interesting is that using this proposed sum (€70 per day), Michels calculated that in 2010, the ICTY would have been liable to pay €790 510 in compensation to ten individuals who had, collectively, spent over 11 000 days in custody.[315] This calculation dispels concerns that such rights would have detrimental financial impact. This would amount to 0.34 per cent of the annual budget of the ICTY. And this is assuming that all persons would qualify for compensation. Schemes based on narrow eligibility or judicial discretion, such as the one established by Article 85(3), are likely to be a 'negligible public expense'.[316]

6.1.4 Delivering financial compensation

While it is not stated explicitly, any awards granted under Article 85(3), as expenses of the Court, would be payable from the funds of the Court.[317] It is likely that any (successful) decision will state a total sum of compensation to be awarded to the claimant. There is no guidance about how such awards should be delivered. The sum could be transferred in a final lump sum. However, it is also possible to consider the use of regular instalments. While the payment of instalments might be considered an unjustifiably paternalistic approach if based on a view that the claimant is incapable of managing their own money,[318] this approach may be warranted on two grounds. First, it may be appropriate where it has been established that the claimant's needs may vary over time or where they cannot be identified or accurately assessed at the time of the claim and therefore require on-going and continuous assessment. In this case, it may be appropriate to award an initial sum to compensate for the time spent in detention and associated costs with further assessed yearly sums to cover on-going and arising needs. Secondly, a regular payment option may be easier for the budget to absorb. This should not be taken to detract from the fact that international organisations have a duty to ensure they have finances in place to provide remedies where they have committed international wrongs.[319]

---

314 Trechsel (n 281) 501.
315 Michels (n 54) 423.
316 Sheehy (n 64) 989.
317 Art. 114 ICCSt.
318 See Lonergan (n 76) 426.
319 See Mulgrew (n 73) 313–14.

6.2 Other Forms of Redress

As the previous section outlined, the rules focus on the determination of an amount (if any) of compensation to be awarded. The current legal framework does not therefore cater for non-compensatory or indeed, non-monetary redress. This differs from the broader approach adopted by the STL rules, which state that other forms of redress may be granted.[320] As the consequences of a miscarriage of justices can be both erosive and cumulative,[321] it may not be possible to restore the status quo ante with recourse to financial compensation alone. While compensation can have an 'ameliorative, restorative and therapeutic function',[322] some feel that when dealing with the complex harm caused by the loss of liberty, this traditional, monetary remedy is inadequate.[323] European penal policy recognises that 'although the damage suffered in many cases will require financial compensation, other forms of reparation may be more appropriate'.[324] International policy states that international organisations should provide a range of remedies including restitution, reparation, compensation and satisfaction.[325] Given the detrimental consequences of wrongful prosecution and detention, it may be necessary to ensure the availability of a form of remedy that can provide, inter alia, reputational repair, rehabilitative support and reintegration assistance. This section advocates moving beyond a solely monetary approach to remedies and proposes the adoption of a more comprehensive redress system.

6.2.1 Remedial responsiveness

Zdenkowski argues for a 'making amends' model of redress for wrongfully convicted persons, as 'it is not possible to reverse history and restore an individual with complete integrity to his former position'.[326] He argues, however, that it is 'possible to take account of what has happened and to attempt to be responsive to those changes'.[327] This idea of being remedially responsive to the impact detention has had on an individual's life course has found expression in human rights law as '*proyecto de vida*'.

The I-ACtHR, basing this concept on autonomy, noted that remedies granted on this ground should reflect the irreparable loss or severe impairment of opportunities for professional and personal development caused by an encroachment on an individual's rights.[328] In other words, claimants should be viewed as more than 'mere agent[s] of economic production'.[329]

---

320 Rule 170(D)–(E) STL RPE.

321 Ewick (n 169) 304.

322 Beresford (n 30) 634.

323 See G. Zdenkowski, 'Remedies for Miscarriage of Justice: Wrongful Imprisonment' (1993) 5(1) *Current Issues in Criminal Justice* 105, 108.

324 Explanatory Memorandum CM(2006)122 Addendum (n 152) para 34.

325 See Mulgrew (n 73) 313–4.

326 Zdenkowski (n 323) 107.

327 Ibid., 108.

328 *Loayza Tamayo v Peru* (Reparations) (27 November 1998) 42 IAmCtHR (series C). See also Shelton (n 215) 314.

329 Separate opinion, Judges Cancado Trindade and Abvell Burelli. See Shelton (n 215) 251.

Disappointingly, however, no award was made on this ground due to the difficulties of translating the concept into monetary terms: access to the court and the decision were held to constitute satisfaction.[330] Despite this, the concept can be and has been utilised to provide a normative basis for non-monetary remedies. For example, in the *Cantoral Benavides* case, Peru was required to pay for a university scholarship and associated living costs to one of the victims.[331] This concept could be developed to provide a principled basis for devising and awarding non-financial remedies at the ICC.

There is already practice of the grant of non-monetary remedies at the ICTR. In the *Rwamakuba* case, the Trial Chamber directed the Registrar to ensure that Mr. Rwamakuba received, in addition to financial compensation, a public apology, assistance with resettlement for him and his family and with his children's education.[332] This approach seems to take a rehabilitative approach to restitution that focuses on restoring a person's reputation and health, and assisting with their reintegration into society.[333]

6.2.2 Reputational repair

The social stigma associated with being a former international detainee will vary with each claimant. For some it has not prevented their appointment or continuation in government positions.[334] An international indictment, arrest, prosecution and detention will often, however, attract global media attention. These actions, and the attendant publicity, can have a punitive and stigmatising effect that endures long after the formal termination of the international criminal justice process.[335] Even for acquitted persons, or persons against whom proceedings have been terminated, the mere existence of formal accusations can result in an enduring presumption of guilt.[336] As a Deputy Registrar at the ICTR noted, although defendants 'can't get more innocent than seven or eight judges telling the world that they are innocent (…) [s]omehow, the fact that they have been indicted haunts them for the rest of their existence'.[337] Heller argues that the international community should ensure that acquitted persons do not continue to 'suffer the legal stigma of being accused'.[338]

Official apologies are often sought as a form of satisfaction. Apologies can both provide an explicit acknowledgement of the harm caused and prevent the same thing

---

330 Judge C.V. de Reux Rengifo dissented on this point, criticising the court for failing to grant an award. He felt that awards under this ground should be limited to changes of such a magnitude that they alter the foundations of life. He would have granted $124 190 under this ground. See Shelton (n 215) 315–6.

331 *Cantoral Benavides Case* (Reparations) (3 December 2001) 88 IAmCtHR (series C) para 6 Disposition.

332 See *Rwamakuba* ICTR-98-44C-T (Decision on Appropriate Remedy, 31 Jan 2007) Disposition.

333 See Shelton (n 215) 275.

334 For example, Delalić (acquitted by the ICTY) is now a deputy justice minister in Herzegovina Neretva canton – see Tinjak (n 65).

335 See B. Steels, 'Forever Guilty: Convict Perceptions of Pre and Post Conviction' (2009) 21(2) *Current Issues in Criminal Justice* 242.

336 See Beresford (n 30) 635.

337 Heller (n 85) 680.

338 Ibid.

from happening again by creating awareness of the causes of the problem.[339] Apologies can assist with reputational repair. So can simple practical steps such as making the fact of the acquittal or termination of proceeding as prominent on the websites of the international courts as the fact of their indictment. Publicity notices can also be placed in international and local media. For example, in Japan a grant of compensation to acquitted accused persons will be published in the official journal and three newspapers of the claimant's choice.[340]

Although it has been argued by international officials that a formal apology can suffice,[341] an apology should be seen as supplementary or additional form of redress only and not a substitute for a proper remedy.

6.2.3 Dealing with trauma

It is necessary to recognise that the mental health needs of claimants 'may be complex and substantial'.[342] Research has shown that wrongful detention can have long-lasting and significant consequences such as long-term personality change, post-traumatic stress and other psychiatric disorders.[343] Accordingly, remedies should include psychological and psychiatric support services that address any trauma caused by the wrongful detention.[344] Treatment needs can be immediate, to address specific conditions such as PTSD or depression, but also longer-term, requiring counselling to come to terms with the time lost on account of their deprivation of liberty.[345] Although this latter form of trauma can have a long-term impact on the claimant's physical and mental health, it can be difficult to assess at the time of release.[346] Rather than continually reassess such needs, the ICC could consider providing relevant persons with long-term or life-long medical insurance to cover the costs of any required interventions.[347]

6.2.4 Reintegration support

Wrongfully convicted persons in domestic criminal justice systems tend to 'fall on the periphery of any existing social service relief measures',[348] with little to nothing being done to 'ease the transition from prison to the real world'.[349] The situation is worse in the international criminal justice system, where there is no support for any released

---

339 Campbell and Denov (n 64) 156; Sheehy (n 64) 992, 998; Grant (n 63) 20; Grounds (n 66) 20.

340 See Michels (n 54) 418; Sheehy (n 64) 984.

341 *Rwamakuba* ICTR-98-44C-A (Decision on Appeal against Decision on Appropriate Remedy, 13 September 2007) para 21.

342 Grounds (n 66) 44.

343 See Norris (n 206) 4; Grounds (n 66).

344 Chinn and Ratliff (n 68) 439.

345 Grounds (n 66) 44.

346 S. Armbrust, 'When Money Isn't Enough: The Case for Holistic Compensation for Wrongfully Convicted' (2004) 41 *American Criminal Law Review* 157, 178; Norris (n 206) 4; Lonergan (n 76) 428–30.

347 Lonergan (n 76) 432; Armbrust (n 346) 174.

348 Chinn and Ratliff (n 68) 417.

349 Armbrust (n 346) 176.

person.[350] Even the new conditional release system instituted by the SCSL fails in this regard, focusing more on supervision than support.[351] This means that acquitted accused persons (or persons against whom proceedings have been terminated) at the ICC will not have access to any established reintegration support measures. This is unfortunate given the lengthy periods of detention likely to be involved in such cases. In addition to the usual reintegration problems faced by released persons (institutionalisation, health and relationship issues), persons released following a grave and manifest miscarriage of justice at the ICC may also have to deal with resettlement in a post-conflict society still in transition.

Acquitted persons in the international context may require access to a scheme that can 'perform a stepping-stone function between prison and society and between war and peace'.[352] Detention at the seat of the Court in The Hague may mean, however, that acquitted accused persons cannot benefit from national demobilisation, peace-building or reconciliation programmes in their country of origin.[353] Moreover, a post-conflict society may not have a functioning probation system to provide support to released persons at a national level. This discussion assumes however, that the released persons can travel to their country of origin. Practice has shown that acquitted accused persons may face significant legal and practical problems that prevent their relocation.

6.2.5 Relocation

Release from detention following an acquittal at an international court has not always resulted in freedom. As the cases outlined in Section 2.5 above demonstrate, release following an acquittal can result in further custody in administrative detention, (threatened) deportation to a country where the individual fears persecution and restricted freedom of movement and association if they remain in the Host State. For Mr. Ngudjolo, his 'acquittal instead became a nightmare. The trauma of his incarceration increased by the day (…) [he was] on the verge of depression as he had trouble understanding how such treatment could be inflicted on an acquitted person'.[354] Serious detrimental consequences of a miscarriage of justice can therefore continue after an acquittal or termination of proceedings in the international criminal justice context. Despite an explicit and negotiated division of responsibility between the ICC and the Dutch Government in relation to the duty to relocate,[355] *de facto* Statelessness and a legal limbo was imposed on the first person to be acquitted by the Court. As Heller argues, while the ICTR 'has proven admirably protective of its acquittees (…) acquitted defendants should not have to choose between living as virtual prisoners

---

[350] See Mulgrew (n 73) 102.

[351] See R. Mulgrew, 'Projet sur vingt-cinq ans: une analyse du système de liberation conditionnelle du Tribunal special pour la Sierra Leone' (2014) 27 *Cahiers de la Sécurité et de la Justice* 142–53.

[352] Jefferson (n 77) 393.

[353] Ibid., 393.

[354] Basila (n 72) 3.

[355] Article 48(1) ICC HQA. See also Rule 185 ICC RPE. The STL has also included this provision in its agreement. See Article 43(1) STL HQA.

under international protection and returning home to face significant physical and legal dangers'.[356]

The ICC, conscious of the need to deal with this issue, drafted a model agreement that can be entered between the Court and States in the 'event that a suspect acquitted by the Court would not be able to return to their State of nationality'.[357] Like the ICTR,[358] however, the ICC cannot oblige a State to grant asylum or residency rights: 'the reception of both an acquitted person and a protected witness is completely reliant on the voluntary cooperation of a State'.[359] Cooperation in this regard remains vitally important, not only to protect the fundamental rights of acquitted accused persons, but also to ensure respect for the Court's judgments.[360]

6.2.6 Re-entry support

A finding of not guilty and subsequent release may only be the beginning of a long and difficult transition period.[361] Persons who can claim under Article 85(3) are likely to have been released suddenly without the preparation, support and supervision normally provided to long-term prisoners due to be released in domestic systems. Such released persons can face the same challenges as other institutionalised persons, such as adapting to their regained freedom, changes in their family life and advances in technology.[362] While most adapt to practical changes, such as new technologies, in relatively short periods of time,[363] dealing with the impact of institutionalisation may take longer. They may also face problems associated with the operational difficulties faced by international courts.

Re-entry support in this context is therefore vital. The re-entry requirements of each individual should be assessed and such assessments should form part of the discussion about the appropriate form of redress to grant. Re-entry assistance will be required immediately before and after release, but also over the longer term.

It is foreseeable that persons who have been declared indigent and detained for long periods of time in a foreign country without access to paid work (or available funds due to asset freezing) will have immediate financial needs upon release. They will have to pay for somewhere to live, food, clothing, insurance, etc. The ICC should consider granting immediate transition loans (which could be deducted from any award made) or a grant to cover reasonable reintegration expenses incurred during this interim period that could be claimed in addition to compensatory damages.[364]

Beyond these immediate basics, it can be more difficult to assess longer-term needs that may require other forms of assistance. It may be necessary to ensure that rather than view such support (only) as a remedy following a judicial decision on eligibility

---

356 Heller (n 85) 677–8.

357 Report of the Court on cooperation ICC-ASP/10/40, 18 November 2011 (Assembly of States Parties, Tenth Session New York, 12–21 December 2011) para 52.

358 See 16th ICTR Annual Report para 54.

359 *Chui* ICC-01/04-02/12, 22 (n 98) para 4.

360 See Henry (n 83) 87; Basila (n 72) 6, 7, 9.

361 See Costa (n 304) 1617.

362 See Norris (n 206) 4.

363 Armbrust (n 346) 176.

364 See Lonergan (n 76) 424–5.

and merit, re-entry support should (also) be seen as an administrative responsibility of the Registry. It is already technically the Registry's responsibility to relocate such persons. Further, both the ICTR and ICC have practice of directly supporting and being responsible for acquitted accused persons who cannot be relocated. But the responsibility is broader than supporting acquitted accused persons stuck in this form of legal stalemate.

The potentially life-altering consequences of international prosecution and detention discussed above will often necessitate more than financial recovery. This duty should be broadened to include all forms of reintegration support. The ICC's Registry along with the Presidency's Enforcement team should establish a Re-entry Team to ensure the enforcement of acquittal decisions and provide support to persons harmed by wrongful prosecutions.

A dedicated re-entry team could provide the coordinated and multi-disciplinary support such persons require.[365] Rather than assess such needs in an adversarial hearing, mediation could be used to discuss compensation claims and negotiate an individualised support package. A specialist team could provide a tailored approach to post-custody transition by assessing and delivering support in relation to both immediate and longer-term reintegration needs. This would involve a range of tasks such as organising access to accommodation upon release, and helping to secure and implement relocation treaties with cooperating States.

6.3 Conclusion

Article 85(3)'s restrictive thresholds mean that persons deemed eligible are likely to have suffered a very significant degree of harm. If the underlying goal is to address the harmful consequences of international remand detention, the remedy should be tailored to provide meaningful support that helps claimants rebuild their lives. The ICC should seek independent and expert advice when assessing the quantity of compensation to award and the method of delivery. Guidelines should be developed to ensure a transparent and principled approach to decision-making. Further, the ICC should adopt a broader approach to remedy than simple compensation. In fact a more holistic scheme would appear to be required by evolving human rights jurisprudence, contemporary penological standards, international principles on international organisation responsibility, the ICJ operational context and an explicit internal regulatory duty to focus on the consequences. Using respect for human dignity as a base line, remedies should help to restore the individual's autonomy and reputation and assist with rehabilitative and reintegrative needs.

---

[365] Chinn and Ratliff (n 68) 407.

7. DEALING WITH THE COSTS OF SUSPICION IN INTERNATIONAL CRIMINAL JUSTICE

Issues related to acquittals in the international criminal justice field are increasingly attracting attention.[366] The inclusion of Article 85(3) ICCSt represented a statutory recognition of the problems faced by such persons at the UN Tribunals and the judicial inability to respond to their situation in the absence of a legal right to compensation under international law.

The lack of political willingness at the UNSC to grant this judicial power to the UN Tribunals (attributed to cost concerns and the temporary nature of these courts) was disappointing due to the priority these institutions placed on protecting the rights of accused persons.[367] The power included in Article 85(3) may be viewed as a 'logical corollary'[368] to the due process approach adopted by the ICCSt that prioritises the presumption of innocence and the right to a fair trial. This new power in international (criminal) law bridges an important remedial gap. It reflects evolving law, policy and practice at both national and regional levels. It essentially provides the ICC with a scheme to address the costs of suspicion and related detention.

While the ability to address the real and harmful consequences of wrongful international prosecution and detention is a welcome addition, both the objectives and the scope of the scheme are uncertain. Is this new judicial power an innovative step towards recognising the harm caused by excessive reliance on, and length of, detention in international criminal justice, or is it a legitimacy lever to be used to respond (or not) to instances of intense political reaction to judgments? On the one hand, Article 85(3) can be viewed as a form of social insurance that (re-)distributes the burden of international criminal justice process across society (and to an institution with means to provide a remedy).[369] By accepting responsibility for mistakes, the legitimacy of international criminal justice process and public confidence in its outcomes can be enhanced.[370] Fairness also dictates the need for such a system on a number of grounds. As Beresford notes, it is illogical to compensate someone for an unlawful arrest but not for the harm caused by spending extended periods of time in detention.[371] Moreover, convicted persons can offset the time they spend in pre-judgment custody against any sentence imposed.[372]

On the other hand, however, acquittals in the international criminal justice context have the propensity to be extremely controversial.[373] The discretionary basis of Article

---

[366] See for example the project 'When Justice is Done' at <http://www.whenjusticeisdone.org/index.php/acquittedd> accessed June 2015.

[367] See Beresford (n 30) 645.

[368] Sheehy (n 64) 984.

[369] See H.S. Master, 'Revisiting the Takings-Based Argument for Compensating the Wrongfully Convicted' (2004) 60 *NYU Annual Survey of American Law* 97, 111; Sheehy (n 64) 985; Doménech-Pascual and Puchades-Navarro (n 156) 1; Michels (n 54) 414–5, 418.

[370] See Doménech-Pascual and Puchades-Navarro (n 156) 2; De Keijser, De Lange and Van Wilsem (n 157) 33; Beresford (n 30) 635; Michels (n 54) 417; Sheehy (n 64) 989.

[371] Beresford (n 30) 643.

[372] See for example Art. 78(2) ICCSt; Rule101(c) ICTY/ICTR RPE.

[373] See Clark (n 183) 400.

85(3) may enable the Court to withhold a remedy in sensitive cases. There is also a danger that the provision can be used to address the costly impact of excessive detention without directly recognising violations of the right to liberty and a fair trial, and thereby as a means to avoid traditional remedies of release or re-trial. The new judicial power should not be used to commodify or pay for infringements of fundamental rights.[374] The scheme should not be used to implicitly invert the illegality of situations of excessive detention in international remand centres.

In relation to the scope of the scheme, the rules on eligibility and procedure will result in a very narrow range of potential claimants and a low likelihood of an award being made. The current eligibility thresholds (GMMOJ and exceptional circumstances) should be removed. Guidelines and practice directions should be developed to define key terms, clarify requirements and set the foundation for principled decision-making. The appointed judges should be able to use their discretion to tailor the remedy to the individual claimant's needs.

In terms of the remedy that can be awarded, this requires independent and expert input. Moreover, the form of the remedy available should be broader than monetary recompense and the ICC should create a body tasked with the design and delivery of a comprehensive redress and support system that assists with reputational repair, rehabilitation and reintegration.

To conclude, Article 85(3) is to be welcomed as an innovative and progressive development in international criminal law. However, it remains unclear in what circumstances and for what purpose this scheme will be used. The scheme requires refinement, the removal of unnecessary obstacles and the form of available redress needs to be reconsidered.

---

[374] See Shelton (n 215) 48, 270, 290, 292, 465.

Conclusion

Róisín Mulgrew and Denis Abels

The goal of this Handbook was to explore and analyse the operation of the international penal system. The contributors examined and assessed a range of issues related to detention, punishment and imprisonment in the international criminal justice system. It is clear from the various contributions that while many of these issues are significant for the authority and legitimacy of international courts, they have typically received scant attention. That is why we, the editors, believed that this book was both a necessary and timely addition to academic literature.

The *Research Handbook on the International Penal System* provides scholars, researchers and practitioners interested in international criminal law, and punishment more generally, with a wealth of information and insights into the legal framework pertaining to and the realities of detaining and imprisoning persons accused and convicted of international crimes. It addresses broader normative issues, such as purposes for international imprisonment and the use of indigenous forms of punishment, as well as more practical questions, such as how to design a rehabilitation programme for international criminals and whether an international prison should be created.

Not only does the Handbook provide the most up-to-date research on contemporary issues related to the operation of the international penal system, it highlights some significant gaps where further research is required and makes suggestions for its reform and development. In this way it is hoped that the Handbook can contribute to the development of law, policy and practice in this field.

The scope of topics discussed pays testament to the diversity and range of scholarship that forms the field of international penal studies. The Handbook's authors come from a range of different backgrounds; contributors include academics who specialise in criminology, transitional justice, (international) criminal law and procedure, international and comparative penal and human rights law, as well as officials, lawyers and judges who work or have worked at international criminal courts.

Drawing on their expertise and experience, the authors have all contributed to this compilation to provide an overview and critical analysis of international penal law. Kress recently suggested that a new sub-field in international criminal law could be identified by 'rapidly increasing levels of detail and refinement of the scholarly studies' and 'indications of internal scholarly specialisation'.[1] The level of detail and specialisation of the contributions to this Handbook signify the emergence of international penal law as a distinct sub-branch of international criminal law, which deserves attention in its own right.

---

[1] C. Kress, *Towards a Truly Universal Invisible College of International Criminal Lawyers* (Torkel Opsahl Academic EPublisher 2014) 10.

Selected bibliography

The legal framework governing this area of law (statutes, rules, regulations, practice directions, treaties, jurisprudence, international human rights law and penal standards) is publicly available and easily accessible online. What has perhaps not been so visible, until now, is the body of scholarly literature in this field. The selected bibliography below draws attention to some important works and is organized around the key themes analysed in this Handbook.

I. INTERNATIONAL REMAND DETENTION

D. Abels, *Prisoners of the International Community. The Legal Position of Persons Detained at the International Criminal Tribunals* (TMC Asser Press 2012)

D. Abels, 'Positive Obligations and the International Criminal Tribunals' Law of Detention: Funding Family Visits and the ICC Presidency's Ngudjolo Decision' (2013) 60 *Netherlands International Law Review* 51

C. Davidson, 'No Shortcuts on Human Rights: Bail and the International Criminal Trial' (2010) 60 *American University Law Review* 1

M. Fairlie, 'The Precedent of Pretrial Release at the ICTY: A Road Better Left Less Travelled' (2010) 33 *Fordham International Law Journal* 1101

F. Gaynor, 'Provisional Release in the Law of the International Criminal Tribunal for the Former Yugoslavia', in J. Doria, H-P. Gasser and M.C. Bassiouni (eds), *The Legal Regime of the International Criminal Court: Essays in Honour of Professor Igor Blishchenko* (Martinus Nijhoff Publishers 2009)

S. Golubok, 'Pre-Conviction Detention before the International Criminal Court: Compliance or Fragmentation' (2010) 8 *The Law and Practice of International Courts and Tribunals* 295

N. Grosselfinger, 'The United Nations Detention Unit', in P.J. van Krieken and D. MacKay (eds), *The Hague: the Legal Capital of the World* (TMC Asser Press 2005)

C. Müller, 'The Law of Interim Release in the Jurisprudence of the International Criminal Tribunals' (2008) 8 *International Criminal Law Review* 589

G. Sluiter, 'Human Rights Protection in the ICC Pre-Trial Phase', in C. Stahn and G. Sluiter (eds), *The Emerging Practice of the International Criminal Court* (Koninklijke Brill 2009)

S. Starygin, 'ECCC in Pre-Trial Action: Was there Good Reason to Order Pre-Trial Detention of the ECCC Defendants' (2011) 9 *Human Rights in the Post-Conflict Context* 9

A. Trotter, 'Innocence, Liberty and Provisional Release at the ICTY: a Post-Mortem of "Compelling Humanitarian Grounds" in Context' (2012) 12 *Human Rights Law Review* 353

R. Vincent, *An Administrative Practices Manual for Internationally Assisted Criminal Justice Institutions* (International Centre for Transitional Justice 2007). Available online at <https://www.ictj.org/sites/default/files/ICTJ-Global-Administrative-Practices-2007-English_0.pdf> accessed on 20 August 2015

P. Wald and J. Martinez, 'Provisional Release at the ICTY: A Work in Progress', in R. May et al (eds), *Essays on ICTY Procedure and Evidence* (Kluwer Law International 2001) 233

II. INTERNATIONAL PENALTIES

K. Ambos, 'Punishment without a Sovereign?' (2013) 33 *Oxford Journal of Legal Studies* 306

K. Ambos, *Treatise on International Criminal Law. Volume I: Foundations and General Part* (Oxford University Press 2013)

R.E. Fife, 'Penalties', in R.S. Lee (ed), *The International Criminal Court: Elements of Crimes and Rules of Procedure and Evidence* (Transnational Publishers 2001)

E. Gumboh, 'The Penalty of Life Imprisonment under International Criminal Law' (2011) 11 *African Human Rights Law Journal* 75

F.P. King and A. La Rosa, 'Penalties under the ICC Statute', in F. Lattanzi and W. Schabas (eds), *Essays on the Rome Statute of the International Criminal Court. Volume I* (Editrice il Sirente 1999)

C. Kress, 'Penalties, Enforcement and Cooperation in the International Criminal Court Statute (Parts VII, IX, X)' (1998) 6 *European Journal of Crime, Criminal Law and Criminal Justice* 442

C. Kress and G. Sluiter, 'Fines and Forfeiture Orders', in A. Cassese, P. Gaeta and J.R.W.D. Jones (eds), *The Rome Statute of the International Criminal Court: A Commentary* (Oxford University Press 2002)

R. May and M. Wierda, 'Is There a Hierarchy of Crimes in International Law?', in L.C. Vordah et al (eds), *Man's Inhumanity to Man: Essays on International Law in Honour of Antonio Cassese* (Kluwer 2003)

J.D. Mujuzi, 'Is There a Need for the ICTY to Clarify the Difference(s) between Life Imprisonment and Imprisonment for the Remainder of the Offender's Life? The *Galic* and *Lukic* Decisions' (2010) 10 *International Criminal Law Review* 855

W. Schabas, 'War Crimes, Crimes against Humanity and the Death Penalty' (1997) 60 *Albany Law Review* 733

W. Schabas, 'Penalties', in A. Cassese, P. Gaeta and J.R.W.D. Jones (eds), *The Rome Statute of the International Criminal Court: A Commentary. Volume II* (Oxford University Press 2002)

W. Schabas, 'Article 109: Enforcement of fines and forfeiture measures', in O. Triffterer (ed), *Commentary on the Rome Statute of the International Criminal Court* (2nd edn, C.H. Beck 2008)

D. van Zyl Smit, 'Punishment and Human Rights in International Criminal Justice' (2002) 2 *Human Rights Law Review* 1

III. INTERNATIONAL SENTENCING

K. Ambos, *Treaties on International Criminal Law. Volume II: The Crimes and Sentencing* (Oxford University Press 2014)

S. D'Ascoli, *Sentencing in International Criminal Law. The UN ad hoc Tribunals and Future Perspectives for the ICC* (Hart Publishing 2011)

M. Bagaric and J. Morss, 'International Sentencing Law: In Search of a Justification and Coherent Framework' (2006) 6 *International Criminal Law Review* 199

S. Beresford, 'Unshackling the Paper Tiger – The Sentencing Practices of the ad hoc International Tribunals for the Former Yugoslavia and Rwanda' (2001) 1 *International Criminal Law Review* 33

A. Carcano, 'Sentencing and the Gravity of the Offence in International Criminal Law' (2002) 51 *International & Comparative Law Quarterly* 583

A.M. Danner, 'Constructing a Hierarchy of Crimes in International Law Sentencing' (2001) 87 *Virginia Law Review* 415

J.L. Ginn, *Sugamo Prison, Tokyo. An Account of the Trial and Sentencing of Japanese War Criminals in 1948, by a US Participant* (McFarland & Co 1992)

M.B. Harmon and F. Gaynor, 'Ordinary Sentences for Extraordinary Crimes' (2007) 5(3) *Journal of International Criminal Justice* 683

R. Haveman and O. Olusanya (eds), *Sentencing and Sanctioning in Supranational Criminal Law* (Intersentia 2006)

R. Henham, 'The Philosophical Foundations of International Sentencing' (2003) 1 *Journal of International Criminal Justice* 64

R. Henham, 'Procedural Justice and Human Rights in International Sentencing' (2004) 4 *International Criminal Law Review* 185

R. Henham, 'Developing Contextualized Rationales for Sentencing in International Criminal Trials: A Plea for Empirical Research' (2007) 5(3) *Journal of International Criminal Justice* 757

B. Holá, C. Bijleveld, A. Smeulers, 'Consistency in international sentencing – ICTY and ICTR case study' (2012) 9(5) *European Journal of Criminology* 539

A.N. Keller, 'Punishment for Violations of International Criminal Law: An Analysis of Sentencing at the ICTY and ICTR' (2001) 12 *Indiana International and Comparative Law Review* 53

J. Meernik and K. King, 'The Sentencing Determinants of the International Criminal Tribunal for the Former Yugoslavia: An Empirical and Doctrinal Analysis' (2003) 16 *Leiden Journal of International Law* 717

J. Nemitz, 'The Law of Sentencing in International Criminal Law: The Purposes of Sentencing and the Applicable Method for the Determination of the Sentence' (2001) *Yearbook of International Humanitarian Law* 87

O. Olusanya, *Sentencing War Crimes and Crimes Against Humanity under the International Criminal Tribunal for the Former Yugoslavia* (Europa Law Publishing 2005)

D.B. Pickard, 'Proposed Sentencing Guidelines for the International Criminal Court' (1997) 20 *Loyola of Los Angeles International and Comparative Law Journal* 123

S.M. Sayers, 'Defence Perspectives on Sentencing Practice in the International Criminal Tribunal for the Former Yugoslavia' (2003) 16 *Leiden Journal of International Law* 751

D. Scalia, 'Long-Term Sentences in International Criminal Law – Do They Meet the Standards Set Out by the European Court of Human Rights?' (2011) *9 Journal of International Criminal Justice* 669

W. Schabas, 'Sentencing by International Tribunals: A Human Rights Approach' (1997) 7 *Duke Journal of Comparative and International Law* 461

W. Schabas, 'International Sentencing: From Leipzig (1923) to Arusha (1996)', in M.C. Bassiouni, *International Criminal Law. Volume III* (2nd edn, Trans-national Publishers 1999)

R. Sloane, 'Sentencing for the "Crime of Crimes": The Evolving "Common Law" of Sentencing of the International Criminal Tribunal for Rwanda' (2007) 5(3) *Journal of International Criminal Justice* 713

R. Sloane, 'The Expressive Capacity of International Punishment: The Limits of the National Law Analogy and the Potential of International Criminal Law' (2007) 43 *Stanford Journal of International Law* 39

S. Szoke-Burke, 'Avoiding Belittlement of Human Suffering: A Retributivist Critique of ICTR Sentencing Practices' (2012) 10 *Journal of International Criminal Justice* 561

IV. INTERNATIONAL TRANSFERS

O. Bekou, 'Rule 11*bis*: An Examination of the Process of Referrals to National Courts in ICTY Jurisprudence' (2010) 33 *Fordham International Law Journal* 723

A.S. Canter, '"For These Reasons, the Chamber Denies the Prosecutor's Request for Referral": The False Hope of Rule 11*bis*' (2009) 32 *Fordham International Law Journal* 1614

J. Melman, 'The Possibility of Transfer (?): A Comprehensive Approach to the ICTR's Rule 11*bis* to Permit Transfer to Rwandan Domestic Courts' (2010) 79 *Fordham Law Review* 1271

R. Mulgrew, 'The International Movement of Prisoners' (2011) 22(1) *Criminal Law Forum* 103

N. Palmer, 'Transfer or Transformation?: A Review of the Rule 11*bis* Decisions of the International Criminal Tribunal for Rwanda' (2012) 20 *African Journal of International and Comparative Law* 1

N. Palmer, *Courts in Conflict: Interpreting the Layers of Justice in Post-Genocide Rwanda* (Oxford University Press 2015)

S. Somers, 'Rule 11*bis* of the International Criminal Tribunal for the Former Yugoslavia: Referral of Indictments to National Courts' (2007) 30 *Boston College International & Comparative Law Review* 175

M.M. El Zeidy, 'From Primacy to Complementarity and Backwards: (Re-visiting Rule 11*bis* of the Ad Hoc Tribunals' (2008) 57(2) *International and Comparative Law Quarterly* 403

V. INTERNATIONAL IMPRISONMENT

H. Abtahi and S.A. Koh, 'The Emerging Enforcement Practice of the International Criminal Court' (2012) 45 *Cornell Law Review* 1

T.B. Chimbia, 'Establishing an Enforcement Regime', in R.S. Lee (ed), *The International Criminal Court: The Making of the Rome Statute* (Kluwer Law International 1999)

J. Fishman, *Long Knives and Short Memories: The Spandau Prison Story* (Richardson & Steirman 1986)

J.W. Goda, *Tales From Spandau – Nazi Criminals and the Cold War* (Cambridge University Press 2007)

F. Hassan, 'The Theoretical Basis for Punishment in International Criminal Law' (1983) 15 *Case Western Reserve Journal of International Law* 39

R. Haveman, 'Supranational Expectations of a Punitive Nature', in R. Haveman and O. Olusanya (eds), *Sentencing and Sanctioning in Supranational Criminal Law* (Intersentia 2006)

K. Hoffman, 'Some Remarks on the Enforcement of International Sentences in Light of the Galic case at the ICTY' (2011) 10 *Zeitschrift für Internationale Strafrechtsdogmatik* 838

B. Holá and J. van Wijk, 'Life after Conviction at International Criminal Tribunals: An Empirical Overview' (2014) 12 *Journal of International Criminal Justice* 109

B. Holá, J. van Wijk and J. Kelder, 'Rehabilitation and Early Release of Perpetrators of International Crimes: A Case Study of the ICTY and ICTR' (2014) 14 *International Criminal Law Review* 1177

A. Klip, 'Enforcement of Sanctions Imposed by the International Criminal Tribunals for Rwanda and the former Yugoslavia' (1997) 5(2) *European Journal of Crime, Criminal Law and Criminal Justice* 144

C. Kress and G. Sluiter, 'Imprisonment', in A. Cassese, P. Gaeta and J.R.W.D. Jones (eds), *The Rome Statute of the International Criminal Court: A Commentary. Volume II* (Oxford University Press 2002)

A. Marchesi, 'The Enforcement of Sentences of the ICC', in F. Lattanzi and W. Schabas (eds), *Essays on the Rome Statute of the International Criminal Court. Volume I* (Editrice il Sirente 1999)

G.K. McDonald, 'The International Criminal Tribunals: Crime and Punishment in the International Arena' (2001) 25 *Nova Law Review* 463

R. Mulgrew, 'On the Enforcement of Sentences Imposed by International Courts: Challenges Faced by the Special Court for Sierra Leone' (2009) 7(2) *Journal of International Criminal Justice* 373

R. Mulgrew, *Towards the Development of the International Penal System* (Cambridge University Press 2013)

R. Mulgrew, 'Releasing International Prisoners', in M. Herzog-Evans (ed), *How to Release: The Role of Courts and the Use of Discretion in Sentence Implementation and Re-entry* (Wolf Legal Publishers 2014)

J. Nemitz, 'Execution of Sanctions Imposed by Supranational Criminal Tribunals', in R. Haveman and O. Olusanya (eds), *Sentencing and Sanctioning in Supranational Criminal Law* (Intersentia 2006)

M.M. Penrose, 'Lest We Fail: The Importance of Enforcement in International Criminal Law' (2000) 15 *American University International Law Review* 321
D. Tolbert, 'The ICTY and the Enforcement of Sentences' (1998) 11 *Leiden Journal of International Law* 655
D. Tolbert and A. Rydberg, 'Enforcement of Sentences', in R. May et al (eds), *Essays on ICTY Procedure and Evidence in Honour of Gabrielle Kirk McDonald* (Kluwer Law International 2001)
D. van Zyl Smit, 'International Imprisonment' (2005) 54 *International Comparative Law Quarterly* 357
G. Vermeulen and E. DeWree, *Offender Reintegration and Rehabilitation as a Component of International Criminal Justice?* (Maklu 2014)
I.M. Weinberg de Roca and C.M. Rassi, 'Sentencing and Incarceration in the Ad Hoc Tribunals' (2008) 44 *Stanford Journal of International Law* 1

VI. INTERNATIONAL STANDARDS, OVERSIGHT AND SUPERVISION

D. Abels, *Prisoners of the International Community. The Legal Position of Persons Detained at the International Criminal Tribunals* (TMC Asser Press 2012) Chs 2 and 3
G. Bitti, 'Article 21 of the Statute of the International Criminal Court and the Treatment of Sources of Law in the Jurisprudence of the ICC', in G. Sluiter and C. Stahn (eds), *The Emerging Practice of the International Criminal Court* (Brill 2009)
A. Cassese, 'The Influence of the European Court of Human Rights on International Criminal Tribunals – Some Methodological Remarks', in M. Bergsmo (ed), *Human Rights and Criminal Justice for the Downtrodden – Essays in Honour of Asbjørn Eide* (Martinus Nijhoff Publishers 2003)
R.S. Clark, 'Article 106', in O. Triffterer (ed), *Commentary on the Rome Statute of the International Criminal Court. Volume II* (2nd edn, C.H. Beck 2008)
R. Culp, 'Enforcement and Monitoring of Sentences in the Modern War Crimes Process: Equal Treatment before the Law?' (2010–2011) John Jay College of Criminal Justice. Available online at <http://www.jjay.cuny.edu/Culp_MonitoringTribunalPunishment_rev_9Apr11_1_.pdf> accessed at 9 April 2011
L. Gradoni, 'International Criminal Courts and Tribunals: Bound by Human Rights Norms … or Tied Down?' (2006) 9 *Leiden Journal of International Law* 19
M. McAuliffe de Guzman, 'Article 21', in O. Triffterer (ed), *Commentary on the Rome Statute of the International Criminal Court* (2nd edn, C.H. Beck 2008)
R. Mulgrew, 'Projet sur vingt-cinq ans: une analyse du système de liberation conditionnelle du Tribunal special pour la Sierra Leone' (June 2014), *Cahiers de la Sécurité et de la Justice*, n° 27 pp. 142–53
A. Pellet, 'Applicable Law', in A. Cassese, P. Gaeta and J.R.W.D. Jones (eds), *The Rome Statute of the International Criminal Court: A Commentary* (Oxford University Press 2002)
W. Schabas, *The International Criminal Court: A Commentary on the Rome Statute* (Oxford University Press 2010)

C. Stahn (ed), *The Law and Practice of the International Criminal Court* (OUP, 2015)

A. Trotter, 'Pre-Conviction Detention in the International Criminal Tribunals' 11(2) *Journal of International Criminal Justice* 351 (2013)

VII. ALTERNATIVES TO CUSTODIAL PUNISHMENT

J. Cockayne, 'Hybrids or Mongrels? Internationalized War Crime Trials as Unsuccessful Degradation Ceremonies' (2005) 4 *Journal of Human Rights* 455

M.A. Drumbl, 'Collective Violence and Individual Punishment: The Criminality of Mass Atrocity' (2005) 99(2) *Northwestern University Law Review* 539

M.A. Drumbl, *Atrocity, Punishment and International Law* (Cambridge University Press 2007)

M. Findlay and R. Henham, *Transforming International Criminal Justice: Retributive and Restorative Justice in the Trial Process* (Willan Publishing 2005)

V. Hancock, '"No-self" at Trial: How to Reconcile Punishing the Khmer Rouge for Crimes Against Humanity with Cambodian Buddhist Principles' (2008) 26(1) *Wisconsin International Law Journal* 87

K.L. King and J.D. Meernik, 'Assessing the Impact of the ICTY: Balancing International and Local Interests While Doing Justice', in R. Haveman and O. Olusanya (eds), *Sentencing and Sanctioning in Supranational Criminal Law* (Intersentia 2006)

C. McCarthy, *Reparations and Victims Support in the International Criminal Court* (Cambridge University Press 2012)

M.G. Martinez, 'Forfeiture of Assets at the ICC: the Short Arm of International Criminal Justice' (2014) 12 *Journal of International Criminal Justice* 193

B. Oomen, 'Rwanda's Gacaca: Objectives, Merits and their Relation to Supranational Criminal Law', in R. Haveman and O. Olusanya (eds), *Sentencing and Sanctioning in Supranational Criminal Law* (Intersentia 2006)

B. Oomen, 'Transitional Justice and its Legitimacy: The Case for a Local Perspective' (2007) 25(1) *Netherlands Quarterly of Human Rights* 141

P. Roberts, 'Restoration and Retribution in International Criminal Justice: An Exploratory Analysis', in A. von Hirsch et al. (eds), *Restorative Justice and Criminal Justice: Competing or Reconcilable Paradigms?* (Hart Publishing 2003)

J. Sarkin, 'Enhancing the Legitimacy, Status, and Role of the International Criminal Court Globally by using Transitional Justice and Restorative Justice Strategies' (2011–2012) 6 *Interdisciplinary Journal of Human Rights Law* 83

M.V.S. Sirleaf, 'Beyond Truth and Punishment in Transitional Justice' (2013) 54(2) *Virginia Journal of International Law* 223

C. Stahn, 'Accommodating Individual Criminal Responsibility and National Reconciliation: The UN Truth Commission for East Timor' (2001) 95 *American Journal of International Law* 952

J.E. Waller, 'The Ordinariness of Extraordinary Evil: the Making of Perpetrators of Collective Violence', in A. Smeulers (ed), *Collective Violence and International Criminal Justice. An Interdisciplinary Approach* (Intersentia 2010)

VIII. DEVELOPING THE INTERNATIONAL PENAL SYSTEM

S. Beresford, 'Redressing the Wrongs of the International Justice System' (2002) 96(3) *American Journal of International Law* 628

G. Bitti, 'Compensation to an Arrest or Convicted Person', in R.S. Lee (ed), *The International Criminal Court: Elements of Crimes and Rules of Procedure and Evidence* (Transnational Publishers 2001)

K.J. Heller, 'What Happens to the Acquitted?' (2008) 21(3) *Leiden Journal of International Law* 663

B. Henry, 'The Acquitted Accused; a Forgotten Party of the ICTR' (2005) *New England Journal of International and Comparative Law* 81

J. Michels, 'Compensating Acquitted Defendants for Detention before International Criminal Courts' (2010) 8 *Journal of International Criminal Justice* 407

R. Mulgrew, *Towards the Development of the International Penal System* (Cambridge University Press 2013)

M.M. Penrose, 'Spandau Revisited: The Question of Detention for International War Crimes' (1999) 16 *New York Law School Journal of Human Rights* 553

M. Penrose, 'No Badges, No Bars: A Conspicuous Oversight in the Development of an International Criminal Court' (2003) 38 *Texas International Law Journal* 621

D.L. Rothe and C.W. Mullins, 'Beyond the Juristic Orientation of International Criminal Justice: The Relevance of Criminological Insights to International Criminal Law and its Control: A Commentary' (2010) 10(1) *International Criminal Law Review* 97

C.J.M. Safferling, 'Can Criminal Prosecution be the Answer to Massive Human Rights Violations?' (2004) 5 *German Law Journal* 1469

S.B. Starr, 'Rethinking "Effective Remedies": Remedial Deterrence in International Courts' (2008) 83 *New York University Law Review* 693

J. van Wijk, 'When International Criminal Justice Collides with Principles of International Protection: Assessing the Consequences of ICC Witnesses Seeking Asylum, Defendants Being Acquitted, and Convicted Being Released' (2013) 26 *Leiden Journal of International Law* 173

S. Zappalà, 'Compensation to an Arrested or Convicted Person', in A. Cassese, P. Gaeta and J.R.W.D. Jones (eds), *The Rome Statute of the International Criminal Court. A Commentary* (Oxford University Press 2002)

Index